Understanding the Linux
Virtual Memory Manager

BRUCE PERENS' OPEN SOURCE SERIES

http://www.phptr.com/perens

- *C++ GUI Programming with Qt 3*
  Jasmin Blanchette, Mark Summerfield

- *Managing Linux Systems with Webmin: System Administration and Module Development*
  Jamie Cameron

- *Understanding the Linux Virtual Memory Manager*
  Mel Gorman

- *Implementing CIFS: The Common Internet File System*
  Christopher R. Hertel

- *Embedded Software Development with eCos*
  Anthony J. Massa

- *Rapid Application Development with Mozilla*
  Nigel McFarlane

- *The Linux Development Platform: Configuring, Using, and Maintaining a Complete Programming Environment*
  Rafeeq Ur Rehman, Christopher Paul

- *Intrusion Detection Systems with Snort: Advanced IDS Techniques with Snort, Apache, MySQL, PHP, and ACID*
  Rafeeq Ur Rehman

- *The Official Samba-3 HOWTO and Reference Guide*
  John H. Terpstra, Jelmer R. Vernooij, Editors

- *Samba-3 by Example: Practical Exercises to Successful Deployment*
  John H. Terpstra

Understanding the Linux® Virtual Memory Manager

Mel Gorman

PRENTICE HALL PTR

PRENTICE HALL
PROFESSIONAL TECHNICAL REFERENCE
UPPER SADDLE RIVER, NJ 07458
WWW.PHPTR.COM

Library of Congress Cataloging-in-Publication Data

Gorman, Mel.
    Understanding the Linux Virtual Memory Manager / Mel Gorman.
        p. cm.—(Bruce Perens' Open source series)
    Includes bibliographical references and index.
    ISBN 0-13-145348-3
    1. Linux. 2. Virtual computer systems. 3. Virtual storage (Computer science) I. Title. II.
Series.
    QA76.9.V5G67 2004
    005.4'3—dc22   2004043864

Editorial/production supervision: *Jane Bonnell*
Composition: *TechBooks*
Cover design director: *Jerry Votta*
Manufacturing buyer: *Maura Zaldivar*
Executive Editor: *Mark L. Taub*
Editorial assistant: *Noreen Regina*
Marketing manager: *Dan DePasquale*

To John O'Gorman (RIP) for teaching me the joys of operating systems and for making memory management interesting.

To my parents and family for their continuous support of my work.

To Karen for making all the work seem worthwhile.

About Prentice Hall Professional Technical Reference

With origins reaching back to the industry's first computer science publishing program in the 1960s, and formally launched as its own imprint in 1986, Prentice Hall Professional Technical Reference (PH PTR) has developed into the leading provider of technical books in the world today. Our editors now publish over 200 books annually, authored by leaders in the fields of computing, engineering, and business.

Our roots are firmly planted in the soil that gave rise to the technical revolution. Our bookshelf contains many of the industry's computing and engineering classics: Kernighan and Ritchie's *C Programming Language*, Nemeth's *UNIX System Administration Handbook*, Horstmann's *Core Java*, and Johnson's *High-Speed Digital Design*.

PH PTR acknowledges its auspicious beginnings while it looks to the future for inspiration. We continue to evolve and break new ground in publishing by providing today's professionals with tomorrow's solutions.

Contents

Preface

Linux is developed with a stronger practical emphasis than a theoretical one. When new algorithms or changes to existing implementations are suggested, it is common to request code to match the argument. Many of the algorithms used in the Virtual Memory (VM) system were designed by theorists, but the implementations have now diverged considerably from the theory. In part, Linux does follow the traditional development cycle of design to implementation, but changes made in reaction to how the system behaved in the "real world" and intuitive decisions by developers are more common.

This means that the VM performs well in practice. However, very little VM documentation is available except for a few incomplete overviews on a small number of Web sites, except the Web site containing an earlier draft of this book, of course! This lack of documentation has led to the situation where the VM is fully understood only by a small number of core developers. New developers looking for information on how VM functions are generally told to read the source. Little or no information is available on the theoretical basis for the implementation. This requires that even a casual observer invest a large amount of time reading the code and studying the field of Memory Management.

This book gives a detailed tour of the Linux VM as implemented in 2.4.22 and gives a solid introduction of what to expect in 2.6. As well as discussing the implementation, the theory that Linux VM is based on will also be introduced. This is not intended to be a memory management theory book, but understanding why the VM is implemented in a particular fashion is often much simpler if the underlying basis is known in advance.

To complement the description, the appendices include a detailed code commentary on a significant percentage of the VM. This should drastically reduce the amount of time a developer or researcher needs to invest in understanding what is happening inside the Linux VM because VM implementations tend to follow similar code patterns even between major versions. This means that, with a solid understanding of the 2.4 VM, the later 2.5 development VMs and the 2.6 final release will be decipherable in a number of weeks.

The Intended Audience

Anyone interested in how the VM, a core kernel subsystem, works will find answers to many of their questions in this book. The VM, more than any other subsystem, affects the overall performance of the operating system. The VM is also one of the most poorly understood and badly documented subsystems in Linux, partially because there is, quite literally, so much of it. It is very difficult to isolate and understand individual parts of the code without first having a strong conceptual model of the whole VM, so this book intends to give a detailed description of what to expect before going to the source.

This material should be of prime interest to new developers who want to adapt the VM to their needs and to readers who simply would like to know how the VM works. It also will benefit other subsystem developers who want to get the most from the VM when they interact with it and operating systems researchers looking for details on how memory management is implemented in a modern operating system. For others, who just want to learn more about a subsystem that is the focus of so much discussion, they will find an easy-to-read description of the VM functionality that covers all the details without the need to plow through source code.

However, it is assumed that the reader has read at least one general operating system book or one general Linux kernel-orientated book and has a general knowledge of C before tackling this book. Although every effort is made to make the material approachable, some prior knowledge of general operating systems is assumed.

Book Overview

In Chapter 1, we go into detail on how the source code may be managed and deciphered. Three tools are introduced that are used for analysis, easy browsing and management of code. The main tools are the *Linux Cross Referencing (LXR)* tool, which allows source code to be browsed as a Web page, and *CodeViz*, which was developed while researching this book, for generating call graphs. The last tool, *PatchSet*, is for managing kernels and the application of patches. Applying patches manually can be time consuming, and using version control software, such as Concurrent Versions Systems (CVS) (*http://www.cvshome.org/*) or BitKeeper (*http://www.bitmover.com*), is not always an option. With PatchSet, a simple specification file determines what source to use, what patches to apply and what kernel configuration to use.

In the subsequent chapters, each part of the Linux VM implementation is discussed in detail, such as how memory is described in an architecture-independent manner, how processes manage their memory, how the specific allocators work and so on. Each chapter will refer to other sources that describe the behavior of Linux, as well as covering in depth the implementation, the functions used and their call graphs so that the reader will have a clear view of how the code is structured. The end of each chapter has a "What's New" section, which introduces what to expect in the 2.6 VM.

The appendices are a code commentary of a significant percentage of the VM. They give a line-by-line description of some of the more complex aspects of the VM. The style of the VM tends to be reasonably consistent, even between major releases of the kernel, so an in-depth understanding of the 2.4 VM will be an invaluable aid to understanding the 2.6 kernel when it is released.

What's New in 2.6

At the time of writing, `2.6.0-test4` has just been released, so `2.6.0-final` is due "any month now." Fortunately, the 2.6 VM, in most ways, is still quite recognizable in comparison with 2.4. However, 2.6 has some new material and concepts, and it would be a pity to ignore them. Therefore the book has the "What's New in 2.6" sections. To some extent, these sections presume you have read the rest of the book, so only glance at them during the first reading. If you decide to start reading 2.5 and 2.6 VM code, the basic description of what to expect from the "What's New" sections should greatly aid your understanding. The sections based on the `2.6.0-test4` kernel should not change significantly before 2.6. Because they are still subject to change, though, you should treat the "What's New" sections as guidelines rather than definite facts.

Companion CD

A companion CD is included with this book, and it is highly recommended the reader become familiar with it, especially as you progress more through the book and are using the code commentary. It is recommended that the CD is used with a GNU/Linux system, but it is not required.

The text of the book is contained on the CD in HTML, PDF and plain text formats so the reader can perform basic text searches if the index does not have the desired information. If you are reading the first edition of the book, you may notice small differences between the CD version and the paper version due to printing deadlines, but the differences are minor.

Almost all the tools used to research the book's material are contained on the CD. Each of the tools may be installed on virtually any GNU/Linux installation, references are included to available documentation and the project home sites, so you can check for further updates.

With many GNU/Linux installations, there is the additional bonus of being able to run a Web server directly from the CD. The server has been tested with Red Hat 7.3 and Debian Woody but should work with any distribution. The small Web site it provides at *http://localhost:10080* offers a number of useful features:

- A searchable index for functions that have a code commentary available. If a function is searched for that does not have a commentary, the browser will be automatically redirected to LXR.

- A Web browsable copy of the Linux 2.4.22 source. This allows code to be browsed and identifiers to be searched for.

- A live version of CodeViz, the tool used to generate call graphs for the book, is available. If you feel that the book's graphs are lacking some detail you want, generate them yourself.

- The **VMRegress**, **CodeViz** and **PatchSet** packages, which are discussed in Chapter 1, are available in `/cdrom/software`. **gcc-3.0.4** is also provided because it is required for building **CodeViz**.

Mount the CD on `/cdrom` as follows:

```
root@joshua:/$ mount /dev/cdrom /cdrom -o exec
```

The Web server is **Apache 1.3.27** (*http://www.apache.org/*) and has been built and configured to run with its root as **/cdrom/**. If your distribution normally uses another directory, you will need to use this one instead. To start it, run the script **/cdrom/start_server**. If no errors occur, the output should look like:

```
mel@joshua:~$ /cdrom/start_server
Starting CodeViz Server: done
Starting Apache Server:  done

The URL to access is http://localhost:10080/
```

When the server starts successfully, point your browser to *http://localhost:10080* to avail of the CD's Web services. To shut down the server, run the script **/cdrom/stop_server**, and the CD may then be unmounted.

Typographic Conventions

The conventions used in this document are simple. New concepts that are introduced, as well as URLs, are in *italicized* font. Binaries and package names are in **bold**. Structures, field names, compile time defines and variables are in a `constant-width` font. At times, when talking about a field in a structure, both the structure and field name will be included as `page→list`, for example. File names are in a constant-width font, but include files have angle brackets around them like `<linux/mm.h>` and may be found in the `include/` directory of the kernel source.

Acknowledgments

The compilation of this book was not a trivial task. This book was researched and developed in the open, and I would be remiss not to mention some of the people who helped me at various intervals. If there is anyone I missed, I apologize now.

First, I would like to thank John O'Gorman, who tragically passed away while the material for this book was being researched. His experience and guidance largely inspired the format and quality of this book.

Second, I would like to thank Mark L. Taub from Prentice Hall PTR for giving me the opportunity to publish this book. It has been a rewarding experience and made trawling through all the code worthwhile. Massive thanks go to my reviewers, who provided clear and detailed feedback long after I thought I had finished writing. Finally, on the publisher's front, I would like to thank Bruce Perens for allowing me to publish in the Bruce Perens' Open Source Series (*http://www.perens.com/Books*).

With the technical research, a number of people provided invaluable insight. Abhishek Nayani was a source of encouragement and enthusiasm early in the research. Ingo Oeser kindly provided invaluable assistance early on with a detailed explanation of how data is copied from userspace to kernel space, and he included some valuable historical context. He also kindly offered to help me if I felt I ever got lost in the twisty maze of kernel code. Scott Kaplan made numerous corrections to a number of systems from noncontiguous memory allocation to page replacement policy. Jonathon Corbet provided the most detailed account of the history of kernel development with the kernel page he writes for *Linux Weekly News*. Zack Brown, the chief behind Kernel Traffic, is the sole reason I did not drown in kernel-related mail. IBM, as part of the Equinox Project, provided an xSeries 350, which was invaluable for running my own test kernels on machines larger than those I previously had access to. Late in the game, Jeffrey Haran found the few remaining technical corrections and more of the ever-present grammar errors. Most importantly, I'm grateful for his enlightenment on some PPC issues. Finally, Patrick Healy was crucial to ensuring that this book was consistent and approachable to people who are familiar with, but not experts on, Linux or memory management.

A number of people helped with smaller technical issues and general inconsistencies where material was not covered in sufficient depth. They are Muli Ben-Yehuda, Parag Sharma, Matthew Dobson, Roger Luethi, Brian Lowe and Scott Crosby. All of them sent corrections and queries on different parts of the document, which ensured that too much prior knowledge was not assumed.

Carl Spalletta sent a number of queries and corrections to every aspect of the book in its earlier online form. Steve Greenland sent a large number of grammar corrections. Philipp Marek went above and beyond being helpful by sending more than 90 separate corrections and queries on various aspects. Long after I thought I was finished, Aris Sotiropoulos sent a large number of small corrections and suggestions. The last person, whose name I cannot remember, but is an editor for a magazine, sent me more than 140 corrections to an early version. You know who you are. Thanks.

Eleven people sent a few corrections. Though small, they were still missed by several of my own checks. They are Marek Januszewski, Amit Shah, Adrian Stanciu, Andy Isaacson, Jean Francois Martinez, Glen Kaukola, Wolfgang Oertl, Michael Babcock, Kirk True, Chuck Luciano and David Wilson.

On the development of VMRegress, nine people helped me keep it together. Danny Faught and Paul Larson both sent me a number of bug reports and helped ensure that VMRegress worked with a variety of different kernels. Cliff White, from the OSDL labs, ensured that VMRegress would have a wider application than my own test box. Dave Olien, also associated with the OSDL labs, was responsible for updating VMRegress to work with `2.5.64` and later kernels. Albert Cahalan sent all the information I needed to make VMRegress function against later proc utilities. Finally, Andrew Morton, Rik van Riel and Scott Kaplan all provided insight on the direction the tool should be developed to be both valid and useful.

The last long list are people who sent me encouragement and thanks at various intervals. They are Martin Bligh, Paul Rolland, Mohamed Ghouse, Samuel Chessman, Ersin Er, Mark Hoy, Michael Martin, Martin Gallwey, Ravi Parimi, Daniel Codt, Adnan Shafi, Xiong Quanren, Dave Airlie, Der Herr Hofrat, Ida Hallgren, Manu Anand, Eugene Teo, Diego Calleja and Ed Cashin. Thanks. The encouragement was heartening.

In conclusion, I would like to thank a few people without whom I would not have completed this book. Thanks to my parents, who kept me going long after I should have been earning enough money to support myself. Thanks to my girlfriend, Karen, who patiently listened to rants, tech babble and angsting over the book and made sure I was the person with the best toys. Kudos to friends who dragged me away from the computer periodically and kept me relatively sane, including Daren, who is cooking me dinner as I write this. Finally, thanks to the thousands of hackers who have contributed to GNU, the Linux kernel and other Free Software projects over the years, without whom I would not have an excellent system to write about. It was an inspiration to see such dedication when I first started programming on my own PC six years ago, after finally figuring out that Linux was not an application that Windows used for reading email.

CHAPTER 1

Introduction

Linux is a relatively new operating system that has begun to enjoy a lot of attention from the business, academic and free software worlds. As the operating system matures, its feature set, capabilities and performance grow, but so, out of necessity does its size and complexity. Table 1.1 shows the size of the kernel source code in bytes and lines of code of the `mm/` part of the kernel tree. This size does not include the machine-dependent code or any of the buffer management code and does not even pretend to be an accurate metric for complexity, but it still serves as a small indicator.

Version	Release Date	Total Size	Size of mm/	Line Count
1.0	March 13, 1992	5.9MiB	96KiB	3,109
1.2.13	February 8, 1995	11MiB	136KiB	4,531
2.0.39	January 9, 2001	35MiB	204KiB	6,792
2.2.22	September 16, 2002	93MiB	292KiB	9,554
2.4.22	August 25, 2003	181MiB	436KiB	15,724
2.6.0-test4	August 22, 2003	261MiB	604KiB	21,714

Table 1.1. Kernel Size as an Indicator of Complexity

Out of habit, open source developers tell new developers with questions to refer directly to the source with the "polite" acronym RTFS[1], or refer them to the kernel newbies mailing list (*http://www.kernelnewbies.org*). With the Linux VM manager, this used to be a suitable response because the time required to understand the VM could be measured in weeks. Moreover, the books available devoted enough time to the memory management chapters to make the relatively small amount of code easy to navigate.

The books that describe the operating system such as *Understanding the Linux Kernel* [BC00] [BC03] tend to cover the entire kernel rather than one topic with the notable exception of device drivers [RC01]. These books, particularly *Understanding the Linux Kernel*, provide invaluable insight into kernel internals, but they miss the details that are specific to the VM and not of general interest. But the book you are holding details why ZONE_NORMAL is exactly 896MiB and exactly how per-cpu caches

---

[1] Read The Flaming Source. It doesn't really stand for Flaming, but children could be reading.

1

are implemented. Other aspects of the VM, such as the boot memory allocator and
the VM filesystem, which are not of general kernel interest, are also covered in this
book.

Increasingly, to get a comprehensive view on how the kernel functions, one is
required to read through the source code line by line. This book tackles the VM
specifically so that this investment of time to understand the kernel functions will
be measured in weeks and not months. The details that are missed by the main
part of the book are caught by the code commentary.

In this chapter, there will be an informal introduction to the basics of acquiring
information on an open source project and some methods for managing, browsing
and comprehending the code. If you do not intend to be reading the actual source,
you may skip to Chapter 2.

1.1 Getting Started

One of the largest initial obstacles to understanding code is deciding where to start
and how to easily manage, browse and get an overview of the overall code structure.
If requested on mailing lists, people will provide some suggestions on how to proceed,
but a comprehensive methodology is rarely offered aside from suggestions to keep
reading the source until it makes sense. The following sections introduce some useful
rules of thumb for open source code comprehension and specific guidelines for how
the rules may be applied to the kernel.

1.1.1 Configuration and Building

With any open source project, the first step is to download the source and read
the installation documentation. By convention, the source will have a `README` or
`INSTALL` file at the top level of the source tree [FF02]. In fact, some automated
build tools such as **automake** require the install file to exist. These files contain
instructions for configuring and installing the package or give a reference to where
more information may be found. Linux is no exception because it includes a `README`
that describes how the kernel may be configured and built.

The second step is to build the software. In earlier days, the requirement for
many projects was to edit the `Makefile` by hand, but this is rarely the case now.
Free software usually uses at least **autoconf**[2] to automate testing of the build
environment and **automake**[3] to simplify the creation of `Makefiles`, so building is
often as simple as:

```
mel@joshua: project $ ./configure && make
```

Some older projects, such as the Linux kernel, use their own configuration tools,
and some large projects such as the Apache Web server have numerous configuration
options, but usually the configure script is the starting point. In the case of the

[2] http://www.gnu.org/software/autoconf/
[3] http://www.gnu.org/software/automake/

kernel, the configuration is handled by the `Makefiles` and supporting tools. The simplest means of configuration is to:

```
mel@joshua: linux-2.4.22 $ make config
```

This asks a long series of questions on what type of kernel should be built. After all the questions have been answered, compiling the kernel is simply:

```
mel@joshua: linux-2.4.22 $ make bzImage && make modules
```

A comprehensive guide on configuring and compiling a kernel is available with the Kernel HOWTO[4] and will not be covered in detail with this book. For now, we will presume you have one fully built kernel, and it is time to begin figuring out how the new kernel actually works.

1.1.2 Sources of Information

Open source projects will usually have a home page, especially because free project hosting sites such as *http://www.sourceforge.net* are available. The home site will contain links to available documentation and instructions on how to join the mailing list, if one is available. Some sort of documentation always exists, even if it is as minimal as a simple `README` file, so read whatever is available. If the project is old and reasonably large, the Web site will probably feature a *Frequently Asked Questions (FAQ)* page.

Next, join the development mailing list and lurk, which means to subscribe to a mailing list and read it without posting. Mailing lists are the preferred form of developer communication followed by, to a lesser extent, *Internet Relay Chat (IRC)* and online newgroups, commonly referred to as *UseNet*. Because mailing lists often contain discussions on implementation details, it is important to read at least the previous months archives to get a feel for the developer community and current activity. The mailing list archives should be the first place to search if you have a question or query on the implementation that is not covered by available documentation. If you have a question to ask the developers, take time to research the questions and ask it the "Right Way" [RM01]. Although people will answer "obvious" questions, you will not help your credibility by constantly asking questions that were answered a week previously or are clearly documented.

Now, how does all this apply to Linux? First, the documentation. A `README` is at the top of the source tree, and a wealth of information is available in the `Documentation/` directory. A number of books on UNIX design [Vah96], Linux specifically [BC00] and of course this book are available to explain what to expect in the code.

One of the best online sources of information available on kernel development is the "Kernel Page" in the weekly edition of *Linux Weekly News (http://www.lwn.net)*. This page also reports on a wide range of Linux-related topics and is worth a regular read. The kernel does not have a home Web site as such, but the closest equivalent is *http://www.kernelnewbies.org*, which is a vast

---

[4] *http://www.tldp.org/HOWTO/Kernel-HOWTO/index.html*

source of information on the kernel that is invaluable to new and experienced people alike.

An FAQ is available for the *Linux Kernel Mailing List (LKML)* at *http://www.tux.org/lkml/* that covers questions ranging from the kernel development process to how to join the list itself. The list is archived at many sites, but a common choice to reference is *http://marc.theaimsgroup.com/?l=linux-kernel*. Be aware that the mailing list is a very high volume list that can be a very daunting read, but a weekly summary is provided by the *Kernel Traffic* site at *http://kt.zork.net/kernel-traffic/*.

The sites and sources mentioned so far contain general kernel information, but memory management-specific sources are available too. A Linux-MM Web site at *http://www.linux-mm.org* contains links to memory management-specific documentation and a linux-mm mailing list. The list is relatively light in comparison to the main list and is archived at *http://mail.nl.linux.org/linux-mm/*.

The last site to consult is the *Kernel Trap* site at *http://www.kerneltrap.org*. The site contains many useful articles on kernels in general. It is not specific to Linux, but it does contain many Linux-related articles and interviews with kernel developers.

As is clear, a vast amount of information is available that may be consulted before resorting to the code. With enough experience, it will eventually be faster to consult the source directly, but, when getting started, check other sources of information first.

1.2   Managing the Source

The mainline or stock kernel is principally distributed as a compressed tape archive (.tar.bz) file that is available from your nearest kernel source repository. In Ireland's case, it is *ftp://ftp.ie.kernel.org/*. The stock kernel is always considered to be the one released by the tree maintainer. For example, at time of writing, the stock kernels for 2.2.x are those released by Alan Cox[5], for 2.4.x by Marcelo Tosatti and for 2.5.x by Linus Torvalds. At each release, the full tar file is available as well as a smaller *patch*, which contains the differences between the two releases. Patching is the preferred method of upgrading because of bandwidth considerations. Contributions made to the kernel are almost always in the form of patches, which are *unified diffs* generated by the GNU tool **diff**.

Why patches Sending patches to the mailing list initially sounds clumsy, but it is remarkably efficient in the kernel development environment. The principal advantage of patches is that it is much easier to read what changes have been made than to compare two full versions of a file side by side. A developer familiar with the code can easily see what impact the changes will have and if it should be merged. In addition, it is very easy to quote the email that includes the patch and request more information about it.

---

[5]Last minute update, Alan just announced he was going on sabbatical and will no longer maintain the 2.2.x tree. There is no maintainer at the moment.

Subtrees   At various intervals, individual influential developers may have their own version of the kernel distributed as a large patch to the main tree. These subtrees generally contain features or cleanups that have not been merged to the mainstream yet or are still being tested. Two notable subtrees are the *-rmap* tree maintained by Rik Van Riel, a long-time influential VM developer, and the *-mm* tree maintained by Andrew Morton, the current maintainer of the stock development VM. The -rmap tree contains a large set of features that, for various reasons, are not available in the mainline. It is heavily influenced by the FreeBSD VM and has a number of significant differences from the stock VM. The -mm tree is quite different from -rmap in that it is a testing tree with patches that are being tested before merging into the stock kernel.

BitKeeper   In more recent times, some developers have started using a source code control system called BitKeeper (*http://www.bitmover.com*), a proprietary version control system that was designed with Linux as the principal consideration. BitKeeper allows developers to have their own distributed version of the tree, and other users may "pull" sets of patches called *changesets* from each others' trees. This distributed nature is a very important distinction from traditional version control software that depends on a central server.

BitKeeper allows comments to be associated with each patch, and these are displayed as part of the release information for each kernel. For Linux, this means that the email that originally submitted the patch is preserved, making the progress of kernel development and the meaning of different patches a lot more transparent. On release, a list of the patch titles from each developer is announced, as well as a detailed list of all patches included.

Because BitKeeper is a proprietary product, email and patches are still considered the only method for generating discussion on code changes. In fact, some patches will not be considered for acceptance unless some discussion occurs first on the main mailing list because code quality is considered to be directly related to the amount of peer review [Ray02]. Because the BitKeeper maintained source tree is exported in formats accessible to open source tools like CVS, patches are still the preferred means of discussion. This means that developers are not required to use BitKeeper for making contributions to the kernel, but the tool is still something that developers should be aware of.

1.2.1   Diff and Patch

The two tools for creating and applying patches are **diff** and **patch**, both of which are GNU utilities available from the GNU website[6]. **diff** is used to generate patches, and **patch** is used to apply them. Although the tools have numerous options, there is a "preferred usage."

Patches generated with **diff** should always be *unified diff*, include the C function that the change affects and be generated from one directory above the kernel source root. A unified diff includes more information that just the differences between two lines. It begins with a two-line header with the names and creation date of the

---
[6]*http://www.gnu.org*

two files that **diff** is comparing. After that, the "diff" will consist of one or more "hunks." The beginning of each hunk is marked with a line beginning with @@, which includes the starting line in the source code and how many lines there are before and after the hunk is applied. The hunk includes "context" lines that show lines above and below the changes to aid a human reader. Each line begins with a +, - or blank. If the mark is +, the line is added. If it is a -, the line is removed, and a blank is to leave the line alone because it is there just to provide context. The reasoning behind generating from one directory above the kernel root is that it is easy to see quickly what version the patch has been applied against. It also makes the scripting of applying patches easier if each patch is generated the same way.

Let us take, for example, a very simple change that has been made to mm/page_alloc.c, which adds a small piece of commentary. The patch is generated as follows. Note that this command should be all on one line minus the backslashes.

```
mel@joshua: kernels/ $ diff -up                          \
            linux-2.4.22-clean/mm/page_alloc.c \
            linux-2.4.22-mel/mm/page_alloc.c   > example.patch
```

This generates a unified context diff (-u switch) between two files and places the patch in `example.patch` as shown in Figure 1.1. It also displays the name of the affected C function.

From this patch, it is clear even at a casual glance which files are affected (`page_alloc.c`) and which line it starts at (76), and the new lines added are clearly marked with a + . In a patch, there may be several "hunks" that are marked with a line starting with @@ . Each hunk will be treated separately during patch application.

Broadly speaking, patches come in two varieties: plain text such as the previous one that is sent to the mailing list and compressed patches that are compressed with either **gzip** (.gz extension) or **bzip2** (.bz2 extension). It is usually safe to assume that patches were generated one directory above the root of the kernel source tree. This means that, although the patch is generated one directory above, it may be applied with the option -p1 while the current directory is the kernel source tree root.

Broadly speaking, this means a plain text patch to a clean tree can be easily applied as follows:

```
mel@joshua: kernels/ $ cd linux-2.4.22-clean/
mel@joshua: linux-2.4.22-clean/ $ patch -p1 < ../example.patch
patching file mm/page_alloc.c
mel@joshua: linux-2.4.22-clean/ $
```

To apply a compressed patch, it is a simple extension to just decompress the patch to standard out (stdout) first.

```
mel@joshua: linux-2.4.22-mel/ $ gzip -dc ../example.patch.gz|patch -p1
```

```
--- linux-2.4.22-clean/mm/page_alloc.c Thu Sep  4 03:53:15 2003
+++ linux-2.4.22-mel/mm/page_alloc.c Thu Sep  3 03:54:07 2003
@@ -76,8 +76,23 @@
  * triggers coalescing into a block of larger size.
  *
  * -- wli
+ *
+ * There is a brief explanation of how a buddy algorithm works at
+ * http://www.memorymanagement.org/articles/alloc.html . A better
+ * idea is to read the explanation from a book like UNIX Internals
+ * by Uresh Vahalia
+ *
  */

+/**
+ *
+ * __free_pages_ok - Returns pages to the buddy allocator
+ * @page: The first page of the block to be freed
+ * @order: 2^order number of pages are freed
+ *
+ * This function returns the pages allocated by __alloc_pages and
+ * tries to merge buddies if possible. Do not call directly, use
+ * free_pages()
+ **/
 static void FASTCALL(__free_pages_ok (struct page *page, unsigned
 int order));
 static void __free_pages_ok (struct page *page, unsigned int order)
 {
```

Figure 1.1. Example Patch

If a hunk can be applied, but the line numbers are different, the hunk number and the number of lines that need to be offset will be output. These are generally safe warnings and may be ignored. If there are slight differences in the context, the hunk will be applied, and the level of fuzziness will be printed, which should be double-checked. If a hunk fails to apply, it will be saved to `filename.c.rej`, and the original file will be saved to `filename.c.orig` and have to be applied manually.

1.2.2 Basic Source Management With PatchSet

The untarring of sources, management of patches and building of kernels is initially interesting, but quickly palls. To cut down on the tedium of patch management, a simple tool was developed while writing this book called **PatchSet**, which is designed to easily manage the kernel source and patches and to eliminate a large amount of the tedium. It is fully documented and freely available from *http://www.csn.ul.ie/∼mel/projects/patchset/* and on the companion CD.

Downloading Downloading kernels and patches in itself is quite tedious, and scripts are provided to make the task simpler. First, the configuration file `etc/patchset.conf` should be edited, and the `KERNEL_MIRROR` parameter should be updated for your local *http://www.kernel.org/* mirror. After that is done, use the script **download** to download patches and kernel sources. A simple use of the script is as follows:

```
mel@joshua: patchset/ $ download 2.4.18
# Will download the 2.4.18 kernel source

mel@joshua: patchset/ $ download -p 2.4.19
# Will download a patch for 2.4.19

mel@joshua: patchset/ $ download -p -b 2.4.20
# Will download a bzip2 patch for 2.4.20
```

After the relevant sources or patches have been downloaded, it is time to configure a kernel build.

Configuring Builds Files called *set configuration files* are used to specify what kernel source tar to use, what patches to apply, what kernel configuration (generated by **make config**) to use and what the resulting kernel is to be called. A sample specification file to build kernel 2.4.20-rmap15f is:

```
linux-2.4.18.tar.gz
2.4.20-rmap15f
config_generic

1 patch-2.4.19.gz
1 patch-2.4.20.bz2
1 2.4.20-rmap15f
```

This first line says to unpack a source tree starting with `linux-2.4.18.tar.gz`. The second line specifies that the kernel will be called `2.4.20-rmap15f`. 2.4.20 was selected for this example because rmap patches against a later stable release were not available at the time of writing. To check for updated rmap patches, see *http://surriel.com/patches/*. The third line specifies which kernel `.config` file to use for compiling the kernel. Each line after that has two parts. The first part says what patch depth to use, that is, what number to use with the -p switch to patch. As discussed earlier in Section 1.2.1, this is usually 1 for applying patches while in the source directory. The second is the name of the patch stored in the patches directory. The previous example will apply two patches to update the kernel from 2.4.18 to 2.4.20 before building the `2.4.20-rmap15f` kernel tree.

If the kernel configuration file required is very simple, use the **createset** script to generate a set file for you. It simply takes a kernel version as a parameter and guesses how to build it based on available sources and patches.

```
mel@joshua: patchset/ $ createset 2.4.20
```

Building a Kernel   The package comes with three scripts. The first script, called **make-kernel.sh**, will unpack the kernel to the `kernels/` directory and build it if requested. If the target distribution is Debian, it can also create Debian packages for easy installation by specifying the `-d` switch. The second script, called **make-gengraph.sh**, will unpack the kernel, but, instead of building an installable kernel, it will generate the files required to use **CodeViz**, discussed in the next section, for creating call graphs. The last, called `make-lxr.sh`, will install a kernel for use with LXR.

Generating Diffs   Ultimately, you will need to see the difference between files in two trees or generate a "diff" of changes you have made yourself. Three small scripts are provided to make this task easier. The first is **setclean**, which sets the source tree to compare from. The second is **setworking** to set the path of the kernel tree you are comparing against or working on. The third is **difftree**, which will generate diffs against files or directories in the two trees. To generate the diff shown in Figure 1.1, the following would have worked:

```
mel@joshua: patchset/ $ setclean linux-2.4.22-clean
mel@joshua: patchset/ $ setworking linux-2.4.22-mel
mel@joshua: patchset/ $ difftree mm/page_alloc.c
```

The generated diff is a unified diff with the C function context included and complies with the recommended use of **diff**. Two additional scripts are available that are very useful when tracking changes between two trees. They are **diffstruct** and **difffunc**. These are for printing out the differences between individual structures and functions. When used first, the `-f` switch must be used to record what source file the structure or function is declared in, but it is only needed the first time.

1.3   Browsing the Code

When code is small and manageable, browsing through the code is not particularly difficult because operations are clustered together in the same file, and there is not much coupling between modules. The kernel, unfortunately, does not always exhibit this behavior. Functions of interest may be spread across multiple files or contained as inline functions in headers. To complicate matters, files of interest may be buried beneath architecture-specific directories, which makes tracking them down time consuming.

One solution for easy code browsing is **ctags**(*http://ctags.sourceforge.net/*), which generates tag files from a set of source files. These tags can be used to jump to the C file and line where the identifier is declared with editors such as **Vi** and **Emacs**. In the event there are multiple instances of the same tag, such as with multiple functions with the same name, the correct one may be selected from a list. This method works best when editing the code because it allows very fast navigation through the code to be confined to one terminal window.

A more friendly browsing method is available with the *LXR* tool hosted at *http://lxr.linux.no/*. This tool provides the ability to represent source code as browsable Web pages. Identifiers such as global variables, macros and functions become hyperlinks. When clicked, the location where the identifier is defined is displayed along with every file and line referencing the definition. This makes code navigation very convenient and is almost essential when reading the code for the first time.

The tool is very simple to install, and a browsable version of the kernel 2.4.22 source is available on the CD included with this book. All code extracts throughout the book are based on the output of LXR so that the line numbers would be clearly visible in excerpts.

1.3.1 Analyzing Code Flow

Because separate modules share code across multiple C files, it can be difficult to see what functions are affected by a given code path without tracing through all the code manually. For a large or deep code path, this can be extremely time consuming to answer what should be a simple question.

One simple, but effective, tool to use is **CodeViz**, which is a call graph generator and is included with the CD. It uses a modified compiler for either C or C++ to collect information necessary to generate the graph. The tool is hosted at *http://www.csn.ul.ie/~mel/projects/codeviz/*.

During compilation with the modified compiler, files with a .cdep extension are generated for each C file. This .cdep file contains all function declarations and calls made in the C file. These files are distilled with a program called **genfull** to generate a full call graph of the entire source code, which can be rendered with **dot**, part of the **GraphViz** project hosted at *http://www.graphviz.org/*.

In the kernel compiled for the computer this book was written on, a total of 40,165 entries were in the full.graph file generated by **genfull**. This call graph is essentially useless on its own because of its size, so a second tool is provided called **gengraph**. This program, at basic usage, takes the name of one or more functions as an argument and generates a postscript file with the call graph of the requested function as the root node. The postscript file may be viewed with **ghostview** or **gv**.

The generated graphs can be to an unnecessary depth or show functions that the user is not interested in, so there are three limiting options to graph generation. The first is limit by depth where functions that are greater than N levels deep in a call chain are ignored. The second is to totally ignore a function so that it will not appear on the call graph or any of the functions it calls. The last is to display a function, but not traverse it, which is convenient when the function is covered on a separate call graph or is a known API with an implementation that is not currently of interest.

All call graphs shown in these documents are generated with the **CodeViz** tool because it is often much easier to understand a subsystem at first glance when a call graph is available. The tool has been tested with a number of other open source projects based on C and has a wider application than just the kernel.

1.3.2   Simple Graph Generation

If both **PatchSet** and **CodeViz** are installed, the first call graph in this book shown in Figure 3.4 can be generated and viewed with the following set of commands. For brevity, the output of the commands is omitted:

```
mel@joshua: patchset $ download 2.4.22
mel@joshua: patchset $ createset 2.4.22
mel@joshua: patchset $ make-gengraph.sh 2.4.22
mel@joshua: patchset $ cd kernels/linux-2.4.22
mel@joshua: linux-2.4.22 $ gengraph -t -s "alloc_bootmem_low_pages \
                              zone_sizes_init" -f paging_init
mel@joshua: linux-2.4.22 $ gv paging_init.ps
```

1.4   Reading the Code

When new developers or researchers ask how to start reading the code, experienced developers often recommend starting with the initialization code and working from there. This may not be the best approach for everyone because initialization is quite architecture dependent and requires detailed hardware knowledge to decipher it. It also gives very little information on how a subsystem like the VM works. It is during the late stages of initialization that memory is set up in the way the running system sees it.

The best starting point to understand the VM is this book and the code commentary. It describes a VM that is reasonably comprehensive without being overly complicated. Later VMs are more complex, but are essentially extensions of the one described here.

For when the code has to be approached afresh with a later VM, it is always best to start in an isolated region that has the minimum number of dependencies. In the case of the VM, the best starting point is the *Out Of Memory (OOM)* manager in `mm/oom_kill.c`. It is a very gentle introduction to one corner of the VM where a process is selected to be killed in the event that memory in the system is low. Because this function touches so many different aspects of the VM, it is covered last in this book. The second subsystem to then examine is the noncontiguous memory allocator located in `mm/vmalloc.c` and discussed in Chapter 7 because it is reasonably contained within one file. The third system should be the physical page allocator located in `mm/page_alloc.c` and discussed in Chapter 6 for similar reasons. The fourth system of interest is the creation of Virtual Memory Addresses (VMAs) and memory areas for processes discussed in Chapter 4. Between these systems, they have the bulk of the code patterns that are prevalent throughout the rest of the kernel code, which makes the deciphering of more complex systems such as the page replacement policy or the buffer Input/Output (I/O) much easier to comprehend.

The second recommendation that is given by experienced developers is to benchmark and test the VM. Many benchmark programs are available, but commonly used ones are **ConTest**(*http://members.optusnet.com.au/ckolivas/contest/*), **SPEC**(*http://www.specbench.org/*), **lmbench**(*http://www.bitmover.com/lmbench/*)

and **dbench**(*http://freshmeat.net/projects/dbench/*).   For many purposes, these benchmarks will fit the requirements.

Unfortunately, it is difficult to test just the VM accurately and benchmarking it is frequently based on timing a task such as a kernel compile. A tool called **VM Regress** is available at *http://www.csn.ul.ie/~mel/projects/vmregress/* that lays the foundation required to build a fully fledged testing, regression and benchmarking tool for the VM. **VM Regress** uses a combination of kernel modules and userspace tools to test small parts of the VM in a reproducible manner and has one benchmark for testing the page replacement policy using a large reference string. It is intended as a framework for the development of a testing utility and has a number of Perl libraries and helper kernel modules to do much of the work. However, it is still in the early stages of development, so use it with care.

1.5   Submitting Patches

Two files, `SubmittingPatches` and `CodingStyle`, are in the `Documentation/` directory that cover the important basics. However, very little documentation describes how to get patches merged. This section will give a brief introduction on how, broadly speaking, patches are managed.

First and foremost, the coding style of the kernel needs to be adhered to because having a style inconsistent with the main kernel will be a barrier to getting merged regardless of the technical merit. After a patch has been developed, the first problem is to decide where to send it. Kernel development has a definite, if nonapparent, hierarchy of who handles patches and how to get them submitted. As an example, we'll take the case of 2.5.x development.

The first check to make is if the patch is very small or trivial. If it is, post it to the main kernel mailing list. If no bad reaction occurs, it can be fed to what is called the *Trivial Patch Monkey*[7]. The trivial patch monkey is exactly what it sounds like. It takes small patches and feeds them en masse to the correct people. This is best suited for documentation, commentary or one-liner patches.

Patches are managed through what could be loosely called a set of rings with Linus in the very middle having the final say on what gets accepted into the main tree. Linus, with rare exceptions, accepts patches only from who he refers to as his "lieutenants," a group of around 10 people who he trusts to "feed" him correct code. An example lieutenant is Andrew Morton, the VM maintainer at time of writing. Any change to the VM has to be accepted by Andrew before it will get to Linus. These people are generally maintainers of a particular system, but sometimes will "feed" him patches from another subsystem if they feel it is important enough.

Each of the lieutenants are active developers on different subsystems. Just like Linus, they have a small set of developers they trust to be knowledgeable about the patch they are sending, but will also pick up patches that affect their subsystem more readily. Depending on the subsystem, the list of people they trust will be heavily influenced by the list of maintainers in the `MAINTAINERS` file. The second major area of influence will be from the subsystem-specific mailing list if there is

---

[7] *http://www.kernel.org/pub/linux/kernel/people/rusty/trivial/*

one. The VM does not have a list of maintainers, but it does have a mailing list[8].

The maintainers and lieutenants are crucial to the acceptance of patches. Linus, broadly speaking, does not appear to want to be convinced with argument alone on the merit for a significant patch, but prefers to hear it from one of his lieutenants, which is understandable considering the volume of patches that exist.

In summary, a new patch should be emailed to the subsystem mailing list and cc'd to the main list to generate discussion. If no reaction occurs, it should be sent to the maintainer for that area of code if there is one and to the lieutenant if there is not. After it has been picked up by a maintainer or lieutenant, chances are it will be merged. The important key is that patches and ideas must be released early and often so developers have a chance to look at them while they are still manageable. There are notable cases where massive patches merged with the main tree because there were long periods of silence with little or no discussion. A recent example of this is the Linux Kernel Crash Dump project, which still has not been merged into the mainstream because there has not been enough favorable feedback from lieutenants or strong support from vendors.

---

[8] *http://www.linux-mm.org/mailinglists.shtml*

CHAPTER 2

Describing Physical Memory

Linux is available for a wide range of architectures, so an architecture-independent way of describing memory is needed. This chapter describes the structures used to keep account of memory banks, pages and flags that affect VM behavior.

The first principal concept prevalent in the VM is *Non Uniform Memory Access (NUMA)*. With large-scale machines, memory may be arranged into banks that incur a different cost to access depending on their distance from the processor. For example, a bank of memory might be assigned to each CPU, or a bank of memory very suitable for Direct Memory Access (DMA) near device cards might be assigned.

Each bank is called a *node*, and the concept is represented under Linux by a `struct pglist_data` even if the architecture is Uniform Memory Access (UMA). This struct is always referenced by its typedef `pg_data_t`. Every node in the system is kept on a NULL terminated list called `pgdat_list`, and each node is linked to the next with the field `pg_data_t→node_next`. For UMA architectures like PC desktops, only one static `pg_data_t` structure called `contig_page_data` is used. Nodes are discussed further in Section 2.1.

Each node is divided into a number of blocks called *zones*, which represent ranges within memory. Zones should not be confused with zone-based allocators because they are unrelated. A zone is described by a `struct zone_struct`, type-deffed to `zone_t`, and each one is of type `ZONE_DMA`, `ZONE_NORMAL` or `ZONE_HIGHMEM`. Each zone type is suitable for a different type of use. `ZONE_DMA` is memory in the lower physical memory ranges that certain Industry Standard Architecture (ISA) devices require. Memory within `ZONE_NORMAL` is directly mapped by the kernel into the upper region of the linear address space, which is discussed further in Section 4.1. `ZONE_HIGHMEM` is the remaining available memory in the system and is not directly mapped by the kernel.

With the x86, the zones are the following:

`ZONE_DMA`	First 16MiB of memory
`ZONE_NORMAL`	16MiB - 896MiB
`ZONE_HIGHMEM`	896 MiB - End

Many kernel operations can only take place using `ZONE_NORMAL`, so it is the most performance-critical zone. Zones are discussed further in Section 2.2. The system's memory is comprised of fixed-size chunks called *page frames*. Each physical page frame is represented by a `struct page`, and all the structs are kept in a global `mem_map` array, which is usually stored at the beginning of `ZONE_NORMAL` or just after

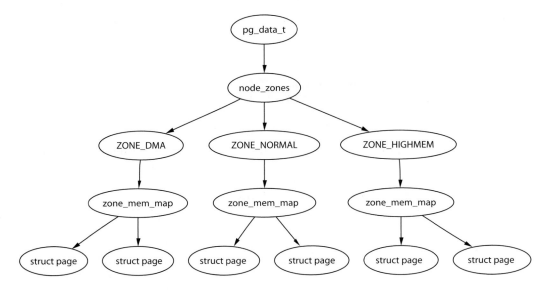

Figure 2.1. Relationship Between Nodes, Zones and Pages

the area reserved for the loaded kernel image in low memory machines. Section 2.4 discusses `struct pages` in detail, and Section 3.7 discusses the global `mem_map` array in detail. The basic relationship between all these structs is illustrated in Figure 2.1.

Because the amount of memory directly accessible by the kernel (`ZONE_NORMAL`) is limited in size, Linux supports the concept of *high memory*, which is discussed further in Section 2.7. This chapter discusses how nodes, zones and pages are represented before introducing high memory management.

2.1 Nodes

As I have mentioned, each node in memory is described by a `pg_data_t`, which is a typedef for a `struct pglist_data`. When allocating a page, Linux uses a *node-local allocation policy* to allocate memory from the node closest to the running CPU. Because processes tend to run on the same CPU, it is likely the memory from the current node will be used. The struct is declared as follows in <`linux/mmzone.h`>:

```
129 typedef struct pglist_data {
130     zone_t node_zones[MAX_NR_ZONES];
131     zonelist_t node_zonelists[GFP_ZONEMASK+1];
132     int nr_zones;
133     struct page *node_mem_map;
134     unsigned long *valid_addr_bitmap;
135     struct bootmem_data *bdata;
136     unsigned long node_start_paddr;
137     unsigned long node_start_mapnr;
```

```
138        unsigned long node_size;
139        int node_id;
140        struct pglist_data *node_next;
141 } pg_data_t;
```

We now briefly describe each of these fields:

node_zones The zones for this node are ZONE_HIGHMEM, ZONE_NORMAL, ZONE_DMA.

node_zonelists This is the order of zones that allocations are preferred from. build_zonelists() in mm/page_alloc.c sets up the order when called by free_area_init_core(). A failed allocation in ZONE_HIGHMEM may fall back to ZONE_NORMAL or back to ZONE_DMA.

nr_zones This is the number of zones in this node between one and three. Not all nodes will have three. A CPU bank may not have ZONE_DMA, for example.

node_mem_map This is the first page of the struct page array that represents each physical frame in the node. It will be placed somewhere within the global mem_map array.

valid_addr_bitmap This is a bitmap that describes "holes" in the memory node that no memory exists for. In reality, this is only used by the Sparc and Sparc64 architectures and is ignored by all others.

bdata This is only of interest to the boot memory allocator discussed in Chapter 5.

node_start_paddr This is the starting physical address of the node. An unsigned long does not work optimally because it breaks for ia32 with *Physical Address Extension (PAE)* and for some PowerPC variants such as the PPC440GP. PAE is discussed further in Section 2.7. A more suitable solution would be to record this as a *Page Frame Number (PFN)*. A PFN is simply an index within physical memory that is counted in page-sized units. PFN for a physical address could be trivially defined as (page_phys_addr >> PAGE_SHIFT).

node_start_mapnr This gives the page offset within the global mem_map. It is calculated in free_area_init_core() by calculating the number of pages between mem_map and the local mem_map for this node called lmem_map.

node_size This is the total number of pages in this zone.

node_id This is the *Node ID (NID)* of the node and starts at 0.

node_next Pointer to next node in a NULL terminated list.

All nodes in the system are maintained on a list called pgdat_list. The nodes are placed on this list as they are initialized by the init_bootmem_core() function, which is described later in Section 5.3. Up until late 2.4 kernels (> 2.4.18), blocks of code that traversed the list looked something like the following:

```
pg_data_t * pgdat;
pgdat = pgdat_list;
do {
      /* do something with pgdata_t */
      ...
} while ((pgdat = pgdat->node_next));
```

In more recent kernels, a macro for_each_pgdat(), which is trivially defined as a for loop, is provided to improve code readability.

2.2 Zones

Each zone is described by a struct zone_struct. zone_structs keep track of information like page usage statistics, free area information and locks. They are declared as follows in <linux/mmzone.h>:

```
37 typedef struct zone_struct {
41      spinlock_t          lock;
42      unsigned long       free_pages;
43      unsigned long       pages_min, pages_low, pages_high;
44      int                 need_balance;
45
49      free_area_t         free_area[MAX_ORDER];
50
76      wait_queue_head_t * wait_table;
77      unsigned long       wait_table_size;
78      unsigned long       wait_table_shift;
79
83      struct pglist_data  *zone_pgdat;
84      struct page         *zone_mem_map;
85      unsigned long       zone_start_paddr;
86      unsigned long       zone_start_mapnr;
87
91      char                *name;
92      unsigned long       size;
93 } zone_t;
```

This is a brief explanation of each field in the struct.

lock Spinlock protects the zone from concurrent accesses.

free_pages The total number of free pages in the zone.

pages_min, pages_low and pages_high These are zone watermarks that are described in the next section.

need_balance This flag tells the pageout **kswapd** to balance the zone. A zone is said to need balance when the number of available pages reaches one of the *zone watermarks*. Watermarks are discussed in the next section.

free_area These are free area bitmaps used by the buddy allocator.

wait_table This is a hash table of wait queues of processes waiting on a page to be freed. This is of importance to `wait_on_page()` and `unlock_page()`. Although processes could all wait on one queue, this would cause all waiting processes to race for pages still locked when woken up. A large group of processes contending for a shared resource like this is sometimes called a thundering herd. Wait tables are discussed further in Section 2.2.3.

wait_table_size This is the number of queues in the hash table, which is a power of 2.

wait_table_shift This is defined as the number of bits in a long minus the binary logarithm of the table size above.

zone_pgdat This points to the parent `pg_data_t`.

zone_mem_map This is the first page in the global `mem_map` that this zone refers to.

zone_start_paddr This uses the same principle as `node_start_paddr`.

zone_start_mapnr This uses the same principle as `node_start_mapnr`.

name This is the string name of the zone: "DMA", "Normal" or "HighMem".

size This is the size of the zone in pages.

2.2.1 Zone Watermarks

When available memory in the system is low, the pageout daemon **kswapd** is woken up to start freeing pages (see Chapter 10). If the pressure is high, the process will free up memory synchronously, sometimes referred to as the *direct-reclaim* path. The parameters affecting pageout behavior are similar to those used by FreeBSD [McK96] and Solaris [MM01].

Each zone has three watermarks called `pages_low`, `pages_min` and `pages_high`, which help track how much pressure a zone is under. The relationship between them is illustrated in Figure 2.2. The number of pages for `pages_min` is calculated in the function `free_area_init_core()` during memory init and is based on a ratio to the size of the zone in pages. It is calculated initially as ZoneSizeInPages/128. The lowest value it will be is 20 pages (80K on a x86), and the highest possible value is 255 pages (1MiB on a x86).

At each watermark a different action is taken to address the memory shortage.

pages_low When the `pages_low` number of free pages is reached, **kswapd** is woken up by the buddy allocator to start freeing pages. This is equivalent to when `lotsfree` is reached in Solaris and `freemin` in FreeBSD. The value is twice the value of `pages_min` by default.

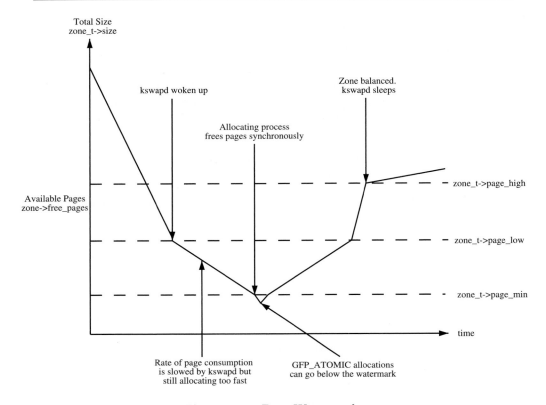

Figure 2.2. Zone Watermarks

pages_min When pages_min is reached, the allocator will do the **kswapd** work in a synchronous fashion, sometimes referred to as the *direct-reclaim* path. Solaris does not have a real equivalent, but the closest is the desfree or minfree, which determine how often the pageout scanner is woken up.

pages_high After **kswapd** has been woken to start freeing pages, it will not consider the zone to be "balanced" when pages_high pages are free. After the watermark has been reached, **kswapd** will go back to sleep. In Solaris, this is called lotsfree, and, in BSD, it is called free_target. The default for pages_high is three times the value of pages_min.

Whatever the pageout parameters are called in each operating system, the meaning is the same. It helps determine how hard the pageout daemon or processes work to free up pages.

2.2.2 Calculating the Size of Zones

The size of each zone is calculated during setup_memory(), shown in Figure 2.3.

The PFN is an offset, counted in pages, within the physical memory map. The first PFN usable by the system, min_low_pfn, is located at the beginning of the

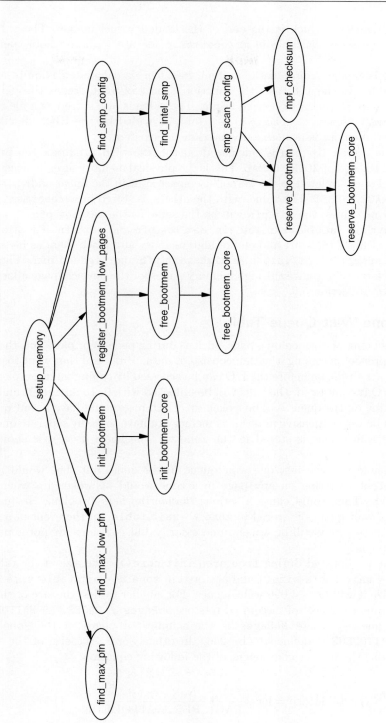

Figure 2.3. Call Graph: setup_memory()

first page after _end, which is the end of the loaded kernel image. The value is stored as a file scope variable in mm/bootmem.c for use with the boot memory allocator.

How the last page frame in the system, max_pfn, is calculated is quite architecture specific. In the x86 case, the function find_max_pfn() reads through the whole *e820* map for the highest page frame. The value is also stored as a file scope variable in mm/bootmem.c. The e820 is a table provided by the BIOS describing what physical memory is available, reserved or nonexistent.

The value of max_low_pfn is calculated on the x86 with find_max_low_pfn(), and it marks the end of ZONE_NORMAL. This is the physical memory directly accessible by the kernel and is related to the kernel/userspace split in the linear address space marked by PAGE_OFFSET. The value, with the others, is stored in mm/bootmem.c. In low memory machines, the max_pfn will be the same as the max_low_pfn.

With the three variables min_low_pfn, max_low_pfn and max_pfn, it is straightforward to calculate the start and end of high memory and place them as file scope variables in arch/i386/mm/init.c as highstart_pfn and highend_pfn. The values are used later to initialize the high memory pages for the physical page allocator, as we will see in Section 5.6.

2.2.3 Zone Wait Queue Table

When I/O is being performed on a page, such as during page-in or page-out, the I/O is locked to prevent accessing it with inconsistent data. Processes that want to use it have to join a wait queue before the I/O can be accessed by calling wait_on_page(). When the I/O is completed, the page will be unlocked with UnlockPage(), and any process waiting on the queue will be woken up. Each page could have a wait queue, but it would be very expensive in terms of memory to have so many separate queues. Instead, the wait queue is stored in the zone_t. The basic process is shown in Figure 2.4.

It is possible to have just one wait queue in the zone, but that would mean that all processes waiting on any page in a zone would be woken up when one was unlocked. This would cause a serious *thundering herd* problem. Instead, a hash table of wait queues is stored in zone_t→wait_table. In the event of a hash collision, processes may still be woken unnecessarily, but collisions are not expected to occur frequently.

The table is allocated during free_area_init_core(). The size of the table is calculated by wait_table_size() and is stored in zone_t→wait_table_size. The maximum size it will be is 4,096 wait queues. For smaller tables, the size of the table is the minimum power of 2 required to store NoPages / PAGES_PER_WAITQUEUE number of queues, where NoPages is the number of pages in the zone and PAGE_PER_WAITQUEUE is defined to be 256. In other words, the size of the table is calculated as the integer component of the following equation:

$$\text{wait\_table\_size} = \log_2(\frac{\text{NoPages} * 2}{\text{PAGE\_PER\_WAITQUEUE}} - 1)$$

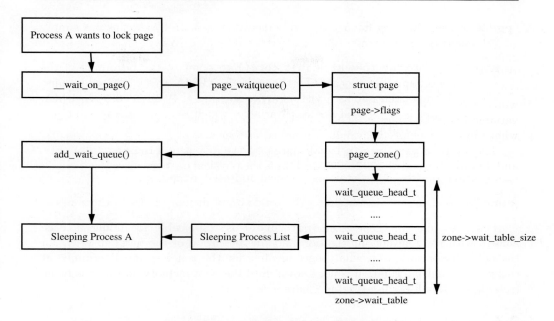

Figure 2.4. Sleeping on a Locked Page

The field `zone_t→wait_table_shift` is calculated as the number of bits a page address must be shifted right to return an index within the table. The function `page_waitqueue()` is responsible for returning which wait queue to use for a page in a zone. It uses a simple multiplicative hashing algorithm based on the virtual address of the `struct page` being hashed.

`page_waitqueue` works by simply multiplying the address by `GOLDEN_RATIO_PRIME` and shifting the result `zone_t→wait_table_shift` bits right to index the result within the hash table. `GOLDEN_RATIO_PRIME`[Lev00] is the largest prime that is closest to the *golden ratio*[Knu68] of the largest integer that may be represented by the architecture.

2.3 Zone Initialization

The zones are initialized after the kernel page tables have been fully set up by `paging_init()`. Page table initialization is covered in Section 3.6. Predictably, each architecture performs this task differently, but the objective is always the same: to determine what parameters to send to either `free_area_init()` for UMA architectures or `free_area_init_node()` for NUMA. The only parameter required for UMA is `zones_size`. The full list of parameters follows:

nid is the NodeID that is the logical identifier of the node whose zones are being initialized.

pgdat is the node's `pg_data_t` that is being initialized. In UMA, this will simply be `contig_page_data`.

pmap is set later by `free_area_init_core()` to point to the beginning of the local `lmem_map` array allocated for the node. In NUMA, this is ignored because NUMA treats `mem_map` as a virtual array starting at `PAGE_OFFSET`. In UMA, this pointer is the global `mem_map` variable, which is now `mem_map`, and gets initialized in UMA.

zones_sizes is an array containing the size of each zone in pages.

zone_start_paddr is the starting physical address for the first zone.

zone_holes is an array containing the total size of memory holes in the zones.

The core function `free_area_init_core()` is responsible for filling in each `zone_t` with the relevant information and the allocation of the `mem_map` array for the node. Information on what pages are free for the zones is not determined at this point. That information is not known until the boot memory allocator is being retired, which will be discussed in Chapter 5.

2.4 Initializing mem_map

The `mem_map` area is created during system startup in one of two fashions. On NUMA systems, the global `mem_map` is treated as a virtual array starting at `PAGE_OFFSET`. `free_area_init_node()` is called for each active node in the system, which allocates the portion of this array for the node being initialized. On UMA systems, `free_area_init()` uses `contig_page_data` as the node and the global `mem_map` as the local `mem_map` for this node. The call graph for both functions is shown in Figure 2.5.

The core function `free_area_init_core()` allocates a local `lmem_map` for the node being initialized. The memory for the array is allocated from the boot memory allocator with `alloc_bootmem_node()` (see Chapter 5). With UMA architectures, this newly allocated memory becomes the global `mem_map`, but it is slightly different for NUMA.

NUMA architectures allocate the memory for `lmem_map` within their own memory node. The global `mem_map` never gets explicitly allocated, but instead is set to `PAGE_OFFSET` where it is treated as a virtual array. The address of the local map is stored in `pg_data_t`→`node_mem_map`, which exists somewhere within the virtual `mem_map`. For each zone that exists in the node, the address within the virtual `mem_map` for the zone is stored in `zone_t`→`zone_mem_map`. All the rest of the code then treats `mem_map` as a real array bacause only valid regions within it will be used by nodes.

2.5 Pages

Every physical page frame in the system has an associated `struct page` that is used to keep track of its status. In the 2.2 kernel [BC00], this structure resembled

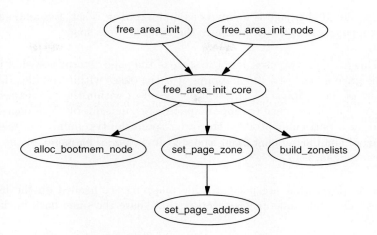

Figure 2.5. Call Graph: `free_area_init()`

its equivalent in System V [GC94], but like the other UNIX variants, the structure changed considerably. It is declared as follows in <`linux/mm.h`>:

```
152 typedef struct page {
153     struct list_head list;
154     struct address_space *mapping;
155     unsigned long index;
156     struct page *next_hash;
158     atomic_t count;
159     unsigned long flags;
161     struct list_head lru;
163     struct page **pprev_hash;
164     struct buffer_head * buffers;
175
176 #if defined(CONFIG_HIGHMEM) || defined(WANT_PAGE_VIRTUAL)
177     void *virtual;
179 #endif /* CONFIG_HIGMEM || WANT_PAGE_VIRTUAL */
180 } mem_map_t;
```

Here is a brief description of each of the fields:

list Pages may belong to many lists, and this field is used as the list head. For example, pages in a mapping will be in one of three circular linked links kept by the `address_space`. These are `clean_pages`, `dirty_pages` and `locked_pages`. In the slab allocator, this field is used to store pointers to the slab and cache structures managing the page when it has been allocated by the slab allocator. It is also used to link blocks of free pages together.

mapping When files or devices are memory mapped, their inode has an associated `address_space`. This field will point to this address space if the page belongs to the file. If the page is anonymous and `mapping` is set, the `address_space` is `swapper_space`, which manages the swap address space.

index This field has two uses, and the state of the page determines what it means. If the page is part of a file mapping, it is the offset within the file. If the page is part of the swap cache, this will be the offset within the `address_space` for the swap address space (`swapper_space`). Second, if a block of pages is being freed for a particular process, the order (power of two number of pages being freed) of the block being freed is stored in `index`. This is set in the function `__free_pages_ok()`.

next_hash Pages that are part of a file mapping are hashed on the inode and offset. This field links pages together that share the same hash bucket.

count This is the reference count to the page. If it drops to zero, it may be freed. If it is any greater, it is in use by one or more processes or is in use by the kernel like when waiting for I/O.

flags These are flags that describe the status of the page. All of them are declared in <`linux/mm.h`> and are listed in Table 2.1. A number of macros defined for testing, clearing and setting the bits are all listed in Table 2.2. The only really interesting flag is `SetPageUptodate()`, which calls an architecture-specific function, `arch_set_page_uptodate()`, if it is defined before setting the bit.

lru For the page replacement policy, pages that may be swapped out will exist on either the `active_list` or the `inactive_list` declared in `page_alloc.c`. This is the list head for these Least Recently Used (LRU) lists. These two lists are discussed in detail in Chapter 10.

pprev_hash This complement to `next_hash` is so that the hash can work as a doubly linked list.

buffers If a page has buffers for a block device associated with it, this field is used to keep track of the `buffer_head`. An anonymous page mapped by a process may also have an associated `buffer_head` if it is backed by a swap file. This is necessary because the page has to be synced with backing storage in block-sized chunks defined by the underlying file system.

virtual Normally only pages from `ZONE_NORMAL` are directly mapped by the kernel. To address pages in `ZONE_HIGHMEM`, `kmap()` is used to map the page for the kernel, which is described further in Chapter 9. Only a fixed number of pages may be mapped. When a page is mapped, this is its virtual address.

The type `mem_map_t` is a typedef for `struct page`, so it can be easily referred to within the `mem_map` array.

Bit Name	Description
PG_active	This bit is set if a page is on the `active_list` LRU and cleared when it is removed. It marks a page as being hot.
PG_arch_1	Quoting directly from the code, `PG_arch_1` is an architecture-specific page state bit. The generic code guarantees that this bit is cleared for a page when it first is entered into the page cache. This allows an architecture to defer the flushing of the D-Cache (See Section 3.9) until the page is mapped by a process.
PG_checked	This is only used by the Ext2 file system.
PG_dirty	This indicates if a page needs to be flushed to disk. When a page is written to that is backed by disk, it is not flushed immediately. This bit is needed to ensure a dirty page is not freed before it is written out.
PG_error	If an error occurs during disk I/O, this bit is set.
PG_fs_1	This bit is reserved for a file system to use for its own purposes. Currently, only NFS uses it to indicate if a page is in sync with the remote server.
PG_highmem	Pages in high memory cannot be mapped permanently by the kernel. Pages that are in high memory are flagged with this bit during `mem_init()`.
PG_launder	This bit is important only to the page replacement policy. When the VM wants to swap out a page, it will set this bit and call the `writepage()` function. When scanning, if it encounters a page with this bit and `PG_locked` set, it will wait for the I/O to complete.
PG_locked	This bit is set when the page must be locked in memory for disk I/O. When I/O starts, this bit is set and released when it completes.
PG_lru	If a page is on either the `active_list` or the `inactive_list`, this bit will be set.
PG_referenced	If a page is mapped and it is referenced through the mapping, index hash table, this bit is set. It is used during page replacement for moving the page around the LRU lists.
PG_reserved	This is set for pages that can never be swapped out. It is set by the boot memory allocator (See Chapter 5) for pages allocated during system startup. Later it is used to flag empty pages or ones that do not even exist.
PG_slab	This will flag a page as being used by the slab allocator.
PG_skip	This was used by some Sparc architectures to skip over parts of the address space but is no longer used. In 2.6, it is totally removed.
PG_unused	This bit is literally unused.
PG_uptodate	When a page is read from disk without error, this bit will be set.

Table 2.1. Flags Describing Page Status

Bit Name	Set	Test	Clear
PG_active	SetPageActive()	PageActive()	ClearPageActive()
PG_arch_1	None	None	None
PG_checked	SetPageChecked()	PageChecked()	None
PG_dirty	SetPageDirty()	PageDirty()	ClearPageDirty()
PG_error	SetPageError()	PageError()	ClearPageError()
PG_highmem	None	PageHighMem()	None
PG_launder	SetPageLaunder()	PageLaunder()	ClearPageLaunder()
PG_locked	LockPage()	PageLocked()	UnlockPage()
PG_lru	TestSetPageLRU()	PageLRU()	TestClearPageLRU()
PG_referenced	SetPageReferenced()	PageReferenced()	ClearPageReferenced()
PG_reserved	SetPageReserved()	PageReserved()	ClearPageReserved()
PG_skip	None	None	None
PG_slab	PageSetSlab()	PageSlab()	PageClearSlab()
PG_unused	None	None	None
PG_uptodate	SetPageUptodate()	PageUptodate()	ClearPageUptodate()

Table 2.2. Macros for Testing, Setting and Clearing page→flags Status Bits

2.6   Mapping Pages to Zones

Up until as recently as kernel `2.4.18`, a `struct page` stored a reference to its zone with page→zone, which was later considered wasteful, because even such a small pointer consumes a lot of memory when thousands of `struct page`s exist. In more recent kernels, the `zone` field has been removed and instead the top `ZONE_SHIFT` (8 in the x86) bits of the page→flags are used to determine the zone that a page belongs to. First, a `zone_table` of zones is set up. It is declared in mm/page_alloc.c as:

```
33 zone_t *zone_table[MAX_NR_ZONES*MAX_NR_NODES];
34 EXPORT_SYMBOL(zone_table);
```

`MAX_NR_ZONES` is the maximum number of zones that can be in a node, i.e., three. `MAX_NR_NODES` is the maximum number of nodes that may exist. The function `EXPORT_SYMBOL()` makes `zone_table` accessible to loadable modules. This table is treated like a multidimensional array. During `free_area_init_core()`, all the pages in a node are initialized. First, it sets the value for the table

```
733              zone_table[nid * MAX_NR_ZONES + j] = zone;
```

Where nid is the node ID, j is the zone index and `zone` is the `zone_t` struct. For each page, the function `set_page_zone()` is called as:

```
788              set_page_zone(page, nid * MAX_NR_ZONES + j);
```

The parameter `page` is the page for which the zone is being set. Therefore, clearly the index in the `zone_table` is stored in the page.

2.7   High Memory

Because the address space usable by the kernel (`ZONE_NORMAL`) is limited in size, the kernel has support for the concept of high memory. Two thresholds of high memory exist on 32-bit x86 systems, one at 4GiB and a second at 64GiB. The 4GiB limit is related to the amount of memory that may be addressed by a 32-bit physical address. To access memory between the range of 1GiB and 4GiB, the kernel temporarily maps pages from high memory into `ZONE_NORMAL` with `kmap()`. This is discussed further in Chapter 9.

The second limit at 64GiB is related to *PAE*, which is an Intel invention to allow more RAM to be used with 32-bit systems. It makes four extra bits available for the addressing of memory, allowing up to 2^{36} bytes (64GiB) of memory to be addressed.

PAE allows a processor to address up to 64GiB in theory but, in practice, processes in Linux still cannot access that much RAM because, the virtual address space is still only 4GiB. This has led to some disappointment from users who have tried to `malloc()` all their RAM with one process.

Second, PAE does not allow the kernel itself to have this much RAM available. The `struct page` used to describe each page frame still requires 44 bytes, and this uses kernel virtual address space in ZONE_NORMAL. That means that to describe 1GiB of memory, approximately 11MiB of kernel memory is required. Thus, with 16GiB, 176MiB of memory is consumed, putting significant pressure on ZONE_NORMAL. This does not sound too bad until other structures are taken into account that use ZONE_NORMAL. Even very small structures, such as *Page Table Entries (PTEs)*, require about 16MiB in the worst case. This makes 16GiB about the practical limit for available physical memory of Linux on an x86. If more memory needs to be accessed, the advice given is simple and straightforward. Buy a 64-bit machine.

2.8   What's New in 2.6

Nodes   At first glance, there have not been many changes made to how memory is described, but the seemingly minor changes are wide reaching. The node descriptor pg_data_t has a few new fields that are as follows:

node_start_pfn replaces the node_start_paddr field. The only difference is that the new field is a PFN instead of a physical address. This was changed because PAE architectures can address more memory than 32 bits can address, so nodes starting over 4GiB would be unreachable with the old field.

kswapd_wait is a new wait queue for **kswapd**. In 2.4, there was a global wait queue for the page swapper daemon. In 2.6, there is one **kswapdN** for each node where N is the node identifier and each **kswapd** has its own wait queue with this field.

The node_size field has been removed and replaced instead with two fields. The change was introduced to recognize the fact that nodes may have holes in them where no physical memory is backing the address.

node_present_pages is the total number of physical pages that are present in the node.

node_spanned_pages is the total area that is addressed by the node, including any holes that may exist.

Zones   Even at first glance, zones look very different. They are no longer called zone_t, but instead are referred to as simply struct zone. The second major difference is the LRU lists. As we'll see in Chapter 10, kernel 2.4 has a global list of pages that determine the order pages are freed or paged out. These lists are now stored in the struct zone. The relevant fields are the following:

lru_lock is the spinlock for the LRU lists in this zone. In 2.4, this is a global lock called pagemap_lru_lock.

active_list is the active list for this zone. This list is the same as described in Chapter 10 except it is now per-zone instead of global.

inactive_list is the inactive list for this zone. In 2.4, it is global.

refill_counter is the number of pages to remove from the `active_list` in one pass and only of interest during page replacement.

nr_active is the number of pages on the `active_list`.

nr_inactive is the number of pages on the `inactive_list`.

all_unreclaimable field is set to 1 if the pageout daemon scans through all the pages in the zone twice and still fails to free enough pages.

pages_scanned is the number of pages scanned since the last bulk amount of pages has been reclaimed. In 2.6, lists of pages are freed at once rather than freeing pages individually, which is what 2.4 does.

pressure measures the scanning intensity for this zone. It is a decaying average that affects how hard a page scanner will work to reclaim pages.

Three other fields are new, but they are related to the dimensions of the zone. They are the following:

zone_start_pfn is the starting PFN of the zone. It replaces the `zone_start_paddr` and `zone_start_mapnr` fields in 2.4.

spanned_pages is the number of pages this zone spans, including holes in memory that exist with some architectures.

present_pages is the number of real pages that exist in the zone. For many architectures, this will be the same value as `spanned_pages`.

The next addition is `struct per_cpu_pageset`, which is used to maintain lists of pages for each CPU to reduce spinlock contention. The `zone→pageset` field is an NR_CPU-sized array of `struct per_cpu_pageset` where NR_CPU is the compiled upper limit of number of CPUs in the system. The per-cpu struct is discussed further at the end of the section.

The last addition to `struct zone` is the inclusion of padding of zeros in the struct. Development of the 2.6 VM recognized that some spinlocks are very heavily contended and are frequently acquired. Because it is known that some locks are almost always acquired in pairs, an effort should be made to ensure they use different cache lines, which is a common cache programming trick [Sea00]. This padding in the `struct zone` is marked with the `ZONE_PADDING()` macro and is used to ensure the `zone→lock`, `zone→lru_lock` and `zone→pageset` fields use different cache lines.

Pages The first noticeable change is that the ordering of fields has been changed so that related items are likely to be in the same cache line. The fields are essentially the same except for two additions. The first is a new union used to create a PTE chain. PTE chains are related to page table management, so will be discussed at the end of Chapter 3. The second addition is the `page→private` field, which contains private information specific to the mapping. For example, the field is used to store a pointer to a `buffer_head` if the page is a buffer page. This means that the `page→buffers` field has also been removed. The last important change is that `page→virtual` is no longer necessary for high memory support and will only exist if the architecture specifically requests it. How high memory pages are supported is discussed further in Chapter 9.

Per-CPU Page Lists   In 2.4, only one subsystem actively tries to maintain per-cpu lists for any object, and that is the Slab Allocator, which is discussed in Chapter 8. In 2.6, the concept is much more widespread, and there is a formalized concept of hot and cold pages.

The `struct per_cpu_pageset`, declared in `<linux/mmzone.h>`, has one field, which is an array with two elements of type `per_cpu_pages`. The zeroth element of this array is for hot pages, and the first element is for cold pages where hot and cold determines how active the page is currently in the cache. When it is known for a fact that the pages are not to be referenced soon, such as with I/O readahead, they will be allocated as cold pages.

The `struct per_cpu_pages` maintains a count of the number of pages currently in the list, a high and low watermark that determines when the set should be refilled or pages freed in bulk, a variable that determines how many pages should be allocated in one block and, finally, the actual list head of pages.

To build upon the per-cpu page lists, there is also a per-cpu page accounting mechanism. A `struct page_state` holds a number of accounting variables, such as the `pgalloc` field, which tracks the number of pages allocated to this CPU, and `pswpin`, which tracks the number of swap readins. The struct is heavily commented in `<linux/page-flags.h>`. A single function `mod_page_state()` is provided for updating fields in the `page_state` for the running CPU, and three helper macros are provided and are called `inc_page_state()`, `dec_page_state()` and `sub_page_state()`.

CHAPTER 3

Page Table Management

Linux layers the machine independent/dependent layer in an unusual manner in comparison to other operating systems [CP99]. Other operating systems have objects that manage the underlying physical pages, such as the `pmap` object in BSD. Linux instead maintains the concept of a three-level page table in the architecture-independent code even if the underlying architecture does not support it. Although this is conceptually easy to understand, it also means that the distinction between different types of pages is very blurry, and page types are identified by their flags or what lists they exist on rather than the objects they belong to.

Architectures that manage their *Memory Management Unit (MMU)* differently are expected to emulate the three-level page tables. For example, on the x86 without PAE enabled, only two page table levels are available. The *Page Middle Directory (PMD)* is defined to be of size 1 and "folds back" directly onto the *Page Global Directory (PGD)*, which is optimized out at compile time. Unfortunately, for architectures that do not manage their cache or *Translation Lookaside Buffer (TLB)* automatically, hooks that are architecture dependent have to be explicitly left in the code for when the TLB and CPU caches need to be altered and flushed, even if they are null operations on some architectures like the x86. These hooks are discussed further in Section 3.8.

This chapter will begin by describing how the page table is arranged and what types are used to describe the three separate levels of the page table. Next is how a virtual address is broken up into its component parts for navigating the table. After this is covered, I discuss the lowest level entry, the *PTE*, and what bits are used by the hardware. After that, the macros used for navigating a page table and setting and checking attributes will be discussed before talking about how the page table is populated and how pages are allocated and freed for the use with page tables. The initialization stage is then discussed, which shows how the page tables are initialized during boot strapping. Finally, I cover how the TLB and CPU caches are utilized.

3.1 Describing the Page Directory

Each process is a pointer (`mm_struct→pgd`) to its own *PGD* which is a physical page frame. This frame contains an array of type `pgd_t`, which is an architecture-specific type defined in `<asm/page.h>`. The page tables are loaded differently

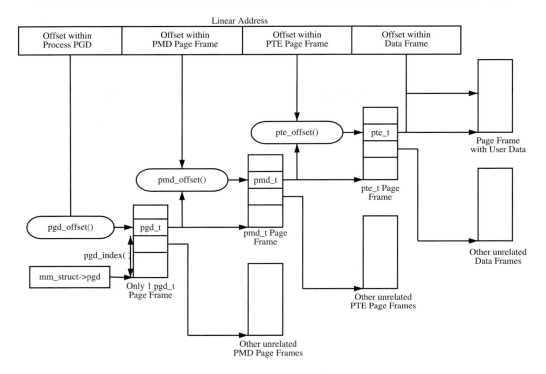

Figure 3.1. Page Table Layout

depending on the architecture. On the x86, the process page table is loaded by copying mm_struct→pgd into the cr3 register, which has the side effect of flushing the TLB. In fact, this is how the function __flush_tlb() is implemented in the architecture-dependent code.

Each active entry in the PGD table points to a page frame containing an array of *PMD* entries of type pmd_t, which in turn points to page frames containing *PTEs* of type pte_t, which finally point to page frames containing the actual user data. In the event that the page has been swapped out to backing storage, the swap entry is stored in the PTE and used by do_swap_page() during page fault to find the swap entry containing the page data. The page table layout is illustrated in Figure 3.1.

Any given linear address may be broken up into parts to yield offsets within these three page table levels and an offset within the actual page. To help break up the linear address into its component parts, a number of macros are provided in triplets for each page table level, namely a SHIFT, a SIZE and a MASK macro. The SHIFT macros specify the length in bits that are mapped by each level of the page tables as illustrated in Figure 3.2.

The MASK values can be ANDd with a linear address to mask out all the upper bits and are frequently used to determine if a linear address is aligned to a given level within the page table. The SIZE macros reveal how many bytes are addressed

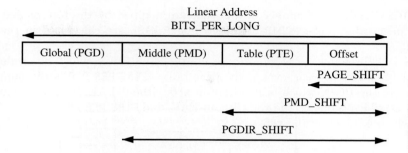

Figure 3.2. Linear Address Bit Size Macros

by each entry at each level. The relationship between the `SIZE` and `MASK` macros is illustrated in Figure 3.3.

For the calculation of each of the triplets, only `SHIFT` is important because the other two are calculated based on it. For example, the three macros for page level on the x86 are:

```
5 #define PAGE_SHIFT        12
6 #define PAGE_SIZE         (1UL << PAGE_SHIFT)
7 #define PAGE_MASK         (~(PAGE_SIZE-1))
```

`PAGE_SHIFT` is the length in bits of the offset part of the linear address space, which is 12 bits on the x86. The size of a page is easily calculated as 2^{PAGE_SHIFT} which is the equivalent of the previous code. Finally, the mask is calculated as the negation of the bits that make up the `PAGE_SIZE - 1`. If a page needs to be aligned on a page boundary, `PAGE_ALIGN()` is used. This macro adds `PAGE_SIZE - 1` to the address before simply ANDing it with the `PAGE_MASK` to zero out the page offset bits.

`PMD_SHIFT` is the number of bits in the linear address that are mapped by the second-level part of the table. The `PMD_SIZE` and `PMD_MASK` are calculated in a similar way to the page-level macros.

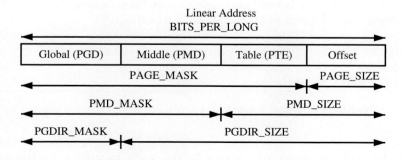

Figure 3.3. Linear Address Size and Mask Macros

PGDIR_SHIFT is the number of bits that are mapped by the top, or first level, of the page table. The PGDIR_SIZE and PGDIR_MASK are calculated in the same manner.

The last three macros of importance are the PTRS_PER_x, which determines the number of entries in each level of the page table. PTRS_PER_PGD is the number of pointers in the PGD, which is 1,024 on an x86 without PAE. PTRS_PER_PMD is for the PMD, which is one on the x86 without PAE, and PTRS_PER_PTE is for the lowest level, which is 1,024 on the x86.

3.2   Describing a Page Table Entry

As mentioned, each entry is described by the structs pte_t, pmd_t and pgd_t for PTEs, PMDs and PGDs respectively. Even though these are often just unsigned integers, they are defined as structs for two reasons. The first is for type protection so that they will not be used inappropriately. The second is for features like PAE on the x86 where an additional 4 bits is used for addressing more than 4GiB of memory. To store the protection bits, pgprot_t is defined, which holds the relevant flags and is usually stored in the lower bits of a page table entry.

For type casting, four macros are provided in asm/page.h, which takes the previous types and returns the relevant part of the structs. They are pte_val(), pmd_val(), pgd_val() and pgprot_val(). To reverse the type casting, four more macros are provided: __pte(), __pmd(), __pgd() and __pgprot().

Where exactly the protection bits are stored is architecture dependent. For illustration purposes, we will examine the case of an x86 architecture without PAE enabled, but the same principles apply across architectures. On an x86 without PAE, the pte_t is simply a 32-bit integer within a struct. Each pte_t points to an address of a page frame, and all the addresses pointed to are guaranteed to be page aligned. Therefore, there are PAGE_SHIFT (12) bits in that 32-bit value that are free for status bits of the page table entry. A number of the protection and status bits are listed in Table 3.1, but what bits exist and what they mean varies between architectures.

Bit	Function
_PAGE_PRESENT	Page is resident in memory and not swapped out.
_PAGE_PROTNONE	Page is resident, but not accessible.
_PAGE_RW	Set if the page may be written to
_PAGE_USER	Set if the page is accessible from userspace
_PAGE_DIRTY	Set if the page is written to
_PAGE_ACCESSED	Set if the page is accessed

Table 3.1. Page Table Entry Protection and Status Bits

These bits are self-explanatory except for the _PAGE_PROTNONE, which I will discuss further. On the x86 with Pentium III and higher, this bit is called the *Page*

Attribute Table (PAT) while earlier architectures such as the Pentium II had this bit reserved. The PAT bit is used to indicate the size of the page that the PTE is referencing. In a PGD entry, this same bit is instead called the *Page Size Extension (PSE)* bit, so obviously these bits are meant to be used in conjunction.

Because Linux does not use the PSE bit for user pages, the PAT bit is free in the PTE for other purposes. There is a requirement for having a page resident in memory, but inaccessible to the user space process, such as when a region is protected with `mprotect()` with the `PROT_NONE` flag. When the region is to be protected, the `_PAGE_PRESENT` bit is cleared, and the `_PAGE_PROTNONE` bit is set. The macro `pte_present()` checks if either of these bits are set, so the kernel itself knows the PTE is present. It is just inaccessible to *userspace*, which is a subtle, but important, point. Because the hardware bit `_PAGE_PRESENT` is clear, a page fault will occur if the page is accessed so that Linux can enforce the protection while still knowing the page is resident if it needs to swap it out or the process exits.

3.3   Using Page Table Entries

Macros are defined in `<asm/pgtable.h>`, which is important for the navigation and examination of page table entries. To navigate the page directories, three macros are provided that break up a linear address space into its component parts. `pgd_offset()` takes an address and the `mm_struct` for the process and returns the PGD entry that covers the requested address. `pmd_offset()` takes a PGD entry and an address and returns the relevant PMD. `pte_offset()` takes a PMD and returns the relevant PTE. The remainder of the linear address provided is the offset within the page. The relationship between these fields is illustrated in Figure 3.1.

The second round of macros determine if the page table entries are present or may be used.

- `pte_none()`, `pmd_none()` and `pgd_none()` return 1 if the corresponding entry does not exist.

- `pte_present()`, `pmd_present()` and `pgd_present()` return 1 if the corresponding page table entries have the `PRESENT` bit set.

- `pte_clear()`, `pmd_clear()` and `pgd_clear()` will clear the corresponding page table entry.

- `pmd_bad()` and `pgd_bad()` are used to check entries when passed as input parameters to functions that may change the value of the entries. Whether they return 1 varies between the few architectures that define these macros. However, for those that actually define it, making sure the page entry is marked as present and accessed are the two most important checks.

Many parts of the VM are littered with page table walk code, and it is important to recognize it. A very simple example of a page table walk is the function `follow_page()` in `mm/memory.c`. The following is an excerpt from that function. The parts unrelated to the page table walk are omitted.

```
407            pgd_t *pgd;
408            pmd_t *pmd;
409            pte_t *ptep, pte;
410
411            pgd = pgd_offset(mm, address);
412            if (pgd_none(*pgd) || pgd_bad(*pgd))
413                    goto out;
414
415            pmd = pmd_offset(pgd, address);
416            if (pmd_none(*pmd) || pmd_bad(*pmd))
417                    goto out;
418
419            ptep = pte_offset(pmd, address);
420            if (!ptep)
421                    goto out;
422
423            pte = *ptep;
```

It simply uses the three offset macros to navigate the page tables and the _none() and _bad() macros to make sure it is looking at a valid page table.

The third set of macros examine and set the permissions of an entry. The permissions determine what a userspace process can and cannot do with a particular page. For example, the kernel page table entries are never readable by a userspace process.

- The read permissions for an entry are tested with pte_read(), set with pte_mkread() and cleared with pte_rdprotect().

- The write permissions are tested with pte_write(), set with pte_mkwrite() and cleared with pte_wrprotect().

- The execute permissions are tested with pte_exec(), set with pte_mkexec() and cleared with pte_exprotect(). It is worth noting that, with the x86 architecture, there is no means of setting execute permissions on pages, so these three macros act the same way as the read macros.

- The permissions can be modified to a new value with pte_modify(), but its use is almost nonexistent. It is only used in the function change_pte_range() in mm/mprotect.c.

The fourth set of macros examine and set the state of an entry. There are only two bits that are important in Linux, the dirty bit and the accessed bit. To check these bits, the macros pte_dirty() and pte_young() are used. To set the bits, the macros pte_mkdirty() and pte_mkyoung() are used. To clear them, the macros pte_mkclean() and pte_old() are available.

3.4   Translating and Setting Page Table Entries

This set of functions and macros deal with the mapping of addresses and pages to PTEs and the setting of the individual entries.

The macro `mk_pte()` takes a `struct page` and protection bits and combines them together to form the `pte_t` that needs to be inserted into the page table. A similar macro `mk_pte_phys()` exists, which takes a physical page address as a parameter.

The macro `pte_page()` returns the `struct page`, which corresponds to the PTE entry.   `pmd_page()` returns the `struct page` containing the set of PTEs.

The macro `set_pte()` takes a `pte_t` such as that returned by `mk_pte()` and places it within the process's page table. `pte_clear()` is the reverse operation. An additional function is provided called `ptep_get_and_clear()`, which clears an entry from the process page table and returns the `pte_t`. This is important when some modification needs to be made to either the PTE protection or the `struct page` itself.

3.5   Allocating and Freeing Page Tables

The last set of functions deal with the allocation and freeing of page tables. Page tables, as stated, are physical pages containing an array of entries, and the allocation and freeing of physical pages is a relatively expensive operation, both in terms of time and the fact that interrupts are disabled during page allocation. The allocation and deletion of page tables, at any of the three levels, is a very frequent operation, so it is important the operation is as quick as possible.

Hence the pages used for the page tables are cached in a number of different lists called *quicklists*. Each architecture implements these caches differently, but the principles used are the same. For example, not all architectures cache PGDs because the allocation and freeing of them only happens during process creation and exit. Because both of these are very expensive operations, the allocation of another page is negligible.

PGDs, PMDs and PTEs have two sets of functions each for the allocation and freeing of page tables. The allocation functions are `pgd_alloc()`, `pmd_alloc()` and `pte_alloc()`, respectively, and the free functions are, predictably enough, called `pgd_free()`, `pmd_free()` and `pte_free()`.

Broadly speaking, the three implement caching with the use of three caches called `pgd_quicklist`, `pmd_quicklist` and `pte_quicklist`. Architectures implement these three lists in different ways, but one method is through the use of a Last In, First Out (LIFO) type structure. Ordinarily, a page table entry contains pointers to other pages containing page tables or data. While cached, the first element of the list is used to point to the next free page table. During allocation, one page is popped off the list, and, during free, one is placed as the new head of the list. A count is kept of how many pages are used in the cache.

The quick allocation function from the `pgd_quicklist` is not externally defined outside of the architecture, although `get_pgd_fast()` is a common choice for the function name. The cached allocation function for PMDs and PTEs are publicly defined as `pmd_alloc_one_fast()` and `pte_alloc_one_fast()`.

If a page is not available from the cache, a page will be allocated using the physical page allocator (see Chapter 6). The functions for the three levels of page tables are `get_pgd_slow()`, `pmd_alloc_one()` and `pte_alloc_one()`.

Obviously, a large number of pages may exist on these caches, so a mechanism is in place for pruning them. Each time the caches grow or shrink, a counter is incremented or decremented, and it has a high and low watermark. `check_pgt_cache()` is called in two places to check these watermarks. When the high watermark is reached, entries from the cache will be freed until the cache size returns to the low watermark. The function is called after `clear_page_tables()` when a large number of page tables are potentially reached and is also called by the system idle task.

3.6   Kernel Page Tables

When the system first starts, paging is not enabled because page tables do not magically initialize themselves. Each architecture implements this differently so only the x86 case will be discussed. The page table initialization is divided into two phases. The bootstrap phase sets up page tables for just 8MiB so that the paging unit can be enabled. The second phase initializes the rest of the page tables. We discuss both of these phases in the following sections.

3.6.1   Bootstrapping

The assembler function `startup_32()` is responsible for enabling the paging unit in `arch/i386/kernel/head.S`. While all normal kernel code in `vmlinuz` is compiled with the base address at `PAGE_OFFSET + 1MiB`, the kernel is actually loaded beginning at the first megabyte (0x00100000) of memory. The first megabyte is used by some devices for communication with the BIOS and is skipped. The bootstrap code in this file treats 1MiB as its base address by subtracting `__PAGE_OFFSET` from any address until the paging unit is enabled. Therefore before the paging unit is enabled, a page table mapping has to be established that translates the 8MiB of physical memory to the virtual address `PAGE_OFFSET`.

Initialization begins at compile time with statically defining an array called `swapper_pg_dir`, which is placed using linker directives at 0x00101000. It then establishes page table entries for two pages, `pg0` and `pg1`. If the processor supports the *Page Size Extension (PSE)* bit, it will be set so that pages that will be translated are 4MiB pages, not 4KiB as is the normal case. The first pointers to `pg0` and `pg1` are placed to cover the region `1-9MiB`; the second pointers to `pg0` and `pg1` are placed at `PAGE_OFFSET+1MiB`. This means that, when paging is enabled, they will map to the correct pages using either physical or virtual addressing for just the kernel image. The rest of the kernel page tables will be initialized by `paging_init()`.

After this mapping has been established, the paging unit is turned on by setting a bit in the `cr0` register, and a jump takes places immediately to ensure the *Instruction Pointer (EIP register)* is correct.

3.6.2 Finalizing

The function responsible for finalizing the page tables is called `paging_init()`. The call graph for this function on the x86 can be seen on Figure 3.4.

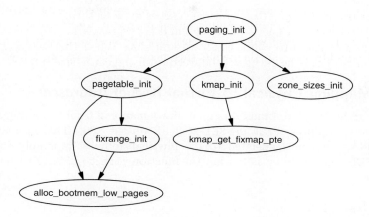

Figure 3.4. Call Graph: `paging_init()`

The function first calls `pagetable_init()` to initialize the page tables necessary to reference all physical memory in `ZONE_DMA` and `ZONE_NORMAL`. Remember that high memory in `ZONE_HIGHMEM` cannot be directly referenced and that mappings are set up for it temporarily. For each `pgd_t` used by the kernel, the boot memory allocator (see Chapter 5) is called to allocate a page for the PGD, and the PSE bit will be set if available to use 4MiB TLB entries instead of 4KiB. If the PSE bit is not supported, a page for PTEs will be allocated for each `pmd_t`. If the CPU supports the PGE flag, it also will be set so that the page table entry will be global and visible to all processes.

Next, `pagetable_init()` calls `fixrange_init()` to set up the fixed address space mappings at the end of the virtual address space starting at `FIXADDR_START`. These mappings are used for purposes such as the local *Advanced Programmable Interrupt Controller (APIC)* and the atomic kmappings between `FIX_KMAP_BEGIN` and `FIX_KMAP_END` required by `kmap_atomic()`. Finally, the function calls `fixrange_init()` to initialize the page table entries required for normal high memory mappings with `kmap()`.

After `pagetable_init()` returns, the page tables for kernel space are now fully initialized, so the static PGD (`swapper_pg_dir`) is loaded into the CR3 register so that the static table is now being used by the paging unit.

The next task of the `paging_init()` is responsible for calling `kmap_init()` to initialize each of the PTEs with the `PAGE_KERNEL` protection flags. The final task is to call `zone_sizes_init()`, which initializes all the zone structures used.

3.7   Mapping Addresses to a struct page

There is a requirement for Linux to have a fast method of mapping virtual addresses to physical addresses and for mapping `struct pages` to their physical address. Linux achieves this by knowing where, in both virtual and physical memory, the global `mem_map` array is because the global array has pointers to all `struct pages` representing physical memory in the system. All architectures achieve this with very similar mechanisms, but, for illustration purposes, we will only examine the x86 carefully. This section will first discuss how physical addresses are mapped to kernel virtual addresses and then what this means to the `mem_map` array.

3.7.1   Mapping Physical to Virtual Kernel Addresses

As we saw in Section 3.6, Linux sets up a direct mapping from the physical address 0 to the virtual address `PAGE_OFFSET` at 3GiB on the x86. This means that any virtual address can be translated to the physical address by simply subtracting `PAGE_OFFSET`, which is essentially what the function `virt_to_phys()` with the macro `__pa()` does:

```
/* from <asm-i386/page.h> */
132 #define __pa(x)                    ((unsigned long)(x)-PAGE_OFFSET)

/* from <asm-i386/io.h> */
 76 static inline unsigned long virt_to_phys(volatile void * address)
 77 {
 78         return __pa(address);
 79 }
```

Obviously, the reverse operation involves simply adding `PAGE_OFFSET`, which is carried out by the function `phys_to_virt()` with the macro `__va()`. Next we see how this helps the mapping of `struct pages` to physical addresses.

There is one exception where `virt_to_phys()` cannot be used to convert virtual addresses to physical ones.[1] Specifically, on the PPC and ARM architectures, `virt_to_phys()` cannot be used to convert addresses that have been returned by the function `consistent_alloc()`. `consistent_alloc()` is used on PPC and ARM architectures to return memory from non-cached for use with DMA.

3.7.2   Mapping struct pages to Physical Addresses

As we saw in Section 3.6.1, the kernel image is located at the physical address 1MiB, which of course translates to the virtual address `PAGE_OFFSET + 0x00100000`, and a virtual region totaling about 8MiB is reserved for the image, which is the region that can be addressed by two PGDs. This would imply that the first available memory to use is located at `0xC0800000`, but that is not the case. Linux tries to reserve the first 16MiB of memory for `ZONE_DMA`, so the first virtual area used

---

[1]This tricky issue was pointed out to me by Jeffrey Haran.

for kernel allocations is actually 0xC1000000. This is where the global mem_map is usually located. ZONE_DMA will still get used, but only when absolutely necessary.

Physical addresses are translated to struct pages by treating them as an index into the mem_map array. Shifting physical address PAGE_SHIFT bits to the right will treat them as a *Page Frame Number (PFN)* from physical address 0, which is *also* an index within the mem_map array. This is exactly what the macro virt_to_page() does, which is declared as follows in <asm-i386/page.h>:

```
#define virt_to_page(kaddr) (mem_map + (__pa(kaddr) >> PAGE_SHIFT))
```

The macro virt_to_page() takes the virtual address kaddr, converts it to the physical address with __pa(), converts it into an array index by bit shifting PAGE_SHIFT bits right and indexing into the mem_map by simply adding them together. No macro is available for converting struct pages to physical addresses, but, at this stage, you should see how it could be calculated.

3.8 Translation Lookaside Buffer (TLB)

Initially, when the processor needs to map a virtual address to a physical address, it must traverse the full page directory searching for the PTE of interest. This would normally imply that each assembly instruction that references memory actually requires several separate memory references for the page table traversal [Tan01]. To avoid this considerable overhead, architectures take advantage of the fact that most processes exhibit a locality of reference, or, in other words, large numbers of memory references tend to be for a small number of pages. They take advantage of this reference locality by providing a *Translation Lookaside Buffer (TLB)*, which is a small associative memory that caches virtual to physical page table resolutions.

Linux assumes that most architectures support some type of TLB, although the architecture-independent code does not care how it works. Instead, architecture-dependent hooks are dispersed throughout the VM code at points where it is known that some hardware with a TLB would need to perform a TLB-related operation. For example, when the page tables have been updated, such as after a page fault has completed, the processor may need to update the TLB for that virtual address mapping.

Not all architectures require these type of operations, but, because some do, the hooks have to exist. If the architecture does not require the operation to be performed, the function for that TLB operation will be a null operation that is optimized out at compile time.

A quite large list of TLB API hooks, most of which are declared in <asm/pgtable.h>, are listed in Tables 3.2 and 3.3, and the APIs are quite well documented in the kernel source by Documentation/cachetlb.txt [Mil00]. It is possible to have just one TLB flush function, but, because both TLB flushes and TLB refills are *very* expensive operations, unnecessary TLB flushes should be avoided if at all possible. For example, when context switching, Linux will avoid loading new page tables using *Lazy TLB Flushing*, discussed further in Section 4.3.

---

void flush_tlb_all(void)

   This flushes the entire TLB on all processors running in the system, which makes it the most expensive TLB flush operation. After it completes, all modifications to the page tables will be visible globally. This is required after the kernel page tables, which are global in nature, have been modified, such as after vfree() (see Chapter 7) completes or after the PKMap is flushed (see Chapter 9).

void flush_tlb_mm(struct mm_struct *mm)

   This flushes all TLB entries related to the userspace portion (i.e., below PAGE_OFFSET) for the requested mm context. In some architectures, such as MIPS, this will need to be performed for all processors, but usually it is confined to the local processor. This is only called when an operation has been performed that affects the entire address space, such as after all the address mapping has been duplicated with dup_mmap() for fork or after all memory mappings have been deleted with exit_mmap().

void flush_tlb_range(struct mm_struct *mm, unsigned long start, unsigned long end)

   As the name indicates, this flushes all entries within the requested user space range for the mm context. This is used after a new region has been moved or changed as during mremap(), which moves regions, or mprotect(), which changes the permissions. The function is also indirectly used during unmapping a region with munmap(), which calls tlb_finish_mmu(), which tries to use flush_tlb_range() intelligently. This API is provided for architectures that can remove ranges of TLB entries quickly rather than iterating with flush_tlb_page().

Table 3.2. Translation Lookaside Buffer Flush API

3.9   Level 1 CPU Cache Management

Because Linux manages the CPU cache in a very similar fashion to the TLB, this section covers how Linux uses and manages the CPU cache. CPU caches, like TLB caches, take advantage of the fact that programs tend to exhibit a locality of reference [Sea00] [CS98]. To avoid having to fetch data from main memory for each reference, the CPU will instead cache very small amounts of data in the CPU cache. Frequently, there are two levels called the Level 1 and Level 2 CPU caches. The Level 2 CPU caches are larger, but slower than the L1 cache, but Linux only concerns itself with the Level 1 or L1 cache.

   CPU caches are organized into *lines*. Each line is typically quite small, usually 32 bytes, and each line is aligned to its boundary size. In other words, a cache line of 32 bytes will be aligned on a 32-byte address. With Linux, the size of the line is L1_CACHE_BYTES, which is defined by each architecture.

   How addresses are mapped to cache lines vary between architectures, but the mappings come under three headings, *direct mapping*, *associative mapping* and *set*

```
void flush_tlb_page(struct vm_area_struct *vma, unsigned long addr)
```
Predictably, this API is responsible for flushing a single page from the TLB. The two most common uses of it are for flushing the TLB after a page has been faulted in or has been paged out.

```
void flush_tlb_pgtables(struct mm_struct *mm, unsigned long start,
unsigned long end)
```
This API is called when the page tables are being torn down and freed. Some platforms cache the lowest level of the page table, i.e., the actual page frame storing entries, which needs to be flushed when the pages are being deleted. This is called when a region is being unmapped and the page directory entries are being reclaimed.

```
void update_mmu_cache(struct vm_area_struct *vma, unsigned long
addr, pte_t pte)
```
This API is only called after a page fault completes. It tells the architecture-dependent code that a new translation now exists at `pte` for the virtual address `addr`. Each architecture decides how this information should be used. For example, Sparc64 uses the information to decide if the local CPU needs to flush its data cache or does it need to send an Inter Processor Interrupt (IPI) to a remote processor.

Table 3.3. Translation Lookaside Buffer Flush API (cont.)

associative mapping. Direct mapping is the simplest approach where each block of memory maps to only one possible cache line. With associative mapping, any block of memory can map to any cache line. Set associative mapping is a hybrid approach where any block of memory can map to any line, but only within a subset of the available lines. Regardless of the mapping scheme, they each have one thing in common. Addresses that are close together and aligned to the cache size are likely to use different lines. Hence Linux employs simple tricks to try and maximize cache use:

- Frequently accessed structure fields are at the start of the structure to increase the chance that only one line is needed to address the common fields.

- Unrelated items in a structure should try to be at least cache-size bytes in part to avoid false sharing between CPUs.

- Objects in the general caches, such as the `mm_struct` cache, are aligned to the L1 CPU cache to avoid false sharing.

If the CPU references an address that is not in the cache, a *cache miss* occurs, and the data is fetched from main memory. The cost of cache misses is quite high because a reference to a cache can typically be performed in less than 10ns where a reference to main memory typically will cost between 100ns and 200ns. The basic objective is then to have as many cache hits and as few cache misses as possible.

Just as some architectures do not automatically manage their TLBs, some do not automatically manage their CPU caches. The hooks are placed in locations where the virtual to physical mapping changes, such as during a page table update. The CPU cache flushes should always take place first because some CPUs require a virtual to physical mapping to exist when the virtual address is being flushed from the cache. The three operations that require proper ordering are important and are listed in Table 3.4.

Flushing Full MM	Flushing Range	Flushing Page
flush_cache_mm()	flush_cache_range()	flush_cache_page()
Change all page tables	Change page table range	Change single PTE
flush_tlb_mm()	flush_tlb_range()	flush_tlb_page()

Table 3.4. Cache and TLB Flush Ordering

The API used for flushing the caches is declared in <asm/pgtable.h> and is listed in Table 3.5. In many respects, it is very similar to the TLB flushing API.

---

void flush_cache_all(void)
    This flushes the entire CPU cache system, which makes it the most severe flush operation to use. It is used when changes to the kernel page tables, which are global in nature, are to be performed.

void flush_cache_mm(struct mm_struct mm)
    This flushes all entries related to the address space. On completion, no cache lines will be associated with mm.

void flush_cache_range(struct mm_struct *mm, unsigned long start, unsigned long end)
    This flushes lines related to a range of addresses in the address space. Like its TLB equivalent, it is provided in case the architecture has an efficient way of flushing ranges instead of flushing each individual page.

void flush_cache_page(struct vm_area_struct *vma, unsigned long vmaddr)
    This is for flushing a single-page-sized region. The VMA is supplied because the mm_struct is easily accessible through vma→vm_mm. Additionally, by testing for the VM_EXEC flag, the architecture will know if the region is executable for caches that separate the instructions and data caches. VMAs are described further in Chapter 4.

Table 3.5. CPU Cache Flush API

It does not end there, though. A second set of interfaces is required to avoid virtual aliasing problems. The problem is that some CPUs select lines based on the virtual address, which means that one physical address can exist on multiple lines leading to cache coherency problems. Architectures with this problem may try and ensure that shared mappings will only use addresses as a stop-gap measure. However, a proper API to address this problem is also supplied, which is listed in Table 3.6.

---

void flush_page_to_ram(unsigned long address)
   This is a deprecated API that should no longer be used and, in fact, will be removed totally for 2.6. It is covered here for completeness and because it is still used. The function is called when a new physical page is about to be placed in the address space of a process. It is required to avoid writes from kernel space being invisible to userspace after the mapping occurs.

void flush_dcache_page(struct page *page)
   This function is called when the kernel writes to or copies from a page cache page because these are likely to be mapped by multiple processes.

void flush_icache_range(unsigned long address, unsigned long endaddr)
   This is called when the kernel stores information in addresses that is likely to be executed, such as when a kernel module has been loaded.

void flush_icache_user_range(struct vm_area_struct *vma, struct page *page, unsigned long addr, int len)
   This is similar to flush_icache_range() except it is called when a userspace range is affected. Currently, this is only used for ptrace() (used when debugging) when the address space is being accessed by access_process_vm().

void flush_icache_page(struct vm_area_struct *vma, struct page *page)
   This is called when a page-cache page is about to be mapped. It is up to the architecture to use the VMA flags to determine whether the I-Cache or D-Cache should be flushed.

Table 3.6. CPU D-Cache and I-Cache Flush API

3.10   What's New in 2.6

Most of the mechanics for page table management are essentially the same for 2.6, but the changes that have been introduced are quite wide reaching and the implementations are in depth.

MMU-less Architecture Support   A new file has been introduced called mm/nommu.c. This source file contains replacement code for functions that assume the existence of a MMU, like mmap() for example. This is to support architectures, usually microcontrollers, that have no MMU. Much of the work in this area was developed by the uCLinux Project (*www.uclinux.org*).

Reverse Mapping The most significant and important change to page table management is the introduction of *Reverse Mapping (rmap)*. Referring to it as "rmap" is
deliberate because it is the common use of the acronym and should not be confused
with the -rmap tree developed by Rik van Riel, which has many more alterations
to the stock VM than just the reverse mapping.

In a single sentence, rmap grants the ability to locate all PTEs that map a
particular page given just the `struct page`. In 2.4, the only way to find all PTEs
that mapped a shared page, such as a memory mapped shared library, is to linearly
search all page tables belonging to all processes. This is far too expensive, and
Linux tries to avoid the problem by using the swap cache (see Section 11.4). This
means that, with many shared pages, Linux may have to swap out entire processes
regardless of the page age and usage patterns. 2.6 instead has a *PTE chain* associated with every `struct page`, which may be traversed to remove a page from all
page tables that reference it. This way, pages in the LRU can be swapped out in
an intelligent manner without resorting to swapping entire processes.

As might be imagined by the reader, the implementation of this simple concept is a little involved. The first step in understanding the implementation is the
`union pte` that is a field in `struct page`. This union has two fields, a pointer
to a `struct pte_chain` called `chain` and a `pte_addr_t` called `direct`. The union
is an optpization whereby `direct` is used to save memory if there is only one PTE
mapping the entry. Otherwise, a chain is used. The type `pte_addr_t` varies between
architectures, but, whatever its type, it can be used to locate a PTE, so we will
treat it as a `pte_t` for simplicity.

The `struct pte_chain` is a little more complex. The struct itself is very simple, but it is *compact* with overloaded fields, and a lot of development effort has
been spent on making it small and efficient. Fortunately, this does not make it
indecipherable.

First, it is the responsibility of the slab allocator to allocate and manage
`struct pte_chains` because it is this type of task that the slab allocator is best at.
Each `struct pte_chain` can hold up to `NRPTE` pointers to PTE structures. After
that many PTEs have been filled, a `struct pte_chain` is allocated and added to
the chain.

The `struct pte_chain` has two fields. The first is `unsigned long`
`next_and_idx`, which has two purposes. When `next_and_idx` is ANDed with `NRPTE`,
it returns the number of PTEs currently in this `struct pte_chain` and indicates
where the next free slot is. When `next_and_idx` is ANDed with the negation of
`NRPTE` (i.e., $\sim$`NRPTE`), a pointer to the next `struct pte_chain` in the chain is returned[2]. This is basically how a PTE chain is implemented.

To give you a taste of the rmap intricacies, I'll give an example of what happens
when a new PTE needs to map a page. The basic process is to have the caller
allocate a new `pte_chain` with `pte_chain_alloc()`. This allocated chain is passed
with the `struct page` and the PTE to `page_add_rmap()`. If the existing PTE
chain associated with the page has slots available, it will be used, and the `pte_chain`

---

[2]I told you it was compact.

allocated by the caller is returned. If no slots were available, the allocated `pte_chain` will be added to the chain, and NULL returned.

There is a quite substantial API associated with rmap for tasks such as creating chains and adding and removing PTEs to a chain, but a full listing is beyond the scope of this section. Fortunately, the API is confined to `mm/rmap.c`, and the functions are heavily commented so that their purpose is clear.

There are two main benefits, both related to pageout, with the introduction of reverse mapping. The first is with the set up and tear down of page tables. As will be seen in Section 11.4, pages being paged out are placed in a swap cache, and information is written into the PTE that is necessary to find the page again. This can lead to multiple minor faults because pages are put into the swap cache and then faulted again by a process. With rmap, the setup and removal of PTEs is atomic. The second major benefit is when pages need to paged out, finding all PTEs referencing the pages is a simple operation, but impractical with 2.4, hence the swap cache.

Reverse mapping is not without its cost, though. The first, and obvious one, is the additional space requirements for the PTE chains. Arguably, the second is a CPU cost associated with reverse mapping, but it has not been proved to be significant. What is important to note, though, is that reverse mapping is only a benefit when pageouts are frequent. If the machines workload does not result in much pageout or memory is ample, reverse mapping is all cost with little or no benefit. At the time of writing, the merits and downsides to rmap are still the subject of a number of discussions.

Object-Based Reverse Mapping   The reverse mapping required for each page can have very expensive space requirements. To compound the problem, many of the reverse mapped pages in a VMA will be essentially identical. One way of addressing this is to reverse map based on the VMAs rather than individual pages. That is, instead of having a reverse mapping for each page, all the VMAs that map a particular page would be traversed and unmap the page from each. Note that objects in this case refer to the VMAs, not an object in the object-orientated sense of the word[3]. At the time of writing, this feature has not been merged yet and was last seen in kernel 2.5.68-mm1, but a strong incentive exists to have it available if the problems with it can be resolved. For the very curious, the patch for just file/device backed objrmap at this release is available[4], but it is only for the very very curious reader.

Two tasks require all PTEs that map a page to be traversed. The first task is `page_referenced()`, which checks all PTEs that map a page to see if the page has been referenced recently. The second task is when a page needs to be unmapped from all processes with `try_to_unmap()`. To complicate matters further, two types of mappings must be reverse mapped, those that are backed by a file or device and those that are anonymous. In both cases, the basic objective is to traverse all

---

[3]Don't blame me, I didn't name it. In fact, the original patch for this feature came with the comment "From Dave. Crappy name."

[4]*ftp://ftp.kernel.org/pub/linux/kernel/people/akpm/patches/2.5/2.5.68/2.5.68-mm2/experimental*

VMAs that map a particular page and then walk the page table for that VMA to get the PTE. The only difference is how it is implemented. The case where it is backed by some sort of file is the easiest case and was implemented first so I'll deal with it first. For the purposes of illustrating the implementation, I'll discuss how `page_referenced()` is implemented.

`page_referenced()` calls `page_referenced_obj()`, which is the top-level function for finding all PTEs within VMAs that map the page. As the page is mapped for a file or device, page→mapping contains a pointer to a valid `address_space`. The `address_space` has two linked lists that contain all VMAs that use the mapping with the address_space→i_mmap and address_space→i_mmap_shared fields. For every VMA that is on these linked lists, `page_referenced_obj_one()` is called with the VMA and the page as parameters. The function `page_referenced_obj_one()` first checks if the page is in an address managed by this VMA and, if so, traverses the page tables of the `mm_struct` using the VMA (vma→vm_mm) until it finds the PTE mapping the page for that `mm_struct`.

Anonymous page tracking is a lot trickier and was implented in a number of stages. It only made a very brief appearance and was removed again in 2.5.65-mm4 because it conflicted with a number of other changes. The first stage in the implementation was to use page→mapping and page→index fields to track `mm_struct` and `address` pairs. These fields previously had been used to store a pointer to `swapper_space` and a pointer to the `swp_entry_t` (See Chapter 11). Exactly how it is addressed is beyond the scope of this section, but the summary is that `swp_entry_t` is stored in page→private.

`try_to_unmap_obj()` works in a similar fashion, but, obviously, all the PTEs that reference a page with this method can do so without needing to reverse map the individual pages. A serious search complexity problem prevents it from being merged. The scenario that describes the problem is as follows.

Take a case where 100 processes have 100 VMAs mapping a single file. To unmap a *single* page in this case with object-based reverse mapping would require 10,000 VMAs to be searched, most of which are totally unnecessary. With page-based reverse mapping, only 100 `pte_chain` slots need to be examined, one for each process. An optimization was introduced to order VMAs in the `address_space` by virtual address, but the search for a single page is still far too expensive for object-based reverse mapping to be merged.

PTEs in High Memory   In 2.4, page table entries exist in ZONE_NORMAL because the kernel needs to be able to address them directly during a page table walk. This was acceptable until it was found that, with high memory machines, ZONE_NORMAL was being consumed by the third-level page table PTEs. The obvious answer is to move PTEs to high memory, which is exactly what 2.6 does.

As we will see in Chapter 9, addressing information in high memory is far from free, so moving PTEs to high memory is a compile-time configuration option. In short, the problem is that the kernel must map pages from high memory into the lower address space before it can be used but a very limited number of slots are available for these mappings, which introduces a troublesome bottleneck. However, for applications with a large number of PTEs, there is little other option. At the time of writing, a proposal has been made for having a User Kernel Virtual Area (UKVA), which would be a region in kernel space private to each process, but it is unclear if it will be merged for 2.6 or not.

To take the possibility of high memory mapping into account, the macro pte_offset() from 2.4 has been replaced with pte_offset_map() in 2.6. If PTEs are in low memory, this will behave the same as pte_offset() and return the address of the PTE. If the PTE is in high memory, it will first be mapped into low memory with kmap_atomic(), so it can be used by the kernel. This PTE must be unmapped as quickly as possible with pte_unmap().

In programming terms, this means that page table walk code looks slightly different. In particular, to find the PTE for a given address, the code now reads as (taken from mm/memory.c):

```
640        ptep = pte_offset_map(pmd, address);
641        if (!ptep)
642                goto out;
643
644        pte = *ptep;
645        pte_unmap(ptep);
```

Additionally, the PTE allocation API has changed. Instead of pte_alloc(), there is now a pte_alloc_kernel() for use with kernel PTE mappings and pte_alloc_map() for userspace mapping. The principal difference between them is that pte_alloc_kernel() will never use high memory for the PTE.

In memory management terms, the overhead of having to map the PTE from high memory should not be ignored. Only one PTE at a time may be mapped per CPU, although a second may be mapped with pte_offset_map_nested(). This introduces a penalty when all PTEs need to be examined, such as during zap_page_range() when all PTEs in a given range need to be unmapped.

At the time of writing, a patch has been submitted that places PMDs in high memory using essentially the same mechanism and API changes. It is likely that it will be merged.

Huge TLB Filesystem   Most modern architectures support more than one page size. For example, on many x86 architectures, there is an option to use 4KiB pages or 4MiB pages. Traditionally, Linux only used large pages for mapping the actual kernel image and nowhere else. Because TLB slots are a scarce resource, it is desirable to be able to take advantage of the large pages, especially on machines with large amounts of physical memory.

In 2.6, Linux allows processes to use huge pages, the size of which is determined by HPAGE_SIZE. The number of available huge pages is determined by the system administrator by using the /proc/sys/vm/nr_hugepages proc interface, which ultimately uses the function set_hugetlb_mem_size(). Because the success of the allocation depends on the availability of physically contiguous memory, the allocation should be made during system startup.

The root of the implementation is a *Huge TLB Filesystem (hugetlbfs)*, which is a pseudofilesystem implemented in fs/hugetlbfs/inode.c. Basically, each file in this filesystem is backed by a huge page. During initialization, `init_hugetlbfs_fs()` registers the file system and mounts it as an internal filesystem with `kern_mount()`.

There are two ways that huge pages may be accessed by a process. The first is by using `shmget()` to set up a shared region backed by huge pages, and the second is the call `mmap()` on a file opened in the huge page filesystem.

When a shared memory region should be backed by huge pages, the process should call `shmget()` and pass `SHM_HUGETLB` as one of the flags. This results in `hugetlb_zero_setup()` being called, which creates a new file in the root of the internal hugetlbfs. A file is created in the root of the internal filesystem. The name of the file is determined by an atomic counter called `hugetlbfs_counter`, which is incremented every time a shared region is set up.

To create a file backed by huge pages, a filesystem of type hugetlbfs must first be mounted by the system administrator. Instructions on how to perform this task are detailed in `Documentation/vm/hugetlbpage.txt`. After the filesystem is mounted, files can be created as normal with the system call `open()`. When `mmap()` is called on the open file, the `file_operations` struct `hugetlbfs_file_operations` ensures that `hugetlbfs_file_mmap()` is called to set up the region properly.

Huge TLB pages have their own function for the management of page tables, address space operations and filesystem operations. The names of the functions for page table management can all be seen in <linux/hugetlb.h>, and they are named very similar to their normal page equivalents. The implementation of the hugetlbfs functions are located near their normal page equivalents, so are easy to find.

Cache Flush Management   The changes here are minimal. The API function `flush_page_to_ram()` has been totally removed, and a new API `flush_dcache_range()` has been introduced.

CHAPTER 4

Process Address Space

One of the principal advantages of virtual memory is that each process has its own virtual address space, which is mapped to physical memory by the operating system. In this chapter I discuss the process address space and how Linux manages it.

The kernel treats the userspace portion of the address space very differently from the kernel portion. For example, allocations for the kernel are satisfied immediately and are visible globally no matter what process is on the CPU. `vmalloc()` is an exception because a minor page fault will occur to sync the process page tables with the reference page tables, but the page will still be allocated immediately upon request. With a process, space is simply reserved in the linear address space by pointing a page table entry to a read-only globally visible page filled with zeros. On writing, a page fault is triggered, which results in a new page being allocated, filled with zeros, placed in the page table entry and marked writable. The new page is filled with zeros so that it will appear exactly the same as the global zero-filled page.

The userspace portion is not trusted or presumed to be constant. After each context switch, the userspace portion of the linear address space can potentially change except when a *Lazy TLB* switch is used as discussed later in Section 4.3. As a result of this, the kernel must be prepared to catch all exceptions and to address errors raised from the userspace. This is discussed in Section 4.5.

This chapter begins with how the linear address space is broken up and what the purpose of each section is. I then cover the structures maintained to describe each process, how they are allocated, initialized and then destroyed. Next, I cover how individual regions within the process space are created and all the various functions associated with them. That will bring us to exception handling related to the process address space, page faulting and the various cases that occur to satisfy a page fault. Finally, I cover how the kernel safely copies information to and from userspace.

4.1 Linear Address Space

From a user perspective, the address space is a flat linear address space, but, predictably, the kernel's perspective is very different. The address space is split into two parts: the userspace part, which potentially changes with each full context switch, and the kernel address space, which remains constant. The location of the

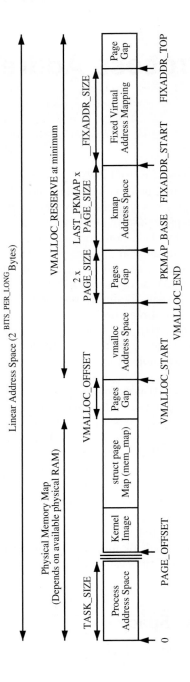

Figure 4.1. Kernel Address Space

split is determined by the value of `PAGE_OFFSET`, which is at `0xC0000000` on the x86. This means that 3GiB is available for the process to use while the remaining 1GiB is always mapped by the kernel. The linear virtual address space as the kernel sees it is illustrated in Figure 4.1.

To load the kernel image to run, 8MiB (the amount of memory addressed by two PGDs) is reserved at `PAGE_OFFSET`. The 8MiB is simply a reasonable amount of space to reserve for the purposes of loading the kernel image. The kernel image is placed in this reserved space during kernel page table initialization as discussed in Section 3.6.1. Somewhere shortly after the image, the `mem_map` for UMA architectures, as discussed in Chapter 2, is stored. The location of the array is usually at the 16MiB mark to avoid using `ZONE_DMA`, but not always. With NUMA architectures, portions of the virtual `mem_map` will be scattered throughout this region. Where they are actually located is architecture dependent.

The region between `PAGE_OFFSET` and `VMALLOC_START` - `VMALLOC_OFFSET` is the physical memory map, and the size of the region depends on the amount of available RAM. As we saw in Section 3.6, page table entries exist to map physical memory to the virtual address range beginning at `PAGE_OFFSET`. Between the physical memory map and the vmalloc address space, there is a gap of space `VMALLOC_OFFSET` in size, which on the x86 is 8MiB, to guard against out-of-bounds errors. For illustration, on a x86 with 32MiB of RAM, `VMALLOC_START` will be located at `PAGE_OFFSET + 0x02000000 + 0x00800000`.

In low memory systems, the remaining amount of the virtual address space, minus a 2 page gap, is used by `vmalloc()` for representing noncontiguous memory allocations in a contiguous virtual address space. In high-memory systems, the vmalloc area extends as far as `PKMAP_BASE` minus the two-page gap, and two extra regions are introduced. The first, which begins at `PKMAP_BASE`, is an area reserved for the mapping of high memory pages into low memory with `kmap()` as discussed in Chapter 9. The second is for fixed virtual address mappings that extend from `FIXADDR_START` to `FIXADDR_TOP`. Fixed virtual addresses are needed for subsystems that need to know the virtual address at compile time such as the *APIC*. `FIXADDR_TOP` is statically defined to be `0xFFFFE000` on the x86 which is one page before the end of the virtual address space. The size of the fixed mapping region is calculated at compile time in `__FIXADDR_SIZE` and used to index back from `FIXADDR_TOP` to give the start of the region `FIXADDR_START`

The region required for `vmalloc()`, `kmap()` and the fixed virtual address mapping is what limits the size of `ZONE_NORMAL`. As the running kernel needs these functions, a region of at least `VMALLOC_RESERVE` will be reserved at the top of the address space. `VMALLOC_RESERVE` is architecture specific but on the x86, it is defined as 128MiB. This is why `ZONE_NORMAL` is generally referred to being only 896MiB in size; it is the 1GiB of the upper potion of the linear address space minus the minimum 128MiB that is reserved for the vmalloc region.

4.2 Managing the Address Space

The address space usable by the process is managed by a high level `mm_struct` which is roughly analogous to the `vmspace` struct in BSD [McK96].

Each address space consists of a number of page-aligned regions of memory that are in use. They never overlap and represent a set of addresses which contain pages that are related to each other in terms of protection and purpose. These regions are represented by a `struct vm_area_struct` and are roughly analogous to the `vm_map_entry` struct in BSD. For clarity, a region may represent the process heap for use with `malloc()`, a memory mapped file such as a shared library or a block of anonymous memory allocated with `mmap()`. The pages for this region may still have to be allocated, be active and resident or have been paged out.

If a region is backed by a file, its `vm_file` field will be set. By traversing `vm_file→f_dentry→d_inode→i_mapping`, the associated `address_space` for the region may be obtained. The `address_space` has all the filesystem specific information required to perform page-based operations on disk.

The relationship between the different address space related structures is illustraed in Figure 4.2. A number of system calls are provided which affect the address space and regions. These are listed in Table 4.1.

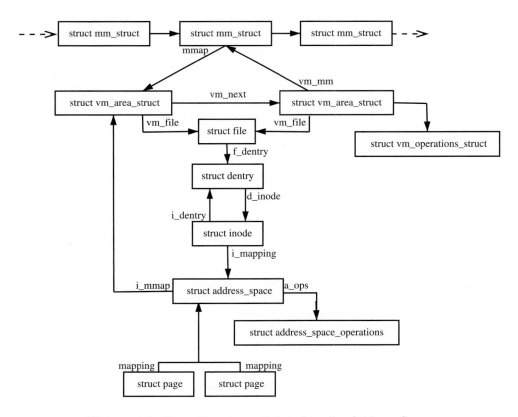

Figure 4.2. Data Structures Related to the Address Space

System Call	Description
`fork()`	Creates a new process with a new address space. All the pages are marked Copy-On-Write (COW) and are shared between the two processes until a page fault occurs. Once a write-fault occurs, a copy is made of the COW page for the faulting process. This is sometimes referred to as breaking a COW page.
`clone()`	`clone()` allows a new process to be created that shares parts of its context with its parent and is how threading is implemented in Linux. `clone()` without the `CLONE_VM` set will create a new address space, which is essentially the same as `fork()`.
`mmap()`	`mmap()` creates a new region within the process linear address space.
`mremap()`	Remaps or resizes a region of memory. If the virtual address space is not available for the mapping, the region may be moved unless the move is forbidden by the caller.
`munmap()`	Destroys part or all of a region. If the region being unmapped is in the middle of an existing region, the existing region is split into two separate regions.
`shmat()`	Attaches a shared memory segment to a process address space.
`shmdt()`	Removes a shared memory segment from an address space.
`execve()`	Loads a new executable file and replaces the current address space.
`exit()`	Destroys an address space and all regions.

Table 4.1. System Calls Related to Memory Regions

4.3 Process Address Space Descriptor

The process address space is described by the `mm_struct` struct, meaning that only one exists for each process and is shared between userspace threads. In fact, threads are identified in the task list by finding all `task_structs` that have pointers to the same `mm_struct`.

A unique `mm_struct` is not needed for kernel threads because they will never page fault or access the userspace portion. The only exception is page faulting within the vmalloc space. The page fault handling code treats this as a special case and updates the current page table with information in the master page table. Because an `mm_struct` is not needed for kernel threads, the `task_struct→mm` field for kernel threads is always NULL. For some tasks, such as the boot idle task, the `mm_struct` is never set up, but, for kernel threads, a call to `daemonize()` will call `exit_mm()` to decrement the usage counter.

Because TLB flushes are extremely expensive, especially with architectures such as the PowerPC (PPC), a technique called *lazy TLB* is employed, which avoids unnecessary TLB flushes by processes that do not access the userspace page tables because the kernel portion of the address space is always visible. The call to `switch_mm()`, which results in a TLB flush, is avoided by borrowing the `mm_struct` used by the previous task and placing it in `task_struct→active_mm`. This technique has made large improvements to context switch times.

When entering lazy TLB, the function `enter_lazy_tlb()` is called to ensure that a `mm_struct` is not shared between processors in Symmetric Multiprocessing (SMP) machines, making it a NULL operation on UP machines. The second-time use of lazy TLB is during process exit when `start_lazy_tlb()` is used briefly while the process is waiting to be reaped by the parent.

The struct has two reference counts called `mm_users` and `mm_count` for two types of users. `mm_users` is a reference count of processes accessing the userspace portion of this `mm_struct`, such as the page tables and file mappings. Threads and the `swap_out()` code, for instance, will increment this count and make sure an `mm_struct` is not destroyed early. When it drops to 0, `exit_mmap()` will delete all mappings and tear down the page tables before decrementing the `mm_count`.

`mm_count` is a reference count of the anonymous users for the `mm_struct` initialized at 1 for the real user. An anonymous user is one that does not necessarily care about the userspace portion and is just borrowing the `mm_struct`. Example users are kernel threads that use lazy TLB switching. When this count drops to 0, the `mm_struct` can be safely destroyed. Both reference counts exist because anonymous users need the `mm_struct` to exist even if the userspace mappings get destroyed and there is no point delaying the teardown of the page tables.

The `mm_struct` is defined in `<linux/sched.h>` as follows:

```
206 struct mm_struct {
207     struct vm_area_struct * mmap;
208     rb_root_t mm_rb;
209     struct vm_area_struct * mmap_cache;
210     pgd_t * pgd;
211     atomic_t mm_users;
212     atomic_t mm_count;
213     int map_count;
214     struct rw_semaphore mmap_sem;
215     spinlock_t page_table_lock;
216
217     struct list_head mmlist;
221
222     unsigned long start_code, end_code, start_data, end_data;
223     unsigned long start_brk, brk, start_stack;
224     unsigned long arg_start, arg_end, env_start, env_end;
225     unsigned long rss, total_vm, locked_vm;
226     unsigned long def_flags;
227     unsigned long cpu_vm_mask;
228     unsigned long swap_address;
229
230     unsigned dumpable:1;
231
232     /* Architecture-specific MM context */
233     mm_context_t context;
234 };
```

The meaning of each of the fields in this sizeable struct is as follows:

mmap The head of a linked list of all VMA regions in the address space.

mm_rb The VMAs are arranged in a linked list and in a red-black tree for fast lookups. This is the root of the tree.

mmap_cache The VMA found during the last call to `find_vma()` is stored in this field on the assumption that the area will be used again soon.

pgd The PGD for this process.

mm_users A reference count of users accessing the userspace portion of the address space as explained at the beginning of the section.

mm_count A reference count of the anonymous users for the `mm_struct` that starts at 1 for the real user as explained at the beginning of this section.

map_count Number of VMAs in use.

mmap_sem This is a long-lived lock that protects the VMA list for readers and writers. Because users of this lock require it for a long time and may need to sleep, a spinlock is inappropriate. A reader of the list takes this semaphore with `down_read()`. If they need to write, it is taken with `down_write()`, and the `page_table_lock` spinlock is later acquired while the VMA linked lists are being updated.

page_table_lock This protects most fields on the `mm_struct`. As well as the page tables, it protects the Resident Set Size (RSS) (see **rss**) count and the VMA from modification.

mmlist All `mm_structs` are linked together by this field.

start_code, end_code The start and end address of the code section.

start_data, end_data The start and end address of the data section.

start_brk, brk The start and end address of the heap.

start_stack Predictably enough, the start of the stack region.

arg_start, arg_end The start and end address of command-line arguments.

env_start, env_end The start and end address of environment variables.

rss *RSS* is the number of resident pages for this process. It should be noted that the global zero page is not accounted for by RSS.

total_vm The total memory space occupied by all VMA regions in the process.

locked_vm The number of resident pages locked in memory.

def_flags Only one possible value, VM_LOCKED. It is used to determine if all future mappings are locked by default.

cpu_vm_mask A bitmask representing all possible CPUs in an SMP system. The mask is used by an *InterProcessor Interrupt (IPI)* to determine if a processor should execute a particular function or not. This is important during TLB flush for each CPU.

swap_address Used by the pageout daemon to record the last address that was swapped from when swapping out entire processes.

dumpable Set by prctl(). This flag is important only when tracing a process.

context Architecture-specific MMU context.

There are a small number of functions for dealing with mm_structs. They are described in Table 4.2.

Function	Description
mm_init()	Initializes an mm_struct by setting starting values for each field, allocating a PGD, initializing spinlocks, etc.
allocate_mm()	Allocates an mm_struct() from the slab allocator
mm_alloc()	Allocates an mm_struct using allocate_mm() and calls mm_init() to initialize it
exit_mmap()	Walks through an mm_struct and unmaps all VMAs associated with it
copy_mm()	Makes an exact copy of the current tasks mm_struct needs for a new task. This is only used during fork.
free_mm()	Returns the mm_struct to the slab allocator

Table 4.2. Functions Related to Memory Region Descriptors

4.3.1 Allocating a Descriptor

Two functions are provided to allocate an mm_struct. To be slightly confusing, they are essentially the same, but with small important differences. allocate_mm() is just a preprocessor macro that allocates an mm_struct from the *slab allocator* (see Chapter 8). mm_alloc() allocates from slab and then calls mm_init() to initialize it.

4.3.2 Initializing a Descriptor

The first mm_struct in the system that is initialized is called init_mm. All subsequent mm_structs are copies of a parent mm_struct. That means that init_mm has to be statically initialized at compile time. This static initialization is performed by the macro INIT_MM().

```
238 #define INIT_MM(name) \
239 {                                                          \
240     mm_rb:          RB_ROOT,                               \
241     pgd:            swapper_pg_dir,                        \
242     mm_users:       ATOMIC_INIT(2),                        \
243     mm_count:       ATOMIC_INIT(1),                        \
244     mmap_sem:       __RWSEM_INITIALIZER(name.mmap_sem), \
245     page_table_lock: SPIN_LOCK_UNLOCKED,                  \
246     mmlist:         LIST_HEAD_INIT(name.mmlist),          \
247 }
```

After it is established, new `mm_structs` are created using their parent `mm_struct` as a template. The function responsible for the copy operation is `copy_mm()`, and it uses `init_mm()` to initialize process-specific fields.

4.3.3 Destroying a Descriptor

While a new user increments the usage count with `atomic_inc(&mm->mm_users)`, it is decremented with a call to `mmput()`. If the `mm_users` count reaches zero, all the mapped regions are destroyed with `exit_mmap()`, and the page tables are destroyed because there are no longer any users of the userspace portions. The `mm_count` count is decremented with `mmdrop()` because all the users of the page tables and VMAs are counted as one `mm_struct` user. When `mm_count` reaches zero, the `mm_struct` will be destroyed.

4.4 Memory Regions

The full address space of a process is rarely used. Only sparse regions are. Each region is represented by a `vm_area_struct`, which never overlaps and represents a set of addresses with the same protection and purpose. Examples of a region include a read-only shared library loaded into the address space or the process heap. A full list of mapped regions that a process has may be viewed using the proc interface at `/proc/PID/maps` where PID is the process ID of the process that is to be examined.

The region may have a number of different structures associated with it as illustrated in Figure 4.2. At the top, there is the `vm_area_struct`, which, on its own, is enough to represent anonymous memory.

If the region is backed by a file, the `struct file` is available through the `vm_file` field, which has a pointer to the `struct inode`. The inode is used to get the `struct address_space`, which has all the private information about the file, including a set of pointers to filesystem functions that perform the filesystem-specific operations, such as reading and writing pages to disk.

The struct `vm_area_struct` is declared as follows in `<linux/mm.h>`:

```
44 struct vm_area_struct {
45     struct mm_struct * vm_mm;
46     unsigned long vm_start;
47     unsigned long vm_end;
49
50     /* linked list of VM areas per task, sorted by address */
51     struct vm_area_struct *vm_next;
52
53     pgprot_t vm_page_prot;
54     unsigned long vm_flags;
55
56     rb_node_t vm_rb;
57
63     struct vm_area_struct *vm_next_share;
64     struct vm_area_struct **vm_pprev_share;
65
66     /* Function pointers to deal with this struct. */
67     struct vm_operations_struct * vm_ops;
68
69     /* Information about our backing store: */
70     unsigned long vm_pgoff;
72     struct file * vm_file;
73     unsigned long vm_raend;
74     void * vm_private_data;
75 };
```

Here is a brief description of the fields.

vm_mm The mm_struct this VMA belongs to.

vm_start The starting address of the region.

vm_end The end address of the region.

vm_next All the VMAs in an address space are linked together in an address-ordered singly linked list by this field It is interesting to note that the VMA list is one of the very rare cases where a singly linked list is used in the kernel.

vm_page_prot The protection flags that are set for each PTE in this VMA. The different bits are described in Table 3.1.

vm_flags A set of flags describing the protections and properties of the VMA. They are all defined in <linux/mm.h> and are described in Table 4.3.

vm_rb As well as being in a linked list, all the VMAs are stored on a *red-black tree* for fast lookups. This is important for page fault handling when finding the correct region quickly is important, especially for a large number of mapped regions.

Protection Flags	
Flags	**Description**
VM_READ	Pages may be read.
VM_WRITE	Pages may be written.
VM_EXEC	Pages may be executed.
VM_SHARED	Pages may be shared.
VM_DONTCOPY	VMA will not be copied on fork.
VM_DONTEXPAND	Prevents a region from being resized. Flag is unused.
mmap Related Flags	
VM_MAYREAD	Allows the VM_READ flag to be set.
VM_MAYWRITE	Allows the VM_WRITE flag to be set.
VM_MAYEXEC	Allows the VM_EXEC flag to be set.
VM_MAYSHARE	Allows the VM_SHARE flag to be set.
VM_GROWSDOWN	Shared segment (probably stack) may grow down.
VM_GROWSUP	Shared segment (probably heap) may grow up.
VM_SHM	Pages are used by shared SHM memory segment.
VM_DENYWRITE	What MAP_DENYWRITE for mmap() translates to. It is now unused.
VM_EXECUTABLE	What MAP_EXECUTABLE for mmap() translates to. It is now unused.
VM_STACK_FLAGS	Flags used by setup_arg_flags() to set up the stack.
Locking Flags	
VM_LOCKED	If set, the pages will not be swapped out. It is set by mlock().
VM_IO	Signals that the area is an mmaped region for I/O to a device. It will also prevent the region from being core dumped.
VM_RESERVED	Do not swap out this region. It is used by device drivers.
madvise() Flags	
VM_SEQ_READ	A hint that pages will be accessed sequentially.
VM_RAND_READ	A hint stating that read-ahead in the region is useless.

Table 4.3. Memory Region Flags

vm_next_share Links together shared VMA regions based on file mappings (such as shared libraries).

vm_pprev_share The complement of vm_next_share.

vm_ops The vm_ops field contains functions pointers for open(), close() and nopage(). These are needed for syncing with information from the disk.

vm_pgoff The page aligned offset within a file that is memory mapped.

vm_file The struct file pointer to the file being mapped.

vm_raend The end address of a read-ahead window. When a fault occurs, a number of additional pages after the desired page will be paged in. This field determines how many additional pages are faulted in.

vm_private_data Used by some device drivers to store private information and
is not of concern to the memory manager.

All the regions are linked together on a linked list ordered by address through the
vm_next field. When searching for a free area, it is a simple matter of traversing the
list, but a frequent operation is to search for the VMA for a particular address, such
as during page faulting, for example. In this case, the red-black tree is traversed
because it has O(log N) search time on average. The tree is ordered so that lower
addresses than the current node are on the left leaf and higher addresses are on the
right.

4.4.1   Memory Region Operations

There are three operations which a VMA may support called open(), close() and
nopage(). VMA supports these with a vm_operations_struct in the VMA called
vma→vm_ops. The struct contains three function pointers and is declared as follows
in <linux/mm.h>:

```
133 struct vm_operations_struct {
134     void (*open)(struct vm_area_struct * area);
135     void (*close)(struct vm_area_struct * area);
136     struct page * (*nopage)(struct vm_area_struct * area,
                                unsigned long address,
                                int unused);
137 };
```

The open() and close() functions are called every time a region is created or
deleted. These functions are only used by a small number of devices, one filesystem
and System V shared regions, which need to perform additional operations when
regions are opened or closed. For example, the System V open() callback will
increment the number of VMAs using a shared segment (shp→shm_nattch).

The main operation of interest is the nopage() callback. This callback is used
during a page-fault by do_no_page(). The callback is responsible for locating the
page in the page cache or allocating a page and populating it with the required data
before returning it.

Most files that are mapped will use a generic vm_operations_struct()
called generic_file_vm_ops. It registers only a nopage() function called
filemap_nopage(). This nopage() function will either locate the page in the
page cache or read the information from disk. The struct is declared as follows
in mm/filemap.c:

```
2243 static struct vm_operations_struct generic_file_vm_ops = {
2244     nopage:          filemap_nopage,
2245 };
```

4.4.2   File/Device-Backed Memory Regions

In the event the region is backed by a file, the vm_file leads to an associated
address_space as shown in Figure 4.2. The struct contains information of relevance

to the filesystem such as the number of dirty pages that must be flushed to disk. It is declared as follows in <linux/fs.h>:

```
406 struct address_space {
407     struct list_head        clean_pages;
408     struct list_head        dirty_pages;
409     struct list_head        locked_pages;
410     unsigned long           nrpages;
411     struct address_space_operations *a_ops;
412     struct inode            *host;
413     struct vm_area_struct   *i_mmap;
414     struct vm_area_struct   *i_mmap_shared;
415     spinlock_t              i_shared_lock;
416     int                     gfp_mask;
417 };
```

A brief description of each field is as follows:

clean_pages is a list of clean pages that need no synchronization with backing storage.

dirty_pages is a list of dirty pages that need synchronization with backing storage.

locked_pages is a list of pages that are locked in memory.

nrpages is the number of resident pages in use by the address space.

a_ops is a struct of function for manipulating the filesystem. Each filesystem provides its own `address_space_operations`, although they sometimes use generic functions.

host is the host inode the file belongs to.

i_mmap is a list of private mappings using this `address_space`.

i_mmap_shared is a list of VMAs that share mappings in this `address_space`.

i_shared_lock is a spinlock to protect this structure.

gfp_mask is the mask to use when calling `__alloc_pages()` for new pages.

Periodically, the memory manager will need to flush information to disk. The memory manager does not know and does not care how information is written to disk, so the `a_ops` struct is used to call the relevant functions. It is declared as follows in <linux/fs.h>:

```
385 struct address_space_operations {
386     int (*writepage)(struct page *);
387     int (*readpage)(struct file *, struct page *);
388     int (*sync_page)(struct page *);
389     /*
390      * ext3 requires that a successful prepare_write() call be
391      * followed by a commit_write() call - they must be balanced
392      */
393     int (*prepare_write)(struct file *, struct page *,
394                          unsigned, unsigned);
        int (*commit_write)(struct file *, struct page *,
                             unsigned, unsigned);
395     /* Unfortunately this kludge is needed for FIBMAP.
         * Don't use it */
396     int (*bmap)(struct address_space *, long);
397     int (*flushpage) (struct page *, unsigned long);
398     int (*releasepage) (struct page *, int);
399 #define KERNEL_HAS_O_DIRECT
400     int (*direct_IO)(int, struct inode *, struct kiobuf *,
                          unsigned long, int);
401 #define KERNEL_HAS_DIRECT_FILEIO
402     int (*direct_fileIO)(int, struct file *, struct kiobuf *,
                             unsigned long, int);
403     void (*removepage)(struct page *);
404 };
```

These fields are all function pointers and are described in the following:

writepage Writes a page to disk. The offset within the file to write to is stored within the page struct. It is up to the filesystem-specific code to find the block. See `buffer.c:block_write_full_page()`.

readpage Reads a page from disk. See `buffer.c:block_read_full_page()`.

sync_page Syncs a dirty page with disk. See `buffer.c:block_sync_page()`.

prepare_write This is called before data is copied from userspace into a page that will be written to disk. With a journaled filesystem, this ensures the filesystem log is up to date. With normal filesystems, it makes sure the needed buffer pages are allocated. See `buffer.c:block_prepare_write()`.

commit_write After the data has been copied from userspace, this function is called to commit the information to disk. See `buffer.c:block_commit_write()`.

bmap Maps a block so that raw I/O can be performed. It is mainly of concern to filesystem-specific code, although it is also used when swapping out pages that are backed by a swap file instead of a swap partition.

flushpage Makes sure there is no I/O pending on a page before releasing it. See `buffer.c:discard_bh_page()`.

releasepage Tries to flush all the buffers associated with a page before freeing the page itself. See `try_to_free_buffers()`.

direct_I/O This function is used when performing direct I/O to an inode. The `#define` exists so that external modules can determine at compile time if the function is available because it was only introduced in 2.4.21.

direct_fileI/O Used to perform direct I/O with a `struct file`. Again, the `#define` exists for external modules because this API was only introduced in 2.4.22.

removepage An optional callback that is used when a page is removed from the page cache in `remove_page_from_inode_queue()`.

4.4.3 Creating a Memory Region

The system call `mmap()` is provided for creating new memory regions within a process. For the x86, the function calls `sys_mmap2()`, which calls `do_mmap2()`, directly with the same parameters. `do_mmap2()` is responsible for acquiring the parameters needed by `do_mmap_pgoff()`, which is the principal function for creating new areas for all architectures.

`do_mmap2()` first clears the `MAP_DENYWRITE` and `MAP_EXECUTABLE` bits from the `flags` parameter because they are ignored by Linux, which is confirmed by the `mmap()` manual page. If a file is being mapped, `do_mmap2()`, shown in Figure 4.3, will look up the `struct file` based on the file descriptor passed as a parameter and will acquire the `mm_struct`→`mmap_sem` semaphore before calling `do_mmap_pgoff()`.

`do_mmap_pgoff()` begins by performing some basic sanity checks. It first checks that the appropriate filesystem or device functions are available if a file or device is being mapped. It then ensures the size of the mapping is page aligned and that it does not attempt to create a mapping in the kernel portion of the address space. It then makes sure the size of the mapping does not overflow the range of `pgoff` and finally that the process does not have too many mapped regions already.

This rest of the function is large, but, broadly speaking, it takes the following steps:

1. Sanity check the parameters.

2. Find a free linear address space large enough for the memory mapping. If a filesystem or device specific `get_unmapped_area()` function is provided, it will be used. Otherwise, `arch_get_unmapped_area()` is called.

3. Calculate the VM flags and check them against the file access permissions.

4. If an old area exists where the mapping is to take place, fix it up so that it is suitable for the new mapping.

5. Allocate a `vm_area_struct` from the slab allocator and fill in its entries.

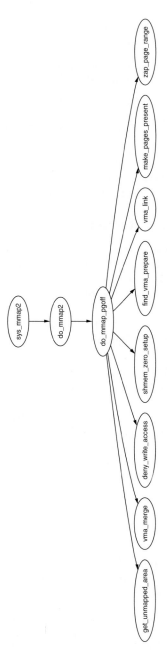

Figure 4.3. Call Graph: sys_mmap2()

6. Link in the new VMA.

7. Call the filesystem or device-specific mmap function.

8. Update statistics and exit.

4.4.4 Finding a Mapped Memory Region

A common operation is to find the VMA that a particular address belongs to, such as during operations like page faulting, and the function responsible for this is `find_vma()`. The function `find_vma()` and other API functions affecting memory regions are listed in Table 4.4.

It first checks the `mmap_cache` field, which caches the result of the last call to `find_vma()` because it is quite likely the same region will be needed a few times in succession. If it is not the desired region, the red-black tree stored in the `mm_rb` field is traversed. If the desired address is not contained within any VMA, the function will return the VMA *closest* to the requested address, so it is important callers double-check to ensure the returned VMA contains the desired address.

A second function called `find_vma_prev()` is provided, which is functionally the same as `find_vma()` except that it also returns a pointer to the VMA preceding the desired VMA, which is required as the list is a singly linked list. `find_vma_prev()` is rarely used, but notably it is used when two VMAs are being compared to determine if they may be merged. It is also used when removing a memory region so that the singly linked list may be updated.

The last function of note for searching VMAs is `find_vma_intersection()`, which is used to find a VMA that overlaps a given address range. The most notable use of this is during a call to `do_brk()` when a region is growing up. It is important to ensure that the growing region will not overlap an old region.

4.4.5 Finding a Free Memory Region

When a new area is to be memory mapped, a free region has to be found that is large enough to contain the new mapping. The function responsible for finding a free area is `get_unmapped_area()`.

As the call graph in Figure 4.4 indicates, little work is involved with finding an unmapped area. The function is passed a number of parameters. A `struct file` is passed that represents the file or device to be mapped as well as `pgoff`, which is the offset within the file that is being mapped. The requested `address` for the mapping is passed as well as its `length`. The last parameter is the protection `flags` for the area.

If a device is being mapped, such as a video card, the associated `f_op`→`get_unmapped_area()` is used. This is because devices or files may have additional requirements for mapping that generic code cannot be aware of, such as the address having to be aligned to a particular virtual address.

If there are no special requirements, the architecture-specific function `arch_get_unmapped_area()` is called. Not all architectures provide their own function. For those that don't, a generic version is provided in `mm/mmap.c`.

---

struct vm_area_struct * find_vma(struct mm_struct * mm, unsigned
long addr)
    Finds the VMA that covers a given address. If the region does not exist, it
returns the VMA closest to the requested address.

struct vm_area_struct * find_vma_prev(struct mm_struct * mm,
unsigned long addr, struct vm_area_struct **pprev)
    The same as find_vma() except that it also also gives the VMA pointing to
the returned VMA. It is not often used, with sys_mprotect() being the notable
exception, because usually find_vma_prepare() is required.

struct vm_area_struct * find_vma_prepare(struct mm_struct * mm,
unsigned long addr, struct vm_area_struct ** pprev, rb_node_t ***
rb_link, rb_node_t ** rb_parent)
    The same as find_vma() except that it will also find the preceeding VMA in
the linked list as well as the red-black tree nodes needed to perform an insertion
into the tree.

struct vm_area_struct * find_vma_intersection(struct mm_struct *
mm, unsigned long start_addr, unsigned long end_addr)
    Returns the VMA that intersects a given address range. It is useful when
checking if a linear address region is in use by any VMA.

int vma_merge(struct mm_struct * mm, struct vm_area_struct * prev,
rb_node_t * rb_parent, unsigned long addr, unsigned long end,
unsigned long vm_flags)
    Attempts to expand the supplied VMA to cover a new address range. If the
VMA cannot be expanded forward, the next VMA is checked to see if it may be
expanded backward to cover the address range instead. Regions may be merged
if there is no file/device mapping and the permissions match.

unsigned long get_unmapped_area(struct file *file, unsigned long
addr, unsigned long len, unsigned long pgoff, unsigned long flags)
    Returns the address of a free region of memory large enough to cover the
requested size of memory. It is used principally when a new VMA is to be
created.

void insert_vm_struct(struct mm_struct *, struct vm_area_struct *)
    Inserts a new VMA into a linear address space.

Table 4.4. Memory Region VMA API

4.4.6 Inserting a Memory Region

The principal function for inserting a new memory region is insert_vm_struct()
that has the call graph seen in Figure 4.5. It is a very simple function that first

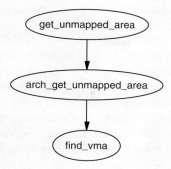

Figure 4.4. Call Graph: `get_unmapped_area()`

calls `find_vma_prepare()` to find the appropriate VMAs that the new region is to be inserted between. It also finds the correct nodes within the red-black tree. It then calls `__vma_link()` to do the work of linking in the new VMA.

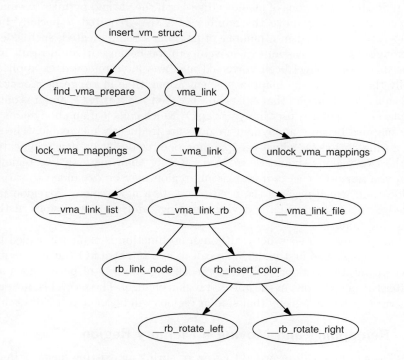

Figure 4.5. Call Graph: `insert_vm_struct()`

The function `insert_vm_struct()` is rarely used because it does not increase the `map_count` field. Instead, the function commonly used is `__insert_vm_struct()`, which performs the same tasks except that it increments `map_count`.

Two varieties of linking functions are provided, `vma_link()` and `__vma_link()`. `vma_link()` is intended for use when no locks are held. It will acquire all the necessary locks, including locking the file if the VMA is a file mapping, before calling `__vma_link()`, which places the VMA in the relevant lists.

Many functions do not use the `insert_vm_struct()` functions, but instead prefer to call `find_vma_prepare()` themselves, followed by a later `vma_link()` to avoid having to traverse the tree multiple times.

The linking in `__vma_link()` consists of three stages that are contained in three separate functions. `__vma_link_list()` inserts the VMA into the linear, singly linked list. If it is the first mapping in the address space (i.e., prev is NULL), it will become the red-black tree root node. The second stage is linking the node into the red-black tree with `__vma_link_rb()`. The final stage is fixing up the file share mapping with `__vma_link_file()`, which basically inserts the VMA into the linked list of VMAs using the `vm_pprev_share` and `vm_next_share` fields.

4.4.7 Merging Contiguous Regions

Linux used to have a function called `merge_segments()` [Hac02] that was responsible for merging adjacent regions of memory together if the file and permissions matched. The objective was to remove the number of VMAs required, especially because many operations resulted in a number of mappings being created, such as calls to `sys_mprotect()`. This was an expensive operation because it could result in large portions of the mappings been traversed and was later removed as applications, especially those with many mappings, spent a long time in `merge_segments()`.

The equivalent function that exists now is called `vma_merge()`, and it is only used in two places. The first is user in `sys_mmap()`, which calls it if an anonymous region is being mapped because anonymous regions are frequently mergeable. The second time is during `do_brk()`, which is expanding one region into a newly allocated one where the two regions should be merged. Rather than merging two regions, the function `vma_merge()` checks if an existing region may be expanded to satisfy the new allocation, which negates the need to create a new region. A region may be expanded if there are no file or device mappings and the permissions of the two areas are the same.

Regions are merged elsewhere, although no function is explicitly called to perform the merging. The first is during a call to `sys_mprotect()` during the fixup of areas where the two regions will be merged if the two sets of permissions are the same after the permissions in the affected region change. The second is during a call to `move_vma()` when it is likely that similar regions will be located beside each other.

4.4.8 Remapping and Moving a Memory Region

`mremap()` is a system call provided to grow or shrink an existing memory mapping. This is implemented by the function `sys_mremap()`, which may move a memory region if it is growing or it would overlap another region and if `MREMAP_FIXED` is not specified in the flags. The call graph is illustrated in Figure 4.6.

If a region is to be moved, `do_mremap()` first calls `get_unmapped_area()` to find a region large enough to contain the new resized mapping and then calls `move_vma()`

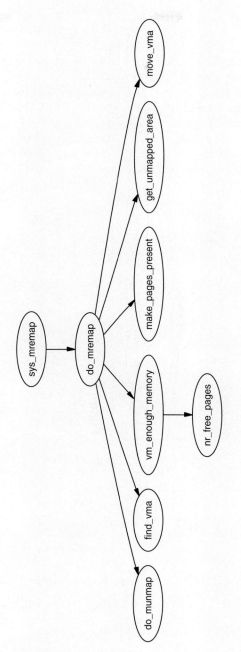

Figure 4.6. Call Graph: sys_mremap()

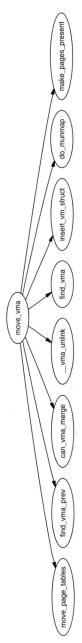

Figure 4.7. Call Graph: move_vma()

to move the old VMA to the new location. See Figure 4.7 for the call graph to `move_vma()`.

First `move_vma()` checks if the new location may be merged with the VMAs adjacent to the new location. If they cannot be merged, a new VMA is allocated literally one PTE at a time. Next `move_page_tables()` is called(see Figure 4.8 for its call graph), which copies all the page table entries from the old mapping to the new one. Although there may be better ways to move the page tables, this method makes error recovery trivial because backtracking is relatively straightforward.

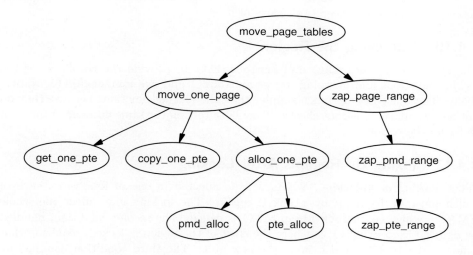

Figure 4.8. Call Graph: `move_page_tables()`

The contents of the pages are not copied. Instead, `zap_page_range()` is called to swap out or remove all the pages from the old mapping, and the normal page fault handling code will swap the pages back in from backing storage or from files or will call the device specific `do_nopage()` function.

4.4.9 Locking a Memory Region

Linux can lock pages from an address range into memory using the system call `mlock()`, which is implemented by `sys_mlock()`, for which the call graph is shown in Figure 4.9. At a high level, the function is simple; it creates a VMA for the address range to be locked, sets the `VM_LOCKED` flag on it and forces all the pages to be present with `make_pages_present()`. A second system call `mlockall()`, which maps to `sys_mlockall()`, is also provided. This is a simple extension to do the same work as `sys_mlock()` except that it affects every VMA on the calling process. Both functions rely on the core function `do_mlock()` to perform the real work of finding the affected VMAs and deciding what function is needed to fix up the regions as described later.

There are some limitations to what memory may be locked. The address range must be page aligned because VMAs are page aligned. This is addressed by simply rounding the range up to the nearest page-aligned range. The second proviso is that the process limit RLIMIT_MLOCK imposed by the system administrator may not be exceeded. The last proviso is that each process may only lock half of physical memory at a time. This is a bit nonfunctional because there is nothing to stop a process forking a number of times and each child locking a portion, but, because only root processes are allowed to lock pages, it does not make much difference. It is safe to presume that a root process is trusted and knows what it is doing. If it does not, the system administrator with the resulting broken system probably deserves it and gets to keep both parts of it.

4.4.10   Unlocking the Region

The system calls munlock() and munlockall() to provide the corollary for the locking functions and mapping to sys_munlock() and sys_munlockall(), respectively. The functions are much simpler than the locking functions because they do not have to make numerous checks. They both rely on the same do_mmap() function to fix up the regions.

4.4.11   Fixing Up Regions After Locking

When locking or unlocking, VMAs will be affected in one of four ways, each of which must be fixed up by mlock_fixup(). The locking may affect the whole VMA, in which case mlock_fixup_all() is called. The second condition, handled by mlock_fixup_start(), is where the start of the region is locked, requiring that a new VMA be allocated to map the new area. The third condition, handled by mlock_fixup_end(), is predictably enough where the end of the region is locked. Finally, mlock_fixup_middle() handles the case where the middle of a region is mapped requiring two new VMAs to be allocated.

It is interesting to note that VMAs created as a result of locking are never merged, even when unlocked. It is presumed that processes that lock regions will need to lock the same regions over and over again, and it is not worth the processor power to constantly merge and split regions.

4.4.12   Deleting a Memory Region

The function responsible for deleting memory regions, or parts thereof, is do_munmap(), which is shown in Figure 4.10. It is a relatively simple operation in comparison with the other memory region-related operations and is basically divided up into three parts. The first is to fix up the red-black tree for the region that is about to be unmapped. The second is to release the pages and PTEs related to the region to be unmapped, and the third is to fix up the regions if a hole has been generated.

To ensure the red-black tree is ordered correctly, all VMAs to be affected by the unmap are placed on a linked list called free and then deleted from the red-black tree with rb_erase(). The regions, if they still exist, will be added with their new

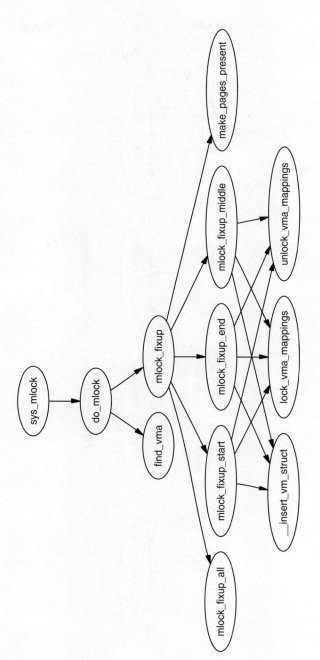

Figure 4.9. Call Graph: sys_mlock()

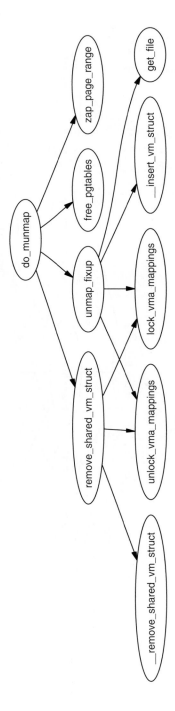

Figure 4.10. Call Graph: do_munmap()

addresses later during the fixup.

Next the linked-list VMAs on `free` are walked through and checked to ensure it is not a partial unmapping. Even if a region is just to be partially unmapped, `remove_shared_vm_struct()` is still called to remove the shared file mapping. Again, if this is a partial unmapping, it will be recreated during fixup. `zap_page_range()` is called to remove all the pages associated with the region about to be unmapped before `unmap_fixup()` is called to handle partial unmappings.

Last, `free_pgtables()` is called to try and free up all the page table entries associated with the unmapped region. It is important to note that the page table entry freeing is not exhaustive. It will only unmap full PGD directories and their entries, so, for example, if only half a PGD was used for the mapping, no page table entries will be freed. This is because a finer grained freeing of page table entries would be too expensive to free up data structures that are both small and likely to be used again.

4.4.13   Deleting All Memory Regions

During process exit, it is necessary to unmap all VMAs associated with an `mm_struct`. The function responsible is `exit_mmap()`. It is a very simple function that flushes the CPU cache before walking through the linked list of VMAs, unmapping each of them in turn and freeing up the associated pages before flushing the TLB and deleting the page table entries. It is covered in detail in the Code Commentary.

4.5   Exception Handling

A very important part of VM is how kernel address space exceptions, which are not bugs, are caught.[1] This section does *not* cover the exceptions that are raised with errors such as divide by zero. I am only concerned with the exception raised as the result of a page fault. There are two situations where a bad reference may occur. The first is where a process sends an invalid pointer to the kernel by a system call, which the kernel must be able to safely trap because the only check made initially is that the address is below `PAGE_OFFSET`. The second is where the kernel uses `copy_from_user()` or `copy_to_user()` to read or write data from userspace.

At compile time, the linker creates an exception table in the `__ex_table` section of the kernel code segment, which starts at `__start___ex_table` and ends at `__stop___ex_table`. Each entry is of type `exception_table_entry`, which is a pair consisting of an execution point and a fixup routine. When an exception occurs that the page fault handler cannot manage, it calls `search_exception_table()` to see if a fixup routine has been provided for an error at the faulting instruction. If module support is compiled, each module's exception table will also be searched.

---

[1]Many thanks go to Ingo Oeser for clearing up the details of how this is implemented.

If the address of the current exception is found in the table, the corresponding location of the fixup code is returned and executed. We will see in Section 4.7 how this is used to trap bad reads and writes to userspace.

4.6   Page Faulting

Pages in the process linear address space are not necessarily resident in memory. For example, allocations made on behalf of a process are not satisfied immediately because the space is just reserved within the vm_area_struct. Other examples of nonresident pages include the page having been swapped out to backing storage or writing a read-only page.

Linux, like most operating systems, has a *Demand Fetch* policy as its fetch policy for dealing with pages that are not resident. This states that the page is only fetched from backing storage when the hardware raises a page fault exception, which the operating system traps and allocates a page. The characteristics of backing storage imply that some sort of page prefetching policy would result in less page faults [MM87], but Linux is fairly primitive in this respect. When a page is paged in from swap space, a number of pages after it, up to $2^{\text{page\_cluster}}$ are read in by swapin_readahead() and placed in the swap cache. Unfortunately, there is only a chance that pages likely to be used soon will be adjacent in the swap area, which makes it a poor prepaging policy. Linux would likely benefit from a prepaging policy that adapts to program behavior [KMC02].

There are two types of page fault, major and minor faults. Major page faults occur when data has to be read from disk, which is an expensive operation, or the fault is referred to as a minor, or soft, page fault. Linux maintains statistics on the number of these types of page faults with the task_struct→maj_flt and task_struct→min_flt fields, respectively.

The page fault handler in Linux is expected to recognize and act on a number of different types of page faults listed in Table 4.5, which will be discussed in detail later in this chapter.

Each architecture registers an architecture-specific function for the handling of page faults. Although the name of this function is arbitrary, a common choice is do_page_fault(), for which the call graph for the x86 is shown in Figure 4.11.

This function is provided with a wealth of information such as the address of the fault, whether the page was simply not found or was a protection error, whether it was a read or write fault and whether it is a fault from user or kernel space. It is responsible for determining which type of fault has occurred and how it should be handled by the architecture-independent code. The flow chart, in Figure 4.12, shows broadly speaking what this function does. In the figure, identifiers with a colon after them correspond to the label as shown in the code.

handle_mm_fault() is the architecture-independent, top-level function for faulting in a page from backing storage, performing Copy-On-Write (COW), and so on. If it returns 1, it was a minor fault, 2 was a major fault, 0 sends a SIGBUS error and any other value invokes the out of memory handler.

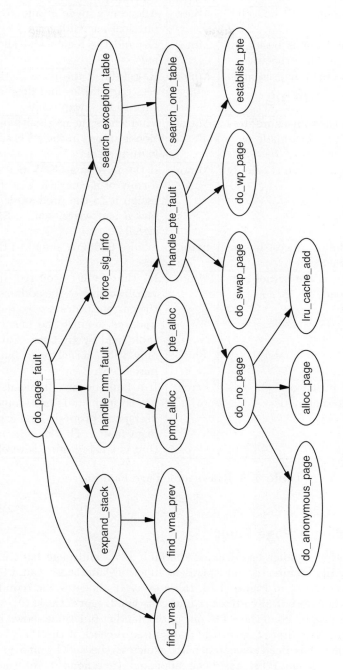

Figure 4.11. Call Graph: do_page_fault()

Exception	Type	Action
Region valid, but page not allocated	Minor	Allocate a page frame from the physical page allocator.
Region not valid but is beside an expandable region like the stack	Minor	Expand the region and allocate a page.
Page swapped out, but present in swap cache	Minor	Re-establish the page in the process page tables and drop a reference to the swap cache.
Page swapped out to backing storage	Major	Find where the page with information is stored in the PTE and read it from disk.
Page write when marked read-only	Minor	If the page is a COW page, make a copy of it, mark it writable and assign it to the process. If it is in fact a bad write, send a SIGSEGV signal.
Region is invalid or process has no permissions to access	Error	Send a SEGSEGV signal to the process.
Fault occurred in the kernel portion address space	Minor	If the fault occurred in the vmalloc area of the address space, the current process page tables are updated against the master page table held by init_mm. This is the only valid kernel page fault that may occur.
Fault occurred in the userspace region while in kernel mode	Error	If a fault occurs, it means a kernel system did not copy from userspace properly and caused a page fault. This is a kernel bug that is treated quite severely.

Table 4.5. Reasons for Page Faulting

4.6.1 Handling a Page Fault

After the exception handler has decided the fault is a valid page fault in a valid memory region, the architecture-independent function handle_mm_fault(), which has its call graph shown in Figure 4.13, takes over. It allocates the required page table entries if they do not already exist and calls handle_pte_fault().

Based on the properties of the PTE, one of the handler functions shown in Figure 4.13 will be used. The first stage of the decision is to check if the PTE is marked not present or if it has been allocated with, which is checked by pte_present() and pte_none(). If no PTE has been allocated (pte_none() returned true), do_no_page() is called, which handles *Demand Allocation*. Otherwise, it is a page that has been swapped out to disk and do_swap_page() performs *Demand Paging*.

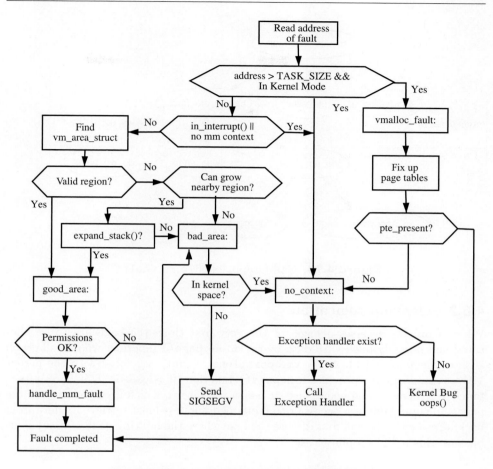

Figure 4.12. do_page_fault() Flow Diagram

There is a rare exception where swapped-out pages belonging to a virtual file are handled by do_no_page(). This particular case is covered in Section 12.4.

The second option is if the page is being written to. If the PTE is write protected, do_wp_page() is called because the page is a COW page. A COW page is one that is shared between multiple processes(usually a parent and child) until a write occurs, after which a private copy is made for the writing process. A COW page is recognized because the VMA for the region is marked writable even though the individual PTE is not. If it is not a COW page, the page is simply marked dirty because it has been written to.

The last option is if the page has been read and is present, but a fault still occurred. This can occur with some architectures that do not have a three-level page table. In this case, the PTE is simply established and marked young.

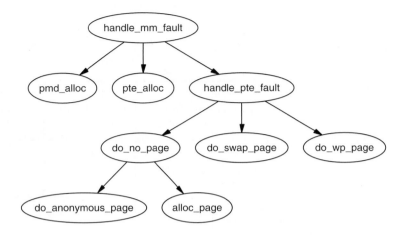

Figure 4.13. Call Graph: `handle_mm_fault()`

4.6.2 Demand Allocation

When a process accesses a page for the very first time, the page has to be allocated and possibly filled with data by the `do_no_page()` function, whose call graph is shown in Figure 4.14. If the `vm_operations_struct` associated with the parent VMA (`vma→vm_ops`) provides a `nopage()` function, it is called. This is of importance to a memory-mapped device such as a video card, which needs to allocate the page and supply data on access or to a mapped file that must retrieve its data from backing storage. We will first discuss the case where the faulting page is anonymous because this is the simplest case.

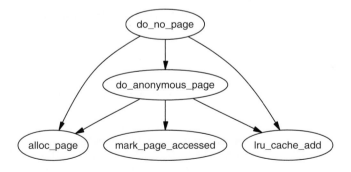

Figure 4.14. Call Graph: `do_no_page()`

Handling Anonymous Pages   If the `vm_area_struct→vm_ops` field is not filled or a `nopage()` function is not supplied, the function `do_anonymous_page()` is called to handle an anonymous access. There are only two cases to handle, first time read and first time write. Because it is an anonymous page, the first read is an easy case because no data exists. In this case, the systemwide `empty_zero_page`, which is just a page of zeros, is mapped for the PTE, and the PTE is write protected. The write protection is set so that another page fault will occur if the process writes to the page. On the x86, the global zero-filled page is zeroed out in the function `mem_init()`.

If this is the first write to the page, `alloc_page()` is called to allocate a free page (see Chapter 6) and is zero filled by `clear_user_highpage()`. Assuming the page was successfully allocated, the RSS field in the `mm_struct` will be incremented; `flush_page_to_ram()` is called as required when a page has been inserted into a userspace process by some architectures to ensure cache coherency. The page is then inserted on the LRU lists so that it may be reclaimed later by the page reclaiming code. Finally the page table entries for the process are updated for the new mapping.

Handling File/Device-Backed Pages If backed by a file or device, a `nopage()` function will be provided within the VMA's `vm_operations_struct`. In the file-backed case, the function `filemap_nopage()` is frequently the `nopage()` function for allocating a page and reading a page-sized amount of data from disk. Pages backed by a virtual file, such as those provided by *shmfs*, will use the function `shmem_nopage()` (See Chapter 12). Each device driver provides a different `nopage()`. Their internals are unimportant to us here as long as it returns a valid `struct page` to use.

On return of the page, a check is made to ensure a page was successfully allocated and appropriate errors were returned if not. A check is then made to see if an early COW break should take place. An early COW break will take place if the fault is a write to the page and the `VM_SHARED` flag is not included in the managing VMA. An early break is a case of allocating a new page and copying the data across before reducing the reference count to the page returned by the `nopage()` function.

In either case, a check is then made with `pte_none()` to ensure a PTE is not already in the page table that is about to be used. It is possible with SMP that two faults would occur for the same page at close to the same time, and because the spinlocks are not held for the full duration of the fault, this check has to be made at the last instant. If there has been no race, the PTE is assigned, statistics are updated and the architecture hooks for cache coherency are called.

4.6.3   Demand Paging

When a page is swapped out to backing storage, the function `do_swap_page()`, shown in Figure 4.15, is responsible for reading the page back in, with the exception of virtual files, which are covered in Section 12. The information needed to find it is stored within the PTE itself. The information within the PTE is enough to find the page in swap. Because pages may be shared between multiple processes, they cannot always be swapped out immediately. Instead, when a page is swapped out, it is placed within the swap cache.

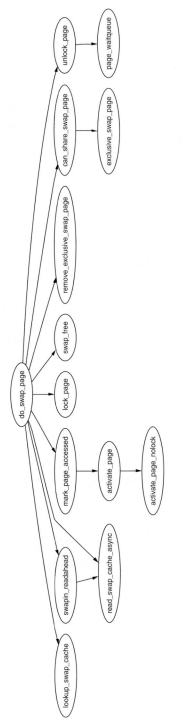

Figure 4.15. Call Graph: do_swap_page()

A shared page cannot be swapped out immediately because there is no way of mapping a **struct page** to the PTEs of each process it is shared between. Searching the page tables of all processes is simply far too expensive. It is worth noting that the late 2.5.x kernels and 2.4.x with a custom patch have what is called *Reverse Mapping (RMAP)*, which is discussed at the end of the chapter.

With the swap cache existing, it is possible that, when a fault occurs, it still exists in the swap cache. If it is, the reference count to the page is simply increased, and it is placed within the process page tables again and registers as a minor page fault.

If the page exists only on disk, **swapin_readahead()** is called, which reads in the requested page and a number of pages after it. The number of pages read in is determined by the variable **page_cluster** defined in **mm/swap.c**. On low memory machines with less than 16MiB of RAM, it is initialized as 2 or 3. The number of pages read in is $2^{\text{page\_cluster}}$ unless a bad or empty swap entry is encountered. This works on the premise that a seek is the most expensive operation in time, so after the seek has completed, the succeeding pages should also be read in.

4.6.4 COW Pages

Once upon a time, the full parent address space was duplicated for a child when a process forked. This was an extremely expensive operation because it is possible a significant percentage of the process would have to be swapped in from backing storage. To avoid this considerable overhead, a technique called COW is employed.

During a fork, the PTEs of the two processes are made read-only so that, when a write occurs, there will be a page fault. Linux recognizes a COW page because, even though the PTE is write protected, the controlling VMA shows the region is writable. It uses the function **do_wp_page()**, shown in Figure 4.16, to handle it by making a copy of the page and assigning it to the writing process. If necessary, a new swap slot will be reserved for the page. With this method, only the page table entries have to be copied during a fork.

4.7   Copying to/from Userspace

It is not safe to access memory in the process address space directly because there is no way to quickly check if the page addressed is resident or not. Linux relies on the MMU to raise exceptions when the address is invalid and have the Page Fault Exception handler catch the exception and fix it up. In the x86 case, an assembler is provided by the **__copy_user()** to trap exceptions where the address is totally useless. The location of the fixup code is found when the function **search_exception_table()** is called. Linux provides an ample API (mainly macros) for copying data to and from the user address space safely as shown in Table 4.6.

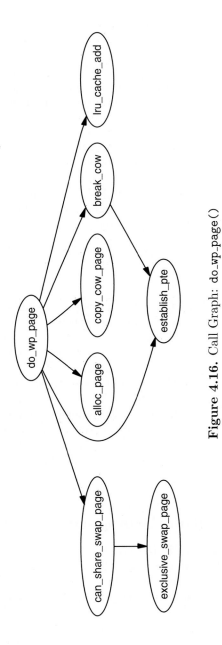

Figure 4.16. Call Graph: do_wp_page()

```
unsigned long copy_from_user(void *to, const void *from, unsigned
long n)
```
Copies n bytes from the user address(`from`) to the kernel address space(`to`).

```
unsigned long copy_to_user(void *to, const void *from, unsigned
long n)
```
Copies n bytes from the kernel address(`from`) to the user address space(`to`).

```
void copy_user_page(void *to, void *from, unsigned long address)
```
Copies data to an anonymous or COW page in userspace. Ports are responsible for avoiding D-cache aliases. It can do this by using a kernel virtual address that would use the same cache lines as the virtual address.

```
void clear_user_page(void *page, unsigned long address)
```
Similar to `copy_user_page()`, except it is for zeroing a page.

```
void get_user(void *to, void *from)
```
Copies an integer value from userspace (`from`) to kernel space (`to`).

```
void put_user(void *from, void *to)
```
Copies an integer value from kernel space (`from`) to userspace (`to`).

```
long strncpy_from_user(char *dst, const char *src, long count)
```
Copies a null terminated string of at most `count` bytes long from userspace (`src`) to kernel space (`dst`).

```
long strlen_user(const char *s, long n)
```
Returns the length, upper bound by `n`, of the userspace string including the terminating NULL.

```
int access_ok(int type, unsigned long addr, unsigned long size)
```
Returns nonzero if the userspace block of memory is valid and zero otherwise.

Table 4.6. Accessing Process Address Space API

All the macros map on to assembler functions, which all follow similar patterns of implementation. For illustration purposes, we'll just trace how `copy_from_user()` is implemented on the x86.

If the size of the copy is known at compile time, `copy_from_user()` calls `__constant_copy_from_user()`, or `__generic_copy_from_user()` is used. If the size is known, there are different assembler optimizations to copy data in 1, 2 or 4 byte strides. Otherwise, the distinction between the two copy functions is not important.

The generic copy function eventually calls the function `__copy_user_zeroing()` in `<asm-i386/uaccess.h>`, which has three important parts. The first part is the assembler for the actual copying of `size` number of bytes from userspace. If any page is not resident, a page fault will occur, and, if the address is valid, it will get swapped in as normal. The second part is fixup code, and the third part is the __ex_table mapping the instructions from the first part to the fixup code in the second part.

These pairings, as described in Section 4.5, copy the location of the copy instructions and the location of the fixup code to the kernel exception handle table by the linker. If an invalid address is read, the function do_page_fault() will fall through, call search_exception_table(), find the Enhanced Instruction Pointer (EIP) where the faulty read took place and jump to the fixup code, which copies zeros into the remaining kernel space, fixes up registers and returns. In this manner, the kernel can safely access userspace with no expensive checks and let the MMU hardware handle the exceptions.

All the other functions that access userspace follow a similar pattern.

4.8   What's New in 2.6

Linear Address Space   The linear address space remains essentially the same as 2.4 with no modifications that cannot be easily recognized. The main change is the addition of a new page usable from userspace that has been entered into the fixed address virtual mappings. On the x86, this page is located at 0xFFFFF000 and called the *vsyscall page*. Code is located at this page, which provides the optimal method for entering kernel space from userspace. A userspace program now should use call 0xFFFFF000 instead of the traditional int 0x80 when entering kernel space.

struct mm_struct   This struct has not changed significantly. The first change is the addition of a free_area_cache field, which is initialized as TASK_UNMAPPED_BASE. This field is used to remember where the first hole is in the linear address space to improve search times. A small number of fields have been added at the end of the struct, which are related to core dumping and are beyond the scope of this book.

struct vm_area_struct   This struct also has not changed significantly. The main difference is that the vm_next_share and vm_pprev_share have been replaced with a proper linked list with a new field called shared. The vm_raend has been removed altogether because file readahead is implemented very differently in 2.6. Readahead is mainly managed by a struct file_ra_state struct stored in struct file→f_ra. How readahead is implemented is described in a lot of detail in mm/readahead.c.

struct address_space   The first change is relatively minor. The gfp_mask field has been replaced with a flags field where the first __GFP_BITS_SHIFT bits are used as the gfp_mask and accessed with mapping_gfp_mask(). The remaining bits are used to store the status of asynchronous I/O. The two flags that may be set are AS_EIO to indicate an I/O error and AS_ENOSPC to indicate the filesystem ran out of space during an asynchronous write.

This struct has a number of significant additions, mainly related to the page cache and file readahead. Because the fields are quite unique, we'll introduce them in detail:

page_tree   This is a radix tree of all pages in the page cache for this mapping indexed by the block that the data is located on the physical disk. In 2.4, searching the page cache involved traversing a linked list. In 2.6, it is a radix tree lookup, which considerably reduces search times. The radix tree is implemented in `lib/radix-tree.c`.

page_lock This is a spinlock that protects `page_tree`.

io_pages When dirty pages are to be written out, they are added to this list before `do_writepages()` is called. As explained in the previous comment, `mpage_writepages()` in `fs/mpage.c`, pages to be written out are placed on this list to avoid deadlocking by locking a page that is already locked for I/O.

dirtied_when This field records, in jiffies, the first time an inode was dirtied. This field determines where the inode is located on the `super_block→s_dirty` list. This prevents a frequently dirtied inode from remaining at the top of the list and starving writeout on other inodes.

backing_dev_info This field records readahead-related information. The struct is declared in `include/linux/backing-dev.h` with comments explaining the fields.

private_list This is a private list available to the `address_space`. If the helper functions `mark_buffer_dirty_inode()` and `sync_mapping_buffers()` are used, this list links `buffer_heads` through the `buffer_head→b_assoc_buffers` field.

private_lock This spinlock is available for the `address_space`. The use of this lock is very convoluted, but some of the uses are explained in the long ChangeLog for 2.5.17 (*lwn.net/2002/0523/a/2.5.17.php3*). It is mainly related to protecting lists in other mappings that share buffers in this mapping. The lock would not protect this `private_list`, but it would protect the `private_list` of another `address_space` sharing buffers with this mapping.

assoc_mapping This is the `address_space` that backs buffers contained in this mapping's `private_list`.

truncate_count This is incremented when a region is being truncated by the function `invalidate_mmap_range()`. The counter is examined during page fault by `do_no_page()` to ensure that a page is not faulted that was just invalidated.

struct address_space_operations Most of the changes to this struct initially look quite simple, but are actually quite involved. The changed fields are the following:

writepage The `writepage()` callback has been changed to take an additional parameter `struct writeback_control`. This struct is responsible for recording information about the writeback, such as if it is congested or not or if the writer is the page allocator for direct reclaim or **kupdated** and contains a handle to the backing `backing_dev_info` to control readahead.

writepages This moves all pages from `dirty_pages` to `io_pages` before writing them all out.

set_page_dirty This is an `address_space`-specific method of dirtying a page. This is mainly used by the backing storage `address_space_operations` and for anonymous shared pages where there are no buffers associated with the page to be dirtied.

readpages This is used when reading in pages so that readahead can be accurately controlled.

bmap This has been changed to deal with disk sectors rather than unsigned longs for devices larger than 2^{32} bytes.

invalidatepage This is a renaming change. `block_flushpage()` and the callback `flushpage()` have been renamed to `block_invalidatepage()` and `invalidatepage()`.

direct_I/O This has been changed to use the new I/O mechanisms in 2.6. The new mechanisms are beyond the scope of this book.

Memory Regions   The operation of `mmap()` has two important changes. The first is that it is possible for security modules to register a callback. This callback is called `security_file_mmap()`, which looks up a `security_ops` struct for the relevant function. By default, this will be a NULL operation.

The second is that much stricter address space accounting code is in place. `vm_area_struct`s that are to be accounted will have the `VM_ACCOUNT` flag set, which will be all userspace mappings. When userspace regions are created or destroyed, the functions `vm_acct_memory()` and `vm_unacct_memory()` update the variable `vm_committed_space`. This gives the kernel a much better view of how much memory has been committed to userspace.

4GiB/4GiB User/Kernel Split   One limitation that exists for the 2.4.x kernels is that the kernel has only 1GiB of virtual address space available, which is visible to all processes. At time of writing, a patch has been developed by Ingo Molnar[2] which allows the kernel to optionally have its own full 4GiB address space. The patches are available from *http://redhat.com/~mingo/4g-patches/* and are included in the -mm test trees, but it is unclear if it will be merged into the mainstream.

This feature is intended for 32-bit systems that have very large amounts (>16GiB) of RAM. The traditional 3/1 split adequately supports up to 1GiB of RAM. After that, high-memory support allows larger amounts to be supported by temporarily mapping high-memory pages. However, with more RAM, this forms a significant bottleneck. For example, as the amount of physical RAM approached the 60GiB range, almost all the low memory is consumed by `mem_map`. By giving the kernel its own 4GiB virtual address space, it is much easier to support the memory. The serious penalty, though, is that there is a per-syscall TLB flush, which heavily impacts performance.

---

[2]See *lwn.net/Articles/39283/* for the first announcement of the patch.

With the patch, only a small 16MiB region of memory is shared between userspace and kernelspace, and this is used to store the Global Descriptor Table (GDT), Interrupt Descriptor Table (IDT), Task State Segments (TSS), Local Descriptor Table (LDT), vsyscall page and the kernel stack. The code for doing the actual switch between the page tables is then contained in the trampoline code for entering/exiting kernelspace. There are a few changes made to the core, such as the removal of direct pointers for accessing userspace buffers, but, by and large, the core kernel is unaffected by this patch.

Nonlinear VMA Population   In 2.4, a VMA backed by a file is populated in a linear fashion. This can be optionally changed in 2.6 with the introduction of the `MAP_POPULATE` flag to `mmap()` and the new system call `remap_file_pages()`, which are implemented by `sys_remap_file_pages()`. This system call allows arbitrary pages in an existing VMA to be remapped to an arbitrary location on the backing file by manipulating the page tables.

On page-out, the nonlinear address for the file is encoded within the PTE so that it can be installed again correctly on page fault. How it is encoded is architecture specific, so two macros are defined, `pgoff_to_pte()` and `pte_to_pgoff()`, for the task.

This feature is largely of benefit to applications with a large number of mappings, such as database servers and virtualizing applications such as emulators. It was introduced for a number of reasons. First, VMAs are per-process and can have considerable space requirements, especially for applications with a large number of mappings. Second, the search `get_unmapped_area()` uses for finding a free area in the virtual address space is a linear search, which is very expensive for large numbers of mappings. Third, nonlinear mappings will prefault most of the pages into memory whereas normal mappings may cause a major fault for each page. This can be avoided though, by using the new `MAP_POPULATE` flag with `mmap()` or by using `mlock()`. The last reason is to avoid sparse mappings, which, at worst case, would require one VMA for every file page mapped.

However, this feature is not without some serious drawbacks. The first is that the system calls, `truncate()` and `mincore()`, are broken with respect to nonlinear mappings. Both system calls depend on `vm_area_struct→vm_pgoff`, which is meaningless for nonlinear mappings. If a file mapped by a nonlinear mapping is truncated, the pages that exist within the VMA will still remain. It has been proposed that the proper solution is to leave the pages in memory, but make them anonymous. At the time of writing, no solution has been implemented.

The second major drawback is TLB invalidations. Each remapped page will require that the MMU be told the remapping took place with `flush_icache_page()`, but the more important penalty is with the call to `flush_tlb_page()`. Some processors are able to invalidate just the TLB entries related to the page, but other processors implement this by flushing the entire TLB. If remappings are frequent, the performance will degrade due to increased TLB misses and the overhead of constantly entering kernel space. In some ways, these penalties are the worst because the impact is heavily processor dependent.

It is currently unclear what the future of this feature, if it remains, will be. At the time of writing, there are still ongoing arguments on how the issues with the feature will be fixed, but it is likely that nonlinear mappings are going to be treated very differently from normal mappings with respect to pageout, truncation and the reverse mapping of pages. Because the main user of this feature is likely to be databases, this special treatment is not likely to be a problem.

Page Faulting   The changes to the page faulting routines are more cosmetic than anything else, other than the necessary changes to support reverse mapping and PTEs in high memory. The main cosmetic change is that the page faulting routines return self-explanatory compile time definitions rather than magic numbers. The possible return values for `handle_mm_fault()` are `VM_FAULT_MINOR`, `VM_FAULT_MAJOR`, `VM_FAULT_SIGBUS` and `VM_FAULT_OOM`.

CHAPTER 5

Boot Memory Allocator

It is impractical to statically initialize all the core kernel memory structures at compile time because there are simply far too many permutations of hardware configurations. To set up even the basic structures, though, requires memory because even the physical page allocator, discussed in the next chapter, needs to allocate memory to initialize itself. But how can the physical page allocator allocate memory to initialize itself?

To address this, a specialized allocator called the *Boot Memory Allocator* is used. It is based on the most basic of allocators, a *First Fit* allocator, which uses a bitmap to represent memory [Tan01] instead of linked lists of free blocks. If a bit is 1, the page is allocated, and if the bit is 0, it is unallocated. To satisfy allocations of sizes smaller than a page, the allocator records the *Page Frame Number (PFN)* of the last allocation and the offset the allocation ended at. Subsequent small allocations are merged together and stored on the same page.

The reader may ask why this allocator is not used for the running system. One compelling reason is that, although the first fit allocator does not suffer badly from fragmentation [JW98], memory frequently has to be linearly searched to satisfy an allocation. Because this is examining bitmaps, it gets very expensive, especially because the first fit algorithm tends to leave many small free blocks at the beginning of physical memory that still get scanned for large allocations, thus making the process very wasteful [WJNB95].

There are two very similar but distinct APIs for the allocator. One is for UMA architectures listed in Table 5.1, and the other is for NUMA listed in Table 5.2. The principal difference is that the NUMA API must be supplied with the node affected by the operation, but, because the callers of these APIs exist in the architecture-dependent layer, it is not a significant problem.

This chapter begins with a description of the structure that the allocator uses to describe the physical memory available for each node. I then illustrate how the limits of physical memory and the sizes of each zone are discovered before talking about how the information is used to initialize the boot memory allocator structures. The allocation and free routines are then discussed before finally talking about how the boot memory allocator is retired.

unsigned long init_bootmem(unsigned long start, unsigned long page)
   Initializes the memory between 0 and the PFN page. The beginning of usable memory is at the PFN start.

void reserve_bootmem(unsigned long addr, unsigned long size)
   Marks the pages between the address addr and addr+size reserved. Requests to partially reserve a page will result in the full page being reserved.

void free_bootmem(unsigned long addr, unsigned long size)
   Marks the pages between the address addr and addr+size as free.

void * alloc_bootmem(unsigned long size)
   Allocates size number of bytes from ZONE_NORMAL. The allocation will be aligned to the L1 hardware cache to get the maximum benefit from the hardware cache.

void * alloc_bootmem_low(unsigned long size)
   Allocates size number of bytes from ZONE_DMA. The allocation will be aligned to the L1 hardware cache.

void * alloc_bootmem_pages(unsigned long size)
   Allocates size number of bytes from ZONE_NORMAL aligned on a page size so that full pages will be returned to the caller.

void * alloc_bootmem_low_pages(unsigned long size)
   Allocates size number of bytes from ZONE_DMA aligned on a page size so that full pages will be returned to the caller.

unsigned long bootmem_bootmap_pages(unsigned long pages)
   Calculates the number of pages required to store a bitmap representing the allocation state of pages number of pages.

unsigned long free_all_bootmem()
   Used at the boot allocator end of life. It cycles through all pages in the bitmap. For each one that is free, the flags are cleared, and the page is freed to the physical page allocator (see next chapter) so that the runtime allocator can set up its free lists.

Table 5.1. Boot Memory Allocator API for UMA Architectures

5.1   Representing the Boot Map

A bootmem_data struct exists for each node of memory in the system. It contains the information needed for the boot memory allocator to allocate memory for a node, such as the bitmap representing allocated pages and where the memory is

unsigned long init_bootmem_node(pg_data_t *pgdat, unsigned long
freepfn, unsigned long startpfn, unsigned long endpfn)
For use with NUMA architectures. It initializes the memory between PFNs
startpfn and endpfn with the first usable PFN at freepfn. After it is initialized, the pgdat node is inserted into the pgdat_list.

void reserve_bootmem_node(pg_data_t *pgdat, unsigned long physaddr,
unsigned long size)
Marks the pages between the address addr and addr+size on the specified
node pgdat reserved. Requests to partially reserve a page will result in the full
page being reserved.

void free_bootmem_node(pg_data_t *pgdat, unsigned long physaddr,
unsigned long size)
Marks the pages between the address addr and addr+size on the specified
node pgdat free.

void * alloc_bootmem_node(pg_data_t *pgdat, unsigned long size)
Allocates size number of bytes from ZONE_NORMAL on the specified node
pgdat. The allocation will be aligned to the L1 hardware cache to get the
maximum benefit from the hardware cache.

void * alloc_bootmem_pages_node(pg_data_t *pgdat, unsigned long
size)
Allocates size number of bytes from ZONE_DMA on the specified node pgdat
aligned on a page size so that full pages will be returned to the caller.

void * alloc_bootmem_low_pages_node(pg_data_t *pgdat, unsigned long
size)
Allocates size number of bytes from ZONE_DMA on the specified node pgdat
aligned on a page size so that full pages will be returned to the caller.

unsigned long free_all_bootmem_node(pg_data_t *pgdat)
Used at the boot allocator end of life. It cycles through all pages in the bitmap
for the specified node. For each one that is free, the page flags are cleared, and
the page is freed to the physical page allocator (see next chapter) so that the
runtime allocator can set up its free lists.

Table 5.2. Boot Memory Allocator API for NUMA Architectures

located. It is declared as follows in <linux/bootmem.h>:

```
25 typedef struct bootmem_data {
26     unsigned long node_boot_start;
27     unsigned long node_low_pfn;
28     void *node_bootmem_map;
```

```
29      unsigned long last_offset;
30      unsigned long last_pos;
31 } bootmem_data_t;
```

The fields of this struct are as follows:

node_boot_start This is the starting physical address of the represented block.

node_low_pfn This is the end physical address, in other words, the end of the
ZONE_NORMAL this node represents.

node_bootmem_map This is the location of the bitmap representing allocated
or free pages with each bit.

last_offset This is the offset within the the page of the end of the last allocation.
If 0, the page used is full.

last_pos This is the the PFN of the page used with the last allocation. By using
this with the last_offset field, a test can be made to see if allocations can
be merged with the page used for the last allocation rather than using up a
full new page.

5.2   Initializing the Boot Memory Allocator

Each architecture is required to supply a setup_arch() function, which, among
other tasks, is responsible for acquiring the necessary parameters to initialize the
boot memory allocator.

Each architecture has its own function to get the necessary parameters. On
the x86, it is called setup_memory() as discussed in Section 2.2.2, but, on other
architectures such as MIPS or Sparc, it is called bootmem_init() or, in the case
of the PPC, do_init_bootmem(). Regardless of the architecture, the tasks are
essentially the same. The parameters it calculates are the following:

min_low_pfn This is the lowest PFN that is available in the system.

max_low_pfn This is the highest PFN that may be addressed by low memory
(ZONE_NORMAL).

highstart_pfn This is the PFN of the beginning of high memory (ZONE_HIGHMEM).

highend_pfn This is the last PFN in high memory.

max_pfn Finally, this is the last PFN available to the system.

5.3   Initializing bootmem_data

After the limits of usable physical memory are discovered by setup_memory(), one
of two boot memory initialization functions is selected and provided with the start
and end PFN for the node to be initialized. init_bootmem(), which initializes

contig_page_data, is used by UMA architectures, while init_bootmem_node() is for NUMA to initialize a specified node. Both functions are trivial and rely on init_bootmem_core() to do the real work.

The first task of the core function is to insert this pgdat_data_t into the pgdat_list because, at the end of this function, the node is ready for use. It then records the starting and end address for this node in its associated bootmem_data_t and allocates the bitmap representing page allocations. The size in bytes, hence the division by eight, of the bitmap required is calculated as:

$$\text{mapsize} = \frac{(\text{end\_pfn} - \text{start\_pfn}) + 7}{8}$$

The bitmap in stored at the physical address pointed to by bootmem_data_t→node_boot_start, and the virtual address to the map is placed in bootmem_data_t→node_bootmem_map. Because there is no architecture-independent way to detect holes in memory, the entire bitmap is initialized to 1, effectively marking all pages allocated. It is up to the architecture-dependent code to set the bits of usable pages to 0, although, in reality, the Sparc architecture is the only one that uses this bitmap. In the case of the x86, the function register_bootmem_low_pages() reads through the e820 map and calls free_bootmem() for each usable page to set the bit to 0 before using reserve_bootmem() to reserve the pages needed by the actual bitmap.

5.4 Allocating Memory

The reserve_bootmem() function may be used to reserve pages for use by the caller, but is very cumbersome to use for general allocations. Four functions are provided for easy allocations on UMA architectures called alloc_bootmem(), alloc_bootmem_low(), alloc_bootmem_pages() and alloc_bootmem_low_pages(), which are fully described in Table 5.1. All of these macros call __alloc_bootmem() with different parameters. The call graph for these functions is shown in in Figure 5.1.

Similar functions exist for NUMA that take the node as an additional

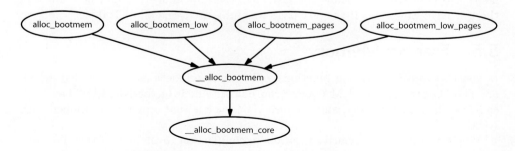

Figure 5.1. Call Graph: alloc_bootmem()

parameter as listed in Table 5.2. They are called `alloc_bootmem_node()`, `alloc_bootmem_pages_node()` and `alloc_bootmem_low_pages_node()`. All of these macros call `__alloc_bootmem_node()` with different parameters.

The parameters to `__alloc_bootmem()` and `__alloc_bootmem_node()` are essentially the same. They are the following:

pgdat This is the node to allocate from. It is omitted in the UMA case because it is assumed to be `contig_page_data`.

size This is the size in bytes of the requested allocation.

align This is the number of bytes that the request should be aligned to. For small allocations, they are aligned to `SMP_CACHE_BYTES`, which, on the x86, will align to the L1 hardware cache.

goal This is the preferred starting address to begin allocating from. The low functions will start from physical address 0 whereas the others will begin from `MAX_DMA_ADDRESS`, which is the maximum address DMA transfers may be made from on this architecture.

The core function for all the allocation APIs is `__alloc_bootmem_core()`. It is a large function, but with simple steps that can be broken down. The function linearly scans memory starting from the **goal** address for a block of memory large enough to satisfy the allocation. With the API, this address will either be 0 for DMA-friendly allocations or `MAX_DMA_ADDRESS` otherwise.

The clever part, and the main bulk of the function, deals with deciding if this new allocation can be merged with the previous one. It may be merged if the following conditions hold:

- The page used for the previous allocation (`bootmem_data→pos`) is adjacent to the page found for this allocation.

- The previous page has some free space in it (`bootmem_data→offset` != 0).

- The alignment is less than `PAGE_SIZE`.

Regardless of whether the allocations may be merged or not, the `pos` and `offset` fields will be updated to show the last page used for allocating and how much of the last page was used. If the last page was fully used, the offset is 0.

5.5 Freeing Memory

In contrast to the allocation functions, only two free functions are provided, which are `free_bootmem()` for UMA and `free_bootmem_node()` for NUMA. They both call `free_bootmem_core()`, and the only difference is that a `pgdat` is supplied with NUMA.

The core function is relatively simple in comparison to the rest of the allocator. For each *full* page affected by the free, the corresponding bit in the bitmap is set to 0. If it already was 0, `BUG()` is called to show a double-free occurred. `BUG()`

is used when an unrecoverable error due to a kernel bug occurs. It terminates the running process and causes a kernel oops, which shows a stack trace and debugging information that a developer can use to fix the bug.

An important restriction with the free functions is that only full pages may be freed. It is never recorded when a page is partially allocated, so, if only partially freed, the full page remains reserved. This is not as major a problem as it appears because the allocations always persist for the lifetime of the system. However, it is still an important restriction for developers during boot time.

5.6 Retiring the Boot Memory Allocator

Late in the bootstrapping process, the function start_kernel() is called, which knows it is safe to remove the boot allocator and all its associated data structures. Each architecture is required to provide a function mem_init(), shown in Figure 5.2, that is responsible for destroying the boot memory allocator and its associated structures.

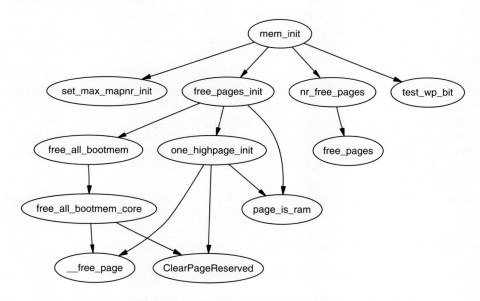

Figure 5.2. Call Graph: mem_init()

The purpose of the function is quite simple. It is responsible for calculating the dimensions of low and high memory and printing out an informational message to the user, as well as performing final initializations of the hardware if necessary. On the x86, the principle function of concern for the VM is the free_pages_init().

This function first tells the boot memory allocator to retire itself by calling free_all_bootmem() for UMA architectures or free_all_bootmem_node() for NUMA. Both call the core function free_all_bootmem_core() with different parameters. The core function is simple in principle and performs the following tasks:

- For all unallocated pages known to the allocator for this node, it does the following:
    - Clear the `PG_reserved` flag in its struct page.
    - Set the count to 1.
    - Call `__free_pages()` so that the buddy allocator (discussed in the next chapter) can build its free lists.

- Free all pages used for the bitmap and give them to the buddy allocator.

At this stage, the buddy allocator now has control of all the pages in low memory, which leaves only the high memory pages. After `free_all_bootmem()` returns, it first counts the number of reserved pages for accounting purposes. The remainder of the `free_pages_init()` function is responsible for the high memory pages. However, at this point, it should be clear how the global `mem_map` array is allocated and initialized and how the pages are given to the main allocator. The basic flow used to initialize pages in low memory in a single node system is shown in Figure 5.3.

After `free_all_bootmem()` returns, all the pages in `ZONE_NORMAL` have been given to the buddy allocator. To initialize the high memory pages, `free_pages_init()` calls `one_highpage_init()` for every page between `highstart_pfn` and `highend_pfn`. `one_highpage_init()` simply clears the `PG_reserved` flag, sets the `PG_highmem` flag, sets the count to 1 and calls `__free_pages()` to release it to the buddy allocator in the same manner `free_all_bootmem_core()` did.

At this point, the boot memory allocator is no longer required, and the buddy allocator is the main physical page allocator for the system. An interesting feature to note is that not only is the data for the boot allocator removed, but also all code that was used to bootstrap the system. All initilization functions that are required only during system start-up are marked `__init`, such as the following:

```
321 unsigned long __init free_all_bootmem (void)
```

All of these functions are placed together in the `.init` section by the linker. On the x86, the function `free_initmem()` walks through all pages from `__init_begin` to `__init_end` and frees up the pages to the buddy allocator. With this method, Linux can free up a considerable amount of memory that is used by bootstrapping code that is no longer required. For example, 27 pages were freed while booting the kernel running on the machine this document was composed on.

5.7   What's New in 2.6

The boot memory allocator has not changed significantly since 2.4 and is mainly concerned with optimizations and some minor NUMA-related modifications. The

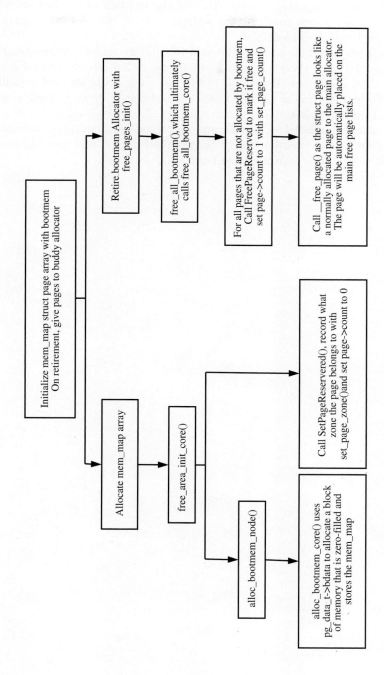

Figure 5.3. Initializing mem_map and the Main Physical Page Allocator

first optimization is the addition of a `last_success` field to the `bootmem_data_t`
struct. As the name suggests, it keeps track of the location of the last successful
allocation to reduce search times. If an address is freed before `last_success`, it
will be changed to the freed location.

The second optimization is also related to the linear search. When searching
for a free page, 2.4 tests every bit, which is expensive. 2.6 instead tests if a block
of `BITS_PER_LONG` is all ones. If it's not, it will test each of the bits individually in
that block. To help the linear search, nodes are ordered in order of their physical
addresses by `init_bootmem()`.

The last change is related to NUMA and contiguous architectures. Contiguous
architectures now define their own `init_bootmem()` function and any architecture
can optionally define their own `reserve_bootmem()` function.

CHAPTER 6

Physical Page Allocation

This chapter describes how physical pages are managed and allocated in Linux. The principal algorithm used is the *Binary Buddy Allocator*, devised by Knowlton [Kno65] and further described by Knuth [Knu68]. The binary buddy allocator is has been shown to be extremely fast in comparison to other allocators [KB85].

This is an allocation scheme that combines a normal power-of-two allocator with free buffer coalescing [Vah96], and the basic concept behind it is quite simple. Memory is broken up into large blocks of pages where each block is a power of two number of pages. If a block of the desired size is not available, a large block is broken up in half, and the two blocks are *buddies* to each other. One half is used for the allocation, and the other is free. The blocks are continuously halved as necessary until a block of the desired size is available. When a block is later freed, the buddy is examined, and the two are coalesced if it is free.

This chapter will begin with describing how Linux remembers what blocks of memory are free. After that the methods for allocating and freeing pages will be discussed in detail. The subsequent section will cover the flags that affect the allocator behavior and finally the problem of fragmentation and how the allocator handles it.

6.1 Managing Free Blocks

As stated, the allocator maintains blocks of free pages where each block is a power of two number of pages. The exponent for the power of two-sized block is referred to as the *order*. An array of `free_area_t` structs are maintained for each order that points to a linked list of blocks of pages that are free as indicated by Figure 6.1.

Hence, the 0th element of the array will point to a list of free page blocks of size 2^0 or 1 page, the 1st element will be a list of 2^1 (2) pages up to $2^{\text{MAX\_ORDER}-1}$ number of pages, where the `MAX_ORDER` is currently defined as 10. This eliminates the chance that a larger block will be split to satisfy a request where a smaller block would have sufficed. The page blocks are maintained on a linear linked list using `page→list`.

Each zone has a `free_area_t` struct array called `free_area[MAX_ORDER]`. It is declared in `<linux/mm.h>` as follows:

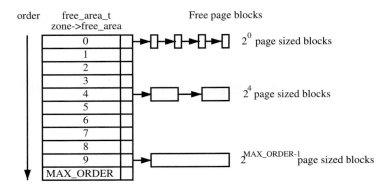

Figure 6.1. Free Page Block Management

```
22 typedef struct free_area_struct {
23          struct list_head          free_list;
24          unsigned long             *map;
25 } free_area_t;
```

The fields in this struct are as follows:

free_list A linked list of free page blocks

map A bitmap representing the state of a pair of buddies

Linux saves memory by only using one bit instead of two to represent each pair of buddies. Each time a buddy is allocated or freed, the bit representing the pair of buddies is toggled so that the bit is zero if the pair of pages are both free or both full and 1 if only one buddy is in use. To toggle the correct bit, the macro MARK_USED() in page_alloc.c is used, which is declared as follows:

```
164 #define MARK_USED(index, order, area) \
165          __change_bit((index) >> (1+(order)), (area)->map)
```

index is the index of the page within the global mem_map array. By shifting it right by 1+order bits, the bit within the map representing the pair of buddies is revealed.

6.2   Allocating Pages

Linux provides a quite sizable API for the allocation of page frames. All of them take a gfp_mask as a parameter, which is a set of flags that determine how the allocator will behave. The flags are discussed in Section 6.4.

As shown in Figure 6.2, the allocation API functions all use the core function __alloc_pages(), but the APIs exist so that the correct node and zone will be chosen. Different users will require different zones, such as ZONE_DMA for certain device drivers or ZONE_NORMAL for disk buffers, and callers should not have to be

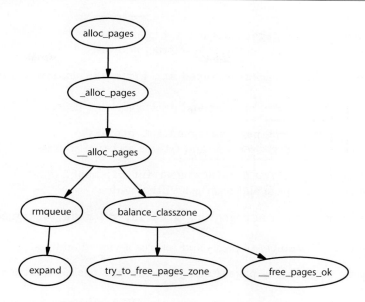

Figure 6.2. Call Graph: `alloc_pages()`

aware of what node is being used. A full list of page allocation APIs are listed in Table 6.1.

Allocations are always for a specified order: 0 in the case where a single page is required. If a free block cannot be found of the requested order, a higher order block is split into two buddies. One is allocated, and the other is placed on the free list for the lower order. Figure 6.3 shows where a 2^4 block is split and how the buddies are added to the free lists until a block for the process is available.

When the block is later freed, the buddy will be checked. If both are free, they are merged to form a higher order block and placed on the higher free list where its buddy is checked and so on. If the buddy is not free, the freed block is added to the free list at the current order. During these list manipulations, interrupts have to be disabled to prevent an interrupt handler manipulating the lists while a process has them in an inconsistent state. This is achieved by using an interrupt safe spinlock.

The second decision to make is which memory node or `pg_data_t` to use. Linux uses a node-local allocation policy, which aims to use the memory bank associated with the CPU running the page-allocating process. Here, the function `_alloc_pages()` is what is important because this function is different depending on whether the kernel is built for a UMA (function in `mm/page_alloc.c`) or NUMA (function in `mm/numa.c`) machine.

Regardless of which API is used, `__alloc_pages()` in `mm/page_alloc.c` is the heart of the allocator. This function, which is never called directly, examines the selected zone and checks if it is suitable to allocate from based on the number of available pages. If the zone is not suitable, the allocator may fall back to other zones. The order of zones to fall back on is decided at boot time by the function

```
struct page * alloc_page(unsigned int gfp_mask)
```
Allocates a single page and returns a struct address.

```
struct page * alloc_pages(unsigned int gfp_mask, unsigned int
order)
```
Allocates 2^{order} number of pages and returns a struct page.

```
unsigned long get_free_page(unsigned int gfp_mask)
```
Allocates a single page, zeros it, and returns a virtual address.

```
unsigned long __get_free_page(unsigned int gfp_mask)
```
Allocates a single page and returns a virtual address.

```
unsigned long __get_free_pages(unsigned int gfp_mask, unsigned int
order)
```
Allocates 2^{order} number of pages and returns a virtual address.

```
struct page * __get_dma_pages(unsigned int gfp_mask, unsigned int
order)
```
Allocates 2^{order} number of pages from the DMA zone and returns a struct page.

Table 6.1. Physical Pages Allocation API

build_zonelists(), but generally ZONE_HIGHMEM will fall back to ZONE_NORMAL and that in turn will fall back to ZONE_DMA. If number of free pages reaches the pages_low watermark, it will wake **kswapd** to begin freeing up pages from zones, and, if memory is extremely tight, the caller will do the work of **kswapd** itself.

After the zone has finally been decided on, the function rmqueue() is called to allocate the block of pages or split higher level blocks if one of the appropriate size is not available.

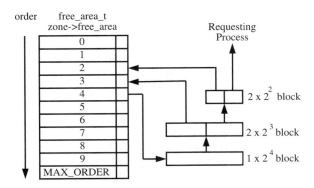

Figure 6.3. Allocating Physical Pages

6.3 Free Pages

The API for the freeing of pages is a lot simpler and exists to help remember the order of the block to free. One disadvantage of a buddy allocator is that the caller has to remember the size of the original allocation. The API for freeing is listed in Table 6.2.

---

void __free_pages(struct page *page, unsigned int order)
    Frees an order number of pages from the given page.

void __free_page(struct page *page)
    Frees a single page.

void free_page(void *addr)
    Frees a page from the given virtual address.

Table 6.2. Physical Pages Free API

The principal function for freeing pages is __free_pages_ok(), and it should not be called directly. Instead the function __free_pages() is provided, which performs simple checks first as indicated in Figure 6.4.

When a buddy is freed, Linux tries to coalesce the buddies together immediately if possible. This is not optimal because the worst-case scenario will have many coalitions followed by the immediate splitting of the same blocks [Vah96].

To detect if the buddies can be merged, Linux checks the bit corresponding to the affected pair of buddies in free_area→map. Because one buddy has just been freed by this function, it is obviously known that at least one buddy is free. If the bit in the map is 0 after toggling, we know that the other buddy must also be free

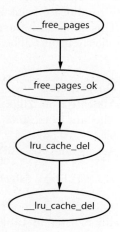

Figure 6.4. Call Graph: __free_pages()

because, if the bit is 0, it means both buddies are either both free or both allocated. If both are free, they may be merged.

Calculating the address of the buddy is a well known concept [Knu68]. Because the allocations are always in blocks of size 2^k, the address of the block, or at least its offset within `zone_mem_map`, will also be a power of 2^k. The end result is that there will always be at least k number of zeros to the right of the address. To get the address of the buddy, the *kth* bit from the right is examined. If it is 0, the buddy will have this bit flipped. To get this bit, Linux creates a `mask`, which is calculated as

$$\text{mask} = (\sim 0 << \text{k})$$

The mask we are interested in is

$$\text{imask} = 1 + \sim \text{mask}$$

Linux takes a shortcut in calculating this by noting that

$$\text{imask} = -\text{mask} = 1 + \sim \text{mask}$$

After the buddy is merged, it is removed for the free list, and the newly coalesced pair moves to the next higher order to see if it may also be merged.

6.4 Get Free Page (GFP) Flags

A persistent concept through the whole VM is the *Get Free Page (GFP)* flags. These flags determine how the allocator and **kswapd** will behave for the allocation and freeing of pages. For example, an interrupt handler may not sleep, so it will *not* have the `__GFP_WAIT` flag set because this flag indicates the caller may sleep. There are three sets of GFP flags, which are all defined in <`linux/mm.h`>.

The first of the three is the set of zone modifiers listed in Table 6.3. These flags indicate that the caller must try to allocate from a particular zone. `ZONE_NORMAL` does not have a zone modifier. This is because the zone modifier flag is used as an offset within an array, and 0 implicitly means allocate from `ZONE_NORMAL`.

Flag	Description
`__GFP_DMA`	Allocate from `ZONE_DMA` if possible.
`__GFP_HIGHMEM`	Allocate from `ZONE_HIGHMEM` if possible.
`GFP_DMA`	Act as alias for `__GFP_DMA`.

Table 6.3. Low-Level GFP Flags Affecting Zone Allocation

The next flags are action modifiers listed in Table 6.4. They change the behavior of the VM and what the calling process may do. The low-level flags on their own are too primitive to be easily used.

Flag	Description
__GFP_WAIT	Indicates that the caller is not high priority and can sleep or reschedule.
__GFP_HIGH	Used by a high priority or kernel process. Kernel 2.2.x used it to determine if a process could access emergency pools of memory. In 2.4.x kernels, it does not appear to be used.
__GFP_IO	Indicates that the caller can perform low-level I/O. In 2.4.x, the main effect this has is determining if try_to_free_buffers() can flush buffers. It is used by at least one journaled filesystem.
__GFP_HIGHIO	Determines that I/O can be performed on pages mapped in high memory. It is only used in try_to_free_buffers().
__GFP_FS	Indicates if the caller can make calls to the filesystem layer. This is used when the caller is filesystem related, the buffer cache, for instance, and wants to avoid recursively calling itself.

Table 6.4. Low-Level GFP Flags Affecting Allocator Behavior

It is difficult to know what the correct combinations are for each instance, so a few high-level combinations are defined and listed in Table 6.5. For clarity the __GFP_ is removed from the table combinations, so the __GFP_HIGH flag will read as HIGH in the table. The combinations to form the high-level flags are listed in Table 6.6. To help understand this, take GFP_ATOMIC as an example. It has only the __GFP_HIGH flag set. This means it is high priority, will use emergency pools (if they exist), but it will not sleep, perform I/O, or access the filesystem. This flag would be used by an interrupt handler, for example.

Flag	Low-Level Flag Combination
GFP_ATOMIC	HIGH
GFP_NOIO	HIGH — WAIT
GFP_NOHIGHIO	HIGH — WAIT — IO
GFP_NOFS	HIGH — WAIT — IO — HIGHIO
GFP_KERNEL	HIGH — WAIT — IO — HIGHIO — FS
GFP_NFS	HIGH — WAIT — IO — HIGHIO — FS
GFP_USER	WAIT — IO — HIGHIO — FS
GFP_HIGHUSER	WAIT — IO — HIGHIO — FS — HIGHMEM
GFP_KSWAPD	WAIT — IO — HIGHIO — FS

Table 6.5. Low-Level GFP Flag Combinations for High-Level Use

6.5 Process Flags

A process may also set flags in the task_struct, which affects allocator behavior. The full list of process flags is defined in <linux/sched.h>, but only the ones affecting VM behavior are listed in Table 6.7.

Flag	Description
GFP_ATOMIC	This flag is used whenever the caller cannot sleep and must be serviced if at all possible. Any interrupt handler that requires memory must use this flag to avoid sleeping or performing I/O. Many subsystems during init will use this system, such as buffer_init() and inode_init().
GFP_NOIO	This is used by callers who are already performing an I/O-related function. For example, when the loopback device is trying to get a page for a buffer head, it uses this flag to make sure it will not perform some action that would result in more I/O. If fact, it appears the flag was introduced specifically to avoid a deadlock in the loopback device.
GFP_NOHIGHIO	This is only used in one place in alloc_bounce_page() during the creating of a bounce buffer for I/O in high memory.
GFP_NOFS	This is only used by the buffer cache and filesystems to make sure they do not recursively call themselves by accident.
GFP_KERNEL	This is the most liberal of the combined flags. It indicates that the caller is free to do whatever it pleases. Strictly speaking the difference between this flag and GFP_USER is that this could use emergency pools of pages, but that is a no-op on 2.4.x kernels.
GFP_USER	This is another flag of historical significance. In the 2.2.x series, an allocation was given a LOW, MEDIUM or HIGH priority. If memory was tight, a request with GFP_USER (low) would fail whereas the others would keep trying. Now it has no significance and is not treated any differently to GFP_KERNEL.
GFP_HIGHUSER	This flag indicates that the allocator should allocate from ZONE_HIGHMEM if possible. It is used when the page is allocated on behalf of a user process.
GFP_NFS	This flag is defunct. In the 2.0.x series, this flag determined what the reserved page size was. Normally, 20 free pages were reserved. If this flag was set, only five would be reserved. Now it is not treated differently anywhere.
GFP_KSWAPD	This has more historical significance. In reality, this is not treated any differently to GFP_KERNEL.

Table 6.6. High-Level GFP Flags Affecting Allocator Behavior

6.6   Avoiding Fragmentation

One important problem that must be addressed with any allocator is the problem of internal and external fragmentation. External fragmentation is the inability to service a request because the available memory exists only in small blocks. Internal fragmentation is defined as the wasted space where a large block had to be assigned to service a small request. In Linux, external fragmentation is not a serious problem because large requests for contiguous pages are rare, and usually vmalloc() (see

Flag	Description
PF_MEMALLOC	This flags the process as a memory allocator. **kswapd** sets this flag, and it is set for any process that is about to be killed by the *OOM* killer, which is discussed in Chapter 13. It tells the buddy allocator to ignore zone watermarks and assigns the pages if at all possible.
PF_MEMDIE	This is set by the OOM killer and functions the same as the PF_MEMALLOC flag by telling the page allocator to give pages if at all possible because the process is about to die.
PF_FREE_PAGES	This is set when the buddy allocator calls try_to_free_pages() itself to indicate that free pages should be reserved for the calling process in __free_pages_ok() instead of returning to the free lists.

Table 6.7. Process Flags Affecting Allocator Behavior

Chapter 7) is sufficient to service the request. The lists of free blocks ensure that large blocks do not have to be split unnecessarily.

Internal fragmentation is the single-most serious failing of the binary buddy system. Although fragmentation is expected to be in the region of 28 percent [WJNB95], it has been shown that it can be in the region of 60 percent, in comparison to just 1 percent with the first fit allocator [JW98]. It has also been shown that using variations of the buddy system will not help the situation significantly [PN77]. To address this problem, Linux uses a *slab allocator* [Bon94] to carve up pages into small blocks of memory for allocation [Tan01], which is discussed further in Chapter 8. With this combination of allocators, the kernel can ensure that the amount of memory wasted due to internal fragmentation is kept to a minimum.

6.7 What's New in 2.6

Allocating Pages The first noticeable difference seems cosmetic at first. The function alloc_pages() is now a macro and is defined in <linux/gfp.h> instead of a function defined in <linux/mm.h>. The new layout is still very recognizable, and the main difference is a subtle, but important one. In 2.4, specific code was dedicated to selecting the correct node to allocate from based on the running CPU, but 2.6 removes this distinction between NUMA and UMA architectures.

In 2.6, the function alloc_pages() calls numa_node_id() to return the logical ID of the node associated with the current running CPU. This NID is passed to _alloc_pages(), which calls NODE_DATA() with the NID as a parameter. On UMA architectures, this will unconditionally result in contig_page_data being returned, but NUMA architectures instead set up an array that NODE_DATA() uses NID as an offset into. In other words, architectures are responsible for setting up a CPU ID to NUMA memory node mapping. This is effectively still a node-local allocation policy as is used in 2.4, but it is a lot more clearly defined.

Per-CPU Page Lists The most important addition to the page allocation is the addition of the per-cpu lists, first discussed in Section 2.8.

In 2.4, a page allocation requires an interrupt-safe spinlock to be held while the allocation takes place. In 2.6, pages are allocated from a `struct per_cpu_pageset` by `buffered_rmqueue()`. If the low watermark (per_cpu_pageset→low) has not been reached, the pages will be allocated from the pageset with no requirement for a spinlock to be held. After the low watermark is reached, a large number of pages will be allocated in bulk with the interrupt-safe spinlock held, added to the per-cpu list and then one returned to the caller.

Higher order allocations, which are relatively rare, still require the interrupt-safe spinlock to be held, and there will be no delay in the splits or coalescing. With 0 order allocations, splits will be delayed until the low watermark is reached in the per-cpu set, and coalescing will be delayed until the high watermark is reached.

However, strictly speaking, this is not a lazy buddy algorithm [BL89]. Although pagesets introduce a merging delay for order-0 allocations, it is a side effect rather than an intended feature, and no method is available to drain the pagesets and merge the buddies. In other words, despite the per-cpu and new accounting code that bulks up the amount of code in `mm/page_alloc.c`, the core of the buddy algorithm remains the same as it was in 2.4.

The implication of this change is straightforward; the number of times the spinlock protecting the buddy lists must be acquired is reduced. Higher order allocations are relatively rare in Linux, so the optimization is for the common case. This change will be noticeable on a large number of CPU machines, but will make little difference to single CPUs. There are a few issues with pagesets, but they are not recognized as a serious problem. The first issue is that high-order allocations may fail if the pagesets hold order-0 pages that would normally be merged into higher order contiguous blocks. The second is that an order-0 allocation may fail if memory is low, the current CPU pageset is empty and other CPUs' pagesets are full because no mechanism exists for reclaiming pages from remote pagesets. The last potential problem is that buddies of newly freed pages could exist in other pagesets, leading to possible fragmentation problems.

Freeing Pages Two new API functions have been introduced for the freeing of pages called `free_hot_page()` and `free_cold_page()`. Predictably, they determine if the freed pages are placed on the hot or cold lists in the per-cpu pagesets. However, although the `free_cold_page()` is exported and available for use, it is actually never called.

Order-0 page frees from `__free_pages()` and frees resulting from page cache releases by `__page_cache_release()` are placed on the hot list whereas higher order allocations are freed immediately with `__free_pages_ok()`. Order-0 are usually related to userspace and are the most common type of allocation and free. By keeping them local to the CPU, lock contention will be reduced because most allocations will also be of order-0.

Eventually, lists of pages must be passed to `free_pages_bulk()`, or the pageset lists would hold all free pages. This `free_pages_bulk()` function takes a list of page block allocations, the **order** of each block and the **count** number of blocks to free from the list. There are two principal cases where this is used. The first is higher order frees passed to `__free_pages_ok()`. In this case, the page block is placed on a linked list of the specified order and a count of 1. The second case is where the high watermark is reached in the pageset for the running CPU. In this case, the pageset is passed with an order of 0 and a count of `pageset→batch`.

After the core function `__free_pages_bulk()` is reached, the mechanisms for freeing pages is very similar to the buddy lists in 2.4.

GFP Flags   There are still only three zones, so the zone modifiers remain the same. However, three new GFP flags have been added that affect how hard the VM will work, or not work, to satisfy a request. The flags are the following:

__GFP_NOFAIL   This flag is used by a caller to indicate that the allocation should never fail and that the allocator should keep trying to allocate indefinitely.

__GFP_REPEAT   This flag is used by a caller to indicate that the request should try to repeat the allocation if it fails. In the current implementation, it behaves the same as `__GFP_NOFAIL`, but later the decision might be made to fail after a while.

__GFP_NORETRY   This flag is almost the opposite of `__GFP_NOFAIL`. It indicates that, if the allocation fails, it should just return immediately.

At time of writing, these flags are not heavily used, but they have just been introduced and are likely to be used more over time. The `__GFP_REPEAT` flag, in particular, is likely to be heavily used because blocks of code which implement this flag's behavior exist throughout the kernel.

The next GFP flag that has been introduced is an allocation modifier called `__GFP_COLD`, which is used to ensure that cold pages are allocated from the per-cpu lists. From the perspective of the VM, the only user of this flag is the function `page_cache_alloc_cold()`, which is mainly used during I/O readahead. Usually, page allocations will be taken from the hot pages list.

The last new flag is `__GFP_NO_GROW`. This is an internal flag used only by the slab allocator (discussed in Chapter 8), which aliases the flag to `SLAB_NO_GROW`. It is used to indicate when new slabs should never be allocated for a particular cache. In reality, the GFP flag has just been introduced to complement the old `SLAB_NO_GROW` flag, which is currently unused in the main kernel.

CHAPTER 7

Noncontiguous Memory Allocation

It is preferable when dealing with large amounts of memory to use physically contiguous pages in memory both for cache-related and memory-access-latency reasons. Unfortunately, due to external fragmentation problems with the buddy allocator, this is not always possible. Linux provides a mechanism through `vmalloc()` where noncontiguous physical memory can be used that is contiguous in virtual memory.

An area is reserved in the virtual address space between `VMALLOC_START` and `VMALLOC_END`. The location of `VMALLOC_START` depends on the amount of available physical memory, but the region will always be at least `VMALLOC_RESERVE` in size, which on the x86 is 128MiB. The exact size of the region is discussed in Section 4.1.

The page tables in this region are adjusted as necessary to point to physical pages, which are allocated with the normal physical page allocator. This means that allocation must be a multiple of the hardware page size. Because allocations require altering the kernel page tables, there is a limitation on how much memory can be mapped with `vmalloc()` because only the virtual addresses space between `VMALLOC_START` and `VMALLOC_END` is available. As a result, `vmalloc()` is used sparingly in the core kernel. In 2.4.22, it is only used for storing the swap map information (see Chapter 11) and for loading kernel modules into memory.

This small chapter begins with a description of how the kernel tracks which areas in the vmalloc address space are used and how regions are allocated and freed.

7.1 Describing Virtual Memory Areas

The vmalloc address space is managed with a resource map allocator [Vah96]. The `struct vm_struct` is responsible for storing the base,size pairs. It is defined in `<linux/vmalloc.h>` as the following:

```
14 struct vm_struct {
15         unsigned long flags;
16         void * addr;
17         unsigned long size;
18         struct vm_struct * next;
19 };
```

A fully-fledged VMA could have been used but it contains extra information that does not apply to vmalloc areas and would be wasteful. Here is a brief description of the fields in this small struct.

flags   These set either to `VM_ALLOC`, in the case of use with `vmalloc()`, or `VM_IOREMAP`, when `ioremap()` is used to map high memory into the kernel virtual address space.

addr   This is the starting address of the memory block.

size   This is, predictably enough, the size in bytes.

next   This is a pointer to the next `vm_struct`. They are ordered by address, and the list is protected by the `vmlist_lock` lock.

As is clear, the areas are linked together by the `next` field and are ordered by address for simple searches. Each area is separated by at least one page to protect against overruns. This is illustrated by the gaps in Figure 7.1.

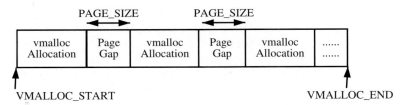

Figure 7.1. vmalloc Address Space

When the kernel wants to allocate a new area, the `vm_struct` list is searched linearly by the function `get_vm_area()`. Space for the struct is allocated with `kmalloc()`. When the virtual area is used for remapping an area for I/O (commonly referred to as *ioremapping*), this function will be called directly to map the requested area.

7.2   Allocating a Noncontiguous Area

The functions `vmalloc()`, `vmalloc_dma()` and `vmalloc_32()` are provided to allocate a memory area that is contiguous in virtual address space, as described in Table 7.1. They all take a single parameter `size`, which is rounded up to the next page alignment. They all return a linear address for the new allocated area.

As is clear from the call graph shown in Figure 7.2, there are two steps to allocating the area. The first step taken by `get_vm_area()` is to find a region large enough to store the request. It searches through a linear linked list of `vm_structs` and returns a new struct describing the allocated region.

The   second   step   is   to   allocate   the   necessary   PGD   entries   with `vmalloc_area_pages()`, PMD entries with `alloc_area_pmd()` and PTE entries with `alloc_area_pte()` before finally allocating the page with `alloc_page()`.

```
void * vmalloc(unsigned long size)
```
   Allocates a number of pages in vmalloc space that satisfy the requested size.

```
void * vmalloc_dma(unsigned long size)
```
   Allocates a number of pages from ZONE_DMA.

```
void * vmalloc_32(unsigned long size)
```
   Allocates memory that is suitable for 32-bit addressing. This ensures that
the physical page frames are in ZONE_NORMAL, which 32-bit devices will require

Table 7.1. Noncontiguous Memory Allocation API

   The page table updated by vmalloc() is not the current process, but the reference page table stored at init_mm→pgd. This means that a process accessing the vmalloc area will cause a page fault exception because its page tables are not pointing to the correct area. There is a special case in the page fault handling code that knows that the fault occured in the vmalloc area and updates the current process page tables using information from the master page table. How the use of vmalloc() relates to the buddy allocator and page faulting is illustrated in Figure 7.3.

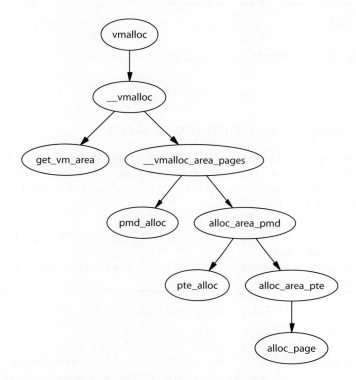

Figure 7.2. Call Graph: vmalloc()

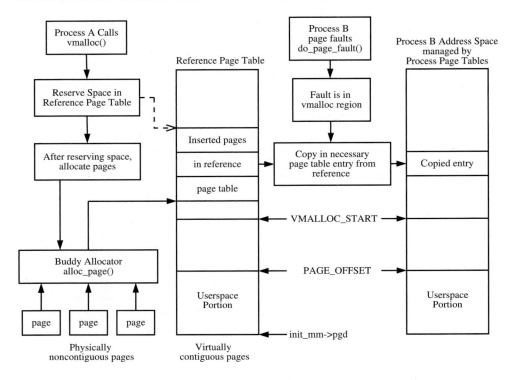

Figure 7.3. Relationship Between `vmalloc()`, `alloc_page()` and Page Faulting

7.3   Freeing a Noncontiguous Area

The function `vfree()` is responsible for freeing a virtual area as described in Table 7.2. It linearly searches the list of `vm_structs` looking for the desired region and then calls `vmfree_area_pages()` on the region of memory to be freed, as shown in Figure 7.4.

```
void vfree(void *addr)
    Frees a region of memory allocated with vmalloc(), vmalloc_dma() or
vmalloc_32()
```

Table 7.2. Noncontiguous Memory Free API

`vmfree_area_pages()` is the exact opposite of `vmalloc_area_pages()`. It walks the page tables and frees up the page table entries and associated pages for the region.

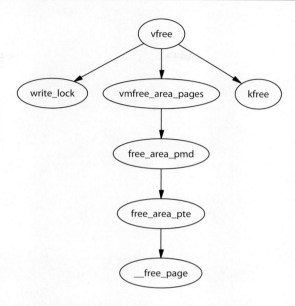

Figure 7.4. Call Graph: `vfree()`

7.4   What's New in 2.6

Noncontiguous memory allocation remains essentially the same in 2.6. The main difference is a slightly different internal API, which affects when the pages are allocated. In 2.4, `vmalloc_area_pages()` is responsible for beginning a page table walk and then allocating pages when the PTE is reached in the function `alloc_area_pte()`. In 2.6, all the pages are allocated in advance by `__vmalloc()` and placed in an array that is passed to `map_vm_area()` for insertion into the kernel page tables.

The `get_vm_area()` API has changed very slightly. When called, it behaves the same as previously because it searches the entire vmalloc virtual address space for a free area. However, a caller can search just a subset of the vmalloc address space by calling `__get_vm_area()` directly and specifying the range. This is only used by the Advance RISC Machine(ARM) architecture when loading modules.

The last significant change is the introduction of a new interface `vmap()` for the insertion of an array of pages in the vmalloc address space and is only used by the sound subsystem core. This interface was backported to 2.4.22, but it is totally unused. It is either the result of an accidental backport or was merged to ease the application of vendor-specific patches that require `vmap()`.

CHAPTER 8

Slab Allocator

In this chapter, the general-purpose allocator is described. It is a slab allocator that is very similar in many respects to the general kernel allocator used in Solaris [MM01]. Linux's implementation is heavily based on the first slab allocator paper by Bonwick [Bon94] with many improvements that bear a close resemblance to those described in his later paper [BA01]. I begin with a quick overview of the allocator, followed by a description of the different structures used before giving an in-depth tour of each task the allocator is responsible for.

The basic idea behind the slab allocator is to have caches of commonly used objects kept in an initialized state available for use by the kernel. Without an object-based allocator, the kernel will spend much of its time allocating, initializing and freeing the same object. The slab allocator aims to cache the freed object so that the basic structure is preserved between uses [Bon94].

The slab allocator consists of a variable number of caches that are linked together on a doubly linked circular list called a *cache chain*. A cache, in the context of the slab allocator, is a manager for a number of objects of a particular type, like the `mm_struct` or `fs_cache` cache, and is managed by a `struct kmem_cache_s` discussed in detail later. The caches are linked by the `next` field in the cache struct.

Each cache maintains blocks of contiguous pages in memory called *slabs* that are carved up into small chunks for the data structures and objects that the cache manages. The relationship between these different structures is illustrated in Figure 8.1.

The slab allocator has three principle aims:

- The allocation of small blocks of memory to help eliminate internal fragmentation that would be otherwise caused by the buddy system.

- The caching of commonly used objects so that the system does not waste time allocating, initializing and destroying objects. Benchmarks on Solaris showed excellent speed improvements for allocations with the slab allocator in use [Bon94].

- Better use of the hardware cache by aligning objects to the L1 or L2 caches.

To help eliminate internal fragmentation normally caused by a binary buddy allocator, two sets of caches of small memory buffers ranging from 2^5 (32) bytes to 2^{17} (131,072) bytes are maintained. One cache set is suitable for use with DMA

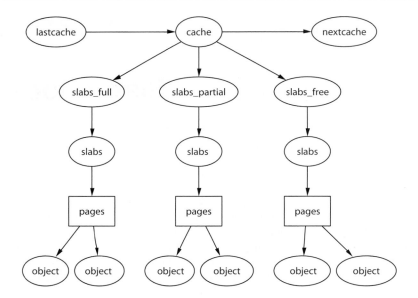

Figure 8.1. Layout of the Slab Allocator

devices. These caches are called size-N and size-N(DMA) where N is the size of the allocation, and a function `kmalloc()` (see Section 8.4.1) is provided for allocating them. With this, the single greatest problem with the low-level page allocator is addressed. The sizes caches are discussed in further detail in Section 8.4.

The second task of the slab allocator is to maintain caches of commonly used objects. For many structures used in the kernel, the time needed to initialize an object is comparable with, or exceeds, the cost of allocating space for it. When a new slab is created, a number of objects are packed into it and initialized using a constructor if available. When an object is freed, it is left in its initialized state so that object allocation will be quick.

The final task of the slab allocator is optimal hardware cache use. If there is space left over after objects are packed into a slab, the remaining space is used to *color* the slab. Slab coloring is a scheme that attempts to have objects in different slabs use different lines in the cache. By placing objects at a different starting offset within the slab, objects will likely use different lines in the CPU cache, which helps ensure that objects from the same slab cache will be unlikely to flush each other. With this scheme, space that would otherwise be wasted fulfills a new function. Figure 8.2 shows how a page allocated from the buddy allocator is used to store objects that use coloring to align the objects to the L1 CPU cache.

Linux does not attempt to color page allocations based on their physical address [Kes91] or to order where objects are placed, such as those described for data [GAV95] or code segments [HK97], but the scheme used does help improve cache line usage. Cache coloring is further discussed in Section 8.1.5. On an SMP system, a further step is taken to help cache utilization where each cache

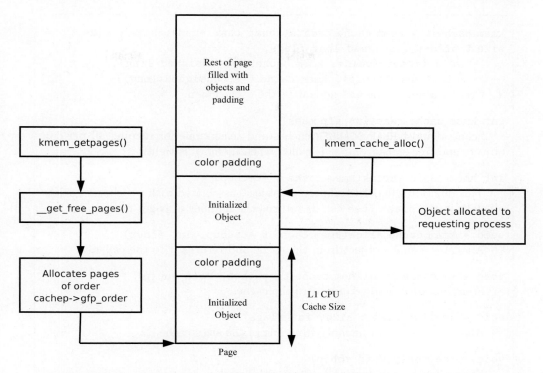

Figure 8.2. Slab Page Containing Objects Aligned to L1 CPU Cache

has a small array of objects reserved for each CPU. This is discussed further in Section 8.5.

The slab allocator provides the additional option of slab debugging if the option is set at compile time with CONFIG_SLAB_DEBUG. Two debugging features are provided called *red zoning* and *object poisoning*. With red zoning, a marker is placed at either end of the object. If this mark is disturbed, the allocator knows the object where a buffer overflow occurred and reports it. Poisoning an object will fill it with a predefined bit pattern (defined 0x5A in mm/slab.c) at slab creation and after a free. At allocation, this pattern is examined, and, if it is changed, the allocator knows that the object was used before it was allocated and flags it.

The small, but powerful, API that the allocator exports is listed in Table 8.1.

8.1 Caches

One cache exists for each type of object that is to be cached. For a full list of caches available on a running system, run cat /proc/slabinfo. This file gives some basic information on the caches. An excerpt from the output of this file looks like the following:

```
kmem_cache_t * kmem_cache_create(const char *name, size_t size,
size_t offset, unsigned long flags,
     void (*ctor)(void*, kmem_cache_t *, unsigned long),
     void (*dtor)(void*, kmem_cache_t *, unsigned long))
```
Creates a new cache and adds it to the cache chain.

`int kmem_cache_reap(int gfp_mask)`
Scans at most **REAP_SCANLEN** caches and selects one for reaping all per-cpu objects and free slabs from. It is called when memory is tight.

`int kmem_cache_shrink(kmem_cache_t *cachep)`
This function will delete all per-cpu objects associated with a cache and delete all slabs in the **slabs_free** list. It returns the number of pages freed.

`void * kmem_cache_alloc(kmem_cache_t *cachep, int flags)`
Allocates a single object from the cache and returns it to the caller.

`void kmem_cache_free(kmem_cache_t *cachep, void *objp)`
Frees an object and returns it to the cache.

`void * kmalloc(size_t size, int flags)`
Allocates a block of memory from one of the sizes cache.

`void kfree(const void *objp)`
Frees a block of memory allocated with kmalloc.

`int kmem_cache_destroy(kmem_cache_t * cachep)`
Destroys all objects in all slabs and frees up all associated memory before removing the cache from the chain.

Table 8.1. Slab Allocator API for Caches

```
slabinfo - version: 1.1 (SMP)
kmem_cache            80      80    248    5    5    1 :  252  126
urb_priv               0       0     64    0    0    1 :  252  126
tcp_bind_bucket       15     226     32    2    2    1 :  252  126
inode_cache         5714    5992    512  856  856    1 :  124   62
dentry_cache        5160    5160    128  172  172    1 :  252  126
mm_struct            240     240    160   10   10    1 :  252  126
vm_area_struct      3911    4480     96  112  112    1 :  252  126
size-64(DMA)           0       0     64    0    0    1 :  252  126
size-64              432    1357     64   23   23    1 :  252  126
size-32(DMA)          17     113     32    1    1    1 :  252  126
size-32              850    2712     32   24   24    1 :  252  126
```

Each of the column fields corresponds to a field in the **struct kmem_cache_s** structure. The columns listed in the previous excerpt are the following:

cache-name A human-readable name such as "tcp_bind_bucket"

num-active-objs Number of objects that are in use

total-objs How many objects are available in total including unused

obj-size The size of each object, typically quite small

num-active-slabs Number of slabs containing objects that are active

total-slabs How many slabs in total exist

num-pages-per-slab The pages required to create one slab, typically 1

If SMP is enabled like in the example excerpt, two more columns will be displayed after a colon. They refer to the per-CPU cache described in Section 8.5. The columns are the following:

limit This is the number of free objects the pool can have before half of it is given to the global free pool.

batchcount This is the number of objects allocated for the processor in a block when no objects are free.

To speed allocation and freeing of objects and slabs, they are arranged into three lists: slabs_full, slabs_partial and slabs_free. slabs_full has all of its objects in use. slabs_partial has free objects in it, so is a prime candidate for allocation of objects. slabs_free has no allocated objects, so is a prime candidate for slab destruction.

8.1.1 Cache Descriptor

All information describing a cache is stored in a struct kmem_cache_s declared in mm/slab.c. This is an extremely large struct, so it will be described in parts.

```
190 struct kmem_cache_s {
193     struct list_head        slabs_full;
194     struct list_head        slabs_partial;
195     struct list_head        slabs_free;
196     unsigned int            objsize;
197     unsigned int            flags;
198     unsigned int            num;
199     spinlock_t              spinlock;
200 #ifdef CONFIG_SMP
201     unsigned int            batchcount;
202 #endif
203
```

Most of these fields are of interest when allocating or freeing objects.

slabs_* These are the three lists where the slabs are stored as described in the previous section.

objsize This is the size of each object packed into the slab.

flags These flags determine how parts of the allocator will behave when dealing with the cache. See Section 8.1.2.

num This is the number of objects contained in each slab.

spinlock This is a spinlock protecting the structure from concurrent accessses.

batchcount This is the number of objects that will be allocated in batch for the per-cpu caches as described in the previous section.

```
206     unsigned int            gfporder;
209     unsigned int            gfpflags;
210
211     size_t                  colour;
212     unsigned int            colour_off;
213     unsigned int            colour_next;
214     kmem_cache_t            *slabp_cache;
215     unsigned int            growing;
216     unsigned int            dflags;
217
219     void (*ctor)(void *, kmem_cache_t *, unsigned long);
222     void (*dtor)(void *, kmem_cache_t *, unsigned long);
223
224     unsigned long           failures;
225
```

This block deals with fields of interest when allocating or freeing slabs from the cache.

gfporder This indicates the size of the slab in pages. Each slab consumes 2^{gfporder} pages because these are the allocation sizes that the buddy allocator provides.

gfpflags The GFP flags used when calling the buddy allocator to allocate pages are stored here. See Section 6.4 for a full list.

colour Each slab stores objects in different cache lines if possible. Cache coloring will be further discussed in Section 8.1.5.

colour_off This is the byte alignment to keep slabs at. For example, slabs for the size-X caches are aligned on the L1 cache.

colour_next This is the next colour line to use. This value wraps back to 0 when it reaches `colour`;

growing This flag is set to indicate if the cache is growing or not. If it is, it is much less likely that this cache will be selected to reap free slabs under memory pressure.

dflags These are the dynamic flags that change during the cache lifetime. See Section 8.1.3.

ctor A complex object has the option of providing a constructor function to be called to initialize each new object. This is a pointer to that function and may be NULL.

dtor This is the complementing object destructor and may be NULL.

failures This field is not used anywhere in the code other than being initialized to 0.

```
227     char                    name[CACHE_NAMELEN];
228     struct list_head        next;
```

These are set during cache creation.

name This is the human-readable name of the cache.

next This is the next cache on the cache chain.

```
229 #ifdef CONFIG_SMP
231     cpucache_t              *cpudata[NR_CPUS];
232 #endif
```

cpudata This is the per-cpu data and is discussed further in Section 8.5.

```
233 #if STATS
234     unsigned long           num_active;
235     unsigned long           num_allocations;
236     unsigned long           high_mark;
237     unsigned long           grown;
238     unsigned long           reaped;
239     unsigned long           errors;
240 #ifdef CONFIG_SMP
241     atomic_t                allochit;
242     atomic_t                allocmiss;
243     atomic_t                freehit;
244     atomic_t                freemiss;
245 #endif
246 #endif
247 };
```

These figures are only available if the CONFIG_SLAB_DEBUG option is set during compile time. They are all bean counters and not of general interest. The statistics for `/proc/slabinfo` are calculated when the proc entry is read by another process by examining every slab used by each cache rather than relying on these fields to be available.

num_active The current number of active objects in the cache is stored here.

num_allocations A running total of the number of objects that have been allocated on this cache is stored in this field.

high_mark This is the highest value `num_active` has had to date.

grown This is the number of times `kmem_cache_grow()` has been called.

reaped The number of times this cache has been reaped is kept here.

errors This field is never used.

allochit This is the total number of times an allocation has used the per-cpu cache.

allocmiss To complement `allochit`, this is the number of times an allocation has missed the per-cpu cache.

freehit This is the number of times a free was placed on a per-cpu cache.

freemiss This is the number of times an object was freed and placed on the global pool.

8.1.2 Cache Static Flags

A number of flags are set at cache creation time that remain the same for the lifetime of the cache. They affect how the slab is structured and how objects are stored within it. All the flags are stored in a bitmask in the `flags` field of the cache descriptor. The full list of possible flags that may be used are declared in <`linux/slab.h`>.

There are three principle sets. The first set is internal flags, which are set only by the slab allocator and are listed in Table 8.2. The only relevant flag in the set is the `CFGS_OFF_SLAB` flag, which determines where the slab descriptor is stored.

Flag	Description
CFGS_OFF_SLAB	Indicates that the slab managers for this cache are kept off-slab. This is discussed further in Section 8.2.1.
CFLGS_OPTIMIZE	This flag is only set and never used.

Table 8.2. Internal Cache Static Flags

The second set is set by the cache creator, and these flags determine how the allocator treats the slab and how objects are stored. They are listed in Table 8.3.

Flag	Description
SLAB_HWCACHE_ALIGN	Aligns the objects to the L1 CPU cache.
SLAB_MUST_HWCACHE_ALIGN	Forces alignment to the L1 CPU cache even if it is very wasteful or slab debugging is enabled.
SLAB_NO_REAP	Never reap slabs in this cache.
SLAB_CACHE_DMA	Allocates slabs with memory from ZONE_DMA.

Table 8.3. Cache Static Flags Set by Caller

The last flags are only available if the compile option CONFIG_SLAB_DEBUG is set; they are listed in Table 8.4. They determine what additional checks will be made to slabs and objects and are primarily of interest only when new caches are being developed.

Flag	Description
SLAB_DEBUG_FREE	Perform expensive checks on free
SLAB_DEBUG_INITIAL	On free, call the constructor as a verifier to ensure the object is still initialized correctly
SLAB_RED_ZONE	This places a marker at either end of objects to trap overflows
SLAB_POISON	Poison objects with a known pattern for trapping changes made to objects not allocated or initialized

Table 8.4. Cache Static Debug Flags

To prevent callers from using the wrong flags, a CREATE_MASK is defined in mm/slab.c that consists of all the allowable flags. When a cache is being created, the requested flags are compared against the CREATE_MASK and reported as a bug if invalid flags are used.

8.1.3 Cache Dynamic Flags

The dflags field has only one flag, DFLGS_GROWN, but it is important. The flag is set during kmem_cache_grow() so that kmem_cache_reap() will be unlikely to choose the cache for reaping. When the function does find a cache with this flag set, it skips the cache and removes the flag.

8.1.4 Cache Allocation Flags

These flags, listed in Table 8.5, correspond to the GFP page flag options for allocating pages for slabs. Callers sometimes call with either SLAB_* or GFP_* flags, but they really should use only SLAB_* flags. They correspond directly to the flags described in Section 6.4 so will not be discussed in detail here. It is presumed that the existence of these flags is for clarity and in case the slab allocator needs to behave differently in response to a particular flag. However, in reality, there is no difference.

Flag	Description
SLAB_ATOMIC	Equivalent to GFP_ATOMIC
SLAB_DMA	Equivalent to GFP_DMA
SLAB_KERNEL	Equivalent to GFP_KERNEL
SLAB_NFS	Equivalent to GFP_NFS
SLAB_NOFS	Equivalent to GFP_NOFS
SLAB_NOHIGHIO	Equivalent to GFP_NOHIGHIO
SLAB_NOIO	Equivalent to GFP_NOIO
SLAB_USER	Equivalent to GFP_USER

Table 8.5. Cache Allocation Flags

A very small number of flags, listed in Table 8.6, may be passed to constructor and destructor functions.

Flag	Description
SLAB_CTOR_CONSTRUCTOR	Set if the function is being called as a constructor for caches that use the same function as a constructor and a destructor.
SLAB_CTOR_ATOMIC	Indicates that the constructor may not sleep.
SLAB_CTOR_VERIFY	Indicates that the constructor should just verify that the object is initialized correctly.

Table 8.6. Cache Constructor Flags

8.1.5   Cache Coloring

To use the hardware cache better, the slab allocator will offset objects in different slabs by different amounts depending on the amount of space left over in the slab. The offset is in units of BYTES_PER_WORD unless SLAB_HWCACHE_ALIGN is set, in which case it is aligned to blocks of L1_CACHE_BYTES for alignment to the L1 hardware cache.

During cache creation, how many objects can fit on a slab (see Section 8.2.7) and how many bytes would be wasted are calculated. Based on wastage, two figures are calculated for the cache descriptor:

colour This is the number of different offsets that can be used.

colour_off This is the multiple to offset each object in the slab.

With the objects offset, they will use different lines on the associative hardware cache. Therefore, objects from slabs are less likely to overwrite each other in memory.

The result of this is best explained by an example. Let us say that s_mem (the address of the first object) on the slab is 0 for convenience, that 100 bytes are wasted on the slab and alignment is to be at 32 bytes to the L1 Hardware Cache on a Pentium II.

In this scenario, the first slab created will have its objects start at 0. The second will start at 32, the third at 64, and the fourth at 96, and the fifth will start back at 0. With this, objects from each of the slabs will not hit the same hardware cache line on the CPU. The value of colour is 3 and colour_off is 32.

8.1.6 Cache Creation

The function kmem_cache_create() is responsible for creating new caches and adding them to the cache chain. The tasks that are taken to create a cache are the following:

- Perform basic sanity checks for bad usage.

- Perform debugging checks if CONFIG_SLAB_DEBUG is set.

- Allocate a kmem_cache_t from the cache_cache slab cache.

- Align the object size to the word size.

- Calculate how many objects will fit on a slab.

- Align the object size to the hardware cache.

- Calculate color offsets.

- Initialize remaining fields in the cache descriptor.

- Add the new cache to the cache chain.

Figure 8.3 shows the call graph relevant to the creation of a cache; each function is fully described in the Code Commentary.

8.1.7 Cache Reaping

When a slab is freed, it is placed on the slabs_free list for future use. Caches do not automatically shrink themselves, so, when **kswapd** notices that memory is tight, it calls kmem_cache_reap() to free some memory. This function is responsible for selecting a cache that will be required to shrink its memory usage. It is worth noting that cache reaping does not take into account what memory node or zone is under pressure. This means that, with a NUMA or high memory machine, it is possible the kernel will spend a lot of time freeing memory from regions that are under no memory pressure, but this is not a problem for architectures like the x86, which has only one bank of memory.

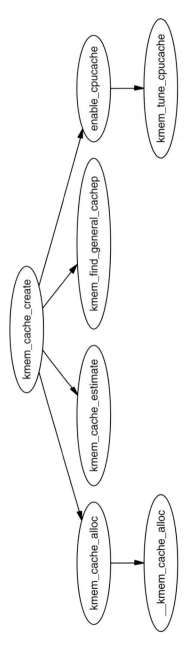

Figure 8.3. Call Graph: kmem_cache_create()

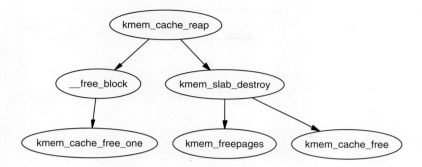

Figure 8.4. Call Graph: `kmem_cache_reap()`

The call graph in Figure 8.4 is deceptively simple because the task of selecting the proper cache to reap is quite long. In the event that the system has numerous caches, only `REAP_SCANLEN` (currently defined as 10) caches are examined in each call. The last cache to be scanned is stored in the variable `clock_searchp` so as not to examine the same caches repeatedly. For each scanned cache, the reaper does the following:

- Check flags for `SLAB_NO_REAP` and skip if set.

- If the cache is growing, skip it.

- If the cache has grown recently or is currently growing, `DFLGS_GROWN` will be set. If this flag is set, the slab is skipped, but the flag is cleared so that it will be a reap candidate the next time.

- Count the number of free slabs in `slabs_free` and calculate how many pages that would free in the variable `pages`.

- If the cache has constructors or large slabs, adjust `pages` to make it less likely for the cache to be selected.

- If the number of pages that would be freed exceeds `REAP_PERFECT`, free half of the slabs in `slabs_free`.

- Otherwise, scan the rest of the caches and select the one that would free the most pages for freeing half of its slabs in `slabs_free`.

8.1.8 Cache Shrinking

When a cache is selected to shrink itself, the steps it takes are simple and brutal:

- Delete all objects in the per-CPU caches.

- Delete all slabs from `slabs_free` unless the growing flag gets set.

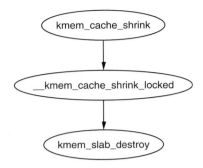

Figure 8.5. Call Graph: `kmem_cache_shrink()`

Linux is nothing, if not subtle.

Two varieties of shrink functions are provided with confusingly similar names. `kmem_cache_shrink()`, shown in Figure 8.5, removes all slabs from **slabs_free** and returns the number of pages freed as a result. This is the principal function exported for use by the slab allocator users.

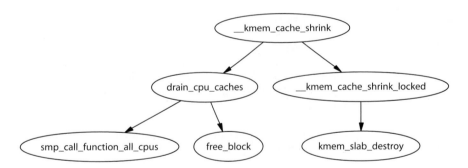

Figure 8.6. Call Graph: `__kmem_cache_shrink()`

The second function, `__kmem_cache_shrink()`, shown in Figure 8.6, frees all slabs from **slabs_free** and then verifies that **slabs_partial** and **slabs_full** are empty. This is for internal use only and is important during cache destruction when it doesn't matter how many pages are freed, just that the cache is empty.

8.1.9   Cache Destroying

When a module is unloaded, it is responsible for destroying any cache with the function `kmem_cache_destroy()`, shown in Figure 8.7. It is important that the cache is properly destroyed because two caches of the same human-readable name are not allowed to exist. Core kernel code often does not bother to destroy its

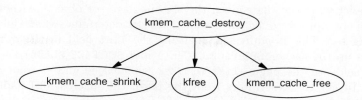

Figure 8.7. Call Graph: `kmem_cache_destroy()`

caches because their existence persists for the life of the system. The steps taken
to destroy a cache are the following:

- Delete the cache from the cache chain.

- Shrink the cache to delete all slabs.

- Free any per-CPU caches (`kfree()`).

- Delete the cache descriptor from the `cache_cache`.

8.2   Slabs

This section will describe how a slab is structured and managed. The struct that
describes it is much simpler than the cache descriptor, but how the slab is arranged
is considerably more complex. It is declared as follows:

```
typedef struct slab_s {
    struct list_head       list;
    unsigned long          colouroff;
    void                   *s_mem;
    unsigned int           inuse;
    kmem_bufctl_t          free;
} slab_t;
```

The fields in this simple struct are as follows:

list This is the linked list the slab belongs to. This will be either `slab_full`,
`slab_partial` or `slab_free` from the cache manager.

colouroff This is the color offset from the base address of the first object within
the slab. The address of the first object is `s_mem + colouroff`.

s_mem This gives the starting address of the first object within the slab.

inuse This gives the number of active objects in the slab.

free This is an array of `bufctls` used for storing locations of free objects. See
Section 8.2.3 for further details.

The reader will note that, given the slab manager or objects within the slab, there does not appear to be an obvious way to determine what slab or cache they belong to. This is addressed by using the `list` field in the `struct page` that makes up the cache. `SET_PAGE_CACHE()` and `SET_PAGE_SLAB()` use the `next` and `prev` fields on the `page→list` to track what cache and slab an object belongs to. To get the descriptors from the page, the macros, `GET_PAGE_CACHE()` and `GET_PAGE_SLAB()`, are available. This set of relationships is illustrated in Figure 8.8.

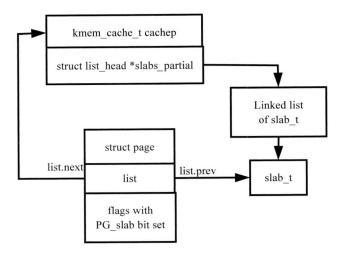

Figure 8.8. Page to Cache and Slab Relationship

The last issue is where the slab management struct is kept. Slab managers are kept either on-(`CFLGS_OFF_SLAB` set in the static flags) or off-slab. Where they are placed are determined by the size of the object during cache creation. In Figure 8.8, the `struct slab_t` could be stored at the beginning of the page frame although the figure implies the `struct slab_` is separate from the page frame.

8.2.1 Storing the Slab Descriptor

If the objects are larger than a threshold (512 bytes on x86), `CFGS_OFF_SLAB` is set in the cache flags, and the *slab descriptor* is kept off-slab in one of the sizes cache (see Section 8.4). The selected sizes cache is large enough to contain the `struct slab_t`, and `kmem_cache_slabmgmt()` allocates from it as necessary. This limits the number of objects that can be stored on the slab because there is limited space for the `bufctls`. However, that is unimportant because the objects are large, so there should not be many stored in a single slab.

Alternatively, the slab manager is reserved at the beginning of the slab. When stored on-slab, enough space is kept at the beginning of the slab to store both the `slab_t` and the `kmem_bufctl_t`, which is an array of unsigned integers. The array is responsible for tracking the index of the next free object that is available for use,

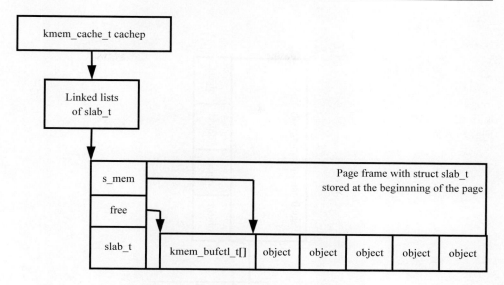

Figure 8.9. Slab With Descriptor On-Slab

which is discussed further in Section 8.2.3. The actual objects are stored after the `kmem_bufctl_t` array.

Figure 8.9 should help clarify what a slab with the descriptor on-slab looks like, and Figure 8.10 illustrates how a cache uses a sizes cache to store the slab descriptor when the descriptor is kept off-slab.

8.2.2 Slab Creation

At this point, we have seen how the cache is created, but, on creation, it is an empty cache with empty lists for its `slab_full`, `slab_partial` and `slabs_free`. New slabs are allocated to a cache by calling the function `kmem_cache_grow()` whose call graph is shown in Figure 8.11. This is frequently called "cache growing" and occurs when no objects are left in the `slabs_partial` list and when there are no slabs in `slabs_free`. The tasks it fulfills are the following:

- Perform basic sanity checks to guard against bad usage.

- Calculate color offset for objects in this slab.

- Allocate memory for the slab and acquire a slab descriptor.

- Link the pages used for the slab to the slab and cache descriptors described in Section 8.2.

- Initialize objects in the slab.

- Add the slab to the cache.

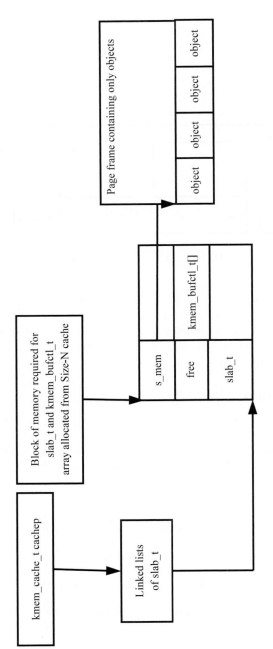

Figure 8.10. Slab With Descriptor Off-Slab

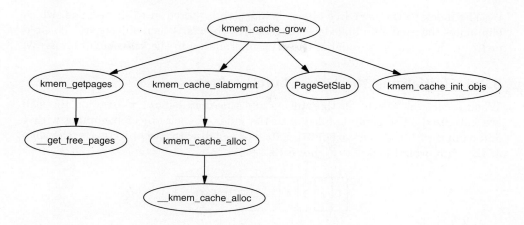

Figure 8.11. Call Graph: `kmem_cache_grow()`

8.2.3   Tracking Free Objects

The slab allocator has got to have a quick and simple means of tracking where free objects are on the partially filled slabs. It achieves this by using an array of unsigned integers called `kmem_bufctl_t` that is associated with each slab manager. Obviously, it is up to the slab manager to know where its free objects are.

Historically, and according to the paper describing the slab allocator [Bon94], `kmem_bufctl_t` was a linked list of objects. In Linux 2.2.x, this struct was a union of three items: a pointer to the next free object, a pointer to the slab manager and a pointer to the object. Which field in the union it was depended on the state of the object.

Today, the slab and cache an object belongs to is determined by the `struct page`, and `kmem_bufctl_t` is simply an integer array of object indices. The number of elements in the array is the same as the number of objects on the slab.

```
141 typedef unsigned int kmem_bufctl_t;
```

Because the array is kept after the slab descriptor and there is no pointer to the first element directly, a helper macro `slab_bufctl()` is provided.

```
163 #define slab_bufctl(slabp) \
164         ((kmem_bufctl_t *)(((slab_t*)slabp)+1))
```

This seemingly cryptic macro is quite simple when broken down. The parameter `slabp` is a pointer to the slab manager. The expression `((slab_t*)slabp)+1` casts `slabp` to a `slab_t` struct and adds 1 to it. This will give a pointer to a `slab_t`, which is actually the beginning of the `kmem_bufctl_t` array. `(kmem_bufctl_t *)` casts the `slab_t` pointer to the required type. The results in blocks of code that contain `slab_bufctl(slabp)[i]`. Translated, that says "take a pointer to a slab descriptor, offset it with `slab_bufctl()` to the beginning of the `kmem_bufctl_t` array and return the *ith* element of the array."

The index to the next free object in the slab is stored in slab_t→free, which eliminates the need for a linked list to track free objects. When objects are allocated or freed, this pointer is updated based on information in the kmem_bufctl_t array.

8.2.4   Initializing the kmem_bufctl_t Array

When a cache is grown, all the objects and the kmem_bufctl_t array on the slab are initialized. The array is filled with the index of each object beginning with 1 and ending with the marker BUFCTL_END. For a slab with five objects, the elements of the array would look like Figure 8.12.

Figure 8.12. Initialized kmem_bufctl_t Array

The value 0 is stored in slab_t→free because the $0th$ object is the first free object to be used. The idea is that, for a given object n, the index of the next free object will be stored in kmem_bufctl_t[n]. Looking at the previous array, the next object free after 0 is 1. After 1, there is two and so on. As the array is used, this arrangement will make the array act as an LIFO for free objects.

8.2.5   Finding the Next Free Object

When allocating an object, kmem_cache_alloc() performs the real work of updating the kmem_bufctl_t() array by calling kmem_cache_alloc_one_tail(). The field slab_t→free has the index of the first free object. The index of the next free object is at kmem_bufctl_t[slab_t→free]. In code terms, this looks like

```
1253      objp = slabp->s_mem + slabp->free*cachep->objsize;
1254      slabp->free=slab_bufctl(slabp)[slabp->free];
```

The field slabp→s_mem is a pointer to the first object on the slab. slabp→free is the index of the object to allocate, and it has to be multiplied by the size of an object.

The index of the next free object is stored at kmem_bufctl_t[slabp→free]. There is no pointer directly to the array, so the helper macro slab_bufctl() is used. Note that the kmem_bufctl_t array is not changed during allocations, but that the elements that are unallocated are unreachable. For example, after two allocations, index 0 and 1 of the kmem_bufctl_t array are not pointed to by any other element.

8.2.6   Updating kmem_bufctl_t

The kmem_bufctl_t list is only updated when an object is freed in the function kmem_cache_free_one(). The array is updated with this block of code:

```
1451        unsigned int objnr = (objp-slabp->s_mem)/cachep->objsize;
1452
1453        slab_bufctl(slabp)[objnr] = slabp->free;
1454        slabp->free = objnr;
```

The pointer `objp` is the object about to be freed, and `objnr` is its index.
`kmem_bufctl_t[objnr]` is updated to point to the current value of `slabp→free`,
effectively placing the object pointed to by `free` on the pseudolinked list.
`slabp→free` is updated to the object being freed so that it will be the next one
allocated.

8.2.7   Calculating the Number of Objects on a Slab

During cache creation, the function `kmem_cache_estimate()` is called to calculate how many objects may be stored on a single slab, which takes into account
whether the slab descriptor must be stored on-slab or off-slab and the size of each
`kmem_bufctl_t` needed to track if an object is free or not. It returns the number of
objects that may be stored and how many bytes are wasted. The number of wasted
bytes is important if cache coloring is to be used.

The calculation is quite basic and takes the following steps:

- Initialize `wastage` to be the total size of the slab, i.e., $PAGE\_SIZE^{gfp\_order}$.

- Subtract the amount of space required to store the slab descriptor.

- Count up the number of objects that may be stored. Include the size of the
  `kmem_bufctl_t` if the slab descriptor is stored on the slab. Keep increasing
  the size of i until the slab is filled.

- Return the number of objects and bytes wasted.

8.2.8   Slab Destroying

When a cache is being shrunk or destroyed, the slabs will be deleted. Because the
objects may have destructors, these must be called, so the tasks of this function are
the following:

- If available, call the destructor for every object in the slab.

- If debugging is enabled, check the red marking and poison pattern.

- Free the pages the slab uses.

The call graph in Figure 8.13 is very simple.

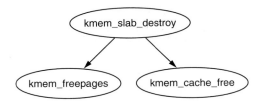

Figure 8.13. Call Graph: `kmem_slab_destroy()`

8.3   Objects

This section will cover how objects are managed. At this point, most of the really hard work has been completed by either the cache or slab managers.

8.3.1   Initializing Objects in a Slab

When a slab is created, all the objects in it are put in an initialized state. If a constructor is available, it is called for each object, and it is expected that objects are left in an initialized state upon free. Conceptually, the initialization is very simple. Cycle through all objects, call the constructor, and initialize the `kmem_bufctl` for it. The function `kmem_cache_init_objs()` is responsible for initializing the objects.

8.3.2   Object Allocation

The function `kmem_cache_alloc()` is responsible for allocating one object to the caller, which behaves slightly different in the UP and SMP cases. Figure 8.14 shows the basic call graph that is used to allocate an object in the SMP case.

There are four basic steps. The first step (`kmem_cache_alloc_head()`) covers basic checking to make sure the allocation is allowable. The second step is to select which slab list to allocate from. This will be one of `slabs_partial` or `slabs_free`. If `slabs_free` does not have any, the cache is grown (see Section 8.2.2) to create a new slab in `slabs_free`. The final step is to allocate the object from the selected slab.

The SMP case takes one further step. Before allocating one object, it will check to see if one is available from the per-CPU cache and will use it if there is. If not, it will allocate `batchcount` number of objects in bulk and place them in its per-cpu cache. See Section 8.5 for more information on the per-cpu caches.

8.3.3   Object Freeing

`kmem_cache_free()`, whose call graph is shown in Figure 8.15, is used to free objects, and it has a relatively simple task. Just like `kmem_cache_alloc()`, it behaves differently in the UP and SMP cases. The principal difference between the two cases

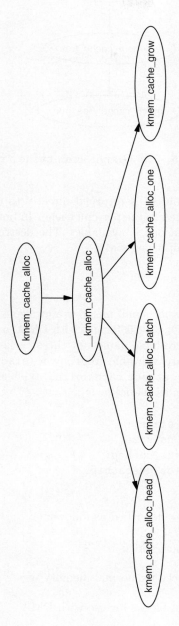

Figure 8.14. Call Graph: kmem_cache_alloc()

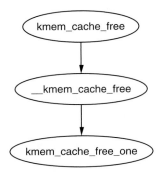

Figure 8.15. Call Graph: `kmem_cache_free()`

is that, in the UP case, the object is returned directly to the slab, but, with the SMP case, the object is returned to the per-cpu cache. In both cases, the destructor for the object will be called if one is available. The destructor is responsible for returning the object to the initialized state.

8.4   Sizes Cache

Linux keeps two sets of caches for small memory allocations for which the physical page allocator is unsuitable. One set is for use with DMA, and the other is suitable for normal use. The human-readable names for these caches are *size-N cache* and *size-N(DMA) cache*, which are viewable from `/proc/slabinfo`. Information for each sized cache is stored in a `struct cache_sizes`, typedeffed to `cache_sizes_t`, which is defined in `mm/slab.c` as the following:

```
331 typedef struct cache_sizes {
332     size_t           cs_size;
333     kmem_cache_t    *cs_cachep;
334     kmem_cache_t    *cs_dmacachep;
335 } cache_sizes_t;
```

The fields in this struct are described as follows:

cs_size The size of the memory block

cs_cachep The cache of blocks for normal memory use

cs_dmacachep The cache of blocks for use with DMA

Because a limited number of these caches exist, a static array called `cache_sizes` is initialized at compile time, beginning with 32 bytes on a 4KiB machine and 64 for greater page sizes.

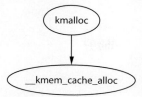

Figure 8.16. Call Graph: `kmalloc()`

```
337 static cache_sizes_t cache_sizes[] = {
338 #if PAGE_SIZE == 4096
339    {     32,        NULL, NULL},
340 #endif
341    {     64,        NULL, NULL},
342    {    128,        NULL, NULL},
343    {    256,        NULL, NULL},
344    {    512,        NULL, NULL},
345    {   1024,        NULL, NULL},
346    {   2048,        NULL, NULL},
347    {   4096,        NULL, NULL},
348    {   8192,        NULL, NULL},
349    {  16384,        NULL, NULL},
350    {  32768,        NULL, NULL},
351    {  65536,        NULL, NULL},
352    {131072,        NULL, NULL},
353    {      0,        NULL, NULL}
```

As is obvious, this is a static array that is zero terminated and that consists of buffers of succeeding powers of 2 from 2^5 to 2^{17}. An array now exists that describes each sized cache, which must be initialized with caches at system startup.

8.4.1   kmalloc()

With the existence of the sizes cache, the slab allocator is able to offer a new allocator function, `kmalloc()`, for use when small memory buffers are required. When a request is received, the appropriate sizes cache is selected, and an object is assigned from it. The call graph in Figure 8.16 is therefore very simple because all the hard work is in cache allocation.

8.4.2   kfree()

Just as there is a `kmalloc()` function to allocate small memory objects for use, there is a `kfree()` for freeing it. As with `kmalloc()`, the real work takes place during object freeing (See Section 8.3.3) so the call graph in Figure 8.17 is very simple.

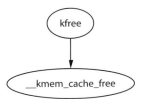

Figure 8.17. Call Graph: `kfree()`

8.5 Per-CPU Object Cache

One of the tasks that the slab allocator is dedicated to is improved hardware cache use. An aim of high performance computing [CS98] in general is to use data on the same CPU for as long as possible. Linux achieves this by trying to keep objects in the same CPU cache with a per-CPU object cache, simply called a *cpucache* for each CPU in the system.

When allocating or freeing objects, they are placed in the cpucache. When no objects are free, a `batch` of objects is placed into the pool. When the pool gets too large, half of them are removed and placed in the global cache. This way the hardware cache will be used for as long as possible on the same CPU.

The second major benefit of this method is that spinlocks do not have to be held when accessing the CPU pool because we are guaranteed another CPU won't access the local data. This is important because, without the caches, the spinlock would have to be acquired for every allocation and free, which is unnecessarily expensive.

8.5.1 Describing the Per-CPU Object Cache

Each cache descriptor has a pointer to an array of cpucaches, described in the cache descriptor as:

```
231     cpucache_t                  *cpudata[NR_CPUS];
```

This structure is very simple.

```
173 typedef struct cpucache_s {
174     unsigned int avail;
175     unsigned int limit;
176 } cpucache_t;
```

The fields are as follows:

avail This is the number of free objects available on this cpucache.

limit This is the total number of free objects that can exist.

A helper macro `cc_data()` is provided to give the cpucache for a given cache and processor. It is defined as:

```
180 #define cc_data(cachep) \
181         ((cachep)->cpudata[smp_processor_id()])
```

This will take a given cache descriptor (`cachep`) and return a pointer from the cpucache array (`cpudata`). The index needed is the ID of the current processor, `smp_processor_id()`.

Pointers to objects on the cpucache are placed immediately after the `cpucache_t` struct. This is very similar to how objects are stored after a slab descriptor.

8.5.2   Adding/Removing Objects From the Per-CPU Cache

To prevent fragmentation, objects are always added or removed from the end of the array. To add an object (`obj`) to the CPU cache (`cc`), the following block of code is used:

```
cc_entry(cc)[cc->avail++] = obj;
```

To remove an object, this block of code is used:

```
obj = cc_entry(cc)[--cc->avail];
```

There is a helper macro called `cc_entry()`, which gives a pointer to the first object in the cpucache. It is defined as:

```
178 #define cc_entry(cpucache) \
179         ((void **)(((cpucache_t*)(cpucache))+1))
```

This takes a pointer to a cpucache and increments the value by the size of the `cpucache_t` descriptor and gives the first object in the cache.

8.5.3   Enabling Per-CPU Caches

When a cache is created, its CPU cache has to be enabled, and memory has to be allocated for it using `kmalloc()`. The function `enable_cpucache()` is responsible for deciding what size to make the cache and for calling `kmem_tune_cpucache()` to allocate memory for it.

Obviously, a CPU cache cannot exist until after the various sizes caches have been enabled, so a global variable `g_cpucache_up` is used to prevent CPU caches from being enabled prematurely. The function `enable_all_cpucaches()` cycles through all caches in the cache chain and enables their cpucache.

After the CPU cache has been set up, it can be accessed without locking because a CPU will never access the wrong cpucache, so it is guaranteed safe access to it.

8.5.4   Updating Per-CPU Information

When the per-cpu caches have been created or changed, each CPU is signalled by an IPI. It is not sufficient to change all the values in the cache descriptor because that would lead to cache coherency issues and spinlocks would have to be used to protect the CPU caches. Instead a `ccupdate_t` struct is populated with all the information that each CPU needs, and each CPU swaps the new data with the old information in the cache descriptor. The struct for storing the new cpucache information is defined as follows:

```
868 typedef struct ccupdate_struct_s
869 {
870     kmem_cache_t *cachep;
871     cpucache_t *new[NR_CPUS];
872 } ccupdate_struct_t;
```

cachep is the cache being updated, and new is the array of the cpucache descriptors for each CPU on the system. The function smp_function_all_cpus() is used to get each CPU to call the do_ccupdate_local() function, which swaps the information from ccupdate_struct_t with the information in the cache descriptor.

After the information has been swapped, the old data can be deleted.

8.5.5 Draining a Per-CPU Cache

When a cache is being shrunk, its first step is to drain the cpucaches of any objects they might have by calling drain_cpu_caches(). This is so that the slab allocator will have a clearer view of what slabs can be freed or not. This is important because, if just one object in a slab is placed in a per-cpu cache, that whole slab cannot be freed. If the system is tight on memory, saving a few milliseconds on allocations has a low priority.

8.6 Slab Allocator Initialization

Here I describe how the slab allocator initializes itself. When the slab allocator creates a new cache, it allocates the kmem_cache_t from the cache_cache or kmem_cache cache. This is an obvious chicken and egg problem, so the cache_cache has to be statically initialized as:

```
357 static kmem_cache_t cache_cache = {
358     slabs_full:     LIST_HEAD_INIT(cache_cache.slabs_full),
359     slabs_partial:  LIST_HEAD_INIT(cache_cache.slabs_partial),
360     slabs_free:     LIST_HEAD_INIT(cache_cache.slabs_free),
361     objsize:        sizeof(kmem_cache_t),
362     flags:          SLAB_NO_REAP,
363     spinlock:       SPIN_LOCK_UNLOCKED,
364     colour_off:     L1_CACHE_BYTES,
365     name:           "kmem_cache",
366 };
```

This code statically initialized the kmem_cache_t struct as follows:

358-360 This initializes the three lists as empty lists.

361 The size of each object is the size of a cache descriptor.

362 The creation and deleting of caches is extremely rare, so do not ever consider it for reaping.

363 This initializes the spinlock unlocked.

364 This aligns the objects to the L1 cache.

365 This records the human-readable name.

This code statically defines all the fields that can be calculated at compile time. To initialize the rest of the struct, `kmem_cache_init()` is called from `start_kernel()`.

8.7 Interfacing With the Buddy Allocator

The slab allocator does not come with pages attached; it must ask the physical page allocator for its pages. Two APIs are provided for this task called `kmem_getpages()` and `kmem_freepages()`. They are basically wrappers around the buddy allocators API so that slab flags will be taken into account for allocations. For allocations, the default flags are taken from `cachep→gfpflags`, and the order is taken from `cachep→gfporder` where `cachep` is the cache requesting the pages. When freeing the pages, `PageClearSlab()` will be called for every page being freed before calling `free_pages()`.

8.8 What's New in 2.6

The first obvious change is that the version of the `/proc/slabinfo` format has changed from 1.1 to 2.0 and is a lot friendlier to read. The most helpful change is that the fields now have a header negating the need to memorize what each column means.

The principal algorithms and ideas remain the same. There are no major algorithm shakeups, but the implementation is quite different. Particularly, there is a greater emphasis on the use of per-cpu objects and the avoidance of locking. Second, a lot more debugging code is mixed in, so keep an eye out for `#ifdef DEBUG` blocks of code because they can be ignored when reading the code first. Last, some changes are purely cosmetic with function name changes, but very similar behavior. For example, `kmem_cache_estimate()` is now called `cache_estimate()` even though they are identical in every other respect.

Cache descriptor The changes to the `kmem_cache_s` are minimal. First, the elements are reordered to have commonly used elements, such as the per-cpu related data, at the beginning of the struct (see Section 3.9 to for the reasoning). Second, the slab lists (e.g. `slabs_full`) and statistics related to them have been moved to a separate `struct kmem_list3`. Comments and the unusual use of macros indicate that there is a plan to make the structure per-node.

Cache Static Flags   The flags in 2.4 still exist, and their use is the same. CFLGS_OPTIMIZE no longer exists, but its use in 2.4 was nonexistent. Two new flags have been introduced, which are the following:

> **SLAB_STORE_USER**   This is a debugging-only flag for recording the function that freed an object. If the object is used after it was freed, the poison bytes will not match, and a kernel error message will be displayed. Because the last function to use the object is known, it can simplify debugging.

> **SLAB_RECLAIM_ACCOUNT**   This flag is set for caches with objects that are easily reclaimable, such as inode caches. A counter is maintained in a variable called slab_reclaim_pages to record how many pages are used in slabs allocated to these caches. This counter is later used in vm_enough_memory() to help determine if the system is truly out of memory.

Cache Reaping   This is one of the most interesting changes made to the slab allocator. kmem_cache_reap() no longer exists because it is very indiscriminate in how it shrinks caches when the cache user could have made a far superior selection. Users of caches can now register a shrink cache callback with set_shrinker() for the intelligent aging and shrinking of slabs. This simple function populates a struct shrinker with a pointer to the callback and a seeks weight, which indicates how difficult it is to recreate an object before placing it in a linked list called shrinker_list.

   During page reclaim, the function shrink_slab() is called, which steps through the full shrinker_list and calls each shrinker callback twice. The first call passes 0 as a parameter, which indicates that the callback should return how many pages it expects it could free if it was called properly. A basic heuristic is applied to determine if it is worth the cost of using the callback. If it is, it is called a second time with a parameter indicating how many objects to free.

   How this mechanism accounts for the number of pages is a little tricky. Each task struct has a field called reclaim_state. When the slab allocator frees pages, this field is updated with the number of pages that is freed. Before calling shrink_slab(), this field is set to 0 and then read again after shrink_cache returns to determine how many pages were freed.

Other changes   The rest of the changes are essentially cosmetic. For example, the slab descriptor is now called struct slab instead of slab_t, which is consistent with the general trend of moving away from typedefs. Per-cpu caches remain essentially the same except the structs and APIs have new names. The same type of points applies to most of the 2.6 slab allocator implementation.

CHAPTER 9

High Memory Management

The kernel may only directly address memory for which it has set up a page table entry. In the most common case, the user/kernel address space split of 3GiB/1GiB implies that, at best, only 896MiB of memory may be directly accessed at any given time on a 32-bit machine as explained in Section 4.1. On 64-bit hardware, this is not really an issue because there is more than enough virtual address space. It is highly unlikely there will be machines running 2.4 kernels with more than terabytes of RAM.

Many high end 32-bit machines have more than 1GiB of memory, and the inconveniently located memory cannot be simply ignored. The solution Linux uses is to temporarily map pages from high memory into the lower page tables. This will be discussed in Section 9.2.

High memory and I/O have a related problem that must be addressed because not all devices are able to address high memory or all the memory available to the CPU. This may be the case if the CPU has PAE extensions enabled, the device is limited to addresses the size of a signed 32-bit integer (2GiB) or a 32-bit device is being used on a 64-bit architecture. Asking the device to write to memory will fail at best and possibly disrupt the kernel at worst. The solution to this problem is to use a *bounce buffer*, and this will be discussed in Section 9.5.

This chapter begins with a brief description of how the *Persistent Kernel Map (PKMap)* address space is managed before talking about how pages are mapped and unmapped from high memory. The subsequent section will deal with the case where the mapping must be atomic before discussing bounce buffers in depth. Finally, we will talk about how emergency pools are used for when memory is very tight.

9.1 Managing the PKMap Address Space

Space is reserved at the top of the kernel page tables from PKMAP_BASE to FIXADDR_START for a PKMap. The size of the space reserved varies slightly. On the x86, PKMAP_BASE is at 0xFE000000, and the address of FIXADDR_START is a compile time constant that varies with configure options, but that is typically only a few pages located near the end of the linear address space. This means that there is slightly below 32MiB of page table space for mapping pages from high memory into usable space.

For mapping pages, a single page set of PTEs is stored at the beginning of the PKMap area to allow 1,024 high pages to be mapped into low memory for short periods with the function `kmap()` and to be unmapped with `kunmap()`. The pool seems very small, but the page is only mapped by `kmap()` for a *very* short time. Comments in the code indicate that there was a plan to allocate contiguous page table entries to expand this area, but it has remained just that, comments in the code, so a large portion of the PKMap is unused.

The page table entry for use with `kmap()` is called `pkmap_page_table`, which is located at `PKMAP_BASE` and which is set up during system initialization. On the x86, this takes place at the end of the `pagetable_init()` function. The pages for the PGD and PMD entries are allocated by the boot memory allocator to ensure they exist.

The current state of the page table entries is managed by a simple array called `pkmap_count`, which has `LAST_PKMAP` entries in it. On an x86 system without PAE, this is 1,024, and, with PAE, it is 512. More accurately, albeit not expressed in code, the `LAST_PKMAP` variable is equivalent to `PTRS_PER_PTE`.

Each element is not exactly a reference count, but it is very close. If the entry is 0, the page is free and has not been used since the last TLB flush. If it is 1, the slot is unused, but a page is still mapped there waiting for a TLB flush. Flushes are delayed until every slot has been used at least once because a global flush is required for all CPUs when the global page tables are modified and is extremely expensive. Any higher value is a reference count of `n-1` users of the page.

9.2 Mapping High Memory Pages

The API for mapping pages from high memory is described in Table 9.1. The main function for mapping a page is `kmap()`, whose call graph is shown in Figure 9.1. For users that do not want to block, `kmap_nonblock()` is available, and interrupt users have `kmap_atomic()`. The kmap pool is quite small, so it is important that users of `kmap()` call `kunmap()` as quickly as possible because the pressure on this small window grows incrementally worse as the size of high memory grows in comparison to low memory.

The `kmap()` function itself is fairly simple. It first checks to make sure an interrupt is not calling this function (because it may sleep) and calls `out_of_line_bug()` if true. An interrupt handler calling `BUG()` would panic the system, so `out_of_line_bug()` prints out bug information and exits cleanly. The second check is that the page is below `highmem_start_page` because pages below this mark are already visible and do not need to be mapped.

It then checks if the page is already in low memory and simply returns the address if it is. This way, users that need `kmap()` may use it unconditionally knowing that, if it is already a low memory page, the function is still safe. If it is a high page to be mapped, `kmap_high()` is called to begin the real work.

The `kmap_high()` function begins with checking the `page→virtual` field, which is set if the page is already mapped. If it is NULL, `map_new_virtual()` provides a mapping for the page.

void * kmap(struct page *page)
  This takes a struct page from high memory and maps it into low memory. The address returned is the virtual address of the mapping.

void * kmap_nonblock(struct page *page)
  This is the same as kmap() except it will not block if slots are not available and will instead return NULL. This is not the same as kmap_atomic(), which uses specially reserved slots.

void * kmap_atomic(struct page *page, enum km_type type)
  There are slots maintained in the map for atomic use by interrupts (see Section 9.4). Their use is heavily discouraged and callers of this function may not sleep or schedule. This function will map a page from high memory atomically for a specific purpose.

Table 9.1. High Memory Mapping API

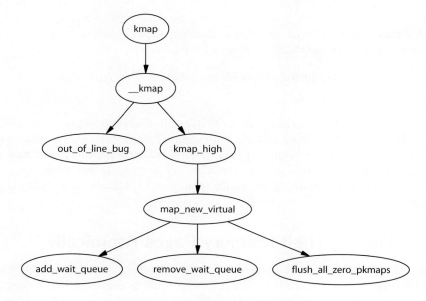

Figure 9.1. Call Graph: kmap()

Creating a new virtual mapping with map_new_virtual() is a simple case of linearly scanning pkmap_count. The scan starts at last_pkmap_nr instead of 0 to prevent searching the same areas repeatedly between kmap()s. When last_pkmap_nr wraps around to 0, flush_all_zero_pkmaps() is called to set all entries from 1 to 0 before flushing the TLB.

If, after another scan, an entry is still not found, the process sleeps on the pkmap_map_wait wait queue until it is woken up after the next kunmap().

After a mapping has been created, the corresponding entry in the `pkmap_count` array is incremented, and the virtual address in low memory is returned.

9.3 Unmapping Pages

The API for unmapping pages from high memory is described in Table 9.2. The `kunmap()` function, like its complement, performs two checks. The first is an identical check to `kmap()` for usage from interrupt context. The second is that the page is below `highmem_start_page`. If it is, the page already exists in low memory and needs no further handling. After it is established that it is a page to be unmapped, `kunmap_high()` is called to perform the unmapping.

`void kunmap(struct page *page)`
    This unmaps a struct page from low memory and frees up the page table entry mapping it.

`void kunmap_atomic(void *kvaddr, enum km_type type)`
    This unmaps a page that was mapped atomically.

Table 9.2. High Memory Unmapping API

The `kunmap_high()` is simple in principle. It decrements the corresponding element for this page in `pkmap_count`. If it reaches 1 (remember this means no more users but a TLB flush is required), any process waiting on the `pkmap_map_wait` is woken up because a slot is now available. The page is not unmapped from the page tables then because that would require a TLB flush. It is delayed until `flush_all_zero_pkmaps()` is called.

9.4 Mapping High Memory Pages Atomically

The use of `kmap_atomic()` is discouraged, but slots are reserved for each CPU for when they are necessary, such as when bounce buffers are used by devices from interrupt. There are a varying number of different requirements an architecture has for atomic high memory mapping, which are enumerated by `km_type`. The total number of uses is KM_TYPE_NR. On the x86, there are a total of six different uses for atomic kmaps.

KM_TYPE_NR entries per processor are reserved at boot time for atomic mapping at the location FIX_KMAP_BEGIN and ending at FIX_KMAP_END. Obviously, a user of an atomic kmap may not sleep or exit before calling `kunmap_atomic()` because the next process on the processor may try to use the same entry and fail.

The function `kmap_atomic()` has the very simple task of mapping the requested page to the slot set aside in the page tables for the requested type of operation and processor. The function `kunmap_atomic()`, whose call graph is shown in Figure 9.2, is interesting because it will only clear the PTE with `pte_clear()` if debugging is enabled. It is considered unnecessary to bother unmapping atomic pages because the next call to `kmap_atomic()` will simply replace it and make TLB flushes unnecessary.

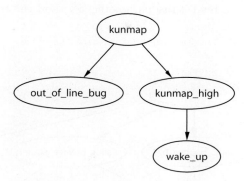

Figure 9.2. Call Graph: `kunmap()`

9.5   Bounce Buffers

Bounce buffers are required for devices that cannot access the full range of memory available to the CPU. An obvious example of this is when a device does not have an address with as many bits as the CPU, such as 32-bit devices on 64-bit architectures or recent Intel processors with PAE enabled.

The basic concept is very simple. A bounce buffer resides in memory low enough for a device to copy from and write data to. It is then copied to the desired user page in high memory. This additional copy is undesirable, but unavoidable. Pages are allocated in low memory, which are used as buffer pages for DMA to and from the device. This is then copied by the kernel to the buffer page in high memory when I/O completes, so the bounce buffer acts as a type of bridge. There is significant overhead to this operation because at the very least, it involves copying a full page, but it is insignificant in comparison to swapping out pages in low memory.

9.5.1   Disk Buffering

Blocks, typically around 1KiB, are packed into pages and managed by a `struct buffer_head` allocated by the slab allocator. Users of buffer heads have the option of registering a callback function. This function is stored in `buffer_head→b_end_io()` and called when I/O completes. It is this mechanism that bounce buffers use to have data copied out of the bounce buffers. The callback registered is the function `bounce_end_io_write()`.

Any other feature of buffer heads or how they are used by the block layer is beyond the scope of this book and more the concern of the I/O layer.

9.5.2 Creating Bounce Buffers

The creation of a bounce buffer is a simple affair, which is started by the
create_bounce() function, shown in Figure 9.3. The principle is very simple: create a new buffer using a provided buffer head as a template. The function takes two
parameters, which are a read/write parameter (rw) and the template buffer head,
to use (bh_orig).

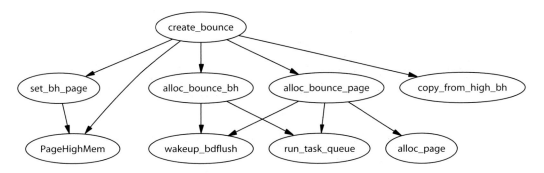

Figure 9.3. Call Graph: create_bounce()

A page is allocated for the buffer itself with the function alloc_bounce_page(),
which is a wrapper around alloc_page() with one important addition. If the
allocation is unsuccessful, there is an emergency pool of pages and buffer heads
available for bounce buffers. This is discussed further in Section 9.6.

The buffer head is, predictably enough, allocated with alloc_bounce_bh(),
which, similar in principle to alloc_bounce_page(), calls the slab allocator for
a buffer_head and uses the emergency pool if one cannot be allocated. Additionally, **bdflush** is woken up to start flushing dirty buffers out to disk so that buffers
are more likely to be freed soon.

After the page and buffer_head have been allocated, information is copied
from the template buffer_head into the new one. Because part of this operation
may use kmap_atomic(), bounce buffers are only created with the Interrupt Request (IRQ) safe io_request_lock held. The I/O completion callbacks are changed
to be either bounce_end_io_write() or bounce_end_io_read()(both shown in
Figure 9.4), depending on whether this is a read or write buffer, so the data will be
copied to and from high memory.

The most important aspect of the allocations to note is that the GFP flags
specify that no I/O operations involving high memory may be used. This is specified
with SLAB_NOHIGHIO to the slab allocator and GFP_NOHIGHIO to the buddy allocator.
This is important because bounce buffers are used for I/O operations with high
memory. If the allocator tries to perform high memory I/O, it will recurse and
eventually crash.

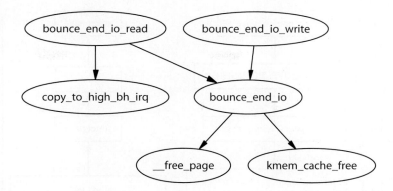

Figure 9.4. Call Graph: `bounce_end_io_read/write()`

9.5.3 Copying via Bounce Buffers

Data is copied via the bounce buffer differently depending on whether it is a read or write buffer. If the buffer is for writes to the device, the buffer is populated with the data from high memory during bounce buffer creation with the function `copy_from_high_bh()`. The callback function `bounce_end_io_write()` will complete the I/O later when the device is ready for the data.

If the buffer is for reading from the device, no data transfer may take place until the device is ready. When it is, the interrupt handler for the device calls the callback function `bounce_end_io_read()` which copies the data to high memory with `copy_to_high_bh_irq()`.

In either case, the buffer head and page may be reclaimed by `bounce_end_io()` after the I/O has completed and the I/O completion function for the template `buffer_head()` is called. If the emergency pools are not full, the resources are added to the pools. Otherwise, they are freed back to the respective allocators.

9.6 Emergency Pools

Two emergency pools of `buffer_heads` and pages are maintained for the express use by bounce buffers. If memory is too tight for allocations, failing to complete I/O requests is going to compound the situation because buffers from high memory cannot be freed until low memory is available. This leads to processes halting, thus preventing the possibility of them freeing up their own memory.

The pools are initialized by `init_emergency_pool()` to contain POOL_SIZE entries, each which is currently defined as 32. The pages are linked by the `page→list` field on a list headed by `emergency_pages`. Figure 9.5 illustrates how pages are stored on emergency pools and acquired when necessary.

The `buffer_heads` are very similar because they are linked by the `buffer_head→inode_buffers` on a list headed by `emergency_bhs`. The number of entries left on the pages and buffer lists are recorded by two counters,

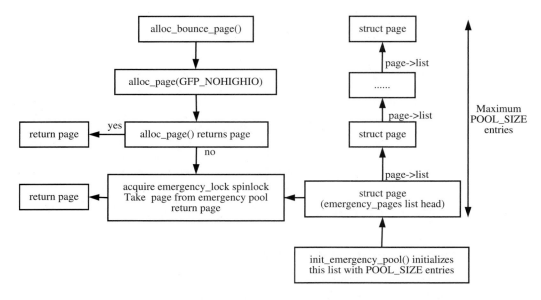

Figure 9.5. Acquiring Pages From Emergency Pools

nr_emergency_pages and nr_emergency_bhs, respectively, and the two lists are protected by the emergency_lock spinlock.

9.7   What's New in 2.6

Memory Pools In 2.4, the high memory manager was the only subsystem that maintained emergency pools of pages. In 2.6, memory pools are implemented as a generic concept when a minimum amount of stuff needs to be reserved for when memory is tight. Stuff in this case can be any type of object, such as pages in the case of the high memory manager or, more frequently, some object managed by the slab allocator. Pools are initialized with mempool_create(), which takes a number of arguments. They are the minimum number of objects that should be reserved (min_nr), an allocator function for the object type (alloc_fn()), a free function (free_fn()) and optional private data that is passed to the allocate and free functions.

The memory pool API provides two generic allocate and free functions called mempool_alloc_slab() and mempool_free_slab(). When the generic functions are used, the private data is the slab cache that objects are to be allocated and freed from.

In the case of the high memory manager, two pools of pages are created. One page pool is for normal use, and the second page pool is for use with ISA devices that must allocate from ZONE_DMA. The allocate function is page_pool_alloc(), and the private data parameter passed indicates the GFP flags to use. The free

function is `page_pool_free()`. The memory pools replace the emergency pool code
that exists in 2.4.

To allocate or free objects from the memory pool, the memory pool API functions `mempool_alloc()` and `mempool_free()` are provided. Memory pools are destroyed with `mempool_destroy()`.

Mapping High Memory Pages   In 2.4, the field `page→virtual` was used to store
the address of the page within the `pkmap_count` array. Due to the number of
`struct pages` that exist in a high memory system, this is a very large penalty to pay
for the relatively small number of pages that need to be mapped into `ZONE_NORMAL`.
2.6 still has this `pkmap_count` array, but it is managed very differently.

In 2.6, a hash table called `page_address_htable` is created. This table is
hashed based on the address of the `struct page`, and the list is used to locate
`struct page_address_slot`. This struct has two fields of interest, a `struct page`
and a virtual address. When the kernel needs to find the virtual address used by a
mapped page, it is located by traversing through this hash bucket. How the page
is actually mapped into lower memory is essentially the same as 2.4 except now
`page→virtual` is no longer required.

Performing I/O   The last major change is that the `struct bio` is now used instead
of the `struct buffer_head` when performing I/O. How `bio` structures work is
beyond the scope of this book. However, the principle reason that `bio` structures
were introduced is so that I/O could be performed in blocks of whatever size the
underlying device supports. In 2.4, all I/O had to be broken up into page-sized
chunks regardless of the transfer rate of the underlying device.

CHAPTER **10**

Page Frame Reclamation

A running system will eventually use all available page frames for purposes like disk buffers, dentries, inode entries, process pages and so on. Linux needs to select old pages that can be freed and invalidated for new uses before physical memory is exhausted. This chapter focuses exclusively on how Linux implements its page replacement policy and how different types of pages are invalidated.

The methods Linux uses to select pages are rather empirical in nature and the theory behind the approach is based on different ideas. It has been shown to work well in practice, and adjustments are made based on user feedback and benchmarks. The basics of the page replacement policy is the first item of discussion in this chapter.

The second topic of discussion is the *page cache*. All data that is read from disk is stored in the page cache to reduce the amount of disk I/O that must be performed. Strictly speaking, this is not directly related to page frame reclamation, but the LRU lists and page cache are closely related. The relevant section will focus on how pages are added to the page cache and quickly located.

This will bring us to the third topic, the LRU lists. With the exception of the slab allocator, all pages in use by the system are stored on LRU lists and linked together by page→lru so that they can be easily scanned for replacement. The slab pages are not stored on the LRU lists because it is considerably more difficult to age a page based on the objects used by the slab. The section focuses on how pages move through the LRU lists before they are reclaimed.

From there, I cover how pages belonging to other caches, such as the dcache and the slab allocator, are reclaimed before talking about how process-mapped pages are removed. Process-mapped pages are not easily swappable because there is no way to map struct pages to PTEs except to search every page table, which is far too expensive. If the page cache has a large number of process-mapped pages in it, process page tables will be walked, and pages will be swapped out by swap_out() until enough pages have been freed, but swap_out() will still have trouble with shared pages. If a page is shared, a swap entry is allocated, the PTE filled with the necessary information to find the page in swap again and the reference count is decremented. Only when the count reaches zero will the page be freed. Pages like this are considered to be in the *swap cache*.

Finally, this chaper will cover the page replacement daemon **kswapd**, how it is implemented and what its responsibilities are.

10.1   Page Replacement Policy

During discussions the page replacement policy is frequently said to be a *LRU-based* algorithm, but this is not strictly speaking true because the lists are not strictly maintained in LRU order. The LRU in Linux consists of two lists called the `active_list` and the `inactive_list`. The objective is for the `active_list` to contain the *working set* [Den70] of all processes and the `inactive_list` to contain reclaim candidates. Because all reclaimable pages are contained in just two lists and pages belonging to any process may be reclaimed, rather than just those belonging to a faulting process, the replacement policy is a global one.

The lists resemble a simplified LRU 2Q [JS94] where two lists called Am and A1 are maintained. With LRU 2Q, pages when first allocated are placed on a First In, First Out (FIFO) queue called A1. If they are referenced while on that queue, they are placed in a normal LRU managed list called Am. This is roughly analogous to using `lru_cache_add()` to place pages on a queue called `inactive_list` (A1) and using `mark_page_accessed()` to get moved to the `active_list` (Am). The algorithm describes how the size of the two lists have to be tuned, but Linux takes a simpler approach by using `refill_inactive()` to move pages from the bottom of `active_list` to `inactive_list` to keep `active_list` about two-thirds the size of the total page cache. Figure 10.1 illustrates how the two lists are structured, how pages are added and how pages move between the lists with `refill_inactive()`.

The lists described for 2Q presumes Am is an LRU list, but the list in Linux closer resembles a clock algorithm [Car84] where the handspread is the size of the

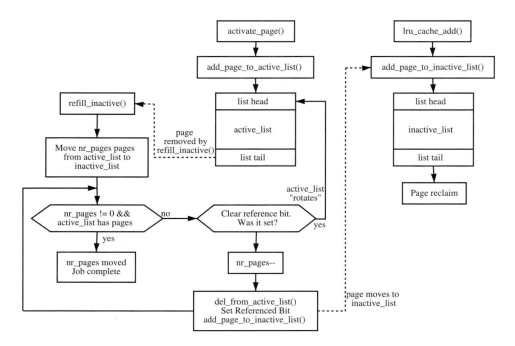

Figure 10.1. Page Cache LRU Lists

active list. When pages reach the bottom of the list, the referenced flag is checked. If it is set, it is moved back to the top of the list, and the next page is checked. If it is cleared, it is moved to the `inactive_list`.

The Move-To-Front heuristic means that the lists behave in an LRU-like manner, but there are too many differences between the Linux replacement policy and LRU to consider it a stack algorithm [MM87]. Even if we ignore the problem of analyzing multiprogrammed systems [CD80] and the fact the memory size for each process is not fixed, the policy does not satisfy the *inclusion property* because the location of pages in the lists depend heavily upon the size of the lists as opposed to the time of last reference. The list priority is also not ordered because that would require list updates with every reference. As a final nail in the stack algorithm coffin, the lists are almost ignored when paging out from processes because pageout decisions are related to their location in the virtual address space of the process rather than the location within the page lists.

In summary, the algorithm does exhibit LRU-like behavior, and it has been shown by benchmarks to perform well in practice. There are only two cases where the algorithm is likely to behave really badly. The first is if the candidates for reclamation are principally anonymous pages. In this case, Linux will keep examining a large number of pages before linearly scanning process page tables searching for pages to reclaim, but this situation is fortunately rare.

The second situation is where there is a single process with many file-backed resident pages in the `inactive_list` that are being written to frequently. Processes and **kswapd** may go into a loop of constantly laundering these pages and placing them at the top of the `inactive_list` without freeing anything. In this case, few pages are moved from the `active_list` to `inactive_list` because the ratio between the two lists, sizes remains do not change significantly.

10.2 Page Cache

The page cache is a set of data structures that contain pages that are backed by regular files, block devices or swap. There are basically four types of pages that exist in the cache:

- One is pages that were faulted in as a result of reading a memory mapped file.

- Blocks read from a block device or filesystem are packed into special pages called buffer pages. The number of blocks that may fit depends on the size of the block and the page size of the architecture.

- Anonymous pages exist in a special aspect of the page cache called the swap cache when slots are allocated in the backing storage for page-out, which is discussed further in Chapter 11.

- Pages belonging to shared memory regions are treated in a similar fashion to anonymous pages. The only difference is that shared pages are added to the swap cache and space reserved in backing storage immediately after the first write to the page.

The principal reason for the existence of this cache is to eliminate unnecessary disk reads. Pages read from disk are stored in a *page hash* table, which is hashed on the `struct address_space`, and the offset, which is always searched before the disk is accessed. An API is provided that is responsible for manipulating the page cache, which is listed in Table 10.1.

---

void add_to_page_cache(struct page * page, struct address_space * mapping, unsigned long offset)
    This adds a page to the LRU with `lru_cache_add()` in addition to adding it to the inode queue and page hash tables.

void add_to_page_cache_unique(struct page * page, struct address_space *mapping, unsigned long offset, struct page **hash)
    This is similar to `add_to_page_cache()` except it checks that the page is not already in the page cache. This is required when the caller does not hold the `pagecache_lock` spinlock.

void remove_inode_page(struct page *page)
    This function removes a page from the inode and hash queues with `remove_page_from_inode_queue()` and `remove_page_from_hash_queue()`, effectively removing the page from the page cache

struct page * page_cache_alloc(struct address_space *x)
    This is a wrapper around `alloc_pages()` that uses x→gfp_mask as the GFP mask.

void page_cache_get(struct page *page)
    This increases the reference count to a page already in the page cache.

int page_cache_read(struct file * file, unsigned long offset)
    This function adds a page corresponding to an `offset` with a `file` if it is not already there. If necessary, the page will be read from disk using an `address_space_operations`→`readpage` function.

void page_cache_release(struct page *page)
    This is an alias for `__free_page()`. The reference count is decremented, and, if it drops to 0, the page will be freed

---

Table 10.1. Page Cache API

10.2.1 Page Cache Hash Table

There is a requirement that pages in the page cache be quickly located. To facilitate this, pages are inserted into a table `page_hash_table`, and the fields page→next_hash and page→pprev_hash are used to handle collisions.

The table is declared as follows in `mm/filemap.c`:

```
45 atomic_t page_cache_size = ATOMIC_INIT(0);
46 unsigned int page_hash_bits;
47 struct page **page_hash_table;
```

The table is allocated during system initialization by `page_cache_init()`, which takes the number of physical pages in the system as a parameter. The desired size of the table (`htable_size`) is enough to hold pointers to every `struct page` in the system and is calculated by:

$$\text{htable\_size} = \text{num\_physpages} * \text{sizeof(struct page *)}$$

To allocate a table, the system begins with an `order` allocation large enough to contain the entire table. It calculates this value by starting at 0 and incrementing it until $2^{\text{order}} > \text{htable\_size}$. This may be roughly expressed as the integer component of the following simple equation:

$$\text{order} = \log_2((\text{htable\_size} * 2) - 1))$$

An attempt is made to allocate this order of pages with `__get_free_pages()`. If the allocation fails, lower orders will be tried, and, if no allocation is satisfied, the system panics.

The value of `page_hash_bits` is based on the size of the table for use with the hashing function `_page_hashfn()`. The value is calculated by successive divides by two, but, in real terms, this is equivalent to:

$$\text{page\_hash\_bits} = \log_2 \left| \frac{\text{PAGE\_SIZE} * 2^{\text{order}}}{\text{sizeof(struct page *)}} \right|$$

This makes the table a power-of-two hash table, which negates the need to use a modulus, which is a common choice for hashing functions.

10.2.2   Inode Queue

The *inode queue* is part of the `struct address_space` introduced in Section 4.4.2. The struct contains three lists. `clean_pages` is a list of clean pages associated with the inode; `dirty_pages` have been written to since the list sync to disk; and `locked_pages` are those currently locked. These three lists in combination are considered to be the inode queue for a given mapping, and the `page→list` field is used to link pages on it. Pages are added to the inode queue with `add_page_to_inode_queue()`, which places pages on the `clean_pages` lists and removes them with `remove_page_from_inode_queue()`.

10.2.3   Adding Pages to the Page Cache

Pages read from a file or block device are generally added to the page cache to avoid further disk I/O. Most filesystems use the high-level function `generic_file_read()`

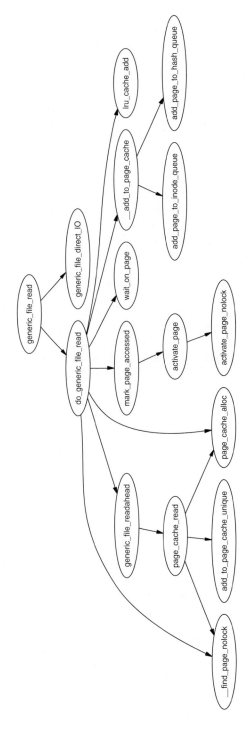

Figure 10.2. Call Graph: generic_file_read()

as their `file_operations`→`read()`, shown in Figure 10.2. The shared memory filesystem, which is covered in Chapter 12, is one noteworthy exception, but, in general, filesystems perform their operations through the page cache. For the purposes of this section, we'll illustrate how `generic_file_read()` operates and how it adds pages to the page cache.

For normal I/O[1], `generic_file_read()` begins with a few basic checks before calling `do_generic_file_read()`. This searches the page cache by calling `__find_page_nolock()` with the `pagecache_lock` held to see if the page already exists in it. If it does not, a new page is allocated with `page_cache_alloc()`, which is a simple wrapper around `alloc_pages()` and is added to the page cache with `__add_to_page_cache()`. After a page frame is present in the page cache, `generic_file_readahead()` is called, which uses `page_cache_read()` to read the page from disk. It reads the page using `mapping`→`a_ops`→`readpage()`, where `mapping` is the `address_space` managing the file. `readpage()` is the filesystem-specific function used to read a page on disk.

Anonymous pages are added to the swap cache when they are unmapped from a process, which will be discussed further in Section 11.4. Until an attempt is made to swap them out, they have no `address_space` acting as a mapping or any offset within a file, which leaves nothing to hash them into the page cache with. Note that these pages still exist on the LRU lists, however. Once in the swap cache, the only real difference between anonymous pages and file-backed pages is that anonymous pages will use `swapper_space` as their `struct address_space`.

Shared memory pages are added during one of two cases. The first is during `shmem_getpage_locked()`, which is called when a page has to be either fetched from swap or allocated because it is the first reference. The second is when the swapout code calls `shmem_unuse()`. This occurs when a swap area is being deactivated and a page, backed by swap space, is found that does not appear to belong to any process. The inodes related to shared memory are exhaustively searched until the correct page is found. In both cases, the page is added with `add_to_page_cache()`, shown in Figure 10.3.

10.3   LRU Lists

As stated in Section 10.1, the LRU lists consist of two lists called `active_list` and `inactive_list`. They are declared in `mm/page_alloc.c` and are protected by the `pagemap_lru_lock` spinlock. They, broadly speaking, store the hot and cold pages respectively, or, in other words, the `active_list` contains all the working sets in the system, and `inactive_list` contains reclaim candidates. The API that deals with the LRU lists is listed in Table 10.2.

10.3.1   Refilling inactive_list

When caches are being shrunk, pages are moved from the `active_list` to the `inactive_list` by the function `refill_inactive()`. It takes as a parameter the

---

[1]Direct I/O is handled differently with `generic_file_direct_IO()`.

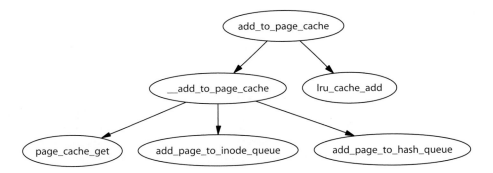

Figure 10.3. Call Graph: add_to_page_cache()

number of pages to move, which is calculated in shrink_caches() as a ratio depending on nr_pages, the number of pages in active_list and the number of pages in inactive_list. The number of pages to move is calculated as:

$$\text{pages} = \text{nr\_pages} * \frac{\text{nr\_active\_pages}}{2 * (\text{nr\_inactive\_pages} + 1)}$$

This keeps the active_list about two-thirds the size of the inactive_list, and the number of pages to move is determined as a ratio based on how many pages we want to swap out (nr_pages).

Pages are taken from the end of the active_list. If the PG_referenced flag is set, it is cleared, and the page is put back at top of the active_list because it has been recently used and is still hot. This is sometimes referred to as rotating the list. If the flag is cleared, it is moved to the inactive_list, and the PG_referenced flag is set so that it will be quickly promoted to the active_list if necessary.

10.3.2 Reclaiming Pages From the LRU Lists

The function shrink_cache() is the part of the replacement algorithm that takes pages from the inactive_list and decides how they should be swapped out. The two starting parameters that determine how much work will be performed are nr_pages and priority. nr_pages starts out as SWAP_CLUSTER_MAX, currently defined as 32 in mm/vmscan.c. The variable priority starts as DEF_PRIORITY, currently defined as 6 in mm/vmscan.c.

Two parameters, max_scan and max_mapped, determine how much work the function will do and are affected by the priority. Each time the function shrink_caches() is called without enough pages being freed, the priority will be decreased until the highest priority 1 is reached.

The variable max_scan is the maximum number of pages that will be scanned by this function and is simply calculated as:

$$\text{max\_scan} = \frac{\text{nr\_inactive\_pages}}{\text{priority}}$$

---

void lru_cache_add(struct page * page)
    Adds a cold page to the inactive_list. It will be moved to active_list with a call to mark_page_accessed() if the page is known to be hot, such as when a page is faulted in.

void lru_cache_del(struct page *page)
    Removes   a   page   from   the   LRU   lists   by   calling   either del_page_from_active_list() or del_page_from_inactive_list(), whichever is appropriate.

void mark_page_accessed(struct page *page)
    Marks that the page has been accessed. If it was not recently referenced (in the inactive_list and PG_referenced flag not set), the referenced flag is set. If it is referenced a second time, activate_page() is called, which marks the page hot, and the referenced flag is cleared.

void activate_page(struct page * page)
    Removes a page from the inactive_list and places it on active_list. It is very rarely called directly because the caller has to know the page is on inactive_list. mark_page_accessed() should be used instead.

Table 10.2. LRU List API

where nr_inactive_pages is the number of pages in the inactive_list. This means that, at lowest priority 6, at most one-sixth of the pages in the inactive_list will be scanned, and, at highest priority, all of them will be.

The second parameter is max_mapped, which determines how many process pages are allowed to exist in the page cache before whole processes will be swapped out. This is calculated as the minimum of either one-tenth of max_scan or

$$\text{max\_mapped} = \text{nr\_pages} * 2^{(10-\text{priority})}$$

In other words, at lowest priority, the maximum number of mapped pages allowed is either one-tenth of max_scan or 16 times the number of pages to swap out (nr_pages), whichever is the lower number. At high priority, it is either one-tenth of max_scan or 512 times the number of pages to swap out.

From there, the function is basically a very large for-loop that scans at most max_scan pages to free up nr_pages pages from the end of the inactive_list or until the inactive_list is empty. After each page, it checks to see whether it should reschedule itself so that the swapper does not monopolize the CPU.

For each type of page found on the list, it makes a different decision on what to do. The different page types and actions taken are handled in this order:

1. *Page is mapped by a process.* This jumps to the page_mapped label, which we will meet again in a later case. The max_mapped count is decremented. If it

reaches 0, the page tables of processes will be linearly searched and swapped out by the function `swap_out()`.

2. *Page is locked, and the PG_launder bit is set.* The page is locked for I/O, so it could be skipped over. However, if the `PG_launder` bit is set, it means that this is the second time that the page has been found locked, so it is better to wait until the I/O completes and get rid of it. A reference to the page is taken with `page_cache_get()` so that the page will not be freed prematurely, and `wait_on_page()` is called, which sleeps until the I/O is complete. After it is completed, the reference count is decremented with `page_cache_release()`. When the count reaches zero, the page will be reclaimed.

3. *Page is dirty, is unmapped by all processes, has no buffers and belongs to a device or file mapping.* Because the page belongs to a file or device mapping, it has a valid `writepage()` function available through `page→mapping→a_ops→writepage`. The `PG_dirty` bit is cleared, and the `PG_launder` bit is set because it is about to start I/O. A reference is taken for the page with `page_cache_get()` before calling the `writepage()` function to synchronize the page with the backing file before dropping the reference with `page_cache_release()`. Be aware that this case will also synchronize anonymous pages that are part of the swap cache with the backing storage because swap cache pages use `swapper_space` as a `page→mapping`. The page remains on the LRU. When it is found again, it will be simply freed if the I/O has completed, and the page will be reclaimed. If the I/O has not completed, the kernel will wait for the I/O to complete as described in the previous case.

4. *Page has buffers associated with data on disk.* A reference is taken to the page, and an attempt is made to free the pages with `try_to_release_page()`. If it succeeds and is an anonymous page (no `page→mapping`), the page is removed from the LRU, and `page_cache_released()` is called to decrement the usage count. There is only one case where an anonymous page has associated buffers and that is when it is backed by a swap file because the page needs to be written out in block-sized chunk. If, on the other hand, it is backed by a file or device, the reference is simply dropped, and the page will be freed as usual when the count reaches 0.

5. *Page is anonymous and is mapped by more than one process.* The LRU is unlocked, and the page is unlocked before dropping into the same `page_mapped` label that was encountered in the first case. In other words, the `max_mapped` count is decremented, and `swap_out` is called when, or if, it reaches 0.

6. *Page has no process referencing it.* This is the final case that is fallen into rather than explicitly checked for. If the page is in the swap cache, it is removed from it because the page is now sychronized with the backing storage and has no process referencing it. If it was part of a file, it is removed from the inode queue, deleted from the page cache and freed.

10.4 Shrinking All Caches

The function responsible for shrinking the various caches is `shrink_caches()`, which takes a few simple steps to free up some memory (see Figure 10.4). The maximum number of pages that will be written to disk in any given pass is `nr_pages`, which is initialized by `try_to_free_pages_zone()` to be `SWAP_CLUSTER_MAX`. The limitation is there so that, if **kswapd** schedules a large number of pages to be written to disk, it will sleep occasionally to allow the I/O to take place. As pages are freed, `nr_pages` is decremented to keep count.

The amount of work that will be performed also depends on the `priority` initialized by `try_to_free_pages_zone()` to be `DEF_PRIORITY`. For each pass that does not free up enough pages, the priority is decremented for the highest priority of 1.

The function first calls `kmem_cache_reap()` (see Section 8.1.7), which selects a slab cache to shrink. If `nr_pages` number of pages are freed, the work is complete, and the function returns. Otherwise, it will try to free `nr_pages` from other caches.

If other caches are to be affected, `refill_inactive()` will move pages from the `active_list` to the `inactive_list` before shrinking the page cache by reclaiming pages at the end of the `inactive_list` with `shrink_cache()`.

Finally, it shrinks three special caches, the *dcache* (`shrink_dcache_memory()`), the *icache* (`shrink_icache_memory()`) and the *dqcache* (`shrink_dqcache_memory()`). These objects are quite small in themselves, but a cascading effect allows a lot more pages to be freed in the form of buffer and disk caches.

10.5 Swapping Out Process Pages

When `max_mapped` pages have been found in the page cache, `swap_out()`, shown in Figure 10.5, is called to start swapping out process pages. Starting from the `mm_struct` pointed to by `swap_mm` and the address mm→`swap_address`, the page tables are searched forward until `nr_pages` have been freed.

All process-mapped pages are examined regardless of where they are in the lists or when they were last referenced, but pages that are part of the `active_list` or have been recently referenced will be skipped over. The examination of hot pages is a bit costly, but insignificant in comparison to linearly searching all processes for the PTEs that reference a particular `struct page`.

After it has been decided to swap out pages from a process, an attempt will be made to swap out at least `SWAP_CLUSTER_MAX` number of pages, and the full list of `mm_structs` will only be examined once to avoid constant looping when no pages are available. Writing out the pages in bulk increases the chance that pages close together in the process address space will be written out to adjacent slots on disk.

The marker `swap_mm` is initialized to point to `init_mm`, and the `swap_address` is initialized to 0 the first time it is used. A task has been fully searched when the `swap_address` is equal to `TASK_SIZE`. After a task has been selected to swap pages from, the reference count to the `mm_struct` is incremented so that it will not be freed early, and `swap_out_mm()` is called with the selected `mm_struct` as a parameter.

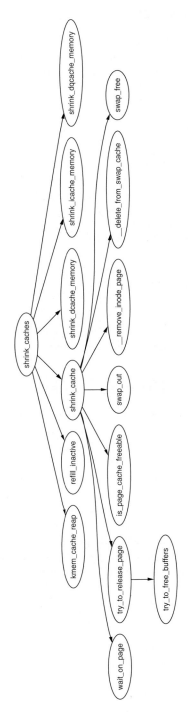

Figure 10.4. Call Graph: `shrink_caches()`

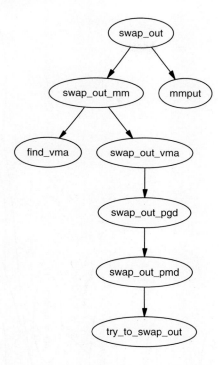

Figure 10.5. Call Graph: `swap_out()`

This function walks each VMA the process holds and calls `swap_out_vma()` for it. This is to avoid having to walk the entire page table, which will be largely sparse. `swap_out_pgd()` and `swap_out_pmd()` walk the page tables for a given VMA until finally `try_to_swap_out()` is called on the actual page and PTE.

The function `try_to_swap_out()` first checks to make sure that the page is not part of the `active_list`, has been recently referenced or belongs to a zone that we are not interested in. After it has been established this is a page to be swapped out, it is removed from the process page tables. The newly removed PTE is then checked to see if it is dirty. If it is, the `struct page` flags will be updated to match so that it will get synchronized with the backing storage. If the page is already a part of the swap cache, the RSS is simply updated, and the reference to the page is dropped. Otherwise, the process is added to the swap cache. How pages are added to the swap cache and synchronized with backing storage is discussed in Chapter 11.

10.6 Pageout Daemon (kswapd)

During system startup, a kernel thread called **kswapd** is started from `kswapd_init()`, which continuously executes the function `kswapd()` in `mm/vmscan.c`, which usually sleeps. This daemon is responsible for reclaiming

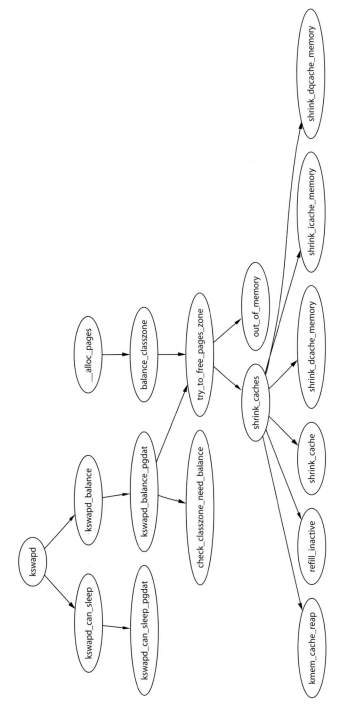

Figure 10.6. Call Graph: `kswapd()`

pages when memory is running low. Historically, **kswapd** used to wake up every 10 seconds, but now it is only woken by the physical page allocator when the `pages_low` number of free pages in a zone is reached (see Section 2.2.1).

It is this daemon that performs most of the tasks needed to maintain the page cache correctly, shrink slab caches and swap out processes if necessary. Unlike swapout daemons such, as Solaris [MM01], which are woken up with increasing frequency because there is memory pressure, **kswapd** keeps freeing pages until the `pages_high` watermark is reached. Under extreme memory pressure, processes will do the work of **kswapd** synchronously by calling `balance_classzone()`, which calls `try_to_free_pages_zone()`. As shown in Figure 10.6, it is at `try_to_free_pages_zone()` where the physical page allocator synchonously performs the same task as **kswapd** when the zone is under heavy pressure.

When **kswapd** is woken up, it performs the following:

- It calls `kswapd_can_sleep()`, which cycles through all zones checking the `need_balance` field in the `struct zone_t`. If any of them are set, it can not sleep.

- If it cannot sleep, it is removed from the `kswapd_wait` wait queue.

- It calls the functions `kswapd_balance()`, which cycles through all zones. It will free pages in a zone with `try_to_free_pages_zone()` if `need_balance` is set and will keep freeing until the `pages_high` watermark is reached.

- The task queue for `tq_disk` is run so that pages queued will be written out.

- It adds **kswapd** back to the `kswapd_wait` queue and goes back to the first step.

10.7 What's New in 2.6

kswapd   As stated in Section 2.8, there is now a **kswapd** for every memory node in the system. These daemons are still started from `kswapd()`, and they all execute the same code, except their work is now confined to their local node. The main changes to the implementation of **kswapd** are related to the `kswapd-per-node` change.

The basic operation of **kswapd** remains the same. Once woken, it calls `balance_pgdat()` for the `pgdat` it is responsible for. `balance_pgdat()` has two modes of operation. When called with `nr_pages == 0`, it will continually try to free pages from each zone in the local `pgdat` until `pages_high` is reached. When `nr_pages` is specified, it will try and free either `nr_pages` or `MAX_CLUSTER_MAX * 8`, whichever is the smaller number of pages.

Balancing Zones   The two main functions called by `balance_pgdat()` to free pages are `shrink_slab()` and `shrink_zone()`. `shrink_slab()` was from Section 8.8 so will not be repeated here. The function `shrink_zone()` is called to free a number of pages based on how urgent it is to free pages. This function behaves very similar to how 2.4 works. `refill_inactive_zone()` will move a number of pages from zone→active_list to zone→inactive_list. Remember from Section 2.8 that LRU lists are now per-zone and not global as they are in 2.4. shrink_cache() is called to remove pages from the LRU and, reclaim pages.

Pageout Pressure   In 2.4, the pageout priority determined how many pages would be scanned.   In 2.6, there is a decaying average that is updated by zone_adj_pressure(). This adjusts the zone→pressure field to indicate how many pages should be scanned for replacement. When more pages are required, this will be pushed up toward the highest value of DEF_PRIORITY << 10 and then decays over time. The value of this average affects how many pages will be scanned in a zone for replacement. The objective is to have page replacement start working and slow gracefully rather than act in a bursty nature.

Manipulating LRU Lists   In 2.4, a spinlock would be acquired when removing pages from the LRU list. This made the lock very heavily contended, so, to relieve contention, operations involving the LRU lists take place using struct pagevec structures. This allows pages to be added or removed from the LRU lists in batches of up to PAGEVEC_SIZE numbers of pages.

To illustrate, when refill_inactive_zone() and shrink_cache() are removing pages, they acquire the zone→lru_lock lock, remove large blocks of pages and store them on a temporary list. After the list of pages to remove is assembled, shrink_list() is called to perform the actual freeing of pages, which can now perform most of its task without needing the zone→lru_lock spinlock.

When adding the pages back, a new page vector struct is initialized with pagevec_init(). Pages are added to the vector with pagevec_add() and then committed to being placed on the LRU list in bulk with pagevec_release().

A sizable API is associated with pagevec structs that can be seen in <linux/pagevec.h> with most of the implementation in mm/swap.c.

CHAPTER 11

Swap Management

Just as Linux uses free memory for purposes such as buffering data from disk, there eventually is a need to free up private or anonymous pages used by a process. These pages, unlike those backed by a file on disk, cannot be simply discarded to be read in later. Instead they have to be carefully copied to *backing storage*, sometimes called the *swap area*. This chapter details how Linux uses and manages its backing storage.

Strictly speaking, Linux does not swap because "swapping" refers to coping an entire process address space to disk and "paging" to copying out individual pages. Linux actually implements paging as modern hardware supports it, but traditionally has called it swapping in discussions and documentation. To be consistent with the Linux usage of the word, we, too, will refer to it as swapping.

There are two principal reasons that the existence of swap space is desirable. First, it expands the amount of memory that a process may use. Virtual memory and swap space allows a large process to run even if the process is only partially resident. Because old pages may be swapped out, the amount of memory addressed may easily exceed RAM because demand paging will ensure the pages are reloaded if necessary.

The casual reader[1] may think that, with a sufficient amount of memory, swap is unnecessary, but this brings me to the second reason. A significant number of the pages referenced by a process early in its life may only be used for initialization and then never used again. It is better to swap out those pages and create more disk buffers than leave them resident and unused.

Swap is not without its drawbacks, and the most important one is the most obvious one. Disk is slow, very very slow. If processes are frequently addressing a large amount of memory, no amount of swap or expensive high-performance disks will make it run within a reasonable time, only more RAM will help. This is why it is very important that the correct page be swapped out as discussed in Chapter 10, but also that related pages be stored close together in the swap space so they are likely to be swapped in at the same time while reading ahead. I start with how Linux describes a swap area.

This chapter begins with describing the structures Linux maintains about each active swap area in the system and how the swap area information is organized on disk. I cover how Linux remembers how to find pages in the swap after they

---

[1]Not to mention the affluent reader.

have been paged out and how swap slots are allocated. After that the *swap cache* is discussed, which is important for shared pages. At that point, there is enough information to begin understanding how swap areas are activated and deactivated, how pages are paged in and paged out and finally how the swap area is read and written to.

11.1   Describing the Swap Area

Each active swap area, be it a file or partition, has a struct `swap_info_struct` describing the area. All the structs in the running system are stored in a statically declared array called `swap_info`, which holds `MAX_SWAPFILES`, which is statically defined as 32, entries. This means that at most 32 swap areas can exist on a running system. The `swap_info_struct` is declared as follows in `<linux/swap.h>`:

```
64 struct swap_info_struct {
65     unsigned int flags;
66     kdev_t swap_device;
67     spinlock_t sdev_lock;
68     struct dentry * swap_file;
69     struct vfsmount *swap_vfsmnt;
70     unsigned short * swap_map;
71     unsigned int lowest_bit;
72     unsigned int highest_bit;
73     unsigned int cluster_next;
74     unsigned int cluster_nr;
75     int prio;
76     int pages;
77     unsigned long max;
78     int next;
79 };
```

Here is a small description of each of the fields in this quite sizable struct.

flags This is a bit field with two possible values. `SWP_USED` is set if the swap area is currently active. `SWP_WRITEOK` is defined as 3, the two lowest significant bits, *including* the `SWP_USED` bit. The flags are set to `SWP_WRITEOK` when Linux is ready to write to the area because it must be active to be written to.

swap_device The device corresponding to the partition used for this swap area is stored here. If the swap area is a file, this is NULL.

sdev_lock As with many structs in Linux, this one has to be protected, too. `sdev_lock` is a spinlock protecting the struct, principally the `swap_map`. It is locked and unlocked with `swap_device_lock()` and `swap_device_unlock()`.

swap_file This is the `dentry` for the actual special file that is mounted as a swap area. This could be the `dentry` for a file in the `/dev/` directory, for example, in the case that a partition is mounted. This field is needed to identify the correct `swap_info_struct` when deactivating a swap area.

vfs_mount This is the `vfs_mount` object corresponding to where the device or file for this swap area is stored.

swap_map This is a large array with one entry for every swap entry, or page-sized slot in the area. An entry is a reference count of the number of users of this page slot. The swap cache counts as one user, and every PTE that has been paged out to the slot counts as a user. If it is equal to `SWAP_MAP_MAX`, the slot is allocated permanently. If equal to `SWAP_MAP_BAD`, the slot will never be used.

lowest_bit This is the lowest possible free slot available in the swap area and is used to start from when linearly scanning to reduce the search space. It is known that there are definitely no free slots below this mark.

highest_bit This is the highest possible free slot available in this swap area. Similar to `lowest_bit`, there are definitely no free slots above this mark.

cluster_next This is the offset of the next cluster of blocks to use. The swap area tries to have pages allocated in cluster blocks to increase the chance related pages will be stored together.

cluster_nr This the number of pages left to allocate in this cluster.

prio Each swap area has a priority, which is stored in this field. Areas are arranged in order of priority and determine how likely the area is to be used. By default the priorities are arranged in order of activation, but the system administrator may also specify it using the `-p` flag when using **swapon**.

pages Because some slots on the swap file may be unusable, this field stores the number of usable pages in the swap area. This differs from `max` in that slots marked `SWAP_MAP_BAD` are not counted.

max This is the total number of slots in this swap area.

next This is the index in the `swap_info` array of the next swap area in the system.

The areas, though stored in an array, are also kept in a pseudolist called `swap_list`, which is a very simple type declared as follows in <linux/swap.h>:

```
153 struct swap_list_t {
154     int head;     /* head of priority-ordered swapfile list */
155     int next;     /* swapfile to be used next */
156 };
```

The field `swap_list_t→head` is the swap area of the highest priority swap area in use, and `swap_list_t→next` is the next swap area that should be used. This is so areas may be arranged in order of priority when searching for a suitable area, but still may be looked up quickly in the array when necessary.

Each swap area is divided up into a number of page-sized slots on disk, which means that each slot is 4,096 bytes on the x86, for example. The first slot is always reserved because it contains information about the swap area that should not be overwritten. The first 1 KiB of the swap area is used to store a disk label for the partition that can be picked up by userspace tools. The remaining space is used for information about the swap area, which is filled when the swap area is created with the system program **mkswap**. The information is used to fill in a **union swap_header**, which is declared as follows in <**linux/swap.h**>:

```
25 union swap_header {
26     struct
27     {
28         char reserved[PAGE_SIZE - 10];
29         char magic[10];
30     } magic;
31     struct
32     {
33         char      bootbits[1024];
34         unsigned int version;
35         unsigned int last_page;
36         unsigned int nr_badpages;
37         unsigned int padding[125];
38         unsigned int badpages[1];
39     } info;
40 };
```

A description of each of the fields follows:

magic The `magic` part of the union is used just for identifying the magic string. The string exists to make sure there is no chance a partition that is not a swap area will be used and to decide what version of swap area is to be used. If the string is SWAP-SPACE, it is version 1 of the swap file format. If it is SWAPSPACE2, it is version 2. The large reserved array is just so that the magic string will be read from the end of the page.

bootbits This is the reserved area containing information about the partition, such as the disk label.

version This is the version of the swap area layout.

last_page This is the last usable page in the area.

nr_badpages The known number of bad pages that exist in the swap area are stored in this field.

padding A disk section is usually about 512 bytes in size. The three fields `version`, `last_page` and `nr_badpages` make up 12 bytes, and the `padding` fills up the remaining 500 bytes to cover one sector.

badpages The remainder of the page is used to store the indices of up to MAX_SWAP_BADPAGES number of bad page slots. These slots are filled in by the **mkswap** system program if the -c switch is specified to check the area.

MAX_SWAP_BADPAGES is a compile time constant that varies if the struct changes, but it is 637 entries in its current form as given by the simple equation.

$$\text{MAX\_SWAP\_BADPAGES} = \frac{\text{PAGE\_SIZE} - 1,024 - 512 - 10}{\text{sizeof(long)}}$$

Where 1,024 is the size of the bootblock, 512 is the size of the padding and 10 is the size of the magic string identifying the format of the swap file.

11.2   Mapping Page Table Entries to Swap Entries

When a page is swapped out, Linux uses the corresponding PTE to store enough information to locate the page on disk again. Obviously, a PTE is not large enough in itself to store precisely where on disk the page is located, but it is more than enough to store an index into the swap_info array and an offset within the swap_map. This is precisely what Linux does.

Each PTE, regardless of architecture, is large enough to store a swp_entry_t, which is declared as follows in <linux/shmem_fs.h>:

```
16 typedef struct {
17     unsigned long val;
18 } swp_entry_t;
```

Two macros are provided for the translation of PTEs to swap entries and vice versa. They are pte_to_swp_entry() and swp_entry_to_pte(), respectively.

Each architecture has to be able to determine if a PTE is present or swapped out. For illustration, I show how this is implemented on the x86. In the swp_entry_t, two bits are always kept free. On the x86, Bit 0 is reserved for the _PAGE_PRESENT flag, and Bit 7 is reserved for _PAGE_PROTNONE. The requirement for both bits is explained in Section 3.2. Bits 1 through 6 are for the *type*, which is the index within the swap_info array and are returned by the SWP_TYPE() macro.

Bits 8 through 31 are used to store the *offset* within the swap_map from the swp_entry_t. On the x86, this means 24 bits are available, which limits the size of the swap area to 64GiB. The macro SWP_OFFSET() is used to extract the offset.

To encode a type and offset into a swp_entry_t, the macro SWP_ENTRY() is available, which simply performs the relevant bit-shifting operations. The relationship between all these macros is illustrated in Figure 11.1.

The six bits for type should allow up to 64 swap areas to exist in a 32-bit architecture instead of the MAX_SWAPFILES restriction of 32. The restriction is due to the consumption of the vmalloc address space. If a swap area is the maximum possible size, 32MiB is required for the swap_map ($2^{24} * \text{sizeof(short)}$); remember that each page uses one short for the reference count. For just MAX_SWAPFILES

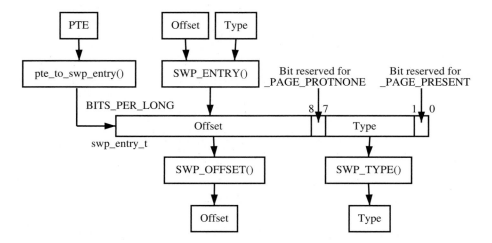

Figure 11.1. Storing Swap Entry Information in `swp_entry_t`

maximum number of swap areas to exist, 1GiB of virtual malloc space is required, which is simply impossible because of the user/kernel linear address space split.

This would imply that supporting 64 swap areas is not worth the additional complexity, but there are cases where a large number of swap areas would be desirable even if the overall swap available does not increase. Some modern machines[2] have many separate disks, which, between them, can create a large number of separate block devices. In this case, it is desirable to create a large number of small swap areas that are evenly distributed across all disks. This would allow a high degree of parallelism in the page swapping behavior, which is important for swap-intensive applications.

11.3   Allocating a Swap Slot

All page-sized slots are tracked by the array `swap_info_struct→swap_map`, which is of type `unsigned short`. Each entry is a reference count of the number of users of the slot, which happens in the case of a shared page and is 0 when free. If the entry is `SWAP_MAP_MAX`, the page is permanently reserved for that slot. It is unlikely, if not impossible, for this condition to occur, but it exists to ensure the reference count does not overflow. If the entry is `SWAP_MAP_BAD`, the slot is unusable.

The task of finding and allocating a swap entry is divided into two major tasks. The first is performed by the high-level function `get_swap_page()`, shown in Figure 11.2. Starting with `swap_list→next`, it searches swap areas for a suitable slot. After a slot has been found, it records what the next swap area to be used will be and returns the allocated entry.

---

[2]A Sun E450 could have in the region of 20 disks in it, for example.

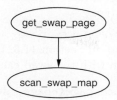

Figure 11.2. Call Graph: get_swap_page()

The task of searching the map is the responsibility of scan_swap_map(). In principle, it is very simple because it linearly scans the array for a free slot and return. Predictably, the implementation is a bit more thorough.

Linux attempts to organize pages into *clusters* on disk of size SWAPFILE_CLUSTER. It allocates SWAPFILE_CLUSTER number of pages sequentially in swap, keeps count of the number of sequentially allocated pages in swap_info_struct→cluster_nr and records the current offset in swap_info_struct→cluster_next. After a sequential block has been allocated, it searches for a block of free entries of size SWAPFILE_CLUSTER. If a block large enough can be found, it will be used as another cluster-sized sequence.

If no free clusters large enough can be found in the swap area, a simple first-free search that starts from swap_info_struct→lowest_bit is performed. The aim is to have pages swapped out at the same time close together on the premise that pages swapped out together are related. This premise, which seems strange at first glance, is quite solid when it is considered that the page replacement algorithm will use swap space most when linearly scanning the process address space swapping out pages. Without scanning for large free blocks and using them, it is likely that the scanning would degenerate to first-free searches and never improve. With it, processes exiting are likely to free up large blocks of slots.

11.4 Swap Cache

Pages that are shared between many processes cannot be easily swapped out because, as mentioned, there is no quick way to map a struct page to every PTE that references it. This leads to the rare condition where a page that is present for one PTE and swapped out for another gets updated without being synced to disk, thereby losing the update.

To address this problem, shared pages that have a reserved slot in backing storage are considered to be part of the *swap cache*. The swap cache has a small API associated with it and is shown in Table 11.1. The swap cache is purely conceptual because it is simply a specialization of the page cache. The first principal difference between pages in the swap cache rather than the page cache is that pages in the swap cache always use swapper_space as their address_space in page→mapping. The second difference is that pages are added to the swap cache with add_to_swap_cache(), shown in Figure 11.3, instead of add_to_page_cache().

---

swp_entry_t get_swap_page()

This function allocates a slot in a **swap_map** by searching active swap areas. This is covered in greater detail in Section 11.3, but included here because it is principally used in conjunction with the swap cache.

int add_to_swap_cache(struct page *page, swp_entry_t entry)

This function adds a page to the swap cache. It first checks if it already exists by calling **swap_duplicate()**, and, if not, it adds it to the swap cache using the normal page cache interface function **add_to_page_cache_unique()**.

struct page * lookup_swap_cache(swp_entry_t entry)

This searches the swap cache and returns the **struct page** corresponding to the supplied **entry**. It works by searching the normal page cache based on **swapper_space** and the **swap_map** offset.

int swap_duplicate(swp_entry_t entry)

This function verifies a swap entry is valid and, if so, increments its swap map count.

void swap_free(swp_entry_t entry)

The complement function to **swap_duplicate()**. It decrements the relevant counter in the **swap_map**. When the count reaches zero, the slot is effectively free.

Table 11.1. Swap Cache API

Anonymous pages are not part of the swap cache *until* an attempt is made to swap them out. The variable **swapper_space** is declared as follows in **swap_state.c**:

```
39 struct address_space swapper_space = {
40     LIST_HEAD_INIT(swapper_space.clean_pages),
41     LIST_HEAD_INIT(swapper_space.dirty_pages),
42     LIST_HEAD_INIT(swapper_space.locked_pages),
43     0,
44     &swap_aops,
45 };
```

A page is identified as being part of the swap cache after the **page→mapping** field has been set to **swapper_space**, which is tested by the **PageSwapCache()** macro. Linux uses the exact same code for keeping pages between swap and memory in sync as it uses for keeping file-backed pages and memory in sync. They both share the page cache code, but the differences are just in the functions used.

The address space for backing storage, **swapper_space**, uses **swap_ops** for its **address_space→a_ops**. The **page→index** field is then used to store the **swp_entry_t** structure instead of a file offset, which is its normal purpose. The **address_space_operations** struct **swap_aops** is declared as follows in

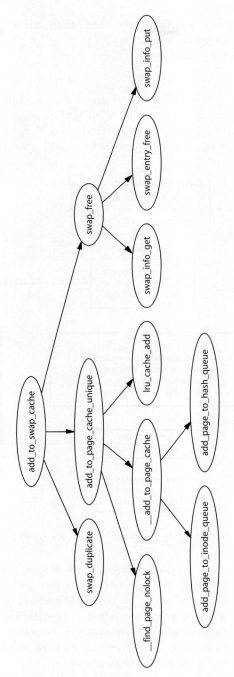

Figure 11.3. Call Graph: add_to_swap_cache()

`swap_state.c`:

```
34 static struct address_space_operations swap_aops = {
35     writepage: swap_writepage,
36     sync_page: block_sync_page,
37 };
```

When a page is being added to the swap cache, a slot is allocated with `get_swap_page()`, added to the page cache with `add_to_swap_cache()` and then marked dirty. When the page is next laundered, it will actually be written to backing storage on disk as the normal page cache would operate. This process is illustrated in Figure 11.4.

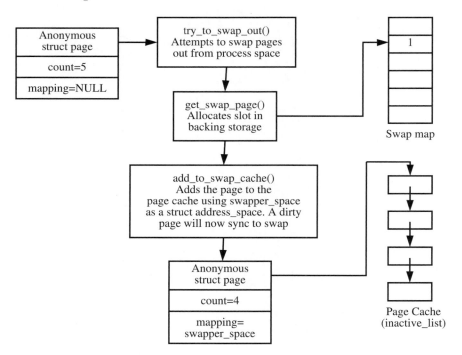

Figure 11.4. Adding a Page to the Swap Cache

Subsequent swapping of the page from shared PTEs results in a call to `swap_duplicate()`, which simply increments the reference to the slot in the `swap_map`. If the PTE is marked dirty by the hardware as a result of a write, the bit is cleared, and the `struct page` is marked dirty with `set_page_dirty()` so that the on-disk copy will be synced before the page is dropped. This ensures that, until all references to the page have been dropped, a check will be made to ensure the data on disk matches the data in the page frame.

When the reference count to the page finally reaches 0, the page is eligible to be dropped from the page cache, and the swap map count will have the count of the number of PTEs the on-disk slot belongs to so that the slot will not be freed prematurely. It is laundered and finally dropped with the same LRU aging and logic described in Chapter 10.

If, on the other hand, a page fault occurs for a page that is swapped out, the logic in `do_swap_page()` will check to see if the page exists in the swap cache by calling `lookup_swap_cache()`. If it does, the PTE is updated to point to the page frame, the page reference count is incremented and the swap slot is decremented with `swap_free()`.

11.5   Reading Pages From Backing Storage

The principal function used when reading in pages is `read_swap_cache_async()`, which is mainly called during page faulting (see Figure 11.5). The function begins searching the swap cache with `find_get_page()`. Normally, swap cache searches are performed by `lookup_swap_cache()`, but that function updates statistics on the number of searches performed. Because the cache may need to be searched multiple times, `find_get_page()` is used instead.

The page can already exist in the swap cache if another process has the same page mapped or if multiple processes are faulting on the same page at the same time. If the page does not exist in the swap cache, one must be allocated and filled with data from backing storage.

After the page is allocated with `alloc_page()`, it is added to the swap cache with `add_to_swap_cache()` because swap cache operations may only be performed on pages in the swap cache. If the page cannot be added to the swap cache, the swap cache will be searched again to make sure another process has not put the data in the swap cache already.

To read information from backing storage, `rw_swap_page()` is called, which is discussed in Section 11.7. After the function completes, `page_cache_release()` is called to drop the reference to the page taken by `find_get_page()`.

11.6   Writing Pages to Backing Storage

When any page is being written to disk, the `address_space`→`a_ops` is consulted to find the appropriate write-out function. In the case of backing storage, the `address_space` is `swapper_space`, and the swap operations are contained in `swap_aops`. The struct `swap_aops` registers `swap_writepage()` because of its write-out function (see Figure 11.6).

The function `swap_writepage()` behaves differently depending on whether the writing process is the last user of the swap cache page or not. It knows this by calling `remove_exclusive_swap_page()`, which checks if there are any other processes using the page. This is a simple case of examining the page count with the `pagecache_lock` held. If no other process is mapping the page, it is removed from the swap cache and freed.

If `remove_exclusive_swap_page()` removed the page from the swap cache and freed it, `swap_writepage()` will unlock the page because it is no longer in use.

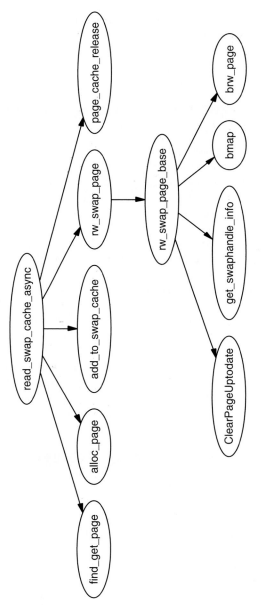

Figure 11.5. Call Graph: read_swap_cache_async()

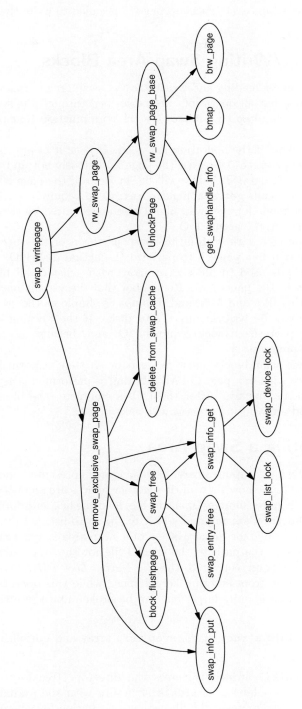

Figure 11.6. Call Graph: swap_writepage()

If it still exists in the swap cache, `rw_swap_page()` is called to write the data to the backing storage.

11.7   Reading/Writing Swap Area Blocks

The top-level function for reading and writing to the swap area is `rw_swap_page()`. This function ensures that all operations are performed through the swap cache to prevent lost updates. `rw_swap_page_base()` is the core function that performs the real work.

It begins by checking if the operation is a read. If it is, it clears the `uptodate` flag with `ClearPageUptodate()` because the page is obviously not up to date if I/O is required to fill it with data. This flag will be set again if the page is successfully read from disk. It then calls `get_swaphandle_info()` to acquire the device for the swap partition of the inode for the swap file. These are required by the block layer, which will be performing the actual I/O.

The core function can work with either swap partition or files because it uses the block layer function `brw_page()` to perform the actual disk I/O. If the swap area is a file, `bmap()` is used to fill a local array with a list of all blocks in the filesystem that contain the page data. Remember that filesystems may have their own method of storing files and disk, and it is not as simple as the swap partition where information may be written directly to disk. If the backing storage is a partition, only one page-sized block requires I/O, and, because no filesystem is involved, `bmap()` is unnecessary.

After it is known what blocks must be read or written, a normal block I/O operation takes place with `brw_page()`. All I/O that is performed is asynchronous, so the function returns quickly. After the I/O is complete, the block layer will unlock the page, and any waiting process will wake up.

11.8   Activating a Swap Area

Now that you know what swap areas are, how they are represented and how pages are tracked, it is time to see how they all tie together to activate an area. Activating an area is conceptually quite simple: Open the file, load the header information from disk, populate a `swap_info_struct` and add it to the swap list.

The function responsible for the activation of a swap area is `sys_swapon()`, and it takes two parameters, the path to the special file for the swap area and a set of flags. While swap is being activated, the *Big Kernel Lock (BKL)* is held, which prevents any application from entering kernel space while this operation is being performed. The function is quite large, but can be broken down into the following simple steps:

1. Find a free `swap_info_struct` in the `swap_info` array and initialize it with default values.

2. Call `user_path_walk()`, which traverses the directory tree for the supplied `specialfile` and populates a `namidata` structure with the available data on the file, such as the `dentry` and the filesystem information for where it is stored (`vfsmount`).

3. Populate `swap_info_struct` fields pertaining to the dimensions of the swap area and how to find it. If the swap area is a partition, the block size will be configured to the `PAGE_SIZE` before calculating the size. If it is a file, the information is obtained directly from the `inode`.

4. Ensure the area is not already activated. If not, allocate a page from memory and read the first page-sized slot from the swap area. This page contains information such as the number of good slots and how to populate the `swap_info_struct`→`swap_map` with the bad entries.

5. Allocate memory with `vmalloc()` for `swap_info_struct`→`swap_map` and initialize each entry with 0 for good slots and `SWAP_MAP_BAD` otherwise. Ideally, the header information will be a version 2 file format because version 1 was limited to swap areas of just under 128MiB for architectures with 4KiB page sizes like the x86.[3]

6. After ensuring the information indicated in the header matches the actual swap area, fill in the remaining information in the `swap_info_struct`, such as the maximum number of pages and the available good pages. Update the global statistics for `nr_swap_pages` and `total_swap_pages`.

7. The swap area is now fully active and initialized, so it is inserted into the swap list in the correct position based on priority of the newly activated area.

At the end of the function, the BKL is released, and the system now has a new swap area available for paging to.

11.9   Deactivating a Swap Area

In comparison to activating a swap area, deactivation is incredibly expensive. The principal problem is that the area cannot be simply removed. Every page that is swapped out must now be swapped back in again. Just as there is no quick way of mapping a `struct page` to every PTE that references it, there is no quick way to map a swap entry to a PTE either. This requires that all process page tables be traversed to find PTEs that reference the swap area to be deactivated and swap them in. This, of course, means that swap deactivation will fail if the physical memory is not available.

The function responsible for deactivating an area is, predictably enough, called `sys_swapoff()`. This function is mainly concerned with updating the `swap_info_struct`. The major task of paging in each paged-out page is the responsibility of `try_to_unuse()`, which is *extremely* expensive. For each slot used in the `swap_map`, the page tables for processes have to be traversed searching for it. In the worst case, all page tables belonging to all `mm_structs` may have to be traversed. Therefore, the tasks taken for deactivating an area are the following, broadly speaking:

1. Call `user_path_walk()` to acquire the information about the special file to be deactivated and then take the BKL.

---

[3]See the Code Commentary for the comprehensive reason for this.

2. Remove the `swap_info_struct` from the swap list and update the global statistics on the number of swap pages available (`nr_swap_pages`) and the total number of swap entries (`total_swap_pages`). After this is acquired, the BKL can be released again.

3. Call `try_to_unuse()`, which will page in all pages from the swap area to be deactivated. This function loops through the swap map using `find_next_to_unuse()` to locate the next used swap slot. For each used slot it finds, it performs the following:

   - Call `read_swap_cache_async()` to allocate a page for the slot saved on disk. Ideally, it exists in the swap cache already, but the page allocator will be called if it is not.

   - Wait on the page to be fully paged in and lock it. Once locked, call `unuse_process()` for every process that has a PTE referencing the page. This function traverses the page table searching for the relevant PTE and then updates it to point to the `struct page`. If the page is a shared memory page with no remaining reference, `shmem_unuse()` is called instead.

   - Free all slots that were permanently mapped. It is believed that slots will never become permanently reserved, so the risk is taken.

   - Delete the page from the swap cache to prevent `try_to_swap_out()` from referencing a page in the event it still somehow has a reference in swap from map.

4. If there was not enough available memory to page in all the entries, the swap area is reinserted back into the running system because it cannot be simply dropped. If it succeeded, the `swap_info_struct` is placed into an uninitialized state, and the `swap_map` memory is freed with `vfree()`

11.10   What's New in 2.6

The most important addition to the `struct swap_info_struct` is the addition of a linked list called `extent_list` and a cache field called `curr_swap_extent` for the implementation of extents.

Extents, which are represented by a `struct swap_extent`, map a contiguous range of pages in the swap area into a contiguous range of disk blocks. These extents are set up at swapon time by the function `setup_swap_extents()`. For block devices, there will only be one swap extent, and it will not improve performance, but the extent it set up so that swap areas backed by block devices or regular files can be treated the same.

It can make a large difference with swap files, which will have multiple extents representing ranges of pages clustered together in blocks. When searching for the page at a particular offset, the extent list will be traversed. To improve search times, the last extent that was searched will be cached in `swap_extent→curr_swap_extent`.

CHAPTER 12

Shared Memory Virtual Filesystem

Sharing a region of memory backed by a file or device is simply a case of calling `mmap()` with the `MAP_SHARED` flag. However, there are two important cases where an anonymous region needs to be shared between processes. The first is when `mmap()` with `MAP_SHARED` is used without file backing. These regions will be shared between a parent and child process after a `fork()` is executed. The second is when a region is explicitly setting them up with `shmget()` and is attached to the virtual address space with `shmat()`.

When pages within a VMA are backed by a file on disk, the interface used is straightforward. To read a page during a page fault, the required `nopage()` function is found in `vm_area_struct→vm_ops`. To write a page to backing storage, the appropriate `writepage()` function is found in the `address_space_operations` using `inode→i_mapping→a_ops` or alternatively using `page→mapping→a_ops`. When normal file operations are taking place, such as `mmap()`, `read()` and `write()`, the `struct file_operations` with the appropriate functions is found using `inode→i_fop` and so on. These relationships were illustrated in Figure 4.2.

This is a very clean interface that is conceptually easy to understand, but it does not help anonymous pages because there is no file backing. To keep this nice interface, Linux creates an artifical file backing for anonymous pages using a RAM-based filesystem where each VMA is backed by a file in this filesystem. Every inode in the filesystem is placed on a linked list called `shmem_inodes` so that it may always be easily located. This allows the same file-based interface to be used without treating anonymous pages as a special case.

The filesystem comes in two variations called *shm* and *tmpfs*. They both share core functionality and mainly differ in what they are used for. `shm` is for use by the kernel for creating file backings for anonymous pages and for backing regions created by `shmget()`. This filesystem is mounted by `kern_mount()` so that it is mounted internally and not visible to users. `tmpfs` is a temporary filesystem that may be optionally mounted on `/tmp/` to have a fast RAM-based temporary filesystem. A secondary use for `tmpfs` is to mount it on `/dev/shm/`. Processes that `mmap()` files in the `tmpfs` filesystem will be able to share information between them as an alternative to System V Inter-Process Communication (IPC) mechanisms. Regardless of the type of use, `tmpfs` must be explicitly mounted by the system administrator.

This chapter begins with a description of how the virtual filesystem is implemented. From there, I discuss how shared regions are set up and destroyed before talking about how the tools are used to implement System V IPC mechanisms.

12.1   Initializing the Virtual Filesystem

The virtual filesystem is initialized by the function `init_tmpfs()`, shown in Figure 12.1, either during system start or when the module is being loaded. This function registers the two filesystems, `tmpfs` and `shm`, and mounts `shm` as an internal filesystem with `kern_mount()`. It then calculates the maximum number of blocks and inodes that can exist in the filesystems. As part of the registration, the function `shmem_read_super()` is used as a callback to populate a `struct super_block` with more information about the filesystems, such as making the block size equal to the page size.

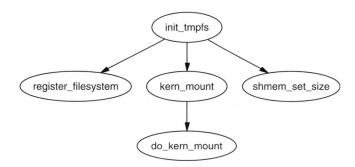

Figure 12.1. Call Graph: `init_tmpfs()`

Every inode created in the filesystem will have a `struct shmem_inode_info` associated with it, which contains private information specific to the filesystem. The function `SHMEM_I()` takes an inode as a parameter and returns a pointer to a struct of this type. It is declared as follows in <linux/shmem_fs.h>:

```
20 struct shmem_inode_info {
21     spinlock_t                  lock;
22     unsigned long               next_index;
23     swp_entry_t                 i_direct[SHMEM_NR_DIRECT];
24     void                      **i_indirect;
25     unsigned long               swapped;
26     unsigned long               flags;
27     struct list_head            list;
28     struct inode               *inode;
29 };
```

The fields are the following:

lock is a spinlock protecting the inode information from concurrent accesses.

next_index is an index of the last page being used in the file. This will be different from `inode→i_size` while a file is being truncated.

i_direct is a direct block containing the first `SHMEM_NR_DIRECT` swap vectors in use by the file. See Section 12.4.1.

i_indirect is a pointer to the first indirect block. See Section 12.4.1.

swapped is a count of the number of pages belonging to the file that are currently swapped out.

flags is currently only used to remember if the file belongs to a shared region set up by `shmget()`. It is set by specifying `SHM_LOCK` with `shmctl()` and unlocked by specifying `SHM_UNLOCK`.

list is a list of all inodes used by the filesystem.

inode is a pointer to the parent inode.

12.2 Using shmem Functions

Different structs contain pointers for shmem specific functions. In all cases, `tmpfs` and `shm` share the same structs.

For faulting in pages and writing them to backing storage, two structs called `shmem_aops` and `shmem_vm_ops` of type `struct address_space_operations` and `struct vm_operations_struct`, respectively, are declared.

The address space operations `struct shmem_aops` contains pointers to a small number of functions of which the most important one is `shmem_writepage()`, which is called when a page is moved from the page cache to the swap cache. `shmem_removepage()` is called when a page is removed from the page cache so that the block can be reclaimed. `shmem_readpage()` is not used by tmpfs, but is provided so that the `sendfile()` system call may be used with tmpfs files. `shmem_prepare_write()` and `shmem_commit_write()` are also unused, but are provided so that tmpfs can be used with the loopback device. `shmem_aops` is declared as follows in `mm/shmem.c`:

```
1500 static struct address_space_operations shmem_aops = {
1501     removepage:     shmem_removepage,
1502     writepage:      shmem_writepage,
1503 #ifdef CONFIG_TMPFS
1504     readpage:       shmem_readpage,
1505     prepare_write:  shmem_prepare_write,
1506     commit_write:   shmem_commit_write,
1507 #endif
1508 };
```

Anonymous VMAs use `shmem_vm_ops` as the `vm_operations_struct` so that `shmem_nopage()` is called when a new page is being faulted in. It is declared as follows:

```
1426 static struct vm_operations_struct shmem_vm_ops = {
1427     nopage: shmem_nopage,
1428 };
```

To perform operations on files and inodes, two structs, `file_operations` and `inode_operations`, are required. The `file_operations`, called `shmem_file_operations`, provides functions that implement `mmap()`, `read()`, `write()` and `fsync()`. It is declared as follows:

```
1510 static struct file_operations shmem_file_operations = {
1511     mmap:           shmem_mmap,
1512 #ifdef CONFIG_TMPFS
1513     read:           shmem_file_read,
1514     write:          shmem_file_write,
1515     fsync:          shmem_sync_file,
1516 #endif
1517 };
```

Three sets of `inode_operations`, are provided. The first is `shmem_inode_operations`, which is used for file inodes. The second, called `shmem_dir_inode_operations`, is for directories. The last pair, called `shmem_symlink_inline_operations` and `shmem_symlink_inode_operations`, is for use with symbolic links.

The two file operations supported are `truncate()` and `setattr()`, which are stored in a `struct inode_operations` called `shmem_inode_operations`. `shmem_truncate()` is used to truncate a file. `shmem_notify_change()` is called when the file attributes change. This allows, among other things, for a file to be grown with `truncate()` and to use the global zero page as the data page. `shmem_inode_operations` is declared as follows:

```
1519 static struct inode_operations shmem_inode_operations = {
1520        truncate:       shmem_truncate,
1521        setattr:        shmem_notify_change,
1522 };
```

The directory `inode_operations` provides functions such as `create()`, `link()` and `mkdir()`. They are declared as follows:

```
1524 static struct inode_operations shmem_dir_inode_operations = {
1525 #ifdef CONFIG_TMPFS
1526     create:         shmem_create,
1527     lookup:         shmem_lookup,
1528     link:           shmem_link,
```

```
1529       unlink:          shmem_unlink,
1530       symlink:         shmem_symlink,
1531       mkdir:           shmem_mkdir,
1532       rmdir:           shmem_rmdir,
1533       mknod:           shmem_mknod,
1534       rename:          shmem_rename,
1535 #endif
1536 };
```

The last pair of operations are for use with symlinks. They are declared as follows:

```
1354 static struct inode_operations shmem_symlink_inline_operations = {
1355         readlink:        shmem_readlink_inline,
1356         follow_link:     shmem_follow_link_inline,
1357 };
1358
1359 static struct inode_operations shmem_symlink_inode_operations = {
1360         truncate:        shmem_truncate,
1361         readlink:        shmem_readlink,
1362         follow_link:     shmem_follow_link,
1363 };
```

The difference between the two `readlink()` and `follow_link()` functions is related to where the link information is stored. A symlink inode does not require the private inode information `struct shmem_inode_information`. If the length of the symbolic link name is smaller than this struct, the space in the inode is used to store the name, and `shmem_symlink_inline_operations` becomes the inode operations struct. Otherwise, a page is allocated with `shmem_getpage()`, the symbolic link is copied to it and `shmem_symlink_inode_operations` is used. The second struct includes a `truncate()` function so that the page will be reclaimed when the file is deleted.

These various structs ensure that the shmem equivalent of inode-related operations will be used when regions are backed by virtual files. When they are used, the majority of the VM sees no difference between pages backed by a real file and ones backed by virtual files.

12.3   Creating Files in tmpfs

Because `tmpfs` is mounted as a proper filesystem that is visible to the user, it must support directory inode operations such as `open()`, `mkdir()` and `link()`. Pointers to functions that implement these for `tmpfs` are provided in `shmem_dir_inode_operations`, which is shown in Section 12.2.

The implementations of most of these functions are quite small, and, at some level, they are all interconnected as can be seen from Figure 12.2. All of them share the same basic principle of performing some work with inodes in the virtual filesystem, and the majority of the inode fields are filled in by `shmem_get_inode()`.

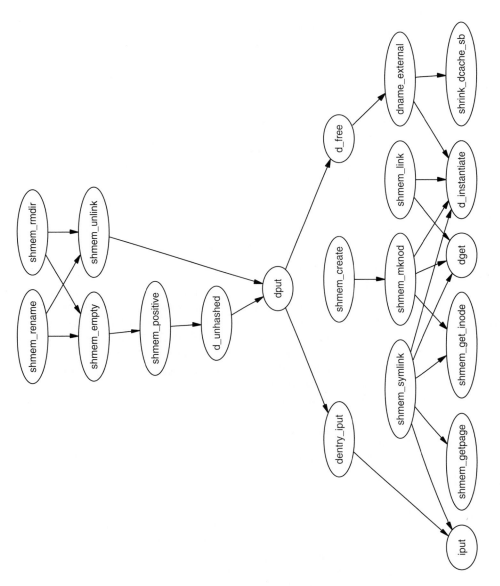

Figure 12.2. Call Graph: shmem_create()

When creating a new file, the top-level function called is `shmem_create()`. This small function calls `shmem_mknod()` with the `S_IFREG` flag added so that a regular file will be created. `shmem_mknod()` is little more than a wrapper around the `shmem_get_inode()`, which, predictably, creates a new inode and fills in the struct fields. The three fields of principal interest that are filled are the `inode→i_mapping→a_ops`, `inode→i_op` and `inode→i_fop` fields. After the inode has been created, `shmem_mknod()` updates the directory inode `size` and `mtime` statistics before instantiating the new inode.

Files are created differently in `shm` even though the filesystems are essentially identical in functionality. How these files are created is covered later in Section 12.7.

12.4   Page Faulting Within a Virtual File

When a page fault occurs, `do_no_page()` will call `vma→vm_ops→nopage` if it exists. In the case of the virtual filesystem, this means the function `shmem_nopage()`, with its call graph shown in Figure 12.3, will be called when a page fault occurs.

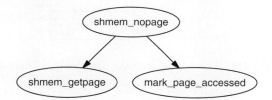

Figure 12.3. Call Graph: `shmem_nopage()`

The core function in this case is `shmem_getpage()`, which is responsible for either allocating a new page or finding it in swap. This overloading of fault types is unusual because `do_swap_page()` is normally responsible for locating pages that have been moved to the swap cache or backing storage using information encoded within the PTE. In this case, pages backed by virtual files have their PTE set to 0 when they are moved to the swap cache. The inode's private filesystem data stores direct and indirect block information, which is used to locate the pages later. This operation is very similar in many respects to normal page faulting.

12.4.1   Locating Swapped Pages

When a page has been swapped out, a `swp_entry_t` will contain information needed to locate the page again. Instead of using the PTEs for this task, the information is stored within the filesystem-specific private information in the inode.

When faulting, the function called to locate the swap entry is `shmem_alloc_entry()`. Its basic task is to perform basic checks and ensure that `shmem_inode_info→next_index` always points to the page index at the end of the virtual file. Its principal task is to call `shmem_swp_entry()`, which searches for the swap vector within the inode information with `shmem_swp_entry()`, and to allocate new pages as necessary to store swap vectors.

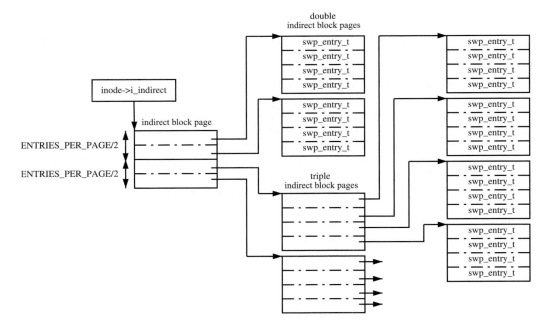

Figure 12.4. Traversing Indirect Blocks in a Virtual File

The first SHMEM_NR_DIRECT entries are stored in inode→i_direct. This means that, for the x86, files that are smaller than 64KiB (SHMEM_NR_DIRECT * PAGE_SIZE) will not need to use indirect blocks. Larger files must use indirect blocks starting with the one located at inode→i_indirect.

The initial indirect block (inode→i_indirect) is broken into two halves. The first half contains pointers to doubly indirect blocks, and the second half contains pointers to triply indirect blocks. The doubly indirect blocks are pages containing swap vectors (swp_entry_t). The triply indirect blocks contain pointers to pages, which in turn are filled with swap vectors. The relationship between the different levels of indirect blocks is illustrated in Figure 12.4. The relationship means that the maximum number of pages in a virtual file (SHMEM_MAX_INDEX) is defined as follows in mm/shmem.c:

```
44 #define SHMEM_MAX_INDEX  (
        SHMEM_NR_DIRECT +
        (ENTRIES_PER_PAGEPAGE/2) *
        (ENTRIES_PER_PAGE+1))
```

12.4.2 Writing Pages to Swap

The function shmem_writepage() is the registered function in the filesystem's address_space_operations for writing pages to swap. The function is responsible for simply moving the page from the page cache to the swap cache. This is implemented with a few simple steps:

1. Record the current `page→mapping` and information about the inode.

2. Allocate a free slot in the backing storage with `get_swap_page()`.

3. Allocate a `swp_entry_t` with `shmem_swp_entry()`.

4. Remove the page from the page cache.

5. Add the page to the swap cache. If it fails, free the swap slot, add back to the page cache and try again.

12.5 File Operations in tmpfs

Four operations, `mmap()`, `read()`, `write()` and `fsync()`, are supported with virtual files. Pointers to the functions are stored in `shmem_file_operations`, which was shown in Section 12.2.

Little is unusual in the implementation of these operations, and they are covered in detail in the Code Commentary. The `mmap()` operation is implemented by `shmem_mmap()`, and it simply updates the VMA that is managing the mapped region. `read()`, implemented by `shmem_read()`, performs the operation of copying bytes from the virtual file to a userspace buffer, faulting in pages as necessary. `write()`, implemented by `shmem_write()`, is essentially the same. The `fsync()` operation is implemented by `shmem_file_sync()`, but is essentially a NULL operation because it performs no task and simply returns 0 for success. Because the files only exist in RAM, they do not need to be synchronized with any disk.

12.6 Inode Operations in tmpfs

The most complex operation that is supported for inodes is truncation and involves four distinct stages. The first, in `shmem_truncate()`, will truncate a partial page at the end of the file and continually calls `shmem_truncate_indirect()` until the file is truncated to the proper size. Each call to `shmem_truncate_indirect()` will only process one indirect block at each pass, which is why it may need to be called multiple times.

The second stage, in `shmem_truncate_indirect()`, understands both doubly and triply indirect blocks. It finds the next indirect block that needs to be truncated. This indirect block, which is passed to the third stage, will contain pointers to pages, which in turn contain swap vectors.

The third stage in `shmem_truncate_direct()` works with pages that contain swap vectors. It selects a range that needs to be truncated and passes the range to the last stage `shmem_swp_free()`. The last stage frees entries with `free_swap_and_cache()`, which frees both the swap entry and the page containing data.

The linking and unlinking of files is very simple because most of the work is performed by the filesystem layer. To link a file, the directory inode size is incremented, the `ctime` and `mtime` of the affected inodes is updated and the number of links to the inode being linked to is incremented. A reference to the new dentry is then taken with `dget()` before instantiating the new `dentry` with `d_instantiate()`. Unlinking updates the same inode statistics before decrementing the reference to the `dentry` with `dput()`. `dput()` will also call `iput()`, which will clear up the inode when its reference count hits zero.

Creating a directory will use `shmem_mkdir()` to perform the task. It simply uses `shmem_mknod()` with the `S_IFDIR` flag before incrementing the parent directory inode's `i_nlink` counter. The function `shmem_rmdir()` will delete a directory by first ensuring it is empty with `shmem_empty()`. If it is, the function then decrements the parent directory inode's `i_nlink` count and calls `shmem_unlink()` to remove the requested directory.

12.7 Setting Up Shared Regions

A shared region is backed by a file created in `shm`. There are two cases where a new file will be created: during the setup of a shared region with `shmget()` and when an anonymous region is set up with `mmap()` with the `MAP_SHARED` flag. Both functions use the core function `shmem_file_setup()` to create a file.

Because the filesystem is internal, the names of the files created do not have to be unique because the files are always located by inode, not name. Therefore, `shmem_zero_setup()` (see Figure 12.5) always says to create a file called `dev/zero`, which is how it shows up in the file `/proc/pid/maps`. Files created by `shmget()` are called `SYSVNN` where the `NN` is the key that is passed as a parameter to `shmget()`.

The core function `shmem_file_setup()` simply creates a new dentry and inode, fills in the relevant fields and instantiates them.

12.8 System V IPC

The full internals of the IPC implementation are beyond the scope of this book. This section will focus just on the implementations of `shmget()` and `shmat()` and how they are affected by the VM. The system call `shmget()` is implemented by `sys_shmget()`, shown in Figure 12.6. It performs basic checks to the parameters and sets up the IPC-related data structures. To create the segment, it calls `newseg()`. This is the function that creates the file in `shmfs` with `shmem_file_setup()` as discussed in the previous section.

The system call `shmat()` is implemented by `sys_shmat()`. There is little remarkable about the function. It acquires the appropriate descriptor and makes sure all the parameters are valid before calling `do_mmap()` to map the shared region into the process address space. Only two points of note are in the function.

The first is that it is responsible for ensuring that VMAs will not overlap if the caller specifies the address. The second is that the shp→`shm_nattch` counter is maintained by a `vm_operations_struct()` called `shm_vm_ops`. It registers `open()` and `close()` callbacks called `shm_open()` and `shm_close()`, respectively. The

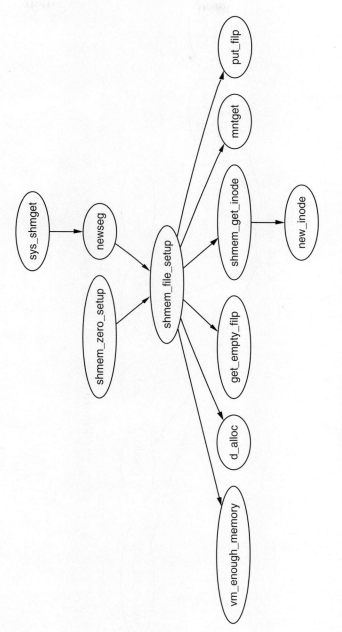

Figure 12.5. Call Graph: shmem_zero_setup()

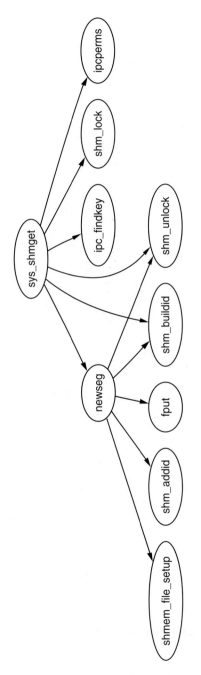

Figure 12.6. Call Graph: sys_shmget ()

shm_close() callback is also responsible for destroyed shared regions if the SHM_DEST flag is specified and the shm_nattch counter reaches zero.

12.9   What's New in 2.6

The core concept and functionality of the filesystem remains the same, and the changes are either optimizations or extensions to the filesystem's functionality. If the reader understands the 2.4 implementation well, the 2.6 implementation will not present much trouble.[1]

A new field has been added to the shmem_inode_info called alloced. The alloced field stores how many data pages are allocated to the file, which had to be calculated on the fly in 2.4 based on inode→i_blocks. It both saves a few clock cycles on a common operation as well as makes the code a bit more readable.

The flags field now uses the VM_ACCOUNT flag as well as the VM_LOCKED flag. The VM_ACCOUNT, always set, means that the VM will carefully account for the amount of memory used to make sure that allocations will not fail.

Extensions to the file operations are the ability to seek with the system call _llseek(), implemented by generic_file_llseek(), and to use sendfile() with virtual files, implemented by shmem_file_sendfile(). An extension has been added to the VMA operations to allow nonlinear mappings, implemented by shmem_populate().

The last major change is that the filesystem is responsible for the allocation and destruction of its own inodes, which are two new callbacks in struct super_operations. It is simply implemented by the creation of a slab cache called shmem_inode_cache. A constructor function init_once() is registered for the slab allocator to use for initializing each new inode.

---

[1]I find that saying "How hard could it possibly be" always helps.

CHAPTER **13**

Out of Memory Management

The last aspect of the VM I am going to discuss is the Out Of Memory (OOM) manager. This intentionally is a very short chapter because it has one simple task: check if there is enough available memory to satisfy, verify that the system is truly out of memory and, if so, select a process to kill. This is a controversial part of the VM and it has been suggested that it be removed on many occasions. Regardless of whether it exists in the latest kernel, it still is a useful system to examine because it touches off a number of other subsystems.

13.1 Checking Available Memory

For certain operations, such as expanding the heap with `brk()` or remapping an address space with `mremap()`, the system will check if there is enough available memory to satisfy a request. Note that this is separate to the `out_of_memory()` path that is covered in the next section. This path is used to avoid the system being in a state of OOM if at all possible.

When checking available memory, the number of required pages is passed as a parameter to `vm_enough_memory()`. Unless the system administrator has specified that the system should overcommit memory, the amount of available memory will be checked. To determine how many pages are potentially available, Linux sums up the following bits of data:

Total page cache because page cache is easily reclaimed.

Total free pages because they are already available.

Total free swap pages because userspace pages may be paged out.

Total pages managed by `swapper_space` However, this double-counts the free swap pages. This is balanced by the fact that slots are sometimes reserved, but not used.

Total pages used by the dentry cache because they are easily reclaimed.

Total pages used by the inode cache because they are easily reclaimed.

If the total number of pages added here is sufficient for the request, `vm_enough_memory()` returns true to the caller. If false is returned, the caller knows that the memory is not available and usually decides to return `-ENOMEM` to userspace.

13.2   Determining OOM Status

When the machine is low on memory, old page frames will be reclaimed (see Chapter 10), but, despite reclaiming pages, it may find that it was unable to free enough pages to satisfy a request even when scanning at highest priority. If it does fail to free page frames, out_of_memory() is called to see if the system is out of memory and needs to kill a process. The function's call graph is shown in Figure 13.1.

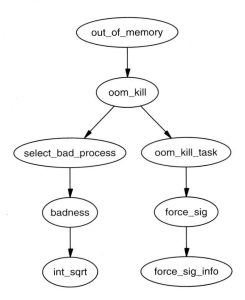

Figure 13.1. Call Graph: out_of_memory()

Unfortunately, it is possible that the system is not out of memory and simply needs to wait for I/O to complete or for pages to be swapped to backing storage. This is unfortunate, not because the system has memory, but because the function is being called unnecessarily, which opens the possibly of processes being unnecessarily killed. Before deciding to kill a process, it goes through the following checklist.

- Is there enough swap space left (nr_swap_pages > 0)? If yes, it is not OOM.

- Has it been more than 5 seconds since the last failure? If yes, it is not OOM.

- Have we failed within the last second? If no, it is not OOM.

- If there have not been 10 failures at least in the last 5 seconds, it is not OOM.

- Has a process been killed within the last 5 seconds? If yes, it is not OOM.

It is only if the previous tests are passed that oom_kill() is called to select a process to kill.

13.3 Selecting a Process

The function `select_bad_process()` is responsible for choosing a process to kill. It decides by stepping through each running task and calculating how suitable it is for killing with the function `badness()`. The badness is calculated as follows. The square roots are integer approximations calculated with `int_sqrt()`:

$$\text{badness\_for\_task} = \frac{\text{total\_vm\_for\_task}}{\sqrt{(\text{cpu\_time\_in\_seconds})} * \sqrt[4]{(\text{cpu\_time\_in\_minutes})}}$$

This has been chosen to select a process that is using a large amount of memory, but is not that long lived. Processes that have been running a long time are unlikely to be the cause of memory shortage, so this calculation is likely to select a process that uses a lot of memory, but has not been running long. If the process is a root process or has `CAP_SYS_ADMIN` capabilities, the points are divided by four because it is assumed that root privilege processes are well behaved. Similarly, if it has `CAP_SYS_RAWIO` capabilities (access to raw devices) privileges, the points are further divided by four because it is undesirable to kill a process that has direct access to hardware.

13.4 Killing the Selected Process

After a task is selected, the list is walked again, and each process that shares the same `mm_struct` as the selected process (i.e., they are threads) is sent a signal. If the process has `CAP_SYS_RAWIO` capabilities, a `SIGTERM` is sent to give the process a chance of exiting cleanly. Otherwise, a `SIGKILL` is sent.

13.5 Is That It?

Yes, that is it. OOM management touches a lot of subsystems, but, otherwise, there is not much to it.

13.6 What's New in 2.6

The majority of OOM management remains essentially the same for 2.6 except for the introduction of VM-accounted objects. These are VMAs that are flagged with the `VM_ACCOUNT` flag, first mentioned in Section 4.8. Additional checks will be made to ensure there is memory available when performing operations on VMAs with this flag set. The principal incentive for this complexity is to avoid the need of an OOM killer.

Some regions that always have the `VM_ACCOUNT` flag set are the process stack, the process heap, regions `mmap()`ed with `MAP_SHARED`, private regions that are writable and regions that set up `shmget()`. In other words, most userspace mappings have the `VM_ACCOUNT` flag set.

Linux accounts for the amount of memory that is committed to these VMAs with `vm_acct_memory()`, which increments a variable called `committed_space`. When the

VMA is freed, the committed space is decremented with vm_unacct_memory(). This is a fairly simple mechanism, but it allows Linux to remember how much memory it has already committed to userspace when deciding if it should commit more.

The checks are performed by calling security_vm_enough_memory(), which introduces another new feature. A feature is available in 2.6 that allows security-related kernel modules to override certain kernel functions. The full list of hooks available is stored in a struct security_operations called security_ops. There are a number of dummy, or default, functions that may be used, which are all listed in security/dummy.c, but the majority do nothing except return. If no security modules are loaded, the security_operations struct used is called dummy_security_ops, which uses all the default functions.

By default, security_vm_enough_memory() calls dummy_vm_enough_memory(), which is declared in security/dummy.c and is very similar to 2.4's vm_enough_memory() function. The new version adds the following pieces of information together to determine available memory:

Total page cache because page cache is easily reclaimed.

Total free pages because they are already available.

Total free swap pages because userspace pages may be paged out.

Slab pages with SLAB_RECLAIM_ACCOUNT **set** because they are easily reclaimed.

These pages, minus a 3 percent reserve for root processes, is the total amount of memory that is available for the request. If the memory is available, it makes a check to ensure the total amount of committed memory does not exceed the allowed threshold. The allowed threshold is TotalRam * (OverCommitRatio/100) + TotalSwapPage, where OverCommitRatio is set by the system administrator. If the total amount of committed space is not too high, 1 will be returned so that the allocation can proceed.

CHAPTER 14

The Final Word

Make no mistake, memory management is a large, complex and time-consuming field to research and difficult to apply to practical implementations. Because it is very difficult to model how systems behave in real multiprogrammed systems [CD80], developers often rely on intuition to guide them, and examination of virtual memory algorithms depends on simulations of specific workloads. Simulations are necessary because modeling how scheduling, paging behavior and multiple processes interact presents a considerable challenge. Page replacement policies, a field that has been the focus of considerable amounts of research, is a good example because it is only ever shown to work well for specified workloads. The problem of adjusting algorithms and policies to different workloads is addressed by having administrators tune systems as much as by research and algorithms.

The Linux kernel is also large, complex and fully understood by a relatively small core group of people. Its development is the result of contributions of thousands of programmers with a varying range of specialties, backgrounds and spare time. The first implementations are developed based on the all-important foundation that theory provides. Contributors built upon this framework with changes based on real-world observations.

It has been asserted on the Linux Memory Management mailing list that the VM is poorly documented and difficult to pick up because "the implementation is a nightmare to follow"[1] and the lack of documentation on practical VMs is not just confined to Linux. Matt Dillon, one of the principal developers of the FreeBSD VM[2] and considered a "VM guru" stated in an interview[3] that documentation can be "hard to come by." One of the principal difficulties with deciphering the implementation is the fact that the developer must have a background in memory management theory to see why implementation decisions were made because a pure understanding of the code is insufficient for any purpose other than microoptimizations.

This book attempted to bridge the gap between memory management theory and the practical implementation in Linux and to tie both fields together in a single place. It tried to describe what life is like in Linux as a memory manager in a

---

[1] *http://mail.nl.linux.org/linux-mm/2002-05/msg00035.html*
[2] His past involvement with the Linux VM is evident from *http://mail.nl.linux.org/linux-mm/2000-05/msg00419.html*.
[3] *http://kerneltrap.com/node.php?id=8*

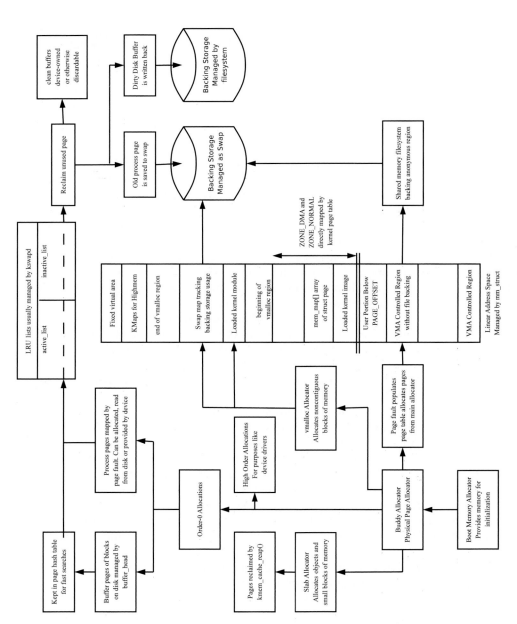

Figure 14.1. Broad Overview of How VM Subsystems Interact

manner that was relatively independent of hardware architecture considerations. I hope after reading this and progressing onto the code commentary that you, the reader, feels a lot more comfortable with tackling the VM subsystem. As a final parting shot, Figure 14.1 broadly illustrates how the subsystems I discussed in detail interact with each other.

On a final personal note, I hope that this book encourages other people to produce similar works for other areas of the kernel. I know I'll buy them!

Introduction

Welcome to the code commentary section of the book. If you are reading this, you are looking for a heavily detailed tour of the code. The commentary presumes you have read the equivalent section in the main part of the book, so, if you just started reading here, you're probably in the wrong place.

Each appendix section corresponds to the order and structure of the book. The order in which the functions are presented is the same order as displayed in the call graphs that are referenced throughout the commentary. At the beginning of each appendix and subsection, there is a mini table of contents to help navigate your way through the commentary. The code coverage is not 100 percent, but all the principal code patterns that are found throughout the VM are here. If the function you are interested in is not commented on, find a function similar to it.

Some of the code has been reformatted slightly for presentation, but the actual code is not changed. It is recommended that you use the companion CD while reading the code commentary. In particular use LXR to browse through the source code so that you get a feel for reading the code with and without the aid of the commentary.

Good Luck!

APPENDIX **B**

Describing Physical Memory

Contents

Describing
Physical Memory

B.1   Initializing Zones

Contents

B.1.1   Function: `setup_memory()`   *(arch/i386/kernel/setup.c)*

The call graph for this function is shown in Figure 2.3. This function gets the necessary information to give to the boot memory allocator to initialize itself. It is broken up into a number of different tasks.

- Find the start and ending PFN for low memory (`min_low_pfn`, `max_low_pfn`), the start and end PFN for high memory (`highstart_pfn`, `highend_pfn`) and the PFN for the last page in the system (`max_pfn`).

- Initialize the `bootmem_data` structure and declare which pages may be used by the boot memory allocator.

- Mark all pages usable by the system as free, and then reserve the pages used by the bitmap representing the pages.

- Reserve pages used by the SMP config or the `initrd` image if one exists.

```
991 static unsigned long __init setup_memory(void)
992 {
993        unsigned long bootmap_size, start_pfn, max_low_pfn;
994
995        /*
996         * partially used pages are not usable - thus
997         * we are rounding upwards:
998         */
999        start_pfn = PFN_UP(__pa(&_end));
1000
1001       find_max_pfn();
1002
1003       max_low_pfn = find_max_low_pfn();
1004
1005 #ifdef CONFIG_HIGHMEM
1006       highstart_pfn = highend_pfn = max_pfn;
1007       if (max_pfn > max_low_pfn) {
1008               highstart_pfn = max_low_pfn;
1009       }
```

```
1010        printk(KERN_NOTICE "%ldMB HIGHMEM available.\n",
1011              pages_to_mb(highend_pfn - highstart_pfn));
1012 #endif
1013        printk(KERN_NOTICE "%ldMB LOWMEM available.\n",
1014              pages_to_mb(max_low_pfn));
```

999 PFN_UP() takes a physical address, rounds it up to the next page and returns the page frame number. _end is the address of the end of the loaded kernel image, so start_pfn is now the offset of the first physical page frame that may be used.

1001 find_max_pfn() loops through the e820 map searching for the highest available PFN.

1003 find_max_low_pfn() finds the highest page frame addressable in ZONE_NORMAL.

1005-1011 If high memory is enabled, start with a high memory region of 0. If it turns out memory is available after max_low_pfn, put the start of high memory (highstart_pfn) there and the end of high memory at max_pfn. Print out an informational message on the availability of high memory.

1013-1014 Print out an informational message on the amount of low memory.

```
1018        bootmap_size = init_bootmem(start_pfn, max_low_pfn);
1019
1020        register_bootmem_low_pages(max_low_pfn);
1021
1028        reserve_bootmem(HIGH_MEMORY, (PFN_PHYS(start_pfn) +
1029              bootmap_size + PAGE_SIZE-1) - (HIGH_MEMORY));
1030
1035        reserve_bootmem(0, PAGE_SIZE);
1036
1037 #ifdef CONFIG_SMP
1043        reserve_bootmem(PAGE_SIZE, PAGE_SIZE);
1044 #endif
1045 #ifdef CONFIG_ACPI_SLEEP
1046        /*
1047         * Reserve low memory region for sleep support.
1048         */
1049        acpi_reserve_bootmem();
1050 #endif
```

1018 init_bootmem()(See Section E.1.1) initializes the bootmem_data struct for the config_page_data node. It sets where physical memory begins and ends for the node, allocates a bitmap representing the pages and sets all pages as reserved initially.

1020 `register_bootmem_low_pages()` reads the e820 map and calls `free_bootmem()` (See Section E.3.1) for all usable pages in the running system. This marks the pages as reserved during initialization as free.

1028-1029 Reserve the pages that are being used to store the bitmap representing the pages.

1035 Reserves page 0 because it is often a special page used by the BIOS.

1043 Reserves an extra page that is required by the trampoline code. The trampoline code deals with how userspace enters kernel space.

1045-1050 If sleep support is added, reserve memory is required for it. This is only of interest to laptops interested in suspending and is beyond the scope of this book.

```
1051 #ifdef CONFIG_X86_LOCAL_APIC
1052        /*
1053         * Find and reserve possible boot-time SMP configuration:
1054         */
1055        find_smp_config();
1056 #endif
1057 #ifdef CONFIG_BLK_DEV_INITRD
1058        if (LOADER_TYPE && INITRD_START) {
1059                if (INITRD_START + INITRD_SIZE <=
1060                    (max_low_pfn << PAGE_SHIFT)) {
1060                        reserve_bootmem(INITRD_START, INITRD_SIZE);
1061                        initrd_start =
1062                         INITRD_START? INITRD_START + PAGE_OFFSET : 0;
1063                        initrd_end = initrd_start+INITRD_SIZE;
1064                }
1065                else {
1066                        printk(KERN_ERR
1066                            "initrd extends beyond end of memory "
1067                            "(0x%081x > 0x%081x)\ndisabling initrd\n",
1068                            INITRD_START + INITRD_SIZE,
1069                            max_low_pfn << PAGE_SHIFT);
1070                        initrd_start = 0;
1071                }
1072        }
1073 #endif
1074
1075        return max_low_pfn;
1076 }
```

1055 This function reserves memory that stores config information about the SMP setup.

1057-1073 If `initrd` is enabled, the memory containing its image will be reserved. `initrd` provides a tiny filesystem image, which is used to boot the system.

1075 Returns the upper limit of addressable memory in `ZONE_NORMAL`.

B.1.2 Function: `zone_sizes_init()` *(arch/i386/mm/init.c)*

This is the top-level function that is used to initialize each of the zones. The size of the zones in PFNs was discovered during `setup_memory()` (See Section B.1.1). This function populates an array of zone sizes for passing to `free_area_init()`.

```
323 static void __init zone_sizes_init(void)
324 {
325     unsigned long zones_size[MAX_NR_ZONES] = {0, 0, 0};
326     unsigned int max_dma, high, low;
327
328     max_dma = virt_to_phys((char *)MAX_DMA_ADDRESS)>>PAGE_SHIFT;
329     low = max_low_pfn;
330     high = highend_pfn;
331
332     if (low < max_dma)
333         zones_size[ZONE_DMA] = low;
334     else {
335         zones_size[ZONE_DMA] = max_dma;
336         zones_size[ZONE_NORMAL] = low - max_dma;
337 #ifdef CONFIG_HIGHMEM
338         zones_size[ZONE_HIGHMEM] = high - low;
339 #endif
340     }
341     free_area_init(zones_size);
342 }
```

325 Initializes the sizes to 0.

328 Calculates the PFN for the maximum possible DMA address. This doubles as the largest number of pages that may exist in `ZONE_DMA`.

329 `max_low_pfn` is the highest PFN available to `ZONE_NORMAL`.

330 `highend_pfn` is the highest PFN available to `ZONE_HIGHMEM`.

332-333 If the highest PFN in `ZONE_NORMAL` is below `MAX_DMA_ADDRESS`, just set the size of `ZONE_DMA` to it. The other zones remain at 0.

335 Sets the number of pages in `ZONE_DMA`.

336 The size of `ZONE_NORMAL` is `max_low_pfn` minus the number of pages in `ZONE_DMA`.

338 The size of `ZONE_HIGHMEM` is the highest possible PFN minus the highest possible PFN in `ZONE_NORMAL` (`max_low_pfn`).

B.1.3 Function: free_area_init() *(mm/page_alloc.c)*

This is the architecture-independent function for setting up a UMA architecture.
It simply calls the core function passing the static `contig_page_data` as the node.
NUMA architectures will use `free_area_init_node()` instead.

```
838 void __init free_area_init(unsigned long *zones_size)
839 {
840     free_area_init_core(0, &contig_page_data, &mem_map,
                            zones_size, 0, 0, 0);
841 }
```

838 The parameters passed to `free_area_init_core()` are the following:

- **0** is the Node Identifier (NID) for the node, which is 0.

- **contig_page_data** is the static global `pg_data_t`.

- **mem_map** is the global `mem_map` used for tracking `struct pages`. The
  function `free_area_init_core()` will allocate memory for this array.

- **zones_sizes** is the array of zone sizes filled by `zone_sizes_init()`.

- **0** This zero is the starting physical address.

- **0** The second zero is an array of memory hole sizes that does not apply
  to UMA architectures.

- **0** The last 0 is a pointer to a local `mem_map` for this node that is used by
  NUMA architectures.

B.1.4 Function: free_area_init_node() *(mm/numa.c)*

This function has two versions. The first is almost identical to `free_area_init()`
except that it uses a different starting physical address. This function is also for
architectures that have only one node (so they use `contig_page_data`), but their
physical address is not at 0.

This version of the function, called after the pagetable initialization, is for initialization of each `pgdat` in the system. The callers have the option of allocating
their own local portion of the `mem_map` and passing it in as a parameter if they
want to optimize its location for the architecture. If they choose not to, it will be
allocated later by `free_area_init_core()`.

```
61 void __init free_area_init_node(int nid,
       pg_data_t *pgdat, struct page *pmap,
62     unsigned long *zones_size, unsigned long zone_start_paddr,
63     unsigned long *zholes_size)
64 {
65     int i, size = 0;
66     struct page *discard;
67
68     if (mem_map == (mem_map_t *)NULL)
69         mem_map = (mem_map_t *)PAGE_OFFSET;
```

```
70
71       free_area_init_core(nid, pgdat, &discard, zones_size,
                       zone_start_paddr,
72                     zholes_size, pmap);
73       pgdat->node_id = nid;
74
75       /*
76        * Get space for the valid bitmap.
77        */
78       for (i = 0; i < MAX_NR_ZONES; i++)
79           size += zones_size[i];
80       size = LONG_ALIGN((size + 7) >> 3);
81       pgdat->valid_addr_bitmap =
                       (unsigned long *)alloc_bootmem_node(pgdat, size);
82       memset(pgdat->valid_addr_bitmap, 0, size);
83 }
```

61 The parameters to the function are the following:

- **nid** is the NID of the `pgdat` passed in.

- **pgdat** is the node to be initialized.

- **pmap** is a pointer to the portion of the `mem_map` for this node to use, which is frequently passed as NULL and allocated later.

- **zones_size** is an array of zone sizes in this node.

- **zone_start_paddr** is the starting physical address for the node.

- **zholes_size** is an array of hole sizes in each zone.

68-69 If the global `mem_map` has not been set, set it to the beginning of the kernel portion of the linear address space. Remember that, with NUMA, `mem_map` is a virtual array with portions filled in by local maps used by each node.

71 Calls `free_area_init_core()`. Note that `discard` is passed in as the third parameter because global `mem_map` does not need to be set for NUMA.

73 Records the `pgdat`'s NID.

78-79 Calculates the total size of the NID.

80 Recalculates size as the number of bits required to have one bit for every byte of the size.

81 Allocates a bitmap to represent where valid areas exist in the node. In reality, this is only used by the Sparc architecture, so it is unfortunate to waste the memory for every other architecture.

82 Initially, all areas are invalid. Valid regions are marked later in the `mem_init()` functions for the Sparc. Other architectures just ignore the bitmap.

Describing Physical Memory

B.1.5   Function: `free_area_init_core()`   *(mm/page_alloc.c)*

This function is responsible for initializing all zones and allocating their local
`lmem_map` within a node. In UMA architectures, this function is called in a way
that will initialize the global `mem_map` array. In NUMA architectures, the array is
treated as a virtual array that is sparsely populated.

```
684 void __init free_area_init_core(int nid,
        pg_data_t *pgdat, struct page **gmap,
685     unsigned long *zones_size, unsigned long zone_start_paddr,
686     unsigned long *zholes_size, struct page *lmem_map)
687 {
688     unsigned long i, j;
689     unsigned long map_size;
690     unsigned long totalpages, offset, realtotalpages;
691     const unsigned long zone_required_alignment =
                                        1UL << (MAX_ORDER-1);
692
693     if (zone_start_paddr & ~PAGE_MASK)
694         BUG();
695
696     totalpages = 0;
697     for (i = 0; i < MAX_NR_ZONES; i++) {
698         unsigned long size = zones_size[i];
699         totalpages += size;
700     }
701     realtotalpages = totalpages;
702     if (zholes_size)
703         for (i = 0; i < MAX_NR_ZONES; i++)
704             realtotalpages -= zholes_size[i];
705
706     printk("On node %d totalpages: %lu\n", nid, realtotalpages);
```

This block is mainly responsible for calculating the size of each zone.

691 The zone must be aligned against the maximum-sized block that can be allocated by the buddy allocator for bitwise operations to work.

693-694 It is a bug if the physical address is not page aligned.

696 Initializes the `totalpages` count for this node to 0.

697-700 Calculates the total size of the node by iterating through `zone_sizes`.

701-704 Calculates the real amount of memory by subtracting the size of the holes in `zholes_size`.

706 Prints an informational message for the user on how much memory is available in this node.

```
708      /*
709       * Some architectures (with lots of mem and discontinous memory
710       * maps) have to search for a good mem_map area:
711       * For discontigmem, the conceptual mem map array starts from
712       * PAGE_OFFSET, we need to align the actual array onto a mem map
713       * boundary, so that MAP_NR works.
714       */
715      map_size = (totalpages + 1)*sizeof(struct page);
716      if (lmem_map == (struct page *)0) {
717          lmem_map = (struct page *) alloc_bootmem_node(pgdat, map_size);
718          lmem_map = (struct page *)(PAGE_OFFSET +
719              MAP_ALIGN((unsigned long)lmem_map - PAGE_OFFSET));
720      }
721      *gmap = pgdat->node_mem_map = lmem_map;
722      pgdat->node_size = totalpages;
723      pgdat->node_start_paddr = zone_start_paddr;
724      pgdat->node_start_mapnr = (lmem_map - mem_map);
725      pgdat->nr_zones = 0;
726
727      offset = lmem_map - mem_map;
```

This block allocates the local lmem_map if necessary and sets the gmap. In UMA architectures, gmap is actually mem_map, so this is where the memory for it is allocated.

715 Calculates the amount of memory required for the array. It is the total number of pages multiplied by the size of a struct page.

716 If the map has not already been allocated, this allocates it.

717 Allocates the memory from the boot memory allocator.

718 MAP_ALIGN() will align the array on a struct page-sized boundary for calculations that locate offsets within the mem_map based on the physical address with the MAP_NR() macro.

721 Sets the gmap and pgdat→node_mem_map variables to the allocated lmem_map. In UMA architectures, this just sets mem_map.

722 Records the size of the node.

723 Records the starting physical address.

724 Records what the offset is within mem_map that this node occupies.

725 Initializes the zone count to 0. This will be set later in the function.

727 offset is now the offset within mem_map that the local portion lmem_map begins at.

```
728        for (j = 0; j < MAX_NR_ZONES; j++) {
729            zone_t *zone = pgdat->node_zones + j;
730            unsigned long mask;
731            unsigned long size, realsize;
732
733            zone_table[nid * MAX_NR_ZONES + j] = zone;
734            realsize = size = zones_size[j];
735            if (zholes_size)
736                realsize -= zholes_size[j];
737
738            printk("zone(%lu): %lu pages.\n", j, size);
739            zone->size = size;
740            zone->name = zone_names[j];
741            zone->lock = SPIN_LOCK_UNLOCKED;
742            zone->zone_pgdat = pgdat;
743            zone->free_pages = 0;
744            zone->need_balance = 0;
745            if (!size)
746                continue;
```

This block starts a loop that initializes every zone_t within the node. The initialization starts with the setting of the simpler fields that values already exist for.

728 Loops through all zones in the node.

733 Records a pointer to this zone in the zone_table. See Section 2.6.

734-736 Calculates the real size of the zone based on the full size in zones_size minus the size of the holes in zholes_size.

738 Prints an informational message saying how many pages are in this zone.

739 Records the size of the zone.

740 zone_names is the string name of the zone for printing purposes.

741-744 Initializes some other fields for the zone such as its parent pgdat.

745-746 If the zone has no memory, this continues to the next zone because nothing further is required.

```
752        zone->wait_table_size = wait_table_size(size);
753        zone->wait_table_shift =
754            BITS_PER_LONG - wait_table_bits(zone->wait_table_size);
755        zone->wait_table = (wait_queue_head_t *)
756            alloc_bootmem_node(pgdat, zone->wait_table_size
757                    * sizeof(wait_queue_head_t));
758
```

```
759            for(i = 0; i < zone->wait_table_size; ++i)
760                init_waitqueue_head(zone->wait_table + i);
```

This block initializes the waitqueue for this zone. Processes waiting on pages in the zone use this hashed table to select a queue to wait on. This means that all processes waiting in a zone will not have to be woken when a page is unlocked, just a smaller subset.

752 `wait_table_size()` calculates the size of the table to use based on the number of pages in the zone and the desired ratio between the number of queues and the number of pages. The table will never be larger than 4KiB.

753-754 Calculates the shift for the hashing algorithm.

755 Allocates a table of `wait_queue_head_t` that can hold zone→`wait_table_size` entries.

759-760 Initializes all of the wait queues.

```
762            pgdat->nr_zones = j+1;
763
764            mask = (realsize / zone_balance_ratio[j]);
765            if (mask < zone_balance_min[j])
766                mask = zone_balance_min[j];
767            else if (mask > zone_balance_max[j])
768                mask = zone_balance_max[j];
769            zone->pages_min = mask;
770            zone->pages_low = mask*2;
771            zone->pages_high = mask*3;
772
773            zone->zone_mem_map = mem_map + offset;
774            zone->zone_start_mapnr = offset;
775            zone->zone_start_paddr = zone_start_paddr;
776
777            if ((zone_start_paddr >> PAGE_SHIFT) &
                                        (zone_required_alignment-1))
778                printk("BUG: wrong zone alignment, it will crash\n");
779
```

This block calculates the watermarks for the zone and records the location of the zone. The watermarks are calculated as ratios of the zone size.

762 First, as a new zone becomes active, this updates the number of zones in this node.

764 Calculates the mask (which will be used as the `pages_min` watermark) as the size of the zone divided by the balance ratio for this zone. The balance ratio is 128 for all zones as declared at the top of `mm/page_alloc.c`.

Describing
Physical Memory

765-766 The `zone_balance_min` ratios are 20 for all zones, which means that `pages_min` will never be below 20.

767-768 Similarly, the `zone_balance_max` ratios are all 255, so `pages_min` will never be over 255.

769 `pages_min` is set to `mask`.

770 `pages_low` is twice the number of pages as `pages_min`.

771 `pages_high` is three times the number of pages as `pages_min`.

773 Records where the first `struct page` for this zone is located within `mem_map`.

774 Records the index within `mem_map` that this zone begins at.

775 Records the starting physical address.

777-778 Ensures that the zone is correctly aligned for use with the buddy allocator. Otherwise, the bitwise operations used for the buddy allocator will break.

```
780          /*
781           * Initially all pages are reserved - free ones are freed
782           * up by free_all_bootmem() once the early boot process is
783           * done. Non-atomic initialization, single-pass.
784           */
785          for (i = 0; i < size; i++) {
786              struct page *page = mem_map + offset + i;
787              set_page_zone(page, nid * MAX_NR_ZONES + j);
788              set_page_count(page, 0);
789              SetPageReserved(page);
790              INIT_LIST_HEAD(&page->list);
791              if (j != ZONE_HIGHMEM)
792                  set_page_address(page, __va(zone_start_paddr));
793              zone_start_paddr += PAGE_SIZE;
794          }
795
```

785-794 Initially, all pages in the zone are marked as reserved because there is no way to know which ones are in use by the boot memory allocator. When the boot memory allocator is retiring in `free_all_bootmem()`, the unused pages will have their `PG_reserved` bit cleared.

786 Gets the page for this offset.

787 The zone the page belongs to is encoded with the page flags. See Section 2.6.

788 Sets the count to 0 because no one is using it.

789 Sets the reserved flag. Later, the boot memory allocator will clear this bit if the page is no longer in use.

790 Initializes the list head for the page.

791-792 Sets the page→virtual field if it is available and the page is in low memory.

793 Increments zone_start_paddr by a page size because this variable will be used to record the beginning of the next zone.

```
796        offset += size;
797        for (i = 0; ; i++) {
798            unsigned long bitmap_size;
799
800            INIT_LIST_HEAD(&zone->free_area[i].free_list);
801            if (i == MAX_ORDER-1) {
802                zone->free_area[i].map = NULL;
803                break;
804            }
805
829            bitmap_size = (size-1) >> (i+4);
830            bitmap_size = LONG_ALIGN(bitmap_size+1);
831            zone->free_area[i].map =
832              (unsigned long *) alloc_bootmem_node(pgdat,
                                                    bitmap_size);
833        }
834    }
835    build_zonelists(pgdat);
836 }
```

This block initializes the free lists for the zone and allocates the bitmap used by the buddy allocator to record the state of page buddies.

797 This will loop from 0 to MAX_ORDER-1.

800 Initializes the linked list for the free_list of the current order i.

801-804 If this is the last order, this sets the free area map to NULL because this is what marks the end of the free lists.

829 Calculates the bitmap_size to be the number of bytes required to hold a bitmap where each bit represents a pair of buddies that are 2^i number of pages.

830 Aligns the size to a long with LONG_ALIGN() because all bitwise operations are on longs.

831-832 Allocates the memory for the map.

Describing Physical Memory

834 Loops back to move to the next zone.

835 Builds the zone fallback lists for this node with `build_zonelists()`.

B.1.6   Function: build_zonelists()   *(mm/page_alloc.c)*

This function builds the list of fallback zones for each zone in the requested node. This is for when an allocation cannot be satisfied and another zone is consulted. When this consultation is finished, allocations from ZONE_HIGHMEM will fall back to ZONE_NORMAL. Allocations from ZONE_NORMAL will fall back to ZONE_DMA, which in turn has nothing to fall back on.

```
589 static inline void build_zonelists(pg_data_t *pgdat)
590 {
591     int i, j, k;
592
593     for (i = 0; i <= GFP_ZONEMASK; i++) {
594         zonelist_t *zonelist;
595         zone_t *zone;
596
597         zonelist = pgdat->node_zonelists + i;
598         memset(zonelist, 0, sizeof(*zonelist));
599
600         j = 0;
601         k = ZONE_NORMAL;
602         if (i & __GFP_HIGHMEM)
603             k = ZONE_HIGHMEM;
604         if (i & __GFP_DMA)
605             k = ZONE_DMA;
606
607         switch (k) {
608             default:
609                 BUG();
610             /*
611              * fallthrough:
612              */
613             case ZONE_HIGHMEM:
614                 zone = pgdat->node_zones + ZONE_HIGHMEM;
615                 if (zone->size) {
616 #ifndef CONFIG_HIGHMEM
617                     BUG();
618 #endif
619                     zonelist->zones[j++] = zone;
620                 }
621             case ZONE_NORMAL:
622                 zone = pgdat->node_zones + ZONE_NORMAL;
623                 if (zone->size)
```

```
624                         zonelist->zones[j++] = zone;
625                case ZONE_DMA:
626                        zone = pgdat->node_zones + ZONE_DMA;
627                        if (zone->size)
628                                zonelist->zones[j++] = zone;
629        }
630        zonelist->zones[j++] = NULL;
631    }
632 }
```

593 Looks through the maximum possible number of zones.

597 Gets the `zonelist` for this zone and zeros it.

600 Starts j at 0, which corresponds to ZONE_DMA.

601-605 Sets k to be the type of zone currently being examined.

614 Gets the `ZONE_HIGHMEM`.

615-620 If the zone has memory, `ZONE_HIGHMEM` is the preferred zone to allocate from for high memory allocations. If `ZONE_HIGHMEM` has no memory, `ZONE_NORMAL` will become the preferred zone when the next case is fallen through to because j is not incremented for an empty zone.

621-624 Sets the next preferred zone to allocate from to be `ZONE_NORMAL`. Again, do not use it if the zone has no memory.

626-628 Sets the final fallback zone to be `ZONE_DMA`. The check is still made for `ZONE_DMA` having memory. Like NUMA architecture, not all nodes will have a `ZONE_DMA`.

Describing
Physical Memory

B.2   Page Operations

Contents

B.2.1   Locking Pages

B.2.1.1   Function: `lock_page()`   *(mm/filemap.c)*

This function tries to lock a page. If the page cannot be locked, it will cause the process to sleep until the page is available.

```
921 void lock_page(struct page *page)
922 {
923     if (TryLockPage(page))
924         __lock_page(page);
925 }
```

923 `TryLockPage()` is just a wrapper around `test_and_set_bit()` for the `PG_locked` bit in page→flags. If the bit was previously clear, the function returns immediately because the page is now locked.

924 Otherwise, `__lock_page()` is called (See Section B.2.1.2) to put the process to sleep.

B.2.1.2   Function: `__lock_page()`   *(mm/filemap.c)*

This is called after a `TryLockPage()` failed. It will locate the waitqueue for this page and sleep on it until the lock can be acquired.

```
897 static void __lock_page(struct page *page)
898 {
899     wait_queue_head_t *waitqueue = page_waitqueue(page);
900     struct task_struct *tsk = current;
901     DECLARE_WAITQUEUE(wait, tsk);
902
903     add_wait_queue_exclusive(waitqueue, &wait);
904     for (;;) {
905         set_task_state(tsk, TASK_UNINTERRUPTIBLE);
906         if (PageLocked(page)) {
```

```
907             sync_page(page);
908             schedule();
909         }
910     if (!TryLockPage(page))
911         break;
912     }
913     __set_task_state(tsk, TASK_RUNNING);
914     remove_wait_queue(waitqueue, &wait);
915 }
```

899 page_waitqueue() is the implementation of the hash algorithm that determines which wait queue this page belongs to in the table zone→wait_table.

900-901 Initializes the waitqueue for this task.

903 Adds this process to the waitqueue returned by page_waitqueue().

904-912 Loops here until the lock is acquired.

905 Sets the process states as being in uninterruptible sleep. When schedule() is called, the process will be put to sleep and will not wake again until the queue is explicitly woken up.

906 If the page is still locked, this calls the sync_page() function to schedule the page to be synchronized with its backing storage. It calls schedule() to sleep until the queue is woken up, such as when the I/O on the page completes.

910-911 Try and lock the page again. If we succeed, exit the loop, otherwise sleep on the queue again.

913-914 The lock is now acquired, so this sets the process state to TASK_RUNNING and removes it from the wait queue. The function now returns with the lock acquired.

B.2.1.3 Function: sync_page() *(mm/filemap.c)*

This calls the filesystem-specific sync_page() to synchronize the page with its backing storage.

```
140 static inline int sync_page(struct page *page)
141 {
142     struct address_space *mapping = page->mapping;
143
144     if (mapping && mapping->a_ops && mapping->a_ops->sync_page)
145         return mapping->a_ops->sync_page(page);
146     return 0;
147 }
```

142 Gets the address_space for the page if it exists.

144-145 If a backing exists, and it has an associated address_space_operations, which provides a sync_page() function, this calls it.

B.2.2 Unlocking Pages

B.2.2.1   Function: unlock_page()   *(mm/filemap.c)*
    This function unlocks a page and wakes up any processes that may be waiting
on it.

```
874 void unlock_page(struct page *page)
875 {
876     wait_queue_head_t *waitqueue = page_waitqueue(page);
877     ClearPageLaunder(page);
878     smp_mb__before_clear_bit();
879     if (!test_and_clear_bit(PG_locked, &(page)->flags))
880         BUG();
881     smp_mb__after_clear_bit();
882
883     /*
884      * Although the default semantics of wake_up() are
885      * to wake all, here the specific function is used
886      * to make it even more explicit that a number of
887      * pages are being waited on here.
888      */
889     if (waitqueue_active(waitqueue))
890         wake_up_all(waitqueue);
891 }
```

876 page_waitqueue() is the implementation of the hash algorithm, which deter-
    mines which wait queue this page belongs to in the table zone→wait_table.

877 Clears the launder bit because I/O has now completed on the page.

878 This is a memory block operation that must be called before performing bit
    operations that may be seen by multiple processors.

879-880 Clears the PG_locked bit. It is a BUG() if the bit was already cleared.

881 Completes the SMP memory block operation.

889-890 If there are processes waiting on the page queue for this page, this wakes
    them.

B.2.3 Waiting on Pages

B.2.3.1   Function: wait_on_page()   *(include/linux/pagemap.h)*

```
94 static inline void wait_on_page(struct page * page)
95 {
96     if (PageLocked(page))
97         ___wait_on_page(page);
98 }
```

96-97 If the page is currently locked, this calls `___wait_on_page()` to sleep until it is unlocked.

B.2.3.2   Function: `___wait_on_page()`   *(mm/filemap.c)*

This function is called after `PageLocked()` has been used to determine that the page is locked. The calling process will probably sleep until the **page** is unlocked.

```
849 void ___wait_on_page(struct page *page)
850 {
851     wait_queue_head_t *waitqueue = page_waitqueue(page);
852     struct task_struct *tsk = current;
853     DECLARE_WAITQUEUE(wait, tsk);
854
855     add_wait_queue(waitqueue, &wait);
856     do {
857         set_task_state(tsk, TASK_UNINTERRUPTIBLE);
858         if (!PageLocked(page))
859             break;
860         sync_page(page);
861         schedule();
862     } while (PageLocked(page));
863     __set_task_state(tsk, TASK_RUNNING);
864     remove_wait_queue(waitqueue, &wait);
865 }
```

851 `page_waitqueue()` is the implementation of the hash algorithm that determines which wait queue this page belongs to in the table `zone→wait_table`.

852-853 Initializes the waitqueue for the current task.

855 Adds this task to the waitqueue returned by `page_waitqueue()`.

857 Sets the process state to be in uninterruptible sleep. When `schedule()` is called, the process will sleep.

858-859 Checks to make sure the page was not unlocked since the last check.

860 Calls `sync_page()` (See Section B.2.1.3) to call the filesystem-specific function to synchronize the page with its backing storage.

861 Calls `schedule()` to go to sleep. The process will be woken when the page is unlocked.

862 Checks if the page is still locked. Remember that multiple pages could be using this wait queue, and there could be processes sleeping that want to lock this page.

863-864 The page has been unlocked. It sets the process to be in the `TASK_RUNNING` state and removes the process from the waitqueue.

Describing
Physical Memory

Page Table Management

Contents

Page Table
Management

C.1   Page Table Initialization

Contents

C.1.1   Function: `paging_init()`   *(arch/i386/mm/init.c)*

This is the top-level function called from **setup_arch()**. When this function returns, the page tables have been fully set up. Be aware that this is all x86 specific.

```
351 void __init paging_init(void)
352 {
353     pagetable_init();
354
355     load_cr3(swapper_pg_dir);
356
357 #if CONFIG_X86_PAE
362     if (cpu_has_pae)
363         set_in_cr4(X86_CR4_PAE);
364 #endif
365
366     __flush_tlb_all();
367
368 #ifdef CONFIG_HIGHMEM
369     kmap_init();
370 #endif
371     zone_sizes_init();
372 }
```

353 `pagetable_init()` is responsible for setting up a static page table using `swapper_pg_dir` as the PGD.

355 Loads the initialized `swapper_pg_dir` into the CR3 register so that the CPU will be able to use it.

362-363 If PAE is enabled, this sets the appropriate bit in the CR4 register.

366 Flushes all TLBs, including the global kernel ones.

369 `kmap_init()` initializes the region of pagetables reserved for use with `kmap()`.

371 `zone_sizes_init()` (See Section B.1.2) records the size of each of the zones before calling `free_area_init()` (See Section B.1.3) to initialize each zone.

C.1.2 Function: pagetable_init() *(arch/i386/mm/init.c)*

This function is responsible for statically initializing a pagetable starting with a statically defined PGD called swapper_pg_dir. At the very least, a PTE will be available that points to every page frame in ZONE_NORMAL.

```
205 static void __init pagetable_init (void)
206 {
207     unsigned long vaddr, end;
208     pgd_t *pgd, *pgd_base;
209     int i, j, k;
210     pmd_t *pmd;
211     pte_t *pte, *pte_base;
212
213     /*
214      * This can be zero as well - no problem, in that case we exit
215      * the loops anyway due to the PTRS_PER_* conditions.
216      */
217     end = (unsigned long)__va(max_low_pfn*PAGE_SIZE);
218
219     pgd_base = swapper_pg_dir;
220 #if CONFIG_X86_PAE
221     for (i = 0; i < PTRS_PER_PGD; i++)
222         set_pgd(pgd_base + i, __pgd(1 + __pa(empty_zero_page)));
223 #endif
224     i = __pgd_offset(PAGE_OFFSET);
225     pgd = pgd_base + i;
```

This first block initializes the PGD. It does this by pointing each entry to the global zero page. Entries needed to reference available memory in ZONE_NORMAL will be allocated later.

217 The variable end marks the end of physical memory in ZONE_NORMAL.

219 pgd_base is set to the beginning of the statically declared PGD.

220-223 If PAE is enabled, it is insufficient to leave each entry simply as 0 (which, in effect, points each entry to the global zero page) because each pgd_t is a struct. Instead, set_pgd must be called for each pgd_t to point the entry to the global zero page.

224 i is initialized as the offset within the PGD that corresponds to PAGE_OFFSET. In other words, this function will only be initializing the kernel portion of the linear address space. The userspace portion is left alone.

225 pgd is initialized to the pgd_t corresponding to the beginning of the kernel portion of the linear address space.

Page Table Management

```
227     for (; i < PTRS_PER_PGD; pgd++, i++) {
228         vaddr = i*PGDIR_SIZE;
229         if (end && (vaddr >= end))
230             break;
231 #if CONFIG_X86_PAE
232         pmd = (pmd_t *) alloc_bootmem_low_pages(PAGE_SIZE);
233         set_pgd(pgd, __pgd(__pa(pmd) + 0x1));
234 #else
235         pmd = (pmd_t *)pgd;
236 #endif
237         if (pmd != pmd_offset(pgd, 0))
238             BUG();
```

This loop begins setting up valid PMD entries to point to. In the PAE case, pages are allocated with `alloc_bootmem_low_pages()`, and the PGD is set appropriately. Without PAE, there is no middle directory, so it is just folded back onto the PGD to preserve the illusion of a three-level pagetable.

227 `i` is already initialized to the beginning of the kernel portion of the linear address space, so this keeps looping until the last `pgd_t` at `PTRS_PER_PGD` is reached.

228 Calculates the virtual address for this PGD.

229-230 If the end of `ZONE_NORMAL` is reached, this exits the loop because further pagetable entries are not needed.

231-234 If PAE is enabled, this allocates a page for the PMD and inserts the page into the pagetable with `set_pgd()`.

235 If PAE is not available, just set `pmd` to the current `pgd_t`. This is the "folding back" trick for emulating three-level pagetables.

237-238 This is a sanity check to make sure the PMD is valid.

```
239         for (j = 0; j < PTRS_PER_PMD; pmd++, j++) {
240             vaddr = i*PGDIR_SIZE + j*PMD_SIZE;
241             if (end && (vaddr >= end))
242                 break;
243             if (cpu_has_pse) {
244                 unsigned long __pe;
245
246                 set_in_cr4(X86_CR4_PSE);
247                 boot_cpu_data.wp_works_ok = 1;
248                 __pe = _KERNPG_TABLE + _PAGE_PSE + __pa(vaddr);
249                 /* Make it "global" too if supported */
250                 if (cpu_has_pge) {
251                     set_in_cr4(X86_CR4_PGE);
```

```
252                          __pe += _PAGE_GLOBAL;
253                     }
254                     set_pmd(pmd, __pmd(__pe));
255                     continue;
256                 }
257
258             pte_base = pte =
                             (pte_t *) alloc_bootmem_low_pages(PAGE_SIZE);
259
```

This block initializes each entry in the PMD. This loop will only execute if PAE is enabled. Remember that, without PAE, PTRS_PER_PMD is 1.

240 Calculates the virtual address for this PMD.

241-242 If the end of ZONE_NORMAL is reached, this finishes.

243-248 If the CPU supports PSE, use large TLB entries. This means that, for kernel pages, a TLB entry will map 4MiB instead of the normal 4KiB, and the third level of PTEs is unnecessary.

258 __pe is set as the flags for a kernel pagetable (_KERNPG_TABLE), as the flag to indicate that this is an entry mapping 4MiB (_PAGE_PSE) and then to the physical address for this virtual address with __pa(). This means that 4MiB of physical memory is not being mapped by the pagetables.

250-253 If the CPU supports PGE, then set it for this page table entry. This marks the entry as being global and visible to all processes.

254-255 Because the third level is not required because of PSE, set the PMD now with set_pmd() and continue to the next PMD.

258 If not, PSE is not supported, and PTEs are required, so allocate a page for them.

```
260             for (k = 0; k < PTRS_PER_PTE; pte++, k++) {
261                 vaddr = i*PGDIR_SIZE + j*PMD_SIZE + k*PAGE_SIZE;
262                 if (end && (vaddr >= end))
263                     break;
264                 *pte = mk_pte_phys(__pa(vaddr), PAGE_KERNEL);
265             }
266             set_pmd(pmd, __pmd(_KERNPG_TABLE + __pa(pte_base)));
267             if (pte_base != pte_offset(pmd, 0))
268                 BUG();
269
270         }
271     }
```

This block initializes the PTEs.

Page Table Management

260-265 For each `pte_t`, calculate the virtual address currently being examined and create a PTE that points to the appropriate physical page frame.

266 The PTEs have been initialized, so set the PMD to point to the page containing them.

267-268 Makes sure that the entry was established correctly.

```
273     /*
274      * Fixed mappings, only the page table structure has to be
275      * created - mappings will be set by set_fixmap():
276      */
277     vaddr = __fix_to_virt(__end_of_fixed_addresses - 1) & PMD_MASK;
278     fixrange_init(vaddr, 0, pgd_base);
279
280 #if CONFIG_HIGHMEM
281     /*
282      * Permanent kmaps:
283      */
284     vaddr = PKMAP_BASE;
285     fixrange_init(vaddr, vaddr + PAGE_SIZE*LAST_PKMAP, pgd_base);
286
287     pgd = swapper_pg_dir + __pgd_offset(vaddr);
288     pmd = pmd_offset(pgd, vaddr);
289     pte = pte_offset(pmd, vaddr);
290     pkmap_page_table = pte;
291 #endif
292
293 #if CONFIG_X86_PAE
294     /*
295      * Add low memory identity-mappings - SMP needs it when
296      * starting up on an AP from real-mode. In the non-PAE
297      * case we already have these mappings through head.S.
298      * All user-space mappings are explicitly cleared after
299      * SMP startup.
300      */
301     pgd_base[0] = pgd_base[USER_PTRS_PER_PGD];
302 #endif
303 }
```

At this point, pagetable entries have been set up that reference all parts of ZONE_NORMAL. The remaining regions needed are those for fixed mappings and those needed for mapping high memory pages with `kmap()`.

277 The fixed address space is considered to start at FIXADDR_TOP and to finish earlier in the address space. `__fix_to_virt()` takes an index as a parameter and returns the index'th pageframe backward (starting from FIXADDR_TOP)

within the fixed virtual address space. `__end_of_fixed_addresses` is the last
index used by the fixed virtual address space. In other words, this line returns
the virtual address of the PMD that corresponds to the beginning of the fixed
virtual address space.

278 By passing 0 as the end to `fixrange_init()`, the function will start at `vaddr`
and build valid PGDs and PMDs until the end of the virtual address space.
PTEs are not needed for these addresses.

280-291 Sets up pagetables for use with `kmap()`.

287-290 Gets the PTE corresponding to the beginning of the region for use with
`kmap()`.

301 This sets up a temporary identity mapping between the virtual address 0 and
the physical address 0.

C.1.3 Function: `fixrange_init()` *(arch/i386/mm/init.c)*

This function creates valid PGDs and PMDs for fixed virtual address mappings.

```
167 static void __init fixrange_init (unsigned long start,
                                      unsigned long end,
                                      pgd_t *pgd_base)
168 {
169     pgd_t *pgd;
170     pmd_t *pmd;
171     pte_t *pte;
172     int i, j;
173     unsigned long vaddr;
174
175     vaddr = start;
176     i = __pgd_offset(vaddr);
177     j = __pmd_offset(vaddr);
178     pgd = pgd_base + i;
179
180     for ( ; (i < PTRS_PER_PGD) && (vaddr != end); pgd++, i++) {
181 #if CONFIG_X86_PAE
182         if (pgd_none(*pgd)) {
183             pmd = (pmd_t *) alloc_bootmem_low_pages(PAGE_SIZE);
184             set_pgd(pgd, __pgd(__pa(pmd) + 0x1));
185             if (pmd != pmd_offset(pgd, 0))
186                 printk("PAE BUG #02!\n");
187         }
188         pmd = pmd_offset(pgd, vaddr);
189 #else
190         pmd = (pmd_t *)pgd;
191 #endif
```

```
192            for (; (j < PTRS_PER_PMD) && (vaddr != end); pmd++, j++) {
193                if (pmd_none(*pmd)) {
194                    pte = (pte_t *) alloc_bootmem_low_pages(PAGE_SIZE);
195                    set_pmd(pmd, __pmd(_KERNPG_TABLE + __pa(pte)));
196                    if (pte != pte_offset(pmd, 0))
197                        BUG();
198                }
199                vaddr += PMD_SIZE;
200            }
201            j = 0;
202    }
203 }
```

175 Sets the starting virtual address (**vadd**) to the requested starting address provided as the parameter.

176 Gets the index within the PGD corresponding to **vaddr**.

177 Gets the index within the PMD corresponding to **vaddr**.

178 Gets the starting **pgd_t**.

180 Keeps cycling until **end** is reached. When **pagetable_init()** passes in 0, this loop will continue until the end of the PGD.

182-187 In the case of PAE, this allocates a page for the PMD if one has not already been allocated.

190 Without PAE, there is no PMD, so this treats the **pgd_t** as the **pmd_t**.

192-200 For each entry in the PMD, this allocates a page for the **pte_t** entries and sets it within the pagetables. Note that **vaddr** is incremented in PMD-sized strides.

C.1.4   Function: kmap_init()   *(arch/i386/mm/init.c)*

This function only exists if **CONFIG_HIGHMEM** is set during compile time. It is responsible for caching where the beginning of the kmap region is, the PTE referencing it and the protection for the page tables. This means the PGD will not have to be checked every time **kmap()** is used.

```
74 #if CONFIG_HIGHMEM
75 pte_t *kmap_pte;
76 pgprot_t kmap_prot;
77
78 #define kmap_get_fixmap_pte(vaddr)                         \
79     pte_offset(pmd_offset(pgd_offset_k(vaddr), (vaddr)), (vaddr))
80
81 void __init kmap_init(void)
```

```
82 {
83     unsigned long kmap_vstart;
84
85     /* cache the first kmap pte */
86     kmap_vstart = __fix_to_virt(FIX_KMAP_BEGIN);
87     kmap_pte = kmap_get_fixmap_pte(kmap_vstart);
e8
89     kmap_prot = PAGE_KERNEL;
90 }
91 #endif /* CONFIG_HIGHMEM */
```

78-79 Because `fixrange_init()` has already set up valid PGDs and PMDs, there is no need to double-check them, so `kmap_get_fixmap_pte()` is responsible for quickly traversing the pagetable.

86 Caches the virtual address for the kmap region in `kmap_vstart`.

87 Caches the PTE for the start of the kmap region in `kmap_pte`.

89 Caches the protection for the pagetable entries with `kmap_prot`.

Page Table
Management

C.2   Page Table Walking

Contents

C.2.1   Function: `follow_page()`   *(mm/memory.c)*

This function returns the **struct page** used by the PTE at **address** in mm's pagetables.

```
405 static struct page * follow_page(struct mm_struct *mm,
                                     unsigned long address,
                                     int write)
406 {
407     pgd_t *pgd;
408     pmd_t *pmd;
409     pte_t *ptep, pte;
410
411     pgd = pgd_offset(mm, address);
412     if (pgd_none(*pgd) || pgd_bad(*pgd))
413         goto out;
414
415     pmd = pmd_offset(pgd, address);
416     if (pmd_none(*pmd) || pmd_bad(*pmd))
417         goto out;
418
419     ptep = pte_offset(pmd, address);
420     if (!ptep)
421         goto out;
422
423     pte = *ptep;
424     if (pte_present(pte)) {
425         if (!write ||
426             (pte_write(pte) && pte_dirty(pte)))
427             return pte_page(pte);
428     }
429
430 out:
431     return 0;
432 }
```

405 The parameters are the **mm** with the pagetables that are about to be walked, the **address** that has the **struct page** of interest and **write**, which indicates if the page is about to be written to.

411 Gets the PGD for the **address** and makes sure it is present and valid.

415-417 Gets the PMD for the **address** and makes sure it is present and valid.

419 Gets the PTE for the `address` and makes sure it exists.

424 If the PTE is currently present, then something can be returned.

425-426 If the caller has indicated a write is about to take place, this checks to make sure that the PTE has write permissions set and, if so, makes the PTE dirty.

427 If the PTE is present and the permissions are fine, this returns the `struct page` mapped by the PTE.

431 Returns 0, indicating that the `address` has no associated `struct page`.

Page Table
Management

Process Address Space

Contents

251

Process Address Space

D.1 Process Memory Descriptors

Contents

This section covers the functions used to allocate, initialize, copy and destroy memory descriptors.

D.1.1 Initializing a Descriptor

The initial `mm_struct` in the system is called `init_mm` and is statically initialized at compile time using the macro `INIT_MM()`.

```
238 #define INIT_MM(name) \
239 {                                                              \
240        mm_rb:            RB_ROOT,                              \
241        pgd:              swapper_pg_dir,                       \
242        mm_users:         ATOMIC_INIT(2),                       \
243        mm_count:         ATOMIC_INIT(1),                       \
244        mmap_sem:         __RWSEM_INITIALIZER(name.mmap_sem),\
245        page_table_lock:  SPIN_LOCK_UNLOCKED,                  \
246        mmlist:           LIST_HEAD_INIT(name.mmlist),         \
247 }
```

After it is established, new `mm_structs` are copies of their parent `mm_struct` and are copied using `copy_mm()` with the process-specific fields initialized with `init_mm()`.

D.1.2 Copying a Descriptor

D.1.2.1 Function: `copy_mm()` *(kernel/fork.c)*

This function makes a copy of the `mm_struct` for the given task. This is only called from `do_fork()` after a new process has been created and needs its own `mm_struct`.

```
315 static int copy_mm(unsigned long clone_flags,
                       struct task_struct * tsk)
316 {
```

```
317        struct mm_struct * mm, *oldmm;
318        int retval;
319
320        tsk->min_flt = tsk->maj_flt = 0;
321        tsk->cmin_flt = tsk->cmaj_flt = 0;
322        tsk->nswap = tsk->cnswap = 0;
323
324        tsk->mm = NULL;
325        tsk->active_mm = NULL;
326
327        /*
328         * Are we cloning a kernel thread?
330         * We need to steal an active VM for that..
331         */
332        oldmm = current->mm;
333        if (!oldmm)
334              return 0;
335
336        if (clone_flags & CLONE_VM) {
337              atomic_inc(&oldmm->mm_users);
338              mm = oldmm;
339              goto good_mm;
340        }
```

This block resets fields that are not inherited by a child mm_struct and finds an mm to copy from.

315 The parameters are the flags passed for clone and the task that is creating a copy of the mm_struct.

320-325 Initializes the task_struct fields related to memory management.

332 Borrows the mm of the current running process to copy from.

333 A kernel thread has no mm, so it can return immediately.

336-341 If the CLONE_VM flag is set, the child process is to share the mm with the parent process. This is required by users like pthreads. The mm_users field is incremented so that the mm is not destroyed prematurely. The good_mm label sets tsk→mm and tsk→active_mm and returns success.

```
342        retval = -ENOMEM;
343        mm = allocate_mm();
344        if (!mm)
345              goto fail_nomem;
346
347        /* Copy the current MM stuff.. */
348        memcpy(mm, oldmm, sizeof(*mm));
```

Process Address Space

```
349          if (!mm_init(mm))
350                  goto fail_nomem;
351
352          if (init_new_context(tsk,mm))
353                  goto free_pt;
354
355          down_write(&oldmm->mmap_sem);
356          retval = dup_mmap(mm);
357          up_write(&oldmm->mmap_sem);
358
```

343 Allocates a new mm.

348-350 Copies the parent mm and initializes the process-specific mm fields with init_mm().

352-353 Initializes the MMU context for architectures that do not automatically manage their MMU.

355-357 Calls dup_mmap(), which is responsible for copying all the VMA's regions in use by the parent process.

```
359          if (retval)
360                  goto free_pt;
361
362          /*
363           * child gets a private LDT (if there was an LDT in the parent)
364           */
365          copy_segments(tsk, mm);
366
367 good_mm:
368          tsk->mm = mm;
369          tsk->active_mm = mm;
370          return 0;
371
372 free_pt:
373          mmput(mm);
374 fail_nomem:
375          return retval;
376 }
```

359 dup_mmap() returns 0 on success. If it failed, the label free_pt will call mmput(), which decrements the use count of the mm.

365 Copies the LDT for the new process based on the parent process.

368-370 Sets the new mm, active_mm, and return success.

D.1.2.2   Function: `mm_init()`   *(kernel/fork.c)*

This function initializes process-specific mm fields.

```
230 static struct mm_struct * mm_init(struct mm_struct * mm)
231 {
232         atomic_set(&mm->mm_users, 1);
233         atomic_set(&mm->mm_count, 1);
234         init_rwsem(&mm->mmap_sem);
235         mm->page_table_lock = SPIN_LOCK_UNLOCKED;
236         mm->pgd = pgd_alloc(mm);
237         mm->def_flags = 0;
238         if (mm->pgd)
239                 return mm;
240         free_mm(mm);
241         return NULL;
242 }
```

232 Sets the number of users to 1.

233 Sets the reference count of the mm to 1.

234 Initializes the semaphore protecting the VMA list.

235 Initializes the spinlock protecting write access to it.

236 Allocates a new PGD for the struct.

237 By default, pages used by the process are not locked in memory.

238 If a PGD exists, this returns the initialized struct.

240 If initialization failed, this deletes the `mm_struct` and returns.

D.1.3   Allocating a Descriptor

Two functions are provided that allocate an `mm_struct`. To be slightly confusing, they are essentially the same. `allocate_mm()` will allocate a `mm_struct` from the slab allocator. `mm_alloc()` will allocate the struct and then call the function `mm_init()` to initialize it.

D.1.3.1   Function: `allocate_mm()`   *(kernel/fork.c)*

```
227 #define allocate_mm()    (kmem_cache_alloc(mm_cachep, SLAB_KERNEL))
```

227 Allocates an `mm_struct` from the slab allocator.

Process Address Space

D.1.3.2   Function: mm_alloc()   *(kernel/fork.c)*

```
248 struct mm_struct * mm_alloc(void)
249 {
250        struct mm_struct * mm;
251
252        mm = allocate_mm();
253        if (mm) {
254                memset(mm, 0, sizeof(*mm));
255                return mm_init(mm);
256        }
257        return NULL;
258 }
```

252 Allocates an mm_struct from the slab allocator.

254 Zeroes out all contents of the struct.

255 Performs basic initialization.

D.1.4   Destroying a Descriptor

A new user to an mm increments the usage count with a simple call:

```
atomic_inc(&mm->mm_users};
```

It is decremented with a call to mmput(). If the mm_users count reaches zero, all the mapped regions are deleted with exit_mmap(), and the pagetables are destroyed because there are no longer any users of the userspace portions. The mm_count count is decremented with mmdrop() because all the users of the pagetables and VMAs are counted as one mm_struct user. When mm_count reaches zero, the mm_struct will be destroyed.

D.1.4.1   Function: mmput()   *(kernel/fork.c)*

```
276 void mmput(struct mm_struct *mm)
277 {
278        if (atomic_dec_and_lock(&mm->mm_users, &mmlist_lock)) {
279                extern struct mm_struct *swap_mm;
280                if (swap_mm == mm)
281                        swap_mm = list_entry(mm->mmlist.next,
                                        struct mm_struct, mmlist);
282                list_del(&mm->mmlist);
283                mmlist_nr--;
284                spin_unlock(&mmlist_lock);
285                exit_mmap(mm);
286                mmdrop(mm);
287        }
288 }
```

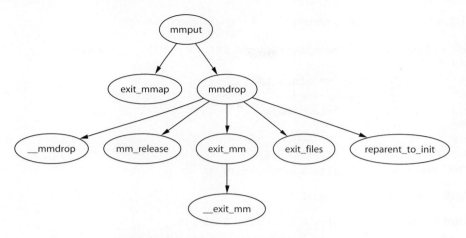

Figure D.1. Call Graph: `mmput()`

278 Atomically decrements the `mm_users` field while holding the `mmlist_lock` lock. It returns with the lock held if the count reaches zero.

279-286 If the usage count reaches zero, the mm and associated structures need to be removed.

279-281 The `swap_mm` is the last mm that was swapped out by the vmscan code. If the current process was the last mm swapped, this moves to the next entry in the list.

282 Removes this mm from the list.

283-284 Reduces the count of mms in the list and releases the `mmlist` lock.

285 Removes all associated mappings.

286 Deletes the mm.

D.1.4.2   Function: `mmdrop()`   *(include/linux/sched.h)*

```
765 static inline void mmdrop(struct mm_struct * mm)
766 {
767         if (atomic_dec_and_test(&mm->mm_count))
768                 __mmdrop(mm);
769 }
```

767 Atomically decrements the reference count. The reference count could be higher if the mm was used by lazy tlb switching tasks.

768 If the reference count reaches zero, this calls `__mmdrop()`.

Process Address Space

D.1.4.3   Function: __mmdrop()   *(kernel/fork.c)*

```
265 inline void __mmdrop(struct mm_struct *mm)
266 {
267         BUG_ON(mm == &init_mm);
268         pgd_free(mm->pgd);
269         destroy_context(mm);
270         free_mm(mm);
271 }
```

267 Makes sure the `init_mm` is not destroyed.

268 Deletes the PGD entry.

269 Deletes the LDT (Local Descriptor Table).

270 Calls `kmem_cache_free()` for the mm, freeing it with the slab allocator.

D.2   Creating Memory Regions

Contents

This large section deals with the creation, deletion and manipulation of memory regions.

D.2.1   Creating a Memory Region

The main call graph for creating a memory region is shown in Figure 4.3.

D.2.1.1   Function: do_mmap()   *(include/linux/mm.h)*

This is a very simple wrapper function around do_mmap_pgoff(), which performs most of the work.

```
557 static inline unsigned long do_mmap(struct file *file,
```

```
                   unsigned long addr,
558                unsigned long len, unsigned long prot,
559                unsigned long flag, unsigned long offset)
560 {
561     unsigned long ret = -EINVAL;
562     if ((offset + PAGE_ALIGN(len)) < offset)
563         goto out;
564     if (!(offset & ~PAGE_MASK))
565         ret = do_mmap_pgoff(file, addr, len, prot, flag,
                                offset >> PAGE_SHIFT);
566 out:
567         return ret;
568 }
```

561 By default, this returns -EINVAL.

562-563 Makes sure that the size of the region will not overflow the total size of the address space.

564-565 Page aligns the offset and calls do_mmap_pgoff() to map the region.

D.2.1.2 Function: do_mmap_pgoff()   *(mm/mmap.c)*
This function is very large, so it is broken up into a number of sections. Broadly speaking the sections are the following:

- Sanity check the parameters.

- Find a free linear address space large enough for the memory mapping. If a filesystem or device-specific get_unmapped_area() function is provided, it will be used. Otherwise, arch_get_unmapped_area() is called.

- Calculate the VM flags and check them against the file access permissions.

- If an old area exists where the mapping is to take place, fix it so it is suitable for the new mapping.

- Allocate a vm_area_struct from the slab allocator and fill in its entries.

- Link in the new VMA.

- Call the filesystem or device-specific mmap() function.

- Update statistics and exit.

```
393 unsigned long do_mmap_pgoff(struct file * file,
                  unsigned long addr,
                  unsigned long len, unsigned long prot,
394               unsigned long flags, unsigned long pgoff)
395 {
396     struct mm_struct * mm = current->mm;
```

```
397     struct vm_area_struct * vma, * prev;
398     unsigned int vm_flags;
399     int correct_wcount = 0;
400     int error;
401     rb_node_t ** rb_link, * rb_parent;
402
403     if (file && (!file->f_op || !file->f_op->mmap))
404         return -ENODEV;
405
406     if (!len)
407         return addr;
408
409     len = PAGE_ALIGN(len);
410
        if (len > TASK_SIZE || len == 0)
            return -EINVAL;
413
414     /* offset overflow? */
415     if ((pgoff + (len >> PAGE_SHIFT)) < pgoff)
416         return -EINVAL;
417
418     /* Too many mappings? */
419     if (mm->map_count > max_map_count)
420         return -ENOMEM;
421
```

393 The parameters that correspond directly to the parameters of the mmap system call are the following:

- **file** The struct file to mmap if this is a file-backed mapping
- **addr** The requested address to map
- **len** The length in bytes to mmap
- **prot** The permissions on the area
- **flags** The flags for the mapping
- **pgoff** The offset within the file to begin the mmap at

403-404 If a file or device is mapped, this makes sure a filesystem or device-specific mmap function is provided. For most filesystems, this will call generic_file_mmap()(See Section D.6.2.1).

406-407 Makes sure a zero length mmap() is not requested.

409 Ensures that the mapping is confined to the userspace portion of the address space. On the x86, kernel space begins at PAGE_OFFSET(3GiB).

415-416 Ensures the mapping will not overflow the end of the largest possible file size.

Process Address
Space

419-420 Only `max_map_count` number of mappings are allowed. By default, this
value is `DEFAULT_MAX_MAP_COUNT` or 65,536 mappings.

```
422        /* Obtain the address to map to. we verify (or select) it and
423         * ensure that it represents a valid section of the address space.
424         */
425        addr = get_unmapped_area(file, addr, len, pgoff, flags);
426        if (addr & ~PAGE_MASK)
427            return addr;
428
```

425 After basic sanity checks, this function will call the device- or file-specific
`get_unmapped_area()` function. If a device-specific one is unavailable,
`arch_get_unmapped_area()` is called. This function is discussed in Section
D.3.2.2.

```
429        /* Do simple checking here so the lower-level routines won't
430         * have to. we assume access permissions have been handled by
431         * the open of the memory object, so we don't do any here.
432         */
433        vm_flags = calc_vm_flags(prot,flags) | mm->def_flags
434                      | VM_MAYREAD | VM_MAYWRITE | VM_MAYEXEC;
435
435        /* mlock MCL_FUTURE? */
436        if (vm_flags & VM_LOCKED) {
437            unsigned long locked = mm->locked_vm << PAGE_SHIFT;
438            locked += len;
439            if (locked > current->rlim[RLIMIT_MEMLOCK].rlim_cur)
440                return -EAGAIN;
441        }
442
```

433 `calc_vm_flags()` translates the `prot` and `flags` from userspace and translates
them to their `VM_` equivalents.

436-440 Checks if it has been requested that all future mappings be locked in
memory. If yes, it makes sure the process isn't locking more memory than it
is allowed to. If it is, it returns `-EAGAIN`.

```
443        if (file) {
444            switch (flags & MAP_TYPE) {
445            case MAP_SHARED:
446                if ((prot & PROT_WRITE) &&
                    !(file->f_mode & FMODE_WRITE))
447                    return -EACCES;
448
449                /* Make sure we don't allow writing to
```

```
                     an append-only file.. */
450            if (IS_APPEND(file->f_dentry->d_inode) &&
                   (file->f_mode & FMODE_WRITE))
451                return -EACCES;
452
453            /* make sure there are no mandatory
                  locks on the file. */
454            if (locks_verify_locked(file->f_dentry->d_inode))
455                return -EAGAIN;
456
457            vm_flags |= VM_SHARED | VM_MAYSHARE;
458            if (!(file->f_mode & FMODE_WRITE))
459                vm_flags &= ~(VM_MAYWRITE | VM_SHARED);
460
461            /* fall through */
462        case MAP_PRIVATE:
463            if (!(file->f_mode & FMODE_READ))
464                return -EACCES;
465            break;
466
467        default:
468            return -EINVAL;
469        }
```

443-469 If a file is memory mapped, this checks the file's access permissions.

446-447 If write access is requested, this makes sure the file is opened for write.

450-451 Similarly, if the file is opened for append, this makes sure it cannot be written to. The **prot** field is not checked because the **prot** field applies only to the mapping whereas the opened file needs to be checked.

453 If the file is mandatory locked, this returns **-EAGAIN** so the caller will try a second type.

457-459 Fixes up the flags to be consistent with the file flags.

463-464 Makes sure the file can be read before mmapping it.

```
470    } else {
471        vm_flags |= VM_SHARED | VM_MAYSHARE;
472        switch (flags & MAP_TYPE) {
473        default:
474            return -EINVAL;
475        case MAP_PRIVATE:
476            vm_flags &= ~(VM_SHARED | VM_MAYSHARE);
477            /* fall through */
478        case MAP_SHARED:
```

```
479              break;
480        }
481    }
```

471-481 If the file is mapped for anonymous use, this fixes up the flags if the
requested mapping is MAP_PRIVATE to make sure the flags are consistent.

```
483    /* Clear old maps */
484 munmap_back:
485    vma = find_vma_prepare(mm, addr, &prev, &rb_link, &rb_parent);
486    if (vma && vma->vm_start < addr + len) {
487        if (do_munmap(mm, addr, len))
488            return -ENOMEM;
489        goto munmap_back;
490    }
```

485 find_vma_prepare() (See Section D.2.2.2) steps through the RB tree for the
VMA corresponding to a given address.

486-488 If a VMA was found and it is part of the new mmaping, this removes the
old mapping because the new one will cover both.

```
491
492    /* Check against address space limit. */
493    if ((mm->total_vm << PAGE_SHIFT) + len
494        > current->rlim[RLIMIT_AS].rlim_cur)
495        return -ENOMEM;
496
497    /* Private writable mapping? Check memory availability.. */
498    if ((vm_flags & (VM_SHARED | VM_WRITE)) == VM_WRITE &&
499        !(flags & MAP_NORESERVE)                    &&
500        !vm_enough_memory(len >> PAGE_SHIFT))
501        return -ENOMEM;
502
503    /* Can we just expand an old anonymous mapping? */
504    if (!file && !(vm_flags & VM_SHARED) && rb_parent)
505        if (vma_merge(mm, prev, rb_parent,
506                addr, addr + len, vm_flags))
506            goto out;
507
```

493-495 Ensures the new mapping will not exceed the total VM that a process is
allowed to have. It is unclear why this check is not made earlier.

498-501 If the caller does not specifically request that free space is not checked
with MAP_NORESERVE and it is a private mapping, this ensures enough memory
is available to satisfy the mapping under current conditions.

504-506 If two adjacent memory mappings are anonymous and can be treated as one, this expands the old mapping rather than creating a new one.

```
508        /* Determine the object being mapped and call the appropriate
509         * specific mapper. the address has already been validated,
510         * but not unmapped, but the maps are removed from the list.
511         */
512        vma = kmem_cache_alloc(vm_area_cachep, SLAB_KERNEL);
513        if (!vma)
514            return -ENOMEM;
515
516        vma->vm_mm = mm;
517        vma->vm_start = addr;
518        vma->vm_end = addr + len;
519        vma->vm_flags = vm_flags;
520        vma->vm_page_prot = protection_map[vm_flags & 0x0f];
521        vma->vm_ops = NULL;
522        vma->vm_pgoff = pgoff;
523        vma->vm_file = NULL;
524        vma->vm_private_data = NULL;
525        vma->vm_raend = 0;
```

512 Allocates a vm_area_struct from the slab allocator.

516-525 Fills in the basic vm_area_struct fields.

```
527        if (file) {
528            error = -EINVAL;
529            if (vm_flags & (VM_GROWSDOWN|VM_GROWSUP))
530                goto free_vma;
531            if (vm_flags & VM_DENYWRITE) {
532                error = deny_write_access(file);
533                if (error)
534                    goto free_vma;
535                correct_wcount = 1;
536            }
537            vma->vm_file = file;
538            get_file(file);
539            error = file->f_op->mmap(file, vma);
540            if (error)
541                goto unmap_and_free_vma;
```

527-541 Fills in the file-related fields if this file has been mapped.

529-530 These are both invalid flags for a file mapping, so it frees the vm_area_struct and returns.

531-536 This flag is cleared by the system call `mmap()`, but is still cleared for kernel modules that call this function directly. Historically, `-ETXTBUSY` was returned to the calling process if the underlying file was written to.

537 Fills in the `vm_file` field.

538 Increments the file usage count.

539 Calls the filesystem or device-specific `mmap()` function. In many filesystem cases, this will call `generic_file_mmap()`(See Section D.6.2.1).

540-541 If an error is called, this goes to `unmap_and_free_vma` to clean up and return the error.

```
542        } else if (flags & MAP_SHARED) {
543            error = shmem_zero_setup(vma);
544            if (error)
545                goto free_vma;
546        }
547
```

543 If this is an anonymous shared mapping, the region is created and set up by `shmem_zero_setup()`(See Section L.7.1). Anonymous shared pages are backed by a virtual tmpfs filesystem so that they can be synchronized properly with swap. The writeback function is `shmem_writepage()`(See Section L.6.1).

```
548        /* Can addr have changed??
549         *
550         * Answer: Yes, several device drivers can do it in their
551         *     f_op->mmap method. -DaveM
552         */
553        if (addr != vma->vm_start) {
554            /*
555             * It is a bit too late to pretend changing the virtual
556             * area of the mapping, we just corrupted userspace
557             * in the do_munmap, so FIXME (not in 2.4 to avoid
558             * breaking the driver API).
559             */
560            struct vm_area_struct * stale_vma;
561            /* Since addr changed, we rely on the mmap op to prevent
562             * collisions with existing vmas and just use
563             * find_vma_prepare to update the tree pointers.
564             */
565            addr = vma->vm_start;
566            stale_vma = find_vma_prepare(mm, addr, &prev,
567                            &rb_link, &rb_parent);
568            /*
569             * Make sure the lowlevel driver did its job right.
570             */
```

```
571            if (unlikely(stale_vma && stale_vma->vm_start <
                   vma->vm_end)) {
572                printk(KERN_ERR "buggy mmap operation: [<%p>]\n",
573                    file ? file->f_op->mmap : NULL);
574                BUG();
575            }
576        }
577
578        vma_link(mm, vma, prev, rb_link, rb_parent);
579        if (correct_wcount)
580            atomic_inc(&file->f_dentry->d_inode->i_writecount);
581
```

553-576 If the address has changed, it means the device-specific mmap operation
moved the VMA address to somewhere else. The function
`find_vma_prepare()` (See Section D.2.2.2) is used to find where the VMA
was moved to.

578 Links in the new `vm_area_struct`.

579-580 Updates the file write count.

```
582 out:
583        mm->total_vm += len >> PAGE_SHIFT;
584        if (vm_flags & VM_LOCKED) {
585            mm->locked_vm += len >> PAGE_SHIFT;
586            make_pages_present(addr, addr + len);
587        }
588        return addr;
589
590 unmap_and_free_vma:
591        if (correct_wcount)
592            atomic_inc(&file->f_dentry->d_inode->i_writecount);
593        vma->vm_file = NULL;
594        fput(file);
595
596        /* Undo any partial mapping done by a device driver. */
597        zap_page_range(mm,
                       vma->vm_start,
                       vma->vm_end - vma->vm_start);
598 free_vma:
599        kmem_cache_free(vm_area_cachep, vma);
600        return error;
601 }
```

583-588 Updates statistics for the process `mm_struct` and returns the new address.

590-597 This is reached if the file has been partially mapped before failing.
The write statistics are updated, and then all user pages are removed with
`zap_page_range()`.

Process Address
Space

598-600 This goto is used if the mapping failed immediately after the `vm_area_struct` is created. It is freed back to the slab allocator before the error is returned.

D.2.2 Inserting a Memory Region

The call graph for `insert_vm_struct()` is shown in Figure 4.5.

D.2.2.1 Function: `__insert_vm_struct()` *(mm/mmap.c)*

This is the top-level function for inserting a new vma into an address space. There is a second function like it called simply `insert_vm_struct()` that is not described in detail here because the only difference is the one line of code increasing the `map_count`.

```
1174 void __insert_vm_struct(struct mm_struct * mm,
                  struct vm_area_struct * vma)
1175 {
1176     struct vm_area_struct * __vma, * prev;
1177     rb_node_t ** rb_link, * rb_parent;
1178
1179     __vma = find_vma_prepare(mm, vma->vm_start, &prev,
                  &rb_link, &rb_parent);
1180     if (__vma && __vma->vm_start < vma->vm_end)
1181         BUG();
1182     __vma_link(mm, vma, prev, rb_link, rb_parent);
1183     mm->map_count++;
1184     validate_mm(mm);
1185 }
```

1174 The arguments are the `mm_struct` that represents the linear address space and the `vm_area_struct` that is to be inserted.

1179 `find_vma_prepare()`(See Section D.2.2.2) locates where the new VMA can be inserted. It will be inserted between `prev` and `__vma`, and the required nodes for the red-black tree are also returned.

1180-1181 This is a check to make sure the returned VMA is invalid. It is virtually impossible for this condition to occur without manually inserting bogus VMAs into the address space.

1182 This function does the actual work of linking the VMA struct into the linear linked list and the red-black tree.

1183 Increases the `map_count` to show a new mapping has been added. This line is not present in `insert_vm_struct()`.

1184 `validate_mm()` is a debugging macro for red-black trees. If `DEBUG_MM_RB` is set, the linear list of VMAs and the tree will be traversed to make sure it is

valid. The tree traversal is a recursive function, so it is very important that
it is used only if really necessary because a large number of mappings could
cause a stack overflow. If it is not set, `validate_mm()` does nothing at all.

D.2.2.2   Function: `find_vma_prepare()`   *(mm/mmap.c)*

This is responsible for finding the correct places to insert a VMA at the supplied
address. It returns a number of pieces of information through the actual return and
the function arguments. The forward VMA to link to is returned with return.
`pprev` is the previous node, which is required because the list is a singly linked list.
`rb_link` and `rb_parent` are the parent and leaf node that the new VMA will be
inserted between.

```
246 static struct vm_area_struct * find_vma_prepare(
                        struct mm_struct * mm,
                        unsigned long addr,
247                     struct vm_area_struct ** pprev,
248                     rb_node_t *** rb_link,
                        rb_node_t ** rb_parent)
249 {
250     struct vm_area_struct * vma;
251     rb_node_t ** __rb_link, * __rb_parent, * rb_prev;
252
253     __rb_link = &mm->mm_rb.rb_node;
254     rb_prev = __rb_parent = NULL;
255     vma = NULL;
256
257     while (*__rb_link) {
258         struct vm_area_struct *vma_tmp;
259
260         __rb_parent = *__rb_link;
261         vma_tmp = rb_entry(__rb_parent,
                    struct vm_area_struct, vm_rb);
262
263         if (vma_tmp->vm_end > addr) {
264             vma = vma_tmp;
265             if (vma_tmp->vm_start <= addr)
266                 return vma;
267             __rb_link = &__rb_parent->rb_left;
268         } else {
269             rb_prev = __rb_parent;
270             __rb_link = &__rb_parent->rb_right;
271         }
272     }
273
274     *pprev = NULL;
275     if (rb_prev)
```

```
276          *pprev = rb_entry(rb_prev, struct vm_area_struct, vm_rb);
277      *rb_link = __rb_link;
278      *rb_parent = __rb_parent;
279      return vma;
280 }
```

246 The function arguments are described previously.

253-255 Initializes the search.

263-272 This is a similar tree walk to what was described for find_vma(). The only real difference is the nodes last traversed are remembered with the __rb_link and __rb_parent variables.

275-276 Gets the back linking VMA through the red-black tree.

279 Returns the forward linking VMA.

D.2.2.3   Function: vma_link()   *(mm/mmap.c)*
This is the top-level function for linking a VMA into the proper lists. It is responsible for acquiring the necessary locks to make a safe insertion.

```
337 static inline void vma_link(struct mm_struct * mm,
                struct vm_area_struct * vma,
                struct vm_area_struct * prev,
338                 rb_node_t ** rb_link, rb_node_t * rb_parent)
339 {
340     lock_vma_mappings(vma);
341     spin_lock(&mm->page_table_lock);
342     __vma_link(mm, vma, prev, rb_link, rb_parent);
343     spin_unlock(&mm->page_table_lock);
344     unlock_vma_mappings(vma);
345
346     mm->map_count++;
347     validate_mm(mm);
348 }
```

337 mm is the address space that the VMA is to be inserted into. prev is the backward-linked VMA for the linear-linked-list of VMAs. rb_link and rb_parent are the nodes required to make the rb insertion.

340 This function acquires the spinlock that protects the address_space representing the file that is memory mapped.

341 Acquires the pagetable lock, which protects the whole mm_struct.

342 Inserts the VMA.

343 Frees the lock protecting the mm_struct.

345 Unlocks the `address_space` for the file.

346 Increases the number of mappings in this mm.

347 If `DEBUG_MM_RB` is set, the RB trees and linked lists will be checked to make sure they are still valid.

D.2.2.4 Function: `__vma_link()` *(mm/mmap.c)*

This simply calls three helper functions that are responsible for linking the VMA into the three linked lists that link VMAs together.

```
329 static void __vma_link(struct mm_struct * mm,
              struct vm_area_struct * vma,
              struct vm_area_struct * prev,
330           rb_node_t ** rb_link, rb_node_t * rb_parent)
331 {
332     __vma_link_list(mm, vma, prev, rb_parent);
333     __vma_link_rb(mm, vma, rb_link, rb_parent);
334     __vma_link_file(vma);
335 }
```

332 Links the VMA into the linear-linked lists of VMAs in this mm through the `vm_next field`.

333 Links the VMA into the red-black tree of VMAs in this mm that has its root stored in the `vm_rb` field.

334 Links the VMA into the shared mapping VMA links. Memory mapped files are linked together over potentially many mms by this function using the `vm_next_share` and `vm_pprev_share` fields.

D.2.2.5 Function: `__vma_link_list()` *(mm/mmap.c)*

```
282 static inline void __vma_link_list(struct mm_struct * mm,
                 struct vm_area_struct * vma,
                 struct vm_area_struct * prev,
283              rb_node_t * rb_parent)
284 {
285     if (prev) {
286         vma->vm_next = prev->vm_next;
287         prev->vm_next = vma;
288     } else {
289         mm->mmap = vma;
290         if (rb_parent)
291             vma->vm_next = rb_entry(rb_parent,
                        struct vm_area_struct,
                        vm_rb);
```

```
292         else
293             vma->vm_next = NULL;
294     }
295 }
```

285 If `prev` is not null, the VMA is simply inserted into the list.

289 If not, this is the first mapping, and the first element of the list has to be stored in the `mm_struct`.

290 The VMA is stored as the parent node.

D.2.2.6 Function: __vma_link_rb() *(mm/mmap.c)*

The principal workings of this function are stored within `<linux/rbtree.h>` and will not be discussed in detail in this book.

```
297 static inline void __vma_link_rb(struct mm_struct * mm,
                    struct vm_area_struct * vma,
298                 rb_node_t ** rb_link,
                    rb_node_t * rb_parent)
299 {
300     rb_link_node(&vma->vm_rb, rb_parent, rb_link);
301     rb_insert_color(&vma->vm_rb, &mm->mm_rb);
302 }
```

D.2.2.7 Function: __vma_link_file() *(mm/mmap.c)*

This function links the VMA into a linked list of shared file mappings.

```
304 static inline void __vma_link_file(struct vm_area_struct * vma)
305 {
306     struct file * file;
307
308     file = vma->vm_file;
309     if (file) {
310         struct inode * inode = file->f_dentry->d_inode;
311         struct address_space *mapping = inode->i_mapping;
312         struct vm_area_struct **head;
313
314         if (vma->vm_flags & VM_DENYWRITE)
315             atomic_dec(&inode->i_writecount);
316
317         head = &mapping->i_mmap;
318         if (vma->vm_flags & VM_SHARED)
319             head = &mapping->i_mmap_shared;
320
321         /* insert vma into inode's share list */
322         if((vma->vm_next_share = *head) != NULL)
```

```
323                    (*head)->vm_pprev_share = &vma->vm_next_share;
324             *head = vma;
325             vma->vm_pprev_share = head;
326     }
327 }
```

309 Checks to see if this VMA has a shared file mapping. If it does not, this function has nothing more to do.

310-312 Extracts the relevant information about the mapping from the VMA.

314-315 If this mapping is not allowed to write even if the permissions are ok for writing, decrement the `i_writecount` field. A negative value to this field indicates that the file is memory mapped and may not be written to. Efforts to open the file for writing will now fail.

317-319 Checks to make sure this is a shared mapping.

322-325 Inserts the VMA into the shared mapping linked list.

D.2.3 Merging Contiguous Regions

D.2.3.1 Function: vma_merge() *(mm/mmap.c)*

This function checks to see if a region pointed to be `prev` may be expanded forward to cover the area from `addr` to `end` instead of allocating a new VMA. If it cannot, the VMA ahead is checked to see whether it can be expanded backward instead.

```
350 static int vma_merge(struct mm_struct * mm,
                 struct vm_area_struct * prev,
351                 rb_node_t * rb_parent,
                 unsigned long addr, unsigned long end,
                 unsigned long vm_flags)
352 {
353     spinlock_t * lock = &mm->page_table_lock;
354     if (!prev) {
355         prev = rb_entry(rb_parent, struct vm_area_struct, vm_rb);
356         goto merge_next;
357     }
```

350 The parameters are as follows:

- **mm** The mm the VMAs belong to
- **prev** The VMA before the address we are interested in
- **rb_parent** The parent RB node as returned by `find_vma_prepare()`
- **addr** The starting address of the region to be merged
- **end** The end of the region to be merged

- **vm_flags** The permission flags of the region to be merged

353 This is the lock to the mm.

354-357 If prev is not passed it, it is taken to mean that the VMA being tested
for merging is in front of the region from addr to end. The entry for that
VMA is extracted from the rb_parent.

```
358     if (prev->vm_end == addr && can_vma_merge(prev, vm_flags)) {
359         struct vm_area_struct * next;
360
361         spin_lock(lock);
362         prev->vm_end = end;
363         next = prev->vm_next;
364         if (next && prev->vm_end == next->vm_start &&
                    can_vma_merge(next, vm_flags)) {
365             prev->vm_end = next->vm_end;
366             __vma_unlink(mm, next, prev);
367             spin_unlock(lock);
368
369             mm->map_count--;
370             kmem_cache_free(vm_area_cachep, next);
371             return 1;
372         }
373         spin_unlock(lock);
374         return 1;
375     }
376
377     prev = prev->vm_next;
378     if (prev) {
379 merge_next:
380         if (!can_vma_merge(prev, vm_flags))
381             return 0;
382         if (end == prev->vm_start) {
383             spin_lock(lock);
384             prev->vm_start = addr;
385             spin_unlock(lock);
386             return 1;
387         }
388     }
389
390     return 0;
391 }
```

358-375 Checks to see if the region pointed to by prev may be expanded to cover
the current region.

358 The function `can_vma_merge()` checks the permissions of `prev` with those in `vm_flags` and that the VMA has no file mappings (i.e., it is anonymous). If it is true, the area at `prev` may be expanded.

361 Locks the mm.

362 Expands the end of the VMA region (`vm_end`) to the end of the new mapping (`end`).

363 `next` is now the VMA in front of the newly expanded VMA.

364 Checks if the expanded region can be merged with the VMA in front of it.

365 If it can, this continues to expand the region to cover the next VMA.

366 Because a VMA has been merged, one region is now defunct and may be unlinked.

367 No further adjustments are made to the mm struct, so the lock is released.

369 There is one less mapped region to reduce the `map_count`.

370 Deletes the struct describing the merged VMA.

371 Returns success.

377 If this line is reached, it means the region pointed to by `prev` could not be expanded forward, so a check is made to see if the region ahead can be merged backward instead.

382-388 The same idea as the previous block except instead of adjusted `vm_end` to cover `end`, `vm_start` is expanded to cover `addr`.

D.2.3.2 Function: `can_vma_merge()` *(include/linux/mm.h)*

This trivial function checks to see if the permissions of the supplied VMA match the permissions in `vm_flags`.

```
582 static inline int can_vma_merge(struct vm_area_struct * vma,
                     unsigned long vm_flags)
583 {
584     if (!vma->vm_file && vma->vm_flags == vm_flags)
585         return 1;
586     else
587         return 0;
588 }
```

584 Self-explanatory. It returns true if there is no file/device mapping (i.e., it is anonymous) and if the VMA flags for both regions match.

D.2.4   Remapping and Moving a Memory Region

D.2.4.1   Function: `sys_mremap()`   *(mm/mremap.c)*
    The call graph for this function is shown in Figure 4.6. This is the system
service call to remap a memory region.

```
347 asmlinkage unsigned long sys_mremap(unsigned long addr,
348     unsigned long old_len, unsigned long new_len,
349     unsigned long flags, unsigned long new_addr)
350 {
351     unsigned long ret;
352
353     down_write(&current->mm->mmap_sem);
354     ret = do_mremap(addr, old_len, new_len, flags, new_addr);
355     up_write(&current->mm->mmap_sem);
356     return ret;
357 }
```

347-349 The parameters are the same as those described in the `mremap()` man
    page.

353 Acquires the mm semaphore.

354 `do_mremap()`(See Section D.2.4.2) is the top-level function for remapping a
    region.

355 Releases the mm semaphore.

356 Returns the status of the remapping.

D.2.4.2   Function: `do_mremap()`   *(mm/mremap.c)*
    This function does most of the actual work required to remap, resize and move
a memory region. It is quite long, but can be broken up into distinct parts, which
will be dealt with separately here. The tasks are, broadly speaking, the following:

- Check usage flags and page align lengths.

- Handle the condition where **MAP_FIXED** has set and the region has been moved
  to a new location.

- If a region is shrinking, allow it to happen unconditionally.

- If the region is growing or moving, perform a number of checks in advance to
  make sure the move is allowed and safe.

- Handle the case where the region has been expanded and cannot be moved.

- Finally, handle the case where the region has to be resized and moved.

```
219 unsigned long do_mremap(unsigned long addr,
220     unsigned long old_len, unsigned long new_len,
221     unsigned long flags, unsigned long new_addr)
222 {
223     struct vm_area_struct *vma;
224     unsigned long ret = -EINVAL;
225
226     if (flags & ~(MREMAP_FIXED | MREMAP_MAYMOVE))
227         goto out;
228
229     if (addr & ~PAGE_MASK)
230         goto out;
231
232     old_len = PAGE_ALIGN(old_len);
233     new_len = PAGE_ALIGN(new_len);
234
```

219 The parameters of the function are the following:

- **addr** is the old starting address.
- **old_len** is the old region length.
- **new_len** is the new region length.
- **flags** is the option flags passed. If MREMAP_MAYMOVE is specified, it means that the region is allowed to move if there is not enough linear address space at the current space. If MREMAP_FIXED is specified, it means that the whole region is to move to the specified new_addr with the new length. The area from new_addr to new_addr+new_len will be unmapped with do_munmap().
- **new_addr** is the address of the new region if it is moved.

224 At this point, the default return is -EINVAL for invalid arguments.

226-227 Makes sure flags other than the two allowed flags are not used.

229-230 The address passed in must be page aligned.

232-233 Page-aligns the passed region lengths.

```
236     if (flags & MREMAP_FIXED) {
237         if (new_addr & ~PAGE_MASK)
238             goto out;
239         if (!(flags & MREMAP_MAYMOVE))
240             goto out;
241
242         if (new_len > TASK_SIZE || new_addr > TASK_SIZE - new_len)
243             goto out;
244
```

```
245            /* Check if the location we're moving into overlaps the
246             * old location at all, and fail if it does.
247             */
248            if ((new_addr <= addr) && (new_addr+new_len) > addr)
249                goto out;
250
251            if ((addr <= new_addr) && (addr+old_len) > new_addr)
252                goto out;
253
254            do_munmap(current->mm, new_addr, new_len);
255        }
```

This block handles the condition where the region location is fixed and must be fully moved. It ensures the area being moved to is safe and definitely unmapped.

236 MREMAP_FIXED is the flag that indicates the location is fixed.

237-238 The specified `new_addr` must be be page-aligned.

239-240 If MREMAP_FIXED is specified, the MAYMOVE flag must be used as well.

242-243 Makes sure the resized region does not exceed TASK_SIZE.

248-249 Just as the comments indicate, the two regions being used for the move may not overlap.

254 Unmaps the region that is about to be used. It is presumed the caller ensures that the region is not in use for anything important.

```
261    ret = addr;
262    if (old_len >= new_len) {
263        do_munmap(current->mm, addr+new_len, old_len - new_len);
264        if (!(flags & MREMAP_FIXED) || (new_addr == addr))
265            goto out;
266    }
```

261 At this point, the address of the resized region is the return value.

262 If the old length is larger than the new length, the region is shrinking.

263 Unmaps the unused region.

264-265 If the region is not to be moved, either because MREMAP_FIXED is not used or the new address matches the old address, goto out, which will return the address.

```
271    ret = -EFAULT;
272    vma = find_vma(current->mm, addr);
273    if (!vma || vma->vm_start > addr)
274        goto out;
```

```
275         /* We can't remap across vm area boundaries */
276         if (old_len > vma->vm_end - addr)
277             goto out;
278         if (vma->vm_flags & VM_DONTEXPAND) {
279             if (new_len > old_len)
280                 goto out;
281         }
282         if (vma->vm_flags & VM_LOCKED) {
283             unsigned long locked = current->mm->locked_vm << PAGE_SHIFT;
284             locked += new_len - old_len;
285             ret = -EAGAIN;
286             if (locked > current->rlim[RLIMIT_MEMLOCK].rlim_cur)
287                 goto out;
288         }
289         ret = -ENOMEM;
290         if ((current->mm->total_vm << PAGE_SHIFT) + (new_len - old_len)
291             > current->rlim[RLIMIT_AS].rlim_cur)
292             goto out;
293         /* Private writable mapping? Check memory availability.. */
294         if ((vma->vm_flags & (VM_SHARED | VM_WRITE)) == VM_WRITE &&
295             !(flags & MAP_NORESERVE) &&
296             !vm_enough_memory((new_len - old_len) >> PAGE_SHIFT))
297             goto out;
```

This block does a number of checks to make sure it is safe to grow or move the region.

271 At this point, the default action is to return -EFAULT, which causes a segmentation fault because the ranges of memory being used are invalid.

272 Finds the VMA responsible for the requested address.

273 If the returned VMA is not responsible for this address, an invalid address was used to return a fault.

276-277 If the old_len passed in exceeds the length of the VMA, it means the user is trying to remap multiple regions, which is not allowed.

278-281 If the VMA has been explicitly marked as nonresizable, this raises a fault.

282-283 If the pages for this VMA must be locked in memory, this recalculates the number of locked pages that will be kept in memory. If the number of pages exceeds the ulimit set for this resource, this returns EAGAIN, which indicated to the caller that the region is locked and cannot be resized.

289 The default return at this point is to indicate there is not enough memory.

290-292 Ensures that the users will not exceed their allowed allocation of memory.

Process Address Space

294-297 Ensures that there is enough memory to satisfy the request after the resizing with vm_enough_memory()(See Section M.1.1).

```
302      if (old_len == vma->vm_end - addr &&
303          !((flags & MREMAP_FIXED) && (addr != new_addr)) &&
304          (old_len != new_len || !(flags & MREMAP_MAYMOVE))) {
305          unsigned long max_addr = TASK_SIZE;
306          if (vma->vm_next)
307              max_addr = vma->vm_next->vm_start;
308          /* can we just expand the current mapping? */
309          if (max_addr - addr >= new_len) {
310              int pages = (new_len - old_len) >> PAGE_SHIFT;
311              spin_lock(&vma->vm_mm->page_table_lock);
312              vma->vm_end = addr + new_len;
313              spin_unlock(&vma->vm_mm->page_table_lock);
314              current->mm->total_vm += pages;
315              if (vma->vm_flags & VM_LOCKED) {
316                  current->mm->locked_vm += pages;
317                  make_pages_present(addr + old_len,
318                              addr + new_len);
319              }
320              ret = addr;
321              goto out;
322          }
323      }
```

This block handles the case where the region is being expanded and cannot be moved.

302 If it is the full region that is being remapped and ...

303 The region is definitely not being moved and ...

304 The region is being expanded and cannot be moved, then ...

305 Sets the maximum address that can be used to TASK_SIZE, which is 3GiB on an x86.

306-307 If there is another region, this sets the max address to be the start of the next region.

309-322 Only allows the expansion if the newly sized region does not overlap with the next VMA.

310 Calculates the number of extra pages that will be required.

311 Locks the mm spinlock.

312 Expands the VMA.

313 Frees the mm spinlock.

314 Updates the statistics for the mm.

315-319 If the pages for this region are locked in memory, this makes them present now.

320-321 Returns the address of the resized region.

```
329     ret = -ENOMEM;
330     if (flags & MREMAP_MAYMOVE) {
331         if (!(flags & MREMAP_FIXED)) {
332             unsigned long map_flags = 0;
333             if (vma->vm_flags & VM_SHARED)
334                 map_flags |= MAP_SHARED;
335
336             new_addr = get_unmapped_area(vma->vm_file, 0,
                        new_len, vma->vm_pgoff, map_flags);
337             ret = new_addr;
338             if (new_addr & ~PAGE_MASK)
339                 goto out;
340         }
341         ret = move_vma(vma, addr, old_len, new_len, new_addr);
342     }
343 out:
344     return ret;
345 }
```

To expand the region, a new one has to be allocated, and the old one moved to it.

329 The default action is to return saying no memory is available.

330 Checks to make sure the region is allowed to move.

331 If MREMAP_FIXED is not specified, it means the new location was not supplied, so one must be found.

333-334 Preserves the MAP_SHARED option.

336 Finds an unmapped region of memory large enough for the expansion.

337 The return value is the address of the new region.

338-339 For the returned address to be not page aligned, get_unmapped_area() would need to be broken. This could possibly be the case with a buggy device driver implementing get_unmapped_area() incorrectly.

341 Calls move_vma() to move the region.

343-344 Returns the address if successful and the error code otherwise.

Process Address Space

D.2.4.3 Function: `move_vma()` (mm/mremap.c)

The call graph for this function is shown in Figure 4.7. This function is responsible for moving all the pagetable entries from one VMA to another region. If necessary, a new VMA will be allocated for the region being moved to. Just like the previous function, it is very long, but may be broken up into the following distinct parts.

- Function preamble finds the VMA preceding the area about to be moved to and the VMA in front of the region to be mapped.

- Handles the case where the new location is between two existing VMAs. It determines if the preceding region can be expanded forward or the next region expanded backward to cover the new mapped region.

- Handles the case where the new location is going to be the last VMA on the list. It determines if the preceding region can be expanded forward.

- If a region could not be expanded, it allocates a new VMA from the slab allocator.

- Calls `move_page_tables()`, fills in the new VMA details if a new one was allocated, and updates statistics before returning.

```
125 static inline unsigned long move_vma(struct vm_area_struct * vma,
126     unsigned long addr, unsigned long old_len, unsigned long
127     new_len, unsigned long new_addr)
128 {
129     struct mm_struct * mm = vma->vm_mm;
130     struct vm_area_struct * new_vma, * next, * prev;
131     int allocated_vma;
132
133     new_vma = NULL;
134     next = find_vma_prev(mm, new_addr, &prev);
```

125-127 The parameters are the following:

- **vma** The VMA that the address being moved belongs to
- **addr** The starting address of the moving region
- **old_len** The old length of the region to move
- **new_len** The new length of the region moved
- **new_addr** The new address to relocate to

134 Finds the VMA preceding the address being moved indicated by `prev` and returns the region after the new mapping as `next`.

```
135     if (next) {
136         if (prev && prev->vm_end == new_addr &&
```

```
137                 can_vma_merge(prev, vma->vm_flags) &&
                !vma->vm_file && !(vma->vm_flags & VM_SHARED)) {
138             spin_lock(&mm->page_table_lock);
139             prev->vm_end = new_addr + new_len;
140             spin_unlock(&mm->page_table_lock);
141             new_vma = prev;
142             if (next != prev->vm_next)
143                 BUG();
144             if (prev->vm_end == next->vm_start &&
                can_vma_merge(next, prev->vm_flags)) {
145                 spin_lock(&mm->page_table_lock);
146                 prev->vm_end = next->vm_end;
147                 __vma_unlink(mm, next, prev);
148                 spin_unlock(&mm->page_table_lock);
149
150                 mm->map_count--;
151                 kmem_cache_free(vm_area_cachep, next);
152             }
153         } else if (next->vm_start == new_addr + new_len &&
154                 can_vma_merge(next, vma->vm_flags) &&
                 !vma->vm_file && !(vma->vm_flags & VM_SHARED)) {
155             spin_lock(&mm->page_table_lock);
156             next->vm_start = new_addr;
157             spin_unlock(&mm->page_table_lock);
158             new_vma = next;
159         }
160     } else {
```

In this block, the new location is between two existing VMAs. Checks are made to see if the preceding region can be expanded to cover the new mapping and then if it can be expanded to cover the next VMA as well. If it cannot be expanded, the next region is checked to see if it can be expanded backward.

136-137 If the preceding region touches the address to be mapped to and may be merged, it enters this block, which will attempt to expand regions.

138 Locks the mm.

139 Expands the preceding region to cover the new location.

140 Unlocks the mm.

141 The new VMA is now the preceding VMA, which was just expanded.

142-143 Makes sure the VMA linked list is intact. It would require a device driver with severe brain damage to cause this situation to occur.

144 Checks if the region can be expanded forward to encompass the next region.

145 If it can, this locks the mm.

146 Expands the VMA further to cover the next VMA.

147 There is now an extra VMA, so this unlinks it.

148 Unlocks the mm.

150 There is one less mapping now, so this updates the `map_count`.

151 Frees the memory used by the memory mapping.

153 If the `prev` region could not be expanded forward, this checks if the region pointed to be `next` may be expanded backward to cover the new mapping instead.

155 If it can, this locks the mm.

156 Expands the mapping backward.

157 Unlocks the mm.

158 The VMA representing the new mapping is now `next`.

```
161            prev = find_vma(mm, new_addr-1);
162            if (prev && prev->vm_end == new_addr &&
163                can_vma_merge(prev, vma->vm_flags) && !vma->vm_file &&
                       !(vma->vm_flags & VM_SHARED)) {
164                spin_lock(&mm->page_table_lock);
165                prev->vm_end = new_addr + new_len;
166                spin_unlock(&mm->page_table_lock);
167                new_vma = prev;
168            }
169        }
```

This block is for the case where the newly mapped region is the last VMA (`next` is NULL), so a check is made to see if the preceding region can be expanded.

161 Gets the previously mapped region.

162-163 Checks if the regions may be mapped.

164 Locks the mm.

165 Expands the preceding region to cover the new mapping.

166 Locks the mm.

167 The VMA representing the new mapping is now `prev`.

```
170
171     allocated_vma = 0;
172     if (!new_vma) {
173         new_vma = kmem_cache_alloc(vm_area_cachep, SLAB_KERNEL);
174         if (!new_vma)
175             goto out;
176         allocated_vma = 1;
177     }
178
```

171 Sets a flag indicating if a new VMA was not allocated.

172 If a VMA has not been expanded to cover the new mapping then...

173 Allocates a new VMA from the slab allocator.

174-175 If it could not be allocated, goto out to return failure.

176 Sets the flag indicating that a new VMA was allocated.

```
179     if (!move_page_tables(current->mm, new_addr, addr, old_len)) {
180         unsigned long vm_locked = vma->vm_flags & VM_LOCKED;
181
182         if (allocated_vma) {
183             *new_vma = *vma;
184             new_vma->vm_start = new_addr;
185             new_vma->vm_end = new_addr+new_len;
186             new_vma->vm_pgoff +=
                        (addr-vma->vm_start) >> PAGE_SHIFT;
187             new_vma->vm_raend = 0;
188             if (new_vma->vm_file)
189                 get_file(new_vma->vm_file);
190             if (new_vma->vm_ops && new_vma->vm_ops->open)
191                 new_vma->vm_ops->open(new_vma);
192             insert_vm_struct(current->mm, new_vma);
193         }
194         do_munmap(current->mm, addr, old_len);
197         current->mm->total_vm += new_len >> PAGE_SHIFT;
198         if (new_vma->vm_flags & VM_LOCKED) {
199             current->mm->locked_vm += new_len >> PAGE_SHIFT;
200             make_pages_present(new_vma->vm_start,
201                     new_vma->vm_end);
202         }
203         return new_addr;
204     }
205     if (allocated_vma)
```

Process Address Space

```
206          kmem_cache_free(vm_area_cachep, new_vma);
207  out:
208      return -ENOMEM;
209  }
```

179 move_page_tables()(See Section D.2.4.6) is responsible for copying all the pagetable entries. It returns 0 on success.

182-193 If a new VMA was allocated, this fills in all the relevant details, including the file/device entries, and inserts it into the various VMA linked lists with insert_vm_struct()(See Section D.2.2.1).

194 Unmaps the old region because it is no longer required.

197 Updates the total_vm size for this process. The size of the old region is not important because it is handled within do_munmap().

198-202 If the VMA has the VM_LOCKED flag, all the pages within the region are made present with mark_pages_present().

203 Returns the address of the new region.

205-206 This is the error path. If a VMA was allocated, it deletes it.

208 Returns an out of memory error.

D.2.4.4 Function: make_pages_present() *(mm/memory.c)*

This function makes all pages between addr and end present. It assumes that the two addresses are within the one VMA.

```
1460  int make_pages_present(unsigned long addr, unsigned long end)
1461  {
1462      int ret, len, write;
1463      struct vm_area_struct * vma;
1464
1465      vma = find_vma(current->mm, addr);
1466      write = (vma->vm_flags & VM_WRITE) != 0;
1467      if (addr >= end)
1468          BUG();
1469      if (end > vma->vm_end)
1470          BUG();
1471      len = (end+PAGE_SIZE-1)/PAGE_SIZE-addr/PAGE_SIZE;
1472      ret = get_user_pages(current, current->mm, addr,
1473                  len, write, 0, NULL, NULL);
1474      return ret == len ? 0 : -1;
1475  }
```

1465 Finds the VMA with find_vma()(See Section D.3.1.1) that contains the starting address.

1466 Records if write-access is allowed in `write`.

1467-1468 If the starting address is after the end address, then `BUG()` runs.

1469-1470 If the range spans more than one VMA, it is a bug.

1471 Calculates the length of the region to fault in.

1472 Calls `get_user_pages()` to fault in all the pages in the requested region. It returns the number of pages that were faulted in.

1474 Returns true if all the requested pages were successfully faulted in.

D.2.4.5 Function: `get_user_pages()` *(mm/memory.c)*

This function is used to fault in user pages and may be used to fault in pages belonging to another process, which is required by `ptrace()`, for example.

```
454 int get_user_pages(struct task_struct *tsk, struct mm_struct *mm,
                        unsigned long start,
455                     int len, int write, int force, struct page
                        **pages, struct vm_area_struct **vmas)
456 {
457     int i;
458     unsigned int flags;
459
460     /*
461      * Require read or write permissions.
462      * If 'force' is set, we only require the "MAY" flags.
463      */
464     flags =  write ? (VM_WRITE | VM_MAYWRITE) : (VM_READ | VM_MAYREAD);
465     flags &= force ? (VM_MAYREAD | VM_MAYWRITE) : (VM_READ | VM_WRITE);
466     i = 0;
467
```

454 The parameters are the following:

- **tsk** is the process that pages are being faulted for.

- **mm** is the `mm_struct` managing the address space being faulted.

- **start** is where to start faulting.

- **len** is the length of the region, in pages, to fault.

- **write** indicates if the pages are being faulted for writing.

- **force** indicates that the pages should be faulted even if the region only has the `VM_MAYREAD` or `VM_MAYWRITE` flags.

- **pages** is an array of struct pages, which may be NULL. If supplied, the array will be filled with `struct pages` that were faulted in.

- **vmas** is similar to the **pages** array. If supplied, it will be filled with VMAs that were affected by the faults.

464 Sets the required flags to VM_WRITE and VM_MAYWRITE flags if the parameter write is set to 1. Otherwise, it uses the read equivalents.

465 If force is specified, this only requires the MAY flags.

```
468     do {
469         struct vm_area_struct * vma;
470
471         vma = find_extend_vma(mm, start);
472
473         if ( !vma ||
                (pages && vma->vm_flags & VM_IO) ||
                !(flags & vma->vm_flags) )
474             return i ? : -EFAULT;
475
476         spin_lock(&mm->page_table_lock);
477         do {
478             struct page *map;
479             while (!(map = follow_page(mm, start, write))) {
480                 spin_unlock(&mm->page_table_lock);
481                 switch (handle_mm_fault(mm, vma, start, write)) {
482                 case 1:
483                     tsk->min_flt++;
484                     break;
485                 case 2:
486                     tsk->maj_flt++;
487                     break;
488                 case 0:
489                     if (i) return i;
490                     return -EFAULT;
491                 default:
492                     if (i) return i;
493                     return -ENOMEM;
494                 }
495                 spin_lock(&mm->page_table_lock);
496             }
497             if (pages) {
498                 pages[i] = get_page_map(map);
499                 /* FIXME: call the correct function,
500                  * depending on the type of the found page
501                  */
502                 if (!pages[i])
503                     goto bad_page;
504                 page_cache_get(pages[i]);
```

```
505                }
506                if (vmas)
507                    vmas[i] = vma;
508                i++;
509                start += PAGE_SIZE;
510                len--;
511         } while(len && start < vma->vm_end);
512         spin_unlock(&mm->page_table_lock);
513     } while(len);
514 out:
515     return i;
```

468-513 This outer loop will move through every VMA affected by the faults.

471 Finds the VMA affected by the current value of `start`. This variable is incremented in `PAGE_SIZE`d strides.

473 If a VMA does not exist for the address, or the caller has requested `struct pages` for a region that is I/O mapped (and therefore not backed by physical memory) or that the VMA does not have the required flags for, this returns `-EFAULT`.

476 Locks the pagetable spinlock.

479-496 `follow_page()`(See Section C.2.1) walks the page tables and returns the `struct page` that represents the frame mapped at `start`. This loop will only be entered if the PTE is not present and will keep looping until the PTE is known to be present with the pagetable spinlock held.

480 Unlocks the page table spinlock because `handle_mm_fault()` is likely to sleep.

481 If the page is not present, this faults it in with `handle_mm_fault()` (See Section D.5.3.1).

482-487 Updates the `task_struct` statistics and indicates if a major or minor fault occured.

488-490 If the faulting address is invalid, this returns `-EFAULT`.

491-493 If the system is out of memory, this returns `-ENOMEM`.

495 Relocks the page tables. The loop will check to make sure the page is actually present.

597-505 If the caller requested it, this populates the `pages` array with `struct pages` affected by this function. Each struct will have a reference to it taken with `page_cache_get()`.

506-507 Similarly, this records VMAs affected.

Process Address Space

508 Increments i, which is a counter for the number of pages present in the requested region.

509 Increments `start` in a page-sized stride.

510 Decrements the number of pages that must be faulted in.

511 Keeps moving through the VMAs until the requested pages have been faulted in.

512 Releases the pagetable spinlock.

515 Returns the number of pages known to be present in the region.

```
516
517     /*
518      * We found an invalid page in the VMA.  Release all we have
519      * so far and fail.
520      */
521 bad_page:
522     spin_unlock(&mm->page_table_lock);
523     while (i--)
524         page_cache_release(pages[i]);
525     i = -EFAULT;
526     goto out;
527 }
```

521 This will only be reached if a `struct page` is found that represents a nonexistant page frame.

523-524 If one is found, it releases references to all pages stored in the `pages` array.

525-526 Returns -EFAULT.

D.2.4.6   **Function:** `move_page_tables()`   *(mm/mremap.c)*

The call graph for this function is shown in Figure 4.8. This function is responsible for copying all the pagetable entries from the region pointed to `old_addr` to `new_addr`. It works by literally copying pagetable entries one at a time. When it is finished, it deletes all the entries from the old area. This is not the most efficient way to perform the operation, but it is very easy to error recover.

```
90 static int move_page_tables(struct mm_struct * mm,
91     unsigned long new_addr, unsigned long old_addr,
       unsigned long len)
92 {
93     unsigned long offset = len;
94
95     flush_cache_range(mm, old_addr, old_addr + len);
```

```
 96
102     while (offset) {
103         offset -= PAGE_SIZE;
104         if (move_one_page(mm, old_addr + offset, new_addr +
                  offset))
105             goto oops_we_failed;
106     }
107     flush_tlb_range(mm, old_addr, old_addr + len);
108     return 0;
109
117 oops_we_failed:
118     flush_cache_range(mm, new_addr, new_addr + len);
119     while ((offset += PAGE_SIZE) < len)
120         move_one_page(mm, new_addr + offset, old_addr + offset);
121     zap_page_range(mm, new_addr, len);
122     return -1;
123 }
```

90 The parameters are the mm for the process, the new location, the old location and the length of the region to move entries for.

95 flush_cache_range() will flush all CPU caches for this range. It must be called first because some architectures, notably Sparc's, require that a virtual to physical mapping exist before flushing the TLB.

102-106 Loops through each page in the region and moves the PTE with move_one_pte()(See Section D.2.4.7). This translates to a lot of pagetable walking and could be performed much better, but it is a rare operation.

107 Flushes the TLB for the old region.

108 Returns success.

118-120 This block moves all the PTEs back. A flush_tlb_range() is not necessary because the region could not have been used yet, so no TLB entries should exist.

121 Zaps any pages that were allocated for the move.

122 Returns failure.

D.2.4.7   Function: move_one_page()   *(mm/mremap.c)*

This function is responsible for acquiring the spinlock before finding the correct PTE with get_one_pte() and copying it with copy_one_pte().

```
77 static int move_one_page(struct mm_struct *mm,
                unsigned long old_addr, unsigned long new_addr)
78 {
```

Process Address Space

```
79    int error = 0;
80    pte_t * src;
81
82    spin_lock(&mm->page_table_lock);
83    src = get_one_pte(mm, old_addr);
84    if (src)
85        error = copy_one_pte(mm, src, alloc_one_pte(mm, new_addr));
86    spin_unlock(&mm->page_table_lock);
87    return error;
88 }
```

82 Acquires the mm lock.

83 Calls get_one_pte()(See Section D.2.4.8), which walks the pagetables to get the correct PTE.

84-85 If the PTE exists, this allocates a PTE for the destination and copies the PTEs with copy_one_pte()(See Section D.2.4.10).

86 Releases the lock.

87 Returns whatever copy_one_pte() returned. It will only return an error if alloc_one_pte()(See Section D.2.4.9) failed on line 85.

D.2.4.8 Function: get_one_pte() *(mm/mremap.c)*
This is a very simple pagetable walk.

```
18 static inline pte_t *get_one_pte(struct mm_struct *mm,
                                    unsigned long addr)
19 {
20     pgd_t * pgd;
21     pmd_t * pmd;
22     pte_t * pte = NULL;
23
24     pgd = pgd_offset(mm, addr);
25     if (pgd_none(*pgd))
26         goto end;
27     if (pgd_bad(*pgd)) {
28         pgd_ERROR(*pgd);
29         pgd_clear(pgd);
30         goto end;
31     }
32
33     pmd = pmd_offset(pgd, addr);
34     if (pmd_none(*pmd))
35         goto end;
36     if (pmd_bad(*pmd)) {
```

```
37            pmd_ERROR(*pmd);
38            pmd_clear(pmd);
39            goto end;
40        }
41
42        pte = pte_offset(pmd, addr);
43        if (pte_none(*pte))
44            pte = NULL;
45 end:
46        return pte;
47 }
```

24 Gets the PGD for this address.

25-26 If no PGD exists, this returns NULL because no PTE will exist either.

27-31 If the PGD is bad, this marks that an error occurred in the region, clears its contents and returns NULL.

33-40 Acquires the correct PMD in the same fashion as for the PGD.

42 Acquires the PTE so it may be returned if it exists.

D.2.4.9 Function: alloc_one_pte() *(mm/mremap.c)*

This trivial function allocates what is necessary for one PTE in a region.

```
49 static inline pte_t *alloc_one_pte(struct mm_struct *mm,
                    unsigned long addr)
50 {
51    pmd_t * pmd;
52    pte_t * pte = NULL;
53
54    pmd = pmd_alloc(mm, pgd_offset(mm, addr), addr);
55    if (pmd)
56        pte = pte_alloc(mm, pmd, addr);
57    return pte;
58 }
```

54 If a PMD entry does not exist, this allocates it.

55-56 If the PMD exists, this allocates a PTE entry. The check to make sure it succeeded is performed later in the function copy_one_pte().

D.2.4.10 Function: copy_one_pte() *(mm/mremap.c)*

This copies the contents of one PTE to another.

```
60 static inline int copy_one_pte(struct mm_struct *mm,
                    pte_t * src, pte_t * dst)
```

```
61 {
62     int error = 0;
63     pte_t pte;
64
65     if (!pte_none(*src)) {
66         pte = ptep_get_and_clear(src);
67         if (!dst) {
68             /* No dest?  We must put it back. */
69             dst = src;
70             error++;
71         }
72         set_pte(dst, pte);
73     }
74     return error;
75 }
```

65 If the source PTE does not exist, this just returns 0 to say the copy was successful.

66 Gets the PTE and removes it from its old location.

67-71 If the `dst` does not exist, it means the call to `alloc_one_pte()` failed, and the copy operation has failed and must be aborted.

72 Moves the PTE to its new location.

74 Returns an error if one occurred.

D.2.5   Deleting a Memory Region

D.2.5.1   Function: do_munmap()   *(mm/mmap.c)*

The call graph for this function is shown in Figure 4.10. This function is responsible for unmapping a region. If necessary, the unmapping can span multiple VMAs, and it can partially unmap one if necessary. Hence, the full unmapping operation is divided into two major operations. This function is responsible for finding what VMAs are affected, and `unmap_fixup()` is responsible for fixing up the remaining VMAs.

This function is divided up in a number of small sections that will be dealt with in turn. They are, broadly speaking, the following:

- Function as a preamble, and find the VMA to start working from.

- Take all VMAs affected by the unmapping out of the mm and place them on a linked list headed by the variable `free`.

- Cycle through the list headed by `free`, unmap all the pages in the region to be unmapped and call `unmap_fixup()` to fix up the mappings.

- Validate the mm and free memory associated with the unmapping.

```
924 int do_munmap(struct mm_struct *mm, unsigned long addr,
                  size_t len)
925 {
926     struct vm_area_struct *mpnt, *prev, **npp, *free, *extra;
927
928     if ((addr & ~PAGE_MASK) || addr > TASK_SIZE ||
                    len  > TASK_SIZE-addr)
929         return -EINVAL;
930
931     if ((len = PAGE_ALIGN(len)) == 0)
932         return -EINVAL;
933
939     mpnt = find_vma_prev(mm, addr, &prev);
940     if (!mpnt)
941         return 0;
942     /* we have  addr < mpnt->vm_end  */
943
944     if (mpnt->vm_start >= addr+len)
945         return 0;
946
948     if ((mpnt->vm_start < addr && mpnt->vm_end > addr+len)
949         && mm->map_count >= max_map_count)
950         return -ENOMEM;
951
956     extra = kmem_cache_alloc(vm_area_cachep, SLAB_KERNEL);
957     if (!extra)
958         return -ENOMEM;
```

924 The parameters are as follows:

- **mm** The mm for the processes performing the unmap operation
- **addr** The starting address of the region to unmap
- **len** The length of the region

928-929 Ensures the address is page aligned and that the area to be unmapped is not in the kernel virtual address space.

931-932 Makes sure the region size to unmap is page aligned.

939 Finds the VMA that contains the starting address and the preceding VMA so it can be easily unlinked later.

940-941 If no `mpnt` was returned, it means the address must be past the last used VMA. Therefore, the address space is unused and just returns.

944-945 If the returned VMA starts past the region you are trying to unmap, the region in unused and just returns.

Process Address
Space

948-950 The first part of the check sees if the VMA is just being partially unmapped. If it is, another VMA will be created later to deal with a region
being broken into, so the `map_count` has to be checked to make sure it is not
too large.

956-958 In case a new mapping is required, it is allocated now because later it
will be much more difficult to back out in event of an error.

```
960     npp = (prev ? &prev->vm_next : &mm->mmap);
961     free = NULL;
962     spin_lock(&mm->page_table_lock);
963     for ( ; mpnt && mpnt->vm_start < addr+len; mpnt = *npp) {
964         *npp = mpnt->vm_next;
965         mpnt->vm_next = free;
966         free = mpnt;
967         rb_erase(&mpnt->vm_rb, &mm->mm_rb);
968     }
969     mm->mmap_cache = NULL;  /* Kill the cache. */
970     spin_unlock(&mm->page_table_lock);
```

This section takes all the VMAs affected by the unmapping and places them on
a separate linked list headed by a variable called `free`. This makes the fixup of the
regions much easier.

960 `npp` becomes the next VMA in the list during the for loop that follows. To
initialize it, it is either the current VMA (`mpnt`), or it becomes the first VMA
in the list.

961 `free` is the head of a linked list of VMAs that are affected by the unmapping.

962 Locks the mm.

963 Cycles through the list until the start of the current VMA is past the end of
the region to be unmapped.

964 `npp` becomes the next VMA in the list.

965-966 Removes the current VMA from the linear linked list within the mm and
places it on a linked list headed by `free`. The current `mpnt` becomes the head
of the free linked list.

967 Deletes `mpnt` from the red-black tree.

969 Removes the cached result in case the last looked-up result is one of the regions
to be unmapped.

970 Frees the mm.

```
971
972      /* Ok - we have the memory areas we should free on the
973       * 'free' list, so release them, and unmap the page range..
974       * If one of the segments is only being partially unmapped,
975       * it will put new vm_area_struct(s) into the address space.
976       * In that case we have to be careful with VM_DENYWRITE.
977       */
978      while ((mpnt = free) != NULL) {
979          unsigned long st, end, size;
980          struct file *file = NULL;
981
982          free = free->vm_next;
983
984          st = addr < mpnt->vm_start ? mpnt->vm_start : addr;
985          end = addr+len;
986          end = end > mpnt->vm_end ? mpnt->vm_end : end;
987          size = end - st;
988
989          if (mpnt->vm_flags & VM_DENYWRITE &&
990              (st != mpnt->vm_start || end != mpnt->vm_end) &&
991              (file = mpnt->vm_file) != NULL) {
992              atomic_dec(&file->f_dentry->d_inode->i_writecount);
993          }
994          remove_shared_vm_struct(mpnt);
995          mm->map_count--;
996
997          zap_page_range(mm, st, size);
998
999          /*
1000          * Fix the mapping, and free the old area
                * if it wasn't reused.
1001          */
1002          extra = unmap_fixup(mm, mpnt, st, size, extra);
1003          if (file)
1004              atomic_inc(&file->f_dentry->d_inode->i_writecount);
1005      }
```

978 Keeps stepping through the list until no VMAs are left.

982 Moves `free` to the next element in the list, leaving `mpnt` as the head about to be removed.

984 `st` is the start of the region to be unmapped. If the `addr` is before the start of the VMA, the starting point is mpnt→vm_start. Otherwise, it is the supplied address.

985-986 Calculates the end of the region to map in a similar fashion.

987 Calculates the size of the region to be unmapped in this pass.

989-993 If the `VM_DENYWRITE` flag is specified, a hole will be created by this unmapping, and a file is mapped. Then, the `i_writecounts` are decremented. When this field is negative, it counts how many users there are protecting this file from being opened for writing.

994 Removes the file mapping. If the file is still partially mapped, it will be acquired again during `unmap_fixup()`(See Section D.2.5.2).

995 Reduces the map count.

997 Removes all pages within this region.

1002 Calls `unmap_fixup()`(See Section D.2.5.2) to fix up the regions after this one is deleted.

1003-1004 Increments the writecount to the file because the region has been unmapped. If it was just partially unmapped, this call will simply balance out the decrement at line 987.

```
1006       validate_mm(mm);
1007
1008       /* Release the extra vma struct if it wasn't used */
1009       if (extra)
1010           kmem_cache_free(vm_area_cachep, extra);
1011
1012       free_pgtables(mm, prev, addr, addr+len);
1013
1014       return 0;
1015 }
```

1006 `validate_mm()` is a debugging function. If enabled, it will ensure the VMA tree for this mm is still valid.

1009-1010 If extra VMA was not required, this deletes it.

1012 Frees all the pagetables that were used for the unmapped region.

1014 Returns success.

D.2.5.2   Function: `unmap_fixup()`   *(mm/mmap.c)*

This function fixes up the regions after a block has been unmapped. It is passed a list of VMAs that are affected by the unmapping, the region and length to be unmapped and a spare VMA that may be required to fix up the region if a whole is created. This function handles four principle cases: the unmapping of a region, partial unmapping from the start to somewhere in the middle, partial unmapping from somewhere in the middle to the end and creation of a hole in the middle of the region. Each case will be taken in turn.

```
787 static struct vm_area_struct * unmap_fixup(struct mm_struct *mm,
788     struct vm_area_struct *area, unsigned long addr, size_t len,
789     struct vm_area_struct *extra)
790 {
791     struct vm_area_struct *mpnt;
792     unsigned long end = addr + len;
793
794     area->vm_mm->total_vm -= len >> PAGE_SHIFT;
795     if (area->vm_flags & VM_LOCKED)
796         area->vm_mm->locked_vm -= len >> PAGE_SHIFT;
797
```

This block is the function preamble.

787 The parameters to the function are the following:

- **mm** is the mm the unmapped region belongs to.
- **area** is the head of the linked list of VMAs affected by the unmapping.
- **addr** is the starting address of the unmapping.
- **len** is the length of the region to be unmapped.
- **extra** is a spare VMA passed in for when a hole in the middle is created.

792 Calculates the end address of the region being unmapped.

794 Reduces the count of the number of pages used by the process.

795-796 If the pages were locked in memory, this reduces the locked page count.

```
798     /* Unmapping the whole area. */
799     if (addr == area->vm_start && end == area->vm_end) {
800         if (area->vm_ops && area->vm_ops->close)
801             area->vm_ops->close(area);
802         if (area->vm_file)
803             fput(area->vm_file);
804         kmem_cache_free(vm_area_cachep, area);
805         return extra;
806     }
```

The first, and easiest, case is where the full region is being unmapped.

799 The full region is unmapped if the `addr` is the start of the VMA and the end is the end of the VMA. This is interesting because, if the unmapping is spanning regions, it is possible that the end is *beyond* the end of the VMA, but the full of this VMA is still being unmapped.

800-801 If a close operation is supplied by the VMA, this calls it.

802-803 If a file or device is mapped, this calls `fput()`, which decrements the usage count and releases it if the count falls to 0.

804 Frees the memory for the VMA back to the slab allocator.

805 Returns the extra VMA because it was unused.

```
809      if (end == area->vm_end) {
810          /*
811           * here area isn't visible to the semaphore-less readers
812           * so we don't need to update it under the spinlock.
813           */
814          area->vm_end = addr;
815          lock_vma_mappings(area);
816          spin_lock(&mm->page_table_lock);
817      }
```

This block handles the case where the middle of the region to the end is been unmapped.

814 Truncates the VMA back to `addr`. At this point, the pages for the region have already freed, and the pagetable entries will be freed later, so no further work is required.

815 If a file/device is being mapped, the lock protecting shared access to it is taken in the function `lock_vm_mappings()`.

816 Locks the mm. Later in the function, the remaining VMA will be reinserted into the mm.

```
817          else if (addr == area->vm_start) {
818          area->vm_pgoff += (end - area->vm_start) >> PAGE_SHIFT;
819          /* same locking considerations of the above case */
820          area->vm_start = end;
821          lock_vma_mappings(area);
822          spin_lock(&mm->page_table_lock);
823      } else {
```

This block handles the case where the VMA is been unmapped from the start to some part in the middle.

818 Increases the offset within the file/device mapped by the number of pages this unmapping represents.

820 Moves the start of the VMA to the end of the region being unmapped.

821-822 Locks the file/device and mm as previously described.

```
823        } else {
825            /* Add end mapping -- leave beginning for below */
826            mpnt = extra;
827            extra = NULL;
828
829            mpnt->vm_mm = area->vm_mm;
830            mpnt->vm_start = end;
831            mpnt->vm_end = area->vm_end;
832            mpnt->vm_page_prot = area->vm_page_prot;
833            mpnt->vm_flags = area->vm_flags;
834            mpnt->vm_raend = 0;
835            mpnt->vm_ops = area->vm_ops;
836            mpnt->vm_pgoff = area->vm_pgoff +
                         ((end - area->vm_start) >> PAGE_SHIFT);
837            mpnt->vm_file = area->vm_file;
838            mpnt->vm_private_data = area->vm_private_data;
839            if (mpnt->vm_file)
840                get_file(mpnt->vm_file);
841            if (mpnt->vm_ops && mpnt->vm_ops->open)
842                mpnt->vm_ops->open(mpnt);
843            area->vm_end = addr;     /* Truncate area */
844
845            /* Because mpnt->vm_file == area->vm_file this locks
846             * things correctly.
847             */
848            lock_vma_mappings(area);
849            spin_lock(&mm->page_table_lock);
850            __insert_vm_struct(mm, mpnt);
851        }
```

This block handles the case where a hole is being created by a partial unmapping. In this case, the extra VMA is required to create a new mapping from the end of the unmapped region to the end of the old VMA.

826-827 Takes the extra VMA and makes VMA NULL so that the calling function will know it is in use and cannot be freed.

828-838 Copies in all the VMA information.

839 If a file/device is mapped, this gets a reference to it with get_file().

841-842 If an open function is provided, this calls it.

843 Truncates the VMA so that it ends at the start of the region to be unmapped.

848-849 Locks the files and mm as with the two previous cases.

850 Inserts the extra VMA into the mm.

Process Address Space

```
852
853        __insert_vm_struct(mm, area);
854        spin_unlock(&mm->page_table_lock);
855        unlock_vma_mappings(area);
856        return extra;
857 }
```

853 Reinserts the VMA into the mm.

854 Unlocks the pagetables.

855 Unlocks the spinlock to the shared mapping.

856 Returns the extra VMA if it was not used and NULL if it was.

D.2.6   Deleting All Memory Regions

D.2.6.1   Function: exit_mmap()   *(mm/mmap.c)*

This function simply steps through all VMAs associated with the supplied mm and unmaps them.

```
1127 void exit_mmap(struct mm_struct * mm)
1128 {
1129      struct vm_area_struct * mpnt;
1130
1131      release_segments(mm);
1132      spin_lock(&mm->page_table_lock);
1133      mpnt = mm->mmap;
1134      mm->mmap = mm->mmap_cache = NULL;
1135      mm->mm_rb = RB_ROOT;
1136      mm->rss = 0;
1137      spin_unlock(&mm->page_table_lock);
1138      mm->total_vm = 0;
1139      mm->locked_vm = 0;
1140
1141      flush_cache_mm(mm);
1142      while (mpnt) {
1143          struct vm_area_struct * next = mpnt->vm_next;
1144          unsigned long start = mpnt->vm_start;
1145          unsigned long end = mpnt->vm_end;
1146          unsigned long size = end - start;
1147
1148          if (mpnt->vm_ops) {
1149              if (mpnt->vm_ops->close)
1150                  mpnt->vm_ops->close(mpnt);
1151          }
1152          mm->map_count--;
1153          remove_shared_vm_struct(mpnt);
```

```
1154          zap_page_range(mm, start, size);
1155          if (mpnt->vm_file)
1156              fput(mpnt->vm_file);
1157          kmem_cache_free(vm_area_cachep, mpnt);
1158          mpnt = next;
1159      }
1160      flush_tlb_mm(mm);
1161
1162      /* This is just debugging */
1163      if (mm->map_count)
1164          BUG();
1165
1166      clear_page_tables(mm, FIRST_USER_PGD_NR, USER_PTRS_PER_PGD);
1167 }
```

1131 `release_segments()` will release memory segments associated with the process on its Local Descriptor Table (LDT) if the architecture supports segments and the process was using them. Some applications, notably WINE, use this feature.

1132 Locks the mm.

1133 `mpnt` becomes the first VMA on the list.

1134 Clears VMA-related information from the mm so that it may be unlocked.

1137 Unlocks the mm.

1138-1139 Clears the mm statistics.

1141 Flushes the CPU for the address range.

1142-1159 Steps through every VMA that was associated with the mm.

1143 Records what the next VMA to clear will be so that this one may be deleted.

1144-1146 Records the start, end and size of the region to be deleted.

1148-1151 If there is a close operation associated with this VMA, this calls it.

1152 Reduces the map count.

1153 Removes the file/device mapping from the shared mappings list.

1154 Frees all pages associated with this region.

1155-1156 If a file/device was mapped in this region, this frees it.

1157 Frees the VMA struct.

1158 Moves to the next VMA.

Process Address Space

1160 Flushes the TLB for this whole mm because it is about to be unmapped.

1163-1164 If the `map_count` is positive, it means the map count was not accounted for properly, so this calls `BUG()` to mark it.

1166 Clears the pagetables associated with this region with `clear_page_tables()` (See Section D.2.6.2).

D.2.6.2 Function: `clear_page_tables()` *(mm/memory.c)*

This is the top-level function used to unmap all PTEs and free pages within a region. It is used when pagetables need to be torn down, such as when the process exits or a region is unmapped.

```
146 void clear_page_tables(struct mm_struct *mm,
                           unsigned long first, int nr)
147 {
148     pgd_t * page_dir = mm->pgd;
149
150     spin_lock(&mm->page_table_lock);
151     page_dir += first;
152     do {
153         free_one_pgd(page_dir);
154         page_dir++;
155     } while (--nr);
156     spin_unlock(&mm->page_table_lock);
157
158     /* keep the pagetable cache within bounds */
159     check_pgt_cache();
160 }
```

148 Gets the PGD for the mm being unmapped.

150 Locks the pagetables.

151-155 Steps through all PGDs in the requested range. For each PGD found, this calls `free_one_pgd()` (See Section D.2.6.3).

156 Unlocks the pagetables.

159 Checks the cache of available PGD structures. If there are too many PGDs in the PGD quicklist, some of them will be reclaimed.

D.2.6.3 Function: `free_one_pgd()` *(mm/memory.c)*

This function tears down one PGD. For each PMD in this PGD, `free_one_pmd()` will be called.

```
109 static inline void free_one_pgd(pgd_t * dir)
110 {
```

```
111     int j;
112     pmd_t * pmd;
113
114     if (pgd_none(*dir))
115         return;
116     if (pgd_bad(*dir)) {
117         pgd_ERROR(*dir);
118         pgd_clear(dir);
119         return;
120     }
121     pmd = pmd_offset(dir, 0);
122     pgd_clear(dir);
123     for (j = 0; j < PTRS_PER_PMD ; j++) {
124         prefetchw(pmd+j+(PREFETCH_STRIDE/16));
125         free_one_pmd(pmd+j);
126     }
127     pmd_free(pmd);
128 }
```

114-115 If no PGD exists here, this returns.

116-120 If the PGD is bad, this flags the error and returns.

1121 Gets the first PMD in the PGD.

122 Clears the PGD entry.

123-126 For each PMD in this PGD, this calls `free_one_pmd()` (See Section D.2.6.4).

127 Frees the PMD page to the PMD quicklist. Later, `check_pgt_cache()` will be called, and, if the cache has too many PMD pages in it, they will be reclaimed.

D.2.6.4   Function: `free_one_pmd()`   *(mm/memory.c)*

```
93 static inline void free_one_pmd(pmd_t * dir)
94 {
95     pte_t * pte;
96
97     if (pmd_none(*dir))
98         return;
99     if (pmd_bad(*dir)) {
100         pmd_ERROR(*dir);
101         pmd_clear(dir);
102         return;
103     }
104     pte = pte_offset(dir, 0);
105     pmd_clear(dir);
```

```
106     pte_free(pte);
107 }
```

97-98 If no PMD exists here, this returns.

99-103 If the PMD is bad, this flags the error and returns.

104 Gets the first PTE in the PMD.

105 Clears the PMD from the pagetable.

106 Frees the PTE page to the PTE quicklist cache with `pte_free()`. Later, `check_pgt_cache()` will be called, and, if the cache has too many PTE pages in it, they will be reclaimed.

D.3   Searching Memory Regions

Contents

The functions in this section deal with searching the virtual address space for mapped and free regions.

D.3.1   Finding a Mapped Memory Region

D.3.1.1   Function: `find_vma()`   *(mm/mmap.c)*

```
661 struct vm_area_struct * find_vma(struct mm_struct * mm,
                                      unsigned long addr)
662 {
663     struct vm_area_struct *vma = NULL;
664
665     if (mm) {
666         /* Check the cache first. */
667         /* (Cache hit rate is typically around 35%.) */
668         vma = mm->mmap_cache;
669         if (!(vma && vma->vm_end > addr &&
              vma->vm_start <= addr)) {
670             rb_node_t * rb_node;
671
672             rb_node = mm->mm_rb.rb_node;
673             vma = NULL;
674
675             while (rb_node) {
676                 struct vm_area_struct * vma_tmp;
677
678                 vma_tmp = rb_entry(rb_node,
                        struct vm_area_struct, vm_rb);
679
680                 if (vma_tmp->vm_end > addr) {
681                     vma = vma_tmp;
682                     if (vma_tmp->vm_start <= addr)
683                         break;
684                     rb_node = rb_node->rb_left;
685                 } else
686                     rb_node = rb_node->rb_right;
```

Process Address Space

```
687                  }
688                  if (vma)
689                          mm->mmap_cache = vma;
690          }
691      }
692      return vma;
693 }
```

661 The two parameters are the top-level `mm_struct` that is to be searched and the address the caller is interested in.

663 Defaults to returning NULL for address not found.

665 Makes sure the caller does not try to search a bogus mm.

668 `mmap_cache` has the result of the last call to `find_vma()`. This has a chance of not having to search at all through the red-black tree.

669 If it is a valid VMA that is being examined, this checks to see if the address being searched is contained within it. If it is, the VMA was the `mmap_cache` one, so it can be returned. Otherwise, the tree is searched.

670-674 Starts at the root of the tree.

675-687 This block is the tree walk.

678 The macro, as the name suggests, returns the VMA that this tree node points to.

680 Checks if the next node is traversed by the left or right leaf.

682 If the current VMA is what is required, this exits the while loop.

689 If the VMA is valid, this sets the `mmap_cache` for the next call to `find_vma()`.

692 Returns the VMA that contains the address or, as a side effect of the tree walk, returns the VMA that is closest to the requested address.

D.3.1.2   Function: `find_vma_prev()`   *(mm/mmap.c)*

```
696 struct vm_area_struct * find_vma_prev(struct mm_struct * mm,
                         unsigned long addr,
697                      struct vm_area_struct **pprev)
698 {
699     if (mm) {
700         /* Go through the RB tree quickly. */
701         struct vm_area_struct * vma;
702         rb_node_t * rb_node, * rb_last_right, * rb_prev;
703
704         rb_node = mm->mm_rb.rb_node;
```

```
705         rb_last_right = rb_prev = NULL;
706         vma = NULL;
707
708         while (rb_node) {
709             struct vm_area_struct * vma_tmp;
710
711             vma_tmp = rb_entry(rb_node,
712                         struct vm_area_struct, vm_rb);
713             if (vma_tmp->vm_end > addr) {
714                 vma = vma_tmp;
715                 rb_prev = rb_last_right;
716                 if (vma_tmp->vm_start <= addr)
717                     break;
718                 rb_node = rb_node->rb_left;
719             } else {
720                 rb_last_right = rb_node;
721                 rb_node = rb_node->rb_right;
722             }
723         }
724         if (vma) {
725             if (vma->vm_rb.rb_left) {
726                 rb_prev = vma->vm_rb.rb_left;
727                 while (rb_prev->rb_right)
728                     rb_prev = rb_prev->rb_right;
729             }
730             *pprev = NULL;
731             if (rb_prev)
732                 *pprev = rb_entry(rb_prev, struct
733                     vm_area_struct, vm_rb);
733             if ((rb_prev ? (*pprev)->vm_next : mm->mmap) !=
vma)
734                 BUG();
735             return vma;
736         }
737     }
738     *pprev = NULL;
739     return NULL;
740 }
```

696-723 This is essentially the same as the find_vma() function already described.
The only difference is that the last right node accessed is remembered because
this will represent the VMA previous to the requested VMA.

725-729 If the returned VMA has a left node, it means that it has to be traversed.
It first takes the left leaf and then follows each right leaf until the bottom of
the tree is found.

Process Address Space

731-732 Extracts the VMA from the red-black tree node.

733-734 A debugging check. If this is the previous node, its next field should point to the VMA being returned. If it is not, it is a bug.

D.3.1.3   Function: `find_vma_intersection()`   *(include/linux/mm.h)*

```
673 static inline struct vm_area_struct * find_vma_intersection(
                         struct mm_struct * mm,
                         unsigned long start_addr, unsigned long end_addr)
674 {
675     struct vm_area_struct * vma = find_vma(mm,start_addr);
676
677     if (vma && end_addr <= vma->vm_start)
678         vma = NULL;
679     return vma;
680 }
```

675 Returns the VMA closest to the starting address.

677 If a VMA is returned and the end address is still less than the beginning of the returned VMA, the VMA does not intersect.

679 Returns the VMA if it does intersect.

D.3.2   Finding a Free Memory Region

D.3.2.1   Function: `get_unmapped_area()`   *(mm/mmap.c)*
The call graph for this function is shown in Figure 4.4.

```
644 unsigned long get_unmapped_area(struct file *file,
                         unsigned long addr,
                         unsigned long len,
                         unsigned long pgoff,
                         unsigned long flags)
645 {
646     if (flags & MAP_FIXED) {
647         if (addr > TASK_SIZE - len)
648             return -ENOMEM;
649         if (addr & ~PAGE_MASK)
650             return -EINVAL;
651         return addr;
652     }
653
654     if (file && file->f_op && file->f_op->get_unmapped_area)
655         return file->f_op->get_unmapped_area(file, addr,
                         len, pgoff, flags);
656
```

```
657        return arch_get_unmapped_area(file, addr, len, pgoff, flags);
658 }
```

644 The parameters passed are the following:

- **file** The file or device being mapped
- **addr** The requested address to map to
- **len** The length of the mapping
- **pgoff** The offset within the file being mapped
- **flags** Protection flags

646-652 A sanity check. If it is required that the mapping be placed at the specified address, this makes sure it will not overflow the address space and that it is page aligned.

654 If the `struct file` provides a `get_unmapped_area()` function, this uses it.

657 Uses `arch_get_unmapped_area()`(See Section D.3.2.2) as an anonymous version of the `get_unmapped_area()` function.

D.3.2.2   Function: `arch_get_unmapped_area()`   *(mm/mmap.c)*

Architectures have the option of specifying this function for themselves by defining `HAVE_ARCH_UNMAPPED_AREA`. If the architectures do not supply one, this version is used.

```
614 #ifndef HAVE_ARCH_UNMAPPED_AREA
615 static inline unsigned long arch_get_unmapped_area(
            struct file *filp,
            unsigned long addr, unsigned long len,
            unsigned long pgoff, unsigned long flags)
616 {
617     struct vm_area_struct *vma;
618
619     if (len > TASK_SIZE)
620         return -ENOMEM;
621
622     if (addr) {
623         addr = PAGE_ALIGN(addr);
624         vma = find_vma(current->mm, addr);
625         if (TASK_SIZE - len >= addr &&
626             (!vma || addr + len <= vma->vm_start))
627             return addr;
628     }
629     addr = PAGE_ALIGN(TASK_UNMAPPED_BASE);
630
631     for (vma = find_vma(current->mm, addr); ; vma = vma->vm_next) {
```

```
632              /* At this point:  (!vma || addr < vma->vm_end). */
633              if (TASK_SIZE - len < addr)
634                  return -ENOMEM;
635              if (!vma || addr + len <= vma->vm_start)
636                  return addr;
637              addr = vma->vm_end;
638          }
639  }
640  #else
641  extern unsigned long arch_get_unmapped_area(struct file *,
                         unsigned long, unsigned long,
                         unsigned long, unsigned long);
642  #endif
```

614 If this is not defined, it means that the architecture does not provide its own arch_get_unmapped_area(), so this one is used instead.

615 The parameters are the same as those for get_unmapped_area() (See Section D.3.2.1).

619-620 A sanity check to make sure the required map length is not too long.

622-628 If an address is provided, this uses it for the mapping.

623 Makes sure the address is page aligned.

624 find_vma()(See Section D.3.1.1) will return the region closest to the requested address.

625-627 Makes sure the mapping will not overlap with another region. If it does not, it returns it because it is safe to use. Otherwise, it gets ignored.

629 TASK_UNMAPPED_BASE is the starting point for searching for a free region to use.

631-638 Starting from TASK_UNMAPPED_BASE, this linearly searches the VMAs until a large enough region between them is found to store the new mapping. This is essentially a first fit search.

641 If an external function is provided, it still needs to be declared here.

D.4   Locking and Unlocking Memory Regions

Contents

This section contains the functions related to locking and unlocking a region. The main complexity in them is how the regions need to be fixed up after the operation takes place.

D.4.1   Locking a Memory Region

D.4.1.1   Function: sys_mlock()   *(mm/mlock.c)*

The call graph for this function is shown in Figure 4.9. This is the system call mlock() for locking a region of memory into physical memory. This function simply checks to make sure that process and user limits are not exceeeded and that the region to lock is page aligned.

```
195 asmlinkage long sys_mlock(unsigned long start, size_t len)
196 {
197     unsigned long locked;
198     unsigned long lock_limit;
199     int error = -ENOMEM;
200
201     down_write(&current->mm->mmap_sem);
202     len = PAGE_ALIGN(len + (start & ~PAGE_MASK));
203     start &= PAGE_MASK;
204
205     locked = len >> PAGE_SHIFT;
206     locked += current->mm->locked_vm;
207
208     lock_limit = current->rlim[RLIMIT_MEMLOCK].rlim_cur;
209     lock_limit >>= PAGE_SHIFT;
210
211     /* check against resource limits */
```

```
212     if (locked > lock_limit)
213         goto out;
214
215     /* we may lock at most half of physical memory... */
216     /* (this check is pretty bogus, but doesn't hurt) */
217     if (locked > num_physpages/2)
218         goto out;
219
220     error = do_mlock(start, len, 1);
221 out:
222     up_write(&current->mm->mmap_sem);
223     return error;
224 }
```

201 Takes the semaphore. We are likely to sleep during this, so a spinlock cannot be used.

202 Rounds the length up to the page boundary.

203 Rounds the start address down to the page boundary.

205 Calculates how many pages will be locked.

206 Calculates how many pages will be locked in total by this process.

208-209 Calculates what the limit is to the number of locked pages.

212-213 Does not allow the process to lock more than it should.

217-218 Does not allow the process to map more than half of physical memory.

220 Calls do_mlock()(See Section D.4.1.4), which starts the real work by finding the VMA clostest to the area to lock before calling mlock_fixup() (See Section D.4.3.1).

222 Frees the semaphore.

223 Returns the error or success code from do_mlock().

D.4.1.2   Function: sys_mlockall()   *(mm/mlock.c)*

This is the system call mlockall(), which attempts to lock all pages in the calling process in memory. If MCL_CURRENT is specified, all current pages will be locked. If MCL_FUTURE is specified, all future mappings will be locked. The flags may be or-ed together. This function makes sure that the flags and process limits are ok before calling do_mlockall().

```
266 asmlinkage long sys_mlockall(int flags)
267 {
268     unsigned long lock_limit;
```

```
269        int ret = -EINVAL;
270
271        down_write(&current->mm->mmap_sem);
272        if (!flags || (flags & ~(MCL_CURRENT | MCL_FUTURE)))
273            goto out;
274
275        lock_limit = current->rlim[RLIMIT_MEMLOCK].rlim_cur;
276        lock_limit >>= PAGE_SHIFT;
277
278        ret = -ENOMEM;
279        if (current->mm->total_vm > lock_limit)
280            goto out;
281
282        /* we may lock at most half of physical memory... */
283        /* (this check is pretty bogus, but doesn't hurt) */
284        if (current->mm->total_vm > num_physpages/2)
285            goto out;
286
287        ret = do_mlockall(flags);
288 out:
289        up_write(&current->mm->mmap_sem);
290        return ret;
291 }
```

269 By default, this returns -EINVAL to indicate invalid parameters.

271 Acquires the current mm_struct semaphore.

272-273 Makes sure that some valid flag has been specified. If not, it uses goto out to unlock the semaphore and returns -EINVAL.

275-276 Checks the process limits to see how many pages may be locked.

278 From here on, the default error is -ENOMEM.

279-280 If the size of the locking would exceed set limits, then it uses goto out.

284-285 Do not allow this process to lock more than half of physical memory. This is a bogus check because four processes locking a quarter of physical memory each will bypass this. It is acceptable though because only root processes are allowed to lock memory and are unlikely to make this type of mistake.

287 Calls the core function do_mlockall()(See Section D.4.1.3).

289-290 Unlocks the semaphore and returns.

Process Address
Space

D.4.1.3   Function: do_mlockall()   *(mm/mlock.c)*

```
238 static int do_mlockall(int flags)
239 {
240     int error;
241     unsigned int def_flags;
242     struct vm_area_struct * vma;
243
244     if (!capable(CAP_IPC_LOCK))
245         return -EPERM;
246
247     def_flags = 0;
248     if (flags & MCL_FUTURE)
249         def_flags = VM_LOCKED;
250     current->mm->def_flags = def_flags;
251
252     error = 0;
253     for (vma = current->mm->mmap; vma ; vma = vma->vm_next) {
254         unsigned int newflags;
255
256         newflags = vma->vm_flags | VM_LOCKED;
257         if (!(flags & MCL_CURRENT))
258             newflags &= ~VM_LOCKED;
259         error = mlock_fixup(vma, vma->vm_start, vma->vm_end,
                                         newflags);
260         if (error)
261             break;
262     }
263     return error;
264 }
```

244-245 The calling process must be either root or have **CAP_IPC_LOCK** capabilities.

248-250 The **MCL_FUTURE** flag says that all future pages should be locked, so, if set, the **def_flags** for VMAs should be **VM_LOCKED**.

253-262 Cycles through all VMAs.

256 Sets the **VM_LOCKED** flag in the current VMA flags.

257-258 If the **MCL_CURRENT** flag has not been set requesting that all current pages be locked, then this clears the **VM_LOCKED** flag. The logic is arranged like this so that the unlock code can use this same function, just with no flags.

259 Calls **mlock_fixup()** (See Section D.4.3.1), which will adjust the regions to match the locking as necessary.

260-261 If a nonzero value is returned at any point, this stops locking. It is interesting to note that VMAs already locked will not be unlocked.

263 Returns the success or error value.

D.4.1.4   Function: do_mlock()   *(mm/mlock.c)*

This function is responsible for starting the work needed to either lock or unlock
a region, depending on the value of the **on** parameter. It is broken up into two
sections. The first makes sure the region is page aligned (despite the fact the
only two callers of this function do the same thing) before finding the VMA that
is to be adjusted. The second part then sets the appropriate flags before calling
`mlock_fixup()` for each VMA that is affected by this locking.

```
148 static int do_mlock(unsigned long start, size_t len, int on)
149 {
150     unsigned long nstart, end, tmp;
151     struct vm_area_struct * vma, * next;
152     int error;
153
154     if (on && !capable(CAP_IPC_LOCK))
155         return -EPERM;
156     len = PAGE_ALIGN(len);
157     end = start + len;
158     if (end < start)
159         return -EINVAL;
160     if (end == start)
161         return 0;
162     vma = find_vma(current->mm, start);
163     if (!vma || vma->vm_start > start)
164         return -ENOMEM;
```

This block page aligns the request and finds the VMA.

154 Only root processes can lock pages.

156 Page aligns the length. This is redundant because the length is page aligned
in the parent functions.

157-159 Calculates the end of the locking and makes sure it is a valid region. It
returns -EINVAL if it is not.

160-161 If locking a region of size 0, this just returns.

162 Finds the VMA that will be affected by this locking.

163-164 If the VMA for this address range does not exist, it returns -ENOMEM.

```
166     for (nstart = start ; ; ) {
167         unsigned int newflags;
168
170
```

```
171              newflags = vma->vm_flags | VM_LOCKED;
172              if (!on)
173                  newflags &= ~VM_LOCKED;
174
175              if (vma->vm_end >= end) {
176                  error = mlock_fixup(vma, nstart, end, newflags);
177                  break;
178              }
179
180              tmp = vma->vm_end;
181              next = vma->vm_next;
182              error = mlock_fixup(vma, nstart, tmp, newflags);
183              if (error)
184                  break;
185              nstart = tmp;
186              vma = next;
187              if (!vma || vma->vm_start != nstart) {
188                  error = -ENOMEM;
189                  break;
190              }
191          }
192      return error;
193 }
```

This block walks through the VMAs affected by this locking and calls
mlock_fixup() for each of them.

166-192 Cycles through as many VMAs as necessary to lock the pages.

171 Sets the VM_LOCKED flag on the VMA.

172-173 If this is an unlock, it removes the flag.

175-177 If this VMA is the last VMA to be affected by the unlocking, this calls
mlock_fixup() with the end address for the locking and exits.

180-190 This is whole VMA that needs to be locked. To lock it, the end of this
VMA is passed as a parameter to mlock_fixup()(See Section D.4.3.1) instead
of the end of the actual locking.

180 tmp is the end of the mapping on this VMA.

181 next is the next VMA that will be affected by the locking.

182 Calls mlock_fixup()(See Section D.4.3.1) for this VMA.

183-184 If an error occurs, this backs out. Note that the VMAs already locked
are not fixed up right.

185 The next start address is the start of the next VMA.

186 Moves to the next VMA.

187-190 If there is no VMA, this returns -ENOMEM. The next condition, though, would require the regions to be extremly broken as a result of a broken implementation of mlock_fixup() or have VMAs that overlap.

192 Returns the error or success value.

D.4.2 Unlocking the Region

D.4.2.1 Function: sys_munlock() *(mm/mlock.c)*
This page aligns the request before calling do_mlock(), which begins the real work of fixing up the regions.

```
226 asmlinkage long sys_munlock(unsigned long start, size_t len)
227 {
228     int ret;
229
230     down_write(&current->mm->mmap_sem);
231     len = PAGE_ALIGN(len + (start & ~PAGE_MASK));
232     start &= PAGE_MASK;
233     ret = do_mlock(start, len, 0);
234     up_write(&current->mm->mmap_sem);
235     return ret;
236 }
```

230 Acquires the semaphore protecting the mm_struct.

231 Rounds the length of the region up to the nearest page boundary.

232 Rounds the start of the region down to the nearest page boundary.

233 Calls do_mlock() (See Section D.4.1.4) with 0 as the third parameter to unlock the region.

234 Releases the semaphore.

235 Returns the success or failure code.

D.4.2.2 Function: sys_munlockall() *(mm/mlock.c)*
This is a trivial function. If the flags to mlockall() are 0, it gets translated as none of the current pages must be present and no future mappings should be locked either, which means the VM_LOCKED flag will be removed on all VMAs.

```
293 asmlinkage long sys_munlockall(void)
294 {
295     int ret;
296
297     down_write(&current->mm->mmap_sem);
```

Process Address
Space

```
298     ret = do_mlockall(0);
299     up_write(&current->mm->mmap_sem);
300     return ret;
301 }
```

297 Acquires the semaphore protecting the `mm_struct`.

298 Calls `do_mlockall()`(See Section D.4.1.3) with 0 as flags, which will remove the `VM_LOCKED` from all VMAs.

299 Releases the semaphore.

300 Returns the error or success code.

D.4.3   Fixing Up Regions After Locking/Unlocking

D.4.3.1   Function: `mlock_fixup()`   *(mm/mlock.c)*

This function identifies four separate types of locking that must be addressed. The first is where the full VMA is to be locked, and it calls `mlock_fixup_all()`. The second is where only the beginning portion of the VMA is affected, which is handled by `mlock_fixup_start()`. The third is the locking of a region at the end, which is handled by `mlock_fixup_end()`, and the last is locking a region in the middle of the VMA with `mlock_fixup_middle()`.

```
117 static int mlock_fixup(struct vm_area_struct * vma,
118    unsigned long start, unsigned long end, unsigned int newflags)
119 {
120     int pages, retval;
121
122     if (newflags == vma->vm_flags)
123         return 0;
124
125     if (start == vma->vm_start) {
126         if (end == vma->vm_end)
127             retval = mlock_fixup_all(vma, newflags);
128         else
129             retval = mlock_fixup_start(vma, end, newflags);
130     } else {
131         if (end == vma->vm_end)
132             retval = mlock_fixup_end(vma, start, newflags);
133         else
134             retval = mlock_fixup_middle(vma, start,
                            end, newflags);
135     }
136     if (!retval) {
137         /* keep track of amount of locked VM */
138         pages = (end - start) >> PAGE_SHIFT;
139         if (newflags & VM_LOCKED) {
```

```
140                 pages = -pages;
141                 make_pages_present(start, end);
142             }
143             vma->vm_mm->locked_vm -= pages;
144         }
145     return retval;
146 }
```

122-123 If no change is to be made, this just returns.

125 If the start of the locking is at the start of the VMA, it means that either the full region is to the locked or only a portion at the beginning.

126-127 If the full VMA is being locked, this calls `mlock_fixup_all()` (See Section D.4.3.2).

128-129 If part of the VMA is being locked with the start of the VMA matching the start of the locking, this calls `mlock_fixup_start()` (See Section D.4.3.3).

130 Means that either a region at the end is to be locked or a region in the middle.

131-132 If the end of the locking matches the end of the VMA, this calls `mlock_fixup_end()` (See Section D.4.3.4).

133-134 If a region in the middle of the VMA is to be locked, this calls `mlock_fixup_middle()` (See Section D.4.3.5).

136-144 For this, the fixup functions return 0 on success. If the fixup of the regions succeed and the regions are now marked as locked, this calls `make_pages_present()`, which makes some basic checks before calling `get_user_pages()`, which faults in all the pages in the same way that the page fault handler does.

D.4.3.2   Function: `mlock_fixup_all()`   *(mm/mlock.c)*

```
15 static inline int mlock_fixup_all(struct vm_area_struct * vma,
                    int newflags)
16 {
17     spin_lock(&vma->vm_mm->page_table_lock);
18     vma->vm_flags = newflags;
19     spin_unlock(&vma->vm_mm->page_table_lock);
20     return 0;
21 }
```

17-19 Trivial. It locks the VMA with the spinlock, sets the new flags, releases the lock and returns success.

Process Address Space

D.4.3.3   **Function:** `mlock_fixup_start()`   *(mm/mlock.c)*

This is slightly more complicated. A new VMA is required to represent the affected region. The start of the old VMA is moved forward.

```
23 static inline int mlock_fixup_start(struct vm_area_struct * vma,
24     unsigned long end, int newflags)
25 {
26     struct vm_area_struct * n;
27
28     n = kmem_cache_alloc(vm_area_cachep, SLAB_KERNEL);
29     if (!n)
30         return -EAGAIN;
31     *n = *vma;
32     n->vm_end = end;
33     n->vm_flags = newflags;
34     n->vm_raend = 0;
35     if (n->vm_file)
36         get_file(n->vm_file);
37     if (n->vm_ops && n->vm_ops->open)
38         n->vm_ops->open(n);
39     vma->vm_pgoff += (end - vma->vm_start) >> PAGE_SHIFT;
40     lock_vma_mappings(vma);
41     spin_lock(&vma->vm_mm->page_table_lock);
42     vma->vm_start = end;
43     __insert_vm_struct(current->mm, n);
44     spin_unlock(&vma->vm_mm->page_table_lock);
45     unlock_vma_mappings(vma);
46     return 0;
47 }
```

28 Allocates a VMA from the slab allocator for the affected region.

31-34 Copies in the necessary information.

35-36 If the VMA has a file or device mapping, `get_file()` will increment the reference count.

37-38 If an `open()` function is provided, this calls it.

39 Updates the offset within the file or device mapping for the old VMA to be the end of the locked region.

40 `lock_vma_mappings()` will lock any files if this VMA is a shared region.

41-44 Locks the parent `mm_struct`, updates its start to be the end of the affected region, inserts the new VMA into the processes linked lists (See Section D.2.2.1) and releases the lock.

45 Unlocks the file mappings with `unlock_vma_mappings()`.

46 Returns success.

D.4.3.4   Function: mlock_fixup_end()   *(mm/mlock.c)*

This function is essentially the same as `mlock_fixup_start()` except the affected region is at the end of the VMA.

```
49 static inline int mlock_fixup_end(struct vm_area_struct * vma,
50     unsigned long start, int newflags)
51 {
52     struct vm_area_struct * n;
53
54     n = kmem_cache_alloc(vm_area_cachep, SLAB_KERNEL);
55     if (!n)
56         return -EAGAIN;
57     *n = *vma;
58     n->vm_start = start;
59     n->vm_pgoff += (n->vm_start - vma->vm_start) >> PAGE_SHIFT;
60     n->vm_flags = newflags;
61     n->vm_raend = 0;
62     if (n->vm_file)
63         get_file(n->vm_file);
64     if (n->vm_ops && n->vm_ops->open)
65         n->vm_ops->open(n);
66     lock_vma_mappings(vma);
67     spin_lock(&vma->vm_mm->page_table_lock);
68     vma->vm_end = start;
69     __insert_vm_struct(current->mm, n);
70     spin_unlock(&vma->vm_mm->page_table_lock);
71     unlock_vma_mappings(vma);
72     return 0;
73 }
```

54 Allocates a VMA from the slab allocator for the affected region.

57-61 Copies in the necessary information and updates the offset within the file or device mapping.

62-63 If the VMA has a file or device mapping, `get_file()` will increment the reference count.

64-65 If an `open()` function is provided, this calls it.

66 `lock_vma_mappings()` will lock any files if this VMA is a shared region.

67-70 Locks the parent `mm_struct`, updates its start to be the end of the affected region, inserts the new VMA into the processes linked lists (See Section D.2.2.1) and releases the lock.

Process Address Space

71 Unlocks the file mappings with `unlock_vma_mappings()`.

72 Returns success.

D.4.3.5   Function: `mlock_fixup_middle()`   *(mm/mlock.c)*

This is similar to the previous two fixup functions except that two new regions are required to fix up the mapping.

```
75 static inline int mlock_fixup_middle(struct vm_area_struct * vma,
76     unsigned long start, unsigned long end, int newflags)
77 {
78     struct vm_area_struct * left, * right;
79
80     left = kmem_cache_alloc(vm_area_cachep, SLAB_KERNEL);
81     if (!left)
82         return -EAGAIN;
83     right = kmem_cache_alloc(vm_area_cachep, SLAB_KERNEL);
84     if (!right) {
85         kmem_cache_free(vm_area_cachep, left);
86         return -EAGAIN;
87     }
88     *left = *vma;
89     *right = *vma;
90     left->vm_end = start;
91     right->vm_start = end;
92     right->vm_pgoff += (right->vm_start - left->vm_start) >>
              PAGE_SHIFT;
93     vma->vm_flags = newflags;
94     left->vm_raend = 0;
95     right->vm_raend = 0;
96     if (vma->vm_file)
97         atomic_add(2, &vma->vm_file->f_count);
98
99     if (vma->vm_ops && vma->vm_ops->open) {
100         vma->vm_ops->open(left);
101         vma->vm_ops->open(right);
102     }
103     vma->vm_raend = 0;
104     vma->vm_pgoff += (start - vma->vm_start) >> PAGE_SHIFT;
105     lock_vma_mappings(vma);
106     spin_lock(&vma->vm_mm->page_table_lock);
107     vma->vm_start = start;
108     vma->vm_end = end;
109     vma->vm_flags = newflags;
110     __insert_vm_struct(current->mm, left);
111     __insert_vm_struct(current->mm, right);
```

```
112         spin_unlock(&vma->vm_mm->page_table_lock);
113         unlock_vma_mappings(vma);
114         return 0;
115 }
```

80-87 Allocates the two new VMAs from the slab allocator.

88-89 Copies in the information from the old VMA into the new VMAs.

90 The end of the left region is the start of the region to be affected.

91 The start of the right region is the end of the affected region.

92 Updates the file offset.

93 The old VMA is now the affected region, so this updates its flags.

94-95 Makes the readahead window 0 to ensure pages not belonging to their regions are not accidently read ahead.

96-97 Increments the reference count to the file/device mapping if there is one.

99-102 Calls the `open()` function for the two new mappings.

103-104 Cancels the readahead window and updates the offset within the file to be the beginning of the locked region.

105 Locks the shared file/device mappings.

106-112 Locks the parent `mm_struct`, updates the VMA and inserts the two new regions into the process before releasing the lock again.

113 Unlocks the shared mappings.

114 Returns success.

Process Address Space

D.5   Page Faulting

Contents

This section deals with the page fault handler. It begins with the architecture-specific function for the x86 and then moves to the architecture-independent layer. The architecture-specific functions all have the same responsibilities.

D.5.1   x86 Page Fault Handler

D.5.1.1   Function: do_page_fault()   *(arch/i386/mm/fault.c)*
The call graph for this function is shown in Figure 4.11. This function is the x86 architecture-dependent function for the handling of page fault exception handlers. Each architecture registers its own, but all of them have similar responsibilities.

```
140 asmlinkage void do_page_fault(struct pt_regs *regs,
                unsigned long error_code)
141 {
142     struct task_struct *tsk;
143     struct mm_struct *mm;
144     struct vm_area_struct * vma;
145     unsigned long address;
146     unsigned long page;
147     unsigned long fixup;
148     int write;
149     siginfo_t info;
150
151     /* get the address */
152     __asm__("movl %%cr2,%0":"=r" (address));
153
154     /* It's safe to allow irq's after cr2 has been saved */
155     if (regs->eflags & X86_EFLAGS_IF)
```

```
156            local_irq_enable();
157
158      tsk = current;
159
```

This is the function preamble. It gets the fault address and enables interrupts.

140 The parameters are the following:

- **regs** is a struct containing what all the registers have at fault time.
- **error_code** indicates what sort of fault occurred.

152 As the comment indicates, the cr2 register holds the fault address.

155-156 If the fault is from within an interrupt, this enables it.

158 Sets the current task.

```
173      if (address >= TASK_SIZE && !(error_code & 5))
174          goto vmalloc_fault;
175
176      mm = tsk->mm;
177      info.si_code = SEGV_MAPERR;
178
183      if (in_interrupt() || !mm)
184          goto no_context;
185
```

This block checks for exceptional faults, kernel faults, fault in interrupt and fault with no memory context.

173 If the fault address is over TASK_SIZE, it is within the kernel address space. If the error code is 5, it means the error happened while in kernel mode and is not a protection error, so this handles a vmalloc fault.

176 Records the working mm.

183 If this is an interrupt or there is no memory context (such as with a kernel thread), there is no way to safely handle the fault, so goto no_context.

```
186      down_read(&mm->mmap_sem);
187
188      vma = find_vma(mm, address);
189      if (!vma)
190          goto bad_area;
191      if (vma->vm_start <= address)
192          goto good_area;
193      if (!(vma->vm_flags & VM_GROWSDOWN))
194          goto bad_area;
```

Process Address
Space

```
195     if (error_code & 4) {
196         /*
197          * accessing the stack below %esp is always a bug.
198          * The "+ 32" is there due to some instructions (like
199          * pusha) doing post-decrement on the stack and that
200          * doesn't show up until later..
201          */
202         if (address + 32 < regs->esp)
203             goto bad_area;
204     }
205     if (expand_stack(vma, address))
206         goto bad_area;
```

If the fault is in userspace, this block finds the VMA for the faulting address and determines if it is a good area, a bad area or if the fault occurred near a region that can be expanded, such as the stack.

186 Takes the long-lived mm semaphore.

188 Finds the VMA that is responsible or is closest to the faulting address.

189-190 If a VMA does not exist at all, goto bad_area.

191-192 If the start of the region is before the address, it means this VMA is the correct VMA for the fault, so goto good_area, which will check the permissions.

193-194 For the region that is closest, this checks if it can grown down (VM_GROWSDOWN). If it does, it means the stack can probably be expanded. If not, goto bad_area.

195-204 Checks to make sure it is not an access below the stack. If the error_code is 4, it means it is running in userspace.

205-206 The stack is the only region with VM_GROWSDOWN set, so, if we reach here, the stack is expanded with expand_stack()(See Section D.5.2.1). If it fails, goto bad_area.

```
211 good_area:
212     info.si_code = SEGV_ACCERR;
213     write = 0;
214     switch (error_code & 3) {
215         default:    /* 3: write, present */
216 #ifdef TEST_VERIFY_AREA
217             if (regs->cs == KERNEL_CS)
218                 printk("WP fault at %08lx\n", regs->eip);
219 #endif
220             /* fall through */
221         case 2:     /* write, not present */
```

```
222              if (!(vma->vm_flags & VM_WRITE))
223                  goto bad_area;
224              write++;
225              break;
226          case 1:    /* read, present */
227              goto bad_area;
228          case 0:    /* read, not present */
229              if (!(vma->vm_flags & (VM_READ | VM_EXEC)))
230                  goto bad_area;
231      }
```

This block is where the first part of a fault in a good area is handled. The permissions need to be checked in case this is a protection fault.

212 By default, this returns an error.

214 Checks the error code against bits 0 and 1 of the error code. Bit 0 at 0 means the page was not present. At 1, it means a protection fault, like a write to a read-only area. Bit 1 is 0 if it was a read fault and 1 if it was a write fault.

215 If it is 3, both bits are 1, so it is a write protection fault.

221 Bit 1 is a 1, so it is a write fault.

222-223 If the region cannot be written to, it is a bad write to goto `bad_area`. If the region can be written to, this is a page that is marked Copy On Write (COW).

224 Flags that a write has occurred.

226-227 This is a read, and the page is present. There is no reason for the fault, so it must be some other type of exception like a divide by zero, or goto `bad_area` where it is handled.

228-230 A read occurred on a missing page. This makes sure it is ok to read or exec this page. If not, goto `bad_area`. The check for exec is made because the x86 cannot exec protect a page and instead uses the read protect flag. This is why both have to be checked.

```
233  survive:
239      switch (handle_mm_fault(mm, vma, address, write)) {
240      case 1:
241          tsk->min_flt++;
242          break;
243      case 2:
244          tsk->maj_flt++;
245          break;
246      case 0:
247          goto do_sigbus;
```

Process Address
Space

```
248    default:
249        goto out_of_memory;
250    }
251
252    /*
253     * Did it hit the DOS screen memory VA from vm86 mode?
254     */
255    if (regs->eflags & VM_MASK) {
256        unsigned long bit = (address - 0xA0000) >> PAGE_SHIFT;
257        if (bit < 32)
258            tsk->thread.screen_bitmap |= 1 << bit;
259    }
260    up_read(&mm->mmap_sem);
261    return;
```

At this point, an attempt is going to be made to handle the fault gracefully with `handle_mm_fault()`.

239 Calls `handle_mm_fault()` with the relevant information about the fault. This is the architecture-independent part of the handler.

240-242 A return of 1 means it was a minor fault. Updates statistics.

243-245 A return of 2 means it was a major fault. Update statistics

246-247 A return of 0 means some I/O error happened during the fault, so it goes to the do_sigbus handler.

248-249 Any other return means memory could not be allocated for the fault, so we are out of memory. In reality, this does not happen because another function `out_of_memory()` is invoked in `mm/oom_kill.c` before this could happen, which is a function that is a lot more graceful about who it kills.

260 Releases the lock to the mm.

261 Returns because the fault has been successfully handled.

```
267 bad_area:
268    up_read(&mm->mmap_sem);
269
270    /* User mode accesses just cause a SIGSEGV */
271    if (error_code & 4) {
272        tsk->thread.cr2 = address;
273        tsk->thread.error_code = error_code;
274        tsk->thread.trap_no = 14;
275        info.si_signo = SIGSEGV;
276        info.si_errno = 0;
277        /* info.si_code has been set above */
278        info.si_addr = (void *)address;
```

```
279              force_sig_info(SIGSEGV, &info, tsk);
280              return;
281      }
282
283      /*
284       * Pentium F0 0F C7 C8 bug workaround.
285       */
286      if (boot_cpu_data.f00f_bug) {
287              unsigned long nr;
288
289              nr = (address - idt) >> 3;
290
291              if (nr == 6) {
292                      do_invalid_op(regs, 0);
293                      return;
294              }
295      }
```

This is the bad area handler, such as using memory with no `vm_area_struct` managing it. If the fault is not by a user process or the f00f bug, the no_context label is fallen through to.

271 An error code of 4 implies userspace, so it is a simple case of sending a `SIGSEGV` to kill the process.

272-274 Sets thread information about what happened, which can be read by a debugger later.

275 Records that a `SIGSEGV` signal was sent.

276 Clears errno, as the `SIGSEGV` is sufficient to explain the error.

278 Records the address.

279 Sends the `SIGSEGV` signal. The process will exit and dump all the relevant information.

280 Returns because the fault has been successfully handled.

286-295 A bug in the first Pentiums was called the f00f bug, which caused the processor to constantly page fault. It was used as a local DoS attack on a running Linux system. This bug was trapped within a few hours, and a patch was released. Now it results in a harmless termination of the process rather than a rebooting system.

```
296
297 no_context:
298     /* Are we prepared to handle this kernel fault?  */
299     if ((fixup = search_exception_table(regs->eip)) != 0) {
```

Process Address Space

```
300        regs->eip = fixup;
301        return;
302    }
```

299-302 Searches the exception table with search_exception_table() to see
if this exception be handled, and, if so, it calls the proper exception handler after returning. This is really important during copy_from_user() and
copy_to_user() when an exception handler is installed to trap reads and
writes to invalid regions in userspace without having to make expensive checks.
It means that a small fixup block of code can be called rather than falling
through to the next block, which causes an oops.

```
304 /*
305  * Oops. The kernel tried to access some bad page. We'll have to
306  * terminate things with extreme prejudice.
307  */
308
309    bust_spinlocks(1);
310
311    if (address < PAGE_SIZE)
312        printk(KERN_ALERT "Unable to handle kernel NULL pointer
                    dereference");
313    else
314        printk(KERN_ALERT "Unable to handle kernel paging
                    request");
315    printk(" at virtual address %08lx\n",address);
316    printk(" printing eip:\n");
317    printk("%08lx\n", regs->eip);
318    asm("movl %%cr3,%0":"=r" (page));
319    page = ((unsigned long *) __va(page))[address >> 22];
320    printk(KERN_ALERT "*pde = %08lx\n", page);
321    if (page & 1) {
322        page &= PAGE_MASK;
323        address &= 0x003ff000;
324        page = ((unsigned long *)
                __va(page))[address >> PAGE_SHIFT];
325        printk(KERN_ALERT "*pte = %08lx\n", page);
326    }
327    die("Oops", regs, error_code);
328    bust_spinlocks(0);
329    do_exit(SIGKILL);
```

This is the no_context handler. Some bad exception occurred, which is going
to end up in the process being terminated in all likelihood. Otherwise, the kernel
faulted when it definitely should have, and an oops report is generated.

309-329 Otherwise, the kernel faulted when it really should not have, and it is a
kernel bug. This block generates an oops report.

309 Forcibly frees spinlocks, which might prevent a message getting to the console.

311-312 If the address is < PAGE_SIZE, it means that a null pointer was used. Linux deliberately has page 0 unassigned to trap this type of fault, which is a common programming error.

313-314 Otherwise, it is just some bad kernel error, such as a driver trying to access userspace incorrectly.

315-320 Prints out information about the fault.

321-326 Prints out information about the page being faulted.

327 Dies and generates an oops report, which can be used later to get a stack trace so that a developer can see more accurately where and how the fault occurred.

329 Forcibly kills the faulting process.

```
335 out_of_memory:
336     if (tsk->pid == 1) {
337         yield();
338         goto survive;
339     }
340     up_read(&mm->mmap_sem);
341     printk("VM: killing process %s\n", tsk->comm);
342     if (error_code & 4)
343         do_exit(SIGKILL);
344     goto no_context;
```

This block is the out of memory handler. It usually ends with the faulting process getting killed unless it is **init**.

336-339 If the process is **init**, just yield and goto survive, which will try to handle the fault gracefully. **init** should never be killed.

340 Frees the mm semaphore.

341 Prints out a helpful "You are Dead" message.

342 If it is from userspace, this just kills the process.

344 If it is in kernel space, go to the no_context handler, which, in this case, will probably result in a kernel oops.

```
345
346 do_sigbus:
347     up_read(&mm->mmap_sem);
348
353     tsk->thread.cr2 = address;
```

```
354        tsk->thread.error_code = error_code;
355        tsk->thread.trap_no = 14;
356        info.si_signo = SIGBUS;
357        info.si_errno = 0;
358        info.si_code = BUS_ADRERR;
359        info.si_addr = (void *)address;
360        force_sig_info(SIGBUS, &info, tsk);
361
362        /* Kernel mode? Handle exceptions or die */
363        if (!(error_code & 4))
364            goto no_context;
365        return;
```

347 Frees the mm lock.

353-359 Fills in information to show a SIGBUS occurred at the faulting address
so that a debugger can trap it later.

360 Sends the signal.

363-364 If in kernel mode, this tries and handles the exception during no_context.

365 If it is in userspace, this just returns, and the process will die in due course.

```
367 vmalloc_fault:
368     {
376         int offset = __pgd_offset(address);
377         pgd_t *pgd, *pgd_k;
378         pmd_t *pmd, *pmd_k;
379         pte_t *pte_k;
380
381         asm("movl %%cr3,%0":"=r" (pgd));
382         pgd = offset + (pgd_t *)__va(pgd);
383         pgd_k = init_mm.pgd + offset;
384
385         if (!pgd_present(*pgd_k))
386             goto no_context;
387         set_pgd(pgd, *pgd_k);
388
389         pmd = pmd_offset(pgd, address);
390         pmd_k = pmd_offset(pgd_k, address);
391         if (!pmd_present(*pmd_k))
392             goto no_context;
393         set_pmd(pmd, *pmd_k);
394
395         pte_k = pte_offset(pmd_k, address);
396         if (!pte_present(*pte_k))
397             goto no_context;
```

```
398          return;
399     }
400 }
```

This is the vmalloc fault handler. When pages are mapped in the vmalloc space, only the reference pagetable is updated. As each process references this area, a fault will be trapped, and the process pagetables will be synchronized with the reference pagetable here.

376 Gets the offset within a PGD.

381 Copies the address of the PGD for the process from the cr3 register to pgd.

382 Calculates the pgd pointer from the process PGD.

383 Calculates for the kernel reference PGD.

385-386 If the pgd entry is invalid for the kernel page table, goto `no_context`.

386 Sets the pagetable entry in the process pagetable with a copy from the kernel reference pagetable.

389-393 This is the same idea for the PMD. Copies the pagetable entry from the kernel reference pagetable to the process pagetables.

395 Checks the PTE.

396-397 If it is not present, it means the page was not valid even in the kernel reference pagetable, so goto `no_context` to handle what is probably a kernel bug or a reference to a random part of unused kernel space.

398 Returns knowing the process pagetables have been updated and are in sync with the kernel pagetables.

D.5.2 Expanding the Stack

D.5.2.1 Function: `expand_stack()` *(include/linux/mm.h)*

This function is called by the architecture-dependent page fault handler. The VMA supplied is guaranteed to be one that can grow to cover the address.

```
640 static inline int expand_stack(struct vm_area_struct * vma,
                                   unsigned long address)
641 {
642     unsigned long grow;
643
644     /*
645      * vma->vm_start/vm_end cannot change under us because
         * the caller is required
646      * to hold the mmap_sem in write mode. We need to get the
647      * spinlock only before relocating the vma range ourself.
```

```
648      */
649      address &= PAGE_MASK;
650      spin_lock(&vma->vm_mm->page_table_lock);
651      grow = (vma->vm_start - address) >> PAGE_SHIFT;
652      if (vma->vm_end - address >
                                 current->rlim[RLIMIT_STACK].rlim_cur ||
653        ((vma->vm_mm->total_vm + grow) << PAGE_SHIFT) >
                                 current->rlim[RLIMIT_AS].rlim_cur) {
654          spin_unlock(&vma->vm_mm->page_table_lock);
655          return -ENOMEM;
656      }
657      vma->vm_start = address;
658      vma->vm_pgoff -= grow;
659      vma->vm_mm->total_vm += grow;
660      if (vma->vm_flags & VM_LOCKED)
661          vma->vm_mm->locked_vm += grow;
662      spin_unlock(&vma->vm_mm->page_table_lock);
663      return 0;
664 }
```

649 Rounds the address down to the nearest page boundary.

650 Locks the pagetables spinlock.

651 Calculates how many pages the stack needs to grow by.

652 Checks to make sure that the size of the stack does not exceed the process limits.

653 Checks to make sure that the size of the address space will not exceed process limits after the stack is grown.

654-655 If either of the limits are reached, this returns -ENOMEM, which will cause the faulting process to segfault.

657-658 Grows the VMA down.

659 Updates the amount of address space used by the process.

660-661 If the region is locked, this updates the number of locked pages used by the process.

662-663 Unlocks the process pagetables and returns success.

D.5.3   Architecture-Independent Page Fault Handler

This is the top-level pair of functions for the architecture-independent page fault handler.

D.5.3.1   Function: `handle_mm_fault()`   *(mm/memory.c)*

The call graph for this function is shown in Figure 4.13. This function allocates the PMD and PTE necessary for this new PTE that is about to be allocated. It takes the necessary locks to protect the pagetables before calling `handle_pte_fault()` to fault in the page itself.

```
1364 int handle_mm_fault(struct mm_struct *mm,
         struct vm_area_struct * vma,
1365     unsigned long address, int write_access)
1366 {
1367     pgd_t *pgd;
1368     pmd_t *pmd;
1369
1370     current->state = TASK_RUNNING;
1371     pgd = pgd_offset(mm, address);
1372
1373     /*
1374      * We need the page table lock to synchronize with kswapd
1375      * and the SMP-safe atomic PTE updates.
1376      */
1377     spin_lock(&mm->page_table_lock);
1378     pmd = pmd_alloc(mm, pgd, address);
1379
1380     if (pmd) {
1381         pte_t * pte = pte_alloc(mm, pmd, address);
1382         if (pte)
1383             return handle_pte_fault(mm, vma, address,
                          write_access, pte);
1384     }
1385     spin_unlock(&mm->page_table_lock);
1386     return -1;
1387 }
```

1364 The parameters of the function are the following:

- **mm** is the `mm_struct` for the faulting process.
- **vma** is the `vm_area_struct` managing the region the fault occurred in.
- **address** is the faulting address.
- **write_access** is 1 if the fault is a write fault.

1370 Sets the current state of the process.

1371 Gets the pgd entry from the top-level pagetable.

1377 Locks the `mm_struct` because the pagetables will change.

1378 `pmd_alloc()` will allocate a `pmd_t` if one does not already exist.

Process Address Space

1380 If the pmd has been successfully allocated, then...

1381 Allocates a PTE for this address if one does not already exist.

1382-1383 Handles the page fault with `handle_pte_fault()` (See Section D.5.3.2) and returns the status code.

1385 Failure path and unlocks the `mm_struct`.

1386 Returns -1, which will be interpreted as an out of memory condition. This is correct because this line is only reached if a PMD or PTE could not be allocated.

D.5.3.2   Function: `handle_pte_fault()`   *(mm/memory.c)*

This function decides what type of fault this is and which function should handle it. `do_no_page()` is called if this is the first time a page is to be allocated. `do_swap_page()` handles the case where the page was swapped out to disk with the exception of pages swapped out from tmpfs. `do_wp_page()` breaks COW pages. If none of them are appropriate, the PTE entry is simply updated. If it was written to, it is marked dirty, and it is marked accessed to show it is a young page.

```
1331 static inline int handle_pte_fault(struct mm_struct *mm,
1332     struct vm_area_struct * vma, unsigned long address,
1333     int write_access, pte_t * pte)
1334 {
1335     pte_t entry;
1336
1337     entry = *pte;
1338     if (!pte_present(entry)) {
1339         /*
1340          * If it truly wasn't present, we know that kswapd
1341          * and the PTE updates will not touch it later. So
1342          * drop the lock.
1343          */
1344         if (pte_none(entry))
1345             return do_no_page(mm, vma, address,
1346                     write_access, pte);
1346         return do_swap_page(mm, vma, address, pte, entry,
1347                 write_access);
1347     }
1348
1349     if (write_access) {
1350         if (!pte_write(entry))
1351             return do_wp_page(mm, vma, address, pte, entry);
1352
1353         entry = pte_mkdirty(entry);
1354     }
```

```
1355        entry = pte_mkyoung(entry);
1356        establish_pte(vma, address, pte, entry);
1357        spin_unlock(&mm->page_table_lock);
1358        return 1;
1359 }
```

1331 The parameters of the function are the same as those for `handle_mm_fault()` except that the PTE for the fault is included.

1337 Records the PTE.

1338 Handles the case where the PTE is not present.

1344 If the PTE has never been filled, this handles the allocation of the PTE with `do_no_page()`(See Section D.5.4.1).

1346 If the page has been swapped out to backing storage, this handles it with `do_swap_page()`(See Section D.5.5.1).

1349-1354 Handles the case where the page is been written to.

1350-1351 If the PTE is marked write-only, it is a COW page, so handle it with `do_wp_page()`(See Section D.5.6.1).

1353 Otherwise, this just simply marks the page as dirty.

1355 Marks the page as accessed.

1356 `establish_pte()` copies the PTE and then updates the TLB and MMU cache. This does not copy in a new PTE, but some architectures require the TLB and MMU update.

1357 Unlocks the `mm_struct` and returns that a minor fault occurred.

D.5.4 Demand Allocation

D.5.4.1 Function: `do_no_page()` *(mm/memory.c)*

The call graph for this function is shown in Figure 4.14. This function is called the first time a page is referenced so that it may be allocated and filled with data if necessary. If it is an anonymous page, which is determined by the lack of a `vm_ops` available to the VMA or the lack of a `nopage()` function, `do_anonymous_page()` is called. Otherwise, the supplied `nopage()` function is called to allocate a page, and it is inserted into the pagetables here. The function has the following tasks:

- Check if `do_anonymous_page()` should be used, and, if so, call it and return the page it allocates. If not, call the supplied `nopage()` function and ensure it allocates a page successfully.

- Break COW early if appropriate.

Process Address Space

- Add the page to the pagetable entries and call the appropriate architecture-dependent hooks.

```
1245 static int do_no_page(struct mm_struct * mm,
         struct vm_area_struct * vma,
1246     unsigned long address, int write_access, pte_t *page_table)
1247 {
1248     struct page * new_page;
1249     pte_t entry;
1250
1251     if (!vma->vm_ops || !vma->vm_ops->nopage)
1252         return do_anonymous_page(mm, vma, page_table,
                       write_access, address);
1253     spin_unlock(&mm->page_table_lock);
1254
1255     new_page = vma->vm_ops->nopage(vma, address & PAGE_MASK, 0);
1256
1257     if (new_page == NULL)   /* no page was available -- SIGBUS */
1258         return 0;
1259     if (new_page == NOPAGE_OOM)
1260         return -1;
```

1245 The parameters supplied are the same as those for `handle_pte_fault()`.

1251-1252 If no `vm_ops` is supplied or no `nopage()` function is supplied, then this calls `do_anonymous_page()`(See Section D.5.4.2) to allocate a page and return it.

1253 Otherwise, this frees the pagetable lock because the `nopage()` function cannot be called with spinlocks held.

1255 Calls the supplied nopage function. In the case of filesystems, this is frequently `filemap_nopage()`(See Section D.6.4.1), but will be different for each device driver.

1257-1258 If NULL is returned, it means some error occurred in the nopage function, such as an I/O error while reading from disk. In this case, 0 is returned which results in a SIGBUS being sent to the faulting process.

1259-1260 If `NOPAGE_OOM` is returned, the physical page allocator failed to allocate a page, and -1 is returned, which will forcibly kill the process.

```
1265     if (write_access && !(vma->vm_flags & VM_SHARED)) {
1266         struct page * page = alloc_page(GFP_HIGHUSER);
1267         if (!page) {
1268             page_cache_release(new_page);
1269             return -1;
1270         }
```

```
1271            copy_user_highpage(page, new_page, address);
1272            page_cache_release(new_page);
1273            lru_cache_add(page);
1274            new_page = page;
1275    }
```

This block breaks COW early in this block if appropriate. COW is broken if the fault is a write fault and the region is not shared with `VM_SHARED`. If COW was not broken in this case, a second fault would occur immediately upon return.

1265 Checks if COW should be broken early.

1266 If so, this allocates a new page for the process.

1267-1270 If the page could not be allocated, this reduces the reference count to the page returned by the `nopage()` function and returns -1 for out of memory.

1271 Otherwise, it copies the contents.

1272 Reduces the reference count to the returned page, which may still be in use by another process.

1273 Adds the new page to the LRU lists so that it may be reclaimed by kswapd later.

```
1277    spin_lock(&mm->page_table_lock);
1288    /* Only go through if we didn't race with anybody else... */
1289    if (pte_none(*page_table)) {
1290        ++mm->rss;
1291        flush_page_to_ram(new_page);
1292        flush_icache_page(vma, new_page);
1293        entry = mk_pte(new_page, vma->vm_page_prot);
1294        if (write_access)
1295            entry = pte_mkwrite(pte_mkdirty(entry));
1296        set_pte(page_table, entry);
1297    } else {
1298        /* One of our sibling threads was faster, back out. */
1299        page_cache_release(new_page);
1300        spin_unlock(&mm->page_table_lock);
1301        return 1;
1302    }
1303
1304    /* no need to invalidate: a not-present page shouldn't
        * be cached
        */
1305    update_mmu_cache(vma, address, entry);
1306    spin_unlock(&mm->page_table_lock);
1307    return 2;      /* Major fault */
1308 }
```

1277 Locks the pagetables again because the allocations have finished and the pagetables are about to be updated.

1289 Checks if there is still no PTE in the entry we are about to use. If two faults hit here at the same time, it is possible another processor has already completed the page fault and that this one should be backed out.

1290-1297 If there is no PTE entered, this completes the fault.

1290 Increases the RSS count because the process is now using another page. A check really should be made here to make sure it isn't the global zero page because the RSS count could be misleading.

1291 As the page is about to be mapped to the process space, it is possible for some architectures that write to the page in kernel space will not be visible to the process. `flush_page_to_ram()` ensures the CPU cache will be coherent.

1292 `flush_icache_page()` is similar in principle except it ensures the icache and dcaches are coherent.

1293 Creates a `pte_t` with the appropriate permissions.

1294-1295 If this is a write, then this makes sure the PTE has write permissions.

1296 Places the new PTE in the process pagetables.

1297-1302 If the PTE is already filled, the page acquired from the `nopage()` function must be released.

1299 Decrements the reference count to the page. If it drops to 0, it will be freed.

1300-1301 Releases the `mm_struct` lock and returns 1 to signal this is a minor page fault because no major work had to be done for this fault because it was all done by the winner of the race.

1305 Updates the MMU cache for architectures that require it.

1306-1307 Releases the `mm_struct` lock and returns 2 to signal this is a major page fault.

D.5.4.2   Function: `do_anonymous_page()`   *(mm/memory.c)*

This function allocates a new page for a process accessing a page for the first time. If it is a read access, a systemwide page containing only zeros is mapped into the process. If it is write, a zero-filled page is allocated and placed within the pagetables.

```
1190 static int do_anonymous_page(struct mm_struct * mm,
                struct vm_area_struct * vma,
                pte_t *page_table, int write_access,
                unsigned long addr)
```

```
1191 {
1192     pte_t entry;
1193
1194     /* Read-only mapping of ZERO_PAGE. */
1195     entry = pte_wrprotect(mk_pte(ZERO_PAGE(addr),
                          vma->vm_page_prot));
1196
1197     /* ..except if it's a write access */
1198     if (write_access) {
1199         struct page *page;
1200
1201         /* Allocate our own private page. */
1202         spin_unlock(&mm->page_table_lock);
1203
1204         page = alloc_page(GFP_HIGHUSER);
1205         if (!page)
1206             goto no_mem;
1207         clear_user_highpage(page, addr);
1208
1209         spin_lock(&mm->page_table_lock);
1210         if (!pte_none(*page_table)) {
1211             page_cache_release(page);
1212             spin_unlock(&mm->page_table_lock);
1213             return 1;
1214         }
1215         mm->rss++;
1216         flush_page_to_ram(page);
1217         entry = pte_mkwrite(
                    pte_mkdirty(mk_pte(page, vma->vm_page_prot)));
1218         lru_cache_add(page);
1219         mark_page_accessed(page);
1220     }
1221
1222     set_pte(page_table, entry);
1223
1224     /* No need to invalidate - it was non-present before */
1225     update_mmu_cache(vma, addr, entry);
1226     spin_unlock(&mm->page_table_lock);
1227     return 1;      /* Minor fault */
1228
1229 no_mem:
1230     return -1;
1231 }
```

1190 The parameters are the same as those passed to handle_pte_fault()
(See Section D.5.3.2).

1195 For read accesses, this simply maps the systemwide `empty_zero_page`, which the `ZERO_PAGE()` macro returns with the given permissions. The page is write protected so that a write to the page will result in a page fault.

1198-1220 If this is a write fault, it allocates a new page and zero-fills it.

1202 Unlocks the `mm_struct` so the allocation of a new page could sleep.

1204 Allocates a new page.

1205 If a page could not be allocated, this returns -1 to handle the OOM situation.

1207 Zero-fills the page.

1209 Reacquires the lock because the pagetables are to be updated.

1215 Updates the RSS for the process. Note that the RSS is not updated if it is the global zero page being mapped as is the case with the read-only fault at line 1195.

1216 Ensures the cache is coherent.

1217 Marks the PTE writable and dirty because it has been written to.

1218 Adds the page to the LRU list so that it may be reclaimed by the swapper later.

1219 Marks the page accessed, which ensures the page is marked hot and on the top of the active list.

1222 Fixes the PTE in the pagetables for this process.

1225 Updates the MMU cache if the architecture needs it.

1226 Frees the pagetable lock.

1227 Returns as a minor fault. Even though it is possible the page allocator spent time writing out pages, data did not have to be read from disk to fill this page.

D.5.5   Demand Paging

D.5.5.1   Function: `do_swap_page()`   *(mm/memory.c)*

The call graph for this function is shown in Figure 4.15. This function handles the case where a page has been swapped out. A swapped-out page may exist in the swap cache if it is shared between a number of processes or recently swapped in during readahead. This function is broken up into three parts:

- Search for the page in swap cache.

- If it does not exist, call `swapin_readahead()` to read in the page.

- Insert the page into the process pagetables.

```
1117 static int do_swap_page(struct mm_struct * mm,
1118     struct vm_area_struct * vma, unsigned long address,
1119     pte_t * page_table, pte_t orig_pte, int write_access)
1120 {
1121     struct page *page;
1122     swp_entry_t entry = pte_to_swp_entry(orig_pte);
1123     pte_t pte;
1124     int ret = 1;
1125
1126     spin_unlock(&mm->page_table_lock);
1127     page = lookup_swap_cache(entry);
```

This block is a function preamble. It checks for the page in the swap cache.

1117-1119 The parameters are the same as those supplied to `handle_pte_fault()` (See Section D.5.3.2).

1122 Gets the swap entry information from the PTE.

1126 Frees the `mm_struct` spinlock.

1127 Looks up the page in the swap cache.

```
1128     if (!page) {
1129         swapin_readahead(entry);
1130         page = read_swap_cache_async(entry);
1131         if (!page) {
1136             int retval;
1137             spin_lock(&mm->page_table_lock);
1138             retval = pte_same(*page_table, orig_pte) ? -1 : 1;
1139             spin_unlock(&mm->page_table_lock);
1140             return retval;
1141         }
1142
1143         /* Had to read the page from swap area: Major fault */
1144         ret = 2;
1145     }
```

If the page did not exist in the swap cache, then this block reads it from backing storage with `swapin_readhead()`, which reads in the requested pages and a number of pages after it. After it completes, `read_swap_cache_async()` should be able to return the page.

1128-1145 This block is executed if the page was not in the swap cache.

1129 `swapin_readahead()`(See Section D.6.6.1) reads in the requested page and a number of pages after it. The number of pages read in is determined by the `page_cluster` variable in `mm/swap.c`, which is initialized to 2 on machines with less than 16MiB of memory and 3 otherwise. $2^{\text{page\_cluster}}$ pages are read in after the requested page unless a bad or empty page entry is encountered.

1130 `read_swap_cache_async()` (See Section K.3.1.1) will look up the requested page and read it from disk if necessary.

1131-1141 If the page does not exist, there was another fault that swapped in this page and removed it from the cache while spinlocks were dropped.

1137 Locks the `mm_struct`.

1138 Compares the two PTEs. If they do not match, -1 is returned to signal an I/O error. If not, 1 is returned to mark a minor page fault because a disk access was not required for this particular page.

1139-1140 Frees the `mm_struct` and returns the status.

1144 The disk had to be accessed to mark that this is a major page fault.

```
1147      mark_page_accessed(page);
1148
1149      lock_page(page);
1150
1151      /*
1152       * Back out if somebody else faulted in this pte while we
1153       * released the page table lock.
1154       */
1155      spin_lock(&mm->page_table_lock);
1156      if (!pte_same(*page_table, orig_pte)) {
1157          spin_unlock(&mm->page_table_lock);
1158          unlock_page(page);
1159          page_cache_release(page);
1160          return 1;
1161      }
1162
1163      /* The page isn't present yet, go ahead with the fault. */
1164
1165      swap_free(entry);
1166      if (vm_swap_full())
1167          remove_exclusive_swap_page(page);
1168
1169      mm->rss++;
1170      pte = mk_pte(page, vma->vm_page_prot);
1171      if (write_access && can_share_swap_page(page))
1172          pte = pte_mkdirty(pte_mkwrite(pte));
1173      unlock_page(page);
1174
```

```
1175        flush_page_to_ram(page);
1176        flush_icache_page(vma, page);
1177        set_pte(page_table, pte);
1178
1179        /* No need to invalidate - it was non-present before */
1180        update_mmu_cache(vma, address, pte);
1181        spin_unlock(&mm->page_table_lock);
1182        return ret;
1183 }
```

This block places the page in the process pagetables.

1147 mark_page_accessed()(See Section J.2.3.1) will mark the page as active so that it will be moved to the top of the active LRU list.

1149 Locks the page, which has the side effect of waiting for the I/O swapping in the page to complete.

1155-1161 If someone else faulted in the page before we could, the reference to the page is dropped, the lock is freed and this returns that this was a minor fault.

1165 The function swap_free()(See Section K.2.2.1) reduces the reference to a swap entry. If it drops to 0, it is actually freed.

1166-1167 Page slots in swap space are reserved for the same page after they have been swapped out to avoid having to search for a free slot each time. If the swap space is full, though, the reservation is broken, and the slot freed up for another page.

1169 The page is now going to be used, so this increments the mm_structs RSS count.

1170 Makes a PTE for this page.

1171 If the page is being written to and is not shared between more than one process, this marks it dirty so that it will be kept in sync with the backing storage and swap cache for other processes.

1173 Unlocks the page.

1175 As the page is about to be mapped to the process space, it is possible for some architectures that write to the page in kernel space that it will not be visible to the process. flush_page_to_ram() ensures the cache will be coherent.

1176 flush_icache_page() is similar in principle except it ensures the icache and dcaches are coherent.

1177 Sets the PTE in the process pagetables.

1180 Updates the MMU cache if the architecture requires it.

Process Address Space

1181-1182 Unlocks the `mm_struct` and returns whether it was a minor or major page fault.

D.5.5.2   **Function:** `can_share_swap_page()`   *(mm/swapfile.c)*

This function determines if the swap cache entry for this page may be used or not. It may be used if there is no other references to it. Most of the work is performed by `exclusive_swap_page()`, but this function first makes a few basic checks to avoid having to acquire too many locks.

```
259 int can_share_swap_page(struct page *page)
260 {
261     int retval = 0;
262
263     if (!PageLocked(page))
264         BUG();
265     switch (page_count(page)) {
266     case 3:
267         if (!page->buffers)
268             break;
269         /* Fallthrough */
270     case 2:
271         if (!PageSwapCache(page))
272             break;
273         retval = exclusive_swap_page(page);
274         break;
275     case 1:
276         if (PageReserved(page))
277             break;
278         retval = 1;
279     }
280     return retval;
281 }
```

263-264 This function is called from the fault path, and the page must be locked.

265 Switch is based on the number of references.

266-268 If the count is 3, but there are no buffers associated with it, there is more than one process using the page. Buffers may be associated for just one process if the page is backed by a swap file instead of a partition.

270-273 If the count is only two, but it is not a member of the swap cache, then it has no slot that may be shared, so it returns false. Otherwise, it performs a full check with `exclusive_swap_page()` (See Section D.5.5.3).

276-277 If the page is reserved, it is the global `ZERO_PAGE`, so it cannot be shared. Otherwise, this page is definitely the only one.

D.5.5.3   Function: `exclusive_swap_page()`   *(mm/swapfile.c)*

This function checks if the process is the only user of a locked swap page.

```
229 static int exclusive_swap_page(struct page *page)
230 {
231     int retval = 0;
232     struct swap_info_struct * p;
233     swp_entry_t entry;
234
235     entry.val = page->index;
236     p = swap_info_get(entry);
237     if (p) {
238         /* Is the only swap cache user the cache itself? */
239         if (p->swap_map[SWP_OFFSET(entry)] == 1) {
240             /* Recheck the page count with the pagecache
                 * lock held.. */
241             spin_lock(&pagecache_lock);
242             if (page_count(page) - !!page->buffers == 2)
243                 retval = 1;
244             spin_unlock(&pagecache_lock);
245         }
246         swap_info_put(p);
247     }
248     return retval;
249 }
```

231 By default, this returns false.

235 The `swp_entry_t` for the page is stored in **page→index** as explained in Section 2.5.

236 Gets the `swap_info_struct` with `swap_info_get()`(See Section K.2.3.1).

237-247 If a slot exists, this checks if we are the exclusive user and returns true if we are.

239 Checks if the slot is only being used by the cache itself. If it is, the page count needs to be checked again with the `pagecache_lock` held.

242-243 `!!page→buffers` will evaluate to 1 if there buffers are present, so this block effectively checks if the process is the only user of the page. If it is, `retval` is set to 1 so that true will be returned.

246 Drops the reference to the slot that was taken with `swap_info_get()` (See Section K.2.3.1).

D.5.6   Copy On Write (COW) Pages

D.5.6.1   Function: do_wp_page()   *(mm/memory.c)*

The call graph for this function is shown in Figure 4.16. This function handles the case where a user tries to write to a private page shared among processes, such as what happens after fork(). Basically what happens is a page is allocated, the contents are copied to the new page and the shared count is decremented in the old page.

```
948 static int do_wp_page(struct mm_struct *mm,
            struct vm_area_struct * vma,
949         unsigned long address, pte_t *page_table, pte_t pte)
950 {
951     struct page *old_page, *new_page;
952
953     old_page = pte_page(pte);
954     if (!VALID_PAGE(old_page))
955         goto bad_wp_page;
956
```

948-950 The parameters are the same as those supplied to handle_pte_fault().

953-955 Gets a reference to the current page in the PTE and makes sure it is valid.

```
957     if (!TryLockPage(old_page)) {
958         int reuse = can_share_swap_page(old_page);
959         unlock_page(old_page);
960         if (reuse) {
961             flush_cache_page(vma, address);
962             establish_pte(vma, address, page_table,
                        pte_mkyoung(pte_mkdirty(pte_mkwrite(pte))));
963             spin_unlock(&mm->page_table_lock);
964             return 1;        /* Minor fault */
965         }
966     }
```

957 First tries to lock the page. If 0 is returned, it means the page was previously unlocked.

958 If we managed to lock it, this calls can_share_swap_page() (See Section D.5.5.2) to see if we are the exclusive user of the swap slot for this page. If we are, it means that we are the last process to break COW and that we can simply use this page rather than allocating a new one.

960-965 If we are the only users of the swap slot, it means we are the only user of this page and are the last process to break COW. Therefore, the PTE is simply re-established, and we return a minor fault.

```
968      /*
969       * Ok, we need to copy. Oh, well..
970       */
971      page_cache_get(old_page);
972      spin_unlock(&mm->page_table_lock);
973
974      new_page = alloc_page(GFP_HIGHUSER);
975      if (!new_page)
976          goto no_mem;
977      copy_cow_page(old_page,new_page,address);
978
```

971 We need to copy this page, so it first gets a reference to the old page so that it doesn't disappear before we are finished with it.

972 Unlocks the spinlock as we are about to call `alloc_page()` (See Section F.2.1), which may sleep.

974-976 Allocates a page and makes sure one was returned.

977 No prizes for guessing what this function does. If the page being broken is the global zero page, `clear_user_highpage()` will be used to zero out the contents of the page. Otherwise, `copy_user_highpage()` copies the actual contents.

```
982      spin_lock(&mm->page_table_lock);
983      if (pte_same(*page_table, pte)) {
984          if (PageReserved(old_page))
985              ++mm->rss;
986          break_cow(vma, new_page, address, page_table);
987          lru_cache_add(new_page);
988
989          /* Free the old page.. */
990          new_page = old_page;
991      }
992      spin_unlock(&mm->page_table_lock);
993      page_cache_release(new_page);
994      page_cache_release(old_page);
995      return 1;        /* Minor fault */
```

982 The pagetable lock was released for `alloc_page()`(See Section F.2.1), so this reacquires it.

983 Makes sure the PTE has not changed in the meantime, which could have happened if another fault occured while the spinlock was released.

984-985 The RSS is only updated if `PageReserved()` is true, which will only happen if the page being faulted is the global `ZERO_PAGE`, which is not accounted for in the RSS. If this was a normal page, the process would be using the same number of physical frames after the fault as it was before, but, against the zero page, it will be using a new frame, so `rss++` reflects the use of a new page.

986 `break_cow()` is responsible for calling the architecture hooks to ensure the CPU cache and TLBs are up to date and then establishes the new page into the PTE. It first calls `flush_page_to_ram()`, which must be called when a `struct page` is about to be placed in userspace. Next is `flush_cache_page()`, which flushes the page from the CPU cache. Last is `establish_pte()`, which establishes the new page into the PTE.

987 Adds the page to the LRU lists.

992 Releases the spinlock.

993-994 Drops the references to the pages.

995 Returns a minor fault.

```
996
997 bad_wp_page:
998     spin_unlock(&mm->page_table_lock);
999     printk("do_wp_page: bogus page at address %08lx (page 0x%lx)\n",
                    address,(unsigned long)old_page);
1000    return -1;
1001 no_mem:
1002    page_cache_release(old_page);
1003    return -1;
1004 }
```

997-1000 This is a false COW break, which will only happen with a buggy kernel. It prints out an informational message and returns.

1001-1003 The page allocation failed, so this releases the reference to the old page and returns -1.

D.6   Page-Related Disk I/O

Contents

D.6.1   Generic File Reading

This is more the domain of the I/O manager than the VM, but, because it performs the operations through the page cache, we will cover it briefly. The operation of `generic_file_write()` is essentially the same, although it is not covered by this book. However, if you understand how the read takes place, the write function will pose no problem to you.

D.6.1.1   Function: `generic_file_read()`   *(mm/filemap.c)*

This is the generic file read function used by any filesystem that reads pages through the page cache. For normal I/O, it is responsible for building a `read_descriptor_t` for use with `do_generic_file_read()` and `file_read_actor()`. For direct I/O, this function is basically a wrapper around `generic_file_direct_IO()`.

```
1695 ssize_t generic_file_read(struct file * filp,
                        char * buf, size_t count,
                        loff_t *ppos)
```

```
1696 {
1697     ssize_t retval;
1698
1699     if ((ssize_t) count < 0)
1700         return -EINVAL;
1701
1702     if (filp->f_flags & O_DIRECT)
1703         goto o_direct;
1704
1705     retval = -EFAULT;
1706     if (access_ok(VERIFY_WRITE, buf, count)) {
1707         retval = 0;
1708
1709         if (count) {
1710             read_descriptor_t desc;
1711
1712             desc.written = 0;
1713             desc.count = count;
1714             desc.buf = buf;
1715             desc.error = 0;
1716             do_generic_file_read(filp, ppos, &desc,
1717                              file_read_actor);
1718
1719             retval = desc.written;
1720             if (!retval)
1721                 retval = desc.error;
1722         }
1723     }
1724 out:
     return retval;
```

This block is concerned with normal file I/O.

1702-1703 If this is direct I/O, it jumps to the o_direct label.

1706 If the access permissions to write to a userspace page are ok, then this proceeds.

1709 If the count is 0, there is no I/O to perform.

1712-1715 Populates a read_descriptor_t structure, which will be used by file_read_actor()(See Section L.3.2.3).

1716 Performs the file read.

1718 Extracts the number of bytes written from the read descriptor struct.

1719-1720 If an error occured, this extracts what the error was.

1724 Returns either the number of bytes read or the error that occured.

```
1725
1726  o_direct:
1727      {
1728          loff_t pos = *ppos, size;
1729          struct address_space *mapping =
                                      filp->f_dentry->d_inode->i_mapping;
1730          struct inode *inode = mapping->host;
1731
1732          retval = 0;
1733          if (!count)
1734              goto out; /* skip atime */
1735          down_read(&inode->i_alloc_sem);
1736          down(&inode->i_sem);
1737          size = inode->i_size;
1738          if (pos < size) {
1739              retval = generic_file_direct_IO(READ, filp, buf,
                                                  count, pos);
1740              if (retval > 0)
1741                  *ppos = pos + retval;
1742          }
1743          UPDATE_ATIME(filp->f_dentry->d_inode);
1744          goto out;
1745      }
1746  }
```

This block is concerned with direct I/O. It is largely responsible for extracting the parameters required for `generic_file_direct_IO()`.

1729 Gets the `address_space` used by this `struct file`.

1733-1734 If no I/O has been requested, this jumps `out` to avoid updating the inodes' access time.

1737 Gets the size of the file.

1738-1739 If the current position is before the end of the file, the read is safe, so this calls `generic_file_direct_IO()`.

1740-1741 If the read was successful, this updates the current position in the file for the reader.

1743 Updates the access time.

1744 Goto out, which just returns `retval`.

Process Address Space

D.6.1.2 Function: `do_generic_file_read()` *(mm/filemap.c)*

This is the core part of the generic file read operation. It is responsible for allocating a page if it doesn't already exist in the page cache. If it does, it must make sure the page is up to date, and it is responsible for making sure that the appropriate readahead window is set.

```
1349 void do_generic_file_read(struct file * filp,
                               loff_t *ppos,
                               read_descriptor_t * desc,
                               read_actor_t actor)
1350 {
1351     struct address_space *mapping =
                                   filp->f_dentry->d_inode->i_mapping;
1352     struct inode *inode = mapping->host;
1353     unsigned long index, offset;
1354     struct page *cached_page;
1355     int reada_ok;
1356     int error;
1357     int max_readahead = get_max_readahead(inode);
1358
1359     cached_page = NULL;
1360     index = *ppos >> PAGE_CACHE_SHIFT;
1361     offset = *ppos & ~PAGE_CACHE_MASK;
1362
```

1357 Gets the maximum readahead window size for this block device.

1360 Calculates the page index, which holds the current file position pointer.

1361 Calculates the offset within the page that holds the current file position pointer.

```
1363 /*
1364  * If the current position is outside the previous read-ahead
1365  * window, we reset the current read-ahead context and set read
1366  * ahead max to zero (will be set to just needed value later),
1367  * otherwise, we assume that the file accesses are sequential
1368  * enough to continue read-ahead.
1369  */
1370     if (index > filp->f_raend ||
                index + filp->f_rawin < filp->f_raend) {
1371         reada_ok = 0;
1372         filp->f_raend = 0;
1373         filp->f_ralen = 0;
1374         filp->f_ramax = 0;
1375         filp->f_rawin = 0;
1376     } else {
```

```
1377            reada_ok = 1;
1378        }
1379 /*
1380  * Adjust the current value of read-ahead max.
1381  * If the read operation stay in the first half page, force no
1382  * readahead. Otherwise try to increase read ahead max just
      * enough to do the read request.
1383  * Then, at least MIN_READAHEAD if read ahead is ok,
1384  * and at most MAX_READAHEAD in all cases.
1385  */
1386     if (!index && offset + desc->count <= (PAGE_CACHE_SIZE >> 1)) {
1387         filp->f_ramax = 0;
1388     } else {
1389         unsigned long needed;
1390
1391         needed = ((offset + desc->count) >> PAGE_CACHE_SHIFT) + 1;
1392
1393         if (filp->f_ramax < needed)
1394             filp->f_ramax = needed;
1395
1396         if (reada_ok && filp->f_ramax < vm_min_readahead)
1397             filp->f_ramax = vm_min_readahead;
1398         if (filp->f_ramax > max_readahead)
1399             filp->f_ramax = max_readahead;
1400     }
```

1370-1378 As the comment suggests, the readahead window gets reset if the current file position is outside the current readahead window. It gets reset to 0 here and adjusted by `generic_file_readahead()`(See Section D.6.1.3) as necessary.

1386-1400 As the comment states, the readahead window gets adjusted slightly if we are in the second half of the current page.

```
1402     for (;;) {
1403         struct page *page, **hash;
1404         unsigned long end_index, nr, ret;
1405
1406         end_index = inode->i_size >> PAGE_CACHE_SHIFT;
1407
1408         if (index > end_index)
1409             break;
1410         nr = PAGE_CACHE_SIZE;
1411         if (index == end_index) {
1412             nr = inode->i_size & ~PAGE_CACHE_MASK;
1413             if (nr <= offset)
1414                 break;
```

```
1415            }
1416
1417            nr = nr - offset;
1418
1419            /*
1420             * Try to find the data in the page cache..
1421             */
1422            hash = page_hash(mapping, index);
1423
1424            spin_lock(&pagecache_lock);
1425            page = __find_page_nolock(mapping, index, *hash);
1426            if (!page)
1427                goto no_cached_page;
```

1402 This loop goes through each of the pages necessary to satisfy the read request.

1406 Calculates where the end of the file is in pages.

1408-1409 If the current index is beyond the end, then this breaks out because we are trying to read beyond the end of the file.

1410-1417 Calculates **nr** to be the number of bytes remaining to be read in the current page. The block takes into account that this might be the last page used by the file and where the current file position is within the page.

1422-1425 Searches for the page in the page cache.

1426-1427 If the page is not in the page cache, goto no_cached_page where it will be allocated.

```
1428 found_page:
1429            page_cache_get(page);
1430            spin_unlock(&pagecache_lock);
1431
1432            if (!Page_Uptodate(page))
1433                goto page_not_up_to_date;
1434            generic_file_readahead(reada_ok, filp, inode, page);
```

In this block, the page was found in the page cache.

1429 Takes a reference to the page in the page cache so it does not get freed prematurely.

1432-1433 If the page is not up to date, goto page_not_up_to_date to update the page with information on the disk.

1434 Performs file readahead with generic_file_readahead() (See Section D.6.1.3).

```
1435 page_ok:
1436          /* If users can be writing to this page using arbitrary
1437           * virtual addresses, take care about potential aliasing
1438           * before reading the page on the kernel side.
1439           */
1440          if (mapping->i_mmap_shared != NULL)
1441              flush_dcache_page(page);
1442
1443          /*
1444           * Mark the page accessed if we read the
1445           * beginning or we just did an lseek.
1446           */
1447          if (!offset || !filp->f_reada)
1448              mark_page_accessed(page);
1449
1450          /*
1451           * Ok, we have the page, and it's up-to-date, so
1452           * now we can copy it to user space...
1453           *
1454           * The actor routine returns how many bytes were actually
1455           * used.. NOTE! This may not be the same as how much of a
1456           * user buffer we filled up (we may be padding etc), so we
1457           * can only update "pos" here (the actor routine has to
1458           * update the user buffer pointers and the remaining count).
1459           */
1460          ret = actor(desc, page, offset, nr);
1461          offset += ret;
1462          index += offset >> PAGE_CACHE_SHIFT;
1463          offset &= ~PAGE_CACHE_MASK;
1464
1465          page_cache_release(page);
1466          if (ret == nr && desc->count)
1467              continue;
1468          break;
```

In this block, the page is present in the page cache and ready to be read by the file read actor function.

1440-1441 Because other users could be writing this page, call `flush_dcache_page()` to make sure the changes are visible.

1447-1448 Because the page has just been accessed, call `mark_page_accessed()` (See Section J.2.3.1) to move it to the `active_list`.

1460 Calls the actor function. In this case, the actor function is `file_read_actor()` (See Section L.3.2.3), which is responsible for copying the bytes from the page to userspace.

Process Address Space

1461 Updates the current offset within the file.

1462 Moves to the next page if necessary.

1463 Updates the offset within the page we are currently reading. Remember that we could have just crossed into the next page in the file.

1465 Releases our reference to this page.

1466-1468 If there is still data to be read, this loops again to read the next page. Otherwise, it breaks because the read operation is complete.

```
1470 /*
1471  * Ok, the page was not immediately readable, so let's try to
       * read ahead while we're at it..
1472  */
1473 page_not_up_to_date:
1474         generic_file_readahead(reada_ok, filp, inode, page);
1475
1476         if (Page_Uptodate(page))
1477             goto page_ok;
1478
1479         /* Get exclusive access to the page ... */
1480         lock_page(page);
1481
1482         /* Did it get unhashed before we got the lock? */
1483         if (!page->mapping) {
1484             UnlockPage(page);
1485             page_cache_release(page);
1486             continue;
1487         }
1488
1489         /* Did somebody else fill it already? */
1490         if (Page_Uptodate(page)) {
1491             UnlockPage(page);
1492             goto page_ok;
1493         }
```

In this block, the page being read was not up to date with information on the disk. `generic_file_readahead()` is called to update the current page and readahead because I/O is required anyway.

1474 Calls `generic_file_readahead()` (See Section D.6.1.3) to sync the current page and readahead if necessary.

1476-1477 If the page is now up to date, goto `page_ok` to start copying the bytes to userspace.

1480 Otherwise, something happened with readahead, so this locks the page for exclusive access.

1483-1487 If the page was somehow removed from the page cache while spinlocks were not held, then this releases the reference to the page and starts all over again. The second time around, the page will get allocated and inserted into the page cache all over again.

1490-1493 If someone updated the page while we did not have a lock on the page, then unlock it again and goto page_ok to copy the bytes to userspace.

```
1495 readpage:
1496          /* ... and start the actual read. The read will
                * unlock the page. */
1497          error = mapping->a_ops->readpage(filp, page);
1498
1499          if (!error) {
1500              if (Page_Uptodate(page))
1501                  goto page_ok;
1502
1503              /* Again, try some read-ahead while waiting for
                    * the page to finish.. */
1504              generic_file_readahead(reada_ok, filp, inode, page);
1505              wait_on_page(page);
1506              if (Page_Uptodate(page))
1507                  goto page_ok;
1508              error = -EIO;
1509          }
1510
1511          /* UHHUH! A synchronous read error occurred. Report it */
1512          desc->error = error;
1513          page_cache_release(page);
1514          break;
```

At this block, readahead failed to synchronously read the page with the address_space supplied readpage() function.

1497 Calls the address_space filesystem-specific readpage() function. In many cases, this will ultimately call the function block_read_full_page() declared in fs/buffer.c().

1499-1501 If no error occurred and the page is now up to date, goto page_ok to begin copying the bytes to userspace.

1504 Otherwise, it schedules some readahead to occur because we are forced to wait on I/O anyway.

1505-1507 Waits for I/O on the requested page to complete. If it finished successfully, then goto page_ok.

Process Address
Space

1508 Otherwise, an error occured, so this sets -EIO to be returned to userspace.

1512-1514 An I/O error occured, so this records it and releases the reference to the current page. This error will be picked up from the read_descriptor_t struct by generic_file_read() (See Section D.6.1.1).

```
1516  no_cached_page:
1517        /*
1518         * Ok, it wasn't cached, so we need to create a new
1519         * page..
1520         *
1521         * We get here with the page cache lock held.
1522         */
1523        if (!cached_page) {
1524            spin_unlock(&pagecache_lock);
1525            cached_page = page_cache_alloc(mapping);
1526            if (!cached_page) {
1527                desc->error = -ENOMEM;
1528                break;
1529            }
1530
1531            /*
1532             * Somebody may have added the page while we
1533             * dropped the page cache lock. Check for that.
1534             */
1535            spin_lock(&pagecache_lock);
1536            page = __find_page_nolock(mapping, index, *hash);
1537            if (page)
1538                goto found_page;
1539        }
1540
1541        /*
1542         * Ok, add the new page to the hash-queues...
1543         */
1544        page = cached_page;
1545        __add_to_page_cache(page, mapping, index, hash);
1546        spin_unlock(&pagecache_lock);
1547        lru_cache_add(page);
1548        cached_page = NULL;
1549
1550        goto readpage;
1551    }
```

In this block, the page does not exist in the page cache, so it allocates one and adds it.

1523-1539 If a cache page has not already been allocated, then allocate one and make sure that someone else did not insert one into the page cache while we were sleeping.

1524 Releases `pagecache_lock` because `page_cache_alloc()` may sleep.

1525-1529 Allocates a page and sets `-ENOMEM` to be returned if the allocation failed.

1535-1536 Acquires `pagecache_lock` again and searches the page cache to make sure another process has not inserted it while the lock was dropped.

1537 If another process added a suitable page to the cache already, this jumps to `found_page` because the one we just allocated is no longer necessary.

1544-1545 Otherwise, this adds the page we just allocated to the page cache.

1547 Adds the page to the LRU lists.

1548 Sets `cached_page` to NULL because it is now in use.

1550 Goto `readpage` to schedule the page to be read from disk.

```
1552
1553        *ppos = ((loff_t) index << PAGE_CACHE_SHIFT) + offset;
1554        filp->f_reada = 1;
1555        if (cached_page)
1556            page_cache_release(cached_page);
1557        UPDATE_ATIME(inode);
1558 }
```

1553 Updates our position within the file.

1555-1556 If a page was allocated for addition to the page cache and then found to be unneeded, it is released it here.

1557 Updates the access time to the file.

D.6.1.3 Function: `generic_file_readahead()` *(mm/filemap.c)*

This function performs generic file readahead. Readahead is one of the few areas that is very heavily commented upon in the code. It is highly recommended that you read the comments in `mm/filemap.c` marked with "Read-ahead context."

```
1222 static void generic_file_readahead(int reada_ok,
1223        struct file * filp, struct inode * inode,
1224        struct page * page)
1225 {
1226        unsigned long end_index;
1227        unsigned long index = page->index;
1228        unsigned long max_ahead, ahead;
1229        unsigned long raend;
```

```
1230        int max_readahead = get_max_readahead(inode);
1231
1232        end_index = inode->i_size >> PAGE_CACHE_SHIFT;
1233
1234        raend = filp->f_raend;
1235        max_ahead = 0;
```

1227 Gets the index to start from based on the supplied **page**.

1230 Gets the maximum-sized readahead for this block device.

1232 Gets the index, in pages, of the end of the file.

1234 Gets the end of the readahead window from the **struct file**.

```
1236
1237 /*
1238  * The current page is locked.
1239  * If the current position is inside the previous read IO request,
1240  * do not try to reread previously read ahead pages.
1241  * Otherwise decide or not to read ahead some pages synchronously.
1242  * If we are not going to read ahead, set the read ahead context
1243  * for this page only.
1244  */
1245     if (PageLocked(page)) {
1246         if (!filp->f_ralen ||
                    index >= raend ||
                    index + filp->f_rawin < raend) {
1247             raend = index;
1248             if (raend < end_index)
1249                 max_ahead = filp->f_ramax;
1250             filp->f_rawin = 0;
1251             filp->f_ralen = 1;
1252             if (!max_ahead) {
1253                 filp->f_raend  = index + filp->f_ralen;
1254                 filp->f_rawin += filp->f_ralen;
1255             }
1256         }
1257     }
```

This block has encountered a page that is locked, so it must decide whether to temporarily disable readahead.

1245 If the current page is locked for I/O, then check if the current page is within the last readahead window. If it is, there is no point trying to readahead again. If it is not or readahead has not been performed previously, update the readahead context.

1246 The first check is if readahead has been performed previously. The second
is to see if the current locked page is after where the the previous readahead
finished. The third check is if the current locked page is within the current
readahead window.

1247 Updates the end of the readahead window.

1248-1249 If the end of the readahead window is not after the end of the file, this
sets `max_ahead` to be the maximum amount of readahead that should be used
with this `struct file(filp→f_ramax)`.

1250-1255 Sets readahead to only occur with the current page, effectively dis-
abling readahead.

```
1258 /*
1259  * The current page is not locked.
1260  * If we were reading ahead and,
1261  * if the current max read ahead size is not zero and,
1262  * if the current position is inside the last read-ahead IO
1263  * request, it is the moment to try to read ahead asynchronously.
1264  * We will later force unplug device in order to force
      * asynchronous read IO.
1265  */
1266     else if (reada_ok && filp->f_ramax && raend >= 1 &&
1267           index <= raend && index + filp->f_ralen >= raend) {
1268 /*
1269  * Add ONE page to max_ahead in order to try to have about the
1270  * same IO maxsize as synchronous read-ahead
      * (MAX_READAHEAD + 1)*PAGE_CACHE_SIZE.
1271  * Compute the position of the last page we have tried to read
1272  * in order to begin to read ahead just at the next page.
1273  */
1274         raend -= 1;
1275         if (raend < end_index)
1276             max_ahead = filp->f_ramax + 1;
1277
1278         if (max_ahead) {
1279             filp->f_rawin = filp->f_ralen;
1280             filp->f_ralen = 0;
1281             reada_ok     = 2;
1282         }
1283     }
```

This is one of the rare cases where the in-code commentary makes the code as
clear as it possibly could be. Basically, it is saying that if the current page is not
locked for I/O, then it extends the readahead window slightly and remembers that
readahead is currently going well.

```
1284 /*
1285  * Try to read ahead pages.
1286  * We hope that ll_rw_blk() plug/unplug, coalescence, requests
1287  * sort and the scheduler, will work enough for us to avoid too
      * bad actuals IO requests.
1288  */
1289     ahead = 0;
1290     while (ahead < max_ahead) {
1291         ahead ++;
1292         if ((raend + ahead) >= end_index)
1293             break;
1294         if (page_cache_read(filp, raend + ahead) < 0)
1295             break;
1296     }
```

This block performs the actual readahead by calling `page_cache_read()` for each of the pages in the readahead window. Note here how `ahead` is incremented for each page that is readahead.

```
1297 /*
1298  * If we tried to read ahead some pages,
1299  * If we tried to read ahead asynchronously,
1300  *   Try to force unplug of the device in order to start an
1301  *   asynchronous read IO request.
1302  * Update the read-ahead context.
1303  * Store the length of the current read-ahead window.
1304  * Double the current max read ahead size.
1305  *   That heuristic avoid to do some large IO for files that are
1306  *   not really accessed sequentially.
1307  */
1308     if (ahead) {
1309         filp->f_ralen += ahead;
1310         filp->f_rawin += filp->f_ralen;
1311         filp->f_raend = raend + ahead + 1;
1312
1313         filp->f_ramax += filp->f_ramax;
1314
1315         if (filp->f_ramax > max_readahead)
1316             filp->f_ramax = max_readahead;
1317
1318 #ifdef PROFILE_READAHEAD
1319         profile_readahead((reada_ok == 2), filp);
1320 #endif
1321     }
1322
1323     return;
1324 }
```

If readahead was successful, then this updates the readahead fields in the `struct file` to mark the progress. This is basically growing the readahead context, but can be reset by `do_generic_file_readahead()` if it is found that the readahead is ineffective.

1309 Updates the `f_ralen` with the number of pages that were readahead in this pass.

1310 Updates the size of the readahead window.

1311 Marks the end of the readahead.

1313 Doubles the current maximum-sized readahead.

1315-1316 Do not let the maximum-sized readahead get larger than the maximum readahead defined for this block device.

D.6.2   Generic File mmap()

D.6.2.1   Function: `generic_file_mmap()`   *(mm/filemap.c)*

This is the generic `mmap()` function used by many `struct files` as their `struct file_operations`. It is mainly responsible for ensuring the appropriate `address_space` functions exist and for setting what VMA operations to use.

```
2249 int generic_file_mmap(struct file * file,
                             struct vm_area_struct * vma)
2250 {
2251     struct address_space *mapping =
                             file->f_dentry->d_inode->i_mapping;
2252     struct inode *inode = mapping->host;
2253
2254     if ((vma->vm_flags & VM_SHARED) &&
             (vma->vm_flags & VM_MAYWRITE)) {
2255         if (!mapping->a_ops->writepage)
2256             return -EINVAL;
2257     }
2258     if (!mapping->a_ops->readpage)
2259         return -ENOEXEC;
2260     UPDATE_ATIME(inode);
2261     vma->vm_ops = &generic_file_vm_ops;
2262     return 0;
2263 }
```

2251 Gets the `address_space` that is managing the file being mapped.

2252 Gets the `struct inode` for this `address_space`.

2254-2257 If the VMA is to be shared and writable, this makes sure an `a_ops→writepage()` function exists. It returns `-EINVAL` if it does not.

2258-2259 Makes sure an a_ops→readpage() function exists.

2260 Updates the access time for the inode.

2261 Uses generic_file_vm_ops for the file operations. The generic VM operations structure, defined in mm/filemap.c, only supplies filemap_nopage() (See Section D.6.4.1) as its nopage() function. No other callback is defined.

D.6.3   Generic File Truncation

This section covers the path where a file is being truncated. The actual system call truncate() is implemented by sys_truncate() in fs/open.c. By the time the top-level function in the VM is called (vmtruncate()), the dentry information for the file has been updated, and the inode's semaphore has been acquired.

D.6.3.1   Function: vmtruncate()   *(mm/memory.c)*

This is the top-level VM function responsible for truncating a file. When it completes, all pagetable entries mapping pages that have been truncated have been unmapped and reclaimed if possible.

```
1042 int vmtruncate(struct inode * inode, loff_t offset)
1043 {
1044     unsigned long pgoff;
1045     struct address_space *mapping = inode->i_mapping;
1046     unsigned long limit;
1047
1048     if (inode->i_size < offset)
1049         goto do_expand;
1050     inode->i_size = offset;
1051     spin_lock(&mapping->i_shared_lock);
1052     if (!mapping->i_mmap && !mapping->i_mmap_shared)
1053         goto out_unlock;
1054
1055     pgoff = (offset + PAGE_CACHE_SIZE - 1) >> PAGE_CACHE_SHIFT;
1056     if (mapping->i_mmap != NULL)
1057         vmtruncate_list(mapping->i_mmap, pgoff);
1058     if (mapping->i_mmap_shared != NULL)
1059         vmtruncate_list(mapping->i_mmap_shared, pgoff);
1060
1061 out_unlock:
1062     spin_unlock(&mapping->i_shared_lock);
1063     truncate_inode_pages(mapping, offset);
1064     goto out_truncate;
1065
1066 do_expand:
1067     limit = current->rlim[RLIMIT_FSIZE].rlim_cur;
1068     if (limit != RLIM_INFINITY && offset > limit)
1069         goto out_sig;
```

```
1070     if (offset > inode->i_sb->s_maxbytes)
1071         goto out;
1072     inode->i_size = offset;
1073
1074 out_truncate:
1075     if (inode->i_op && inode->i_op->truncate) {
1076         lock_kernel();
1077         inode->i_op->truncate(inode);
1078         unlock_kernel();
1079     }
1080     return 0;
1081 out_sig:
1082     send_sig(SIGXFSZ, current, 0);
1083 out:
1084     return -EFBIG;
1085 }
```

1042 The parameters passed are the `inode` being truncated and the new `offset` marking the new end of the file. The old length of the file is stored in inode→i_size.

1045 Gets the `address_space` responsible for the inode.

1048-1049 If the new file size is larger than the old size, then goto `do_expand`, where the limits for the process will be checked before the file is grown.

1050 Here, the file is being shrunk, so it updates inode→i_size to match.

1051 Locks the spinlock, protecting the two lists of VMAs using this inode.

1052-1053 If no VMAs are mapping the inode, goto `out_unlock`, where the pages used by the file will be reclaimed by `truncate_inode_pages()` (See Section D.6.3.6).

1055 Calculates `pgoff` as the offset within the file in pages where the truncation will begin.

1056-1057 Truncates pages from all private mappings with `vmtruncate_list()` (See Section D.6.3.2).

1058-1059 Truncates pages from all shared mappings.

1062 Unlocks the spinlock protecting the VMA lists.

1063 Calls `truncate_inode_pages()` (See Section D.6.3.6) to reclaim the pages if they exist in the page cache for the file.

1064 Goto `out_truncate` to call the filesystem-specific `truncate()` function so the blocks used on disk will be freed.

Process Address Space

1066-1071 If the file is being expanded, this makes sure that the process limits for maximum file size are not being exceeded and that the hosting filesystem is able to support the new filesize.

1072 If the limits are fine, this updates the inodes size and falls through to call the filesystem-specific truncate function, which will fill the expanded filesize with zeros.

1075-1079 If the filesystem provides a `truncate()` function, then this locks the kernel, calls it and unlocks the kernel again. Filesystems do not acquire the proper locks to prevent races between file truncation and file expansion due to writing or faulting so the big kernel lock is needed.

1080 Returns success.

1082-1084 If the file size grows too big, this sends the `SIGXFSZ` signal to the calling process and returns `-EFBIG`.

D.6.3.2 Function: vmtruncate_list() *(mm/memory.c)*

This function cycles through all VMAs in an `address_spaces` list and calls `zap_page_range()` for the range of addresses that map a file that is being truncated.

```
1006 static void vmtruncate_list(struct vm_area_struct *mpnt,
                                 unsigned long pgoff)
1007 {
1008     do {
1009         struct mm_struct *mm = mpnt->vm_mm;
1010         unsigned long start = mpnt->vm_start;
1011         unsigned long end = mpnt->vm_end;
1012         unsigned long len = end - start;
1013         unsigned long diff;
1014
1015         /* mapping wholly truncated? */
1016         if (mpnt->vm_pgoff >= pgoff) {
1017             zap_page_range(mm, start, len);
1018             continue;
1019         }
1020
1021         /* mapping wholly unaffected? */
1022         len = len >> PAGE_SHIFT;
1023         diff = pgoff - mpnt->vm_pgoff;
1024         if (diff >= len)
1025             continue;
1026
1027         /* Ok, partially affected.. */
1028         start += diff << PAGE_SHIFT;
1029         len = (len - diff) << PAGE_SHIFT;
```

```
1030            zap_page_range(mm, start, len);
1031    } while ((mpnt = mpnt->vm_next_share) != NULL);
1032 }
```

1008-1031 Loops through all VMAs in the list.

1009 Gets the `mm_struct` that hosts this VMA.

1010-1012 Calculates the start, end and length of the VMA.

1016-1019 If the whole VMA is being truncated, this calls the function `zap_page_range()` (See Section D.6.3.3) with the start and length of the full VMA.

1022 Calculates the length of the VMA in pages.

1023-1025 Checks if the VMA maps any of the region being truncated. If the VMA in unaffected, it continues to the next VMA.

1028-1029 If the VMA is being partially truncated this calculates where the start and length of the region to truncate is in pages.

1030 Calls `zap_page_range()` (See Section D.6.3.3) to unmap the affected region.

D.6.3.3   Function: `zap_page_range()`   *(mm/memory.c)*

This function is the top-level pagetable-walk function, which unmaps userpages in the specified range from an `mm_struct`.

```
360 void zap_page_range(struct mm_struct *mm,
                        unsigned long address, unsigned long size)
361 {
362     mmu_gather_t *tlb;
363     pgd_t * dir;
364     unsigned long start = address, end = address + size;
365     int freed = 0;
366
367     dir = pgd_offset(mm, address);
368
369     /*
370      * This is a long-lived spinlock. That's fine.
371      * There's no contention, because the page table
372      * lock only protects against kswapd anyway, and
373      * even if kswapd happened to be looking at this
374      * process we _want_ it to get stuck.
375      */
376     if (address >= end)
377         BUG();
378     spin_lock(&mm->page_table_lock);
```

```
379        flush_cache_range(mm, address, end);
380        tlb = tlb_gather_mmu(mm);
381
382        do {
383            freed += zap_pmd_range(tlb, dir, address, end - address);
384            address = (address + PGDIR_SIZE) & PGDIR_MASK;
385            dir++;
386        } while (address && (address < end));
387
388        /* this will flush any remaining tlb entries */
389        tlb_finish_mmu(tlb, start, end);
390
391        /*
392         * Update rss for the mm_struct (not necessarily current->mm)
393         * Notice that rss is an unsigned long.
394         */
395        if (mm->rss > freed)
396            mm->rss -= freed;
397        else
398            mm->rss = 0;
399        spin_unlock(&mm->page_table_lock);
400 }
```

364 Calculates the `start` and `end` address for zapping.

367 Calculates the PGD (`dir`) that contains the starting `address`.

376-377 Makes sure the start address is not after the end address.

378 Acquires the spinlock protecting the page tables. This is a very longheld lock and would normally be considered a bad idea, but the comment prior to the block explains why it is ok in this case.

379 Flushes the CPU cache for this range.

380 `tlb_gather_mmu()` records the MM that is being altered. Later, `tlb_remove_page()` will be called to unmap the PTE that stores the PTEs in a `struct free_pte_ctx` until the zapping is finished. This is to avoid having to constantly flush the TLB as PTEs are freed.

382-386 For each PMD affected by the zapping, this calls `zap_pmd_range()` until the end address has been reached. Note that `tlb` is passed as well for `tlb_remove_page()` to use later.

389 `tlb_finish_mmu()` frees all the PTEs that were unmapped by `tlb_remove_page()` and then flushes the TLBs. Doing the flushing this way avoids a storm of TLB flushing that would be otherwise required for each PTE unmapped.

395-398 Updates RSS count.

399 Releases the pagetable lock.

D.6.3.4   Function: `zap_pmd_range()`   *(mm/memory.c)*

This function is unremarkable. It steps through the PMDs that are affected by the requested range and calls `zap_pte_range()` for each one.

```
331 static inline int zap_pmd_range(mmu_gather_t *tlb, pgd_t * dir,
                                    unsigned long address,
      unsigned long size)
332 {
333     pmd_t * pmd;
334     unsigned long end;
335     int freed;
336
337     if (pgd_none(*dir))
338         return 0;
339     if (pgd_bad(*dir)) {
340         pgd_ERROR(*dir);
341         pgd_clear(dir);
342         return 0;
343     }
344     pmd = pmd_offset(dir, address);
345     end = address + size;
346     if (end > ((address + PGDIR_SIZE) & PGDIR_MASK))
347         end = ((address + PGDIR_SIZE) & PGDIR_MASK);
348     freed = 0;
349     do {
350         freed += zap_pte_range(tlb, pmd, address, end - address);
351         address = (address + PMD_SIZE) & PMD_MASK;
352         pmd++;
353     } while (address < end);
354     return freed;
355 }
```

337-338 If no PGD exists, this returns.

339-343 If the PGD is bad, it flags the error and returns.

344 Gets the starting `pmd`.

345-347 Calculates the `end` address of the zapping. If it is beyond the end of this PGD, then set `end` to the end of the PGD.

349-353 Steps through all PMDs in this PGD. For each PMD, it calls `zap_pte_range()` (See Section D.6.3.5) to unmap the PTEs.

354 Returns how many pages were freed.

Process Address Space

D.6.3.5   Function: `zap_pte_range()`   *(mm/memory.c)*

This function calls `tlb_remove_page()` for each PTE in the requested `pmd` within the requested address range.

```
294 static inline int zap_pte_range(mmu_gather_t *tlb, pmd_t * pmd,
                                    unsigned long address,
        unsigned long size)
295 {
296     unsigned long offset;
297     pte_t * ptep;
298     int freed = 0;
299
300     if (pmd_none(*pmd))
301         return 0;
302     if (pmd_bad(*pmd)) {
303         pmd_ERROR(*pmd);
304         pmd_clear(pmd);
305         return 0;
306     }
307     ptep = pte_offset(pmd, address);
308     offset = address & ~PMD_MASK;
309     if (offset + size > PMD_SIZE)
310         size = PMD_SIZE - offset;
311     size &= PAGE_MASK;
312     for (offset=0; offset < size; ptep++, offset += PAGE_SIZE) {
313         pte_t pte = *ptep;
314         if (pte_none(pte))
315             continue;
316         if (pte_present(pte)) {
317             struct page *page = pte_page(pte);
318             if (VALID_PAGE(page) && !PageReserved(page))
319                 freed ++;
320             /* This will eventually call __free_pte on the pte. */
321             tlb_remove_page(tlb, ptep, address + offset);
322         } else {
323             free_swap_and_cache(pte_to_swp_entry(pte));
324             pte_clear(ptep);
325         }
326     }
327
328     return freed;
329 }
```

300-301 If the PMD does not exist, this returns.

302-306 If the PMD is bad, it flags the error and returns.

307 Gets the starting PTE offset.

308 Aligns the offset to a PMD boundary.

309 If the size of the region to unmap is past the PMD boundary, this fixes the size so that only this PMD will be affected.

311 Aligns `size` to a page boundary.

312-326 Steps through all PTEs in the region.

314-315 If no PTE exists, this continues to the next one.

316-322 If the PTE is present, this calls `tlb_remove_page()` to unmap the page. If the page is reclaimable, it increments the `freed` count.

322-325 If the PTE is in use, but the page is paged out or in the swap cache, this frees the swap slot and page with `free_swap_and_cache()` (See Section K.3.2.3). It is possible that a page is reclaimed if it was in the swap cache that is unaccounted for here, but it is not of paramount importance.

328 Returns the number of pages that were freed.

D.6.3.6 Function: `truncate_inode_pages()` *(mm/filemap.c)*
This is the top-level function responsible for truncating all pages from the page cache that occured after `lstart` in a `mapping`.

```
327 void truncate_inode_pages(struct address_space * mapping,
                              loff_t lstart)
328 {
329     unsigned long start = (lstart + PAGE_CACHE_SIZE - 1) >>
                                                PAGE_CACHE_SHIFT;
330     unsigned partial = lstart & (PAGE_CACHE_SIZE - 1);
331     int unlocked;
332
333     spin_lock(&pagecache_lock);
334     do {
335         unlocked = truncate_list_pages(&mapping->clean_pages,
                                    start, &partial);
336         unlocked |= truncate_list_pages(&mapping->dirty_pages,
                                    start, &partial);
337         unlocked |= truncate_list_pages(&mapping->locked_pages,
                                    start, &partial);
338     } while (unlocked);
339     /* Traversed all three lists without dropping the lock */
340     spin_unlock(&pagecache_lock);
341 }
```

329 Calculates where to `start` the truncation as an index in pages.

330 Calculates `partial` as an offset within the last page if it is being partially truncated.

333 Locks the page cache.

334 This will loop until none of the calls to `truncate_list_pages()` returns that a page was found that should have been reclaimed.

335 Uses `truncate_list_pages()` (See Section D.6.3.7) to truncate all pages in the `clean_pages` list.

336 Similarly, truncates pages in the `dirty_pages` list.

337 Similarly, truncates pages in the `locked_pages` list.

340 Unlocks the page cache.

D.6.3.7 Function: `truncate_list_pages()` *(mm/filemap.c)*

This function searches the requested list (`head`), which is part of an `address_space`. If pages are found after `start`, they will be truncated.

```
259 static int truncate_list_pages(struct list_head *head,
                                   unsigned long start,
                                   unsigned *partial)
260 {
261     struct list_head *curr;
262     struct page * page;
263     int unlocked = 0;
264
265 restart:
266     curr = head->prev;
267     while (curr != head) {
268         unsigned long offset;
269
270         page = list_entry(curr, struct page, list);
271         offset = page->index;
272
273         /* Is one of the pages to truncate? */
274         if ((offset >= start) ||
                (*partial && (offset + 1) == start)) {
275             int failed;
276
277             page_cache_get(page);
278             failed = TryLockPage(page);
279
280             list_del(head);
281             if (!failed)
282                 /* Restart after this page */
```

```
283                        list_add_tail(head, curr);
284                else
285                        /* Restart on this page */
286                        list_add(head, curr);
287
288                spin_unlock(&pagecache_lock);
289                unlocked = 1;
290
291                if (!failed) {
292                        if (*partial && (offset + 1) == start) {
293                                truncate_partial_page(page, *partial);
294                                *partial = 0;
295                        } else
296                                truncate_complete_page(page);
297
298                        UnlockPage(page);
299                } else
300                        wait_on_page(page);
301
302                page_cache_release(page);
303
304                if (current->need_resched) {
305                        __set_current_state(TASK_RUNNING);
306                        schedule();
307                }
308
309                spin_lock(&pagecache_lock);
310                goto restart;
311            }
312        curr = curr->prev;
313    }
314    return unlocked;
315 }
```

266-267 Records the start of the list and loops until the full list has been scanned.

270-271 Gets the page for this entry and what `offset` within the file it represents.

274 If the current page is after `start` or is a page that is to be partially truncated, this truncates this page or moves to the next one.

277-278 Takes a reference to the page and tries to lock it.

280 Removes the page from the list.

281-283 If we locked the page, this adds it back to the list where it will be skipped over on the next iteration of the loop.

284-286 If not, it adds it back where it will be found again immediately. Later in the function, `wait_on_page()` is called until the page is unlocked.

288 Releases the pagecache lock.

299 Sets locked to 1 to indicate a page was found that had to be truncated. This will force `truncate_inode_pages()` to call this function again to make sure there are no pages left behind. This looks like an oversight and was intended to have the functions recalled only if a *locked* page was found. However the way it is implemented means that it will be called whether the page was locked or not.

291-299 If we locked the page, this truncates it.

292-294 If the page is to be partially truncated, this calls `truncate_partial_page()` (See Section D.6.3.10) with the offset within the page where the truncation begins (`partial`).

296 If not, it calls `truncate_complete_page()` (See Section D.6.3.8) to truncate the whole page.

298 Unlocks the page.

300 If the page locking failed, this calls `wait_on_page()` to wait until the page can be locked.

302 Releases the reference to the page. If there are no more mappings for the page, it will be reclaimed.

304-307 Checks if the process should call `schedule()` before continuing. This is to prevent a truncating process from hogging the CPU.

309 Reacquires the spinlock and restarts the scanning for pages to reclaim.

312 The current page should not be reclaimed, so this moves to the next page.

314 Returns 1 if a page was found in the list that had to be truncated.

D.6.3.8 Function: `truncate_complete_page()` *(mm/filemap.c)*
This function truncates a full page, frees associates resoures and reclaims the page.

```
239 static void truncate_complete_page(struct page *page)
240 {
241     /* Leave it on the LRU if it gets converted into
        * anonymous buffers */
242     if (!page->buffers || do_flushpage(page, 0))
243         lru_cache_del(page);
244
245     /*
246      * We remove the page from the page cache _after_ we have
```

```
247        * destroyed all buffer-cache references to it. Otherwise
248        * some other process might think this inode page is not in
249        * the page cache and creates a buffer-cache alias to it
250        * causing all sorts of fun problems ...
251        */
252       ClearPageDirty(page);
253       ClearPageUptodate(page);
254       remove_inode_page(page);
255       page_cache_release(page);
256   }
```

242 If the page has buffers, this calls do_flushpage() (See Section D.6.3.9) to flush all buffers associated with the page. The comments in the following lines describe the problem concisely.

243 Deletes the page from the LRU.

252-253 Clears the dirty and uptodate flags for the page.

254 Calls remove_inode_page() (See Section J.1.2.1) to delete the page from the page cache.

255 Drops the reference to the page. The page will be later reclaimed when truncate_list_pages() drops its own private reference to it.

D.6.3.9   Function: do_flushpage()   *(mm/filemap.c)*
This function is responsible for flushing all buffers associated with a page.

```
223 static int do_flushpage(struct page *page, unsigned long offset)
224 {
225     int (*flushpage) (struct page *, unsigned long);
226     flushpage = page->mapping->a_ops->flushpage;
227     if (flushpage)
228         return (*flushpage)(page, offset);
229     return block_flushpage(page, offset);
230 }
```

226-228 If the page→mapping provides a flushpage() function, this calls it.

229 If not, this calls block_flushpage(), which is the generic function for flushing buffers associated with a page.

D.6.3.10   Function: truncate_partial_page()   *(mm/filemap.c)*
This function partially truncates a page by zeroing out the higher bytes no longer in use and flushing any associated buffers.

```
232 static inline void truncate_partial_page(struct page *page,
                                             unsigned partial)
```

```
233 {
234     memclear_highpage_flush(page, partial, PAGE_CACHE_SIZE-partial);
235     if (page->buffers)
236         do_flushpage(page, partial);
237 }
```

234 `memclear_highpage_flush()` fills an address range with zeros. In this case, it will zero from `partial` to the end of the page.

235-236 If the page has any associated buffers, this flushes any buffers containing data in the truncated region.

D.6.4   Reading Pages for the Page Cache

D.6.4.1   Function: `filemap_nopage()`   *(mm/filemap.c)*

This is the generic `nopage()` function used by many VMAs. This loops around itself with a large number of goto's, which can be difficult to trace, but there is nothing novel here. It is principally responsible for fetching the faulting page from either the pagecache or reading it from disk. If appropriate, it will also perform file readahead.

```
1994 struct page * filemap_nopage(struct vm_area_struct * area,
                                   unsigned long address,
                                   int unused)
1995 {
1996     int error;
1997     struct file *file = area->vm_file;
1998     struct address_space *mapping =
                         file->f_dentry->d_inode->i_mapping;
1999     struct inode *inode = mapping->host;
2000     struct page *page, **hash;
2001     unsigned long size, pgoff, endoff;
2002
2003     pgoff = ((address - area->vm_start) >> PAGE_CACHE_SHIFT) +
                 area->vm_pgoff;
2004     endoff = ((area->vm_end - area->vm_start) >> PAGE_CACHE_SHIFT) +
                  area->vm_pgoff;
2005
```

This block acquires the `struct file`, `addres_space` and `inode`, which are important for this page fault. It then acquires the starting offset within the file needed for this fault and the offset that corresponds to the end of this VMA. The offset is the end of the VMA instead of the end of the page in case file readahead is performed.

1997-1999 Acquires the `struct file`, `address_space` and `inode` required for this fault.

2003 Calculates `pgoff`, which is the offset within the file corresponding to the beginning of the fault.

2004 Calculates the offset within the file corresponding to the end of the VMA.

```
2006 retry_all:
2007     /*
2008      * An external ptracer can access pages that normally aren't
2009      * accessible..
2010      */
2011     size = (inode->i_size + PAGE_CACHE_SIZE - 1) >> PAGE_CACHE_SHIFT;
2012     if ((pgoff >= size) && (area->vm_mm == current->mm))
2013         return NULL;
2014
2015     /* The "size" of the file, as far as mmap is concerned, isn't
              bigger than the mapping */
2016     if (size > endoff)
2017         size = endoff;
2018
2019     /*
2020      * Do we have something in the page cache already?
2021      */
2022     hash = page_hash(mapping, pgoff);
2023 retry_find:
2024     page = __find_get_page(mapping, pgoff, hash);
2025     if (!page)
2026         goto no_cached_page;
2027
2028     /*
2029      * Ok, found a page in the page cache, now we need to check
2030      * that it's up-to-date.
2031      */
2032     if (!Page_Uptodate(page))
2033         goto page_not_uptodate;
```

2011 Calculates the size of the file in pages.

2012 If the faulting `pgoff` is beyond the end of the file and this is not a tracing process, this returns NULL.

2016-2017 If the VMA maps beyond the end of the file, this sets the size of the file to be the end of the mapping.

2022-2024 Searches for the page in the page cache.

2025-2026 If it does not exist, goto `no_cached_page` where `page_cache_read()` will be called to read the page from backing storage.

Process Address Space

2032-2033 If the page is not up to date, goto `page_not_uptodate` where the page will either be declared invalid or the data in the page will be updated.

```
2035 success:
2036     /*
2037      * Try read-ahead for sequential areas.
2038      */
2039     if (VM_SequentialReadHint(area))
2040         nopage_sequential_readahead(area, pgoff, size);
2041
2042     /*
2043      * Found the page and have a reference on it, need to check
2044      * sharing and possibly copy it over to another page..
2045      */
2046     mark_page_accessed(page);
2047     flush_page_to_ram(page);
2048     return page;
2049
```

2039-2040 If this mapping specified the `VM_SEQ_READ` hint, the pages of the current fault will be prefaulted with `nopage_sequential_readahead()`.

2046 Marks the faulted-in page as accessed, so it will be moved to the `active_list`.

2047 As the page is about to be installed into a process page table, this calls `flush_page_to_ram()` so that recent stores by the kernel to the page will definitely be visible to userspace.

2048 Returns the faulted-in page.

```
2050 no_cached_page:
2051     /*
2052      * If the requested offset is within our file, try to read
2053      * a whole cluster of pages at once.
2054      *
2055      * Otherwise, we're off the end of a privately mapped file,
2056      * so we need to map a zero page.
2057      */
2058     if ((pgoff < size) && !VM_RandomReadHint(area))
2059         error = read_cluster_nonblocking(file, pgoff, size);
2060     else
2061         error = page_cache_read(file, pgoff);
2062
2063     /*
2064      * The page we want has now been added to the page cache.
2065      * In the unlikely event that someone removed it in the
2066      * meantime, we'll just come back here and read it again.
```

```
2067        */
2068        if (error >= 0)
2069            goto retry_find;
2070
2071        /*
2072         * An error return from page_cache_read can result if the
2073         * system is low on memory, or a problem occurs while trying
2074         * to schedule I/O.
2075         */
2076        if (error == -ENOMEM)
2077            return NOPAGE_OOM;
2078        return NULL;
```

2058-2059 If the end of the file has not been reached and the random-read hint has not been specified, this calls `read_cluster_nonblocking()` to prefault in just a few pages near ths faulting page.

2061 If not, the file is being accessed randomly, so it just calls `page_cache_read()` (See Section D.6.4.2) to read in just the faulting page.

2068-2069 If no error occurred, goto `retry_find` at line 1958, which will check to make sure the page is in the page cache before returning.

2076-2077 If the error was due to being out of memory, this returns so that the fault handler can act accordingly.

2078 If not, this returns NULL to indicate that a nonexistant page was faulted, resulting in a `SIGBUS` signal being sent to the faulting process.

```
2080 page_not_uptodate:
2081        lock_page(page);
2082
2083        /* Did it get unhashed while we waited for it? */
2084        if (!page->mapping) {
2085            UnlockPage(page);
2086            page_cache_release(page);
2087            goto retry_all;
2088        }
2089
2090        /* Did somebody else get it up-to-date? */
2091        if (Page_Uptodate(page)) {
2092            UnlockPage(page);
2093            goto success;
2094        }
2095
2096        if (!mapping->a_ops->readpage(file, page)) {
2097            wait_on_page(page);
2098            if (Page_Uptodate(page))
```

```
2099                goto success;
2100     }
```

In this block, the page was found, but it was not up to date so the reasons for the page not being up to date are checked. If it looks ok, the appropriate `readpage()` function is called to resync the page.

2081 Locks the page for I/O.

2084-2088 If the page was removed from the mapping (possible because of a file truncation) and is now anonymous, then goto `retry_all`, which will try and fault in the page again.

2090-2094 Checks again for the `Uptodate` flag in case the page was updated just before we locked the page for I/O.

2096 Calls the `address_space`→`readpage()` function to schedule the data to be read from disk.

2097 Waits for the I/O to complete and if it is now up to date, goto `success` to return the page. If the `readpage()` function failed, it falls through to the error recovery path.

```
2101
2102     /*
2103      * Umm, take care of errors if the page isn't up-to-date.
2104      * Try to re-read it _once_. We do this synchronously,
2105      * because there really aren't any performance issues here
2106      * and we need to check for errors.
2107      */
2108     lock_page(page);
2109
2110     /* Somebody truncated the page on us? */
2111     if (!page->mapping) {
2112         UnlockPage(page);
2113         page_cache_release(page);
2114         goto retry_all;
2115     }
2116
2117     /* Somebody else successfully read it in? */
2118     if (Page_Uptodate(page)) {
2119         UnlockPage(page);
2120         goto success;
2121     }
2122     ClearPageError(page);
2123     if (!mapping->a_ops->readpage(file, page)) {
2124         wait_on_page(page);
2125         if (Page_Uptodate(page))
```

```
2126              goto success;
2127     }
2128
2129     /*
2130      * Things didn't work out. Return zero to tell the
2131      * mm layer so, possibly freeing the page cache page first.
2132      */
2133     page_cache_release(page);
2134     return NULL;
2135 }
```

In this path, the page is not up to date due to some I/O error. A second attempt is made to read the page data, and, if it fails, it returns.

2110-2127 This is almost identical to the previous block. The only difference is that `ClearPageError()` is called to clear the error caused by the previous I/O.

2133 If it still failed, this releases the reference to the page because it is useless.

2134 Returns NULL because the fault failed.

D.6.4.2 Function: page_cache_read() *(mm/filemap.c)*
This function adds the page corresponding to the `offset` within the `file` to the pagecache if it does not exist there already.

```
702 static int page_cache_read(struct file * file,
                                unsigned long offset)
703 {
704     struct address_space *mapping =
                                file->f_dentry->d_inode->i_mapping;
705     struct page **hash = page_hash(mapping, offset);
706     struct page *page;
707
708     spin_lock(&pagecache_lock);
709     page = __find_page_nolock(mapping, offset, *hash);
710     spin_unlock(&pagecache_lock);
711     if (page)
712         return 0;
713
714     page = page_cache_alloc(mapping);
715     if (!page)
716         return -ENOMEM;
717
718     if (!add_to_page_cache_unique(page, mapping, offset, hash)) {
719         int error = mapping->a_ops->readpage(file, page);
720         page_cache_release(page);
```

```
721            return error;
722      }
723      /*
724       * We arrive here in the unlikely event that someone
725       * raced with us and added our page to the cache first.
726       */
727      page_cache_release(page);
728      return 0;
729 }
```

704 Acquires the `address_space` mapping managing the file.

705 The page cache is a hash table, and `page_hash()` returns the first page in the bucket for this `mapping` and `offset`.

708-709 Searches the page cache with `__find_page_nolock()` (See Section J.1.4.3). This basically will traverse the list starting at `hash` to see if the requested page can be found.

711-712 If the page is already in the page cache, this returns.

714 Allocates a new page for insertion into the page cache. `page_cache_alloc()` will allocate a page from the buddy allocator using GFP mask information contained in `mapping`.

718 Inserts the page into the page cache with `add_to_page_cache_unique()` (See Section J.1.1.2). This function is used because a second check needs to be made to make sure the page was not inserted into the page cache while the `pagecache_lock` spinlock was not acquired.

719 If the allocated page was inserted into the page cache, it needs to be populated with data, so the `readpage()` function for the `mapping` is called. This schedules the I/O to take place, and the page will be unlocked when the I/O completes.

720 The path in `add_to_page_cache_unique()` (See Section J.1.1.2) takes an extra reference to the page being added to the page cache, which is dropped here. The page will not be freed.

727 If another process added the page to the page cache, it is released here by `page_cache_release()` because there will be no users of the page.

D.6.5   File Readahead for nopage()

D.6.5.1   Function: `nopage_sequential_readahead()`   *(mm/filemap.c)*

This function is only called by `filemap_nopage()` when the **VM_SEQ_READ** flag has been specified in the VMA. When half of the current readahead window has been faulted in, the next readahead window is scheduled for I/O, and pages from the previous window are freed.

```
1936 static void nopage_sequential_readahead(
        struct vm_area_struct * vma,
1937    unsigned long pgoff, unsigned long filesize)
1938 {
1939    unsigned long ra_window;
1940
1941    ra_window = get_max_readahead(vma->vm_file->f_dentry->d_inode);
1942    ra_window = CLUSTER_OFFSET(ra_window + CLUSTER_PAGES - 1);
1943
1944    /* vm_raend is zero if we haven't read ahead
         * in this area yet.  */
1945    if (vma->vm_raend == 0)
1946        vma->vm_raend = vma->vm_pgoff + ra_window;
1947
```

1941 get_max_readahead() returns the maximum-sized readahead window for the block that device the specified inode resides on.

1942 CLUSTER_PAGES is the number of pages that are paged-in or paged-out in bulk. The macro CLUSTER_OFFSET() will align the readahead window to a cluster boundary.

1945-1946 If readahead has not occurred yet, this sets the end of the readahead window (vm_reend).

```
1948    /*
1949     * If we've just faulted the page half-way through our window,
1950     * then schedule reads for the next window, and release the
1951     * pages in the previous window.
1952     */
1953    if ((pgoff + (ra_window >> 1)) == vma->vm_raend) {
1954        unsigned long start = vma->vm_pgoff + vma->vm_raend;
1955        unsigned long end = start + ra_window;
1956
1957        if (end > ((vma->vm_end >> PAGE_SHIFT) + vma->vm_pgoff))
1958            end = (vma->vm_end >> PAGE_SHIFT) + vma->vm_pgoff;
1959        if (start > end)
1960            return;
1961
1962        while ((start < end) && (start < filesize)) {
1963            if (read_cluster_nonblocking(vma->vm_file,
1964                            start, filesize) < 0)
1965                break;
1966            start += CLUSTER_PAGES;
1967        }
1968        run_task_queue(&tq_disk);
1969
```

```
1970          /* if we're far enough past the beginning of this area,
1971             recycle pages that are in the previous window. */
1972          if (vma->vm_raend >
                             (vma->vm_pgoff + ra_window + ra_window)) {
1973              unsigned long window = ra_window << PAGE_SHIFT;
1974
1975              end = vma->vm_start + (vma->vm_raend << PAGE_SHIFT);
1976              end -= window + window;
1977              filemap_sync(vma, end - window, window, MS_INVALIDATE);
1978          }
1979
1980          vma->vm_raend += ra_window;
1981      }
1982
1983      return;
1984 }
```

1953 If the fault has occurred halfway through the readahead window, this schedules the next readahead window to be read in from disk and frees the pages for
the first half of the current window because they are presumably not required
any more.

1954-1955 Calculates the `start` and `end` of the next readahead window because
we are about to schedule it for I/O.

1957 If the end of the readahead window is after the end of the VMA, this sets
`end` to the end of the VMA.

1959-1960 If we are at the end of the mapping, this just returns because there is
no more readahead to perform.

1962-1967 Schedules the next readahead window to be paged in by calling
`read_cluster_nonblocking()` (See Section D.6.5.2).

1968 Calls `run_task_queue()` to start the I/O.

1972-1978 Recycles the pages in the previous readahead window with
`filemap_sync()` as they are no longer required.

1980 Updates where the end of the readahead window is.

D.6.5.2   Function: `read_cluster_nonblocking()`   *(mm/filemap.c)*
This function schedules the next readahead window to be paged in.

```
737 static int read_cluster_nonblocking(struct file * file,
                                        unsigned long offset,
738     unsigned long filesize)
739 {
740     unsigned long pages = CLUSTER_PAGES;
```

```
741
742     offset = CLUSTER_OFFSET(offset);
743     while ((pages-- > 0) && (offset < filesize)) {
744         int error = page_cache_read(file, offset);
745         if (error < 0)
746             return error;
747         offset ++;
748     }
749
750     return 0;
751 }
```

740 CLUSTER_PAGES will be four pages in low memory systems and eight pages in larger ones. This means that, on an x86 with ample memory, 32KiB will be read in one cluster.

742 CLUSTER_OFFSET() will align the offset to a cluster-sized alignment.

743-748 Reads the full cluster into the page cache by calling page_cache_read() (See Section D.6.4.2) for each page in the cluster.

745-746 If an error occurs during readahead, this returns the error.

750 Returns success.

D.6.6   Swap-Related Read-Ahead

D.6.6.1   Function: swapin_readahead()   *(mm/memory.c)*
This function will fault in a number of pages after the current entry. It will stop when either CLUSTER_PAGES have been swapped in or an unused swap entry is found.

```
1093 void swapin_readahead(swp_entry_t entry)
1094 {
1095     int i, num;
1096     struct page *new_page;
1097     unsigned long offset;
1098
1099     /*
1100      * Get the number of handles we should do readahead io to.
1101      */
1102     num = valid_swaphandles(entry, &offset);
1103     for (i = 0; i < num; offset++, i++) {
1104         /* Ok, do the async read-ahead now */
1105         new_page =
1106             read_swap_cache_async(SWP_ENTRY(SWP_TYPE(entry),
                                                  offset));
1106         if (!new_page)
```

```
1107                 break;
1108             page_cache_release(new_page);
1109         }
1110     return;
1111 }
```

1102 valid_swaphandles() is what determines how many pages should be swapped in. It will stop at the first empty entry or when CLUSTER_PAGES is reached.

1103-1109 Swaps in the pages.

1105 Attempts to swap the page into the swap cache with read_swap_cache_async() (See Section K.3.1.1).

1106-1107 If the page could not be paged in, this breaks and returns.

1108 Drops the reference to the page that read_swap_cache_async() takes.

1110 Returns.

D.6.6.2   Function: valid_swaphandles()   *(mm/swapfile.c)*

This function determines how many pages should be readahead from swap starting from offset. It will readahead to the next unused swap slot, but, at most, it will return CLUSTER_PAGES.

```
1238 int valid_swaphandles(swp_entry_t entry, unsigned long *offset)
1239 {
1240     int ret = 0, i = 1 << page_cluster;
1241     unsigned long toff;
1242     struct swap_info_struct *swapdev = SWP_TYPE(entry) + swap_info;
1243
1244     if (!page_cluster)        /* no readahead */
1245         return 0;
1246     toff = (SWP_OFFSET(entry) >> page_cluster) << page_cluster;
1247     if (!toff)            /* first page is swap header */
1248         toff++, i--;
1249     *offset = toff;
1250
1251     swap_device_lock(swapdev);
1252     do {
1253         /* Don't read-ahead past the end of the swap area */
1254         if (toff >= swapdev->max)
1255             break;
1256         /* Don't read in free or bad pages */
1257         if (!swapdev->swap_map[toff])
1258             break;
1259         if (swapdev->swap_map[toff] == SWAP_MAP_BAD)
```

```
1260              break;
1261          toff++;
1262          ret++;
1263      } while (--i);
1264      swap_device_unlock(swapdev);
1265      return ret;
1266 }
```

1240 i is set to CLUSTER_PAGES, which is the equivalent of the bitshift shown here.

1242 Gets the swap_info_struct that contains this entry.

1244-1245 If readahead has been disabled, this returns.

1246 Calculates toff to be entry rounded down to the nearest CLUSTER_PAGES-sized boundary.

1247-1248 If toff is 0, it moves it to 1 because the first page contains information about the swap area.

1251 Locks the swap device as we are about to scan it.

1252-1263 Loops at most i, which is initialized to CLUSTER_PAGES, times.

1254-1255 If the end of the swap area is reached, that is as far as can be readahead.

1257-1258 If an unused entry is reached, this just returns because it is as far as we want to readahead.

1259-1260 Likewise, this returns if a bad entry is discovered.

1261 Moves to the next slot.

1262 Increments the number of pages to be readahead.

1264 Unlocks the swap device.

1265 Returns the number of pages that should be readahead.

Process Address Space

Boot Memory Allocator

Contents

E.1   Initializing the Boot Memory Allocator

Contents

The functions in this section are responsible for bootstrapping the boot memory allocator. It starts with the architecture-specific function `setup_memory()` (See Section B.1.1), but all architectures cover the same basic tasks in the architecture-specific function before calling the architecture-independent function `init_bootmem()`.

E.1.1   Function: `init_bootmem()`   *(mm/bootmem.c)*

This is called by UMA architectures to initialize their boot memory allocator structures.

```
304 unsigned long __init init_bootmem (unsigned long start,
                                       unsigned long pages)
305 {
306     max_low_pfn = pages;
307     min_low_pfn = start;
308     return(init_bootmem_core(&contig_page_data, start, 0, pages));
309 }
```

304 Confusingly, the `pages` parameter is actually the end PFN of the memory addressable by this node, not the number of pages as the name implies.

306 Sets the max PFN addressable by this node in case the architecture-dependent code did not.

307 Sets the min PFN addressable by this node in case the architecture-dependent code did not.

308 Calls `init_bootmem_core()`(See Section E.1.3), which does the real work of initializing the `bootmem_data`.

E.1.2   Function: `init_bootmem_node()`   *(mm/bootmem.c)*

This is called by NUMA architectures to initialize boot memory allocator data for a given node.

```
284 unsigned long __init init_bootmem_node (pg_data_t *pgdat,
                                            unsigned long freepfn,
                                            unsigned long startpfn,
                                            unsigned long endpfn)
285 {
286     return(init_bootmem_core(pgdat, freepfn, startpfn, endpfn));
287 }
```

286 Just calls `init_bootmem_core()`(See Section E.1.3) directly.

E.1.3   Function: `init_bootmem_core()`   *(mm/bootmem.c)*

This initializes the appropriate `struct bootmem_data_t` and inserts the node into the linked list of nodes `pgdat_list`.

```
46 static unsigned long __init init_bootmem_core (
        pg_data_t *pgdat,
47      unsigned long mapstart,
        unsigned long start,
        unsigned long end)
48 {
49      bootmem_data_t *bdata = pgdat->bdata;
50      unsigned long mapsize = ((end - start)+7)/8;
51
52      pgdat->node_next = pgdat_list;
53      pgdat_list = pgdat;
54
55      mapsize = (mapsize + (sizeof(long) - 1UL)) &
                    ~(sizeof(long) - 1UL);
56      bdata->node_bootmem_map = phys_to_virt(mapstart << PAGE_SHIFT);
57      bdata->node_boot_start = (start << PAGE_SHIFT);
58      bdata->node_low_pfn = end;
59
60      /*
61       * Initially all pages are reserved - setup_arch() has to
62       * register free RAM areas explicitly.
63       */
64      memset(bdata->node_bootmem_map, 0xff, mapsize);
65
66      return mapsize;
67 }
```

46 The parameters are the following:

- **pgdat** is the node descriptor being initialized.

- **mapstart** is the beginning of the memory that will be usable.

- **start** is the beginning PFN of the node.

- **end** is the end PFN of the node.

50 Each page requires one bit to represent it, so the size of the map required is the number of pages in this node rounded up to the nearest multiple of 8 and then divided by 8 to give the number of bytes required.

52-53 Because the node will be shortly considered initialized, this inserts it into the global `pgdat_list`.

55 Rounds the mapsize up to the closest word boundary.

56 Converts the `mapstart` to a virtual address and stores it in bdata→node_bootmem_map.

57 Converts the starting PFN to a physical address and stores it on node_boot_start.

58 Stores the end PFN of ZONE_NORMAL in node_low_pfn.

64 Fills the full map with 1s that mark all pages as allocated. It is up to the architecture-dependent code to mark the usable pages.

E.2 Allocating Memory

Contents

E.2.1 Reserving Large Regions of Memory

E.2.1.1 Function: `reserve_bootmem()` *(mm/bootmem.c)*

```
311 void __init reserve_bootmem (unsigned long addr, unsigned long size)
312 {
313     reserve_bootmem_core(contig_page_data.bdata, addr, size);
314 }
```

313 Just calls `reserve_bootmem_core()`(See Section E.2.1.3). Because this is for a NUMA architecture, the node to allocate from is the static `contig_page_data` node.

E.2.1.2 Function: `reserve_bootmem_node()` *(mm/bootmem.c)*

```
289 void __init reserve_bootmem_node (pg_data_t *pgdat,
                    unsigned long physaddr,
                    unsigned long size)
290 {
291     reserve_bootmem_core(pgdat->bdata, physaddr, size);
292 }
```

291 Just calls `reserve_bootmem_core()`(See Section E.2.1.3) and passes it the bootmem data of the requested node.

E.2.1.3 Function: `reserve_bootmem_core()` *(mm/bootmem.c)*

```
74 static void __init reserve_bootmem_core(bootmem_data_t *bdata,
                    unsigned long addr,
                    unsigned long size)
75 {
76     unsigned long i;
```

```
77      /*
78       * round up, partially reserved pages are considered
79       * fully reserved.
80       */
81      unsigned long sidx = (addr - bdata->node_boot_start)/PAGE_SIZE;
82      unsigned long eidx = (addr + size - bdata->node_boot_start +
83                  PAGE_SIZE-1)/PAGE_SIZE;
84      unsigned long end = (addr + size + PAGE_SIZE-1)/PAGE_SIZE;
85
86      if (!size) BUG();
87
88      if (sidx < 0)
89          BUG();
90      if (eidx < 0)
91          BUG();
92      if (sidx >= eidx)
93          BUG();
94      if ((addr >> PAGE_SHIFT) >= bdata->node_low_pfn)
95          BUG();
96      if (end > bdata->node_low_pfn)
97          BUG();
98      for (i = sidx; i < eidx; i++)
99          if (test_and_set_bit(i, bdata->node_bootmem_map))
100             printk("hm, page %08lx reserved twice.\n",
                    i*PAGE_SIZE);
101 }
```

81 The `sidx` is the starting index to serve pages from. The value is obtained by subtracting the starting address from the requested address and dividing by the size of a page.

82 A similar calculation is made for the ending index `eidx` except that the allocation is rounded up to the nearest page. This means that requests to partially reserve a page will result in the full page being reserved.

84 end is the last PFN that is affected by this reservation.

86 Checks that a nonzero value has been given.

88-89 Checks that the starting index is not before the start of the node.

90-91 Checks that the end index is not before the start of the node.

92-93 Checks that the starting index is not after the end index.

94-95 Checks that the starting address is not beyond the memory that this boot-mem node represents.

96-97 Checks that the ending address is not beyond the memory that this boot-mem node represents.

88-100 Starting with `sidx` and finishing with `eidx`, this tests and sets the bit in the bootmem map that represents the page marking it as allocated. If the bit was already set to 1, it prints out a message saying it was reserved twice.

E.2.2 Allocating Memory at Boot Time

E.2.2.1 Function: `alloc_bootmem()` *(mm/bootmem.c)*
The call graph for these macros is shown in Figure 5.1.

```
38 #define alloc_bootmem(x) \
39     __alloc_bootmem((x), SMP_CACHE_BYTES, __pa(MAX_DMA_ADDRESS))
40 #define alloc_bootmem_low(x) \
41     __alloc_bootmem((x), SMP_CACHE_BYTES, 0)
42 #define alloc_bootmem_pages(x) \
43     __alloc_bootmem((x), PAGE_SIZE, __pa(MAX_DMA_ADDRESS))
44 #define alloc_bootmem_low_pages(x) \
45     __alloc_bootmem((x), PAGE_SIZE, 0)
```

39 `alloc_bootmem()` will align to the L1 hardware cache and start searching for a page after the maximum address usable for DMA.

40 `alloc_bootmem_low()` will align to the L1 hardware cache and start searching from page 0.

42 `alloc_bootmem_pages()` will align the allocation to a page size so that full pages will be allocated starting from the maximum address usable for DMA.

44 `alloc_bootmem_pages()` will align the allocation to a page size so that full pages will be allocated starting from physical address 0.

E.2.2.2 Function: `__alloc_bootmem()` *(mm/bootmem.c)*

```
326 void * __init __alloc_bootmem (unsigned long size,
                    unsigned long align, unsigned long goal)
327 {
328     pg_data_t *pgdat;
329     void *ptr;
330
331     for_each_pgdat(pgdat)
332         if ((ptr = __alloc_bootmem_core(pgdat->bdata, size,
333                     align, goal)))
334             return(ptr);
335
336     /*
337      * Whoops, we cannot satisfy the allocation request.
```

```
338      */
339      printk(KERN_ALERT "bootmem alloc of %lu bytes failed!\n", size);
340      panic("Out of memory");
341      return NULL;
342 }
```

326 The parameters are the following:

- **size** is the size of the requested allocation.
- **align** is the desired alignment and must be a power of 2. Currently, it is either SMP_CACHE_BYTES or PAGE_SIZE.
- **goal** is the starting address to begin searching from.

331-334 Cycles through all available nodes and tries allocating from each in turn. In the UMA case, this will just allocate from the contig_page_data node.

339-340 If the allocation fails, the system is not going to be able to boot, so the kernel panics.

E.2.2.3 Function: alloc_bootmem_node() *(mm/bootmem.c)*

```
53 #define alloc_bootmem_node(pgdat, x) \
54     __alloc_bootmem_node((pgdat), (x), SMP_CACHE_BYTES, \
                  __pa(MAX_DMA_ADDRESS))
55 #define alloc_bootmem_pages_node(pgdat, x) \
56     __alloc_bootmem_node((pgdat), (x), PAGE_SIZE, \
                  __pa(MAX_DMA_ADDRESS))
57 #define alloc_bootmem_low_pages_node(pgdat, x) \
58     __alloc_bootmem_node((pgdat), (x), PAGE_SIZE, 0)
```

53-54 alloc_bootmem_node() will allocate from the requested node, align to the L1 hardware cache and start searching for a page beginning with ZONE_NORMAL (i.e., at the end of ZONE_DMA, which is at MAX_DMA_ADDRESS).

55-56 alloc_bootmem_pages() will allocate from the requested node and align the allocation to a page size so that full pages will be allocated starting from the ZONE_NORMAL.

57-58 alloc_bootmem_pages() will allocate from the requested node and align the allocation to a page size so that full pages will be allocated starting from physical address 0 so that ZONE_DMA will be used.

E.2.2.4 Function: __alloc_bootmem_node() *(mm/bootmem.c)*

```
344 void * __init __alloc_bootmem_node (pg_data_t *pgdat,
                    unsigned long size,
                    unsigned long align,
```

```
                            unsigned long goal)
345 {
346     void *ptr;
347
348     ptr = __alloc_bootmem_core(pgdat->bdata, size, align, goal);
349     if (ptr)
350         return (ptr);
351
352     /*
353      * Whoops, we cannot satisfy the allocation request.
354      */
355     printk(KERN_ALERT "bootmem alloc of %lu bytes failed!\n", size);
356     panic("Out of memory");
357     return NULL;
358 }
```

344 The parameters are the same as for `__alloc_bootmem_node()` (See Section E.2.2.4) except that the node to allocate from is specified.

348 Calls the core function `__alloc_bootmem_core()` (See Section E.2.2.5) to perform the allocation.

349-350 Returns a pointer if it was successful.

355-356 Otherwise, this prints out a message and panics the kernel because the system will not boot if memory cannot be allocated even now.

E.2.2.5 Function: `__alloc_bootmem_core()` *(mm/bootmem.c)*

This is the core function for allocating memory from a specified node with the boot memory allocator. It is quite large and broken up into the following tasks:

- The function preamble makes sure the parameters are sane.

- It calculates the starting address to scan from based on the `goal` parameter.

- It checks to see if this allocation may be merged with the page used for the previous allocation to save memory.

- It marks the pages allocated as 1 in the bitmap and zeros-out the contents of the pages.

```
144 static void * __init __alloc_bootmem_core (bootmem_data_t *bdata,
145     unsigned long size, unsigned long align, unsigned long goal)
146 {
147     unsigned long i, start = 0;
148     void *ret;
149     unsigned long offset, remaining_size;
150     unsigned long areasize, preferred, incr;
```

```
151        unsigned long eidx = bdata->node_low_pfn -
152                    (bdata->node_boot_start >> PAGE_SHIFT);
153
154        if (!size) BUG();
155
156        if (align & (align-1))
157            BUG();
158
159        offset = 0;
160        if (align &&
161            (bdata->node_boot_start & (align - 1UL)) != 0)
162            offset = (align - (bdata->node_boot_start &
                            (align - 1UL)));
163        offset >>= PAGE_SHIFT;
```

This is the function preamble, which makes sure the parameters are sane.

144 The parameters are the following:

- **bdata** is the bootmem for the struct being allocated from.
- **size** is the size of the requested allocation.
- **align** is the desired alignment for the allocation. It must be a power of 2.
- **goal** is the preferred address to allocate above if possible.

151 Calculates the ending bit index `eidx`, which returns the highest page index that may be used for the allocation.

154 Calls `BUG()` if a request size of 0 is specified.

156-157 If the alignment is not a power of 2, this calls `BUG()`.

159 The default offset for alignments is 0.

160 If an alignment has been specified and...

161 The requested alignment is the same alignment as the start of the node, this calculates the offset to use.

162 The offset to use is the requested alignment masked against the lower bits of the starting address. In reality, this `offset` will likely be identical to `align` for the prevalent values of `align`.

```
169        if (goal && (goal >= bdata->node_boot_start) &&
170                ((goal >> PAGE_SHIFT) < bdata->node_low_pfn)) {
171            preferred = goal - bdata->node_boot_start;
172        } else
173            preferred = 0;
```

```
174
175     preferred = ((preferred + align - 1) & ~(align - 1))
                >> PAGE_SHIFT;
176     preferred += offset;
177     areasize = (size+PAGE_SIZE-1)/PAGE_SIZE;
178     incr = align >> PAGE_SHIFT ? : 1;
```

This block calculates the starting PFN to start scanning from based on the `goal` parameter.

169 If a goal has been specified and the goal is after the starting address for this node and the PFN of the goal is less than the last PFN adressable by this node, then ....

170 The preferred offset to start from is the goal minus the beginning of the memory addressable by this node.

173 If not, the preferred offset is 0.

175-176 Adjusts the preferred address to take the offset into account so that the address will be correctly aligned.

177 The number of pages that will be affected by this allocation is stored in `areasize`.

178 `incr` is the number of pages that have to be skipped to satisfy alignment requirements if they are more than one page.

```
179
180 restart_scan:
181     for (i = preferred; i < eidx; i += incr) {
182         unsigned long j;
183         if (test_bit(i, bdata->node_bootmem_map))
184             continue;
185         for (j = i + 1; j < i + areasize; ++j) {
186             if (j >= eidx)
187                 goto fail_block;
188             if (test_bit (j, bdata->node_bootmem_map))
189                 goto fail_block;
190         }
191         start = i;
192         goto found;
193     fail_block:;
194     }
195     if (preferred) {
196         preferred = offset;
197         goto restart_scan;
198     }
199     return NULL;
```

This block scans through memory looking for a large enough block to satisfy this request.

180 If the allocation could not be satisifed starting from `goal`, this label is jumped to so that the map will be rescanned.

181-194 Starting from `preferred`, this scans linearly searching for a free block large enough to satisfy the request. It walks the address space in `incr` steps to satisfy alignments greater than one page. If the alignment is less than a page, `incr` will just be 1.

183-184 Tests the bit. If it is already 1, it is not free, so it moves to the next page.

185-190 Scans the next `areasize` number of pages and sees if they are also free. It fails if the end of the addressable space is reached (`eidx`) or one of the pages is already in use.

191-192 A free block is found, so this records the `start` and jumps to the found block.

195-198 The allocation failed, so it starts again from the beginning.

199 If that also failed, it returns NULL, which will result in a kernel panic.

```
200 found:
201     if (start >= eidx)
202         BUG();
203
209     if (align <= PAGE_SIZE
210         && bdata->last_offset && bdata->last_pos+1 == start) {
211         offset = (bdata->last_offset+align-1) & ~(align-1);
212         if (offset > PAGE_SIZE)
213             BUG();
214         remaining_size = PAGE_SIZE-offset;
215         if (size < remaining_size) {
216             areasize = 0;
217             // last_pos unchanged
218             bdata->last_offset = offset+size;
219             ret = phys_to_virt(bdata->last_pos*PAGE_SIZE + offset +
220                     bdata->node_boot_start);
221         } else {
222             remaining_size = size - remaining_size;
223             areasize = (remaining_size+PAGE_SIZE-1)/PAGE_SIZE;
224             ret = phys_to_virt(bdata->last_pos*PAGE_SIZE +
225                     offset +
                        bdata->node_boot_start);
226             bdata->last_pos = start+areasize-1;
```

```
227                    bdata->last_offset = remaining_size;
228            }
229            bdata->last_offset &= ~PAGE_MASK;
230      } else {
231            bdata->last_pos = start + areasize - 1;
232            bdata->last_offset = size & ~PAGE_MASK;
233            ret = phys_to_virt(start * PAGE_SIZE +
                           bdata->node_boot_start);
234      }
```

This block tests to see if this allocation may be merged with the previous allocation.

201-202 Checks that the start of the allocation is not after the addressable memory. This check was just made, so it is redundant.

209-230 Tries and merges with the previous allocation if the alignment is less than a PAGE_SIZE, the previous page has space in it (last_offset != 0) and the previously used page is adjacent to the page found for this allocation.

231-234 If not, this records the pages and offset used for this allocation to be used for merging with the next allocation.

211 Updates the offset to use to be aligned correctly for the requested align.

212-213 If the offset now goes over the edge of a page, BUG() is called. This condition would require a very poor choice of alignment to be used. Because the only alignment commonly used is a factor of PAGE_SIZE, it is impossible for normal usage.

214 remaining_size is the remaining free space in the previously used page.

215-221 If there is enough space left in the old page, this uses the old page and updates the bootmem_data struct to reflect it.

221-228 If not, this calculates how many pages in addition to this one will be required and updates the bootmem_data.

216 The number of pages used by this allocation is now 0.

218 Updates the last_offset to be the end of this allocation.

219 Calculates the virtual address to return for the successful allocation.

222 remaining_size is how space will be used in the last page used to satisfy the allocation.

223 Calculates how many more pages are needed to satisfy the allocation.

224 Records the address that the allocation starts from.

226 The last page used is the `start` page plus the number of additional pages required to satisfy this allocation `areasize`.

227 The end of the allocation has already been calculated.

229 If the offset is at the end of the page, this makes it 0.

231 No merging took place, so this records the last page used to satisfy this allocation.

232 Records how much of the last page was used.

233 Records the starting virtual address of the allocation.

```
238        for (i = start; i < start+areasize; i++)
239            if (test_and_set_bit(i, bdata->node_bootmem_map))
240                BUG();
241        memset(ret, 0, size);
242        return ret;
243 }
```

This block marks the pages allocated as 1 in the bitmap and zeros-out the contents of the pages.

238-240 Cycles through all pages used for this allocation and sets the bit to 1 in the bitmap. If any of them are already 1, a double allocation took place, so it calls `BUG()`.

241 Zero-fills the pages.

242 Returns the address of the allocation.

E.3   Freeing Memory

Contents

E.3.1   Function: `free_bootmem()`   *(mm/bootmem.c)*

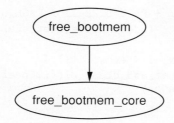

Figure E.1. Call Graph: `free_bootmem()`

```
294 void __init free_bootmem_node (pg_data_t *pgdat,
                     unsigned long physaddr, unsigned long size)
295 {
296         return(free_bootmem_core(pgdat->bdata, physaddr, size));
297 }

316 void __init free_bootmem (unsigned long addr, unsigned long size)
317 {
318         return(free_bootmem_core(contig_page_data.bdata, addr, size));
319 }
```

296 Calls the core function with the corresponding bootmem data for the requested
node.

318 Calls the core function with the bootmem data for `contig_page_data`.

E.3.2   Function: `free_bootmem_core()`   *(mm/bootmem.c)*

```
103 static void __init free_bootmem_core(bootmem_data_t *bdata,
                     unsigned long addr,
                     unsigned long size)
104 {
105       unsigned long i;
106       unsigned long start;
111       unsigned long sidx;
112       unsigned long eidx = (addr + size -
                     bdata->node_boot_start)/PAGE_SIZE;
```

```
113        unsigned long end = (addr + size)/PAGE_SIZE;
114
115        if (!size) BUG();
116        if (end > bdata->node_low_pfn)
117                BUG();
118
119        /*
120         * Round up the beginning of the address.
121         */
122        start = (addr + PAGE_SIZE-1) / PAGE_SIZE;
123        sidx = start - (bdata->node_boot_start/PAGE_SIZE);
124
125        for (i = sidx; i < eidx; i++) {
126                if (!test_and_clear_bit(i, bdata->node_bootmem_map))
127                        BUG();
128        }
129 }
```

112 Calculates the end index affected as `eidx`.

113 The end address is the end of the affected area rounded down to the nearest page if it is not already page aligned.

115 If a size of 0 is freed, this calls `BUG`.

116-117 If the end PFN is after the memory addressable by this node, this calls BUG.

122 Rounds the starting address up to the nearest page if it is not already page aligned.

123 Calculates the starting index to free.

125-127 For all full pages that are freed by this action, this clears the bit in the boot bitmap. If it is already 0, it is a double free or is memory that was never used, so it calls `BUG`.

E.4   Retiring the Boot Memory Allocator

Contents

After the system is started, the boot memory allocator is no longer needed, so these functions are responsible for removing unnecessary boot memory allocator structures and passing the remaining pages to the normal physical page allocator.

E.4.1   Function: `mem_init()`   *(arch/i386/mm/init.c)*

The call graph for this function is shown in Figure 5.2. The important part of this function for the boot memory allocator is that it calls `free_pages_init()`(See Section E.4.2). The function is broken up into the following tasks:

- The function preamble sets the PFN within the global `mem_map` for the location of high memory and zeros-out the systemwide zero page.

- Calls `free_pages_init()`(See Section E.4.2).

- Prints out an informational message on the availability of memory in the system.

- Checks to see if the CPU supports PAE if the config option is enabled and tests the WP bit on the CPU. This is important because, without the WP bit, the function `verify_write()` has to be called for every write to userspace from the kernel. This only applies to old processors like the 386.

- Fills in entries for the userspace portion of the PGD for `swapper_pg_dir`, which are the kernel page tables. The zero page is mapped for all entries.

```
507 void __init mem_init(void)
508 {
509     int codesize, reservedpages, datasize, initsize;
510
511     if (!mem_map)
512         BUG();
513
514     set_max_mapnr_init();
515
516     high_memory = (void *) __va(max_low_pfn * PAGE_SIZE);
517
518     /* clear the zero-page */
519     memset(empty_zero_page, 0, PAGE_SIZE);
```

514 This function records that the PFN high memory starts in mem_map (highmem_start_page), the maximum number of pages in the system (max_mapnr and num_physpages) and finally the maximum number of pages that may be mapped by the kernel (num_mappedpages).

516 high_memory is the virtual address where high memory begins.

519 Zeros-out the systemwide zero page.

```
520
521     reservedpages = free_pages_init();
522
```

521 Calls free_pages_init()(See Section E.4.2), which tells the boot memory allocator to retire itself as well as initializing all pages in high memory for use with the buddy allocator.

```
523     codesize =  (unsigned long) &_etext - (unsigned long) &_text;
524     datasize =  (unsigned long) &_edata - (unsigned long) &_etext;
525     initsize =  (unsigned long) &__init_end - (unsigned long)
                             &__init_begin;
526
527     printk(KERN_INFO "Memory: %luk/%luk available (%dk kernel code,
            %dk reserved, %dk data, %dk init, %ldk highmem)\n",
528         (unsigned long) nr_free_pages() << (PAGE_SHIFT-10),
529         max_mapnr << (PAGE_SHIFT-10),
530         codesize >> 10,
531         reservedpages << (PAGE_SHIFT-10),
532         datasize >> 10,
533         initsize >> 10,
534         (unsigned long) (totalhigh_pages << (PAGE_SHIFT-10))
535     );
```

This block prints out an informational message.

523 Calculates the size of the code segment, data segment and memory used by initialization code and data (all functions marked __init will be in this section).

527-535 Prints out a nice message on the availability of memory and the amount of memory consumed by the kernel.

```
536
537 #if CONFIG_X86_PAE
538     if (!cpu_has_pae)
539         panic("cannot execute a PAE-enabled kernel on a PAE-less
CPU!");
540 #endif
```

```
541        if (boot_cpu_data.wp_works_ok < 0)
542            test_wp_bit();
543
```

538-539 If PAE is enabled, but the processor does not support it, this panics.

541-542 Tests for the availability of the WP bit.

```
550 #ifndef CONFIG_SMP
551        zap_low_mappings();
552 #endif
553
554 }
```

551 Cycles through each PGD used by the userspace portion of `swapper_pg_dir` and maps the zero page to it.

E.4.2 Function: `free_pages_init()` *(arch/i386/mm/init.c)*

This function has three important functions: to call `free_all_bootmem()` (See Section E.4.4), to retire the boot memory allocator and to free all high memory pages to the buddy allocator.

```
481 static int __init free_pages_init(void)
482 {
483     extern int ppro_with_ram_bug(void);
484     int bad_ppro, reservedpages, pfn;
485
486     bad_ppro = ppro_with_ram_bug();
487
488     /* this will put all low memory onto the freelists */
489     totalram_pages += free_all_bootmem();
490
491     reservedpages = 0;
492     for (pfn = 0; pfn < max_low_pfn; pfn++) {
493         /*
494          * Only count reserved RAM pages
495          */
496         if (page_is_ram(pfn) && PageReserved(mem_map+pfn))
497             reservedpages++;
498     }
499 #ifdef CONFIG_HIGHMEM
500     for (pfn = highend_pfn-1; pfn >= highstart_pfn; pfn--)
501         one_highpage_init((struct page *) (mem_map + pfn), pfn,
bad_ppro);
502     totalram_pages += totalhigh_pages;
503 #endif
504     return reservedpages;
505 }
```

486 There is a bug in the Pentium Pros that prevents certain pages in high memory from being used. The function `ppro_with_ram_bug()` checks for its existence.

489 Calls `free_all_bootmem()` to retire the boot memory allocator.

491-498 Cycles through all of memory and counts the number of reserved pages that were left over by the boot memory allocator.

500-501 For each page in high memory, this calls `one_highpage_init()` (See Section E.4.3). This function clears the `PG_reserved` bit, sets the `PG_high` bit, sets the count to 1, calls `__free_pages()` to give the page to the buddy allocator and increments the `totalhigh_pages` count. Pages that kill buggy Pentium Pros are skipped.

E.4.3   Function: `one_highpage_init()`   *(arch/i386/mm/init.c)*

This function initializes the information for one page in high memory and checks to make sure that the page will not trigger a bug with some Pentium Pros. It only exists if `CONFIG_HIGHMEM` is specified at compile time.

```
449 #ifdef CONFIG_HIGHMEM
450 void __init one_highpage_init(struct page *page, int pfn,
                                 int bad_ppro)
451 {
452     if (!page_is_ram(pfn)) {
453         SetPageReserved(page);
454         return;
455     }
456
457     if (bad_ppro && page_kills_ppro(pfn)) {
458         SetPageReserved(page);
459         return;
460     }
461
462     ClearPageReserved(page);
463     set_bit(PG_highmem, &page->flags);
464     atomic_set(&page->count, 1);
465     __free_page(page);
466     totalhigh_pages++;
467 }
468 #endif /* CONFIG_HIGHMEM */
```

452-455 If a page does not exist at the PFN, this marks the `struct page` as reserved, so it will not be used.

457-460 If the running CPU is susceptible to the Pentium Pro bug and this page is a page that would cause a crash (`page_kills_ppro()` performs the check), this marks the page as reserved so that it will never be allocated.

462 From here on, the page is a high memory page that should be used, so this first clears the reserved bit so that it will be given to the buddy allocator later.

463 Sets the `PG_highmem` bit to show it is a high memory page.

464 Initialize the usage count of the page to 1, which will be set to 0 by the buddy allocator.

465 Frees the page with `__free_page()`(See Section F.4.2) so that the buddy allocator will add the high memory page to its free lists.

466 Increments the total number of available high memory pages (`totalhigh_pages`).

E.4.4   Function: free_all_bootmem()   *(mm/bootmem.c)*

```
299 unsigned long __init free_all_bootmem_node (pg_data_t *pgdat)
300 {
301     return(free_all_bootmem_core(pgdat));
302 }

321 unsigned long __init free_all_bootmem (void)
322 {
323     return(free_all_bootmem_core(&contig_page_data));
324 }
```

299-302 For NUMA, this simply calls the core function with the specified `pgdat`.

321-324 For UMA, this calls the core function with only the node `contig_page_data`.

E.4.5   Function: free_all_bootmem_core()   *(mm/bootmem.c)*

This is the core function that retires the boot memory allocator. It is divided into two major tasks:

- For all unallocated pages known to the allocator for this node, it does the following:

  - Clear the `PG_reserved` flag in its struct page.
  - Set the count to 1.
  - Call `__free_pages()` so that the buddy allocator can build its free lists.

- Frees all pages used for the bitmap and frees them to the buddy allocator.

```
245 static unsigned long __init free_all_bootmem_core(pg_data_t *pgdat)
246 {
247     struct page *page = pgdat->node_mem_map;
248     bootmem_data_t *bdata = pgdat->bdata;
```

```
249        unsigned long i, count, total = 0;
250        unsigned long idx;
251
252        if (!bdata->node_bootmem_map) BUG();
253
254        count = 0;
255        idx = bdata->node_low_pfn -
                  (bdata->node_boot_start >> PAGE_SHIFT);
256        for (i = 0; i < idx; i++, page++) {
257            if (!test_bit(i, bdata->node_bootmem_map)) {
258                count++;
259                ClearPageReserved(page);
260                set_page_count(page, 1);
261                __free_page(page);
262            }
263        }
264        total += count;
```

252 If no map is available, it means that this node has already been freed and that something woeful is wrong with the architecture-dependent code, so it calls BUG().

254 Keeps running count of the number of pages given to the buddy allocator.

255 idx is the last index that is addressable by this node.

256-263 Cycles through all pages addressable by this node.

257 If the page is marked free, then...

258 Increases the running count of pages given to the buddy allocator.

259 Clears the PG_reserved flag.

260 Sets the count to 1 so that the buddy allocator will think this is the last user of the page and place it in its free lists.

261 Calls the buddy allocator free function so that the page will be added to its free lists.

264 total will give the total number of pages given over by this function.

```
270        page = virt_to_page(bdata->node_bootmem_map);
271        count = 0;
272        for (i = 0;
           i < ((bdata->node_low_pfn - (bdata->node_boot_start >> PAGE_SHIFT)
                      )/8 + PAGE_SIZE-1)/PAGE_SIZE;
           i++,page++) {
273            count++;
```

```
274              ClearPageReserved(page);
275              set_page_count(page, 1);
276              __free_page(page);
277          }
278      total += count;
279      bdata->node_bootmem_map = NULL;
280
281      return total;
282 }
```

This block frees the allocator bitmap and returns.

270 Gets the `struct page` that is at the beginning of the bootmem map.

271 The count of pages freed by the bitmap.

272-277 For all pages used by the bitmap, this frees them to the buddy allocator in the same way the previous block of code did.

279 Sets the bootmem map to NULL to prevent it from being freed a second time by accident.

281 Returns the total number of pages freed by this function, or, in other words, returns the number of pages that were added to the buddy allocator's free lists.

Boot Memory
Allocator

Physical Page Allocation

Contents

Physical Page
Allocation

F.1 Allocating Pages

Contents

F.1.1 Function: alloc_pages() *(include/linux/mm.h)*
The call graph for this function is shown in Figure 6.2. It is declared as follows:

```
439 static inline struct page * alloc_pages(unsigned int gfp_mask,
                                 unsigned int order)
440 {
444      if (order >= MAX_ORDER)
445          return NULL;
446      return _alloc_pages(gfp_mask, order);
447 }
```

439 The `gfp_mask` (Get Free Pages) flags tell the allocator how it may behave. For example, if `GFP_WAIT` is not set, the allocator will not block and instead will return NULL if memory is tight. The order is the power of two number of pages to allocate.

444-445 A simple debugging check optimized away at compile time.

446 This function is described next.

F.1.2 Function: _alloc_pages() *(mm/page_alloc.c)*
The function _alloc_pages() comes in two varieties. The first is designed to only work with UMA architectures such as the x86 and is in mm/page_alloc.c. It only refers to the static node contig_page_data. The second is in mm/numa.c and is a simple extension. It uses a node-local allocation policy, which means that memory will be allocated from the bank closest to the processor. For the purposes of this book, only the mm/page_alloc.c version will be examined, but developers on NUMA architectures should read _alloc_pages() and _alloc_pages_pgdat() as well in mm/numa.c

```
244 #ifndef CONFIG_DISCONTIGMEM
245 struct page *_alloc_pages(unsigned int gfp_mask,
                             unsigned int order)
246 {
247     return __alloc_pages(gfp_mask, order,
```

```
248        contig_page_data.node_zonelists+(gfp_mask & GFP_ZONEMASK));
249 }
250 #endif
```

244 The ifndef is for UMA architectures like the x86. NUMA architectures used
the _alloc_pages() function in mm/numa.c, which employs a node local policy
for allocations.

245 The gfp_mask flags tell the allocator how it may behave. The order is the
power of two number of pages to allocate.

247 node_zonelists is an array of preferred fallback zones to allocate from. It
is initialized in build_zonelists()(See Section B.1.6). The lower 16 bits of
gfp_mask indicate what zone is preferable to allocate from. Applying the
bitmask gfp_mask & GFP_ZONEMASK will give the index in node_zonelists
that we prefer to allocate from.

F.1.3 Function: _alloc_pages() *(mm/page_alloc.c)*

At this stage, we've reached what is described as the "heart of the zoned buddy
allocator," the _alloc_pages() function. It is responsible for cycling through the
fallback zones and selecting one suitable for the allocation. If memory is tight, it
will take some steps to address the problem. It will wake **kswapd**, and, if necessary,
it will do the work of **kswapd** manually.

```
327 struct page * __alloc_pages(unsigned int gfp_mask,
                                unsigned int order,
                                zonelist_t *zonelist)
328 {
329      unsigned long min;
330      zone_t **zone, * classzone;
331      struct page * page;
332      int freed;
333
334      zone = zonelist->zones;
335      classzone = *zone;
336      if (classzone == NULL)
337           return NULL;
338      min = 1UL << order;
339      for (;;) {
340           zone_t *z = *(zone++);
341           if (!z)
342                break;
343
344           min += z->pages_low;
345           if (z->free_pages > min) {
346                page = rmqueue(z, order);
347                if (page)
```

Physical Page Allocation

```
348                        return page;
349            }
350    }
```

334 Sets the zone to be the preferred zone to allocate from.

335 The preferred zone is recorded as the classzone. If one of the pages' low watermarks is reached later, the classzone is marked as needing balance.

336-337 An unnecessary sanity check. `build_zonelists()` would need to be seriously broken for this to happen.

338-350 This style of block appears a number of times in this function. It reads as "cycle through all zones in this fallback list and see if the allocation can be satisfied without violating watermarks." The `pages_low` for each fallback zone is added together. This is deliberate to reduce the probability that a fallback zone will be used.

340 `z` is the zone currently been examined. The `zone` variable is moved to the next fallback zone.

341-342 If this is the last zone in the fallback list, break.

344 Increments the number of pages to be allocated by the watermark for easy comparisons. This happens for each zone in the fallback zones. Although this appears at first to be a bug, this behavior is actually intended to reduce the probability that a fallback zone is used.

345-349 Allocates the page block if it can be assigned without reaching the `pages_min` watermark. `rmqueue()`(See Section F.1.4) is responsible for removing the block of pages from the zone.

347-348 If the pages could be allocated, this returns a pointer to them.

```
352        classzone->need_balance = 1;
353        mb();
354        if (waitqueue_active(&kswapd_wait))
355            wake_up_interruptible(&kswapd_wait);
356
357        zone = zonelist->zones;
358        min = 1UL << order;
359        for (;;) {
360            unsigned long local_min;
361            zone_t *z = *(zone++);
362            if (!z)
363                break;
364
365            local_min = z->pages_min;
366            if (!(gfp_mask & __GFP_WAIT))
```

```
367                         local_min >>= 2;
368                 min += local_min;
369                 if (z->free_pages > min) {
370                         page = rmqueue(z, order);
371                         if (page)
372                                 return page;
373                 }
374         }
375
```

352 Marks the preferred zone as needing balance. This flag will be read later by **kswapd**.

353 This is a memory barrier. It ensures that all CPUs will see any changes made to variables before this line of code. This is important because **kswapd** could be running on a different processor than the memory allocator.

354-355 Wakes up **kswapd** if it is asleep.

357-358 Begins again with the first preferred zone and min value.

360-374 Cycles through all the zones. This time, it allocates the pages if they can be allocated without hitting the pages_min watermark.

365 local_min indicates how low a number of free pages that this zone can have.

366-367 If the process cannot wait or reschedule (__GFP_WAIT is clear), this allows the zone to be put in further memory pressure than the watermark normally allows.

```
376         /* here we're in the low on memory slow path */
377
378 rebalance:
379      if (current->flags & (PF_MEMALLOC | PF_MEMDIE)) {
380           zone = zonelist->zones;
381           for (;;) {
382                zone_t *z = *(zone++);
383                if (!z)
384                     break;
385
386                page = rmqueue(z, order);
387                if (page)
388                     return page;
389           }
390           return NULL;
391      }
```

378 This label is returned to after an attempt is made to synchronously free pages. From this line on, the low on memory path has been reached. It is likely the process will sleep.

379-391 These two flags are only set by the OOM killer. Because the process is trying to kill itself cleanly, this allocates the pages if at all possible because it is known they will be freed very soon.

```
393         /* Atomic allocations - we can't balance anything */
394         if (!(gfp_mask & __GFP_WAIT))
395                 return NULL;
396
397         page = balance_classzone(classzone, gfp_mask, order, &freed);
398         if (page)
399                 return page;
400
401         zone = zonelist->zones;
402         min = 1UL << order;
403         for (;;) {
404                 zone_t *z = *(zone++);
405                 if (!z)
406                         break;
407
408                 min += z->pages_min;
409                 if (z->free_pages > min) {
410                         page = rmqueue(z, order);
411                         if (page)
412                                 return page;
413                 }
414         }
415
416         /* Don't let big-order allocations loop */
417         if (order > 3)
418                 return NULL;
419
420         /* Yield for kswapd, and try again */
421         yield();
422         goto rebalance;
423 }
```

394-395 If the calling process cannot sleep, this returns NULL because the only way to allocate the pages from here involves sleeping.

397 balance_classzone()(See Section F.1.6) performs the work of **kswapd** in a synchronous fashion. The principal difference is that, instead of freeing the memory into a global pool, it is kept for the process using the current→local_pages linked list.

398-399 If a page block of the right order has been freed, this returns it. Just because this is NULL does not mean an allocation will fail because it could be a higher order of pages that was released.

403-414 This is identical to the previous block. It allocates the page blocks if it can be done without hitting the `pages_min` watermark.

417-418 Satisifing a large allocation like 2^4 number of pages is difficult. If it has not been satisfied by now, it is better to simply return NULL.

421 Yields the processor to give **kswapd** a chance to work.

422 Attempts to balance the zones again and to allocate.

F.1.4   Function: rmqueue()   *(mm/page_alloc.c)*

This function is called from `__alloc_pages()`. It is responsible for finding a block of memory large enough to be used for the allocation. If a block of memory of the requested size is not available, it will look for a larger order that may be split into two buddies. The actual splitting is performed by the `expand()` (See Section F.1.5) function.

```
198 static FASTCALL(struct page *rmqueue(zone_t *zone,
                                         unsigned int order));
199 static struct page * rmqueue(zone_t *zone, unsigned int order)
200 {
201         free_area_t * area = zone->free_area + order;
202         unsigned int curr_order = order;
203         struct list_head *head, *curr;
204         unsigned long flags;
205         struct page *page;
206
207         spin_lock_irqsave(&zone->lock, flags);
208         do {
209                 head = &area->free_list;
210                 curr = head->next;
211
212                 if (curr != head) {
213                         unsigned int index;
214
215                         page = list_entry(curr, struct page, list);
216                         if (BAD_RANGE(zone,page))
217                                 BUG();
218                         list_del(curr);
219                         index = page - zone->zone_mem_map;
220                         if (curr_order != MAX_ORDER-1)
221                                 MARK_USED(index, curr_order, area);
222                         zone->free_pages -= 1UL << order;
223
224                         page = expand(zone, page, index, order,
                                         curr_order, area);
225                         spin_unlock_irqrestore(&zone->lock, flags);
```

```
226
227                        set_page_count(page, 1);
228                        if (BAD_RANGE(zone,page))
229                              BUG();
230                        if (PageLRU(page))
231                              BUG();
232                        if (PageActive(page))
233                              BUG();
234                        return page;
235                }
236                curr_order++;
237                area++;
238        } while (curr_order < MAX_ORDER);
239        spin_unlock_irqrestore(&zone->lock, flags);
240
241        return NULL;
242 }
```

199 The parameters are the zone to allocate from and what order of pages are required.

201 Because the `free_area` is an array of linked lists, the order may be used as an an index within the array.

207 Acquires the zone lock.

208-238 This while block is responsible for finding what order of pages we will need to allocate from. If a free block is not at the order we are interested in, this checks the higher blocks until a suitable one is found.

209 `head` is the list of free page blocks for this order.

210 `curr` is the first block of pages.

212-235 If a free page block is at this order, this allocates it.

215 The page is set to be a pointer to the first page in the free block.

216-217 A sanity check that checks to make sure this page belongs to this zone and is within the `zone_mem_map`. It is unclear how this could possibly happen without severe bugs in the allocator itself that would place blocks in the wrong zones.

218 Because the block is going to be allocated, this removes it from the free list.

219 `index` treats the `zone_mem_map` as an array of pages so that index will be the offset within the array.

220-221 Toggles the bit that represents this pair of buddies. MARK_USED() is a macro that calculates which bit to toggle.

222 Updates the statistics for this zone. 1UL<<order is the number of pages being allocated.

224 expand()(See Section F.1.5) is the function responsible for splitting page blocks of higher orders.

225 No other updates to the zone need to take place, so this releases the lock.

227 Shows that the page is in use.

228-233 Performs a sanity check.

234 Page block has been successfully allocated, so this returns it.

236-237 If a page block was not free of the correct order, this moves to a higher order of page blocks and sees what can be found there.

239 No other updates to the zone need to take place, so this releases the lock.

241 No page blocks of the requested or higher order are availables, so this returns failure.

F.1.5 Function: expand() *(mm/page_alloc.c)*

This function splits page blocks of higher orders until a page block of the needed order is available.

```
177 static inline struct page * expand (zone_t *zone,
                          struct page *page,
                          unsigned long index,
                          int low,
                          int high,
                          free_area_t * area)
179 {
180      unsigned long size = 1 << high;
181
182      while (high > low) {
183              if (BAD_RANGE(zone,page))
184                  BUG();
185          area--;
186          high--;
187          size >>= 1;
188          list_add(&(page)->list, &(area)->free_list);
189          MARK_USED(index, high, area);
190          index += size;
191          page += size;
192      }
```

```
193          if (BAD_RANGE(zone,page))
194                  BUG();
195          return page;
196 }
```

177 The parameters are the following:

> **zone** is where the allocation is coming from.
>
> **page** is the first page of the block being split.
>
> **index** is the index of page within `mem_map`.
>
> **low** is the order of pages needed for the allocation.
>
> **high** is the order of pages that is being split for the allocation.
>
> **area** is the `free_area_t` representing the high order block of pages.

180 `size` is the number of pages in the block that is to be split.

182-192 Keeps splitting until a block of the needed page order is found.

183-184 A sanity check that checks to make sure this page belongs to this zone and is within the `zone_mem_map`.

185 `area` is now the next `free_area_t` representing the lower order of page blocks.

186 `high` is the next order of page blocks to be split.

187 The size of the block being split is now half as big.

188 Of the pair of buddies, the one lower in the `mem_map` is added to the free list for the lower order.

189 Toggles the bit representing the pair of buddies.

190 `index` is now the index of the second buddy of the newly created pair.

191 `page` now points to the second buddy of the newly created pair.

193-194 A sanity check.

195 The blocks have been successfully split, so this returns the page.

F.1.6   Function: `balance_classzone()`   *(mm/page_alloc.c)*

This function is part of the direct-reclaim path. Allocators that can sleep will call this function to start performing the work of **kswapd** in a synchronous fashion. Because the process is performing the work itself, the pages it frees of the desired order are reserved in a linked list in `current→local_pages`, and the number of page blocks in the list is stored in `current→nr_local_pages`. Note that page blocks are not the same as number of pages. A page block could be of any order.

```
253 static struct page * balance_classzone(zone_t * classzone,
                                            unsigned int gfp_mask,
                                            unsigned int order,
                                            int * freed)
254 {
255     struct page * page = NULL;
256     int __freed = 0;
257
258     if (!(gfp_mask & __GFP_WAIT))
259         goto out;
260     if (in_interrupt())
261         BUG();
262
263     current->allocation_order = order;
264     current->flags |= PF_MEMALLOC | PF_FREE_PAGES;
265
266     __freed = try_to_free_pages_zone(classzone, gfp_mask);
267
268     current->flags &= ~(PF_MEMALLOC | PF_FREE_PAGES);
269
```

258-259 If the caller is not allowed to sleep, goto out to exit the function. For this
to occur, the function would have to be called directly, or __alloc_pages()
would need to be deliberately broken.

260-261 This function may not be used by interrupts. Again, deliberate damage
would have to be introduced for this condition to occur.

263 Records the desired size of the allocation in current→allocation_order.
This is actually unused although it could have been used to only add pages of
the desired order to the local_pages list. As it is, the order of pages in the
list is stored in page→index.

264 Sets the flags that will the free functions to add the pages to the local_list.

266 Frees pages directly from the desired zone with try_to_free_pages_zone()
(See Section J.5.3). This is where the direct-reclaim path intersects with
kswapd.

268 Clears the flags again so that the free functions do not continue to add pages
to the local_pages list.

```
270     if (current->nr_local_pages) {
271         struct list_head * entry, * local_pages;
272         struct page * tmp;
273         int nr_pages;
274
275         local_pages = &current->local_pages;
```

Physical Page Allocation

```
276
277              if (likely(__freed)) {
278                   /* pick from the last inserted so we're lifo */
279                   entry = local_pages->next;
280                   do {
281                        tmp = list_entry(entry, struct page, list);
282                        if (tmp->index == order &&
                                 memclass(page_zone(tmp), classzone)) {
283                             list_del(entry);
284                             current->nr_local_pages--;
285                             set_page_count(tmp, 1);
286                             page = tmp;
287
288                             if (page->buffers)
289                                  BUG();
290                             if (page->mapping)
291                                  BUG();
292                             if (!VALID_PAGE(page))
293                                  BUG();
294                             if (PageLocked(page))
295                                  BUG();
296                             if (PageLRU(page))
297                                  BUG();
298                             if (PageActive(page))
299                                  BUG();
300                             if (PageDirty(page))
301                                  BUG();
302
303                             break;
304                        }
305                   } while ((entry = entry->next) != local_pages);
306              }
```

Presuming that pages exist in the local_pages list, this function will cycle through the list looking for a page block belonging to the desired zone and order.

270 Only enter this block if pages are stored in the local list.

275 Starts at the beginning of the list.

277 If pages were freed with try_to_free_pages_zone(), then...

279 The last one inserted is chosen first because it is likely to be cache hot, and it is desirable to use pages that have been recently referenced.

280-305 Cycles through the pages in the list until we find one of the desired order and zone.

281 Gets the page from this list entry.

282 The order of the page block is stored in `page→index`, so this checks if the order matches the desired order and that it belongs to the right zone. It is unlikely that pages from another zone are on this list, but it could occur if `swap_out()` is called to free pages directly from process page tables.

283 This is a page of the right order and zone, so it removes it from the list.

284 Decrements the number of page blocks in the list.

285 Sets the page count to 1 because it is about to be freed.

286 Sets `page` because it will be returned. `tmp` is needed for the next block for freeing the remaining pages in the local list.

288-301 Performs the same checks that are performed in `__free_pages_ok()` to ensure it is safe to free this page.

305 Moves to the next page in the list if the current one was not of the desired order and zone.

```
308        nr_pages = current->nr_local_pages;
309        /* free in reverse order so that the global
            * order will be lifo */
310        while ((entry = local_pages->prev) != local_pages) {
311            list_del(entry);
312            tmp = list_entry(entry, struct page, list);
313            __free_pages_ok(tmp, tmp->index);
314            if (!nr_pages--)
315                BUG();
316        }
317        current->nr_local_pages = 0;
318    }
319 out:
320    *freed = __freed;
321    return page;
322 }
```

This block frees the remaining pages in the list.

308 Gets the number of page blocks that are to be freed.

310 Loops until the `local_pages` list is empty.

311 Removes this page block from the list.

312 Gets the `struct page` for the entry.

313 Frees the page with `__free_pages_ok()` (See Section F.3.2).

314-315 If the count of page blocks reaches zero and pages are still in the list, it means that the accounting is seriously broken somewhere or that someone added pages to the `local_pages` list manually, so it calls `BUG()`.

317 Sets the number of page blocks to 0 because they have all been freed.

320 Updates the `freed` parameter to tell the caller how many pages were freed in total.

321 Returns the page block of the requested order and zone. If the freeing failed, this will be returning NULL.

F.2   Allocation Helper Functions

Contents

This section will cover miscellaneous helper functions and macros that the Buddy Allocator uses to allocate pages. Very few of them do "real" work and are available just for the convenience of the programmer.

F.2.1   Function: `alloc_page()`   *(include/linux/mm.h)*

This trivial macro just calls `alloc_pages()` with an order of 0 to return one page. It is declared as follows:

```
449 #define alloc_page(gfp_mask) alloc_pages(gfp_mask, 0)
```

F.2.2   Function: `__get_free_page()`   *(include/linux/mm.h)*

This trivial function calls `__get_free_pages()` with an order of 0 to return one page. It is declared as follows:

```
454 #define __get_free_page(gfp_mask) \
455            __get_free_pages((gfp_mask),0)
```

F.2.3   Function: `__get_free_pages()`   *(mm/page_alloc.c)*

This function is for callers who do not want to worry about pages and only want to get back an address they can use. It is declared as follows:

```
428 unsigned long __get_free_pages(unsigned int gfp_mask,
                         unsigned int order)
428 {
430      struct page * page;
431
432      page = alloc_pages(gfp_mask, order);
433      if (!page)
434            return 0;
435      return (unsigned long) page_address(page);
436 }
```

431 `alloc_pages()` does the work of allocating the page block. See Section F.1.1.

433-434 Makes sure -the page is valid.

435 `page_address()` returns the physical address of the page.

Physical Page Allocation

F.2.4   Function: __get_dma_pages()   *(include/linux/mm.h)*

This is of principal interest to device drivers. It will return memory from ZONE_DMA suitable for use with DMA devices. It is declared as follows:

```
457 #define __get_dma_pages(gfp_mask, order) \
458         __get_free_pages((gfp_mask) | GFP_DMA,(order))
```

458 The gfp_mask is or-ed with GFP_DMA to tell the allocator to allocate from ZONE_DMA.

F.2.5   Function: get_zeroed_page()   *(mm/page_alloc.c)*

This function will allocate one page and then zeros out the contents of it. It is declared as follows:

```
438 unsigned long get_zeroed_page(unsigned int gfp_mask)
439 {
440         struct page * page;
441
442         page = alloc_pages(gfp_mask, 0);
443         if (page) {
444                 void *address = page_address(page);
445                 clear_page(address);
446                 return (unsigned long) address;
447         }
448         return 0;
449 }
```

438 gfp_mask are the flags that affect allocator behavior.

442 alloc_pages() does the work of allocating the page block. See Section F.1.1.

444 page_address() returns the physical address of the page.

445 clear_page() will fill the contents of a page with zero.

446 Returns the address of the zeroed page.

F.3   Free Pages

Contents

F.3.1   Function: __free_pages()   *(mm/page_alloc.c)*

The call graph for this function is shown in Figure 6.4. Just to be confusing, the opposite to alloc_pages() is not free_pages(); it is __free_pages(). free_pages() is a helper function that takes an address as a parameter. It will be discussed in a later section.

```
451 void __free_pages(struct page *page, unsigned int order)
452 {
453         if (!PageReserved(page) && put_page_testzero(page))
454                 __free_pages_ok(page, order);
455 }
```

451 The parameters are the page that we want to free and what order block it is.

453 A sanity check. PageReserved() indicates that the page is reserved by the boot memory allocator. put_page_testzero() is just a macro wrapper around atomic_dec_and_test() that decrements the usage count and makes sure it is zero.

454 Calls the function that does all the hard work.

F.3.2   Function: __free_pages_ok()   *(mm/page_alloc.c)*

This function will do the actual freeing of the page and coalesce the buddies if possible.

```
81 static void FASTCALL(__free_pages_ok (struct page *page,
                          unsigned int order));
82 static void __free_pages_ok (struct page *page, unsigned int order)
83 {
84      unsigned long index, page_idx, mask, flags;
85      free_area_t *area;
86      struct page *base;
87      zone_t *zone;
88
93      if (PageLRU(page)) {
94              if (unlikely(in_interrupt()))
95                      BUG();
96              lru_cache_del(page);
97      }
98
```

Physical Page Allocation

```
99          if (page->buffers)
100                 BUG();
101         if (page->mapping)
102                 BUG();
103         if (!VALID_PAGE(page))
104                 BUG();
105         if (PageLocked(page))
106                 BUG();
107         if (PageActive(page))
108                 BUG();
109         page->flags &= ~((1<<PG_referenced) | (1<<PG_dirty));
```

82 The parameters are the beginning of the page block to free and what order number of pages are to be freed.

93-97 A dirty page on the LRU will still have the LRU bit set when pinned for I/O. On I/O completion, it is freed, so it must now be removed from the LRU list.

99-108 Sanity checks.

109 The flags showing a page has been referenced and is dirty have to be cleared because the page is now free and not in use.

```
110
111         if (current->flags & PF_FREE_PAGES)
112                 goto local_freelist;
113  back_local_freelist:
114
115         zone = page_zone(page);
116
117         mask = (~0UL) << order;
118         base = zone->zone_mem_map;
119         page_idx = page - base;
120         if (page_idx & ~mask)
121                 BUG();
122         index = page_idx >> (1 + order);
123
124         area = zone->free_area + order;
125
```

111-112 If this flag is set, the pages freed are to be kept for the process doing the freeing. This is set by balance_classzone()(See Section F.1.6) during page allocation if the caller is freeing the pages itself rather than waiting for **kswapd** to do the work.

115 The zone that the page belongs to is encoded within the page flags. The **page_zone()** macro returns the zone.

117 The calculation of mask is discussed in the companion document. It is basically related to the address calculation of the buddy.

118 base is the beginning of this zone_mem_map. For the buddy calculation to work, it was to be relative to an address 0 so that the addresses will be a power of two.

119 page_idx treats the zone_mem_map as an array of pages. This is the index page within the map.

120-121 If the index is not the proper power of two, things are severely broken, and calculation of the buddy will not work.

122 This index is the bit index within free_area→map.

124 area is the area storing the free lists and map for the order block that the pages are been freed from.

```
126        spin_lock_irqsave(&zone->lock, flags);
127
128        zone->free_pages -= mask;
129
130        while (mask + (1 << (MAX_ORDER-1))) {
131            struct page *buddy1, *buddy2;
132
133            if (area >= zone->free_area + MAX_ORDER)
134                BUG();
135            if (!__test_and_change_bit(index, area->map))
136                /*
137                 * the buddy page is still allocated.
138                 */
139                break;
140            /*
141             * Move the buddy up one level.
142             * This code is taking advantage of the identity:
143             *      -mask = 1+~mask
144             */
145            buddy1 = base + (page_idx ^ -mask);
146            buddy2 = base + page_idx;
147            if (BAD_RANGE(zone,buddy1))
148                BUG();
149            if (BAD_RANGE(zone,buddy2))
150                BUG();
151
152            list_del(&buddy1->list);
153            mask <<= 1;
154            area++;
155            index >>= 1;
```

```
156                 page_idx &= mask;
157        }
```

126 The zone is about to be altered, so this takes out the lock. The lock is an interrupt-safe lock because it is possible for interrupt handlers to allocate a page in this path.

128 Another side effect of the calculation of mask is that -mask is the number of pages that are to be freed.

130-157 The allocator will keep trying to coalesce blocks together until it either cannot merge or reaches the highest order that can be merged. mask will be adjusted for each order block that is merged. When the highest order that can be merged is reached, this while loop will evaluate to 0 and exit.

133-134 If by some miracle, mask is corrupt, this check will make sure the free_area array will not not be read beyond the end.

135 Toggles the bit representing this pair of buddies. If the bit was previously zero, both buddies were in use. Because this buddy is being freed, one is still in use and cannot be merged.

145-146 The calculation of the two addresses is discussed in Chapter 6.

147-150 A sanity check to make sure the pages are within the correct zone_mem_map and actually belong to this zone.

152 The buddy has been freed, so it removes it from any list it was part of.

153-156 Prepares to examine the higher order buddy for merging.

153 Moves the mask one bit to the left for order 2^{k+1}.

154 area is a pointer within an array, so area++ moves to the next index.

155 The index in the bitmap of the higher order.

156 The page index within the zone_mem_map for the buddy to merge.

```
158        list_add(&(base + page_idx)->list, &area->free_list);
159
160        spin_unlock_irqrestore(&zone->lock, flags);
161        return;
162
163  local_freelist:
164        if (current->nr_local_pages)
165             goto back_local_freelist;
166        if (in_interrupt())
167             goto back_local_freelist;
168
```

```
169         list_add(&page->list, &current->local_pages);
170         page->index = order;
171         current->nr_local_pages++;
172 }
```

158 As much merging as possible is completed and a new page block is free, so this adds it to the `free_list` for this order.

160-161 Changes to the zone are complete, so this frees the lock and returns.

163 This is the code path taken when the pages are not freed to the main pool, but instead are reserved for the process doing the freeing.

164-165 If the process already has reserved pages, it is not allowed to reserve any more, so it returns back. This is unusual because `balance_classzone()` assumes that more than one page block may be returned on this list. It is likely to be an oversight but may still work if the first page block freed is the same order and zone as required by `balance_classzone()`.

166-167 An interrupt does not have process context, so it has to free in the normal fashion. It is unclear how an interrupt could end up here at all. This check is likely to be bogus and impossible to be true.

169 Adds the page block to the list for the processes `local_pages`.

170 Records what order allocation it was for freeing later.

171 Increases the use count for `nr_local_pages`.

F.4   Free Helper Functions

Contents

These functions are very similar to the page allocation helper functions in that they do no "real" work themselves and depend on the `__free_pages()` function to perform the actual free.

F.4.1   Function: `free_pages()`   *(mm/page_alloc.c)*

This function takes an address instead of a page as a parameter to free. It is declared as follows:

```
457 void free_pages(unsigned long addr, unsigned int order)
458 {
459     if (addr != 0)
460         __free_pages(virt_to_page(addr), order);
461 }
```

460 The function is discussed in Section F.3.1. The macro `virt_to_page()` returns the `struct page` for the `addr`.

F.4.2   Function: `__free_page()`   *(include/linux/mm.h)*

This trivial macro just calls the function `__free_pages()` (See Section F.3.1) with an order 0 for one page. It is declared as follows:

```
472 #define __free_page(page) __free_pages((page), 0)
```

F.4.3   Function: `free_page()`   *(include/linux/mm.h)*

This trivial macro just calls the function `free_pages()`. The essential difference between this macro and `__free_page()` is that this function takes a virtual address as a parameter and `__free_page()` takes a `struct page`. It is declared as follows:

```
472 #define free_page(addr) free_pages((addr),0)
```

Noncontiguous Memory Allocation

Contents

Noncontiguous
Memory Allocation

G.1   Allocating a Noncontiguous Area

Contents

G.1.1   Function: `vmalloc()`   *(include/linux/vmalloc.h)*

The call graph for this function is shown in Figure 7.2. The following macros differ only by the `GFP_` flags (See Section 6.4) used. The size parameter is page aligned by `__vmalloc()`(See Section G.1.2).

```
37 static inline void * vmalloc (unsigned long size)
38 {
39     return __vmalloc(size, GFP_KERNEL | __GFP_HIGHMEM, PAGE_KERNEL);
40 }
45
46 static inline void * vmalloc_dma (unsigned long size)
47 {
48     return __vmalloc(size, GFP_KERNEL|GFP_DMA, PAGE_KERNEL);
49 }
54
55 static inline void * vmalloc_32(unsigned long size)
56 {
57     return __vmalloc(size, GFP_KERNEL, PAGE_KERNEL);
58 }
```

37 The flags indicate to use either `ZONE_NORMAL` or `ZONE_HIGHMEM` as necessary.

46 The flag indicates to only allocate from `ZONE_DMA`.

55 Only physical pages from `ZONE_NORMAL` will be allocated.

G.1.2   Function: `__vmalloc()`   *(mm/vmalloc.c)*

This function has three tasks. It page aligns the size request, asks `get_vm_area()` to find an area for the request and uses `vmalloc_area_pages()` to allocate the PTEs for the pages.

```
261 void * __vmalloc (unsigned long size, int gfp_mask, pgprot_t prot)
262 {
263     void * addr;
264     struct vm_struct *area;
```

```
265
266     size = PAGE_ALIGN(size);
267     if (!size || (size >> PAGE_SHIFT) > num_physpages)
268         return NULL;
269     area = get_vm_area(size, VM_ALLOC);
270     if (!area)
271         return NULL;
272     addr = area->addr;
273     if (__vmalloc_area_pages(VMALLOC_VMADDR(addr), size, gfp_mask,
274                             prot, NULL)) {
275         vfree(addr);
276         return NULL;
277     }
278     return addr;
279 }
```

261 The parameters are the size to allocate, the `GFP_` flags to use for allocation and what protection to give the PTE.

266 Aligns the `size` to a page size.

267 A sanity check. It makes sure the size is not 0 and that the size requested is not larger than the number of physical pages that has been requested.

269 Finds an area of virtual address space to store the allocation with `get_vm_area()` (See Section G.1.3).

272 The addr field has been filled by `get_vm_area()`.

273 Allocates the PTE entries needed for the allocation with `__vmalloc_area_pages()` (See Section G.1.5). If it fails, a nonzero value `-ENOMEM` is returned.

275-276 If the allocation fails, this frees any PTEs, pages and descriptions of the area.

278 Returns the address of the allocated area.

G.1.3   Function: get_vm_area()   *(mm/vmalloc.c)*

To allocate an area for the `vm_struct`, the slab allocator is asked to provide the necessary memory using `kmalloc()`. It then searches the `vm_struct` list linearly looking for a region large enough to satisfy a request, including a page pad at the end of the area.

```
195 struct vm_struct * get_vm_area(unsigned long size,
                                    unsigned long flags)
196 {
197     unsigned long addr, next;
```

```
198     struct vm_struct **p, *tmp, *area;
199
200     area = (struct vm_struct *) kmalloc(sizeof(*area), GFP_KERNEL);
201     if (!area)
202         return NULL;
203
204     size += PAGE_SIZE;
205     if(!size) {
206         kfree (area);
207         return NULL;
208     }
209
210     addr = VMALLOC_START;
211     write_lock(&vmlist_lock);
212     for (p = &vmlist; (tmp = *p) ; p = &tmp->next) {
213         if ((size + addr) < addr)
214             goto out;
215         if (size + addr <= (unsigned long) tmp->addr)
216             break;
217         next = tmp->size + (unsigned long) tmp->addr;
218         if (next > addr)
219             addr = next;
220         if (addr > VMALLOC_END-size)
221             goto out;
222     }
223     area->flags = flags;
224     area->addr = (void *)addr;
225     area->size = size;
226     area->next = *p;
227     *p = area;
228     write_unlock(&vmlist_lock);
229     return area;
230
231 out:
232     write_unlock(&vmlist_lock);
233     kfree(area);
234     return NULL;
235 }
```

195 The parameters are the size of the requested region, which should be a multiple
of the page size and the area flags, either VM_ALLOC or VM_IOREMAP.

200-202 Allocates space for the vm_struct description struct.

204 Pads the request so a page gap is between areas. This is to guard against
overwrites.

205-206 Ensures that the size is not 0 after the padding due to an overflow. If something does go wrong, this frees the `area` just allocated and returns NULL.

210 Starts the search at the beginning of the vmalloc address space.

211 Locks the list.

212-222 Walks through the list searching for an area large enough for the request.

213-214 Checks to make sure the end of the addressable range has not been reached.

215-216 If the requested area would fit between the current address and the next area, the search is complete.

217 Makes sure the address would not go over the end of the vmalloc address space.

223-225 Copies in the area information.

226-227 Links the new area into the list.

228-229 Unlocks the list and returns.

231 This label is reached if the request could not be satisfied.

232 Unlocks the list.

233-234 Frees the memory used for the area descriptor and returns.

G.1.4   Function: `vmalloc_area_pages()`   *(mm/vmalloc.c)*

This is just a wrapper around `__vmalloc_area_pages()`. This function exists for compatibility with older kernels. The name change was made to reflect that the new function `__vmalloc_area_pages()` is able to take an array of pages to use for insertion into the pagetables.

```
189 int vmalloc_area_pages(unsigned long address, unsigned long size,
190                     int gfp_mask, pgprot_t prot)
191 {
192         return __vmalloc_area_pages(address, size, gfp_mask,
                                    prot, NULL);
193 }
```

192 Calls `__vmalloc_area_pages()` with the same parameters. The `pages` array is passed as NULL because the pages will be allocated as necessary.

G.1.5   Function: __vmalloc_area_pages()   *(mm/vmalloc.c)*

This is the beginning of a standard pagetable walk function. This top-level function will step through all PGDs within an address range. For each PGD, it will call pmd_alloc() to allocate a PMD directory and call alloc_area_pmd() for the directory.

```
155 static inline int __vmalloc_area_pages (unsigned long address,
156                                          unsigned long size,
157                                          int gfp_mask,
158                                          pgprot_t prot,
159                                          struct page ***pages)
160 {
161     pgd_t * dir;
162     unsigned long end = address + size;
163     int ret;
164
165     dir = pgd_offset_k(address);
166     spin_lock(&init_mm.page_table_lock);
167     do {
168         pmd_t *pmd;
169
170         pmd = pmd_alloc(&init_mm, dir, address);
171         ret = -ENOMEM;
172         if (!pmd)
173             break;
174
175         ret = -ENOMEM;
176         if (alloc_area_pmd(pmd, address, end - address,
177                     gfp_mask, prot, pages))
                    break;
178
179         address = (address + PGDIR_SIZE) & PGDIR_MASK;
180         dir++;
181
182         ret = 0;
183     } while (address && (address < end));
184     spin_unlock(&init_mm.page_table_lock);
185     flush_cache_all();
186     return ret;
187 }
```

155 The parameters are the following:

> **address** is the starting address to allocate PMDs for.
>
> **size** is the size of the region.
>
> **gfp_mask** is the GFP_ flags for alloc_pages() (See Section F.1.1).

prot is the protection to give the PTE entry.

pages is an array of pages to use for insertion instead of having `alloc_area_pte()` allocate them one at a time. Only the `vmap()` interface passes in an array.

162 The end address is the starting address plus the size.

165 Gets the PGD entry for the starting address.

166 Locks the kernel reference pagetable.

167-183 For every PGD within this address range, this allocates a PMD directory and calls `alloc_area_pmd()` (See Section G.1.6).

170 Allocates a PMD directory.

176 Calls `alloc_area_pmd()` (See Section G.1.6), which will allocate a PTE for each PTE slot in the PMD.

179 `address` becomes the base address of the next PGD entry.

180 Moves `dir` to the next PGD entry.

184 Releases the lock to the kernel pagetable.

185 `flush_cache_all()` will flush all CPU caches. This is necessary because the kernel pagetables have changed.

186 Returns success.

G.1.6 Function: `alloc_area_pmd()` *(mm/vmalloc.c)*

This is the second stage of the standard pagetable walk to allocate PTE entries for an address range. For every PMD within a given address range on a PGD, `pte_alloc()` will create a PTE directory and then `alloc_area_pte()` will be called to allocate the physical pages.

```
132 static inline int alloc_area_pmd(pmd_t * pmd, unsigned long
133                          address, unsigned long size, int gfp_mask,
134                          pgprot_t prot, struct page ***pages)
135 {
136     unsigned long end;
137
138     address &= ~PGDIR_MASK;
139     end = address + size;
140     if (end > PGDIR_SIZE)
141         end = PGDIR_SIZE;
142     do {
143         pte_t * pte = pte_alloc(&init_mm, pmd, address);
144         if (!pte)
145             return -ENOMEM;
146         if (alloc_area_pte(pte, address, end - address,
```

```
147                         gfp_mask, prot, pages))
148               return -ENOMEM;
149           address = (address + PMD_SIZE) & PMD_MASK;
150           pmd++;
151      } while (address < end);
152      return 0;
152  }
```

132 The parameters are the following:

> **pmd** is the PMD that needs the allocations.
>
> **address** is the starting address to start from.
>
> **size** is the size of the region within the PMD to allocate for.
>
> **gfp_mask** is the GFP_ flags for `alloc_pages()` (See Section F.1.1).
>
> **prot** is the protection to give the PTE entry.
>
> **pages** is an optional array of pages to use instead of allocating each page individually.

138 Aligns the starting address to the PGD.

139-141 Calculates the end to be the end of the allocation or the end of the PGD, whichever occurs first.

142-151 For every PMD within the given address range, this allocates a PTE directory and calls `alloc_area_pte()`(See Section G.1.7).

143 Allocates the PTE directory.

146-147 Calls `alloc_area_pte()`, which will allocate the physical pages if an array of pages is not already supplied with **pages**.

149 **address** becomes the base address of the next PMD entry.

150 Moves **pmd** to the next PMD entry.

152 Returns success.

G.1.7   Function: `alloc_area_pte()`   *(mm/vmalloc.c)*

This is the last stage of the pagetable walk. For every PTE in the given PTE directory and address range, a page will be allocated and associated with the PTE.

```
95 static inline int alloc_area_pte (pte_t * pte, unsigned long address,
96                        unsigned long size, int gfp_mask,
97                        pgprot_t prot, struct page ***pages)
98 {
99     unsigned long end;
100
101     address &= ~PMD_MASK;
```

```
102     end = address + size;
103     if (end > PMD_SIZE)
104         end = PMD_SIZE;
105     do {
106         struct page * page;
107
108         if (!pages) {
109             spin_unlock(&init_mm.page_table_lock);
110             page = alloc_page(gfp_mask);
111             spin_lock(&init_mm.page_table_lock);
112         } else {
113             page = (**pages);
114             (*pages)++;
115
116             /* Add a reference to the page so we can free later */
117             if (page)
118                 atomic_inc(&page->count);
119
120         }
121         if (!pte_none(*pte))
122             printk(KERN_ERR "alloc_area_pte: page already exists\n");
123         if (!page)
124             return -ENOMEM;
125         set_pte(pte, mk_pte(page, prot));
126         address += PAGE_SIZE;
127         pte++;
128     } while (address < end);
129     return 0;
130 }
```

101 Aligns the address to a PMD directory.

103-104 The end address is the end of the request or the end of the directory, whichever occurs first.

105-128 Loops through every PTE in this page. If a `pages` array is supplied, it uses pages from it to populate the table. Otherwise, it allocates each one individually.

108-111 If an array of `pages` is not supplied, this unlocks the kernel reference pagetable, allocates a page with `alloc_page()` and reacquires the spinlock.

112-120 If not, it takes one page from the array and increments its usage count as it is about to be inserted into the reference pagetable.

121-122 If the PTE is already in use, it means that the areas in the vmalloc region are overlapping somehow.

Noncontiguous
Memory Allocation

123-124 Returns failure if physical pages are not available.

125 Sets the `page` with the desired protection bits (`prot`) into the PTE.

126 `address` becomes the address of the next PTE.

127 Moves to the next PTE.

129 Returns success.

G.1.8 Function: vmap()   *(mm/vmalloc.c)*
This function allows a caller-supplied array of `pages` to be inserted into the vmalloc address space. This is unused in 2.4.22, and I suspect it is an accidental backport from 2.6.x where it is used by the sound subsystem core.

```
281 void * vmap(struct page **pages, int count,
282              unsigned long flags, pgprot_t prot)
283 {
284     void * addr;
285     struct vm_struct *area;
286     unsigned long size = count << PAGE_SHIFT;
287
288     if (!size || size > (max_mapnr << PAGE_SHIFT))
289         return NULL;
290     area = get_vm_area(size, flags);
291     if (!area) {
292         return NULL;
293     }
294     addr = area->addr;
295     if (__vmalloc_area_pages(VMALLOC_VMADDR(addr), size, 0,
296                             prot, &pages)) {
297         vfree(addr);
298         return NULL;
299     }
300     return addr;
301 }
```

281 The parameters are the following:

> **pages** is the caller-supplied array of pages to insert.
>
> **count** is the number of pages in the array.
>
> **flags** is the flags to use for the `vm_struct`.
>
> **prot** is the protection bits to set the PTE with.

286 Calculates the size in bytes of the region to create based on the size of the array.

288-289 Makes sure the size of the region does not exceed limits.

290-293 Uses `get_vm_area()` to find a region large enough for the mapping. If one is not found, it returns NULL.

294 Gets the virtual address of the area.

295 Inserts the array into the pagetable with `__vmalloc_area_pages()` (See Section G.1.4).

297 If the insertion fails, this frees the region and returns NULL.

298 Returns the virtual address of the newly mapped region.

G.2   Freeing a Noncontiguous Area

Contents

G.2.1   Function: `vfree()`   *(mm/vmalloc.c)*

The call graph for this function is shown in Figure 7.4. This is the top-level function responsible for freeing a noncontiguous area of memory. It performs basic sanity checks before finding the `vm_struct` for the requested `addr`. Once found, it calls `vmfree_area_pages()`.

```
237 void vfree(void * addr)
238 {
239     struct vm_struct **p, *tmp;
240
241     if (!addr)
242         return;
243     if ((PAGE_SIZE-1) & (unsigned long) addr) {
244         printk(KERN_ERR
                "Trying to vfree() bad address (%p)\n", addr);
245         return;
246     }
247     write_lock(&vmlist_lock);
248     for (p = &vmlist ; (tmp = *p) ; p = &tmp->next) {
249         if (tmp->addr == addr) {
250             *p = tmp->next;
251             vmfree_area_pages(VMALLOC_VMADDR(tmp->addr),
                        tmp->size);
252             write_unlock(&vmlist_lock);
253             kfree(tmp);
254             return;
255         }
256     }
257     write_unlock(&vmlist_lock);
258     printk(KERN_ERR
            "Trying to vfree() nonexistent vm area (%p)\n", addr);
259 }
```

237 The parameter is the address returned by `get_vm_area()` (See Section G.1.3) to either `vmalloc()` or `ioremap()`.

241-243 Ignores NULL addresses.

243-246 Checks to see if the address is page aligned and is a reasonable quick guess to see if the area is valid.

247 Acquires a write lock to the `vmlist`.

248 Cycles through the `vmlist` looking for the correct `vm_struct` for `addr`.

249 If this is the correct address, then ...

250 Removes this area from the `vmlist` linked list.

251 Frees all pages associated with the address range.

252 Releases the `vmlist` lock.

253 Frees the memory used for the `vm_struct` and returns.

257-258 The `vm_struct` was not found. This releases the lock and prints a message about the failed free.

G.2.2 Function: `vmfree_area_pages()` *(mm/vmalloc.c)*

This is the first stage of the pagetable walk to free all pages and PTEs associated with an address range. It is responsible for stepping through the relevant PGDs and for flushing the TLB.

```
80 void vmfree_area_pages(unsigned long address, unsigned long size)
81 {
82     pgd_t * dir;
83     unsigned long end = address + size;
84
85     dir = pgd_offset_k(address);
86     flush_cache_all();
87     do {
88         free_area_pmd(dir, address, end - address);
89         address = (address + PGDIR_SIZE) & PGDIR_MASK;
90         dir++;
91     } while (address && (address < end));
92     flush_tlb_all();
93 }
```

80 The parameters are the starting `address` and the `size` of the region.

82 The address space end is the starting address plus its size.

85 Gets the first PGD for the address range.

86 Flushes the cache CPU so that cache hits will not occur on pages that are to be deleted. This is a null operation on many architectures, including the x86.

87 Calls `free_area_pmd()` (See Section G.2.3) to perform the second stage of the pagetable walk.

89 `address` becomes the starting address of the next PGD.

90 Moves to the next PGD.

92 Flushes the TLB because the pagetables have now changed.

G.2.3   Function: `free_area_pmd()`   *(mm/vmalloc.c)*

This is the second stage of the pagetable walk. For every PMD in this directory, it calls `free_area_pte()` to free up the pages and PTEs.

```
56 static inline void free_area_pmd(pgd_t * dir,
                      unsigned long address,
                      unsigned long size)
57 {
58     pmd_t * pmd;
59     unsigned long end;
60
61     if (pgd_none(*dir))
62         return;
63     if (pgd_bad(*dir)) {
64         pgd_ERROR(*dir);
65         pgd_clear(dir);
66         return;
67     }
68     pmd = pmd_offset(dir, address);
69     address &= ~PGDIR_MASK;
70     end = address + size;
71     if (end > PGDIR_SIZE)
72         end = PGDIR_SIZE;
73     do {
74         free_area_pte(pmd, address, end - address);
75         address = (address + PMD_SIZE) & PMD_MASK;
76         pmd++;
77     } while (address < end);
78 }
```

56 The parameters are the PGD being stepped through, the starting address and the length of the region.

61-62 If there is no PGD, this returns. This can occur after `vfree()` (See Section G.2.1) is called during a failed allocation.

63-67 A PGD can be bad if the entry is not present, it is marked read-only or it is marked accessed or dirty.

68 Gets the first PMD for the address range.

69 Makes the address PGD aligned.

70-72 `end` is either the end of the space to free or the end of this PGD, whichever is first.

73-77 For every PMD, this calls `free_area_pte()` (See Section G.2.4) to free the PTE entries.

75 `address` is the base address of the next PMD.

76 Moves to the next PMD.

G.2.4 Function: `free_area_pte()` *(mm/vmalloc.c)*

This is the final stage of the pagetable walk. For every PTE in the given PMD within the address range, it will free the PTE and the associated page.

```
22 static inline void free_area_pte(pmd_t * pmd, unsigned long address,
                unsigned long size)
23 {
24     pte_t * pte;
25     unsigned long end;
26
27     if (pmd_none(*pmd))
28         return;
29     if (pmd_bad(*pmd)) {
30         pmd_ERROR(*pmd);
31         pmd_clear(pmd);
32         return;
33     }
34     pte = pte_offset(pmd, address);
35     address &= ~PMD_MASK;
36     end = address + size;
37     if (end > PMD_SIZE)
38         end = PMD_SIZE;
39     do {
40         pte_t page;
41         page = ptep_get_and_clear(pte);
42         address += PAGE_SIZE;
43         pte++;
44         if (pte_none(page))
45             continue;
46         if (pte_present(page)) {
47             struct page *ptpage = pte_page(page);
48             if (VALID_PAGE(ptpage) &&
                (!PageReserved(ptpage)))
49                 __free_page(ptpage);
50             continue;
51         }
52         printk(KERN_CRIT
```

```
                "Whee.. Swapped out page in kernel page table\n");
53    } while (address < end);
54 }
```

22 The parameters are the PMD that PTEs are being freed from, the starting address and the size of the region to free.

27-28 The PMD could be absent if this region is from a failed `vmalloc()`.

29-33 A PMD can be bad if it is not in main memory, it is read only or it is marked dirty or accessed.

34 `pte` is the first PTE in the address range.

35 Aligns the address to the PMD.

36-38 The end is either the end of the requested region or the end of the PMD, whichever occurs first.

38-53 Steps through all PTEs, performs checks and frees the PTE with its associated page.

41 `ptep_get_and_clear()` will remove a PTE from a pagetable and return it to the caller.

42 `address` will be the base address of the next PTE.

43 Moves to the next PTE.

44 If there was no PTE, this simply continues.

46-51 If the page is present, this performs basic checks and then frees it.

47 `pte_page()` uses the global `mem_map` to find the `struct page` for the PTE.

48-49 Makes sure the page is a valid page and that it is not reserved before calling `__free_page()` to free the physical page.

50 Continues to the next PTE.

52 If this line is reached, a PTE within the kernel address space was somehow swapped out. Kernel memory is not swappable, so this is a critical error.

Slab Allocator

Contents

Slab Allocator

H.1   Cache Manipulation

Contents

H.1.1   Cache Creation

H.1.1.1   Function: `kmem_cache_create()`   *(mm/slab.c)*

The call graph for this function is shown in Figure 8.3. This function is responsible for the creation of a new cache and will be dealt with in chunks due to its size. The chunks roughly are the following:

- Perform basic sanity checks for bad usage.

- Perform debugging checks if `CONFIG_SLAB_DEBUG` is set.

- Allocate a `kmem_cache_t` from the `cache_cache` slab cache.

- Align the object size to the word size.

- Calculate how many objects will fit on a slab.

- Align the slab size to the hardware cache.

- Calculate color offsets.

- Initialize remaining fields in cache descriptor.

- Add the new cache to the cache chain.

```
621 kmem_cache_t *
622 kmem_cache_create (const char *name, size_t size,
623     size_t offset, unsigned long flags,
        void (*ctor)(void*, kmem_cache_t *, unsigned long),
624     void (*dtor)(void*, kmem_cache_t *, unsigned long))
625 {
626     const char *func_nm = KERN_ERR "kmem_create: ";
627     size_t left_over, align, slab_size;
```

```
628        kmem_cache_t *cachep = NULL;
629
633        if ((!name) ||
634            ((strlen(name) >= CACHE_NAMELEN - 1)) ||
635            in_interrupt() ||
636            (size < BYTES_PER_WORD) ||
637            (size > (1<<MAX_OBJ_ORDER)*PAGE_SIZE) ||
638            (dtor && !ctor) ||
639            (offset < 0 || offset > size))
640                BUG();
641
```

This block performs basic sanity checks for bad usage.

622 The parameters of the function are the following:

- **name** The human readable name of the cache

- **size** The size of an object

- **offset** Used to specify a specific alignment for objects in the cache, but usually left as 0

- **flags** Static cache flags

- **ctor** A constructor function to call for each object during slab creation

- **dtor** The corresponding destructor function. The destructor function is expected to leave an object in an initialized state.

633-640 These are all serious usage bugs that prevent the cache from even attempting to create.

634 This is used if the human-readable name is greater than the maximum size for a cache name (CACHE_NAMELEN).

635 An interrupt handler cannot create a cache because access to interrupt-safe spinlocks and semaphores are needed.

636 The object size must be at least a word in size. The slab allocator is not suitable for objects with size measured in individual bytes.

637 The largest possible slab that can be created is $2^{\mathrm{MAX\_OBJ\_ORDER}}$ number of pages, which provides 32 pages.

638 A destructor cannot be used if a constructor is available.

639 The offset cannot be before the slab or beyond the boundary of the first page.

640 Calls BUG() to exit.

```
642 #if DEBUG
643     if ((flags & SLAB_DEBUG_INITIAL) && !ctor) {
645         printk("%sNo con, but init state check
                 requested - %s\n", func_nm, name);
646         flags &= ~SLAB_DEBUG_INITIAL;
647     }
648
649     if ((flags & SLAB_POISON) && ctor) {
651         printk("%sPoisoning requested, but con given - %s\n",
                                              func_nm, name);
652         flags &= ~SLAB_POISON;
653     }
654 #if FORCED_DEBUG
655     if ((size < (PAGE_SIZE>>3)) &&
        !(flags & SLAB_MUST_HWCACHE_ALIGN))
660         flags |= SLAB_RED_ZONE;
661     if (!ctor)
662         flags |= SLAB_POISON;
663 #endif
664 #endif
670     BUG_ON(flags & ~CREATE_MASK);
```

This block performs debugging checks if CONFIG_SLAB_DEBUG is set.

643-646 The flag SLAB_DEBUG_INITIAL requests that the constructor check the objects to make sure they are in an initialized state. For this, a constructor must exist. If it does not, the flag is cleared.

649-653 A slab can be poisoned with a known pattern to make sure an object was not used before it was allocated, but a constructor would ruin this pattern by falsely reporting a bug. If a constructor exists, this removes the SLAB_POISON flag if set.

655-660 Only small objects will be red-zoned for debugging. Red-zoning large objects would cause severe fragmentation.

661-662 If there is no constructor, this sets the poison bit.

670 The CREATE_MASK is set with all the allowable flags kmem_cache_create() (See Section H.1.1.1) that it can be called with. This prevents callers from using debugging flags when they are not available and BUG()s it instead.

```
673     cachep =
        (kmem_cache_t *) kmem_cache_alloc(&cache_cache,
                    SLAB_KERNEL);
674     if (!cachep)
675         goto opps;
676     memset(cachep, 0, sizeof(kmem_cache_t));
```

Slab Allocator

Allocates a `kmem_cache_t` from the `cache_cache` slab cache.

673 Allocates a cache descriptor object from the `cache_cache` with `kmem_cache_alloc()` (See Section H.3.2.1).

674-675 If out of memory, goto `opps`, which handles the OOM situation.

676 Zero-fills the object to prevent surprises with uninitialized data.

```
682      if (size & (BYTES_PER_WORD-1)) {
683          size += (BYTES_PER_WORD-1);
684          size &= ~(BYTES_PER_WORD-1);
685          printk("%sForcing size word alignment
                  - %s\n", func_nm, name);
686      }
687
688 #if DEBUG
689      if (flags & SLAB_RED_ZONE) {
694          flags &= ~SLAB_HWCACHE_ALIGN;
695          size += 2*BYTES_PER_WORD;
696      }
697 #endif
698      align = BYTES_PER_WORD;
699      if (flags & SLAB_HWCACHE_ALIGN)
700          align = L1_CACHE_BYTES;
701
703      if (size >= (PAGE_SIZE>>3))
708          flags |= CFLGS_OFF_SLAB;
709
710      if (flags & SLAB_HWCACHE_ALIGN) {
714          while (size < align/2)
715              align /= 2;
716          size = (size+align-1)&(~(align-1));
717      }
```

Aligns the object size to some word-sized boundary.

682 If the size is not aligned to the size of a word, then...

683-684 Increases the object by the size of a word and then masks out the lower bits. This will effectively round the object size up to the next word boundary.

685 Prints out an informational message for debugging purposes.

688-697 If debugging is enabled, the alignments have to change slightly.

694 Do not bother trying to align things to the hardware cache if the slab will be red-zoned. The red-zoning of the object is going to offset it by moving the object one word away from the cache boundary.

695 The size of the object increases by two `BYTES_PER_WORD` to store the red-zone mark at either end of the object.

698 Initializes the alignment to be to a word boundary. This will change if the caller has requested a CPU cache alignment.

699-700 If requested, this aligns the objects to the L1 CPU cache.

703 If the objects are large, this stores the slab descriptors off-slab. This will allow better packing of objects into the slab.

710 If hardware cache alignment is requested, the size of the objects must be adjusted to align themselves to the hardware cache.

714-715 Tries and packs objects into one cache line if they fit while still keeping the alignment. This is important to arches (e.g., Alpha or Pentium 4) with large L1 cache bytes. `align` will be adjusted to be the smallest that will give hardware cache alignment. For machines with large L1 cache lines, two or more small objects may fit into each line. For example, two objects from the size-32 cache will fit on one cache line from a Pentium 4.

716 Rounds the cache size up to the hardware cache alignment.

```
724     do {
725         unsigned int break_flag = 0;
726 cal_wastage:
727         kmem_cache_estimate(cachep->gfporder,
                size, flags,
728             &left_over,
                &cachep->num);
729         if (break_flag)
730             break;
731         if (cachep->gfporder >= MAX_GFP_ORDER)
732             break;
733         if (!cachep->num)
734             goto next;
735         if (flags & CFLGS_OFF_SLAB &&
            cachep->num > offslab_limit) {
737             cachep->gfporder--;
738             break_flag++;
739             goto cal_wastage;
740         }
741
746         if (cachep->gfporder >= slab_break_gfp_order)
747             break;
748
749         if ((left_over*8) <= (PAGE_SIZE<<cachep->gfporder))
750             break;
```

```
751 next:
752         cachep->gfporder++;
753     } while (1);
754
755     if (!cachep->num) {
756         printk("kmem_cache_create: couldn't
                 create cache %s.\n", name);
757         kmem_cache_free(&cache_cache, cachep);
758         cachep = NULL;
759         goto opps;
760     }
```

Calculates how many objects will fit on a slab and adjusts the slab size as necessary.

727-728 kmem_cache_estimate() (See Section H.1.2.1) calculates the number of objects that can fit on a slab at the current gfp order and what the amount of leftover bytes will be.

729-730 The break_flag is set if the number of objects fitting on the slab exceeds the number that can be kept when offslab slab descriptors are used.

731-732 The order number of pages used must not exceed MAX_GFP_ORDER (5).

733-734 If even one object did not fill, goto next, which will increase the gfporder used for the cache.

735 If the slab descriptor is kept off-cache, but the number of objects exceeds the number that can be tracked with bufctl's off-slab, then ...

737 Reduces the order number of pages used.

738 Sets the break_flag so that the loop will exit.

739 Calculates the new wastage figures.

746-747 The slab_break_gfp_order is the order to not exceed unless 0 objects fit on the slab. This check ensures the order is not exceeded.

749-759 A rough check for internal fragmentation. If the wastage as a fraction of the total size of the cache is less than one-eighth, it is acceptable.

752 If the fragmentation is too high, this increases the gfp order and recalculates the number of objects that can be stored and the wastage.

755 If, after adjustments, objects still do not fit in the cache, it cannot be created.

757-758 Frees the cache descriptor and sets the pointer to NULL.

758 Goto opps, which simply returns the NULL pointer.

```
761        slab_size = L1_CACHE_ALIGN(
                 cachep->num*sizeof(kmem_bufctl_t) +
                 sizeof(slab_t));
762
767        if (flags & CFLGS_OFF_SLAB && left_over >= slab_size) {
768            flags &= ~CFLGS_OFF_SLAB;
769            left_over -= slab_size;
770        }
```

This block aligns the slab size to the hardware cache.

761 slab_size is the total size of the slab descriptor, *not* the size of the slab itself. It is the size slab_t struct and the `number of objects * size of the bufctl`.

767-769 If enough space is left over for the slab descriptor and it was specified to place the descriptor off-slab, this removes the flag and updates the amount of left_over bytes. This will impact the cache coloring, but, with the large objects associated with off-slab descriptors, this is not a problem.

```
773        offset += (align-1);
774        offset &= ~(align-1);
775        if (!offset)
776            offset = L1_CACHE_BYTES;
777        cachep->colour_off = offset;
778        cachep->colour = left_over/offset;
```

Calculates color offsets.

773-774 offset is the offset within the page that the caller requested. This will make sure the offset requested is at the correct alignment for cache usage.

775-776 If somehow the offset is 0, this sets it to be aligned for the CPU cache.

777 The offset to use to keep objects on different cache lines. Each slab created will be given a different color offset.

778 The number of different offsets that can be used.

```
781        if (!cachep->gfporder && !(flags & CFLGS_OFF_SLAB))
782            flags |= CFLGS_OPTIMIZE;
783
784        cachep->flags = flags;
785        cachep->gfpflags = 0;
786        if (flags & SLAB_CACHE_DMA)
787            cachep->gfpflags |= GFP_DMA;
788        spin_lock_init(&cachep->spinlock);
789        cachep->objsize = size;
```

```
790        INIT_LIST_HEAD(&cachep->slabs_full);
791        INIT_LIST_HEAD(&cachep->slabs_partial);
792        INIT_LIST_HEAD(&cachep->slabs_free);
793
794        if (flags & CFLGS_OFF_SLAB)
795            cachep->slabp_cache =
                   kmem_find_general_cachep(slab_size,0);
796        cachep->ctor = ctor;
797        cachep->dtor = dtor;
799        strcpy(cachep->name, name);
800
801 #ifdef CONFIG_SMP
802        if (g_cpucache_up)
803            enable_cpucache(cachep);
804 #endif
```

This block initializes remaining fields in the cache descriptor.

781-782 For caches with slabs of only one page, the CFLGS_OPTIMIZE flag is set. In reality, it makes no difference because the flag is unused.

784 Sets the cache static flags.

785 Zeroes out the gfpflags. This is a defunct operation, as memset() is used to clear these flags after the cache descriptor is allocated.

786-787 If the slab is for DMA use, this sets the GFP_DMA flag so that the buddy allocator will use ZONE_DMA.

788 Initializes the spinlock for accessing the cache.

789 Copies in the object size, which now takes hardware cache alignment if necessary.

790-792 Initializes the slab lists.

794-795 If the descriptor is kept off-slab, this allocates a slab manager and places it for use in slabp_cache (See Section H.2.1.2).

796-797 Sets the pointers to the constructor and destructor functions.

799 Copies in the human-readable name.

802-803 If per-CPU caches are enabled, this creates a set for this cache (See Section 8.5).

```
806        down(&cache_chain_sem);
807        {
808            struct list_head *p;
809
```

```
810          list_for_each(p, &cache_chain) {
811              kmem_cache_t *pc = list_entry(p,
                     kmem_cache_t, next);
812
814              if (!strcmp(pc->name, name))
815                  BUG();
816          }
817      }
818
822      list_add(&cachep->next, &cache_chain);
823      up(&cache_chain_sem);
824 opps:
825      return cachep;
826 }
```

This block adds the new cache to the cache chain.

806 Acquires the semaphore used to synchronize access to the cache chain.

810-816 Checks every cache on the cache chain and makes sure no other cache has the same name. If one does, it means two caches of the same type are being created, which is a serious bug.

811 Gets the cache from the list.

814-815 Compares the names, and if they match, it uses BUG(). It is worth noting that the new cache is not deleted, but this error is the result of sloppy programming during development and is not a normal scenario.

822 Links the cache into the chain.

823 Releases the cache chain semaphore.

825 Returns the new cache pointer.

H.1.2   Calculating the Number of Objects on a Slab

H.1.2.1   Function: kmem_cache_estimate()   *(mm/slab.c)*

During cache creation, it is determined how many objects can be stored in a slab and how much waste there will be. The following function calculates how many objects may be stored, taking into account if the slab and bufctls must be stored on-slab.

```
388 static void kmem_cache_estimate (unsigned long gfporder,
            size_t size,
389         int flags, size_t *left_over, unsigned int *num)
390 {
391     int i;
392     size_t wastage = PAGE_SIZE<<gfporder;
```

Slab Allocator

```
393     size_t extra = 0;
394     size_t base = 0;
395
396     if (!(flags & CFLGS_OFF_SLAB)) {
397         base = sizeof(slab_t);
398         extra = sizeof(kmem_bufctl_t);
399     }
400     i = 0;
401     while (i*size + L1_CACHE_ALIGN(base+i*extra) <= wastage)
402         i++;
403     if (i > 0)
404         i--;
405
406     if (i > SLAB_LIMIT)
407         i = SLAB_LIMIT;
408
409     *num = i;
410     wastage -= i*size;
411     wastage -= L1_CACHE_ALIGN(base+i*extra);
412     *left_over = wastage;
413 }
```

388 The parameters of the function are as follows:

- **gfporder** The 2^{gfporder} number of pages to allocate for each slab
- **size** The size of each object
- **flags** The cache flags
- **left_over** The number of bytes left over in the slab, which is returned to caller
- **num** The number of objects that will fit in a slab, which is returned to caller

392 wastage is decremented through the function. It starts with the maximum possible amount of wastage.

393 extra is the number of bytes needed to store kmem_bufctl_t.

394 base is where usable memory in the slab starts.

396 If the slab descriptor is kept on cache, the base begins at the end of the slab_t struct and the number of bytes needed to store the bufctl is the size of kmem_bufctl_t.

400 i becomes the number of objects that the slab can hold.

401-402 Counts up the number of objects that the cache can store. i*size is the size of the object itself. L1_CACHE_ALIGN(base+i*extra) is slightly trickier.

This is calculating the amount of memory needed to store the `kmem_bufctl_t` needed for every object in the slab. Because it is at the beginning of the slab, it is L1 cache-aligned so that the first object in the slab will be aligned to the hardware cache. `i*extra` will calculate the amount of space needed to hold a `kmem_bufctl_t` for this object. Because wastage starts out as the size of the slab, its use is overloaded here.

403-404 Because the previous loop counts until the slab overflows, the number of objects that can be stored is `i-1`.

406-407 `SLAB_LIMIT` is the absolute largest number of objects a slab can store. It is defined as 0xffffFFFE because this is the largest number that `kmem_bufctl_t()`, which is an unsigned integer, can hold.

409 `num` is now the number of objects a slab can hold.

410 Takes away the space taken up by all the objects from wastage.

411 Takes away the space taken up by the `kmem_bufctl_t`.

412 Wastage has now been calculated as the leftover space in the slab.

H.1.3   Cache Shrinking

The call graph for `kmem_cache_shrink()` is shown in Figure 8.5. Two varieties of shrink functions are provided. `kmem_cache_shrink()` removes all slabs from `slabs_free` and returns the number of pages freed as a result. `__kmem_cache_shrink()` frees all slabs from `slabs_free` and then verifies that `slabs_partial` and `slabs_full` are empty. This is important during cache destruction when it doesn't matter how many pages are freed, just that the cache is empty.

H.1.3.1   Function: `kmem_cache_shrink()`   *(mm/slab.c)*

This function performs basic debugging checks and then acquires the cache descriptor lock before freeing slabs. At one time, it also used to call `drain_cpu_caches()` to free up objects on the per-CPU cache. It is curious that this was removed because it is possible slabs could not be freed due to an object being allocated on a per-CPU cache, but not in use.

```
966 int kmem_cache_shrink(kmem_cache_t *cachep)
967 {
968     int ret;
969
970     if (!cachep || in_interrupt() ||
        !is_chained_kmem_cache(cachep))
971         BUG();
972
973     spin_lock_irq(&cachep->spinlock);
974     ret = __kmem_cache_shrink_locked(cachep);
```

```
975        spin_unlock_irq(&cachep->spinlock);
976
977        return ret << cachep->gfporder;
978 }
```

966 The parameter is the cache being shrunk.

970 Checks the following:

- The cache pointer is not NULL.
- An interrupt is not the caller.
- The cache is on the cache chain and is not a bad pointer.

973 Acquires the cache descriptor lock and disables interrupts.

974 Shrinks the cache.

975 Releases the cache lock and enables interrupts.

976 Returns the number of pages freed, but does not take into account the objects
freed by draining the CPU.

H.1.3.2   Function: __kmem_cache_shrink()   *(mm/slab.c)*
This function is identical to kmem_cache_shrink() except it returns if the cache
is empty. This is important during cache destruction when it is not important how
much memory was freed, just that it is safe to delete the cache and not leak memory.

```
945 static int __kmem_cache_shrink(kmem_cache_t *cachep)
946 {
947        int ret;
948
949        drain_cpu_caches(cachep);
950
951        spin_lock_irq(&cachep->spinlock);
952        __kmem_cache_shrink_locked(cachep);
953        ret = !list_empty(&cachep->slabs_full) ||
954            !list_empty(&cachep->slabs_partial);
955        spin_unlock_irq(&cachep->spinlock);
956        return ret;
957 }
```

949 Removes all objects from the per-CPU objects cache.

951 Acquires the cache descriptor lock and disables interrupts.

952 Frees all slabs in the slabs_free list.

953-954 Checks that the slabs_partial and slabs_full lists are empty.

955 Releases the cache descriptor lock and re-enables interrupts.

956 Returns if the cache has all its slabs free.

H.1.3.3   Function: __kmem_cache_shrink_locked()   *(mm/slab.c)*

This does the dirty work of freeing slabs. It will keep destroying them until the growing flag gets set, indicating the cache is in use or until no more slabs are in slabs_free.

```
917 static int __kmem_cache_shrink_locked(kmem_cache_t *cachep)
918 {
919     slab_t *slabp;
920     int ret = 0;
921
923     while (!cachep->growing) {
924         struct list_head *p;
925
926         p = cachep->slabs_free.prev;
927         if (p == &cachep->slabs_free)
928             break;
929
930         slabp = list_entry(cachep->slabs_free.prev,
                        slab_t, list);
931 #if DEBUG
932         if (slabp->inuse)
933             BUG();
934 #endif
935         list_del(&slabp->list);
936
937         spin_unlock_irq(&cachep->spinlock);
938         kmem_slab_destroy(cachep, slabp);
939         ret++;
940         spin_lock_irq(&cachep->spinlock);
941     }
942     return ret;
943 }
```

923 While the cache is not growing, this frees slabs.

926-930 Gets the last slab on the slabs_free list.

932-933 If debugging is available, this makes sure it is not in use. If it is not in use, it should not be on the slabs_free list in the first place.

935 Removes the slab from the list.

937 Re-enables interrupts. This function is called with interrupts disabled, and this is to free the interrupt as quickly as possible.

938 Deletes the slab with kmem_slab_destroy() (See Section H.2.3.1).

939 Records the number of slabs freed.

940 Acquires the cache descriptor lock and disables interrupts.

Slab Allocator

H.1.4   Cache Destroying

When a module is unloaded, it is responsible for destroying any cache it has created. As during module loading, it is ensured two caches do not have the same name. Core kernel code often does not destroy its caches because their existence persists for the life of the system. The steps taken to destroy a cache are the following:

1. Delete the cache from the cache chain.

2. Shrink the cache to delete all slabs (See Section 8.1.8).

3. Free any per-CPU caches (kfree()).

4. Delete the cache descriptor from the cache_cache (See Section 8.3.3).

H.1.4.1   Function: kmem_cache_destroy()   *(mm/slab.c)*
    The call graph for this function is shown in Figure 8.7.

```
 997 int kmem_cache_destroy (kmem_cache_t * cachep)
 998 {
 999     if (!cachep || in_interrupt() || cachep->growing)
1000         BUG();
1001
1002     /* Find the cache in the chain of caches. */
1003     down(&cache_chain_sem);
1004     /* the chain is never empty, cache_cache is never destroyed */
1005     if (clock_searchp == cachep)
1006         clock_searchp = list_entry(cachep->next.next,
1007                         kmem_cache_t, next);
1008     list_del(&cachep->next);
1009     up(&cache_chain_sem);
1010
1011     if (__kmem_cache_shrink(cachep)) {
1012         printk(KERN_ERR
               "kmem_cache_destroy: Can't free all objects %p\n",
1013         cachep);
1014         down(&cache_chain_sem);
1015         list_add(&cachep->next,&cache_chain);
1016         up(&cache_chain_sem);
1017         return 1;
1018     }
1019 #ifdef CONFIG_SMP
1020     {
1021         int i;
1022         for (i = 0; i < NR_CPUS; i++)
1023             kfree(cachep->cpudata[i]);
1024     }
1025 #endif
```

```
1026        kmem_cache_free(&cache_cache, cachep);
1027
1028        return 0;
1029 }
```

999-1000 A sanity check. It makes sure the `cachep` is not null, that an interrupt is not trying to do this and that the cache has not been marked as growing, indicating it is in use.

1003 Acquires the semaphore for accessing the cache chain.

1005-1007 Acquires the list entry from the cache chain.

1008 Deletes this cache from the cache chain.

1009 Releases the cache chain semaphore.

1011 Shrinks the cache to free all slabs with `__kmem_cache_shrink()` (See Section H.1.3.2).

1012-1017 The shrink function returns true if slabs are still in the cache. If they are, the cache cannot be destroyed, so it is added back into the cache chain, and the error is reported.

1022-1023 If SMP is enabled, the per-CPU data structures are deleted with `kfree()` (See Section H.4.3.1).

1026 Deletes the cache descriptor from the `cache_cache` with `kmem_cache_free()` (See Section H.3.3.1).

H.1.5   Cache Reaping

H.1.5.1   Function: `kmem_cache_reap()`   *(mm/slab.c)*

The call graph for this function is shown in Figure 8.4. Because of the size of this function, it will be broken up into three separate sections. The first is a simple function preamble. The second is the selection of a cache to reap, and the third is the freeing of the slabs. The basic tasks were described in Section 8.1.7.

```
1738 int kmem_cache_reap (int gfp_mask)
1739 {
1740        slab_t *slabp;
1741        kmem_cache_t *searchp;
1742        kmem_cache_t *best_cachep;
1743        unsigned int best_pages;
1744        unsigned int best_len;
1745        unsigned int scan;
1746        int ret = 0;
1747
1748        if (gfp_mask & __GFP_WAIT)
```

Slab Allocator

```
1749              down(&cache_chain_sem);
1750         else
1751              if (down_trylock(&cache_chain_sem))
1752                   return 0;
1753
1754         scan = REAP_SCANLEN;
1755         best_len = 0;
1756         best_pages = 0;
1757         best_cachep = NULL;
1758         searchp = clock_searchp;
```

1738 The only parameter is the GFP flag. The only check made is against the __GFP_WAIT flag. As the only caller, **kswapd**, can sleep. This parameter is virtually worthless.

1748-1749 Can the caller sleep? If yes, then this acquires the semaphore.

1751-1752 If not, this tries and acquires the semaphore. If it is not available, this returns.

1754 REAP_SCANLEN (10) is the number of caches to examine.

1758 Sets searchp to be the last cache that was examined at the last reap.

```
1759     do {
1760          unsigned int pages;
1761          struct list_head* p;
1762          unsigned int full_free;
1763
1765          if (searchp->flags & SLAB_NO_REAP)
1766               goto next;
1767          spin_lock_irq(&searchp->spinlock);
1768          if (searchp->growing)
1769               goto next_unlock;
1770          if (searchp->dflags & DFLGS_GROWN) {
1771               searchp->dflags &= ~DFLGS_GROWN;
1772               goto next_unlock;
1773          }
1774 #ifdef CONFIG_SMP
1775          {
1776               cpucache_t *cc = cc_data(searchp);
1777               if (cc && cc->avail) {
1778                    __free_block(searchp, cc_entry(cc),
                              cc->avail);
1779                    cc->avail = 0;
1780               }
1781          }
1782 #endif
```

```
1783
1784          full_free = 0;
1785          p = searchp->slabs_free.next;
1786          while (p != &searchp->slabs_free) {
1787              slabp = list_entry(p, slab_t, list);
1788 #if DEBUG
1789              if (slabp->inuse)
1790                  BUG();
1791 #endif
1792              full_free++;
1793              p = p->next;
1794          }
1795
1801          pages = full_free * (1<<searchp->gfporder);
1802          if (searchp->ctor)
1803              pages = (pages*4+1)/5;
1804          if (searchp->gfporder)
1805              pages = (pages*4+1)/5;
1806          if (pages > best_pages) {
1807              best_cachep = searchp;
1808              best_len = full_free;
1809              best_pages = pages;
1810              if (pages >= REAP_PERFECT) {
1811                  clock_searchp =
1812                    list_entry(searchp->next.next,
1813                      kmem_cache_t,next);
1814                  goto perfect;
1815              }
1816          }
1816 next_unlock:
1817          spin_unlock_irq(&searchp->spinlock);
1818 next:
1819          searchp =
                   list_entry(searchp->next.next,kmem_cache_t,next);
1820      } while (--scan && searchp != clock_searchp);
```

This block examines REAP_SCANLEN number of caches to select one to free.

1767 Acquires an interrupt-safe lock to the cache descriptor.

1768-1769 If the cache is growing, this skips it.

1770-1773 If the cache has grown recently, this skips it and clears the flag.

1775-1781 Frees any per-CPU objects to the global pool.

1786-1794 Counts the number of slabs in the slabs_free list.

1801 Calculates the number of pages that all the slabs hold.

1802-1803 If the objects have constructors, this reduces the page count by one-fifth to make it less likely to be selected for reaping.

1804-1805 If the slabs consist of more than one page, this reduces the page count by one-fifth. This is because high-order pages are hard to acquire.

1806 If this is the best candidate found for reaping so far, this checks if it is perfect for reaping.

1807-1809 Records the new maximums.

1808 `best_len` is recorded so that it is easy to know how many slabs are half of the slabs in the free list.

1810 If this cache is perfect for reaping, then. . .

1811 Updates `clock_searchp`.

1812 Goto perfect where half the slabs will be freed.

1816 This label is reached if it was found that the cache was growing after acquiring the lock.

1817 Releases the cache descriptor lock.

1818 Moves to the next entry in the cache chain.

1820 Scans while `REAP_SCANLEN` has not been reached and while we have not cycled around the whole cache chain.

```
1822      clock_searchp = searchp;
1823
1824      if (!best_cachep)
1826          goto out;
1827
1828      spin_lock_irq(&best_cachep->spinlock);
1829 perfect:
1830      /* free only 50% of the free slabs */
1831      best_len = (best_len + 1)/2;
1832      for (scan = 0; scan < best_len; scan++) {
1833          struct list_head *p;
1834
1835          if (best_cachep->growing)
1836              break;
1837          p = best_cachep->slabs_free.prev;
1838          if (p == &best_cachep->slabs_free)
1839              break;
1840          slabp = list_entry(p,slab_t,list);
```

```
1841 #if DEBUG
1842         if (slabp->inuse)
1843             BUG();
1844 #endif
1845         list_del(&slabp->list);
1846         STATS_INC_REAPED(best_cachep);
1847
1848         /* Safe to drop the lock. The slab is no longer
1849          * lined to the cache.
1850          */
1851         spin_unlock_irq(&best_cachep->spinlock);
1852         kmem_slab_destroy(best_cachep, slabp);
1853         spin_lock_irq(&best_cachep->spinlock);
1854     }
1855     spin_unlock_irq(&best_cachep->spinlock);
1856     ret = scan * (1 << best_cachep->gfporder);
1857 out:
1858     up(&cache_chain_sem);
1859     return ret;
1860 }
```

This block will free half of the slabs from the selected cache.

1822 Updates `clock_searchp` for the next cache reap.

1824-1826 If a cache was not found, goto out to free the cache chain and exit.

1828 Acquires the cache chain spinlock and disables interrupts. The `cachep` descriptor has to be held by an interrupt-safe lock because some caches may be used from interrupt context. The slab allocator has no way to differentiate between interrupt-safe and -unsafe caches.

1831 Adjusts `best_len` to be the number of slabs to free.

1832-1854 Frees `best_len` number of slabs.

1835-1847 If the cache is growing, this exits.

1837 Gets a slab from the list.

1838-1839 If no slabs are left in the list, this exits.

1840 Gets the slab pointer.

1842-1843 If debugging is enabled, this makes sure no active objects are in the slab.

1845 Removes the slab from the `slabs_free` list.

1846 Updates statistics if enabled.

1851 Frees the cache descriptor and enables interrupts.

1852 Destroys the slab (See Section 8.2.8).

1851 Reacquires the cache descriptor spinlock and disables interrupts.

1855 Frees the cache descriptor and enables interrupts.

1856 `ret` is the number of pages that were freed.

1858-1859 Frees the cache semaphore and returns the number of pages freed.

H.2 Slabs

Contents

H.2.1 Storing the Slab Descriptor

H.2.1.1 Function: `kmem_cache_slabmgmt()` *(mm/slab.c)*

This function will either allocate space to keep the slab descriptor off cache or reserve enough space at the beginning of the slab for the descriptor and the `bufctls`.

```
1032 static inline slab_t * kmem_cache_slabmgmt (
             kmem_cache_t *cachep,
1033         void *objp,
             int colour_off,
             int local_flags)
1034 {
1035     slab_t *slabp;
1036
1037     if (OFF_SLAB(cachep)) {
1039         slabp = kmem_cache_alloc(cachep->slabp_cache,
                     local_flags);
1040         if (!slabp)
1041             return NULL;
1042     } else {
1047         slabp = objp+colour_off;
1048         colour_off += L1_CACHE_ALIGN(cachep->num *
1049                 sizeof(kmem_bufctl_t) +
                     sizeof(slab_t));
1050     }
1051     slabp->inuse = 0;
1052     slabp->colouroff = colour_off;
1053     slabp->s_mem = objp+colour_off;
1054
1055     return slabp;
1056 }
```

1032 The parameters of the function are the following:

- **cachep** The cache the slab is to be allocated to.

- **objp** When the function is called, this points to the beginning of the slab.

- **colour_off** The color offset for this slab.

- **local_flags** These are the flags for the cache.

1037-1042 If the slab descriptor is kept off cache, then...

1039 Allocates memory from the sizes cache. During cache creation, `slabp_cache` is set to the appropriate size cache to allocate from.

1040 If the allocation failed, this returns.

1042-1050 Reserves space at the beginning of the slab.

1047 The address of the slab will be the beginning of the slab (`objp`) plus the color offset.

1048 `colour_off` is calculated to be the offset where the first object will be placed. The address is L1 cache-aligned. `cachep->num * sizeof(kmem_bufctl_t)` is the amount of space needed to hold the bufctls for each object in the slab, and `sizeof(slab_t)` is the size of the slab descriptor. This effectively has reserved the space at the beginning of the slab.

1051 The number of objects in use on the slab is 0.

1052 The `colouroff` is updated for placement of the new object.

1053 The address of the first object is calculated as the address of the beginning of the slab plus the offset.

H.2.1.2   Function: `kmem_find_general_cachep()`   *(mm/slab.c)*

If the slab descriptor is to be kept off-slab, this function, called during cache creation, will find the appropriate size cache to use and will be stored within the cache descriptor in the field `slabp_cache`.

```
1620 kmem_cache_t * kmem_find_general_cachep (size_t size,
                          int gfpflags)
1621 {
1622     cache_sizes_t *csizep = cache_sizes;
1623
1628     for ( ; csizep->cs_size; csizep++) {
1629         if (size > csizep->cs_size)
1630             continue;
1631         break;
1632     }
1633     return (gfpflags & GFP_DMA) ? csizep->cs_dmacachep :
                    csizep->cs_cachep;
1634 }
```

1620 `size` is the size of the slab descriptor. `gfpflags` is always 0 because DMA memory is not needed for a slab descriptor.

1628-1632 Starting with the smallest size, this keeps increasing the size until a cache is found with buffers large enough to store the slab descriptor.

1633 Returns either a normal or DMA-sized cache, depending on the `gfpflags` passed in. In reality, only the `cs_cachep` is ever passed back.

H.2.2   Slab Creation

H.2.2.1   Function: `kmem_cache_grow()`   *(mm/slab.c)*

The call graph for this function is shown in Figure 8.11. The basic tasks for this function are the following:

- Perform basic sanity checks to guard against bad usage.

- Calculate color offset for objects in this slab.

- Allocate memory for the slab and acquire a slab descriptor.

- Link the pages used for the slab to the slab and cache descriptors.

- Initialize objects in the slab.

- Add the slab to the cache.

```
1105 static int kmem_cache_grow (kmem_cache_t * cachep, int flags)
1106 {
1107     slab_t  *slabp;
1108     struct page     *page;
1109     void         *objp;
1110     size_t        offset;
1111     unsigned int    i, local_flags;
1112     unsigned long    ctor_flags;
1113     unsigned long    save_flags;
```

These are basic declarations. The parameters of the function are the following:

- **cachep** The cache to allocate a new slab to

- **flags** The flags for a slab creation

```
1118     if (flags & ~(SLAB_DMA|SLAB_LEVEL_MASK|SLAB_NO_GROW))
1119         BUG();
1120     if (flags & SLAB_NO_GROW)
1121         return 0;
1122
1129     if (in_interrupt() &&
             (flags & SLAB_LEVEL_MASK) != SLAB_ATOMIC)
```

```
1130        BUG();
1131
1132    ctor_flags = SLAB_CTOR_CONSTRUCTOR;
1133    local_flags = (flags & SLAB_LEVEL_MASK);
1134    if (local_flags == SLAB_ATOMIC)
1139        ctor_flags |= SLAB_CTOR_ATOMIC;
```

This performs basic sanity checks to guard against bad usage. The checks are made here rather than kmem_cache_alloc() to protect the speed-critical path. There is no point in checking the flags every time an object needs to be allocated.

1118-1119 Makes sure only allowable flags are used for allocation.

1120-1121 Do not grow the cache if this is set. In reality, it is never set.

1129-1130 If this is called within interrupt context, make sure the ATOMIC flag is set, so we do not sleep when kmem_getpages()(See Section H.7.1.1) is called.

1132 This flag tells the constructor it is to init the object.

1133 The local_flags are just those relevant to the page allocator.

1134-1139 If the SLAB_ATOMIC flag is set, the constructor needs to know about it in case it wants to make new allocations.

```
1142    spin_lock_irqsave(&cachep->spinlock, save_flags);
1143
1145    offset = cachep->colour_next;
1146    cachep->colour_next++;
1147    if (cachep->colour_next >= cachep->colour)
1148        cachep->colour_next = 0;
1149    offset *= cachep->colour_off;
1150    cachep->dflags |= DFLGS_GROWN;
1151
1152    cachep->growing++;
1153    spin_unlock_irqrestore(&cachep->spinlock, save_flags);
```

Calculates color offset for objects in this slab.

1142 Acquires an interrupt-safe lock for accessing the cache descriptor.

1145 Gets the offset for objects in this slab.

1146 Moves to the next color offset.

1147-1148 If colour has been reached, no more offsets are available, so this resets colour_next to 0.

1149 colour_off is the size of each offset, so offset * colour_off will give how many bytes to offset the objects to.

1150 Marks the cache that it is growing so that `kmem_cache_reap()` (See Section H.1.5.1) will ignore this cache.

1152 Increases the count for callers growing this cache.

1153 Frees the spinlock and re-enables interrupts.

```
1165        if (!(objp = kmem_getpages(cachep, flags)))
1166            goto failed;
1167
1169        if (!(slabp = kmem_cache_slabmgmt(cachep,
                              objp, offset,
                              local_flags)))
1160            goto opps1;
```

Allocates memory for the slab and acquires a slab descriptor.

1165-1166 Allocates pages from the page allocator for the slab with `kmem_getpages()` (See Section H.7.1.1).

1169 Acquires a slab descriptor with `kmem_cache_slabmgmt()` (See Section H.2.1.1).

```
1173        i = 1 << cachep->gfporder;
1174        page = virt_to_page(objp);
1175        do {
1176            SET_PAGE_CACHE(page, cachep);
1177            SET_PAGE_SLAB(page, slabp);
1178            PageSetSlab(page);
1179            page++;
1180        } while (--i);
```

Links the pages for the slab used to the slab and cache descriptors.

1173 `i` is the number of pages used for the slab. Each page has to be linked to the slab and cache descriptors.

1174 `objp` is a pointer to the beginning of the slab. The macro `virt_to_page()` will give the `struct page` for that address.

1175-1180 Links each pages list field to the slab and cache descriptors.

1176 `SET_PAGE_CACHE()` links the page to the cache descriptor using the `page→list.next` field.

1177 `SET_PAGE_SLAB()` links the page to the slab descriptor using the `page→list.prev` field.

1178 Sets the `PG_slab` page flag. The full set of `PG_` flags is listed in Table 2.1.

1179 Moves to the next page for this slab to be linked.

```
1182        kmem_cache_init_objs(cachep, slabp, ctor_flags);
```

1182 Initializes all objects (See Section H.3.1.1).

```
1184        spin_lock_irqsave(&cachep->spinlock, save_flags);
1185        cachep->growing--;
1186
1188        list_add_tail(&slabp->list, &cachep->slabs_free);
1189        STATS_INC_GROWN(cachep);
1190        cachep->failures = 0;
1191
1192        spin_unlock_irqrestore(&cachep->spinlock, save_flags);
1193        return 1;
```

Adds the slab to the cache.

1184 Acquires the cache descriptor spinlock in an interrupt-safe fashion.

1185 Decreases the growing count.

1188 Adds the slab to the end of the slabs_free list.

1189 If STATS is set, this increases the cachep→grown field STATS_INC_GROWN().

1190 Sets failures to 0. This field is never used elsewhere.

1192 Unlocks the spinlock in an interrupt-safe fashion.

1193 Returns success.

```
1194 opps1:
1195        kmem_freepages(cachep, objp);
1196 failed:
1197        spin_lock_irqsave(&cachep->spinlock, save_flags);
1198        cachep->growing--;
1199        spin_unlock_irqrestore(&cachep->spinlock, save_flags);
1300        return 0;
1301 }
```

This block is for error handling.

1194-1195 opps1 is reached if the pages for the slab were allocated. They must be freed.

1197 Acquires the spinlock for accessing the cache descriptor.

1198 Reduces the growing count.

1199 Releases the spinlock.

1300 Returns failure.

H.2.3 Slab Destroying

H.2.3.1 Function: `kmem_slab_destroy()` *(mm/slab.c)*

The call graph for this function is shown in Figure 8.13. For readability, the debugging sections have been omitted from this function, but they are almost identical to the debugging section during object allocation. See Section H.3.1.1 for how the markers and poison pattern are checked.

```
555 static void kmem_slab_destroy (kmem_cache_t *cachep, slab_t *slabp)
556 {
557     if (cachep->dtor
561     ) {
562         int i;
563         for (i = 0; i < cachep->num; i++) {
564             void* objp = slabp->s_mem+cachep->objsize*i;

565-574 DEBUG: Check red zone markers

575             if (cachep->dtor)
576                 (cachep->dtor)(objp, cachep, 0);

577-584 DEBUG: Check poison pattern

585         }
586     }
587
588     kmem_freepages(cachep, slabp->s_mem-slabp->colouroff);
589     if (OFF_SLAB(cachep))
590         kmem_cache_free(cachep->slabp_cache, slabp);
591 }
```

557-586 If a destructor is available, this calls it for each object in the slab.

563-585 Cycles through each object in the slab.

564 Calculates the address of the object to destroy.

575-576 Calls the destructor.

588 Frees the pages being used for the slab.

589 If the slab descriptor is off-slab, then this frees the memory being used for it.

Slab Allocator

H.3 Objects

Contents

This section will cover how objects are managed. At this point, most of the real hard work has been completed by either the cache or slab managers.

H.3.1 Initializing Objects in a Slab

H.3.1.1 Function: kmem_cache_init_objs() *(mm/slab.c)*

The vast part of this function is involved with debugging, so I start with the function without the debugging and explain that in detail before handling the debugging part. The two sections that are debugging are marked in the code excerpt that follows as Part 1 and Part 2.

```
1058 static inline void kmem_cache_init_objs (kmem_cache_t * cachep,
1059          slab_t * slabp, unsigned long ctor_flags)
1060 {
1061     int i;
1062
1063     for (i = 0; i < cachep->num; i++) {
1064         void* objp = slabp->s_mem+cachep->objsize*i;

1065-1072        /* Debugging Part 1 */

1079        if (cachep->ctor)
1080            cachep->ctor(objp, cachep, ctor_flags);

1081-1094        /* Debugging Part 2 */

1095        slab_bufctl(slabp)[i] = i+1;
```

```
1096         }
1097         slab_bufctl(slabp)[i-1] = BUFCTL_END;
1098         slabp->free = 0;
1099 }
```

1058 The parameters of the function are the following:

- **cachep** The cache the objects are initialized for
- **slabp** The slab the objects are in
- **ctor_flags** Flags the constructor needs whether this is an atomic allocation or not

1063 Initializes cache→num number of objects.

1064 The base address for objects in the slab is s_mem. The address of the object to allocate is then i * (size of a single object).

1079-1080 If a constructor is available, this calls it.

1095 The macro slab_bufctl() casts slabp to a slab_t slab descriptor and adds one to it. This brings the pointer to the end of the slab descriptor and then casts it back to a kmem_bufctl_t, effectively giving the beginning of the bufctl array.

1098 The index of the first free object is 0 in the bufctl array.

That covers the core of initializing objects. Next, I cover the first debugging part.

```
1065 #if DEBUG
1066         if (cachep->flags & SLAB_RED_ZONE) {
1067             *((unsigned long*)(objp)) = RED_MAGIC1;
1068             *((unsigned long*)(objp + cachep->objsize -
1069                 BYTES_PER_WORD)) = RED_MAGIC1;
1070             objp += BYTES_PER_WORD;
1071         }
1072 #endif
```

1066 If the cache is to be red-zoned, this places a marker at either end of the object.

1067 Places the marker at the beginning of the object.

1068 Places the marker at the end of the object. Remember that the size of the object takes into account the size of the red markers when red-zoning is enabled.

1070 Increases the objp pointer by the size of the marker for the benefit of the constructor, which is called after this debugging block.

```
1081 #if DEBUG
1082          if (cachep->flags & SLAB_RED_ZONE)
1083              objp -= BYTES_PER_WORD;
1084          if (cachep->flags & SLAB_POISON)
1086              kmem_poison_obj(cachep, objp);
1087          if (cachep->flags & SLAB_RED_ZONE) {
1088              if (*((unsigned long*)(objp)) != RED_MAGIC1)
1089                  BUG();
1090              if (*((unsigned long*)(objp + cachep->objsize -
1091                      BYTES_PER_WORD)) != RED_MAGIC1)
1092                  BUG();
1093          }
1094 #endif
```

This is the debugging block that takes place after the constructor, if it exists, has been called.

1082-1083 The `objp` pointer was increased by the size of the red marker in the previous debugging block, so it moves it back again.

1084-1086 If there was no constructor, this poisons the object with a known pattern that can be examined later to trap uninitialized writes.

1088 Checks to make sure the red marker at the beginning of the object was preserved to trap writes before the object.

1090-1091 Checks to make sure writes did not take place past the end of the object.

H.3.2 Object Allocation

H.3.2.1 Function: `kmem_cache_alloc()` *(mm/slab.c)*

The call graph for this function is shown in Figure 8.14. This trivial function simply calls `__kmem_cache_alloc()`.

```
1529 void * kmem_cache_alloc (kmem_cache_t *cachep, int flags)
1531 {
1532     return __kmem_cache_alloc(cachep, flags);
1533 }
```

H.3.2.2 Function: `__kmem_cache_alloc` (UP Case)() *(mm/slab.c)*

This will take the parts of the function specific to the UP case. The SMP case will be dealt with in the next section.

```
1338 static inline void * __kmem_cache_alloc (kmem_cache_t *cachep,
                                                 int flags)
1339 {
1340     unsigned long save_flags;
```

```
1341     void* objp;
1342
1343     kmem_cache_alloc_head(cachep, flags);
1344 try_again:
1345     local_irq_save(save_flags);

1367     objp = kmem_cache_alloc_one(cachep);

1369     local_irq_restore(save_flags);
1370     return objp;
1371 alloc_new_slab:

1376     local_irq_restore(save_flags);
1377     if (kmem_cache_grow(cachep, flags))
1381         goto try_again;
1382     return NULL;
1383 }
```

1338 The parameters are the cache to allocate from and allocation-specific flags.

1343 This function makes sure the appropriate combination of DMA flags are in use.

1345 Disables interrupts and saves the flags. This function is used by interrupts, so this is the only way to provide synchronization in the UP case.

1367 kmem_cache_alloc_one() (See Section H.3.2.5) allocates an object from one of the lists and returns it. If no objects are free, this macro (note it is not a function) will goto alloc_new_slab at the end of this function.

1369-1370 Restores interrupts and returns.

1376 At this label, no objects were free in slabs_partial and slabs_free is empty, so a new slab is needed.

1377 Allocates a new slab (See Section 8.2.2).

1381 A new slab is available, so it tries again.

1382 No slabs could be allocated, so this returns failure.

H.3.2.3   Function: __kmem_cache_alloc (SMP Case)()   *(mm/slab.c)*
This is what the function looks like in the SMP case.

```
1338 static inline void * __kmem_cache_alloc (kmem_cache_t *cachep,
                                               int flags)

1339 {
1340     unsigned long save_flags;
1341     void* objp;
```

```
1342
1343      kmem_cache_alloc_head(cachep, flags);
1344 try_again:
1345      local_irq_save(save_flags);
1347      {
1348          cpucache_t *cc = cc_data(cachep);
1349
1350          if (cc) {
1351              if (cc->avail) {
1352                  STATS_INC_ALLOCHIT(cachep);
1353                  objp = cc_entry(cc)[--cc->avail];
1354              } else {
1355                  STATS_INC_ALLOCMISS(cachep);
1356                  objp =
                     kmem_cache_alloc_batch(cachep,cc,flags);
1357                  if (!objp)
1358                      goto alloc_new_slab_nolock;
1359              }
1360          } else {
1361              spin_lock(&cachep->spinlock);
1362              objp = kmem_cache_alloc_one(cachep);
1363              spin_unlock(&cachep->spinlock);
1364          }
1365      }
1366      local_irq_restore(save_flags);
1370      return objp;
1371 alloc_new_slab:
1373      spin_unlock(&cachep->spinlock);
1374 alloc_new_slab_nolock:
1375      local_irq_restore(save_flags);
1377      if (kmem_cache_grow(cachep, flags))
1381          goto try_again;
1382      return NULL;
1383 }
```

1338-1347 The same as the UP case.

1349 Obtains the per-CPU data for this CPU.

1350-1360 If a per-CPU cache is available, then ....

1351 If an object is available, then ....

1352 Updates statistics for this cache if enabled.

1353 Gets an object and updates the `avail` figure.

1354 If not, an object is not available, so ....

1355 Updates statistics for this cache if enabled.

1356 Allocates `batchcount` number of objects, places all but one of them in the per-CPU cache and returns the last one to `objp`.

1357-1358 The allocation failed, so goto `alloc_new_slab_nolock` to grow the cache and to allocate a new slab.

1360-1364 If a per-CPU cache is not available, this takes out the cache spinlock and allocates one object in the same way the UP case does. This is the case during the initialization for the `cache_cache`, for example.

1363 Objects was successfully assigned, so it releases the cache spinlock.

1366-1370 Re-enables interrupts and returns the allocated object.

1371-1373 If `kmem_cache_alloc_one()` failed to allocate an object, it will goto here with the spinlock still held, so it must be released.

1375-1383 This is the same as the UP case.

H.3.2.4   Function: `kmem_cache_alloc_head()`   *(mm/slab.c)*

This simple function ensures the right combination of slab and GFP flags are used for allocation from a slab. If a cache is for DMA use, this function will make sure the caller does not accidently request normal memory and vice-versa.

```
1231 static inline void kmem_cache_alloc_head(kmem_cache_t *cachep,
                                              int flags)
1232 {
1233     if (flags & SLAB_DMA) {
1234         if (!(cachep->gfpflags & GFP_DMA))
1235             BUG();
1236     } else {
1237         if (cachep->gfpflags & GFP_DMA)
1238             BUG();
1239     }
1240 }
```

1231 The parameters are the cache that we are allocating from, and the flags are requested for the allocation.

1233 If the caller has requested memory for DMA use and ...

1234 The cache is not using DMA memory, then this uses `BUG()`.

1237 If not, if the caller has not requested DMA memory and this cache is for DMA use, it uses `BUG()`.

H.3.2.5   Function: `kmem_cache_alloc_one()`   *(mm/slab.c)*

This is a preprocessor macro.   It may seem strange to not make this an inline function, but it is a preprocessor macro for a goto optimization in `__kmem_cache_alloc()` (See Section H.3.2.2).

```
1283 #define kmem_cache_alloc_one(cachep)                    \
1284 ({                                                       \
1285     struct list_head * slabs_partial, * entry;           \
1286     slab_t *slabp;                                        \
1287                                                           \
1288     slabs_partial = &(cachep)->slabs_partial;            \
1289     entry = slabs_partial->next;                         \
1290     if (unlikely(entry == slabs_partial)) {              \
1291         struct list_head * slabs_free;                   \
1292         slabs_free = &(cachep)->slabs_free;              \
1293         entry = slabs_free->next;                        \
1294         if (unlikely(entry == slabs_free))               \
1295             goto alloc_new_slab;                         \
1296         list_del(entry);                                 \
1297         list_add(entry, slabs_partial);                  \
1298     }                                                    \
1299                                                           \
1300     slabp = list_entry(entry, slab_t, list);             \
1301     kmem_cache_alloc_one_tail(cachep, slabp);            \
1302 })
```

1288-1289 Gets the first slab from the `slabs_partial` list.

1290-1298 If a slab is not available from this list, this executes this block.

1291-1293 Gets the first slab from the `slabs_free` list.

1294-1295 If no slabs are on `slabs_free`, then goto `alloc_new_slab()`. This goto label is in `__kmem_cache_alloc()`, and it will grow the cache by one slab.

1296-1297 If not, this removes the slab from the free list and places it on the `slabs_partial` list because an object is about to be removed from it.

1300 Obtains the slab from the list.

1301 Allocates one object from the slab.

H.3.2.6   Function: `kmem_cache_alloc_one_tail()`   *(mm/slab.c)*

This function is responsible for the allocation of one object from a slab. Much of it is debugging code.

```
1242 static inline void * kmem_cache_alloc_one_tail (
                          kmem_cache_t *cachep,
```

```
1243                        slab_t *slabp)
1244 {
1245     void *objp;
1246
1247     STATS_INC_ALLOCED(cachep);
1248     STATS_INC_ACTIVE(cachep);
1249     STATS_SET_HIGH(cachep);
1250
1252     slabp->inuse++;
1253     objp = slabp->s_mem + slabp->free*cachep->objsize;
1254     slabp->free=slab_bufctl(slabp)[slabp->free];
1255
1256     if (unlikely(slabp->free == BUFCTL_END)) {
1257         list_del(&slabp->list);
1258         list_add(&slabp->list, &cachep->slabs_full);
1259     }
1260 #if DEBUG
1261     if (cachep->flags & SLAB_POISON)
1262         if (kmem_check_poison_obj(cachep, objp))
1263             BUG();
1264     if (cachep->flags & SLAB_RED_ZONE) {
1266         if (xchg((unsigned long *)objp, RED_MAGIC2) !=
1267                         RED_MAGIC1)
1268             BUG();
1269         if (xchg((unsigned long *)(objp+cachep->objsize -
1270             BYTES_PER_WORD), RED_MAGIC2) != RED_MAGIC1)
1271             BUG();
1272         objp += BYTES_PER_WORD;
1273     }
1274 #endif
1275     return objp;
1276 }
```

1242 The parameters are the cache and slab being allocated from.

1247-1249 If stats are enabled, this will set three statistics. ALLOCED is the total
number of objects that have been allocated. ACTIVE is the number of active
objects in the cache. HIGH is the maximum number of objects that were active
at a single time.

1252 inuse is the number of objects active on this slab.

1253 Gets a pointer to a free object. s_mem is a pointer to the first object on the
slab. free is an index of a free object in the slab. index * object size
gives an offset within the slab.

1254 Updates the free pointer to be an index of the next free object.

1256-1259 If the slab is full, this removes it from the `slabs_partial` list and places it on `slabs_full`.

1260-1274 Debugging code.

1275 Without debugging, the object is returned to the caller.

1261-1263 If the object was poisoned with a known pattern, this checks it to guard against uninitialized access.

1266-1267 If red-zoning was enabled, this checks the marker at the beginning of the object and confirms it is safe. It changes the red marker to check for writes before the object later.

1269-1271 Checks the marker at the end of the object and changes it to check for writes after the object later.

1272 Updates the object pointer to point to after the red marker.

1275 Returns the object.

H.3.2.7   Function: kmem_cache_alloc_batch()   *(mm/slab.c)*

This function allocates a batch of objects to a CPU cache of objects. It is only used in the SMP case. In many ways, it is very similar to `kmem_cache_alloc_one()` (See Section H.3.2.5).

```
1305 void* kmem_cache_alloc_batch(kmem_cache_t* cachep,
                  cpucache_t* cc, int flags)
1306 {
1307     int batchcount = cachep->batchcount;
1308
1309     spin_lock(&cachep->spinlock);
1310     while (batchcount--) {
1311         struct list_head * slabs_partial, * entry;
1312         slab_t *slabp;
1313         /* Get slab alloc is to come from. */
1314         slabs_partial = &(cachep)->slabs_partial;
1315         entry = slabs_partial->next;
1316         if (unlikely(entry == slabs_partial)) {
1317             struct list_head * slabs_free;
1318             slabs_free = &(cachep)->slabs_free;
1319             entry = slabs_free->next;
1320             if (unlikely(entry == slabs_free))
1321                 break;
1322             list_del(entry);
1323             list_add(entry, slabs_partial);
1324         }
1325
```

```
1326              slabp = list_entry(entry, slab_t, list);
1327              cc_entry(cc)[cc->avail++] =
1328                    kmem_cache_alloc_one_tail(cachep, slabp);
1329          }
1330      spin_unlock(&cachep->spinlock);
1331
1332      if (cc->avail)
1333          return cc_entry(cc)[--cc->avail];
1334      return NULL;
1335 }
```

1305 The parameters are the cache to allocate from, the per-CPU cache to fill and the allocation flags.

1307 batchcount is the number of objects to allocate.

1309 Obtains the spinlock for access to the cache descriptor.

1310-1329 Loops batchcount times.

1311-1324 This example is the same as kmem_cache_alloc_one() (See Section H.3.2.5). It selects a slab from either slabs_partial or slabs_free to allocate from. If none are available, it breaks out of the loop.

1326-1327 Calls kmem_cache_alloc_one_tail() (See Section H.3.2.6) and places it in the per-CPU cache.

1330 Releases the cache descriptor lock.

1332-1333 Takes one of the objects allocated in this batch and returns it.

1334 If no object was allocated, this returns. __kmem_cache_alloc() (See Section H.3.2.2) will grow the cache by one slab and try again.

H.3.3   Object Freeing

H.3.3.1   Function: kmem_cache_free()   *(mm/slab.c)*
The call graph for this function is shown in Figure 8.15.

```
1576 void kmem_cache_free (kmem_cache_t *cachep, void *objp)
1577 {
1578     unsigned long flags;
1579 #if DEBUG
1580     CHECK_PAGE(virt_to_page(objp));
1581     if (cachep != GET_PAGE_CACHE(virt_to_page(objp)))
1582         BUG();
1583 #endif
1584
1585     local_irq_save(flags);
```

Slab Allocator

```
1586        __kmem_cache_free(cachep, objp);
1587        local_irq_restore(flags);
1588 }
```

1576 The parameter is the cache that the object is being freed from and the object
itself.

1579-1583 If debugging is enabled, the page will first be checked with
CHECK_PAGE() to make sure it is a slab page. Second, the page list will be
examined to make sure it belongs to this cache (See Figure 8.8).

1585 Interrupts are disabled to protect the path.

1586 __kmem_cache_free() (See Section H.3.3.2) will free the object to the per-
CPU cache for the SMP case and to the global pool in the normal case.

1587 Re-enables interrupts.

H.3.3.2   Function: __kmem_cache_free (UP Case)()   *(mm/slab.c)*
This covers what the function looks like in the UP case. Clearly, it simply
releases the object to the slab.

```
1493 static inline void __kmem_cache_free (kmem_cache_t *cachep,
                                                  void* objp)
1494 {
1517     kmem_cache_free_one(cachep, objp);
1519 }
```

H.3.3.3   Function: __kmem_cache_free (SMP Case)()   *(mm/slab.c)*
This case is slightly more interesting. In this case, the object is released to the
per-CPU cache if it is available.

```
1493 static inline void __kmem_cache_free (kmem_cache_t *cachep,
                                                  void* objp)
1494 {
1496     cpucache_t *cc = cc_data(cachep);
1497
1498     CHECK_PAGE(virt_to_page(objp));
1499     if (cc) {
1500         int batchcount;
1501         if (cc->avail < cc->limit) {
1502             STATS_INC_FREEHIT(cachep);
1503             cc_entry(cc)[cc->avail++] = objp;
1504             return;
1505         }
1506         STATS_INC_FREEMISS(cachep);
1507         batchcount = cachep->batchcount;
```

```
1508            cc->avail -= batchcount;
1509            free_block(cachep,
1510                 &cc_entry(cc)[cc->avail],batchcount);
1511            cc_entry(cc)[cc->avail++] = objp;
1512            return;
1513        } else {
1514            free_block(cachep, &objp, 1);
1515        }
1519 }
```

1496 Gets the data for this per-CPU cache (See Section 8.5.1).

1498 Makes sure the page is a slab page.

1499-1513 If a per-CPU cache is available, this tries to use it. This is not always available. During cache destruction, for instance, the per-CPU caches are already gone.

1501-1505 If the number available in the per-CPU cache is below limit, this adds the object to the free list and returns.

1506 Updates statistics if enabled.

1507 The pool has overflowed, so batchcount number of objects is going to be freed to the global pool.

1508 Updates the number of available (`avail`) objects.

1509-1510 Frees a block of objects to the global cache.

1511 Frees the requested object and places it in the per-CPU pool.

1513 If the per-CPU cache is not available, this frees this object to the global pool.

H.3.3.4   Function: kmem_cache_free_one()   *(mm/slab.c)*

```
1414 static inline void kmem_cache_free_one(kmem_cache_t *cachep,
                                            void *objp)
1415 {
1416     slab_t* slabp;
1417
1418     CHECK_PAGE(virt_to_page(objp));
1425     slabp = GET_PAGE_SLAB(virt_to_page(objp));
1426
1427 #if DEBUG
1428     if (cachep->flags & SLAB_DEBUG_INITIAL)
1433         cachep->ctor(objp, cachep,
             SLAB_CTOR_CONSTRUCTOR|SLAB_CTOR_VERIFY);
```

```
1434
1435      if (cachep->flags & SLAB_RED_ZONE) {
1436            objp -= BYTES_PER_WORD;
1437            if (xchg((unsigned long *)objp, RED_MAGIC1) !=
                               RED_MAGIC2)
1438                  BUG();
1440            if (xchg((unsigned long *)(objp+cachep->objsize -
1441                  BYTES_PER_WORD), RED_MAGIC1) !=
                               RED_MAGIC2)
1443                  BUG();
1444      }
1445      if (cachep->flags & SLAB_POISON)
1446            kmem_poison_obj(cachep, objp);
1447      if (kmem_extra_free_checks(cachep, slabp, objp))
1448            return;
1449 #endif
1450      {
1451            unsigned int objnr = (objp-slabp->s_mem)/cachep->objsize;
1452
1453            slab_bufctl(slabp)[objnr] = slabp->free;
1454            slabp->free = objnr;
1455      }
1456      STATS_DEC_ACTIVE(cachep);
1457
1459      {
1460            int inuse = slabp->inuse;
1461            if (unlikely(!--slabp->inuse)) {
1462                  /* Was partial or full, now empty. */
1463                  list_del(&slabp->list);
1464                  list_add(&slabp->list, &cachep->slabs_free);
1465            } else if (unlikely(inuse == cachep->num)) {
1466                  /* Was full. */
1467                  list_del(&slabp->list);
1468                  list_add(&slabp->list, &cachep->slabs_part
1469            }
1470      }
1471 }
```

1418 Makes sure the page is a slab page.

1425 Gets the slab descriptor for the page.

1427-1449 Debugging material. It is discussed at end of the section.

1451 Calculates the index for the object being freed.

1454 Because this object is now free, it updates the bufctl to reflect that.

1456 If statistics are enabled, this disables the number of active objects in the slab.

1461-1464 If `inuse` reaches 0, the slab is free and is moved to the `slabs_free` list.

1465-1468 If the number in use equals the number of objects in a slab, it is full, so this moves it to the `slabs_full` list.

1471 End of the function.

1428-1433 If `SLAB_DEBUG_INITIAL` is set, the constructor is called to verify the object is in an initialized state.

1435-1444 Verifies the red marks at either end of the object are still there. This will check for writes beyond the boundaries of the object and for double frees.

1445-1446 Poisons the freed object with a known pattern.

1447-1448 This function will confirm the object is a part of this slab and cache. It will then check the free list (`bufctl`) to make sure this is not a double free.

H.3.3.5   Function: `free_block()`   *(mm/slab.c)*

This function is only used in the SMP case when the per-CPU cache gets too full. It is used to free a batch of objects in bulk.

```
1481 static void free_block (kmem_cache_t* cachep, void** objpp,
                             int len)
1482 {
1483     spin_lock(&cachep->spinlock);
1484     __free_block(cachep, objpp, len);
1485     spin_unlock(&cachep->spinlock);
1486 }
```

1481 The parameters are the following:

   cachep The cache that objects are being freed from

   objpp The pointer to the first object to free

   len The number of objects to free

1483 Acquires a lock to the cache descriptor.

1484 `__free_block()`(See Section H.3.3.6) performs the actual task of freeing up each of the pages.

1485 Releases the lock.

H.3.3.6   Function: `__free_block()`   *(mm/slab.c)*

This function is responsible for freeing each of the objects in the per-CPU array
`objpp`.

```
1474 static inline void __free_block (kmem_cache_t* cachep,
1475                     void** objpp, int len)
1476 {
1477     for ( ; len > 0; len--, objpp++)
1478         kmem_cache_free_one(cachep, *objpp);
1479 }
```

1474 The parameters are the `cachep` the objects belong to, the list of objects
(`objpp`) and the number of objects to free (`len`).

1477 Loops `len` number of times.

1478 Frees an object from the array.

H.4   Sizes Cache

Contents

H.4.1   Initializing the Sizes Cache

H.4.1.1   Function: `kmem_cache_sizes_init()`   *(mm/slab.c)*

This function is responsible for creating pairs of caches for small memory buffers suitable for either normal or DMA memory.

```
436 void __init kmem_cache_sizes_init(void)
437 {
438     cache_sizes_t *sizes = cache_sizes;
439     char name[20];
440
444     if (num_physpages > (32 << 20) >> PAGE_SHIFT)
445         slab_break_gfp_order = BREAK_GFP_ORDER_HI;
446     do {
452         snprintf(name, sizeof(name), "size-%Zd",
                    sizes->cs_size);
453         if (!(sizes->cs_cachep =
454             kmem_cache_create(name, sizes->cs_size,
455                     0, SLAB_HWCACHE_ALIGN, NULL, NULL))) {
456             BUG();
457         }
458
460         if (!(OFF_SLAB(sizes->cs_cachep))) {
461             offslab_limit = sizes->cs_size-sizeof(slab_t);
462             offslab_limit /= 2;
463         }
464         snprintf(name, sizeof(name), "size-%Zd(DMA)",
                    sizes->cs_size);
465         sizes->cs_dmacachep = kmem_cache_create(name,
                    sizes->cs_size, 0,
466                 SLAB_CACHE_DMA|SLAB_HWCACHE_ALIGN,
                    NULL, NULL);
467         if (!sizes->cs_dmacachep)
468             BUG();
469         sizes++;
470     } while (sizes->cs_size);
471 }
```

438 Gets a pointer to the `cache_sizes` array.

439 The human-readable name of the cache. It should be sized `CACHE_NAMELEN`, which is defined to be 20 bytes long.

444-445 `slab_break_gfp_order` determines how many pages a slab may use unless 0 objects fit into the slab. It is statically initialized to `BREAK_GFP_ORDER_LO` (1). This check sees if more than 32MiB of memory is available, and, if it is, it allows `BREAK_GFP_ORDER_HI` number of pages to be used because internal fragmentation is more acceptable when more memory is available.

446-470 Creates two caches for each size of memory allocation needed.

452 Stores the human-readable cache name in `name`.

453-454 Creates the cache, aligned to the L1 cache.

460-463 Calculates the off-slab `bufctl` limit, which determines the number of objects that can be stored in a cache when the slab descriptor is kept off-cache.

464 The human-readable name for the cache for DMA use.

465-466 Creates the cache, aligned to the L1 cache and suitable for the DMA user.

467 If the cache failed to allocate, it is a bug. If memory is unavailable this early, the machine will not boot.

469 Moves to the next element in the `cache_sizes` array.

470 The array is terminated with a 0 as the last element.

H.4.2 `kmalloc()`

H.4.2.1 Function: `kmalloc()`   *(mm/slab.c)*

The call graph for this function is shown in Figure 8.16.

```
1555 void * kmalloc (size_t size, int flags)
1556 {
1557     cache_sizes_t *csizep = cache_sizes;
1558
1559     for (; csizep->cs_size; csizep++) {
1560         if (size > csizep->cs_size)
1561             continue;
1562         return __kmem_cache_alloc(flags & GFP_DMA ?
1563             csizep->cs_dmacachep :
1564             csizep->cs_cachep, flags);
1564     }
1565     return NULL;
1566 }
```

1557 `cache_sizes` is the array of caches for each size (See Section 8.4).

1559-1564 Starting with the smallest cache, this examines the size of each cache until one large enough to satisfy the request is found.

1562 If the allocation is for use with DMA, this allocates an object from `cs_dmacachep`. If not, it uses the `cs_cachep`.

1565 If a sizes cache of sufficient size was not available or an object could not be allocated, this returns failure.

H.4.3 `kfree()`

H.4.3.1 **Function: `kfree()`** *(mm/slab.c)*
The call graph for this function is shown in Figure 8.17. It is worth noting that the work this function does is almost identical to the function `kmem_cache_free()` with debugging enabled (See Section H.3.3.1).

```
1597 void kfree (const void *objp)
1598 {
1599     kmem_cache_t *c;
1600     unsigned long flags;
1601
1602     if (!objp)
1603         return;
1604     local_irq_save(flags);
1605     CHECK_PAGE(virt_to_page(objp));
1606     c = GET_PAGE_CACHE(virt_to_page(objp));
1607     __kmem_cache_free(c, (void*)objp);
1608     local_irq_restore(flags);
1609 }
```

1602 Returns if the pointer is NULL. This is possible if a caller used `kmalloc()` and had a catch-all failure routine that called `kfree()` immediately.

1604 Disables interrupts.

1605 Makes sure the page that this object is in is a slab page.

1606 Gets the cache that this pointer belongs to (See Section 8.2).

1607 Frees the memory object.

1608 Re-enables interrupts.

Slab Allocator

H.5   Per-CPU Object Cache

Contents

The structure of the per-CPU object cache and how objects are added or removed from it is covered in detail in Sections 8.5.1 and 8.5.2.

H.5.1   Enabling Per-CPU Caches

H.5.1.1   Function: `enable_all_cpucaches()`   *(mm/slab.c)*

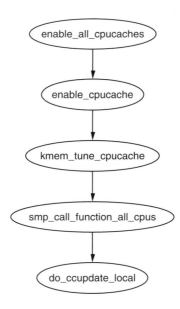

Figure H.1. Call Graph: `enable_all_cpucaches()`

This function locks the cache chain and enables the cpucache for every cache. This is important after the `cache_cache` and sizes cache have been enabled.

```
1714 static void enable_all_cpucaches (void)
1715 {
1716     struct list_head* p;
1717
1718     down(&cache_chain_sem);
1719
1720     p = &cache_cache.next;
1721     do {
1722         kmem_cache_t* cachep = list_entry(p, kmem_cache_t, next);
1723
1724         enable_cpucache(cachep);
1725         p = cachep->next.next;
1726     } while (p != &cache_cache.next);
1727
1728     up(&cache_chain_sem);
1729 }
```

1718 Obtains the semaphore to the cache chain.

1719 Gets the first cache on the chain.

1721-1726 Cycles through the whole chain.

1722 Gets a cache from the chain. This code will skip the first cache on the chain,
but cache_cache does not need a cpucache because it is so rarely used.

1724 Enables the cpucache.

1725 Moves to the next cache on the chain.

1726 Releases the cache chain semaphore.

H.5.1.2 Function: enable_cpucache() *(mm/slab.c)*

This function calculates what the size of a cpucache should be based on the size
of the objects the cache contains before calling kmem_tune_cpucache(), which does
the actual allocation.

```
1693 static void enable_cpucache (kmem_cache_t *cachep)
1694 {
1695     int err;
1696     int limit;
1697
1699     if (cachep->objsize > PAGE_SIZE)
1700         return;
1701     if (cachep->objsize > 1024)
1702         limit = 60;
1703     else if (cachep->objsize > 256)
1704         limit = 124;
```

```
1705        else
1706            limit = 252;
1707
1708        err = kmem_tune_cpucache(cachep, limit, limit/2);
1709        if (err)
1710            printk(KERN_ERR
               "enable_cpucache failed for %s, error %d.\n",
1711                        cachep->name, -err);
1712 }
```

1699-1700 If an object is larger than a page, return to avoid creating a per-CPU cache for this object type because per-CPU caches are too expensive.

1701-1702 If an object is larger than 1KiB, this keeps the cpucache lower than 3MiB in size. The limit is set to 124 objects to take the size of the cpucache descriptors into account.

1703-1704 For smaller objects, this just makes sure the cache does not go above 3MiB in size.

1708 Allocates the memory for the cpucache.

1710-1711 Prints out an error message if the allocation failed.

H.5.1.3   Function: kmem_tune_cpucache()   *(mm/slab.c)*

This function is responsible for allocating memory for the cpucaches. For each CPU on the system, kmalloc gives a block of memory large enough for one cpucache and fills a ccupdate_struct_t struct. The function smp_call_function_all_cpus() then calls do_ccupdate_local(), which swaps the new information with the old information in the cache descriptor.

```
1639 static int kmem_tune_cpucache (kmem_cache_t* cachep,
                     int limit, int batchcount)
1640 {
1641     ccupdate_struct_t new;
1642     int i;
1643
1644     /*
1645      * These are admin-provided, so we are more graceful.
1646      */
1647     if (limit < 0)
1648         return -EINVAL;
1649     if (batchcount < 0)
1650         return -EINVAL;
1651     if (batchcount > limit)
1652         return -EINVAL;
1653     if (limit != 0 && !batchcount)
```

```
1654            return -EINVAL;
1655
1656        memset(&new.new,0,sizeof(new.new));
1657        if (limit) {
1658            for (i = 0; i< smp_num_cpus; i++) {
1659                cpucache_t* ccnew;
1660
1661                ccnew = kmalloc(sizeof(void*)*limit+
1662                        sizeof(cpucache_t),
1663                        GFP_KERNEL);
1663                if (!ccnew)
1664                    goto oom;
1665                ccnew->limit = limit;
1666                ccnew->avail = 0;
1667                new.new[cpu_logical_map(i)] = ccnew;
1668            }
1669        }
1670        new.cachep = cachep;
1671        spin_lock_irq(&cachep->spinlock);
1672        cachep->batchcount = batchcount;
1673        spin_unlock_irq(&cachep->spinlock);
1674
1675        smp_call_function_all_cpus(do_ccupdate_local, (void *)&new);
1676
1677        for (i = 0; i < smp_num_cpus; i++) {
1678            cpucache_t* ccold = new.new[cpu_logical_map(i)];
1679            if (!ccold)
1680                continue;
1681            local_irq_disable();
1682            free_block(cachep, cc_entry(ccold), ccold->avail);
1683            local_irq_enable();
1684            kfree(ccold);
1685        }
1686        return 0;
1687 oom:
1688        for (i--; i >= 0; i--)
1689            kfree(new.new[cpu_logical_map(i)]);
1690        return -ENOMEM;
1691 }
```

1639 The parameters of the function are the following:

- **cachep** The cache this cpucache is being allocated for

- **limit** The total number of objects that can exist in the cpucache

- **batchcount** The number of objects to allocate in one batch when the
  cpucache is empty

1647 The number of objects in the cache cannot be negative.

1649 A negative number of objects cannot be allocated.

1651 A batch of objects greater than the limit cannot be allocated.

1653 A batchcount must be provided if the limit is positive.

1656 Zero-fills the update struct.

1657 If a limit is provided, this allocates memory for the cpucache.

1658-1668 For every CPU, this allocates a cpucache.

1661 The amount of memory needed is limit number of pointers and the size of the cpucache descriptor.

1663 If out of memory, this cleans up and exits.

1665-1666 Fills in the fields for the cpucache descriptor.

1667 Fills in the information for ccupdate_update_t struct.

1670 Tells the ccupdate_update_t struct what cache is being updated.

1671-1673 Acquires an interrupt-safe lock to the cache descriptor and sets its batchcount.

1675 Gets each CPU to update its cpucache information for itself. This swaps the old cpucaches in the cache descriptor with the new ones in new using do_ccupdate_local() (See Section H.5.2.2).

1677-1685 After smp_call_function_all_cpus() (See Section H.5.2.1), the old cpucaches are in new. This block of code cycles through them all, frees any objects in them and deletes the old cpucache.

1686 Returns success.

1688 In the event there is no memory, this deletes all cpucaches that have been allocated up until this point and returns failure.

H.5.2   Updating Per-CPU Information

H.5.2.1   Function: smp_call_function_all_cpus()   *(mm/slab.c)*

This calls the function func() for all CPUs. In the context of the slab allocator, the function is do_ccupdate_local(), and the argument is ccupdate_struct_t.

```
859 static void smp_call_function_all_cpus(void (*func) (void *arg),
                     void *arg)
860 {
861     local_irq_disable();
862     func(arg);
```

```
863        local_irq_enable();
864
865        if (smp_call_function(func, arg, 1, 1))
866            BUG();
867 }
```

861-863 Disables interrupts locally and calls the function for this CPU.

865 For all other CPUs, this calls the function. `smp_call_function()` is an architecture-specific function and will not be discussed further here.

H.5.2.2   Function: do_ccupdate_local()   *(mm/slab.c)*

This function swaps the cpucache information in the cache descriptor with the information in `info` for this CPU.

```
874 static void do_ccupdate_local(void *info)
875 {
876        ccupdate_struct_t *new = (ccupdate_struct_t *)info;
877        cpucache_t *old = cc_data(new->cachep);
878
879        cc_data(new->cachep) = new->new[smp_processor_id()];
880        new->new[smp_processor_id()] = old;
881 }
```

876 `info` is a pointer to the `ccupdate_struct_t`, which is then passed to `smp_call_function_all_cpus()`(See Section H.5.2.1).

877 Part of the `ccupdate_struct_t` is a pointer to the cache that this cpucache belongs to. `cc_data()` returns the `cpucache_t` for this processor.

879 Places the new cpucache in the cache descriptor. `cc_data()` returns the pointer to the cpucache for this CPU.

880 Replaces the pointer in `new` with the old cpucache so that it can be deleted later by the caller of `smp_call_function_call_cpus()`, `kmem_tune_cpucache()`, for example.

H.5.3   Draining a Per-CPU Cache

This function is called to drain all objects in a per-CPU cache. It is called when a cache needs to be shrunk for the freeing up of slabs. A slab would not be freeable if an object was in the per-CPU cache, even though it is not in use.

H.5.3.1   Function: drain_cpu_caches()   *(mm/slab.c)*

```
885 static void drain_cpu_caches(kmem_cache_t *cachep)
886 {
887        ccupdate_struct_t new;
888        int i;
```

Slab Allocator

```
889
890    memset(&new.new,0,sizeof(new.new));
891
892    new.cachep = cachep;
893
894    down(&cache_chain_sem);
895    smp_call_function_all_cpus(do_ccupdate_local, (void *)&new);
896
897    for (i = 0; i < smp_num_cpus; i++) {
898        cpucache_t* ccold = new.new[cpu_logical_map(i)];
899        if (!ccold || (ccold->avail == 0))
900            continue;
901        local_irq_disable();
902        free_block(cachep, cc_entry(ccold), ccold->avail);
903        local_irq_enable();
904        ccold->avail = 0;
905    }
906    smp_call_function_all_cpus(do_ccupdate_local, (void *)&new);
907    up(&cache_chain_sem);
908 }
```

890 Blanks the update structure because it is going to be clearing all data.

892 Sets `new.cachep` to `cachep` so that `smp_call_function_all_cpus()` knows what cache it is affecting.

894 Acquires the cache descriptor semaphore.

895 `do_ccupdate_local()`(See Section H.5.2.2) swaps the `cpucache_t` information in the cache descriptor with the ones in `new` so they can be altered here.

897-905 For each CPU in the system,...

898 Gets the cpucache descriptor for this CPU.

899 If the structure does not exist for some reason or no objects are available in it, this moves to the next CPU.

901 Disables interrupts on this processor. It is possible an allocation from an interrupt handler elsewhere would try to access the per-CPU cache.

902 Frees the block of objects with `free_block()` (See Section H.3.3.5).

903 Re-enables interrupts.

904 Shows that no objects are available.

906 The information for each CPU has been updated, so this calls `do_ccupdate_local()` (See Section H.5.2.2) for each CPU to put the information back into the cache descriptor.

907 Releases the semaphore for the cache chain.

H.6 Slab Allocator Initialization

Contents

H.6.1.1   Function: `kmem_cache_init()`   *(mm/slab.c)*
This function will do the following:

- Initialize the cache chain linked list.

- Initialize a `mutex` for accessing the cache chain.

- Calculate the `cache_cache` color.

```
416 void __init kmem_cache_init(void)
417 {
418     size_t left_over;
419
420     init_MUTEX(&cache_chain_sem);
421     INIT_LIST_HEAD(&cache_chain);
422
423     kmem_cache_estimate(0, cache_cache.objsize, 0,
424             &left_over, &cache_cache.num);
425     if (!cache_cache.num)
426         BUG();
427
428     cache_cache.colour = left_over/cache_cache.colour_off;
429     cache_cache.colour_next = 0;
430 }
```

420 Initializes the semaphore for access to the cache chain.

421 Initializes the cache chain linked list.

423 `kmem_cache_estimate()`(See Section H.1.2.1) calculates the number of objects and amount of bytes wasted.

425 If even one `kmem_cache_t` cannot be stored in a page, something is seriously wrong.

428 `colour` is the number of different cache lines that can be used while still keeping the L1 cache alignment.

429 `colour_next` indicates which line to use next. It starts at 0.

Slab Allocator

H.7   Interfacing with the Buddy Allocator

Contents

H.7.1.1   Function: `kmem_getpages()`   *(mm/slab.c)*
This allocates pages for the slab allocator.

```
486 static inline void * kmem_getpages (kmem_cache_t *cachep,
                                        unsigned long flags)
487 {
488     void    *addr;
495     flags |= cachep->gfpflags;
496     addr = (void*) __get_free_pages(flags, cachep->gfporder);
503     return addr;
504 }
```

495 Whatever flags were requested for the allocation, this appends the cache flags to it. The only flag it may append is `ZONE_DMA` if the cache requires DMA memory.

496 Allocates from the buddy allocator with `__get_free_pages()` (See Section F.2.3).

503 Returns the pages or NULL if it failed.

H.7.1.2   Function: `kmem_freepages()`   *(mm/slab.c)*
This frees pages for the slab allocator. Before it calls the buddy allocator API, it will remove the `PG_slab` bit from the page flags.

```
507 static inline void kmem_freepages (kmem_cache_t *cachep, void *addr)
508 {
509     unsigned long i = (1<<cachep->gfporder);
510     struct page *page = virt_to_page(addr);
511
517     while (i--) {
518         PageClearSlab(page);
519         page++;
520     }
521     free_pages((unsigned long)addr, cachep->gfporder);
522 }
```

509 Retrieves the order used for the original allocation.

510 Gets the struct page for the address.

517-520 Clears the `PG_slab` bit on each page.

521 Frees the pages to the buddy allocator with `free_pages()` (See Section F.4.1).

High Memory Management

Contents

I.1 Mapping High Memory Pages

Contents

I.1.1   Function: kmap()   *(include/asm-i386/highmem.c)*
This API is used by callers willing to block.

```
62 #define kmap(page) __kmap(page, 0)
```

62 The core function __kmap() is called with the second parameter indicating that
the caller is willing to block.

I.1.2   Function: kmap_nonblock()   *(include/asm-i386/highmem.c)*

```
63 #define kmap_nonblock(page) __kmap(page, 1)
```

63 The core function __kmap() is called with the second parameter indicating that
the caller is not willing to block.

I.1.3   Function: __kmap()   *(include/asm-i386/highmem.h)*
The call graph for this function is shown in Figure 9.1.

```
65 static inline void *kmap(struct page *page, int nonblocking)
66 {
67     if (in_interrupt())
68         out_of_line_bug();
69     if (page < highmem_start_page)
70         return page_address(page);
71     return kmap_high(page);
72 }
```

67-68 This function may not be used from interrupt because it may sleep. Instead of BUG(), out_of_line_bug() calls do_exit() and returns an error code.
BUG() is not used because BUG() kills the process with extreme prejudice,
which would result in the fabled "Aiee, killing interrupt handler!" kernel
panic.

69-70 If the page is already in low memory, this returns a direct mapping.

71 Calls kmap_high()(See Section I.1.4) for the beginning of the architecture-
independent work.

I.1.4   Function: kmap_high()   *(mm/highmem.c)*

```
132 void *kmap_high(struct page *page, int nonblocking)
133 {
134     unsigned long vaddr;
135
142     spin_lock(&kmap_lock);
143     vaddr = (unsigned long) page->virtual;
144     if (!vaddr) {
145         vaddr = map_new_virtual(page, nonblocking);
146         if (!vaddr)
147             goto out;
148     }
149     pkmap_count[PKMAP_NR(vaddr)]++;
150     if (pkmap_count[PKMAP_NR(vaddr)] < 2)
151         BUG();
152 out:
153     spin_unlock(&kmap_lock);
154     return (void*) vaddr;
155 }
```

142 The `kmap_lock` protects the `virtual` field of a page and the `pkmap_count` array.

143 Gets the virtual address of the page.

144-148 If it is not already mapped, this calls `map_new_virtual()`, which will map the page and returns the virtual address. If it fails, goto `out` to free the spinlock and return NULL.

149 Increases the reference count for this page mapping.

150-151 If the count is currently less than 2, it is a serious bug. In reality, severe breakage would have to be introduced to cause this to happen.

153 Frees the `kmap_lock`.

I.1.5   Function: map_new_virtual()   *(mm/highmem.c)*

This function is divided into three principal parts: scanning for a free slot, waiting on a queue if none is available and mapping the page.

```
80 static inline unsigned long map_new_virtual(struct page *page)
81 {
82     unsigned long vaddr;
83     int count;
84
85 start:
86     count = LAST_PKMAP;
```

```
87        /* Find an empty entry */
88        for (;;) {
89            last_pkmap_nr = (last_pkmap_nr + 1) & LAST_PKMAP_MASK;
90            if (!last_pkmap_nr) {
91                flush_all_zero_pkmaps();
92                count = LAST_PKMAP;
93            }
94            if (!pkmap_count[last_pkmap_nr])
95                break;  /* Found a usable entry */
96            if (--count)
97                continue;
98
99            if (nonblocking)
100               return 0;
```

86 Starts scanning at the last possible slot.

88-122 This look keeps scanning and waiting until a slot becomes free. This allows
the possibility of an infinite loop for some processes if they were unlucky.

89 last_pkmap_nr is the last pkmap that was scanned. To prevent searching over
the same pages, this value is recorded so that the list is searched circularly.
When it reaches LAST_PKMAP, it wraps around to 0.

90-93 When last_pkmap_nr wraps around, this calls flush_all_zero_pkmaps()
(See Section I.1.6), which will set all entries from 1 to 0 in the pkmap_count
array before flushing the TLB. The count is set back to LAST_PKMAP to restart
scanning.

94-95 If this element is 0, a usable slot has been found for the page.

96-97 Moves to the next index to scan.

99-100 The next block of code is going to sleep while waiting for a slot to be free.
If the caller requested that the function not block, it returns now.

```
105           {
106               DECLARE_WAITQUEUE(wait, current);
107
108               current->state = TASK_UNINTERRUPTIBLE;
109               add_wait_queue(&pkmap_map_wait, &wait);
110               spin_unlock(&kmap_lock);
111               schedule();
112               remove_wait_queue(&pkmap_map_wait, &wait);
113               spin_lock(&kmap_lock);
114
115               /* Somebody else might have mapped it while we
                     slept */
```

```
116               if (page->virtual)
117                   return (unsigned long) page->virtual;
118
119               /* Re-start */
120               goto start;
121           }
122       }
```

If a slot is not available after scanning all the pages once, we sleep on the `pkmap_map_wait` queue until we are woken up after an unmap.

106 Declares the wait queue.

108 Sets the task as interruptible because we are sleeping in kernel space.

109 Adds ourselves to the `pkmap_map_wait` queue.

110 Frees the `kmap_lock` spinlock.

111 Calls `schedule()`, which will put us to sleep. We are woken up after a slot becomes free after an unmap.

112 Removes ourselves from the wait queue.

113 Reacquires `kmap_lock`.

116-117 If someone else mapped the page while we slept, this just returns the address, and the reference count will be incremented by `kmap_high()`.

120 Restarts the scanning.

```
123      vaddr = PKMAP_ADDR(last_pkmap_nr);
124      set_pte(&(pkmap_page_table[last_pkmap_nr]), mk_pte(page,
             kmap_prot));
125
126      pkmap_count[last_pkmap_nr] = 1;
127      page->virtual = (void *) vaddr;
128
129      return vaddr;
130 }
```

This block is when a slot has been found, and it maps the page.

123 Gets the virtual address for the slot found.

124 Makes the PTE entry with the page and required protection and places it in the pagetables at the found slot.

126 Initializes the value in the `pkmap_count` array to 1. The count is incremented in the parent function, and we are sure this is the first mapping if we are in this function in the first place.

127 Sets the `virtual` field for the page.

129 Returns the virtual address.

I.1.6   Function: `flush_all_zero_pkmaps()`   *(mm/highmem.c)*
This function cycles through the `pkmap_count` array and sets all entries from 1 to 0 before flushing the TLB.

```
42 static void flush_all_zero_pkmaps(void)
43 {
44     int i;
45
46     flush_cache_all();
47
48     for (i = 0; i < LAST_PKMAP; i++) {
49         struct page *page;
50
57         if (pkmap_count[i] != 1)
58             continue;
59         pkmap_count[i] = 0;
60
61         /* sanity check */
62         if (pte_none(pkmap_page_table[i]))
63             BUG();
64
72         page = pte_page(pkmap_page_table[i]);
73         pte_clear(&pkmap_page_table[i]);
74
75         page->virtual = NULL;
76     }
77     flush_tlb_all();
78 }
```

46 As the global pagetables are about to change, the CPU caches of all processors have to be flushed.

48-76 Cycles through the entire `pkmap_count` array.

57-58 If the element is not 1, this moves to the next element.

59 Sets from 1 to 0.

62-63 Makes sure the PTE is not somehow mapped.

72-73 Unmaps the page from the PTE and clears the PTE.

75 Updates the `virtual` field as the page is unmapped.

77 Flushes the TLB.

I.2   Mapping High Memory Pages Atomically

Contents

The following is an example `km_type` enumeration for the x86. It lists the different uses interrupts have for atomically calling `kmap`. Note how `KM_TYPE_NR` is the last element, so it doubles up as a count of the number of elements.

```
 4 enum km_type {
 5     KM_BOUNCE_READ,
 6     KM_SKB_SUNRPC_DATA,
 7     KM_SKB_DATA_SOFTIRQ,
 8     KM_USER0,
 9     KM_USER1,
10     KM_BH_IRQ,
11     KM_TYPE_NR
12 };
```

I.2.1   Function: `kmap_atomic()`   *(include/asm-i386/highmem.h)*

This is the atomic version of `kmap()`. Note that, at no point, is a spinlock held or does it sleep. A spinlock is not required because every processor has its own reserved space.

```
 89 static inline void *kmap_atomic(struct page *page,
                                    enum km_type type)
 90 {
 91     enum fixed_addresses idx;
 92     unsigned long vaddr;
 93
 94     if (page < highmem_start_page)
 95         return page_address(page);
 96
 97     idx = type + KM_TYPE_NR*smp_processor_id();
 98     vaddr = __fix_to_virt(FIX_KMAP_BEGIN + idx);
 99 #if HIGHMEM_DEBUG
100     if (!pte_none(*(kmap_pte-idx)))
101         out_of_line_bug();
102 #endif
103     set_pte(kmap_pte-idx, mk_pte(page, kmap_prot));
104     __flush_tlb_one(vaddr);
105
106     return (void*) vaddr;
107 }
```

89 The parameters are the page to map and the type of usage required. One slot per usage per processor is maintained.

94-95 If the page is in low memory, this returns a direct mapping.

97 `type` gives which slot to use. `KM_TYPE_NR * smp_processor_id()` gives the set of slots reserved for this processor.

98 Gets the virtual address.

100-101 For debugging code. In reality, a PTE will always exist.

103 Sets the PTE into the reserved slot.

104 Flushes the TLB for this slot.

106 Returns the virtual address.

I.3 Unmapping Pages

Contents

I.3.1   Function: `kunmap()`   *(include/asm-i386/highmem.h)*

```
74 static inline void kunmap(struct page *page)
75 {
76     if (in_interrupt())
77         out_of_line_bug();
78     if (page < highmem_start_page)
79         return;
80     kunmap_high(page);
81 }
```

76-77 `kunmap()` cannot be called from interrupt, so it exits gracefully.

78-79 If the page is already in low memory, there is no need to unmap.

80 Calls the architecture-independent function `kunmap_high()`.

I.3.2   Function: `kunmap_high()`   *(mm/highmem.c)*
This is the architecture-independent part of the `kunmap()` operation.

```
157 void kunmap_high(struct page *page)
158 {
159     unsigned long vaddr;
160     unsigned long nr;
161     int need_wakeup;
162
163     spin_lock(&kmap_lock);
164     vaddr = (unsigned long) page->virtual;
165     if (!vaddr)
166         BUG();
167     nr = PKMAP_NR(vaddr);
168
173     need_wakeup = 0;
174     switch (--pkmap_count[nr]) {
175     case 0:
176         BUG();
177     case 1:
188         need_wakeup = waitqueue_active(&pkmap_map_wait);
189     }
190     spin_unlock(&kmap_lock);
```

```
191
192     /* do wake-up, if needed, race-free outside of the spin lock */
193     if (need_wakeup)
194         wake_up(&pkmap_map_wait);
195 }
```

163 Acquires `kmap_lock`, protecting the `virtual` field and the `pkmap_count` array.

164 Gets the virtual page.

165-166 If the virtual field is not set, it is a double unmapping or unmapping of a nonmapped page, so it uses `BUG()`.

167 Gets the index within the `pkmap_count` array.

173 By default, a wakeup call to processes calling `kmap()` is not needed.

174 Checks the value of the index after decrement.

175-176 Falling to 0 is a bug because the TLB needs to be flushed to make 0 a valid entry.

177-188 If it has dropped to 1 (the entry is now free, but needs a TLB flush), this checks to see if anyone is sleeping on the `pkmap_map_wait` queue. If necessary, the queue will be woken up after the spinlock is freed.

190 Frees `kmap_lock`.

193-194 If waiters are on the queue and a slot has been freed, this wakes them up.

I.4   Unmapping High Memory Pages Atomically

Contents

I.4.1   Function: `kunmap_atomic()`   *(include/asm-i386/highmem.h)*

This entire function is debug code. The reason is that, because pages are only mapped here atomically, they will only be used in a tiny place for a short time before being unmapped. It is safe to leave the page there because it will not be referenced after unmapping, and another mapping to the same slot will simply replace it.

```
109 static inline void kunmap_atomic(void *kvaddr, enum km_type type)
110 {
111 #if HIGHMEM_DEBUG
112     unsigned long vaddr = (unsigned long) kvaddr & PAGE_MASK;
113     enum fixed_addresses idx = type + KM_TYPE_NR*smp_processor_id();
114
115     if (vaddr < FIXADDR_START) // FIXME
116         return;
117
118     if (vaddr != __fix_to_virt(FIX_KMAP_BEGIN+idx))
119         out_of_line_bug();
120
121     /*
122      * force other mappings to Oops if they'll try to access
123      * this pte without first remap it
124      */
125     pte_clear(kmap_pte-idx);
126     __flush_tlb_one(vaddr);
127 #endif
128 }
```

112 Gets the virtual address and ensures it is aligned to a page boundary.

115-116 If the address supplied is not in the fixed area, this returns.

118-119 If the address does not correspond to the reserved slot for this type of usage and processor, this declares it.

125-126 Unmaps the page now so that, if it is referenced again, it will cause an Oops.

I.5   Bounce Buffers

Contents

I.5.1   Creating Bounce Buffers

I.5.1.1   Function: `create_bounce()`   *(mm/highmem.c)*

The call graph for this function is shown in Figure 9.3. It is a high-level function for the creation of bounce buffers. It is broken into two major parts, the allocation of the necessary resources and the copying of data from the template.

```
405 struct buffer_head * create_bounce(int rw,
                                        struct buffer_head * bh_orig)
406 {
407     struct page *page;
408     struct buffer_head *bh;
409
410     if (!PageHighMem(bh_orig->b_page))
411         return bh_orig;
412
413     bh = alloc_bounce_bh();
420     page = alloc_bounce_page();
421
422     set_bh_page(bh, page, 0);
423
```

405 The parameters of the function are the following:

- **rw** is set to 1 if this is a write buffer.
- **bh_orig** is the template buffer head to copy from.

410-411 If the template buffer head is already in low memory, this simply returns it.

413 Allocates a buffer head from the slab allocator or from the emergency pool if it fails.

420 Allocates a page from the buddy allocator or the emergency pool if it fails.

422 Associates the allocated page with the allocated `buffer_head`.

```
424        bh->b_next = NULL;
425        bh->b_blocknr = bh_orig->b_blocknr;
426        bh->b_size = bh_orig->b_size;
427        bh->b_list = -1;
428        bh->b_dev = bh_orig->b_dev;
429        bh->b_count = bh_orig->b_count;
430        bh->b_rdev = bh_orig->b_rdev;
431        bh->b_state = bh_orig->b_state;
432 #ifdef HIGHMEM_DEBUG
433        bh->b_flushtime = jiffies;
434        bh->b_next_free = NULL;
435        bh->b_prev_free = NULL;
436        /* bh->b_this_page */
437        bh->b_reqnext = NULL;
438        bh->b_pprev = NULL;
439 #endif
440        /* bh->b_page */
441        if (rw == WRITE) {
442            bh->b_end_io = bounce_end_io_write;
443            copy_from_high_bh(bh, bh_orig);
444        } else
445            bh->b_end_io = bounce_end_io_read;
446        bh->b_private = (void *)bh_orig;
447        bh->b_rsector = bh_orig->b_rsector;
448 #ifdef HIGHMEM_DEBUG
449        memset(&bh->b_wait, -1, sizeof(bh->b_wait));
450 #endif
451
452        return bh;
453 }
```

This block populates the newly created `buffer_head`.

431 Copies in information essentially verbatim, except for the `b_list` field because this buffer is not directly connected to the others on the list.

433-438 For debugging-only information.

441-444 If this is a buffer that is to be written to, then the callback function to end the I/O is `bounce_end_io_write()` (See Section I.5.2.1), which is called when the device has received all the information. Because the data exists in high memory, it is copied "down" with `copy_from_high_bh()` (See Section I.5.2.3).

437-438 If we are waiting for a device to write data into the buffer, the callback function `bounce_end_io_read()` (See Section I.5.2.2) is used.

446-447 Copies the remaining information from the template `buffer_head`.

452 Returns the new bounce buffer.

I.5.1.2   Function: `alloc_bounce_bh()`   *(mm/highmem.c)*

This function first tries to allocate a `buffer_head` from the slab allocator, and, if that fails, an emergency pool will be used.

```
369 struct buffer_head *alloc_bounce_bh (void)
370 {
371     struct list_head *tmp;
372     struct buffer_head *bh;
373
374     bh = kmem_cache_alloc(bh_cachep, SLAB_NOHIGHIO);
375     if (bh)
376         return bh;
380
381     wakeup_bdflush();
```

374 Tries to allocate a new `buffer_head` from the slab allocator. Note how the request is made to *not* use I/O operations that involve high I/O to avoid recursion.

375-376 If the allocation was successful, this returns.

381 If it was not, this wakes up **bdflush** to launder pages.

```
383 repeat_alloc:
387     tmp = &emergency_bhs;
388     spin_lock_irq(&emergency_lock);
389     if (!list_empty(tmp)) {
390         bh = list_entry(tmp->next, struct buffer_head,
                        b_inode_buffers);
391         list_del(tmp->next);
392         nr_emergency_bhs--;
393     }
394     spin_unlock_irq(&emergency_lock);
395     if (bh)
396         return bh;
397
398     /* we need to wait I/O completion */
399     run_task_queue(&tq_disk);
400
401     yield();
402     goto repeat_alloc;
403 }
```

The allocation from the slab failed, so this allocates from the emergency pool.

387 Gets the end of the emergency buffer head list.

388 Acquires the lock protecting the pools.

389-393 If the pool is not empty, this takes a `buffer_head` from the list and decrements the `nr_emergency_bhs` counter.

394 Releases the lock.

395-396 If the allocation was successful, this returns it.

399 If not, we are seriously short of memory, and the only way the pool will replenish is if high memory I/O completes. Therefore, requests on `tq_disk` are started so that the data will be written to disk, probably freeing up pages in the process.

401 Yields the processor.

402 Attempts to allocate from the emergency pools again.

I.5.1.3 Function: `alloc_bounce_page()` *(mm/highmem.c)*

This function is essentially identical to `alloc_bounce_bh()`. It first tries to allocate a page from the buddy allocator, and, if that fails, an emergency pool will be used.

```
333 struct page *alloc_bounce_page (void)
334 {
335     struct list_head *tmp;
336     struct page *page;
337
338     page = alloc_page(GFP_NOHIGHIO);
339     if (page)
340         return page;
344
345     wakeup_bdflush();
```

338-340 Allocates from the buddy allocator and returns the page if successful.

345 Wakes **bdflush** to launder pages.

```
347 repeat_alloc:
351     tmp = &emergency_pages;
352     spin_lock_irq(&emergency_lock);
353     if (!list_empty(tmp)) {
354         page = list_entry(tmp->next, struct page, list);
355         list_del(tmp->next);
356         nr_emergency_pages--;
357     }
358     spin_unlock_irq(&emergency_lock);
```

```
359     if (page)
360         return page;
361
362     /* we need to wait I/O completion */
363     run_task_queue(&tq_disk);
364
365     yield();
366     goto repeat_alloc;
367 }
```

351 Gets the end of the emergency buffer head list.

352 Acquires the lock protecting the pools.

353-357 If the pool is not empty, this takes a page from the list and decrements the number of available nr_emergency_pages.

358 Releases the lock.

359-360 If the allocation was successful, this returns it.

363 Runs the I/O task queue to try and replenish the emergency pool.

365 Yields the processor.

366 Attempts to allocate from the emergency pools again.

I.5.2   Copying Using Bounce Buffers

I.5.2.1   Function: bounce_end_io_write()   *(mm/highmem.c)*
This function is called when a bounce buffer used for writing to a device completes I/O. Because the buffer is copied *from* high memory and to the device, there is nothing left to do except reclaim the resources.

```
319 static void bounce_end_io_write (struct buffer_head *bh,
                                     int uptodate)
320 {
321     bounce_end_io(bh, uptodate);
322 }
```

I.5.2.2   Function: bounce_end_io_read()   *(mm/highmem.c)*
This is called when data has been read from the device and needs to be copied to high memory. It is called from interrupt, so it has to be more careful.

```
324 static void bounce_end_io_read (struct buffer_head *bh,
                                    int uptodate)
325 {
326     struct buffer_head *bh_orig =
                (struct buffer_head *)(bh->b_private);
```

```
327
328    if (uptodate)
329        copy_to_high_bh_irq(bh_orig, bh);
330    bounce_end_io(bh, uptodate);
331 }
```

328-329 The data is just copied to the bounce buffer to be moved to high memory with `copy_to_high_bh_irq()` (See Section I.5.2.4).

330 Reclaims the resources.

I.5.2.3 Function: `copy_from_high_bh()` *(mm/highmem.c)*

This function copies data from a high memory `buffer_head` to a bounce buffer.

```
215 static inline void copy_from_high_bh (struct buffer_head *to,
216             struct buffer_head *from)
217 {
218    struct page *p_from;
219    char *vfrom;
220
221    p_from = from->b_page;
222
223    vfrom = kmap_atomic(p_from, KM_USER0);
224    memcpy(to->b_data, vfrom + bh_offset(from), to->b_size);
225    kunmap_atomic(vfrom, KM_USER0);
226 }
```

223 Maps the high-memory page into low memory. This path is protected by the IRQ safe lock `io_request_lock`, so it is safe to call `kmap_atomic()` (See Section I.2.1).

224 Copies the data.

225 Unmaps the page.

I.5.2.4 Function: `copy_to_high_bh_irq()` *(mm/highmem.c)*

This is called from interrupt after the device has finished writing data to the bounce buffer. This function copies data to high memory.

```
228 static inline void copy_to_high_bh_irq (struct buffer_head *to,
229             struct buffer_head *from)
230 {
231    struct page *p_to;
232    char *vto;
233    unsigned long flags;
234
235    p_to = to->b_page;
```

```
236      __save_flags(flags);
237      __cli();
238      vto = kmap_atomic(p_to, KM_BOUNCE_READ);
239      memcpy(vto + bh_offset(to), from->b_data, to->b_size);
240      kunmap_atomic(vto, KM_BOUNCE_READ);
241      __restore_flags(flags);
242 }
```

236-237 Saves the flags and disables interrupts.

238 Maps the high-memory page into low memory.

239 Copies the data.

240 Unmaps the page.

241 Restores the interrupt flags.

I.5.2.5   **Function:** bounce_end_io()   *(mm/highmem.c)*

This reclaims the resources used by the bounce buffers. If emergency pools are depleted, the resources are added to it.

```
244 static inline void bounce_end_io (struct buffer_head *bh,
                                      int uptodate)
245 {
246      struct page *page;
247      struct buffer_head *bh_orig =
                    (struct buffer_head *)(bh->b_private);
248      unsigned long flags;
249
250      bh_orig->b_end_io(bh_orig, uptodate);
251
252      page = bh->b_page;
253
254      spin_lock_irqsave(&emergency_lock, flags);
255      if (nr_emergency_pages >= POOL_SIZE)
256          __free_page(page);
257      else {
258          /*
259           * We are abusing page->list to manage
260           * the highmem emergency pool:
261           */
262          list_add(&page->list, &emergency_pages);
263          nr_emergency_pages++;
264      }
265
266      if (nr_emergency_bhs >= POOL_SIZE) {
```

```
267 #ifdef HIGHMEM_DEBUG
268         /* Don't clobber the constructed slab cache */
269         init_waitqueue_head(&bh->b_wait);
270 #endif
271         kmem_cache_free(bh_cachep, bh);
272     } else {
273         /*
274          * Ditto in the bh case, here we abuse b_inode_buffers:
275          */
276         list_add(&bh->b_inode_buffers, &emergency_bhs);
277         nr_emergency_bhs++;
278     }
279     spin_unlock_irqrestore(&emergency_lock, flags);
280 }
```

250 Calls the I/O completion callback for the original `buffer_head`.

252 Gets the pointer to the buffer page to free.

254 Acquires the lock to the emergency pool.

255-256 If the page pool is full, this just returns the page to the buddy allocator.

257-264 Otherwise, it adds this page to the emergency pool.

266-272 If the `buffer_head` pool is full, this just returns it to the slab allocator.

272-278 Otherwise, this adds this `buffer_head` to the pool.

279 Releases the lock.

I.6   Emergency Pools

Contents

Only one function is of relevance to the emergency pools, and that is the init function. It is called during system startup, and then the code is deleted because it is never needed again.

I.6.1   Function: `init_emergency_pool()`   *(mm/highmem.c)*

This creates a pool for emergency pages and for emergency `buffer_heads`.

```
282 static __init int init_emergency_pool(void)
283 {
284     struct sysinfo i;
285     si_meminfo(&i);
286     si_swapinfo(&i);
287
288     if (!i.totalhigh)
289         return 0;
290
291     spin_lock_irq(&emergency_lock);
292     while (nr_emergency_pages < POOL_SIZE) {
293         struct page * page = alloc_page(GFP_ATOMIC);
294         if (!page) {
295             printk("couldn't refill highmem emergency pages");
296             break;
297         }
298         list_add(&page->list, &emergency_pages);
299         nr_emergency_pages++;
300     }
```

288-289 If no high memory is available, this does not bother.

291 Acquires the lock protecting the pools.

292-300 Allocates `POOL_SIZE` pages from the buddy allocator and adds them to a linked list. It keeps a count of the number of pages in the pool with `nr_emergency_pages`.

```
301     while (nr_emergency_bhs < POOL_SIZE) {
302         struct buffer_head * bh =
                kmem_cache_alloc(bh_cachep, SLAB_ATOMIC);
303         if (!bh) {
304             printk("couldn't refill highmem emergency bhs");
305             break;
306         }
```

```
307            list_add(&bh->b_inode_buffers, &emergency_bhs);
308            nr_emergency_bhs++;
309        }
310        spin_unlock_irq(&emergency_lock);
311        printk("allocated %d pages and %d bhs reserved for the
               highmem bounces\n",
312            nr_emergency_pages, nr_emergency_bhs);
313
314        return 0;
315 }
```

301-309 Allocates POOL_SIZE buffer_heads from the slab allocator and adds them
to a linked list linked by b_inode_buffers. It keeps track of how many heads
are in the pool with nr_emergency_bhs.

310 Releases the lock protecting the pools.

314 Returns success.

Page Frame Reclamation

Contents

J.1   Page Cache Operations

Contents

Page Frame Reclamation

This section addresses how pages are added and removed from the page cache and LRU lists, both of which are heavily intertwined.

J.1.1   Adding Pages to the Page Cache

J.1.1.1   Function: `add_to_page_cache()`   *(mm/filemap.c)*

This acquires the lock protecting the page cache before calling `__add_to_page_cache()`, which will add the page to the page hash table and inode queue, which allows the pages belonging to files to be found quickly.

```
667 void add_to_page_cache(struct page * page,
                  struct address_space * mapping,
                  unsigned long offset)
668 {
669     spin_lock(&pagecache_lock);
670     __add_to_page_cache(page, mapping,
                    offset, page_hash(mapping, offset));
671     spin_unlock(&pagecache_lock);
672     lru_cache_add(page);
673 }
```

669 Acquires the lock protecting the page hash and inode queues.

670 Calls the function that performs the real work.

671 Releases the lock protecting the hash and inode queue.

672 Adds the page to the page cache. `page_hash()` hashes into the page hash table based on the `mapping` and the `offset` within the file. If a page is returned, there was a collision, and the colliding pages are chained with the page→`next_hash` and page→`pprev_hash` fields.

J.1.1.2   Function: `add_to_page_cache_unique()`   *(mm/filemap.c)*

In many respects, this function is very similar to `add_to_page_cache()`. The principal difference is that this function will check the page cache with the `pagecache_lock` spinlock held before adding the page to the cache. It is for callers that may race with another process for inserting a page in the cache, such as `add_to_swap_cache()`(See Section K.2.1.1).

```
675 int add_to_page_cache_unique(struct page * page,
676         struct address_space *mapping, unsigned long offset,
677         struct page **hash)
678 {
679     int err;
680     struct page *alias;
681
682     spin_lock(&pagecache_lock);
683     alias = __find_page_nolock(mapping, offset, *hash);
684
685     err = 1;
686     if (!alias) {
687         __add_to_page_cache(page,mapping,offset,hash);
688         err = 0;
689     }
690
691     spin_unlock(&pagecache_lock);
692     if (!err)
693         lru_cache_add(page);
694     return err;
695 }
```

682 Acquires the `pagecache_lock` for examining the cache.

683 Checks if the page already exists in the cache with `__find_page_nolock()` (See Section J.1.4.3).

686-689 If the page does not exist in the cache, this adds it with `__add_to_page_cache()` (See Section J.1.1.3).

691 Releases the `pagecache_lock`.

692-693 If the page did not already exist in the page cache, it adds it to the LRU lists with `lru_cache_add()`(See Section J.2.1.1).

694 Returns 0 if this call entered the page into the page cache and 1 if it already existed.

J.1.1.3 Function: __add_to_page_cache() *(mm/filemap.c)*

This clears all page flags, locks the page, increments the reference count for the page and adds the page to the inode and hash queues.

```
653 static inline void __add_to_page_cache(struct page * page,
654       struct address_space *mapping, unsigned long offset,
655       struct page **hash)
656 {
657       unsigned long flags;
658
659       flags = page->flags & ~(1 << PG_uptodate |
                              1 << PG_error | 1 << PG_dirty |
                              1 << PG_referenced | 1 << PG_arch_1 |
                              1 << PG_checked);
660       page->flags = flags | (1 << PG_locked);
661       page_cache_get(page);
662       page->index = offset;
663       add_page_to_inode_queue(mapping, page);
664       add_page_to_hash_queue(page, hash);
665 }
```

659 Clears all page flags.

660 Locks the page.

661 Takes a reference to the page in case it gets freed prematurely.

662 Updates the index so it is known what file offset this page represents.

663 Adds the page to the inode queue with add_page_to_inode_queue() (See Section J.1.1.4). This links the page using the page→list to the clean_pages list in the address_space and points the page→mapping to the same address_space.

664 Adds it to the page hash with add_page_to_hash_queue() (See Section J.1.1.5). The hash page was returned by page_hash() in the parent function. The page hash allows pagecache pages without having to linearly search the inode queue.

J.1.1.4 Function: add_page_to_inode_queue() *(mm/filemap.c)*

```
85 static inline void add_page_to_inode_queue(
                     struct address_space *mapping, struct page * page)
86 {
87     struct list_head *head = &mapping->clean_pages;
```

```
88
89      mapping->nrpages++;
90      list_add(&page->list, head);
91      page->mapping = mapping;
92 }
```

87 When this function is called, the page is clean, so `mapping`→`clean_pages` is the list of interest.

89 Increments the number of pages that belong to this `mapping`.

90 Adds the page to the clean list.

91 Sets the `page`→`mapping` field.

J.1.1.5   Function: `add_page_to_hash_queue()`   *(mm/filemap.c)*

This adds `page` to the top of the hash bucket headed by `p`. Bear in mind that `p` is an element of the array `page_hash_table`.

```
71 static void add_page_to_hash_queue(struct page * page,
                                      struct page **p)
72 {
73      struct page *next = *p;
74
75      *p = page;
76      page->next_hash = next;
77      page->pprev_hash = p;
78      if (next)
79          next->pprev_hash = &page->next_hash;
80      if (page->buffers)
81          PAGE_BUG(page);
82      atomic_inc(&page_cache_size);
83 }
```

73 Records the current head of the hash bucket in `next`.

75 Updates the head of the hash bucket to be `page`.

76 Points `page`→`next_hash` to the old head of the hash bucket.

77 Points `page`→`pprev_hash` to point to the array element in `page_hash_table`.

78-79 This will point the `pprev_hash` field to the head of the hash bucket, completing the insertion of the `page` into the linked list.

80-81 Checks that the page entered has no associated buffers.

82 Increments `page_cache_size`, which is the size of the page cache.

J.1.2   Deleting Pages From the Page Cache

J.1.2.1   Function: remove_inode_page()   *(mm/filemap.c)*

```
130 void remove_inode_page(struct page *page)
131 {
132     if (!PageLocked(page))
133         PAGE_BUG(page);
134
135     spin_lock(&pagecache_lock);
136     __remove_inode_page(page);
137     spin_unlock(&pagecache_lock);
138 }
```

132-133 If the page is not locked, it is a bug.

135 Acquires the lock, protecting the page cache.

136 __remove_inode_page() (See Section J.1.2.2) is the top-level function for when the pagecache lock is held.

137 Releases the pagecache lock.

J.1.2.2   Function: __remove_inode_page()   *(mm/filemap.c)*
   This is the top-level function for removing a page from the pagecache for callers with the **pagecache_lock** spinlock held. Callers that do not have this lock acquired should call **remove_inode_page()**.

```
124 void __remove_inode_page(struct page *page)
125 {
126         remove_page_from_inode_queue(page);
127         remove_page_from_hash_queue(page);
128
```

126 remove_page_from_inode_queue() (See Section J.1.2.3) removes the page from its **address_space** at **page→mapping**.

127 remove_page_from_hash_queue() removes the page from the hash table in **page_hash_table**.

J.1.2.3   Function: remove_page_from_inode_queue()   *(mm/filemap.c)*

```
94 static inline void remove_page_from_inode_queue(struct page * page)
95 {
96     struct address_space * mapping = page->mapping;
97
98     if (mapping->a_ops->removepage)
99         mapping->a_ops->removepage(page);
```

```
100     list_del(&page->list);
101     page->mapping = NULL;
102     wmb();
103     mapping->nr_pages--;
104 }
```

96 Gets the associated `address_space` for this `page`.

98-99 Calls the filesystem-specific `removepage()` function if one is available.

100 Deletes the page from whatever list it belongs to in the `mapping`, such as the `clean_pages` list in most cases or the `dirty_pages` in rarer cases.

101 Sets the page→mapping to NULL because it is no longer backed by any `address_space`.

103 Decrements the number of pages in the `mapping`.

J.1.2.4   Function: `remove_page_from_hash_queue()`   *(mm/filemap.c)*

```
107 static inline void remove_page_from_hash_queue(struct page * page)
108 {
109     struct page *next = page->next_hash;
110     struct page **pprev = page->pprev_hash;
111
112     if (next)
113         next->pprev_hash = pprev;
114     *pprev = next;
115     page->pprev_hash = NULL;
116     atomic_dec(&page_cache_size);
117 }
```

109 Gets the `next` page after the `page` being removed.

110 Gets the `pprev` page before the `page` being removed. When the function completes, `pprev` will be linked to `next`.

112 If this is not the end of the list, this updates next→pprev_hash to point to `pprev`.

114 Similarly, this points `pprev` forward to `next`. `page` is now unlinked.

116 Decrements the size of the pagecache.

J.1.3   Acquiring/Releasing Page Cache Pages

J.1.3.1   Function: `page_cache_get()`   *(include/linux/pagemap.h)*

```
31 #define page_cache_get(x)        get_page(x)
```

31 A simple call `get_page()`, which uses `atomic_inc()` to increment the page reference count.

J.1.3.2   Function: `page_cache_release()`   *(include/linux/pagemap.h)*

```
32 #define page_cache_release(x)   __free_page(x)
```

32 Calls `__free_page()`, which decrements the page count. If the count reaches 0, the page will be freed.

J.1.4   Searching the Page Cache

J.1.4.1   Function: `find_get_page()`   *(include/linux/pagemap.h)*
This is a top-level macro for finding a page in the page cache. It simply looks up the page hash.

```
75 #define find_get_page(mapping, index) \
76     __find_get_page(mapping, index, page_hash(mapping, index))
```

76 `page_hash()` locates an entry in the `page_hash_table` based on the `address_space` and offsets.

J.1.4.2   Function: `__find_get_page()`   *(mm/filemap.c)*
This function is responsible for finding a struct page given an entry in `page_hash_table` as a starting point.

```
931 struct page * __find_get_page(struct address_space *mapping,
932                 unsigned long offset, struct page **hash)
933 {
934     struct page *page;
935
936     /*
937      * We scan the hash list read-only. Addition to and removal from
938      * the hash-list needs a held write-lock.
939      */
940     spin_lock(&pagecache_lock);
941     page = __find_page_nolock(mapping, offset, *hash);
942     if (page)
943         page_cache_get(page);
944     spin_unlock(&pagecache_lock);
945     return page;
946 }
```

940 Acquires the read-only pagecache lock.

941 Calls the pagecache traversal function, which presumes a lock is held.

942-943 If the page was found, this obtains a reference to it with `page_cache_get()` (See Section J.1.3.1) so that it is not freed prematurely.

944 Releases the pagecache lock.

945 Returns the page or NULL if not found.

Page Frame Reclamation

J.1.4.3   Function: __find_page_nolock()   *(mm/filemap.c)*

This function traverses the hash collision list looking for the page specified by the `address_space` and `offset`.

```
443 static inline struct page * __find_page_nolock(
                 struct address_space *mapping,
                 unsigned long offset,
                 struct page *page)
444 {
445     goto inside;
446
447     for (;;) {
448         page = page->next_hash;
449 inside:
450         if (!page)
451             goto not_found;
452         if (page->mapping != mapping)
453             continue;
454         if (page->index == offset)
455             break;
456     }
457
458 not_found:
459     return page;
460 }
```

445 Begins by examining the first page in the list.

450-451 If the page is NULL, the right one could not be found, so it returns NULL.

452 If the `address_space` does not match, this moves to the next page on the collision list.

454 If the `offset` matchs, this returns it or moves on.

448 Moves to the next page on the hash list.

459 Returns the found page or NULL if not.

J.1.4.4   Function: find_lock_page()   *(include/linux/pagemap.h)*

This is the top-level function for searching the pagecache for a page and having it returned in a locked state.

```
84 #define find_lock_page(mapping, index) \
85     __find_lock_page(mapping, index, page_hash(mapping, index))
```

85 Calls the core function `__find_lock_page()` after looking up what hash bucket this page is using with `page_hash()`.

J.1.4.5   Function: __find_lock_page()   *(mm/filemap.c)*

This function acquires the `pagecache_lock` spinlock before calling the core function __find_lock_page_helper() to locate the page and lock it.

```
1005 struct page * __find_lock_page (struct address_space *mapping,
1006                     unsigned long offset, struct page **hash)
1007 {
1008     struct page *page;
1009
1010     spin_lock(&pagecache_lock);
1011     page = __find_lock_page_helper(mapping, offset, *hash);
1012     spin_unlock(&pagecache_lock);
1013     return page;
1014 }
```

1010 Acquires the `pagecache_lock` spinlock.

1011 Calls __find_lock_page_helper(), which will search the pagecache and lock the page if it is found.

1012 Releases the `pagecache_lock` spinlock.

1013 If the page was found, it returns it in a locked state or, if not, it returns NULL.

J.1.4.6   Function: __find_lock_page_helper()   *(mm/filemap.c)*

This function uses __find_page_nolock() to locate a page within the pagecache. If it is found, the page will be locked for returning to the caller.

```
972 static struct page * __find_lock_page_helper(
                             struct address_space *mapping,
973                          unsigned long offset, struct page *hash)
974 {
975     struct page *page;
976
977     /*
978      * We scan the hash list read-only. Addition to and removal
979      * from the hash-list needs a held write-lock.
980      */
981 repeat:
982     page = __find_page_nolock(mapping, offset, hash);
983     if (page) {
984         page_cache_get(page);
985         if (TryLockPage(page)) {
986             spin_unlock(&pagecache_lock);
987             lock_page(page);
988             spin_lock(&pagecache_lock);
```

```
989
990                 /* Has the page been re-allocated while we slept?  */
991                 if (page->mapping != mapping || page->index != offset) {
992                         UnlockPage(page);
993                         page_cache_release(page);
994                         goto repeat;
995                 }
996         }
997     }
998     return page;
999 }
```

982 Uses `__find_page_nolock()`(See Section J.1.4.3) to locate the page in the pagecache.

983-984 If the page was found, this takes a reference to it.

985 Tries and locks the page with `TryLockPage()`. This macro is just a wrapper around `test_and_set_bit()`, which attempts to set the `PG_locked` bit in the page→`flags`.

986-988 If the lock failed, this releases the `pagecache_lock` spinlock and calls `lock_page()` (See Section B.2.1.1) to lock the page. It is likely this function will sleep until the page lock is acquired. When the page is locked, it acquires the `pagecache_lock` spinlock again.

991 If the `mapping` and `index` no longer match, it means that this page was reclaimed while we were asleep. The page is unlocked, and the reference dropped before searching the pagecache again.

998 Returns the page in a locked state or NULL if it was not in the pagecache.

J.2 LRU List Operations

Contents

Page Frame
Reclamation

J.2.1 Adding Pages to the LRU Lists

J.2.1.1 Function: `lru_cache_add()` *(mm/swap.c)*
    This adds a page to the LRU `inactive_list`.

```
58 void lru_cache_add(struct page * page)
59 {
60        if (!PageLRU(page)) {
61                spin_lock(&pagemap_lru_lock);
62                if (!TestSetPageLRU(page))
63                        add_page_to_inactive_list(page);
64                spin_unlock(&pagemap_lru_lock);
65        }
66 }
```

60 If the page is not already part of the LRU lists, this adds it.

61 Acquires the LRU lock.

62-63 Tests and sets the LRU bit. If it was clear, it calls
    `add_page_to_inactive_list()`.

64 Releases the LRU lock.

J.2.1.2 Function: `add_page_to_active_list()` *(include/linux/swap.h)*
    This adds the page to the `active_list`.

```
178 #define add_page_to_active_list(page)            \
179 do {                                            \
```

```
180             DEBUG_LRU_PAGE(page);                    \
181             SetPageActive(page);                     \
182             list_add(&(page)->lru, &active_list);    \
183             nr_active_pages++;                       \
184 } while (0)
```

180 The `DEBUG_LRU_PAGE()` macro will call `BUG()` if the page is already on the LRU list or is marked active.

181 Updates the flags of the page to show it is active.

182 Adds the page to the `active_list`.

183 Updates the count of the number of pages in the `active_list`.

J.2.1.3   Function: `add_page_to_inactive_list()`   *(include/linux/swap.h)*
This adds the page to the `inactive_list`.

```
186 #define add_page_to_inactive_list(page)           \
187 do {                                              \
188         DEBUG_LRU_PAGE(page);                     \
189         list_add(&(page)->lru, &inactive_list);   \
190         nr_inactive_pages++;                      \
191 } while (0)
```

188 The `DEBUG_LRU_PAGE()` macro will call `BUG()` if the page is already on the LRU list or is marked active.

189 Adds the page to the `inactive_list`.

190 Updates the count of the number of inactive pages on the list.

J.2.2   Deleting Pages From the LRU Lists

J.2.2.1   Function: `lru_cache_del()`   *(mm/swap.c)*
This acquires the lock protecting the LRU lists before calling `__lru_cache_del()`.

```
90 void lru_cache_del(struct page * page)
91 {
92         spin_lock(&pagemap_lru_lock);
93         __lru_cache_del(page);
94         spin_unlock(&pagemap_lru_lock);
95 }
```

92 Acquires the LRU lock.

93 `__lru_cache_del()` does the real work of removing the page from the LRU lists.

94 Releases the LRU lock.

J.2.2.2   Function: `__lru_cache_del()`   *(mm/swap.c)*

This selects which function is needed to remove the page from the LRU list.

```
75 void __lru_cache_del(struct page * page)
76 {
77         if (TestClearPageLRU(page)) {
78                 if (PageActive(page)) {
79                         del_page_from_active_list(page);
80                 } else {
81                         del_page_from_inactive_list(page);
82                 }
83         }
84 }
```

77 Tests and clears the flag indicating that the page is in the LRU.

78-82 If the page is in the LRU, this selects the appropriate removal function.

78-79 If the page is active, this calls `del_page_from_active_list()` or, if not, it deletes it from the inactive list with `del_page_from_inactive_list()`.

J.2.2.3   Function: `del_page_from_active_list()`   *(include/linux/swap.h)*

This removes the page from the `active_list`.

```
193 #define del_page_from_active_list(page)     \
194 do {                                        \
195         list_del(&(page)->lru);             \
196         ClearPageActive(page);              \
197         nr_active_pages--;                  \
198 } while (0)
```

195 Deletes the page from the list.

196 Clears the flag, indicating it is part of `active_list`. The flag indicating it is part of the LRU list has already been cleared by `__lru_cache_del()`.

197 Updates the count of the number of pages in the `active_list`.

J.2.2.4   Function: `del_page_from_inactive_list()`   *(include/linux/swap.h)*

```
200 #define del_page_from_inactive_list(page) \
201 do {                                      \
202         list_del(&(page)->lru);           \
203         nr_inactive_pages--;              \
204 } while (0)
```

202 Removes the page from the LRU list.

203 Updates the count of the number of pages in the `inactive_list`.

Page Frame Reclamation

J.2.3   Activating Pages

J.2.3.1   Function: `mark_page_accessed()`   *(mm/filemap.c)*

This marks that a page has been referenced. If the page is already on the `active_list` or the referenced flag is clear, the referenced flag will be set. If it is in the `inactive_list` and the referenced flag has been set, `activate_page()` will be called to move the page to the top of the `active_list`.

```
1332 void mark_page_accessed(struct page *page)
1333 {
1334        if (!PageActive(page) && PageReferenced(page)) {
1335                activate_page(page);
1336                ClearPageReferenced(page);
1337        } else
1338                SetPageReferenced(page);
1339 }
```

1334-1337 If the page is on the `inactive_list` (`!PageActive()`) and has been referenced recently (`PageReferenced()`), `activate_page()` is called to move it to the `active_list`.

1338 Otherwise, it marks the page as being referenced.

J.2.3.2   Function: `activate_lock()`   *(mm/swap.c)*

This acquires the LRU lock before calling `activate_page_nolock()`, which moves the page from the `inactive_list` to the `active_list`.

```
47 void activate_page(struct page * page)
48 {
49        spin_lock(&pagemap_lru_lock);
50        activate_page_nolock(page);
51        spin_unlock(&pagemap_lru_lock);
52 }
```

49 Acquires the LRU lock.

50 Calls the main work function.

51 Releases the LRU lock.

J.2.3.3   Function: `activate_page_nolock()`   *(mm/swap.c)*

This moves the page from the `inactive_list` to the `active_list`.

```
39 static inline void activate_page_nolock(struct page * page)
40 {
41        if (PageLRU(page) && !PageActive(page)) {
42                del_page_from_inactive_list(page);
43                add_page_to_active_list(page);
44        }
45 }
```

41 Makes sure the page is on the LRU and is not already on the `active_list`.

42-43 Deletes the page from the `inactive_list` and adds it to the `active_list`.

J.3   Refilling inactive_list

Contents

This section covers how pages are moved from the active lists to the inactive
lists.

J.3.1   Function: refill_inactive()   *(mm/vmscan.c)*

This moves nr_pages from the `active_list` to the `inactive_list`. The parameter nr_pages is calculated by `shrink_caches()` and is a number that tries to keep
the active list two-thirds the size of the pagecache.

```
533 static void refill_inactive(int nr_pages)
534 {
535         struct list_head * entry;
536
537         spin_lock(&pagemap_lru_lock);
538         entry = active_list.prev;
539         while (nr_pages && entry != &active_list) {
540                 struct page * page;
541
542                 page = list_entry(entry, struct page, lru);
543                 entry = entry->prev;
544                 if (PageTestandClearReferenced(page)) {
545                         list_del(&page->lru);
546                         list_add(&page->lru, &active_list);
547                         continue;
548                 }
549
550                 nr_pages--;
551
552                 del_page_from_active_list(page);
553                 add_page_to_inactive_list(page);
554                 SetPageReferenced(page);
555         }
556         spin_unlock(&pagemap_lru_lock);
557 }
```

537 Acquires the lock protecting the LRU list.

538 Takes the last entry in the `active_list`.

539-555 Keeps moving pages until nr_pages are moved or the `active_list` is
empty.

542 Gets the struct page for this entry.

544-548 Tests and clears the referenced flag. If it has been referenced, it is moved back to the top of the `active_list`.

550-553 Moves one page from the `active_list` to the `inactive_list`.

554 Marks it referenced so that, if it is referenced again soon, it will be promoted back to the `active_list` without requiring a second reference.

556 Releases the lock that protects the LRU list.

Page Frame
Reclamation

J.4   Reclaiming Pages From the LRU Lists

Contents

This section covers how a page is reclaimed after it has been selected for pageout.

J.4.1   Function: shrink_cache()   *(mm/vmscan.c)*

```
338 static int shrink_cache(int nr_pages, zone_t * classzone,
                            unsigned int gfp_mask, int priority)
339 {
340     struct list_head * entry;
341     int max_scan = nr_inactive_pages / priority;
342     int max_mapped = min((nr_pages << (10 - priority)),
                            max_scan / 10);
343
344     spin_lock(&pagemap_lru_lock);
345     while (--max_scan >= 0 &&
                (entry = inactive_list.prev) != &inactive_list) {
```

338 The parameters are as follows:

- **nr_pages** The number of pages to swap out

- **classzone** The zone we are interested in swapping pages out for. Pages not belonging to this zone are skipped.

- **gfp_mask** The gfp mask determining what actions may be taken, such as if filesystem operations may be performed

- **priority** The priority of the function, which starts at DEF_PRIORITY (6) and decreases to the highest priority of 1

341 The maximum number of pages to scan is the number of pages in the active_list divided by the priority. At lowest priority, one-sixth of the list may be scanned. At highest priority, the full list may be scanned.

342 The maximum amount of process-mapped pages allowed is either one-tenth of the max_scan value or $nr\_pages*2^{10-priority}$. If this number of pages is found, whole processes will be swapped out.

344 Locks the LRU list.

345 Keeps scanning until max_scan pages have been scanned or the inactive_list is empty.

```
346         struct page * page;
347
348         if (unlikely(current->need_resched)) {
```

```
349                    spin_unlock(&pagemap_lru_lock);
350                    __set_current_state(TASK_RUNNING);
351                    schedule();
352                    spin_lock(&pagemap_lru_lock);
353                    continue;
354            }
355
```

348-354 Reschedules if the quanta has been used up.

349 Frees the LRU lock because it is about to sleep.

350 Shows that we are still running.

351 Calls `schedule()` so another process can be context-switched in.

352 Reacquires the LRU lock.

353 Reiterates through the loop and takes an entry `inactive_list` again. As we slept, another process could have changed what entries are on the list, which is why another entry has to be taken with the spinlock held.

```
356            page = list_entry(entry, struct page, lru);
357
358            BUG_ON(!PageLRU(page));
359            BUG_ON(PageActive(page));
360
361            list_del(entry);
362            list_add(entry, &inactive_list);
363
364            /*
365             * Zero page counts can happen because we unlink the pages
366             * _after_ decrementing the usage count..
367             */
368            if (unlikely(!page_count(page)))
369                continue;
370
371            if (!memclass(page_zone(page), classzone))
372                continue;
373
374            /* Racy check to avoid trylocking when not worthwhile */
375            if (!page->buffers && (page_count(page) != 1 || !page->mapping))
376                goto page_mapped;
```

356 Gets the `struct page` for this entry in the LRU.

358-359 It is a bug if the page either belongs to the `active_list` or is currently marked as active.

361-362 Moves the page to the top of the `inactive_list` so that, if the page is not freed, we can just continue knowing that it will be simply examined later.

368-369 If the page count has already reached 0, this skips over it. In `__free_pages()`, the page count is dropped with `put_page_testzero()` before `__free_pages_ok()` is called to free it. This leaves a window where a page with a zero count is left on the LRU before it is freed. A special case to trap this is at the beginning of `__free_pages_ok()`.

371-372 Skips over this page if it belongs to a zone we are not currently interested in.

375-376 If the page is mapped by a process, goto `page_mapped` where the `max_mapped` is decremented and the next page is examined. If `max_mapped` reaches 0, process pages will be swapped out.

```
382        if (unlikely(TryLockPage(page))) {
383            if (PageLaunder(page) && (gfp_mask & __GFP_FS)) {
384                page_cache_get(page);
385                spin_unlock(&pagemap_lru_lock);
386                wait_on_page(page);
387                page_cache_release(page);
388                spin_lock(&pagemap_lru_lock);
389            }
390            continue;
391        }
```

In this block, a page is locked, and the launder bit is set. In this case, it is the second time this page has been found dirty. The first time it was scheduled for I/O and placed back on the list. This time we wait until the I/O is complete and then try to free the page.

382-383 If we could not lock the page, the `PG_launder` bit is set, and the GFP flags allow the caller to perform FS operations. Then...

384 Takes a reference to the page so that it does not disappear while we sleep.

385 Frees the LRU lock.

386 Waits until the I/O is complete.

387 Releases the reference to the page. If it reaches 0, the page will be freed.

388 Reacquires the LRU lock.

390 Moves to the next page.

```
392
393        if (PageDirty(page) &&
                is_page_cache_freeable(page) &&
                page->mapping) {
```

```
394                 /*
395                  * It is not critical here to write it only if
396                  * the page is unmapped beause any direct writer
397                  * like O_DIRECT would set the PG_dirty bitflag
398                  * on the physical page after having successfully
399                  * pinned it and after the I/O to the page is finished,
400                  * so the direct writes to the page cannot get lost.
401                  */
402                 int (*writepage)(struct page *);
403
404                 writepage = page->mapping->a_ops->writepage;
405                 if ((gfp_mask & __GFP_FS) && writepage) {
406                     ClearPageDirty(page);
407                     SetPageLaunder(page);
408                     page_cache_get(page);
409                     spin_unlock(&pagemap_lru_lock);
410
411                     writepage(page);
412                     page_cache_release(page);
413
414                     spin_lock(&pagemap_lru_lock);
415                     continue;
416                 }
417             }
```

This handles the case where a page is dirty, is not mapped by any process, has no buffers and is backed by a file or device mapping. The page is cleaned and will be reclaimed by the previous block of code when the I/O is complete.

393 PageDirty() checks the PG_dirty bit. is_page_cache_freeable() will return true if it is not mapped by any process and has no buffers.

404 Gets a pointer to the necessary writepage() function for this mapping or device.

405-416 This block of code can only be executed if a writepage() function is available and the GFP flags allow file operations.

406-407 Clears the dirty bit and marks that the page is being laundered.

408 Takes a reference to the page so that it will not be freed unexpectedly.

409 Unlocks the LRU list.

411 Calls the filesystem-specific writepage() function, which is taken from the address_space_operations belonging to page→mapping.

412 Releases the reference to the page.

414-415 Reacquires the LRU list lock and moves to the next page.

```
424            if (page->buffers) {
425                 spin_unlock(&pagemap_lru_lock);
426
427                 /* avoid to free a locked page */
428                 page_cache_get(page);
429
430                 if (try_to_release_page(page, gfp_mask)) {
431                     if (!page->mapping) {
438                         spin_lock(&pagemap_lru_lock);
439                         UnlockPage(page);
440                         __lru_cache_del(page);
441
442                         /* effectively free the page here */
443                         page_cache_release(page);
444
445                         if (--nr_pages)
446                             continue;
447                         break;
448                     } else {
454                         page_cache_release(page);
455
456                         spin_lock(&pagemap_lru_lock);
457                     }
458                 } else {
459                     /* failed to drop the buffers so stop here */
460                     UnlockPage(page);
461                     page_cache_release(page);
462
463                     spin_lock(&pagemap_lru_lock);
464                     continue;
465                 }
466            }
```

Page has buffers associated with it that must be freed.

425 Releases the LRU lock because we may sleep.

428 Takes a reference to the page.

430 Calls `try_to_release_page()`, which will attempt to release the buffers associated with the page. It returns 1 if it succeeds.

431-447 This is a case where an anonymous page that was in the swap cache has now had its buffers cleared and removed. Because it was on the swap cache, it was placed on the LRU by `add_to_swap_cache()`, so it removes it now from the LRU and drops the reference to the page. In `swap_writepage()`, it calls `remove_exclusive_swap_page()`, which will delete the page from the swap cache when no more processes are mapping the page. This block will free the page after the buffers have been written out if it was backed by a swap file.

438-440 Takes the LRU list lock, unlocks the page, deletes it from the pagecache and frees it.

445-446 Updates `nr_pages` to show a page has been freed and moves to the next page.

447 If `nr_pages` drops to 0, this exits the loop as the work is completed.

449-456 If the page does have an associated mapping, this drops the reference to the page and reacquires the LRU lock. More work will be performed later to remove the page from the pagecache at line 499.

459-464 If the buffers could not be freed, this unlocks the page, drops the reference to it, reacquires the LRU lock and moves to the next page.

```
468            spin_lock(&pagecache_lock);
469
470            /*
471             * this is the non-racy check for busy page.
472             */
473            if (!page->mapping || !is_page_cache_freeable(page)) {
474                    spin_unlock(&pagecache_lock);
475                    UnlockPage(page);
476 page_mapped:
477                    if (--max_mapped >= 0)
478                        continue;
479
484                    spin_unlock(&pagemap_lru_lock);
485                    swap_out(priority, gfp_mask, classzone);
486                    return nr_pages;
487            }
```

468 From this point on, pages in the swapcache are likely to be examined, which is protected by the `pagecache_lock`, which must be now held.

473-487 An anonymous page with no buffers is mapped by a process.

474-475 Releases the pagecache lock and the page.

477-478 Decrements `max_mapped`. If it has not reached 0, it moves to the next page.

484-485 Too many mapped pages have been found in the page cache. The LRU lock is released, and `swap_out()` is called to begin swapping out whole processes.

Page Frame Reclamation

```
493          if (PageDirty(page)) {
494                spin_unlock(&pagecache_lock);
495                UnlockPage(page);
496                continue;
497          }
```

493-497 The page has no references, but could have been dirtied by the last process to free it if the dirty bit was set in the PTE. It is left in the pagecache and will get laundered later. After it has been cleaned, it can be safely deleted.

```
498
499          /* point of no return */
500          if (likely(!PageSwapCache(page))) {
501                __remove_inode_page(page);
502                spin_unlock(&pagecache_lock);
503          } else {
504              swp_entry_t swap;
505              swap.val = page->index;
506              __delete_from_swap_cache(page);
507              spin_unlock(&pagecache_lock);
508              swap_free(swap);
509          }
510
511          __lru_cache_del(page);
512          UnlockPage(page);
513
514          /* effectively free the page here */
515          page_cache_release(page);
516
517          if (--nr_pages)
518                continue;
519          break;
520      }
```

500-503 If the page does not belong to the swapcache, it is part of the inode queue so it is removed.

504-508 Removes it from the swapcache because there are no more references to it.

511 Deletes it from the pagecache.

512 Unlocks the page.

515 Frees the page.

517-518 Decrements nr_page and moves to the next page if it is not 0.

519 If it reaches 0, the work of the function is complete.

```
521     spin_unlock(&pagemap_lru_lock);
522
523     return nr_pages;
524 }
```

521-524 Makes the function exit. It frees the LRU lock and returns the number
of pages left to free.

J.5   Shrinking All Caches

Contents

J.5.1   Function: `shrink_caches()`   *(mm/vmscan.c)*

The call graph for this function is shown in Figure 10.4.

```
560 static int shrink_caches(zone_t * classzone, int priority,
                  unsigned int gfp_mask, int nr_pages)
561 {
562     int chunk_size = nr_pages;
563     unsigned long ratio;
564
565     nr_pages -= kmem_cache_reap(gfp_mask);
566     if (nr_pages <= 0)
567         return 0;
568
569     nr_pages = chunk_size;
570     /* try to keep the active list 2/3 of the size of the cache */
571     ratio = (unsigned long) nr_pages *
                  nr_active_pages / ((nr_inactive_pages + 1) * 2);
572     refill_inactive(ratio);
573
574     nr_pages = shrink_cache(nr_pages, classzone, gfp_mask, priority);
575     if (nr_pages <= 0)
576         return 0;
577
578     shrink_dcache_memory(priority, gfp_mask);
579     shrink_icache_memory(priority, gfp_mask);
580 #ifdef CONFIG_QUOTA
581     shrink_dqcache_memory(DEF_PRIORITY, gfp_mask);
582 #endif
583
584     return nr_pages;
585 }
```

560 The parameters are as follows:

- **classzone** is the zone that pages should be freed from.

- **priority** determines how much work will be done to free pages.

- **gfp_mask** determines what sort of actions may be taken.

- **nr_pages** is the number of pages remaining to be freed.

565-567 Asks the slab allocator to free up some pages with `kmem_cache_reap()` (See Section H.1.5.1). If enough are freed, the function returns. Otherwise, `nr_pages` will be freed from other caches.

571-572 Moves pages from the `active_list` to the `inactive_list` by calling `refill_inactive()` (See Section J.3.1). The number of pages moved depends on how many pages need to be freed and need to have `active_list` about two-thirds the size of the page cache.

574-575 Shrinks the pagecache. If enough pages are freed, this returns.

578-582 Shrinks the dcache, icache and dqcache. These are small objects in themselves, but the cascading effect frees up a lot of disk buffers.

584 Returns the number of pages remaining to be freed.

J.5.2 Function: `try_to_free_pages()` *(mm/vmscan.c)*

This function cycles through all `pgdats` and tries to balance the preferred allocation zone (usually `ZONE_NORMAL`) for each of them. This function is only called from one place, `buffer.c:free_more_memory()`, when the buffer manager fails to create new buffers or grow existing ones. It calls `try_to_free_pages()` with `GFP_NOIO` as the `gfp_mask`.

This results in the first zone in `pg_data_t→node_zonelists` having pages freed so that buffers can grow. This array is the preferred order of zones to allocate from and usually will begin with `ZONE_NORMAL`, which is required by the buffer manager. On NUMA architectures, some nodes may have `ZONE_DMA` as the preferred zone if the memory bank is dedicated to I/O devices. UML also uses only this zone. Because the buffer manager is restricted in the zones it uses, there is no point balancing other zones.

```
607 int try_to_free_pages(unsigned int gfp_mask)
608 {
609     pg_data_t *pgdat;
610     zonelist_t *zonelist;
611     unsigned long pf_free_pages;
612     int error = 0;
613
614     pf_free_pages = current->flags & PF_FREE_PAGES;
615     current->flags &= ~PF_FREE_PAGES;
616
617     for_each_pgdat(pgdat) {
618         zonelist = pgdat->node_zonelists +
                    (gfp_mask & GFP_ZONEMASK);
619         error |= try_to_free_pages_zone(
                    zonelist->zones[0], gfp_mask);
620     }
621
```

Page Frame
Reclamation

```
622     current->flags |= pf_free_pages;
623     return error;
624 }
```

614-615 This clears the `PF_FREE_PAGES` flag if it is set so that pages freed by the process will be returned to the global pool rather than reserved for the process itself.

617-620 Cycles through all nodes and calls `try_to_free_pages()` for the preferred zone in each node.

618 This function is only called with `GFP_NOIO` as a parameter. When ANDed with `GFP_ZONEMASK`, it will always result in 0.

622-623 Restores the process flags and returns the result.

J.5.3   Function: `try_to_free_pages_zone()`   *(mm/vmscan.c)*
This tries to free `SWAP_CLUSTER_MAX` pages from the requested zone. As well as being used by **kswapd**, this function is the entry for the buddy allocator's direct-reclaim path.

```
587 int try_to_free_pages_zone(zone_t *classzone,
                                unsigned int gfp_mask)
588 {
589     int priority = DEF_PRIORITY;
590     int nr_pages = SWAP_CLUSTER_MAX;
591
592     gfp_mask = pf_gfp_mask(gfp_mask);
593     do {
594         nr_pages = shrink_caches(classzone, priority,
                        gfp_mask, nr_pages);
595         if (nr_pages <= 0)
596             return 1;
597     } while (--priority);
598
599     /*
600      * Hmm.. Cache shrink failed - time to kill something?
601      * Mwahahhaha! This is the part I really like. Giggle.
602      */
603     out_of_memory();
604     return 0;
605 }
```

589 Starts with the lowest priority. This is statically defined to be 6.

590 Tries and frees `SWAP_CLUSTER_MAX` pages. This is statically defined to be 32.

592 `pf_gfp_mask()` checks the `PF_NOIO` flag in the current process flags. If no I/O can be performed, it ensures no incompatible flags are in the GFP mask.

593-597 Starting with the lowest priority and increasing with each pass, this calls `shrink_caches()` until `nr_pages` have been freed.

595-596 If enough pages were freed, this returns, indicating that the work is complete.

603 If enough pages could not be freed even at highest priority (where at worst the full `inactive_list` is scanned), this checks to see if we are out of memory. If we are, a process will be selected to be killed.

604 Returns indicating that we failed to free enough pages.

J.6   Swapping Out Process Pages

Contents

This section covers the path where too many process-mapped pages have been found in the LRU lists. This path will start scanning whole processes and reclaiming the mapped pages.

J.6.1   Function: swap_out()   *(mm/vmscan.c)*

The call graph for this function is shown in Figure 10.5. This function linearly searches through every process' pagetables trying to swap out SWAP_CLUSTER_MAX number of pages. The process it starts with is the swap_mm, and the starting address is mm→swap_address.

```
296 static int swap_out(unsigned int priority, unsigned int gfp_mask,
            zone_t * classzone)
297 {
298     int counter, nr_pages = SWAP_CLUSTER_MAX;
299     struct mm_struct *mm;
300
301     counter = mmlist_nr;
302     do {
303         if (unlikely(current->need_resched)) {
304             __set_current_state(TASK_RUNNING);
305             schedule();
306         }
307
308         spin_lock(&mmlist_lock);
309         mm = swap_mm;
310         while (mm->swap_address == TASK_SIZE || mm == &init_mm) {
311             mm->swap_address = 0;
312             mm = list_entry(mm->mmlist.next,
                    struct mm_struct, mmlist);
313             if (mm == swap_mm)
314                 goto empty;
315             swap_mm = mm;
316         }
317
318         /* Make sure the mm doesn't disappear
             when we drop the lock.. */
319         atomic_inc(&mm->mm_users);
```

```
320            spin_unlock(&mmlist_lock);
321
322            nr_pages = swap_out_mm(mm, nr_pages, &counter, classzone);
323
324            mmput(mm);
325
326            if (!nr_pages)
327                return 1;
328        } while (--counter >= 0);
329
330        return 0;
331
332 empty:
333        spin_unlock(&mmlist_lock);
334        return 0;
335 }
```

301 Sets the counter so that the process list is only scanned once.

303-306 Reschedules if the quanta has been used up to prevent CPU hogging.

308 Acquires the lock protecting the mm list.

309 Starts with the `swap_mm`. It is interesting that this is never checked to make sure it is valid. It is possible, albeit unlikely, that the process with the `mm` has exited since the last scan *and* the slab holding the `mm_struct` has been reclaimed during a cache shrink, making the pointer totally invalid. The lack of bug reports might be because the slab rarely gets reclaimed and would be difficult to trigger in reality.

310-316 Moves to the next process if the `swap_address` has reached the `TASK_SIZE` or if the mm is the `init_mm`.

311 Starts at the beginning of the process space.

312 Gets the mm for this process.

313-314 If it is the same, no running processes can be examined.

315 Records the `swap_mm` for the next pass.

319 Increases the reference count so that the mm does not get freed while we are scanning.

320 Releases the mm lock.

322 Begins scanning the mm with `swap_out_mm()`(See Section J.6.2).

324 Drops the reference to the mm.

326-327 If the required number of pages has been freed, this returns success.

328 If we failed on this pass, this increases the priority so more processes will be scanned.

330 Returns failure.

J.6.2 Function: swap_out_mm() *(mm/vmscan.c)*
This walks through each VMA and calls swap_out_mm() for each one.

```
256 static inline int swap_out_mm(struct mm_struct * mm, int count,
                int * mmcounter, zone_t * classzone)
257 {
258     unsigned long address;
259     struct vm_area_struct* vma;
260
265     spin_lock(&mm->page_table_lock);
266     address = mm->swap_address;
267     if (address == TASK_SIZE || swap_mm != mm) {
268         /* We raced: don't count this mm but try again */
269         ++*mmcounter;
270         goto out_unlock;
271     }
272     vma = find_vma(mm, address);
273     if (vma) {
274         if (address < vma->vm_start)
275             address = vma->vm_start;
276
277         for (;;) {
278             count = swap_out_vma(mm, vma, address,
                        count, classzone);
279             vma = vma->vm_next;
280             if (!vma)
281                 break;
282             if (!count)
283                 goto out_unlock;
284             address = vma->vm_start;
285         }
286     }
287     /* Indicate that we reached the end of address space */
288     mm->swap_address = TASK_SIZE;
289
290 out_unlock:
291     spin_unlock(&mm->page_table_lock);
292     return count;
293 }
```

265 Acquires the pagetable lock for this mm.

266 Starts with the address contained in `swap_address`.

267-271 If the address is `TASK_SIZE`, it means that a thread raced and scanned this process already. It increases mmcounter so that `swap_out_mm()` knows to go to another process.

272 Finds the VMA for this address.

273 Presuming a VMA was found, then ...

274-275 Starts at the beginning of the VMA.

277-285 Scans through this and each subsequent VMA calling `swap_out_vma()` (See Section J.6.3) for each one. If the requisite number of pages (count) is freed, this finishes scanning and returns.

288 After the last VMA has been scanned, this sets `swap_address` to `TASK_SIZE` so that this process will be skipped over by `swap_out_mm()` next time.

J.6.3   Function: `swap_out_vma()`   *(mm/vmscan.c)*
This walks through this VMA, and, for each PGD in it, calls `swap_out_pgd()`.

```
227 static inline int swap_out_vma(struct mm_struct * mm,
                    struct vm_area_struct * vma,
                    unsigned long address, int count,
                    zone_t * classzone)
228 {
229     pgd_t *pgdir;
230     unsigned long end;
231
232     /* Don't swap out areas which are reserved */
233     if (vma->vm_flags & VM_RESERVED)
234         return count;
235
236     pgdir = pgd_offset(mm, address);
237
238     end = vma->vm_end;
239     BUG_ON(address >= end);
240     do {
241         count = swap_out_pgd(mm, vma, pgdir,
                    address, end, count, classzone);
242         if (!count)
243             break;
244         address = (address + PGDIR_SIZE) & PGDIR_MASK;
245         pgdir++;
246     } while (address && (address < end));
247     return count;
248 }
```

Page Frame Reclamation

233-234 Skips over this VMA if the VM_RESERVED flag is set. This is used by some device drivers, such as the Small Computer System Interface (SCSI) generic driver.

236 Gets the starting PGD for the address.

238 Marks where the end is and uses BUG() if the starting address is somehow past the end.

240 Cycles through PGDs until the end address is reached.

241 Calls swap_out_pgd()(See Section J.6.4) to keep count of how many more pages need to be freed.

242-243 If enough pages have been freed, this breaks and returns.

244-245 Moves to the next PGD and moves the address to the next PGD-aligned address.

247 Returns the remaining number of pages to be freed.

J.6.4   Function: swap_out_pgd()   *(mm/vmscan.c)*
This steps through all PMDs in the supplied PGD and calls swap_out_pmd().

```
197 static inline int swap_out_pgd(struct mm_struct * mm,
                  struct vm_area_struct * vma, pgd_t *dir,
                  unsigned long address, unsigned long end,
                  int count, zone_t * classzone)
198 {
199     pmd_t * pmd;
200     unsigned long pgd_end;
201
202     if (pgd_none(*dir))
203         return count;
204     if (pgd_bad(*dir)) {
205         pgd_ERROR(*dir);
206         pgd_clear(dir);
207         return count;
208     }
209
210     pmd = pmd_offset(dir, address);
211
212     pgd_end = (address + PGDIR_SIZE) & PGDIR_MASK;
213     if (pgd_end && (end > pgd_end))
214         end = pgd_end;
215
216     do {
217         count = swap_out_pmd(mm, vma, pmd,
```

```
                                   address, end, count, classzone);
218         if (!count)
219             break;
220         address = (address + PMD_SIZE) & PMD_MASK;
221         pmd++;
222     } while (address && (address < end));
223     return count;
224 }
```

202-203 If there is no PGD, this returns.

204-208 If the PGD is bad, this flags it as such and returns.

210 Gets the starting PMD.

212-214 Calculates the end to be the end of this PGD or the end of the VMA being scanned, whichever is closer.

216-222 For each PMD in this PGD, this calls `swap_out_pmd()` (See Section J.6.5). If enough pages get freed, it breaks and returns.

223 Returns the number of pages remaining to be freed.

J.6.5   Function: swap_out_pmd()   *(mm/vmscan.c)*

For each PTE in this PMD, this calls `try_to_swap_out()`. On completion, mm→swap_address is updated to show where we finished to prevent the same page being examined soon after this scan.

```
158 static inline int swap_out_pmd(struct mm_struct * mm,
                   struct vm_area_struct * vma, pmd_t *dir,
                   unsigned long address, unsigned long end,
                   int count, zone_t * classzone)
159 {
160     pte_t * pte;
161     unsigned long pmd_end;
162
163     if (pmd_none(*dir))
164         return count;
165     if (pmd_bad(*dir)) {
166         pmd_ERROR(*dir);
167         pmd_clear(dir);
168         return count;
169     }
170
171     pte = pte_offset(dir, address);
172
173     pmd_end = (address + PMD_SIZE) & PMD_MASK;
174     if (end > pmd_end)
```

```
175            end = pmd_end;
176
177     do {
178         if (pte_present(*pte)) {
179             struct page *page = pte_page(*pte);
180
181             if (VALID_PAGE(page) && !PageReserved(page)) {
182                 count -= try_to_swap_out(mm, vma,
                                      address, pte,
                                      page, classzone);
183                 if (!count) {
184                     address += PAGE_SIZE;
185                     break;
186                 }
187             }
188         }
189         address += PAGE_SIZE;
190         pte++;
191     } while (address && (address < end));
192     mm->swap_address = address;
193     return count;
194 }
```

163-164 Returns if there is no PMD.

165-169 If the PMD is bad, this flags it as such and returns.

171 Gets the starting PTE.

173-175 Calculates the end to be the end of the PMD or the end of the VMA, whichever is closer.

177-191 Cycles through each PTE.

178 Makes sure the PTE is marked present.

179 Gets the struct page for this PTE.

181 If it is a valid page and it is not reserved, then ...

182 Calls try_to_swap_out().

183-186 If enough pages have been swapped out, this moves the address to the next page and breaks to return.

189-190 Moves to the next page and PTE.

192 Updates the swap_address to show where we last finished off.

193 Returns the number of pages remaining to be freed.

J.6.6   Function: `try_to_swap_out()`   *(mm/vmscan.c)*

This function tries to swap out a page from a process. It is quite a large function, so it will be dealt with in parts. Broadly speaking, they are the following:

- Ensure this is a page that should be swapped out (function preamble).

- Remove the page and PTE from the pagetables.

- Handle the case where the page is already in the swap cache.

- Handle the case where the page is dirty or has associated buffers.

- Handle the case where the page is being added to the swap cache.

```
47 static inline int try_to_swap_out(struct mm_struct * mm,
                      struct vm_area_struct* vma,
                      unsigned long address,
                      pte_t * page_table,
                      struct page *page,
                      zone_t * classzone)
48 {
49     pte_t pte;
50     swp_entry_t entry;
51
52     /* Don't look at this pte if it's been accessed recently. */
53     if ((vma->vm_flags & VM_LOCKED) ||
       ptep_test_and_clear_young(page_table)) {
54         mark_page_accessed(page);
55         return 0;
56     }
57
58     /* Don't bother unmapping pages that are active */
59     if (PageActive(page))
60         return 0;
61
62     /* Don't bother replenishing zones not under pressure.. */
63     if (!memclass(page_zone(page), classzone))
64         return 0;
65
66     if (TryLockPage(page))
67         return 0;
```

53-56 If the page is locked (for tasks like I/O) or the PTE shows the page has been accessed recently, then this clears the referenced bit and calls `mark_page_accessed()` (See Section J.2.3.1) to make the struct page reflect the age. It returns 0 to show it was not swapped out.

59-60 If the page is on the `active_list`, do not swap it out.

63-64 If the page belongs to a zone we are not interested in, do not swap it out.

66-67 If the page is already locked for I/O, this skips it.

```
74      flush_cache_page(vma, address);
75      pte = ptep_get_and_clear(page_table);
76      flush_tlb_page(vma, address);
77
78      if (pte_dirty(pte))
79          set_page_dirty(page);
80
```

74 Calls the architecture hook to flush this page from all CPUs.

75 Gets the PTE from the pagetables and clears it.

76 Calls the architecture hook to flush the TLB.

78-79 If the PTE was marked dirty, this marks the **struct page** dirty so that it will be laundered correctly.

```
86      if (PageSwapCache(page)) {
87          entry.val = page->index;
88          swap_duplicate(entry);
89 set_swap_pte:
90          set_pte(page_table, swp_entry_to_pte(entry));
91 drop_pte:
92          mm->rss--;
93          UnlockPage(page);
94          {
95              int freeable =
                 page_count(page) - !!page->buffers <= 2;
96              page_cache_release(page);
97              return freeable;
98          }
99      }
```

Handles the case where the page is already in the swap cache.

86 Enters this block only if the page is already in the swap cache. Note that it can also be entered by calling goto to the **set_swap_pte** and **drop_pte** labels.

87-88 Fills in the index value for the swap entry. **swap_duplicate()** verifies the swap identifier is valid and increases the counter in the **swap_map** if it is.

90 Fills the PTE with information needed to get the page from swap.

92 Updates RSS to show one less page is being mapped by the process.

93 Unlocks the page.

95 The page is freeable if the count is currently 2 or less and has no buffers. If the count is higher, it is either being mapped by other processes or is a file-backed page, and the "user" is the pagecache.

96 Decrements the reference count and frees the page if it reaches 0. Note that, if this is a file-backed page, it will not reach 0 even if no processes are mapping it. The page will be later reclaimed from the page cache by `shrink_cache()` (See Section J.4.1).

97 Returns if the page was freed.

```
115     if (page->mapping)
116         goto drop_pte;
117     if (!PageDirty(page))
118         goto drop_pte;
124     if (page->buffers)
125         goto preserve;
```

115-116 If the page has an associated mapping, this drops it from the pagetables. When no processes are mapping it, it will be reclaimed from the pagecache by `shrink_cache()`.

117-118 If the page is clean, it is safe to drop it.

124-125 If it has associated buffers due to a truncate followed by a page fault, this reattaches the page and PTE to the pagetables because it cannot be handled yet.

```
126
127     /*
128      * This is a dirty, swappable page.  First of all,
129      * get a suitable swap entry for it, and make sure
130      * we have the swap cache set up to associate the
131      * page with that swap entry.
132      */
133     for (;;) {
134         entry = get_swap_page();
135         if (!entry.val)
136             break;
137         /* Add it to the swap cache and mark it dirty
138          * (adding to the page cache will clear the dirty
139          * and uptodate bits, so we need to do it again)
140          */
141         if (add_to_swap_cache(page, entry) == 0) {
142             SetPageUptodate(page);
143             set_page_dirty(page);
144             goto set_swap_pte;
145         }
```

```
146            /* Raced with "speculative" read_swap_cache_async */
147            swap_free(entry);
148        }
149
150        /* No swap space left */
151    preserve:
152        set_pte(page_table, pte);
153        UnlockPage(page);
154        return 0;
155    }
```

134 Allocates a swap entry for this page.

135-136 If one could not be allocated, it breaks out where the PTE and page will be reattached to the process pagetables.

141 Adds the page to the swap cache.

142 Marks the page as up to date in memory.

143 Marks the page dirty so that it will be written out to swap soon.

144 Goto set_swap_pte, which will update the PTE with information needed to get the page from swap later.

147 If the add to swap cache failed, it means that the page was placed in the swap cache already by a readahead, so it drops the work done here.

152 Reattaches the PTE to the page tables.

153 Unlocks the page.

154 Returns that no page was freed.

J.7 Page Swap Daemon

Contents

This section details the main loops used by the **kswapd** daemon, which is woken up when memory is low. The main functions covered are the ones that determine if **kswapd** can sleep and how it determines which nodes need balancing.

J.7.1 Initializing kswapd

J.7.1.1 Function: kswapd_init() *(mm/vmscan.c)*
This starts the kswapd kernel thread.

```
767 static int __init kswapd_init(void)
768 {
769     printk("Starting kswapd\n");
770     swap_setup();
771     kernel_thread(kswapd, NULL, CLONE_FS
                                | CLONE_FILES
                                | CLONE_SIGNAL);
772     return 0;
773 }
```

770 `swap_setup()`(See Section K.4.2) sets up how many pages will be prefetched when reading from backing storage based on the amount of physical memory.

771 Starts the **kswapd** kernel thread.

J.7.2 kswapd Daemon

J.7.2.1 Function: kswapd() *(mm/vmscan.c)*
This is the main function of the **kswapd** kernel thread.

```
720 int kswapd(void *unused)
721 {
722     struct task_struct *tsk = current;
723     DECLARE_WAITQUEUE(wait, tsk);
724
725     daemonize();
726     strcpy(tsk->comm, "kswapd");
```

```
727        sigfillset(&tsk->blocked);
728
741        tsk->flags |= PF_MEMALLOC;
742
746        for (;;) {
747            __set_current_state(TASK_INTERRUPTIBLE);
748            add_wait_queue(&kswapd_wait, &wait);
749
750            mb();
751            if (kswapd_can_sleep())
752                schedule();
753
754            __set_current_state(TASK_RUNNING);
755            remove_wait_queue(&kswapd_wait, &wait);
756
762            kswapd_balance();
763            run_task_queue(&tq_disk);
764        }
765 }
```

725 Calls `daemonize()`, which will make this a kernel thread, remove the mm context, close all files and reparent the process.

726 Sets the name of the process.

727 Ignores all signals.

741 By setting this flag, the physical page allocator will always try to satisfy requests for pages. Because this process will always be trying to free pages, it is worth satisfying requests.

746-764 Endlessly loops.

747-748 This adds **kswapd** to the wait queue in preparation to sleep.

750 The memory block function (`mb()`) ensures that all reads and writes that occurred before this line will be visible to all CPUs.

751 `kswapd_can_sleep()`(See Section J.7.2.2) cycles through all nodes and zones checking the **need_balance** field. If any of them are set to 1, kswapd cannot sleep.

752 By calling `schedule()`, **kswapd** will now sleep until woken again by the physical page allocator in `__alloc_pages()` (See Section F.1.3).

754-755 After it is woken up, **kswapd** is removed from the wait queue because it is now running.

762 `kswapd_balance()`(See Section J.7.2.4) cycles through all zones and calls `try_to_free_pages_zone()`(See Section J.5.3) for each zone that requires balance.

763 Runs the I/O task queue to start writing data out to disk.

J.7.2.2 Function: `kswapd_can_sleep()` *(mm/vmscan.c)*

This is a simple function to cycle through all `pgdats` to call `kswapd_can_sleep_pgdat()` on each.

```
695 static int kswapd_can_sleep(void)
696 {
697     pg_data_t * pgdat;
698
699     for_each_pgdat(pgdat) {
700         if (!kswapd_can_sleep_pgdat(pgdat))
701             return 0;
702     }
703
704     return 1;
705 }
```

699-702 `for_each_pgdat()` does exactly as the name implies. It cycles through all available `pgdats` and, in this case, calls `kswapd_can_sleep_pgdat()` (See Section J.7.2.3) for each. On the x86, there will only be one `pgdat`.

J.7.2.3 Function: `kswapd_can_sleep_pgdat()` *(mm/vmscan.c)*

This cycles through all zones to make sure none of them need balance. The `zone`→`need_balanace` flag is set by `__alloc_pages()` when the number of free pages in the zone reaches the **pages_low** watermark.

```
680 static int kswapd_can_sleep_pgdat(pg_data_t * pgdat)
681 {
682     zone_t * zone;
683     int i;
684
685     for (i = pgdat->nr_zones-1; i >= 0; i--) {
686         zone = pgdat->node_zones + i;
687         if (!zone->need_balance)
688             continue;
689         return 0;
690     }
691
692     return 1;
693 }
```

685-689 A simple for loop to cycle through all zones.

686 The `node_zones` field is an array of all available zones, so adding `i` gives the index.

687-688 If the zone does not need balance, this continues.

689 0 is returned if any zone needs balance, indicating **kswapd** cannot sleep.

692 Returns indicating **kswapd** can sleep if the for loop completes.

J.7.2.4 Function: `kswapd_balance()` *(mm/vmscan.c)*
This continuously cycles through each `pgdat` until none require balancing.

```
667 static void kswapd_balance(void)
668 {
669     int need_more_balance;
670     pg_data_t * pgdat;
671
672     do {
673         need_more_balance = 0;
674
675         for_each_pgdat(pgdat)
676             need_more_balance |= kswapd_balance_pgdat(pgdat);
677     } while (need_more_balance);
678 }
```

672-677 Cycles through all `pgdats` until none of them report that they need balancing.

675 For each `pgdat`, this calls `kswapd_balance_pgdat()` to check if the node requires balancing. If any node required balancing, `need_more_balance` will be set to 1.

J.7.2.5 Function: `kswapd_balance_pgdat()` *(mm/vmscan.c)*
This function will check if a node requires balance by examining each of the nodes in it. If any zone requires balancing, `try_to_free_pages_zone()` will be called.

```
641 static int kswapd_balance_pgdat(pg_data_t * pgdat)
642 {
643     int need_more_balance = 0, i;
644     zone_t * zone;
645
646     for (i = pgdat->nr_zones-1; i >= 0; i--) {
647         zone = pgdat->node_zones + i;
648         if (unlikely(current->need_resched))
649             schedule();
650         if (!zone->need_balance)
```

```
651              continue;
652          if (!try_to_free_pages_zone(zone, GFP_KSWAPD)) {
653              zone->need_balance = 0;
654              __set_current_state(TASK_INTERRUPTIBLE);
655              schedule_timeout(HZ);
656              continue;
657          }
658          if (check_classzone_need_balance(zone))
659              need_more_balance = 1;
660          else
661              zone->need_balance = 0;
662      }
663
664      return need_more_balance;
665 }
```

646-662 Cycles through each zone and calls `try_to_free_pages_zone()` (See Section J.5.3) if it needs rebalancing.

647 `node_zones` is an array, and i is an index within it.

648-649 Calls `schedule()` if the quanta is expired to prevent **kswapd** from hogging the CPU.

650-651 If the zone does not require balance, this moves to the next one.

652-657 If the function returns 0, it means the `out_of_memory()` function was called because a sufficient number of pages could not be freed. **kswapd** sleeps for 1 second to give the system a chance to reclaim the killed processes' pages and to perform I/O. The zone is marked as balanced, so **kswapd** will ignore this zone until the allocator function `__alloc_pages()` complains again.

658-661 If it was successful, `check_classzone_need_balance()` is called to see if the zone requires further balancing.

664 Returns 1 if one zone requires further balancing.

Page Frame Reclamation

Swap Management

Contents

K.1 Scanning for Free Entries

Contents

K.1.1   Function: get_swap_page()   *(mm/swapfile.c)*

The call graph for this function is shown in Figure 11.2. This is the high-level API function for searching the swap areas for a free swap lot and returning the resulting swp_entry_t.

```
 99 swp_entry_t get_swap_page(void)
100 {
101     struct swap_info_struct * p;
102     unsigned long offset;
103     swp_entry_t entry;
104     int type, wrapped = 0;
105
106     entry.val = 0;  /* Out of memory */
107     swap_list_lock();
108     type = swap_list.next;
109     if (type < 0)
110         goto out;
111     if (nr_swap_pages <= 0)
112         goto out;
113
114     while (1) {
115         p = &swap_info[type];
116         if ((p->flags & SWP_WRITEOK) == SWP_WRITEOK) {
117             swap_device_lock(p);
118             offset = scan_swap_map(p);
119             swap_device_unlock(p);
120             if (offset) {
121                 entry = SWP_ENTRY(type,offset);
122                 type = swap_info[type].next;
123                 if (type < 0 ||
124                     p->prio != swap_info[type].prio) {
125                     swap_list.next = swap_list.head;
126                 } else {
127                     swap_list.next = type;
128                 }
129                 goto out;
130             }
131         }
132         type = p->next;
```

Swap Management

```
133          if (!wrapped) {
134              if (type < 0 || p->prio != swap_info[type].prio) {
135                  type = swap_list.head;
136                  wrapped = 1;
137              }
138          } else
139              if (type < 0)
140                  goto out;      /* out of swap space */
141      }
142 out:
143      swap_list_unlock();
144      return entry;
145 }
```

107 Locks the list of swap areas.

108 Gets the next swap area that is to be used for allocating from. This list will be ordered depending on the priority of the swap areas.

109-110 If there are no swap areas, this returns NULL.

111-112 If the accounting says no swap slots are available, this returns NULL.

114-141 Cycles through all swap areas.

115 Gets the current swap info struct from the **swap_info** array.

116 If this swap area is available for writing to and is active, then...

117 Locks the swap area.

118 Calls **scan_swap_map()** (See Section K.1.2), which searches the requested swap map for a free slot.

119 Unlocks the swap device.

120-130 If a slot was free, then...

121 Encodes an identifier for the entry with **SWP_ENTRY()**.

122 Records the next swap area to use.

123-126 If the next area is the end of the list or the priority of the next swap area does not match the current one, this moves back to the head.

126-128 Otherwise, it moves to the next area.

129 Goto out.

132 Moves to the next swap area.

133-138 Checks for wrapaound. It sets `wrapped` to 1 if we get to the end of the list of swap areas.

139-140 If no swap areas are available, goto out.

142 The exit to this function.

143 Unlocks the swap area list.

144 Returns the entry if one was found and returns NULL otherwise.

K.1.2 Function: `scan_swap_map()` *(mm/swapfile.c)*

This function tries to allocate `SWAPFILE_CLUSTER` number of pages sequentially in swap. When it has allocated that many, it searches for another block of free slots of size `SWAPFILE_CLUSTER`. If it fails to find one, it resorts to allocating the first free slot. This clustering attempts to make sure that slots are allocated and freed in `SWAPFILE_CLUSTER`-sized chunks.

```
36 static inline int scan_swap_map(struct swap_info_struct *si)
37 {
38     unsigned long offset;
47     if (si->cluster_nr) {
48         while (si->cluster_next <= si->highest_bit) {
49             offset = si->cluster_next++;
50             if (si->swap_map[offset])
51                 continue;
52             si->cluster_nr--;
53             goto got_page;
54         }
55     }
```

This block allocates `SWAPFILE_CLUSTER` pages sequentially. `cluster_nr` is initialized to `SWAPFILE_CLUTER` and decrements with each allocation.

47 If `cluster_nr` is still postive, this allocates the next available sequential slot.

48 When the current offset to use (`cluster_next`) is less then the highest known free slot (`highest_bit`), then ...

49 Records the offset and updates `cluster_next` to the next free slot.

50-51 If the slot is not actually free, this moves to the next one.

52 If a slot has been found, this decrements the `cluster_nr` field.

53 Goto the `out` path.

```
56        si->cluster_nr = SWAPFILE_CLUSTER;
57
58        /* try to find an empty (even not aligned) cluster. */
59        offset = si->lowest_bit;
60  check_next_cluster:
61        if (offset+SWAPFILE_CLUSTER-1 <= si->highest_bit)
62        {
63            int nr;
64            for (nr = offset; nr < offset+SWAPFILE_CLUSTER; nr++)
65                if (si->swap_map[nr])
66                {
67                    offset = nr+1;
68                    goto check_next_cluster;
69                }
70            /* We found a completly empty cluster, so start
71             * using it.
72             */
73            goto got_page;
74        }
```

At this stage, SWAPFILE_CLUSTER pages have been allocated sequentially, so this finds the next free block of SWAPFILE_CLUSTER pages.

56 Reinitializes the count of sequential pages to allocate to SWAPFILE_CLUSTER.

59 Starts searching at the lowest known free slot.

61 If the offset plus the cluster size is less than the known last free slot, this examines all the pages to see if this is a large free block.

64 Scans from offset to offset + SWAPFILE_CLUSTER.

65-69 If this slot is used, this starts searching again for a free slot, beginning after this known allocated one.

73 A large cluster was found, so this uses it.

```
75        /* No luck, so now go finegrined as usual. -Andrea */
76        for (offset = si->lowest_bit; offset <= si->highest_bit ;
                                offset++) {
77            if (si->swap_map[offset])
78                continue;
79            si->lowest_bit = offset+1;
```

This unusual for loop extract starts scanning for a free page starting from lowest_bit.

77-78 If the slot is in use, this moves to the next one.

79 Updates the `lowest_bit` known probable free slot to the succeeding one.

```
80      got_page:
81          if (offset == si->lowest_bit)
82              si->lowest_bit++;
83          if (offset == si->highest_bit)
84              si->highest_bit--;
85          if (si->lowest_bit > si->highest_bit) {
86              si->lowest_bit = si->max;
87              si->highest_bit = 0;
88          }
89          si->swap_map[offset] = 1;
90          nr_swap_pages--;
91          si->cluster_next = offset+1;
92          return offset;
93      }
94      si->lowest_bit = si->max;
95      si->highest_bit = 0;
96      return 0;
97 }
```

If a slot has been found, this does some housekeeping and returns it.

81-82 If this offset is the known lowest free slot(`lowest_bit`), this increments it.

83-84 If this offset is the highest known likely free slot, this decrements it.

85-88 If the low and high mark meet, the swap area is not worth searching any more because these marks represent the lowest and highest known free slots. This sets the low slot to be the highest possible slot and the high mark to 0 to cut down on search time later. This will be fixed up the next time a slot is freed.

89 Sets the reference count for the slot.

90 Updates the accounting for the number of available swap pages (`nr_swap_pages`).

91 Sets `cluster_next` to the adjacent slot, so the next search will start here.

92 Returns the free slot.

94-96 If a free slot is not available, this marks the area unsearchable and returns 0.

K.2   Swap Cache

Contents

K.2.1   Adding Pages to the Swap Cache

K.2.1.1   Function: `add_to_swap_cache()`   *(mm/swap_state.c)*

The call graph for this function is shown in Figure 11.3. This function wraps around the normal page cache handler. It first checks if the page is already in the swap cache with `swap_duplicate()`, and, if it is not, it calls `add_to_page_cache_unique()` instead.

```
70 int add_to_swap_cache(struct page *page, swp_entry_t entry)
71 {
72     if (page->mapping)
73         BUG();
74     if (!swap_duplicate(entry)) {
75         INC_CACHE_INFO(noent_race);
76         return -ENOENT;
77     }
78     if (add_to_page_cache_unique(page, &swapper_space, entry.val,
79             page_hash(&swapper_space, entry.val)) != 0) {
80         swap_free(entry);
81         INC_CACHE_INFO(exist_race);
82         return -EEXIST;
83     }
84     if (!PageLocked(page))
85         BUG();
86     if (!PageSwapCache(page))
87         BUG();
88     INC_CACHE_INFO(add_total);
89     return 0;
90 }
```

72-73 A check is made with `PageSwapCache()` before this function is called to make sure the page is not already in the swap cache. This check here ensures the page has no other existing mapping in case the caller was careless and did not make the check.

74-77 Uses `swap_duplicate()` (See Section K.2.1.2) to try and increment the count for this entry. If a slot already exists in the `swap_map`, this increments the statistic recording the number of races involving adding pages to the swap cache and returns `-ENOENT`.

78 Tries and adds the page to the page cache with `add_to_page_cache_unique()` (See Section J.1.1.2). This function is similar to `add_to_page_cache()` (See Section J.1.1.1) except it searches the page cache for a duplicate entry with `__find_page_nolock()`. The managing address space is `swapper_space`. The "offset within the file" in this case is the offset within `swap_map`, so `entry.val`, and finally the page, is hashed based on `address_space` and is offset within `swap_map`.

80-83 If it already existed in the page cache, we raced, so this increments the statistic recording the number of races to insert an existing page into the swap cache and returns `EEXIST`.

84-85 If the page is locked for I/O, it is a bug.

86-87 If it is not now in the swap cache, something went seriously wrong.

88 Increments the statistic recording the total number of pages in the swap cache.

89 Returns success.

K.2.1.2 Function: `swap_duplicate()` *(mm/swapfile.c)*

This function verifies a swap entry is valid and, if so, increments its swap map count.

```
1161 int swap_duplicate(swp_entry_t entry)
1162 {
1163     struct swap_info_struct * p;
1164     unsigned long offset, type;
1165     int result = 0;
1166
1167     type = SWP_TYPE(entry);
1168     if (type >= nr_swapfiles)
1169         goto bad_file;
1170     p = type + swap_info;
1171     offset = SWP_OFFSET(entry);
1172
1173     swap_device_lock(p);
1174     if (offset < p->max && p->swap_map[offset]) {
1175         if (p->swap_map[offset] < SWAP_MAP_MAX - 1) {
1176             p->swap_map[offset]++;
```

```
1177                        result = 1;
1178            } else if (p->swap_map[offset] <= SWAP_MAP_MAX) {
1179                if (swap_overflow++ < 5)
1180                    printk(KERN_WARNING "swap_dup: swap entry
                               overflow\n");
1181                p->swap_map[offset] = SWAP_MAP_MAX;
1182                result = 1;
1183            }
1184        }
1185        swap_device_unlock(p);
1186 out:
1187        return result;
1188
1189 bad_file:
1190        printk(KERN_ERR "swap_dup: %s%081x\n", Bad_file, entry.val);
1191        goto out;
1192 }
```

1161 The parameter is the swap entry to increase the swap_map count for.

1167-1169 Gets the offset within the swap_info for the swap_info_struct containing this entry. If it is greater than the number of swap areas, goto bad_file.

1170-1171 Gets the relevant swap_info_struct and gets the offset within its swap_map.

1173 Locks the swap device.

1174 Makes a quick sanity check to ensure the offset is within the swap_map and that the slot indicated has a positive count. A 0 count would mean that the slot is not free, and this is a bogus swp_entry_t.

1175-1177 If the count is not SWAP_MAP_MAX, this increments it and returns 1 for success.

1178-1183 If not, the count would overflow, so this sets it to SWAP_MAP_MAX and reserves the slot permanently. In reality, this condition is virtually impossible.

1185-1187 Unlocks the swap device and returns.

1190-1191 If a bad device was used, this prints out the error message and returns failure.

K.2.2   Deleting Pages From the Swap Cache

K.2.2.1   Function: swap_free()   *(mm/swapfile.c)*

This decrements the corresponding swap_map entry for the swp_entry_t.

```
214 void swap_free(swp_entry_t entry)
215 {
216     struct swap_info_struct * p;
217
218     p = swap_info_get(entry);
219     if (p) {
220         swap_entry_free(p, SWP_OFFSET(entry));
221         swap_info_put(p);
222     }
223 }
```

218 swap_info_get() (See Section K.2.3.1) fetches the correct swap_info_struct and performs a number of debugging checks to ensure it is a valid area and a valid swap_map entry. If all is sane, it will lock the swap device.

219-222 If it is valid, the corresponding swap_map entry is decremented with swap_entry_free() (See Section K.2.2.2) and swap_info_put() (See Section K.2.3.2) is called to free the device.

K.2.2.2 Function: swap_entry_free() *(mm/swapfile.c)*

```
192 static int swap_entry_free(struct swap_info_struct *p,
                unsigned long offset)
193 {
194     int count = p->swap_map[offset];
195
196     if (count < SWAP_MAP_MAX) {
197         count--;
198         p->swap_map[offset] = count;
199         if (!count) {
200             if (offset < p->lowest_bit)
201                 p->lowest_bit = offset;
202             if (offset > p->highest_bit)
203                 p->highest_bit = offset;
204             nr_swap_pages++;
205         }
206     }
207     return count;
208 }
```

194 Gets the current count.

196 If the count indicates the slot is not permanently reserved, then...

197-198 Decrements the count and stores it in the swap_map.

199 If the count reaches 0, the slot is free, so it updates some information.

200-201 If this freed slot is below `lowest_bit`, this updates `lowest_bit`, which indicates the lowest known free slot.

202-203 Similarly, this updates the `highest_bit` if this newly freed slot is above it.

204 Increments the count indicating the number of free swap slots.

207 Returns the current count.

K.2.3   Acquiring/Releasing Swap Cache Pages

K.2.3.1   Function: `swap_info_get()`   *(mm/swapfile.c)*

This function finds the `swap_info_struct` for the given entry, performs some basic checking and then locks the device.

```
147 static struct swap_info_struct * swap_info_get(swp_entry_t entry)
148 {
149     struct swap_info_struct * p;
150     unsigned long offset, type;
151
152     if (!entry.val)
153         goto out;
154     type = SWP_TYPE(entry);
155     if (type >= nr_swapfiles)
156         goto bad_nofile;
157     p = & swap_info[type];
158     if (!(p->flags & SWP_USED))
159         goto bad_device;
160     offset = SWP_OFFSET(entry);
161     if (offset >= p->max)
162         goto bad_offset;
163     if (!p->swap_map[offset])
164         goto bad_free;
165     swap_list_lock();
166     if (p->prio > swap_info[swap_list.next].prio)
167         swap_list.next = type;
168     swap_device_lock(p);
169     return p;
170
171 bad_free:
172     printk(KERN_ERR "swap_free: %s%08lx\n", Unused_offset,
                                                entry.val);
173     goto out;
174 bad_offset:
175     printk(KERN_ERR "swap_free: %s%08lx\n", Bad_offset,
                                                entry.val);
176     goto out;
```

```
177 bad_device:
178     printk(KERN_ERR "swap_free: %s%081x\n", Unused_file,
                                            entry.val);
179     goto out;
180 bad_nofile:
181     printk(KERN_ERR "swap_free: %s%081x\n", Bad_file,
                                            entry.val);
182 out:
183     return NULL;
184 }
```

152-153 If the supplied entry is NULL, this returns.

154 Gets the offset within the `swap_info` array.

155-156 Ensures it is a valid area.

157 Gets the address of the area.

158-159 If the area is not active yet, this prints a bad device error and returns.

160 Gets the offset within the `swap_map`.

161-162 Makes sure the offset is not after the end of the map.

163-164 Makes sure the slot is currently in use.

165 Locks the swap area list.

166-167 If this area is of higher priority than the area that would be next, this ensures the current area is used.

168-169 Locks the swap device and returns the swap area descriptor.

K.2.3.2   Function: `swap_info_put()`   *(mm/swapfile.c)*
This function simply unlocks the area and list.

```
186 static void swap_info_put(struct swap_info_struct * p)
187 {
188     swap_device_unlock(p);
189     swap_list_unlock();
190 }
```

188 Unlocks the device.

189 Unlocks the swap area list.

Swap Management

K.2.4   Searching the Swap Cache

K.2.4.1   Function: `lookup_swap_cache()`   *(mm/swap_state.c)*
This is a top-level function for finding a page in the swap cache.

```
161 struct page * lookup_swap_cache(swp_entry_t entry)
162 {
163     struct page *found;
164
165     found = find_get_page(&swapper_space, entry.val);
166     /*
167      * Unsafe to assert PageSwapCache and mapping on page found:
168      * if SMP nothing prevents swapoff from deleting this page from
169      * the swap cache at this moment.  find_lock_page would prevent
170      * that, but no need to change: we _have_ got the right page.
171      */
172     INC_CACHE_INFO(find_total);
173     if (found)
174         INC_CACHE_INFO(find_success);
175     return found;
176 }
```

165 `find_get_page()`(See Section J.1.4.1) is the principal function for returning the **struct page**. It uses the normal page hashing and cache functions for quickly finding it.

172 Increases the statistic recording the number of times a page was searched for in the cache.

173-174 If one was found, this increments the successful find count.

175 Returns the **struct page** or NULL if it did not exist.

K.3 Swap Area I/O

Contents

K.3.1 Reading Backing Storage

K.3.1.1 Function: read_swap_cache_async() *(mm/swap_state.c)*

This function will return the requested page from the swap cache. If it does not exist, a page will be allocated and placed in the swap cache. The data is then scheduled to be read from disk with `rw_swap_page()`.

```
184 struct page * read_swap_cache_async(swp_entry_t entry)
185 {
186     struct page *found_page, *new_page = NULL;
187     int err;
188
189     do {
196         found_page = find_get_page(&swapper_space, entry.val);
197         if (found_page)
198             break;
199
200         /*
201          * Get a new page to read into from swap.
202          */
203         if (!new_page) {
204             new_page = alloc_page(GFP_HIGHUSER);
205             if (!new_page)
206                 break;          /* Out of memory */
207         }
208
209         /*
210          * Associate the page with swap entry in the swap cache.
211          * May fail (-ENOENT) if swap entry has been freed since
212          * our caller observed it.  May fail (-EEXIST) if there
213          * is already a page associated with this entry in the
214          * swap cache: added by a racing read_swap_cache_async,
```

```
215              * or by try_to_swap_out (or shmem_writepage) re-using
216              * the just freed swap entry for an existing page.
217              */
218             err = add_to_swap_cache(new_page, entry);
219             if (!err) {
220                 /*
221                  * Initiate read into locked page and return.
222                  */
223                 rw_swap_page(READ, new_page);
224                 return new_page;
225             }
226         } while (err != -ENOENT);
227
228         if (new_page)
229             page_cache_release(new_page);
230         return found_page;
231 }
```

189 Loops in case `add_to_swap_cache()` fails to add a page to the swap cache.

196 First searches the swap cache with `find_get_page()`(See Section J.1.4.1)
to see if the page is already available.   Ordinarily, `lookup_swap_cache()`
(See Section K.2.4.1) would be called, but it updates statistics (such as the
number of cache searches), so `find_get_page()` (See Section J.1.4.1) is called
directly.

203-207 If the page is not in the swap cache and we have not allocated one yet,
this allocates one with `alloc_page()`.

218 Adds the newly allocated page to the swap cache with `add_to_swap_cache()`
(See Section K.2.1.1).

223 Schedules the data to be read with `rw_swap_page()`(See Section K.3.3.1). The
page will be returned locked and will be unlocked when I/O completes.

224 Returns the new page.

226 Loops until `add_to_swap_cache()` succeeds or another process successfully
inserts the page into the swap cache.

228-229 This is either the error path, or another process added the page to
the swap cache for us. If a new page was allocated, this frees it with
`page_cache_release()` (See Section J.1.3.2).

230 Returns either the page found in the swap cache or an error.

K.3.2 Writing Backing Storage

K.3.2.1 Function: `swap_writepage()` *(mm/swap_state.c)*

This is the function registered in `swap_aops` for writing out pages. Its function is pretty simple. First, it calls `remove_exclusive_swap_page()` to try and free the page. If the page was freed, the page will be unlocked here before returning because no I/O is pending on the page. Otherwise, `rw_swap_page()` is called to sync the page with backing storage.

```
24 static int swap_writepage(struct page *page)
25 {
26     if (remove_exclusive_swap_page(page)) {
27         UnlockPage(page);
28         return 0;
29     }
30     rw_swap_page(WRITE, page);
31     return 0;
32 }
```

26-29 `remove_exclusive_swap_page()` (See Section K.3.2.2) will reclaim the page from the swap cache if possible. If the page is reclaimed, this unlocks it before returning.

30 Otherwise, the page is still in the swap cache, so this synchronizes it with backing storage by calling `rw_swap_page()` (See Section K.3.3.1).

K.3.2.2 Function: `remove_exclusive_swap_page()` *(mm/swapfile.c)*

This function will try to work out if other processes are sharing this page. If possible, the page will be removed from the swap cache and freed. After it is removed from the swap cache, `swap_free()` is decremented to indicate that the swap cache is no longer using the slot. The count will instead reflect the number of PTEs that contain a `swp_entry_t` for this slot.

```
287 int remove_exclusive_swap_page(struct page *page)
288 {
289     int retval;
290     struct swap_info_struct * p;
291     swp_entry_t entry;
292
293     if (!PageLocked(page))
294         BUG();
295     if (!PageSwapCache(page))
296         return 0;
297     if (page_count(page) - !!page->buffers != 2) /* 2: us + cache */
298         return 0;
299
300     entry.val = page->index;
```

Swap Management

```
301        p = swap_info_get(entry);
302        if (!p)
303            return 0;
304
305        /* Is the only swap cache user the cache itself? */
306        retval = 0;
307        if (p->swap_map[SWP_OFFSET(entry)] == 1) {
308            /* Recheck the page count with the pagecache lock held.. */
309            spin_lock(&pagecache_lock);
310            if (page_count(page) - !!page->buffers == 2) {
311                __delete_from_swap_cache(page);
312                SetPageDirty(page);
313                retval = 1;
314            }
315            spin_unlock(&pagecache_lock);
316        }
317        swap_info_put(p);
318
319        if (retval) {
320            block_flushpage(page, 0);
321            swap_free(entry);
322            page_cache_release(page);
323        }
324
325        return retval;
326 }
```

293-294 This operation should only be made with the page locked.

295-296 If the page is not in the swap cache, then there is nothing to do.

297-298 If there are other users of the page, then it cannot be reclaimed, so it returns.

300 The `swp_entry_t` for the page is stored in `page→index` as explained in Section 2.5.

301 Gets the `swap_info_struct` with `swap_info_get()` (See Section K.2.3.1).

307 If the only user of the swap slot is the swap cache itself (i.e, no process is mapping it), this deletes this page from the swap cache to free the slot. Later, the swap slot usage count will be decremented because the swap cache is no longer using it.

310 If the current user is the only user of this page, it is safe to remove from the swap cache. If another process is sharing it, it must remain here.

311 Deletes from the swap cache.

313 Sets `retval` to 1 so that the caller knows the page was freed and so that `swap_free()` (See Section K.2.2.1) will be called to decrement the usage count in the `swap_map`.

317 Drops the reference to the swap slot that was taken with `swap_info_get()` (See Section K.2.3.1).

320 The slot is being freed to call `block_flushpage()` so that all I/O will complete and any buffers associated with the page will be freed.

321 Frees the swap slot with `swap_free()`.

322 Drops the reference to the page.

K.3.2.3 Function: `free_swap_and_cache()` *(mm/swapfile.c)*
This function frees an entry from the swap cache and tries to reclaim the page. Note that this function only applies to the swap cache.

```
332 void free_swap_and_cache(swp_entry_t entry)
333 {
334     struct swap_info_struct * p;
335     struct page *page = NULL;
336
337     p = swap_info_get(entry);
338     if (p) {
339         if (swap_entry_free(p, SWP_OFFSET(entry)) == 1)
340             page = find_trylock_page(&swapper_space, entry.val);
341         swap_info_put(p);
342     }
343     if (page) {
344         page_cache_get(page);
345         /* Only cache user (+us), or swap space full? Free it! */
346         if (page_count(page) - !!page->buffers == 2 ||
                vm_swap_full()) {
347             delete_from_swap_cache(page);
348             SetPageDirty(page);
349         }
350         UnlockPage(page);
351         page_cache_release(page);
352     }
353 }
```

337 Gets the `swap_info` struct for the requsted `entry`.

338-342 Presuming the swap area information struct exists, this calls `swap_entry_free()` to free the swap entry. The page for the `entry` is then located in the swap cache using `find_trylock_page()`. Note that the page is returned locked.

341 Drops the reference taken to the swap info struct at line 337.

343-352 If the page was located, then we try to reclaim it.

344 Takes a reference to the page so that it will not be freed prematurely.

346-349 The page is deleted from the swap cache if no processes are mapping the page or if the swap area is more than 50 percent full (checked by `vm_swap_full()`).

350 Unlocks the page again.

351 Drops the local reference to the page taken at line 344.

K.3.3   Block I/O

K.3.3.1   Function: `rw_swap_page()`   *(mm/page_io.c)*
This is the main function used for reading data from backing storage into a page or writing data from a page to backing storage. Which operation it performs depends on the first parameter `rw`. It is basically a wrapper function around the core function `rw_swap_page_base()`. This simply enforces that the operations are only performed on pages in the swap cache.

```
85 void rw_swap_page(int rw, struct page *page)
86 {
87     swp_entry_t entry;
88
89     entry.val = page->index;
90
91     if (!PageLocked(page))
92         PAGE_BUG(page);
93     if (!PageSwapCache(page))
94         PAGE_BUG(page);
95     if (!rw_swap_page_base(rw, entry, page))
96         UnlockPage(page);
97 }
```

85 `rw` indicates whether a read or write is taking place.

89 Gets the `swp_entry_t` from the `index` field.

91-92 If the page is not locked for I/O, it is a bug.

93-94 If the page is not in the swap cache, it is a bug.

95 Calls the core function `rw_swap_page_base()`. If it returns failure, the page is unlocked with `UnlockPage()` so that it can be freed.

K.3.3.2   Function: `rw_swap_page_base()`   *(mm/page_io.c)*

This is the core function for reading or writing data to the backing storage. Whether it is writing to a partition or a file, the block layer `brw_page()` function is used to perform the actual I/O. This function sets up the necessary buffer information for the block layer to do its job. The `brw_page()` performs asynchronous I/O, so it is likely it will return with the page locked, which will be unlocked when the I/O completes.

```
36  static int rw_swap_page_base(int rw, swp_entry_t entry,
                                  struct page *page)
37  {
38      unsigned long offset;
39      int zones[PAGE_SIZE/512];
40      int zones_used;
41      kdev_t dev = 0;
42      int block_size;
43      struct inode *swapf = 0;
44
45      if (rw == READ) {
46          ClearPageUptodate(page);
47          kstat.pswpin++;
48      } else
49          kstat.pswpout++;
50
```

36 The parameters are the following:

- **rw** indicates whether the operation is a read or a write.
- **entry** is the swap entry for locating the data in backing storage.
- **page** is the page that is being read or written to.

39 zones is a parameter required by the block layer for `brw_page()`. It is expected to contain an array of block numbers that are to be written to. This is primarily of importance when the backing storage is a file rather than a partition.

45-47 If the page is to be read from disk, this clears the `Uptodate` flag because the page is obviously not up to date if we are reading information from the disk. It increments the pages-swapped-in (`pswpin`) statistic.

49 If not, it just updates the pages-swapped-out (`pswpout`) statistic.

```
51          get_swaphandle_info(entry, &offset, &dev, &swapf);
52          if (dev) {
53              zones[0] = offset;
54              zones_used = 1;
55              block_size = PAGE_SIZE;
```

```
56      } else if (swapf) {
57          int i, j;
58          unsigned int block =
59              offset << (PAGE_SHIFT - swapf->i_sb->s_blocksize_bits);
60
61          block_size = swapf->i_sb->s_blocksize;
62          for (i=0, j=0; j< PAGE_SIZE ; i++, j += block_size)
63              if (!(zones[i] = bmap(swapf,block++))) {
64                  printk("rw_swap_page: bad swap file\n");
65                  return 0;
66              }
67          zones_used = i;
68          dev = swapf->i_dev;
69      } else {
70          return 0;
71      }
72
73      /* block_size == PAGE_SIZE/zones_used */
74      brw_page(rw, page, dev, zones, block_size);
75      return 1;
76 }
```

51 get_swaphandle_info()(See Section K.3.3.3) returns either the kdev_t or struct inode that represents the swap area, whichever is appropriate.

52-55 If the storage area is a partition, then there is only one block to be written, which is the size of a page. Hence, zones only has one entry, which is the offset within the partition to be written, and the block_size is PAGE_SIZE.

56 If not, it is a swap file, so each of the blocks in the file that make up the page has to be mapped with bmap() before calling brw_page().

58-59 Calculates what the starting block is.

61 The size of individual block is stored in the superblock information for the filesystem the file resides on.

62-66 Calls bmap() for every block that makes up the full page. Each block is stored in the zones array for passing to brw_page(). If any block fails to be mapped, 0 is returned.

67 Records how many blocks make up the page in zones_used.

68 Records which device is being written to.

74 Calls brw_page() from the block layer to schedule the I/O to occur. This function returns immediately because the I/O is asynchronous. When the I/O is completed, a callback function (end_buffer_io_async()) is called, which unlocks the page. Any process waiting on the page will be woken up at that point.

75 Returns success.

K.3.3.3   Function: `get_swaphandle_info()`   *(mm/swapfile.c)*

This function is responsible for returning either the `kdev_t` or `struct inode` that is managing the swap area that `entry` belongs to.

```
1197 void get_swaphandle_info(swp_entry_t entry, unsigned long *offset,
1198                          kdev_t *dev, struct inode **swapf)
1199 {
1200     unsigned long type;
1201     struct swap_info_struct *p;
1202
1203     type = SWP_TYPE(entry);
1204     if (type >= nr_swapfiles) {
1205         printk(KERN_ERR "rw_swap_page: %s%08lx\n", Bad_file,
                                                       entry.val);
1206         return;
1207     }
1208
1209     p = &swap_info[type];
1210     *offset = SWP_OFFSET(entry);
1211     if (*offset >= p->max && *offset != 0) {
1212         printk(KERN_ERR "rw_swap_page: %s%08lx\n", Bad_offset,
                                                       entry.val);
1213         return;
1214     }
1215     if (p->swap_map && !p->swap_map[*offset]) {
1216         printk(KERN_ERR "rw_swap_page: %s%08lx\n", Unused_offset,
                                                       entry.val);
1217         return;
1218     }
1219     if (!(p->flags & SWP_USED)) {
1220         printk(KERN_ERR "rw_swap_page: %s%08lx\n", Unused_file,
                                                       entry.val);
1221         return;
1222     }
1223
1224     if (p->swap_device) {
1225         *dev = p->swap_device;
1226     } else if (p->swap_file) {
1227         *swapf = p->swap_file->d_inode;
1228     } else {
1229         printk(KERN_ERR "rw_swap_page: no swap file or device\n");
1230     }
1231     return;
1232 }
```

Swap Management

1203 Extracts which area within `swap_info` this `entry` belongs to.

1204-1206 If the index is for an area that does not exist, this prints out an information message and returns. `Bad_file` is a static array declared near the top of `mm/swapfile.c` that says "Bad swap file entry."

1209 Gets the `swap_info_struct` from `swap_info`.

1210 Extracts the offset within the swap area for this `entry`.

1211-1214 Makes sure the offset is not after the end of the file. It prints out the message in `Bad_offset` if it is.

1215-1218 If the offset is currently not being used, it means that `entry` is a stale entry, so it prints out the error message in `Unused_offset`.

1219-1222 If the swap area is currently not active, this prints out the error message in `Unused_file`.

1224 If the swap area is a device, this returns the `kdev_t` in `swap_info_struct`→`swap_device`.

1226-1227 If it is a swap file, this returns the `struct inode`, which is available through `swap_info_struct`→`swap_file`→`d_inode`.

1229 If not, there is no swap file or device for this `entry`, so it prints out the error message and returns.

K.4   Activating a Swap Area

Contents

K.4.1   Function: `sys_swapon()`   *(mm/swapfile.c)*

This quite large function is responsible for the activating of swap space. Broadly speaking, the tasks it takes are as follows:

- Find a free `swap_info_struct` in the `swap_info` array and initialize it with default values.

- Call `user_path_walk()`, which traverses the directory tree for the supplied `specialfile` and populates a `namidata` structure with the available data on the file, such as the `dentry` and the filesystem information for where it is stored (`vfsmount`).

- Populate `swap_info_struct` fields pertaining to the dimensions of the swap area and how to find it. If the swap area is a partition, the block size will be configured to the `PAGE_SIZE` before calculating the size. If it is a file, the information is obtained directly from the `inode`.

- Ensure the area is not already activated. If not, allocate a page from memory and read the first page-sized slot from the swap area. This page contains information, such as the number of good slots and how to populate the `swap_info_struct`→`swap_map` with the bad entries.

- Allocate memory with `vmalloc()` for `swap_info_struct`→`swap_map` and initialize each entry with 0 for good slots and `SWAP_MAP_BAD` otherwise. Ideally, the header information will be a version 2 file format because version 1 was limited to swap areas of just under 128MiB for architectures with 4KiB page sizes like the x86.

- After ensuring the information indicated in the header matches the actual swap area, fill in the remaining information in the `swap_info_struct`, such as the maximum number of pages and the available good pages. Update the global statistics for `nr_swap_pages` and `total_swap_pages`.

- The swap area is now fully active and initialized, so it is inserted into the swap list in the correct position based on priority of the newly activated area.

```
855 asmlinkage long sys_swapon(const char * specialfile,
                               int swap_flags)
856 {
857        struct swap_info_struct * p;
858        struct nameidata nd;
859        struct inode * swap_inode;
```

```
860        unsigned int type;
861        int i, j, prev;
862        int error;
863        static int least_priority = 0;
864        union swap_header *swap_header = 0;
865        int swap_header_version;
866        int nr_good_pages = 0;
867        unsigned long maxpages = 1;
868        int swapfilesize;
869        struct block_device *bdev = NULL;
870        unsigned short *swap_map;
871
872        if (!capable(CAP_SYS_ADMIN))
873          return -EPERM;
874        lock_kernel();
875        swap_list_lock();
876        p = swap_info;
```

855 The two parameters are the path to the swap area and the flags for activation.

872-873 The activating process must have the CAP_SYS_ADMIN capability or be the superuser to activate a swap area.

874 Acquires the Big Kernel Lock (BKL).

875 Locks the list of swap areas.

876 Gets the first swap area in the swap_info array.

```
877        for (type = 0 ; type < nr_swapfiles ; type++,p++)
878          if (!(p->flags & SWP_USED))
879            break;
880        error = -EPERM;
881        if (type >= MAX_SWAPFILES) {
882          swap_list_unlock();
883          goto out;
884        }
885        if (type >= nr_swapfiles)
886          nr_swapfiles = type+1;
887        p->flags = SWP_USED;
888        p->swap_file = NULL;
889        p->swap_vfsmnt = NULL;
890        p->swap_device = 0;
891        p->swap_map = NULL;
892        p->lowest_bit = 0;
893        p->highest_bit = 0;
894        p->cluster_nr = 0;
895        p->sdev_lock = SPIN_LOCK_UNLOCKED;
```

```
896        p->next = -1;
897        if (swap_flags & SWAP_FLAG_PREFER) {
898          p->prio =
899            (swap_flags & SWAP_FLAG_PRIO_MASK)>>SWAP_FLAG_PRIO_SHIFT;
900        } else {
901          p->prio = --least_priority;
902        }
903        swap_list_unlock();
```

Finds a free `swap_info_struct` and initializes it with default values.

877-879 Cycles through the `swap_info` until a struct is found that is not in use.

880 By default, the error returned is Permission Denied, which indicates the caller did not have the proper permissions or too many swap areas are already in use.

881 If no struct was free, `MAX_SWAPFILE` areas have already been activated, so this unlocks the swap list and returns.

885-886 If the selected swap area is after the last known active area (`nr_swapfiles`), this updates `nr_swapfiles`.

887 Sets the flag, indicating the area is in use.

888-896 Initializes fields to default values.

897-902 If the caller has specified a priority, this uses it or sets it to `least_priority` and decrements it. This way, the swap areas will be prioritized in order of activation.

903 Releases the swap list lock.

```
904        error = user_path_walk(specialfile, &nd);
905        if (error)
906          goto bad_swap_2;
907
908        p->swap_file = nd.dentry;
909        p->swap_vfsmnt = nd.mnt;
910        swap_inode = nd.dentry->d_inode;
911        error = -EINVAL;
912
```

This block traverses the VFS and gets some information about the special file.

904 `user_path_walk()` traverses the directory structure to obtain a `nameidata` structure describing the `specialfile`.

905-906 If it failed, this returns failure.

Swap Management

908 Fills in the `swap_file` field with the returned `dentry`.

909 Similarly, fills in the `swap_vfsmnt`.

910 Records the inode of the special file.

911 Now the default error is `-EINVAL`, indicating that the special file was found but it was not a block device or a regular file.

```
913       if (S_ISBLK(swap_inode->i_mode)) {
914         kdev_t dev = swap_inode->i_rdev;
915         struct block_device_operations *bdops;
916         devfs_handle_t de;
917
918         p->swap_device = dev;
919         set_blocksize(dev, PAGE_SIZE);
920
921         bd_acquire(swap_inode);
922         bdev = swap_inode->i_bdev;
923         de = devfs_get_handle_from_inode(swap_inode);
924         bdops = devfs_get_ops(de);
925         if (bdops) bdev->bd_op = bdops;
926
927         error = blkdev_get(bdev, FMODE_READ|FMODE_WRITE, 0,
                      BDEV_SWAP);
928         devfs_put_ops(de);/* Decrement module use count
                              * now we're safe*/
929         if (error)
930           goto bad_swap_2;
931         set_blocksize(dev, PAGE_SIZE);
932         error = -ENODEV;
933         if (!dev || (blk_size[MAJOR(dev)] &&
934          !blk_size[MAJOR(dev)][MINOR(dev)]))
935           goto bad_swap;
936         swapfilesize = 0;
937         if (blk_size[MAJOR(dev)])
938           swapfilesize = blk_size[MAJOR(dev)][MINOR(dev)]
939             >> (PAGE_SHIFT - 10);
940       } else if (S_ISREG(swap_inode->i_mode))
941         swapfilesize = swap_inode->i_size >> PAGE_SHIFT;
942       else
943         goto bad_swap;
```

If a partition, this code configures the block device before calculating the size of the area, or it obtains it from the inode for the file.

913 Checks if the special file is a block device.

914-939 This code segment handles the case where the swap area is a partition.

914 Records a pointer to the device structure for the block device.

918 Stores a pointer to the device structure describing the special file that will be needed for block I/O operations.

919 Sets the block size on the device to be `PAGE_SIZE` because it will be page-sized chunks swap is interested in.

921 The `bd_acquire()` function increments the usage count for this block device.

922 Gets a pointer to the `block_device` structure, which is a descriptor for the device file, which is needed to open it.

923 Gets a devfs handle if it is enabled. devfs is beyond the scope of this book.

924-925 Increments the usage count of this device entry.

927 Opens the block device in read/write mode and sets the `BDEV_SWAP` flag, which is an enumerated type, but is ignored when `do_open()` is called.

928 Decrements the use count of the devfs entry.

929-930 If an error occured on open, this returns failure.

931 Sets the block size again.

932 After this point, the default error is to indicate no device could be found.

933-935 Ensures the returned device is ok.

937-939 Calculates the size of the swap file as the number of page-sized chunks that exist in the block device as indicated by `blk_size`. The size of the swap area is calculated to make sure the information in the swap area is sane.

941 If the swap area is a regular file, this obtains the size directly from the inode and calculates how many page-sized chunks exist.

943 If the file is not a block device or regular file, this returns error.

```
945        error = -EBUSY;
946        for (i = 0 ; i < nr_swapfiles ; i++) {
947          struct swap_info_struct *q = &swap_info[i];
948          if (i == type || !q->swap_file)
949            continue;
950          if (swap_inode->i_mapping ==
             q->swap_file->d_inode->i_mapping)
951            goto bad_swap;
952        }
953
954        swap_header = (void *) __get_free_page(GFP_USER);
```

```
955        if (!swap_header) {
956          printk("Unable to start swapping: out of memory :-)\n");
957          error = -ENOMEM;
958          goto bad_swap;
959        }
960
961        lock_page(virt_to_page(swap_header));
962        rw_swap_page_nolock(READ, SWP_ENTRY(type,0),
             (char *) swap_header);
963
964        if (!memcmp("SWAP-SPACE",swap_header->magic.magic,10))
965          swap_header_version = 1;
966        else if (!memcmp("SWAPSPACE2",swap_header->magic.magic,10))
967          swap_header_version = 2;
968        else {
969          printk("Unable to find swap-space signature\n");
970          error = -EINVAL;
971          goto bad_swap;
972        }
```

945 The next check makes sure the area is not already active. If it is, the error -EBUSY will be returned.

946-962 Reads through the while swap_info struct and ensures the area to be activated if not already active.

954-959 Allocates a page for reading the swap area information from disk.

961 The function lock_page() locks a page and makes sure it is synced with the disk if it is file backed. In this case, it will just mark the page as locked, which is required for the rw_swap_page_nolock() function.

962 Reads the first page slot in the swap area into swap_header.

964-672 Checks the version based on the swap area information and sets swap_header_version variable with it. If the swap area could not be identified, it returns -EINVAL.

```
974        switch (swap_header_version) {
975        case 1:
976          memset(((char *) swap_header)+PAGE_SIZE-10,0,10);
977          j = 0;
978          p->lowest_bit = 0;
979          p->highest_bit = 0;
980          for (i = 1 ; i < 8*PAGE_SIZE ; i++) {
981            if (test_bit(i,(char *) swap_header)) {
982              if (!p->lowest_bit)
983                  p->lowest_bit = i;
```

```
984            p->highest_bit = i;
985            maxpages = i+1;
986            j++;
987          }
988        }
989        nr_good_pages = j;
990        p->swap_map = vmalloc(maxpages * sizeof(short));
991        if (!p->swap_map) {
992          error = -ENOMEM;
993          goto bad_swap;
994        }
995        for (i = 1 ; i < maxpages ; i++) {
996          if (test_bit(i,(char *) swap_header))
997            p->swap_map[i] = 0;
998          else
999            p->swap_map[i] = SWAP_MAP_BAD;
1000       }
1001       break;
1002
```

This block reads in the information needed to populate the swap_map when the swap area is version 1.

976 Zeros-out the magic string identifying the version of the swap area.

978-979 Initializes fields in swap_info_struct to 0.

980-988 A bitmap with 8*PAGE_SIZE entries is stored in the swap area. The full page, minus 10 bits for the magic string, is used to describe the swap map and limits swap areas to just under 128MiB in size. If the bit is set to 1, a slot on disk is available. This pass will calculate how many slots are available, so a swap_map may be allocated.

981 Tests if the bit for this slot is set.

982-983 If the lowest_bit field is not yet set, this sets it to this slot. In most cases, lowest_bit will be initialized to 1.

984 As long as new slots are found, this keeps updating the highest_bit.

985 Counts the number of pages.

986 j is the count of good pages in the area.

990 Allocates memory for the swap_map with vmalloc().

991-994 If memory could not be allocated, this returns ENOMEM.

995-1000 For each slot, this checks if the slot is "good." If yes, it initializes the slot count to 0, or sets it to SWAP_MAP_BAD, so it will not be used.

Swap Management

1001 Exits the switch statement.

```
1003        case 2:
1006          if (swap_header->info.version != 1) {
1007            printk(KERN_WARNING
1008              "Unable to handle swap header version %d\n",
1009              swap_header->info.version);
1010            error = -EINVAL;
1011            goto bad_swap;
1012          }
1013
1014          p->lowest_bit  = 1;
1015          maxpages = SWP_OFFSET(SWP_ENTRY(0,~OUL)) - 1;
1016          if (maxpages > swap_header->info.last_page)
1017            maxpages = swap_header->info.last_page;
1018          p->highest_bit = maxpages - 1;
1019
1020          error = -EINVAL;
1021          if (swap_header->info.nr_badpages > MAX_SWAP_BADPAGES)
1022            goto bad_swap;
1023
1025          if (!(p->swap_map = vmalloc(maxpages * sizeof(short)))) {
1026            error = -ENOMEM;
1027            goto bad_swap;
1028          }
1029
1030          error = 0;
1031          memset(p->swap_map, 0, maxpages * sizeof(short));
1032          for (i=0; i<swap_header->info.nr_badpages; i++) {
1033            int page = swap_header->info.badpages[i];
1034            if (page <= 0 ||
                 page >= swap_header->info.last_page)
1035              error = -EINVAL;
1036            else
1037              p->swap_map[page] = SWAP_MAP_BAD;
1038          }
1039          nr_good_pages = swap_header->info.last_page -
1040              swap_header->info.nr_badpages -
1041              1 /* header page */;
1042          if (error)
1043            goto bad_swap;
1044        }
```

This block reads the header information when the file format is version 2.

1006-1012 Makes absolutely sure we can handle this swap file format and returns
-EINVAL if we cannot. Remember that, with this version, the swap_header
struct is placed nicely on disk.

1014 Initializes `lowest_bit` to the known lowest available slot.

1015-1017 Calculates the `maxpages` initially as the maximum possible size of a `swap_map` and then sets it to the size indicated by the information on disk. This ensures the `swap_map` array is not accidently overloaded.

1018 Initializes `highest_bit`.

1020-1022 Makes sure the number of bad pages that exists does not exceed `MAX_SWAP_BADPAGES`.

1025-1028 Allocates memory for the `swap_map` with `vmalloc()`.

1031 Initializes the full `swap_map` to 0 indicating all slots are available.

1032-1038 Using the information loaded from disk, this sets each slot that is unusable to `SWAP_MAP_BAD`.

1039-1041 Calculates the number of available good pages.

1042-1043 Returns if an error occurred.

```
1045
1046      if (swapfilesize && maxpages > swapfilesize) {
1047        printk(KERN_WARNING
1048          "Swap area shorter than signature indicates\n");
1049        error = -EINVAL;
1050        goto bad_swap;
1051      }
1052      if (!nr_good_pages) {
1053        printk(KERN_WARNING "Empty swap-file\n");
1054        error = -EINVAL;
1055        goto bad_swap;
1056      }
1057      p->swap_map[0] = SWAP_MAP_BAD;
1058      swap_list_lock();
1059      swap_device_lock(p);
1060      p->max = maxpages;
1061      p->flags = SWP_WRITEOK;
1062      p->pages = nr_good_pages;
1063      nr_swap_pages += nr_good_pages;
1064      total_swap_pages += nr_good_pages;
1065      printk(KERN_INFO "Adding Swap:
                          %dk swap-space (priority %d)\n",
1066        nr_good_pages<<(PAGE_SHIFT-10), p->prio);
```

1046-1051 Ensures the information loaded from disk matches the actual dimensions of the swap area. If they do not match, this prints a warning and returns an error.

1052-1056 If no good pages were available, this returns an error.

1057 Makes sure the first page in the map containing the swap header information is not used. If it was, the header information would be overwritten the first time this area was used.

1058-1059 Locks the swap list and the swap device.

1060-1062 Fills in the remaining fields in the `swap_info_struct`.

1063-1064 Updates global statistics for the number of available swap pages (`nr_swap_pages`) and the total number of swap pages (`total_swap_pages`).

1065-1066 Prints an informational message about the swap activation.

```
1068        /* insert swap space into swap_list: */
1069        prev = -1;
1070        for (i = swap_list.head; i >= 0; i = swap_info[i].next) {
1071          if (p->prio >= swap_info[i].prio) {
1072            break;
1073          }
1074          prev = i;
1075        }
1076        p->next = i;
1077        if (prev < 0) {
1078          swap_list.head = swap_list.next = p - swap_info;
1079        } else {
1080          swap_info[prev].next = p - swap_info;
1081        }
1082        swap_device_unlock(p);
1083        swap_list_unlock();
1084        error = 0;
1085        goto out;
```

1070-1080 Inserts the new swap area into the correct slot in the swap list based on priority.

1082 Unlocks the swap device.

1083 Unlocks the swap list.

1084-1085 Returns success.

```
1086 bad_swap:
1087        if (bdev)
1088          blkdev_put(bdev, BDEV_SWAP);
1089 bad_swap_2:
1090        swap_list_lock();
1091        swap_map = p->swap_map;
```

```
1092            nd.mnt = p->swap_vfsmnt;
1093            nd.dentry = p->swap_file;
1094            p->swap_device = 0;
1095            p->swap_file = NULL;
1096            p->swap_vfsmnt = NULL;
1097            p->swap_map = NULL;
1098            p->flags = 0;
1099            if (!(swap_flags & SWAP_FLAG_PREFER))
1100               ++least_priority;
1101            swap_list_unlock();
1102            if (swap_map)
1103               vfree(swap_map);
1104            path_release(&nd);
1105 out:
1106            if (swap_header)
1107               free_page((long) swap_header);
1108            unlock_kernel();
1109            return error;
1110 }
```

1087-1088 Drops the reference to the block device.

1090-1104 This is the error path where the swap list needs to be unlocked, the slot in swap_info reset to being unused and the memory allocated for swap_map freed if it was assigned.

1104 Drops the reference to the special file.

1106-1107 Releases the page containing the swap header information because it is no longer needed.

1108 Drops the Big Kernel Lock.

1109 Returns the error or success value.

K.4.2 Function: swap_setup() *(mm/swap.c)*

This function is called during the initialization of kswapd to set the size of page_cluster. This variable determines how many pages readahead from files and from backing storage when paging in data.

```
100 void __init swap_setup(void)
101 {
102     unsigned long megs = num_physpages >> (20 - PAGE_SHIFT);
103
104     /* Use a smaller cluster for small-memory machines */
105     if (megs < 16)
106         page_cluster = 2;
107     else
```

```
108         page_cluster = 3;
109     /*
110      * Right now other parts of the system means that we
111      * _really_ don't want to cluster much more
112      */
113 }
```

102 Calculates how much memory the system has in megabytes.

105 In low memory systems, this sets page_cluster to 2, which means that, at most, four pages will be paged in from disk during readahead.

108 If not, readahead will be eight pages.

K.5   Deactivating a Swap Area

Contents

K.5.1   Function: `sys_swapoff()`   *(mm/swapfile.c)*

This function is principally concerned with updating the `swap_info_struct` and the swap lists. The main task of paging in all pages in the area is the responsibility of `try_to_unuse()`. The function tasks are broadly the following:

- Call `user_path_walk()` to acquire the information about the special file to be deactivated and then take the BKL.

- Remove the `swap_info_struct` from the swap list and update the global statistics on the number of swap pages available (`nr_swap_pages`) and the total number of swap entries (`total_swap_pages`). After this is acquired, the BKL can be released again.

- Call `try_to_unuse()`, which will page in all pages from the swap area to be deactivated.

- If there was not enough available memory to page in all the entries, the swap area is reinserted back into the running system because it cannot be simply dropped. If it succeeded, the `swap_info_struct` is placed into an uninitialized state, and the `swap_map` memory freed with `vfree()`.

```
720 asmlinkage long sys_swapoff(const char * specialfile)
721 {
722     struct swap_info_struct * p = NULL;
723     unsigned short *swap_map;
724     struct nameidata nd;
725     int i, type, prev;
726     int err;
727
728     if (!capable(CAP_SYS_ADMIN))
729         return -EPERM;
730
731     err = user_path_walk(specialfile, &nd);
732     if (err)
733         goto out;
734
```

728-729 Only the superuser or a process with CAP_SYS_ADMIN capabilities may deactivate an area.

731-732 Acquires information about the special file representing the swap area with user_path_walk(). Goto out if an error occured.

```
735        lock_kernel();
736        prev = -1;
737        swap_list_lock();
738        for (type = swap_list.head; type >= 0;
            type = swap_info[type].next) {
739            p = swap_info + type;
740            if ((p->flags & SWP_WRITEOK) == SWP_WRITEOK) {
741                if (p->swap_file == nd.dentry)
742                    break;
743            }
744            prev = type;
745        }
746        err = -EINVAL;
747        if (type < 0) {
748            swap_list_unlock();
749            goto out_dput;
750        }
751
752        if (prev < 0) {
753            swap_list.head = p->next;
754        } else {
755            swap_info[prev].next = p->next;
756        }
757        if (type == swap_list.next) {
758            /* just pick something that's safe... */
759            swap_list.next = swap_list.head;
760        }
761        nr_swap_pages -= p->pages;
762        total_swap_pages -= p->pages;
763        p->flags = SWP_USED;
```

Acquires the BKL, finds the swap_info_struct for the area to be deactivated and removes it from the swap list.

735 Acquires the BKL.

737 Locks the swap list.

738-745 Traverses the swap list and finds the swap_info_struct for the requested area. It uses the dentry to identify the area.

747-750 If the struct could not be found, this returns.

752-760 Removes from the swap list, making sure that this is not the head.

761 Updates the total number of free swap slots.

762 Updates the total number of existing swap slots.

763 Marks the area as active, but may not be written to.

```
764        swap_list_unlock();
765        unlock_kernel();
766        err = try_to_unuse(type);
```

764 Unlocks the swap list.

765 Releases the BKL.

766 Pages in all pages from this swap area.

```
767        lock_kernel();
768        if (err) {
769            /* re-insert swap space back into swap_list */
770            swap_list_lock();
771            for (prev = -1, i = swap_list.head;
                     i >= 0;
                     prev = i, i = swap_info[i].next)
772                if (p->prio >= swap_info[i].prio)
773                    break;
774            p->next = i;
775            if (prev < 0)
776                swap_list.head = swap_list.next = p - swap_info;
777            else
778                swap_info[prev].next = p - swap_info;
779            nr_swap_pages += p->pages;
780            total_swap_pages += p->pages;
781            p->flags = SWP_WRITEOK;
782            swap_list_unlock();
783            goto out_dput;
784        }
```

This block acquires the BKL. If we failed to page in all pages, then it reinserts the area into the swap list.

767 Acquires the BKL.

770 Locks the swap list.

771-778 Reinserts the area into the swap list. The position it is inserted at depends on the swap area priority.

779-780 Updates the global statistics.

Swap Management

781 Marks the area as safe to write to again.

782-783 Unlocks the swap list and returns.

```
785     if (p->swap_device)
786         blkdev_put(p->swap_file->d_inode->i_bdev, BDEV_SWAP);
787     path_release(&nd);
788
789     swap_list_lock();
790     swap_device_lock(p);
791     nd.mnt = p->swap_vfsmnt;
792     nd.dentry = p->swap_file;
793     p->swap_vfsmnt = NULL;
794     p->swap_file = NULL;
795     p->swap_device = 0;
796     p->max = 0;
797     swap_map = p->swap_map;
798     p->swap_map = NULL;
799     p->flags = 0;
800     swap_device_unlock(p);
801     swap_list_unlock();
802     vfree(swap_map);
803     err = 0;
804
805 out_dput:
806     unlock_kernel();
807     path_release(&nd);
808 out:
809     return err;
810 }
```

This block is used if the swap area was successfully deactivated to close the block device and mark the **swap_info_struct** free.

785-786 Closes the block device.

787 Releases the path information.

789-790 Acquires the swap list and swap device lock.

791-799 Resets the fields in **swap_info_struct** to default values.

800-801 Releases the swap list and swap device.

801 Frees the memory used for the **swap_map**.

806 Releases the BKL.

807 Releases the path information in the event we reached here by the error path.

809 Returns success or failure.

K.5.2   Function: `try_to_unuse()`   *(mm/swapfile.c)*

This function is heavily commented in the source code, albeit it consists of speculation or is slightly inaccurate at parts. The comments are omitted here for brevity.

```
513 static int try_to_unuse(unsigned int type)
514 {
515     struct swap_info_struct * si = &swap_info[type];
516     struct mm_struct *start_mm;
517     unsigned short *swap_map;
518     unsigned short swcount;
519     struct page *page;
520     swp_entry_t entry;
521     int i = 0;
522     int retval = 0;
523     int reset_overflow = 0;
525
540     start_mm = &init_mm;
541     atomic_inc(&init_mm.mm_users);
542
```

540-541 The starting `mm_struct` to page in pages for is `init_mm`. The count is incremented even though this particular struct will not disappear to prevent having to write special cases in the remainder of the function.

```
556     while ((i = find_next_to_unuse(si, i))) {
557         /*
558          * Get a page for the entry, using the existing swap
559          * cache page if there is one.  Otherwise, get a clean
560          * page and read the swap into it.
561          */
562         swap_map = &si->swap_map[i];
563         entry = SWP_ENTRY(type, i);
564         page = read_swap_cache_async(entry);
565         if (!page) {
572             if (!*swap_map)
573                 continue;
574             retval = -ENOMEM;
575             break;
576         }
577
578         /*
579          * Don't hold on to start_mm if it looks like exiting.
580          */
581         if (atomic_read(&start_mm->mm_users) == 1) {
582             mmput(start_mm);
583             start_mm = &init_mm;
```

```
584                atomic_inc(&init_mm.mm_users);
585           }
```

556 This is the beginning of the major loop in this function. Starting from the beginning of the `swap_map`, it searches for the next entry to be freed with `find_next_to_unuse()` until all swap map entries have been paged in.

562-564 Gets the `swp_entry_t` and calls `read_swap_cache_async()` (See Section K.3.1.1) to find the page in the swap cache or to have a new page allocated for reading in from the disk.

565-576 If we failed to get the page, it means the slot has already been freed independently by another process or thread (process could be exiting elsewhere) or we are out of memory. If independently freed, we continue to the next map, or we return `-ENOMEM`.

581 Checks to make sure this mm is not exiting. If it is, it decrements its count and goes back to `init_mm`.

```
587           /*
588            * Wait for and lock page.  When do_swap_page races with
589            * try_to_unuse, do_swap_page can handle the fault much
590            * faster than try_to_unuse can locate the entry.  This
591            * apparently redundant "wait_on_page" lets try_to_unuse
592            * defer to do_swap_page in such a case - in some tests,
593            * do_swap_page and try_to_unuse repeatedly compete.
594            */
595           wait_on_page(page);
596           lock_page(page);
597
598           /*
599            * Remove all references to entry, without blocking.
600            * Whenever we reach init_mm, there's no address space
601            * to search, but use it as a reminder to search shmem.
602            */
603           shmem = 0;
604           swcount = *swap_map;
605           if (swcount > 1) {
606               flush_page_to_ram(page);
607               if (start_mm == &init_mm)
608                   shmem = shmem_unuse(entry, page);
609               else
610                   unuse_process(start_mm, entry, page);
611           }
```

595 Waits on the page to complete I/O. After it returns, we know for a fact the page exists in memory with the same information as that on disk.

596 Locks the page.

604 Gets the swap map reference count.

605 If the count is positive, then...

606 As the page is about to be inserted into process pagetables, it must be freed from the D-Cache, or the process may not "see" changes made to the page by the kernel.

607-608 If we are using the `init_mm`, this calls `shmem_unuse()` (See Section L.6.2), which will free the page from any shared memory regions that are in use.

610 If not, this updates the PTE in the current mm, which references this page.

```
612            if (*swap_map > 1) {
613                    int set_start_mm = (*swap_map >= swcount);
614                    struct list_head *p = &start_mm->mmlist;
615                    struct mm_struct *new_start_mm = start_mm;
616                    struct mm_struct *mm;
617
618                    spin_lock(&mmlist_lock);
619                    while (*swap_map > 1 &&
620                        (p = p->next) != &start_mm->mmlist) {
621                        mm = list_entry(p, struct mm_struct,
                                    mmlist);
622                        swcount = *swap_map;
623                        if (mm == &init_mm) {
624                            set_start_mm = 1;
625                            spin_unlock(&mmlist_lock);
626                            shmem = shmem_unuse(entry, page);
627                            spin_lock(&mmlist_lock);
628                        } else
629                            unuse_process(mm, entry, page);
630                        if (set_start_mm && *swap_map < swcount) {
631                            new_start_mm = mm;
632                            set_start_mm = 0;
633                        }
634                    }
635                    atomic_inc(&new_start_mm->mm_users);
636                    spin_unlock(&mmlist_lock);
637                    mmput(start_mm);
638                    start_mm = new_start_mm;
639            }
```

612-637 If an entry still exists, this begins traversing through all `mm_structs` to find references to this page and updates the respective PTE.

618 Locks the mm list.

619-632 Keeps searching until all `mm_structs` have been found. Do not traverse the full list more than once.

621 Gets the `mm_struct` for this list entry.

623-627 Calls `shmem_unuse()`(See Section L.6.2) if the mm is `init_mm` because that indicates that is a page from the virtual filesystem. If not, it calls `unuse_process()` (See Section K.5.3) to traverse the current process's pagetables searching for the swap entry. If found, the entry will be freed, and the page reinstantiated in the PTE.

630-633 Records if we need to start searching `mm_structs` starting from `init_mm` again.

```
654             if (*swap_map == SWAP_MAP_MAX) {
655                     swap_list_lock();
656                     swap_device_lock(si);
657                     nr_swap_pages++;
658                     *swap_map = 1;
659                     swap_device_unlock(si);
660                     swap_list_unlock();
661                     reset_overflow = 1;
662             }
```

654 If the swap map entry is permanently mapped, we have to hope that all processes have their PTEs updated to point to the page and, in reality, that the swap map entry is free. In reality, it is highly unlikely a slot would be permanently reserved in the first place.

654-661 Locks the list and swap device, sets the swap map entry to 1, unlocks them again and records that a reset overflow occured.

```
683             if ((*swap_map > 1) && PageDirty(page) &&
                        PageSwapCache(page)) {
684                     rw_swap_page(WRITE, page);
685                     lock_page(page);
686             }
687             if (PageSwapCache(page)) {
688                     if (shmem)
689                             swap_duplicate(entry);
690                     else
691                             delete_from_swap_cache(page);
692             }
```

683-686 In the very rare event a reference still exists to the page, this writes the page back to disk so, at least if another process really has a reference to it, it will copy the page back in from disk correctly.

687-689 If the page is in the swap cache and belongs to the shared memory filesystem, a new reference is taken to it with `swap_duplicate()` so that we can try and remove it again later with `shmem_unuse()`.

691 If not, for normal pages, this just deletes them from the swap cache.

```
699        SetPageDirty(page);
700        UnlockPage(page);
701        page_cache_release(page);
```

699 Marks the page dirty so that the swap out code will preserve the page, and, if it needs to remove it again, it will write it correctly to a new swap area.

700 Unlocks the page.

701 Releases our reference to it in the pagecache.

```
708        if (current->need_resched)
714            schedule();
715    }
716
717    mmput(start_mm);
718    if (reset_overflow) {
719        printk(KERN_WARNING "swapoff: cleared swap entry
                    overflow\n");
720        swap_overflow = 0;
721    }
722    return retval;
723 }
```

708-709 Calls `schedule()` if necessary so that the deactivation of swap does not hog the entire CPU.

717 Drops our reference to the mm.

718-721 If a permanently mapped page had to be removed, this prints out a warning so that, in the very unlikely event an error occurs later, there will be a hint to what might have happened.

717 Returns success or failure.

K.5.3 Function: `unuse_process()` *(mm/swapfile.c)*

This function begins the pagetable walk required to remove the requested **page** and **entry** from the process pagetables managed by **mm**. This is only required when a swap area is being deactivated, so, although expensive, it is a very rare operation. This set of functions should be instantly recognizable as a standard pagetable walk.

Swap Management

```
454 static void unuse_process(struct mm_struct * mm,
455                           swp_entry_t entry, struct page* page)
456 {
457     struct vm_area_struct* vma;
458
459     /*
460      * Go through process' page directory.
461      */
462     spin_lock(&mm->page_table_lock);
463     for (vma = mm->mmap; vma; vma = vma->vm_next) {
464         pgd_t * pgd = pgd_offset(mm, vma->vm_start);
465         unuse_vma(vma, pgd, entry, page);
466     }
467     spin_unlock(&mm->page_table_lock);
468     return;
469 }
```

462 Locks the process pagetables.

463 Moves through every VMA managed by this `mm`. Remember that one page
frame could be mapped in multiple locations.

462 Gets the PGD managing the beginning of this VMA.

465 Calls `unuse_vma()` (See Section K.5.4) to search the VMA for the `page`.

467-468 The full `mm` has been searched, so this unlocks the process pagetables and
returns.

K.5.4   Function: unuse_vma()   *(mm/swapfile.c)*

This function searches the requested VMA for pagetable entries mapping the
`page` and using the given swap `entry`. It calls `unuse_pgd()` for every PGD that
this VMA maps.

```
440 static void unuse_vma(struct vm_area_struct * vma, pgd_t *pgdir,
441                       swp_entry_t entry, struct page* page)
442 {
443     unsigned long start = vma->vm_start, end = vma->vm_end;
444
445     if (start >= end)
446         BUG();
447     do {
448         unuse_pgd(vma, pgdir, start, end - start, entry, page);
449         start = (start + PGDIR_SIZE) & PGDIR_MASK;
450         pgdir++;
451     } while (start && (start < end));
452 }
```

443 Gets the virtual addresses for the `start` and `end` of the VMA.

445-446 Checks that the `start` is not after the `end`. There would need to be serious brain damage in the kernel for this to occur.

447-451 Walks through the VMA in `PGDIR_SIZE`-sized strides until the end of the VMA is reached. This effectively walks through every PGD that maps portions of this VMA.

448 Calls `unuse_pgd()`(See Section K.5.5) to walk through just this PGD to unmap `page`.

449 Moves the virtual address `start` to the beginning of the next PGD.

450 Moves `pgdir` to the next PGD in the VMA.

K.5.5 Function: unuse_pgd() *(mm/swapfile.c)*

This function searches the requested PGD for pagetable entries mapping the `page` and using the given swap `entry`. It calls `unuse_pmd()` for every PMD this PGD maps.

```
409 static inline void unuse_pgd(struct vm_area_struct * vma, pgd_t *dir,
410         unsigned long address, unsigned long size,
411         swp_entry_t entry, struct page* page)
412 {
413     pmd_t * pmd;
414     unsigned long offset, end;
415
416     if (pgd_none(*dir))
417         return;
418     if (pgd_bad(*dir)) {
419         pgd_ERROR(*dir);
420         pgd_clear(dir);
421         return;
422     }
423     pmd = pmd_offset(dir, address);
424     offset = address & PGDIR_MASK;
425     address &= ~PGDIR_MASK;
426     end = address + size;
427     if (end > PGDIR_SIZE)
428         end = PGDIR_SIZE;
429     if (address >= end)
430         BUG();
431     do {
432         unuse_pmd(vma, pmd, address, end - address, offset, entry,
433                 page);
434         address = (address + PMD_SIZE) & PMD_MASK;
435         pmd++;
```

Swap Management

```
436        } while (address && (address < end));
437 }
```

416-417 If there is no PGD here, this returns.

418-422 If the PGD is bad, this sets the appropriate error, clears the PGD and
returns. There are very few architectures where this condition can occur.

423 Gets the address of the first PMD in this PGD.

424 Calculates `offset` as the offset within the PGD the `address` is for. Remember
that on the first time this function is called, it might be searching a partial
PGD.

425 Aligns the `address` to the PGD.

426 Calculates the `end` address of the search.

427-428 If the `end` is beyond this PGD, this sets the `end` just to the end of this
PGD.

429-430 If the starting address is after the end address, something is very seriously
wrong.

431-436 Steps through the PGD in `PMD_SIZE`-sized strides and calls `unuse_pmd()`
(See Section K.5.6) for every PMD in this PGD.

K.5.6   Function: unuse_pmd()   *(mm/swapfile.c)*
This function searches the requested PMD for pagetable entries mapping the
`page` and using the given swap `entry`. It calls `unuse_pte()` for every PTE this
PMD maps.

```
381 static inline void unuse_pmd(struct vm_area_struct * vma, pmd_t *dir,
382     unsigned long address, unsigned long size, unsigned long offset,
383     swp_entry_t entry, struct page* page)
384 {
385     pte_t * pte;
386     unsigned long end;
387
388     if (pmd_none(*dir))
389         return;
390     if (pmd_bad(*dir)) {
391         pmd_ERROR(*dir);
392         pmd_clear(dir);
393         return;
394     }
395     pte = pte_offset(dir, address);
396     offset += address & PMD_MASK;
397     address &= ~PMD_MASK;
```

```
398        end = address + size;
399        if (end > PMD_SIZE)
400            end = PMD_SIZE;
401        do {
402            unuse_pte(vma, offset+address-vma->vm_start, pte, entry, page);
403            address += PAGE_SIZE;
404            pte++;
405        } while (address && (address < end));
406 }
```

388-389 Returns if no PMD exists.

390-394 Sets the appropriate error and clears the PMD if it is bad. There are
very few architectures where this condition can occur.

395 Calculates the starting PTE for this `address`.

396 Sets `offset` to be the offset within the PMD we are starting at.

397 Aligns `address` to the PMD.

398-400 Calculates the `end` address. If it is beyond the end of this PMD, it sets
it to the end of this PMD.

401-405 Steps through this PMD in `PAGE_SIZE`-sized chunks and calls
`unuse_pte()` (See Section K.5.7) for each PTE.

K.5.7   Function: unuse_pte()   *(mm/swapfile.c)*
This function checks if the PTE at `dir` matches the `entry` we are searching for.
If it does, the swap entry is freed, and a reference is taken to the page representing
the PTE that will be updated to map it.

```
365 static inline void unuse_pte(struct vm_area_struct * vma,
            unsigned long address,
366            pte_t *dir, swp_entry_t entry, struct page* page)
367 {
368     pte_t pte = *dir;
369
370     if (likely(pte_to_swp_entry(pte).val != entry.val))
371         return;
372     if (unlikely(pte_none(pte) || pte_present(pte)))
373         return;
374     get_page(page);
375     set_pte(dir, pte_mkold(mk_pte(page, vma->vm_page_prot)));
376     swap_free(entry);
377     ++vma->vm_mm->rss;
378 }
```

370-371 If the `entry` does not match the PTE, this returns.

372-373 If there is no PTE or it is already present (meaning there is no way this `entry` is mapped here), this returns.

374 Otherwise, we have found the entry we are looking for, so it takes a reference to the page because a new PTE is about to map it.

375 Updates the PTE to map `page`.

376 Frees the swap entry.

377 Increments the RSS count for this process.

Shared Memory Virtual Filesystem

Contents

Shared Memory
Virtual Filesystem

L.1   Initializing shmfs

Contents

L.1.1   Function: `init_tmpfs()`   *(mm/shmem.c)*

This function is responsible for registering and mounting the `tmpfs` and `shmemfs`
filesystems.

```
1451 #ifdef CONFIG_TMPFS
1453 static DECLARE_FSTYPE(shmem_fs_type, "shm",
                         shmem_read_super, FS_LITTER);
1454 static DECLARE_FSTYPE(tmpfs_fs_type, "tmpfs",
                         shmem_read_super, FS_LITTER);
1455 #else
1456 static DECLARE_FSTYPE(tmpfs_fs_type, "tmpfs",
                         shmem_read_super, FS_LITTER|FS_NOMOUNT);
1457 #endif

1560 static int __init init_tmpfs(void)
1561 {
1562         int error;
1563
1564         error = register_filesystem(&tmpfs_fs_type);
1565         if (error) {
1566                 printk(KERN_ERR "Could not register tmpfs\n");
1567                 goto out3;
1568         }
1569 #ifdef CONFIG_TMPFS
1570         error = register_filesystem(&shmem_fs_type);
1571         if (error) {
1572                 printk(KERN_ERR "Could not register shm fs\n");
1573                 goto out2;
1574         }
1575         devfs_mk_dir(NULL, "shm", NULL);
1576 #endif
1577         shm_mnt = kern_mount(&tmpfs_fs_type);
1578         if (IS_ERR(shm_mnt)) {
1579                 error = PTR_ERR(shm_mnt);
1580                 printk(KERN_ERR "Could not kern_mount tmpfs\n");
1581                 goto out1;
1582         }
1583
1584         /* The internal instance should not do size checking */
```

```
1585          shmem_set_size(SHMEM_SB(shm_mnt->mnt_sb),
                              ULONG_MAX, ULONG_MAX);
1586          return 0;
1587
1588 out1:
1589 #ifdef CONFIG_TMPFS
1590          unregister_filesystem(&shmem_fs_type);
1591 out2:
1592 #endif
1593          unregister_filesystem(&tmpfs_fs_type);
1594 out3:
1595          shm_mnt = ERR_PTR(error);
1596          return error;
1597 }
1598 module_init(init_tmpfs)
```

1551 The shm filesystem is only mountable if CONFIG_TMPFS is defined at compile time. Even if it is not specified, a tmpfs will still be set up for anonymous shared memory resulting from a fork().

1553 DECLARE_FSTYPE(), declared in <linux/fs.h>, declares tmpfs_fs_type as type struct file_system_type and fills in four fields. "tmpfs" is its human-readable name. shmem_read_super() is the function that is used to read the superblock for the filesystem (a detailed description of superblocks and how they pertain to filesystems is beyond the scope of this book). FS_LITTER is a flag that indicates the filesystem tree should be maintained in the dcache. Finally, the macro sets the module owner of the filesystem to be the module loading the filesystem.

1560 __init places this function in the init section. This means that, after the kernel has finished bootstrapping, the code for the function will be removed.

1564-1568 Registers the filesystem tmpfs_fs_type, which was declared in line 1433. If it fails, goto out3 where the appropriate error will be returned.

1569-1574 If tmpfs is specified at configure time, this registers the shmem filesystem. If it fails, goto out2 where tmpfs_fs_type will be unregistered before returning the error.

1575 If /dev/ is being managed by the device filesystem (devfs), this creates a new shm directory. If the kernel does not use devfs, the system administrator must manually create the directory.

1577 kern_mount() mounts a filesystem internally. In other words, the filesystem is mounted and active, but it is not visible to the user anywhere in the VFS. The mount point is shm_mnt, which is local to the shmem.c file and of type struct vfsmount. This variable is needed for searching the filesystem and for unmounting it later.

1578-1582 Ensures the filesystem is mounted correctly, but, if it did not, goto `out1` where the filesystems will be unregistered before returning the error.

1585 The function `shmem_set_size()` (See Section L.1.3) is responsible for setting the maximum number of blocks and inodes that may be created in this filesystem.

1598 `module_init()` in this instance indicates that `init_shmem_fs()` should be called when the module is loaded. If it is compiled directly into the kernel, the function will be called on system startup.

L.1.2 Function: `shmem_read_super()` *(mm/shmem.c)*

This is the callback function provided for the filesystem that reads the superblock. With an ordinary filesystem, this would entail reading the information from the disk, but, because this is a RAM-based filesystem, it instead populates a `struct super_block`.

```
1452 static struct super_block *shmem_read_super(struct super_block *sb,
                                                 void* data, int silent)
1453 {
1454     struct inode *inode;
1455     struct dentry *root;
1456     unsigned long blocks, inodes;
1457     int mode   = S_IRWXUGO | S_ISVTX;
1458     uid_t uid = current->fsuid;
1459     gid_t gid = current->fsgid;
1460     struct shmem_sb_info *sbinfo = SHMEM_SB(sb);
1461     struct sysinfo si;
1462
1463     /*
1464      * Per default we only allow half of the physical ram per
1465      * tmpfs instance
1466      */
1467     si_meminfo(&si);
1468     blocks = inodes = si.totalram / 2;
1469
1470 #ifdef CONFIG_TMPFS
1471     if (shmem_parse_options(data, &mode, &uid,
                                 &gid, &blocks, &inodes))
1472         return NULL;
1473 #endif
1474
1475     spin_lock_init(&sbinfo->stat_lock);
1476     sbinfo->max_blocks = blocks;
1477     sbinfo->free_blocks = blocks;
1478     sbinfo->max_inodes = inodes;
1479     sbinfo->free_inodes = inodes;
```

Shared Memory Virtual Filesystem

```
1480        sb->s_maxbytes = SHMEM_MAX_BYTES;
1481        sb->s_blocksize = PAGE_CACHE_SIZE;
1482        sb->s_blocksize_bits = PAGE_CACHE_SHIFT;
1483        sb->s_magic = TMPFS_MAGIC;
1484        sb->s_op = &shmem_ops;
1485        inode = shmem_get_inode(sb, S_IFDIR | mode, 0);
1486        if (!inode)
1487            return NULL;
1488
1489        inode->i_uid = uid;
1490        inode->i_gid = gid;
1491        root = d_alloc_root(inode);
1492        if (!root) {
1493            iput(inode);
1494            return NULL;
1495        }
1496        sb->s_root = root;
1497        return sb;
1498 }
```

1471 The parameters are the following:

- **sb** is the super_block to populate.

- **data** contains the mount arguments.

- **silent** is unused in this function.

1457-1459 Sets the default mode, uid and gid. These may be overridden with the parameters passed as mount options.

1460 Each super_block is allowed to have a filesystem-specific struct that is contained within a union called super_block→u. The macro SHMEM_SB() returns the struct shmem_sb_info contained within this union.

1467 si_meminfo() populates struct sysinfo with total memory, available memory and usage statistics. The function is defined in arch/i386/mm/init.c and is architecture dependent.

1468 By default, this only allows the filesystem to consume half of total available physical memory.

1471-1472 If tmpfs is available, this parses the mount options and allows them to override the defaults.

1475 Acquires the lock protecting sbinfo, which is the struct shmem_sb_info in the super_block.

1483 Populates the sb and sbinfo fields.

1484 The `shmem_ops` is a struct of function pointers for super block operations, such as remounting the filesystem and deleting an inode.

1485-1487 This block allocates a special inode, that represents the root of the filesystem.

1489-1490 Sets the uid and gid of the root of the new filesystem.

1496 Sets the root inode into the `super_block`.

1497 Returns the populated superblock.

L.1.3   Function: `shmem_set_size()`   *(mm/shmem.c)*

This function updates the number of available blocks and inodes in the filesystem. It is set while the filesystem is being mounted or remounted.

```
861 static int shmem_set_size(struct shmem_sb_info *info,
862                             unsigned long max_blocks,
                                unsigned long max_inodes)
863 {
864     int error;
865     unsigned long blocks, inodes;
866
867     spin_lock(&info->stat_lock);
868     blocks = info->max_blocks - info->free_blocks;
869     inodes = info->max_inodes - info->free_inodes;
870     error = -EINVAL;
871     if (max_blocks < blocks)
872         goto out;
873     if (max_inodes < inodes)
874         goto out;
875     error = 0;
876     info->max_blocks  = max_blocks;
877     info->free_blocks = max_blocks - blocks;
878     info->max_inodes  = max_inodes;
879     info->free_inodes = max_inodes - inodes;
880 out:
881     spin_unlock(&info->stat_lock);
882     return error;
883 }
```

861 The parameters are the `info` representing the filesystem superblock, the maximum number of blocks (`max_blocks`) and the maximum number of inodes (`max_inodes`).

867 Locks the superblock info spinlock.

868 Calculates the number of `blocks` currently in use by the filesystem. On initial mount, this is unimportant, but, if the filesystem is being remounted, the function must ensure that the new filesystem is not too small.

869 Calculates the number of `inodes` currently in use.

871-872 If the remounted filesystem would have too few blocks to store the current information, goto `out` to return `-EINVAL`.

873-874 Similarly, makes sure there are enough available inodes or returns `-EINVAL`.

875 It is safe to mount the filesystem, so this sets `error` to 0 indicating that this operation will be successful.

876-877 Sets the maximum number of blocks and number of available blocks in the filesystems' superblock `info` struct.

878-879 Sets the maximum and available number of inodes.

881 Unlocks the filesystems' superblock `info` struct.

882 Returns 0 if successful or `-EINVAL` if not.

L.2   Creating Files in tmpfs

Contents

L.2.1   Function: shmem_create()   *(mm/shmem.c)*

This is the top-level function called when creating a new file.

```
1164 static int shmem_create(struct inode *dir,
                 struct dentry *dentry,
                 int mode)
1165 {
1166     return shmem_mknod(dir, dentry, mode | S_IFREG, 0);
1167 }
```

1164 The parameters are the following:

- **dir** is the inode of the directory the new file is being created in.
- **entry** is the dentry of the new file being created.
- **mode** is the flags passed to the **open** system call.

1166 Calls shmem_mknod()(See Section L.2.2) and adds the S_IFREG flag to the mode flags so that a regular file will be created.

L.2.2   Function: shmem_mknod()   *(mm/shmem.c)*

```
1139 static int shmem_mknod(struct inode *dir,
                 struct dentry *dentry,
                 int mode, int dev)
1140 {
1141     struct inode *inode = shmem_get_inode(dir->i_sb, mode, dev);
1142     int error = -ENOSPC;
1143
1144     if (inode) {
1145         dir->i_size += BOGO_DIRENT_SIZE;
1146         dir->i_ctime = dir->i_mtime = CURRENT_TIME;
1147         d_instantiate(dentry, inode);
1148         dget(dentry); /* Extra count - pin the dentry in core */
1149         error = 0;
1150     }
1151     return error;
1152 }
```

1141 Calls shmem_get_inode() (See Section L.2.3) to create a new inode.

Shared Memory
Virtual Filesystem

1144 If the inode was successfully created, this updates the directory statistics and instantiates the new file.

1145 Updates the size of the directory.

1146 Updates the `ctime` and `mtime` fields.

1147 Instantiates the inode.

1148 Takes a reference to the dentry so that it will be pinned and not accidentally reclaimed during pageout. Unlike normal files, there is no automatic way of recreating dentries after they are deleted.

1149 Indicates the call ended successfully.

1151 Returns success or `-ENOSPC` on error.

L.2.3   Function: shmem_get_inode()   *(mm/shmem.c)*

```
809 struct inode *shmem_get_inode(struct super_block *sb,
                                 int mode,
                                 int dev)
810 {
811     struct inode *inode;
812     struct shmem_inode_info *info;
813     struct shmem_sb_info *sbinfo = SHMEM_SB(sb);
814
815     spin_lock(&sbinfo->stat_lock);
816     if (!sbinfo->free_inodes) {
817         spin_unlock(&sbinfo->stat_lock);
818         return NULL;
819     }
820     sbinfo->free_inodes--;
821     spin_unlock(&sbinfo->stat_lock);
822
823     inode = new_inode(sb);
```

This preamble section is responsible for updating the free inode count and allocating an inode with `new_inode()`.

815 Acquires the `sbinfo` spinlock because it is about to be updated.

816-819 Makes sure there are free inodes, and if not, it returns NULL.

820-821 Updates the free inode count and frees the lock.

823 `new_inode()` is part of the filesystem layer and declared in `<linux/fs.h>`. Exactly how it works is beyond the scope of this document, but the summary is simple. It allocates an inode from the slab allocator, zeros most fields and populates inode→i_sb, inode→i_dev and inode→i_blkbits based on information in the super block.

```
824     if (inode) {
825         inode->i_mode = mode;
826         inode->i_uid = current->fsuid;
827         inode->i_gid = current->fsgid;
828         inode->i_blksize = PAGE_CACHE_SIZE;
829         inode->i_blocks = 0;
830         inode->i_rdev = NODEV;
831         inode->i_mapping->a_ops = &shmem_aops;
832         inode->i_atime = inode->i_mtime
                            = inode->i_ctime
                            = CURRENT_TIME;
833         info = SHMEM_I(inode);
834         info->inode = inode;
835         spin_lock_init(&info->lock);
836         switch (mode & S_IFMT) {
837         default:
838             init_special_inode(inode, mode, dev);
839             break;
840         case S_IFREG:
841             inode->i_op = &shmem_inode_operations;
842             inode->i_fop = &shmem_file_operations;
843             spin_lock(&shmem_ilock);
844             list_add_tail(&info->list, &shmem_inodes);
845             spin_unlock(&shmem_ilock);
846             break;
847         case S_IFDIR:
848             inode->i_nlink++;
849             /* Some things misbehave if size == 0 on a directory */
850             inode->i_size = 2 * BOGO_DIRENT_SIZE;
851             inode->i_op = &shmem_dir_inode_operations;
852             inode->i_fop = &dcache_dir_ops;
853             break;
854         case S_IFLNK:
855             break;
856         }
857     }
858     return inode;
859 }
```

824-858 Fills in the inode fields if created successfully.

825-830 Fills in the basic inode information.

831 Sets the `address_space_operations` to use `shmem_aops`, which sets up the function `shmem_writepage()`(See Section L.6.1) to be used as a page writeback callback for the `address_space`.

832-834 Fills in more basic information.

835-836 Initializes the inodes semaphore and spinlock.

836-856 Determines how to fill the remaining fields based on the mode flags passed in.

838 In this case, a special inode is being created. Specifically, this is while the filesystem is being mounted and the root inode is being created.

840-846 Creates an inode for a regular file. The main point to note here is that the inode→i_op and inode→i_fop fields are set to shmem_inode_operations, and shmem_file_operations, respectively.

847-852 Creates an inode for a new directory. The i_nlink and i_size fields are updated to show the increased number of files and the size of the directory. The main point to note here is that the inode→i_op and inode→i_fop fields are set to shmem_dir_inode_operations and dcach_dir_ops, respectively.

854-855 If linking a file, this does nothing for now because it is handled by the parent function shmem_link().

858 Returns the new inode or NULL if it could not be created.

L.3 File Operations in tmpfs

Contents

L.3.1 Memory Mapping

The tasks for memory mapping a virtual file are simple. The only changes that need to be made are to update the VMAs `vm_operations_struct` field (vma→vm_ops) to use the shmfs equivalents for faulting.

L.3.1.1 Function: shmem_mmap() *(mm/shmem.c)*

```
796 static int shmem_mmap(struct file * file, struct vm_area_struct * vma)
797 {
798     struct vm_operations_struct *ops;
799     struct inode *inode = file->f_dentry->d_inode;
800
801     ops = &shmem_vm_ops;
802     if (!S_ISREG(inode->i_mode))
803         return -EACCES;
804     UPDATE_ATIME(inode);
805     vma->vm_ops = ops;
806     return 0;
807 }
```

801 ops is now the `vm_operations_struct` to be used for the virtual filesystem.

802 Makes sure that the inode being mapped is a regular file. If not, it returns -EACCESS.

804 Updates the `atime` for the inode to show it was accessed.

805 Updates vma→vm_ops so that `shmem_nopage()` (See Section L.5.1.1) will be used to handle page faults within the mapping.

L.3.2   Reading Files

L.3.2.1   Function: `shmem_file_read()`   *(mm/shmem.c)*

This is the top-level function called for **read()**ing a tmpfs file.

```
1088 static ssize_t shmem_file_read(struct file *filp, char *buf,
                                    size_t count, loff_t *ppos)
1089 {
1090     read_descriptor_t desc;
1091
1092     if ((ssize_t) count < 0)
1093         return -EINVAL;
1094     if (!access_ok(VERIFY_WRITE, buf, count))
1095         return -EFAULT;
1096     if (!count)
1097         return 0;
1098
1099     desc.written = 0;
1100     desc.count = count;
1101     desc.buf = buf;
1102     desc.error = 0;
1103
1104     do_shmem_file_read(filp, ppos, &desc);
1105     if (desc.written)
1106         return desc.written;
1107     return desc.error;
1108 }
```

1088 The parameters are the following:

- **filp** is a pointer to the **struct file** being read.
- **buf** is the buffer that should be filled.
- **count** is the number of bytes that should be read.
- **ppos** is the current position.

1092-1093 count cannot be negative.

1094-1095 access_ok() ensures that it is safe to write count number of bytes to the userspace buffer. If it can't, -EFAULT will be returned.

1099-1102 Initializes a read_descriptor_t struct, which will eventually be passed to file_read_actor()(See Section L.3.2.3).

1104 Calls do_shmem_file_read() to start performing the actual read.

1105-1106 Returns the number of bytes that were written to the userspace buffer.

1107 If none were written, it returns the error.

L.3.2.2   Function: do_shmem_file_read()   *(mm/shmem.c)*

This function retrieves the pages needed for the file read with shmem_getpage()
and calls file_read_actor() to copy the data to userspace.

```
1003 static void do_shmem_file_read(struct file *filp,
                                    loff_t *ppos,
        read_descriptor_t *desc)
1004 {
1005     struct inode *inode = filp->f_dentry->d_inode;
1006     struct address_space *mapping = inode->i_mapping;
1007     unsigned long index, offset;
1008
1009     index = *ppos >> PAGE_CACHE_SHIFT;
1010     offset = *ppos & ~PAGE_CACHE_MASK;
1011
1012     for (;;) {
1013         struct page *page = NULL;
1014         unsigned long end_index, nr, ret;
1015
1016         end_index = inode->i_size >> PAGE_CACHE_SHIFT;
1017         if (index > end_index)
1018             break;
1019         if (index == end_index) {
1020             nr = inode->i_size & ~PAGE_CACHE_MASK;
1021             if (nr <= offset)
1022                 break;
1023         }
1024
1025         desc->error = shmem_getpage(inode, index, &page, SGP_READ);
1026         if (desc->error) {
1027             if (desc->error == -EINVAL)
1028                 desc->error = 0;
1029             break;
1030         }
1031
1036         nr = PAGE_CACHE_SIZE;
1037         end_index = inode->i_size >> PAGE_CACHE_SHIFT;
1038         if (index == end_index) {
1039             nr = inode->i_size & ~PAGE_CACHE_MASK;
1040             if (nr <= offset) {
1041                 page_cache_release(page);
1042                 break;
1043             }
1044         }
1045         nr -= offset;
1046
```

```
1047              if (page != ZERO_PAGE(0)) {
1053                  if (mapping->i_mmap_shared != NULL)
1054                      flush_dcache_page(page);
1055                  /*
1056                   * Mark the page accessed if we read the
1057                   * beginning or we just did an lseek.
1058                   */
1059                  if (!offset || !filp->f_reada)
1060                      mark_page_accessed(page);
1061              }
1062
1073              ret = file_read_actor(desc, page, offset, nr);
1074              offset += ret;
1075              index += offset >> PAGE_CACHE_SHIFT;
1076              offset &= ~PAGE_CACHE_MASK;
1077
1078              page_cache_release(page);
1079              if (ret != nr || !desc->count)
1080                  break;
1081          }
1082
1083          *ppos = ((loff_t) index << PAGE_CACHE_SHIFT) + offset;
1084          filp->f_reada = 1;
1085          UPDATE_ATIME(inode);
1086 }
```

1005-1006 Retrieves the `inode` and `mapping` using the `struct file`.

1009 `index` is the page index within the file that contains the data.

1010 `offset` is the offset within the page that is currently being read.

1012-1081 Loops until the requested number of bytes has been read. `nr` is the number of bytes that are still to be read within the current page. `desc`→`count` starts as the number of bytes to read and is decremented by `file_read_actor()` (See Section L.3.2.3).

1016-1018 `end_index` is the index of the last page in the file. It breaks when the end of the file is reached.

1019-1023 When the last page is reached, this sets `nr` to be the number of bytes to be read within this page. If the file pointer is after `nr`, this breaks because there is no more data to be read. This could happen after the file was truncated.

1025-1030 `shmem_getpage()` (See Section L.5.1.2) will locate the requested page in the page cache, swap cache or page it in. If an error occurs, this records it in `desc`→`error` and returns.

1036 **nr** is the number of pages that must be read from the page so it initializes it to the size of a page because this full page is being read.

1037 Initializes **end_index**, which is index of the page at the end of the file.

1038-1044 If this is the last page in the file, this updates **nr** to be the number of bytes in the page. If **nr** is currently after the end of the file (could happen after truncate), this releases the reference to the page (taken by **shmem_getpage()**) and exits the loop.

1045 Updates the number of bytes to be read. Remember that **offset** is where the file reader is currently within the page.

1047-1061 If the page being read is not the global zero page, this takes care of potential aliasing problems by calling **flush_dcache_page()**. If the page is being read the first time or an **lseek()** just occured (**f_reada** is zero), this marks the page accessed with **mark_page_accesssed()**.

1073 Calls **file_read_actor()**(See Section L.3.2.3) to copy the data to userspace. It returns the number of bytes that were copied and updates the user buffer pointers and remaining count.

1074 Updates the offset within the page being read.

1075 Moves the **index** to the next page if necessary.

1076 Ensures that **offset** is an offset within a page.

1078 Releases the reference to the page being copied. The reference was taken by **shmem_getpage()**.

1079-1080 If the requested bytes have been read, this returns.

1083 Updates the file pointer.

1084 Enables file readahead.

1085 Updates the access time for the inode because it has just been read from.

L.3.2.3 Function: **file_read_actor()** *(mm/filemap.c)*

This function is responsible for copying data from a page to a userspace buffer. It is ultimately called by a number of functions, including **generic_file_read()** and **shmem_file_read()**.

```
1669 int file_read_actor(read_descriptor_t * desc,
                         struct page *page,
                         unsigned long offset,
                         unsigned long size)
1670 {
1671     char *kaddr;
```

```
1672        unsigned long left, count = desc->count;
1673
1674        if (size > count)
1675            size = count;
1676
1677        kaddr = kmap(page);
1678        left = __copy_to_user(desc->buf, kaddr + offset, size);
1679        kunmap(page);
1680
1681        if (left) {
1682            size -= left;
1683            desc->error = -EFAULT;
1684        }
1685        desc->count = count - size;
1686        desc->written += size;
1687        desc->buf += size;
1688        return size;
1689 }
```

1669 The parameters are the following:

- **desc** is a structure containing information about the read, including the buffer and the total number of bytes that are to be read from this file.

- **page** is the page containing file data that is to be copied to userspace.

- **offset** is the offset within the page that is being copied.

- **size** is the number of bytes to be read from **page**.

1672 count is now the number of bytes that are to be read from the file.

1674-1675 Makes sure to not read more bytes than are requested.

1677 Maps the page into low memory with kmap(). See Section I.1.1.

1678 Copies the data from the kernel page to the userspace buffer.

1679 Unmaps the page. See Section I.3.1.

1681-1684 If all the bytes were not copied, it must be because the buffer was not accessible. This updates size so that desc→count will reflect how many bytes are still to be copied by the read. -EFAULT will be returned to the process performing the read.

1685-1687 Updates the desc struct to show the current status of the read.

1688 Returns the number of bytes that were written to the userspace buffer.

L.3.3 Writing

L.3.3.1 Function: shmem_file_write() *(mm/shmem.c)*

```
925 shmem_file_write(struct file *file, const char *buf,
                    size_t count, loff_t *ppos)
926 {
927     struct inode    *inode = file->f_dentry->d_inode;
928     loff_t        pos;
929     unsigned long   written;
930     int           err;
931
932     if ((ssize_t) count < 0)
933         return -EINVAL;
934
935     if (!access_ok(VERIFY_READ, buf, count))
936         return -EFAULT;
937
938     down(&inode->i_sem);
939
940     pos = *ppos;
941     written = 0;
942
943     err = precheck_file_write(file, inode, &count, &pos);
944     if (err || !count)
945         goto out;
946
947     remove_suid(inode);
948     inode->i_ctime = inode->i_mtime = CURRENT_TIME;
949
```

This block is the function preamble.

927 Gets the inode that represents the file being written.

932-933 Returns -EINVAL if the user tries to write a negative number of bytes.

935-936 Returns -EFAULT if the userspace buffer is inaccessible.

938 Acquires the semaphore protecting the inode.

940 Records the beginning of where the write is taking place.

941 Initializes the written number of bytes to 0.

943 precheck_file_write() performs a number of checks to make sure the write is ok to proceed. This includes updating pos to be the end of the file if opened in append mode and checking that the process limits will not be exceeded.

944-945 If the write cannot proceed, goto out.

Shared Memory
Virtual Filesystem

947 Clears the SUID bit if it is set.

948 Updates the inodes ctime and mtime.

```
950     do {
951         struct page *page = NULL;
952         unsigned long bytes, index, offset;
953         char *kaddr;
954         int left;
955
956         offset = (pos & (PAGE_CACHE_SIZE -1)); /* Within page */
957         index = pos >> PAGE_CACHE_SHIFT;
958         bytes = PAGE_CACHE_SIZE - offset;
959         if (bytes > count)
960             bytes = count;
961
962         /*
963          * We don't hold page lock across copy from user -
964          * what would it guard against? - so no deadlock here.
965          */
966
967         err = shmem_getpage(inode, index, &page, SGP_WRITE);
968         if (err)
969             break;
970
971         kaddr = kmap(page);
972         left = __copy_from_user(kaddr + offset, buf, bytes);
973         kunmap(page);
974
975         written += bytes;
976         count -= bytes;
977         pos += bytes;
978         buf += bytes;
979         if (pos > inode->i_size)
980             inode->i_size = pos;
981
982         flush_dcache_page(page);
983         SetPageDirty(page);
984         SetPageReferenced(page);
985         page_cache_release(page);
986
987         if (left) {
988             pos -= left;
989             written -= left;
990             err = -EFAULT;
991             break;
992         }
```

```
993      } while (count);
994
995      *ppos = pos;
996      if (written)
997          err = written;
998 out:
999      up(&inode->i_sem);
1000     return err;
1001 }
```

950-993 Loops until all the requested bytes have been written.

956 Sets `offset` to be the offset within the current page being written.

957 `index` is the page index within the file currently being written.

958 `bytes` is the number of bytes within the current page remaining to be written.

959-960 If `bytes` indicates that more bytes should be written than was requested (`count`), this sets `bytes` to `count`.

967-969 Locates the page to be written to. The `SGP_WRITE` flag indicates that a page should be allocated if one does not already exist. If the page could not be found or allocated, this breaks out of the loop.

971-973 Maps the page to be written to and copies the bytes from the userspace buffer before unmapping the page again.

975 Updates the number of bytes written.

976 Updates the number of bytes remaining to write.

977 Updates the position within the file.

978 Updates the pointer within the userspace buffer.

979-980 If the file is now bigger, this updates inode→i_size.

982 Flushes the dcache to avoid aliasing problems.

983-984 Sets the page as dirty and referenced.

985 Releases the reference to the page taken by `shmem_getpage()`.

987-992 If all the requested bytes were not read from the userspace buffer, this updates the written statistics and the postition within the file and buffer.

995 Updates the file pointer.

996-997 If all the requested bytes were not written, this sets the error return variable.

999 Releases the inodes semaphore.

1000 Returns success or else returns the number of bytes remaining to be written.

Shared Memory
Virtual Filesystem

L.3.4   Symbolic Linking

L.3.4.1   Function: `shmem_symlink()`   *(mm/shmem.c)*

   This function is responsible for creating a symbolic link **symname** and for deciding where to store the information. The name of the link will be stored in the inode if the name is small enough and in a pageframe otherwise.

```
1272 static int shmem_symlink(struct inode * dir,
                              struct dentry *dentry,
                              const char * symname)
1273 {
1274     int error;
1275     int len;
1276     struct inode *inode;
1277     struct page *page = NULL;
1278     char *kaddr;
1279     struct shmem_inode_info *info;
1280
1281     len = strlen(symname) + 1;
1282     if (len > PAGE_CACHE_SIZE)
1283         return -ENAMETOOLONG;
1284
1285     inode = shmem_get_inode(dir->i_sb, S_IFLNK|S_IRWXUGO, 0);
1286     if (!inode)
1287         return -ENOSPC;
1288
1289     info = SHMEM_I(inode);
1290     inode->i_size = len-1;
```

This block performs basic sanity checks and creates a new inode for the symbolic link.

1272 The parameter **symname** is the name of the link to create.

1281 Calculates the length (**len**) of the link.

1282-1283 If the name is larger than a page, this returns **-ENAMETOOLONG**.

1285-1287 Allocates a new **inode**. Returns **-ENOSPC** if it fails.

1289 Gets the private information struct.

1290 The size of the inode is the length of the link.

```
1291     if (len <= sizeof(struct shmem_inode_info)) {
1292         /* do it inline */
1293         memcpy(info, symname, len);
1294         inode->i_op = &shmem_symlink_inline_operations;
1295     } else {
```

```
1296            error = shmem_getpage(inode, 0, &page, SGP_WRITE);
1297            if (error) {
1298                    iput(inode);
1299                    return error;
1300            }
1301            inode->i_op = &shmem_symlink_inode_operations;
1302            spin_lock(&shmem_ilock);
1303            list_add_tail(&info->list, &shmem_inodes);
1304            spin_unlock(&shmem_ilock);
1305            kaddr = kmap(page);
1306            memcpy(kaddr, symname, len);
1307            kunmap(page);
1308            SetPageDirty(page);
1309            page_cache_release(page);
1310    }
```

This block is responsible for storing the link information.

1291-1295 If the length of the name is smaller than the space used for the `shmem_inode_info`, this copies the name into the space reserved for the private struct.

1294 Sets the `inode→i_op` to `shmem_symlink_inline_operations`, which has functions that know the link name is in the inode.

1296 Allocates a page with `shmem_getpage_locked`.

1297-1300 If an error occured, this drops the reference to the inode and returns the error.

1301 Uses `shmem_symlink_inode_operations`, which understands that the link information is contained within a page.

1302 `shmem_ilock` is a global spinlock that protects a global linked list of inodes, which are linked by the private information structs `info→list` field.

1303 Adds the new inode to the global list.

1304 Releases `shmem_ilock`.

1305 Maps the page.

1306 Copies in the link information.

1307 Unmaps the page.

1308 Sets the page dirty.

1309 Releases our reference to it.

Shared Memory
Virtual Filesystem

```
1311        dir->i_size += BOGO_DIRENT_SIZE;
1312        dir->i_ctime = dir->i_mtime = CURRENT_TIME;
1313        d_instantiate(dentry, inode);
1314        dget(dentry);
1315        return 0;
1316 }
```

1311 Increments the size of the directory as a new inode has been added. BOGO_DIRENT_SIZE is just a pseudosize of inodes so that **ls** output looks nice.

1312 Updates the i_ctime and i_mtime.

1313-1314 Instantiates the inode.

1315 Returns success.

L.3.4.2   Function: shmem_readlink_inline()   *(mm/shmem.c)*

```
1318 static int shmem_readlink_inline(struct dentry *dentry,
                                      char *buffer, int buflen)
1319 {
1320        return vfs_readlink(dentry, buffer, buflen,
                               (const char *)SHMEM_I(dentry->d_inode));
1321 }
```

1320 The link name is contained within the inode, so it passes it as a parameter to the VFS layer with **vfs_readlink()**.

L.3.4.3   Function: shmem_follow_link_inline()   *(mm/shmem.c)*

```
1323 static int shmem_follow_link_inline(struct dentry *dentry,
                                         struct nameidata *nd)
1324 {
1325        return vfs_follow_link(nd,
                                  (const char *)SHMEM_I(dentry->d_inode));
1326 }
```

1325 The link name is contained within the inode, so it passes it as a parameter to the VFS layer with **vfs_followlink()**.

L.3.4.4   Function: shmem_readlink()   *(mm/shmem.c)*

```
1328 static int shmem_readlink(struct dentry *dentry,
                              char *buffer, int buflen)
1329 {
1330        struct page *page - NULL;
1331        int res = shmem_getpage(dentry->d_inode, 0, &page, SGP_READ);
1332        if (res)
```

```
1333            return res;
1334        res = vfs_readlink(dentry,buffer,buflen, kmap(page));
1335        kunmap(page);
1336        mark_page_accessed(page);
1337        page_cache_release(page);
1338        return res;
1339 }
```

1331 The link name is contained in a page associated with the symlink, so it calls shmem_getpage()(See Section L.5.1.2) to get a pointer to it.

1332-1333 If an error occurred, this returns NULL.

1334 Maps the page with kmap() (See Section I.1.1) and passes it as a pointer to vfs_readlink(). The link is at the beginning of the page.

1335 Unmaps the page.

1336 Marks the page accessed.

1337 Drops our reference to the page taken by shmem_getpage().

1338 Returns the link.

```
1231 static int shmem_follow_link(struct dentry *dentry,
                                   struct nameidata *nd)
1232 {
1233        struct page * page;
1234        int res = shmem_getpage(dentry->d_inode, 0, &page);
1235        if (res)
1236                return res;
1237
1238        res = vfs_follow_link(nd, kmap(page));
1239        kunmap(page);
1240        page_cache_release(page);
1241        return res;
1242 }
```

1234 The link name is within a page, so it gets the page with shmem_getpage().

1235-1236 Returns the error if one occurred.

1238 Maps the page and passes it as a pointer to vfs_follow_link().

1239 Unmaps the page.

1240 Drops our reference to the page.

1241 Returns success.

Shared Memory
Virtual Filesystem

L.3.5   Synchronizing

L.3.5.1   Function: `shmem_sync_file()`   *(mm/shmem.c)*

This function simply returns 0 because the file exists only in memory and does not need to be synchronized with a file on disk.

```
1446 static int shmem_sync_file(struct file * file,
                                struct dentry *dentry,
                                int datasync)
1447 {
1448     return 0;
1449 }
```

L.4   Inode Operations in tmpfs

Contents

L.4.1   Truncating

L.4.1.1   Function: `shmem_truncate()`   *(mm/shmem.c)*

By the time this function has been called, the inode→i_size has been set to the new size by `vmtruncate()`. It is the job of this function to either create or remove pages as necessary to set the size of the file.

```
351 static void shmem_truncate(struct inode *inode)
352 {
353     struct shmem_inode_info *info = SHMEM_I(inode);
354     struct shmem_sb_info *sbinfo = SHMEM_SB(inode->i_sb);
355     unsigned long freed = 0;
356     unsigned long index;
357
358     inode->i_ctime = inode->i_mtime = CURRENT_TIME;
359     index = (inode->i_size + PAGE_CACHE_SIZE - 1)
                    >> PAGE_CACHE_SHIFT;
360     if (index >= info->next_index)
361         return;
362
363     spin_lock(&info->lock);
364     while (index < info->next_index)
365             freed += shmem_truncate_indirect(info, index);
366     BUG_ON(info->swapped > info->next_index);
367     spin_unlock(&info->lock);
368
369     spin_lock(&sbinfo->stat_lock);
```

```
370        sbinfo->free_blocks += freed;
371        inode->i_blocks -= freed*BLOCKS_PER_PAGE;
372        spin_unlock(&sbinfo->stat_lock);
373 }
```

353 Gets the private filesystem information for this inode with SHMEM_I().

354 Gets the superblock private information.

358 Updates the ctime and mtime for the inode.

359 Gets the index of the page that is the new end of the file. The old size is stored in info→next_index.

360-361 If the file is being expanded, this just returns because the global zero page will be used to represent the expanded region.

363 Acquires the private info spinlock.

364-365 Continually calls shmem_truncate_indirect() until the file is truncated to the desired size.

366 It is a bug if the shmem_info_info struct indicates that more pages are swapped out than there are pages in the file.

367 Releases the private info spinlock.

369 Acquires the superblock private info spinlock.

370 Updates the number of free blocks available.

371 Updates the number of blocks being used by this inode.

372 Releases the superblock private info spinlock.

L.4.1.2 Function: shmem_truncate_indirect() *(mm/shmem.c)*
    This function locates the last doubly-indirect block in the inode and calls shmem_truncate_direct() to truncate it.

```
308 static inline unsigned long
309 shmem_truncate_indirect(struct shmem_inode_info *info,
                            unsigned long index)
310 {
311     swp_entry_t ***base;
312     unsigned long baseidx, start;
313     unsigned long len = info->next_index;
314     unsigned long freed;
315
316     if (len <= SHMEM_NR_DIRECT) {
317         info->next_index = index;
```

```
318            if (!info->swapped)
319                return 0;
320            freed = shmem_free_swp(info->i_direct + index,
321                                   info->i_direct + len);
322            info->swapped -= freed;
323            return freed;
324        }
325
326        if (len <= ENTRIES_PER_PAGEPAGE/2 + SHMEM_NR_DIRECT) {
327            len -= SHMEM_NR_DIRECT;
328            base = (swp_entry_t ***) &info->i_indirect;
329            baseidx = SHMEM_NR_DIRECT;
330        } else {
331            len -= ENTRIES_PER_PAGEPAGE/2 + SHMEM_NR_DIRECT;
332            BUG_ON(len > ENTRIES_PER_PAGEPAGE*ENTRIES_PER_PAGE/2);
333            baseidx = len - 1;
334            baseidx -= baseidx % ENTRIES_PER_PAGEPAGE;
335            base = (swp_entry_t ***) info->i_indirect +
336                    ENTRIES_PER_PAGE/2 + baseidx/ENTRIES_PER_PAGEPAGE;
337            len -= baseidx;
338            baseidx += ENTRIES_PER_PAGEPAGE/2 + SHMEM_NR_DIRECT;
339        }
340
341        if (index > baseidx) {
342            info->next_index = index;
343            start = index - baseidx;
344        } else {
345            info->next_index = baseidx;
346            start = 0;
347        }
348        return *base? shmem_truncate_direct(info, base, start, len): 0;
349 }
```

313 len is the second to last page that is currently in use by the file.

316-324 If the file is small and all entries are stored in the direct block information, this calls shmem_free_swp() and passes it the first swap entry in info→i_direct and the number of entries to truncate.

326-339 The pages to be truncated are in the indirect blocks somewhere. This section of code is dedicated to calculating three variables, base, baseidx and len. base is the beginning of the page that contains pointers to swap entries to be truncated. baseidx is the page index of the first entry within the indirect block being used and len is the number of entries to be truncated from in this pass.

326-330 Calculates the variables for a doubly-indirect block. The base is then set to the swap entry at the beginnning of info→i_indirect.

baseidx is SHMEM_NR_DIRECT, which is the page index at the beginning of info→i_indirect. At this point, len is the number of pages in the file, so the number of direct blocks is subtracted to leave the remaining number of pages.

330-339 If not, this is a triply-indexed block, so the next level must be traversed before the base, baseidx and len are calculated.

341-344 If the file is going to be bigger after the truncation, this updates next_index to the new end of the file and makes start the beginning of the indirect block.

344-347 If the file is being made smaller, this moves the current end of the file to the beginning of this indirect block that is about to be truncated.

348 If there is a block at base, this calls shmem_truncate_direct() to truncate pages in it.

L.4.1.3   Function: shmem_truncate_direct()   *(mm/shmem.c)*

This function is responsible for cycling through an indirect block and calling shmem_free_swp for each page that contains swap vectors that are to be truncated.

```
264 static inline unsigned long
265 shmem_truncate_direct(struct shmem_inode_info *info,
             swp_entry_t ***dir,
             unsigned long start, unsigned long len)
266 {
267     swp_entry_t **last, **ptr;
268     unsigned long off, freed_swp, freed = 0;
269
270     last = *dir + (len + ENTRIES_PER_PAGE - 1) / ENTRIES_PER_PAGE;
271     off = start % ENTRIES_PER_PAGE;
272
273     for (ptr = *dir + start/ENTRIES_PER_PAGE;
             ptr < last;
             ptr++, off = 0) {
274         if (!*ptr)
275             continue;
276
277         if (info->swapped) {
278             freed_swp = shmem_free_swp(*ptr + off,
279                         *ptr + ENTRIES_PER_PAGE);
280             info->swapped -= freed_swp;
281             freed += freed_swp;
282         }
283
284         if (!off) {
285             freed++;
286             free_page((unsigned long) *ptr);
```

```
287                *ptr = 0;
288            }
289        }
290
291    if (!start) {
292        freed++;
293        free_page((unsigned long) *dir);
294        *dir = 0;
295    }
296    return freed;
297 }
```

270 `last` is the last page within the indirect block that is to be truncated.

271 `off` is the offset within the page that the truncation is if this is a partial truncation rather than a full-page truncation.

273-289 Beginning with the `start`th block in `dir`, this truncates pages until `last` is reached.

274-275 If no page is here, this continues to the next one.

277-282 If the `info` struct indicates that pages are swapped out belonging to this inode, it calls `shmem_free_swp()` to free any swap slot associated with this page. If one was freed, this updates `info`swapped and increments the count of the `freed` number of pages.

284-288 If this is not a partial truncate, it frees the page.

291-295 If this whole indirect block is now free, this reclaims the page.

296 Returns the number of pages `freed`.

L.4.1.4   Function: shmem_free_swp()   *(mm/shmem.c)*

This frees `count` number of swap entries starting with the entry at `dir`.

```
240 static int shmem_free_swp(swp_entry_t *dir, swp_entry_t *edir)
241 {
242     swp_entry_t *ptr;
243     int freed = 0;
244
245     for (ptr = dir; ptr < edir; ptr++) {
246         if (ptr->val) {
247             free_swap_and_cache(*ptr);
248             *ptr = (swp_entry_t){0};
249             freed++;
250         }
251     }
252     return freed;
254 }
```

245-251 Loops through each of the swap entries to be freed.

246-250 If a swap entry exists, this frees it with `free_swap_and_cache()` and sets the swap entry to 0. It increments the number of pages freed.

252 Returns the total number of pages freed.

L.4.2   Linking

L.4.2.1   Function: `shmem_link()`   *(mm/shmem.c)*
   This function creates a hard link with `dentry` to `old_dentry`.

```
1172 static int shmem_link(struct dentry *old_dentry,
                           struct inode *dir,
                           struct dentry *dentry)
1173 {
1174     struct inode *inode = old_dentry->d_inode;
1175
1176     if (S_ISDIR(inode->i_mode))
1177         return -EPERM;
1178
1179     dir->i_size += BOGO_DIRENT_SIZE;
1180     inode->i_ctime = dir->i_ctime = dir->i_mtime = CURRENT_TIME;
1181     inode->i_nlink++;
1182     atomic_inc(&inode->i_count);
1183     dget(dentry);
1184     d_instantiate(dentry, inode);
1185         return 0;
1186 }
```

1174 Gets the inode corresponding to `old_dentry`.

1176-1177 If it is linking to a directory, this returns `-EPERM`. Strictly speaking, root should be allowed to hard-link directories, although it is not recommended because of the possibility of creating a loop within the filesystem that utilities like **find** get lost in. `tmpfs` simply does not allow the hard-linking of directories.

1179 Increments the size of the directory with the new link.

1180 Updates the directories `mtime` and `ctime` and updates the inode `ctime`.

1181 Increments the number of links leading to `inode`.

1183 Gets an extra reference to the new `dentry` with `dget()`.

1184 Instantiates the new dentry.

1185 Returns success.

L.4.3 Unlinking

L.4.3.1   Function: shmem_unlink()   *(mm/shmem.c)*

```
1221 static int shmem_unlink(struct inode* dir,
                             struct dentry *dentry)
1222 {
1223     struct inode *inode = dentry->d_inode;
1224
1225     dir->i_size -= BOGO_DIRENT_SIZE;
1226     inode->i_ctime = dir->i_ctime = dir->i_mtime = CURRENT_TIME;
1227     inode->i_nlink--;
1228     dput(dentry);
1229     return 0;
1230 }
```

1223 Gets the inode for the dentry being unlinked.

1225 Updates the directory inode's size.

1226 Updates the various ctime and mtime variables.

1227 Decrements the number of links to the inode.

1228 Calls dput() to decrement the reference to the dentry. This function will also call iput() to clear up the inode if its reference count reaches zero.

L.4.4   Making Directories

L.4.4.1   Function: shmem_mkdir()   *(mm/shmem.c)*

```
1154 static int shmem_mkdir(struct inode *dir,
                           struct dentry *dentry,
                           int mode)
1155 {
1156     int error;
1157
1158     if ((error = shmem_mknod(dir, dentry, mode | S_IFDIR, 0)))
1159         return error;
1160     dir->i_nlink++;
1161     return 0;
1162 }
```

1158 Calls shmem_mknod() (See Section L.2.2) to create a special file. By specifying the S_IFDIR flag, a directory will be created.

1160 Increments the parent directory's i_nlink field.

Shared Memory Virtual Filesystem

L.4.5   Removing Directories

L.4.5.1   Function: shmem_rmdir()   *(mm/shmem.c)*

```
1232 static int shmem_rmdir(struct inode *dir, struct dentry *dentry)
1233 {
1234         if (!shmem_empty(dentry))
1235                 return -ENOTEMPTY;
1236
1237         dir->i_nlink--;
1238         return shmem_unlink(dir, dentry);
1239 }
```

1234-1235 Checks to see if the directory is empty with shmem_empty() (See Section L.4.5.2). If it is not, it returns -ENOTEMPTY.

1237 Decrements the parent directory's i_nlink field.

1238 Returns the result of shmem_unlink()(See Section L.4.3.1), which should delete the directory.

L.4.5.2   Function: shmem_empty()   *(mm/shmem.c)*
This function checks to see if a directory is empty or not.

```
1201 static int shmem_empty(struct dentry *dentry)
1202 {
1203     struct list_head *list;
1204
1205     spin_lock(&dcache_lock);
1206     list = dentry->d_subdirs.next;
1207
1208     while (list != &dentry->d_subdirs) {
1209         struct dentry *de = list_entry(list,
                                            struct dentry, d_child);
1210
1211         if (shmem_positive(de)) {
1212             spin_unlock(&dcache_lock);
1213             return 0;
1214         }
1215         list = list->next;
1216     }
1217     spin_unlock(&dcache_lock);
1218     return 1;
1219 }
```

1205 The dcache_lock protects many things, but it mainly protects dcache lookups, which is what will be required for this function, so this acquires it.

1208 Cycles through the subdirs list, which contains all children dentries and sees one active dentry can be found. If it is, 0 will be returned, indicating the directory is not empty.

1209 Gets the dentry for this child.

1211 `shmem_positive()`(See Section L.4.5.3) returns if the dentry has a valid inode associated with it and is currently hashed. If it is hashed, it means that the dentry is active, and the directory is not empty.

1212-1213 If the directory is not empty, this frees the spinlock and returns.

1215 Moves to the next child.

1217-1218 The directory is empty. This frees the spinlock and returns.

L.4.5.3 Function: `shmem_positive()` *(mm/shmem.c)*

```
1188 static inline int shmem_positive(struct dentry *dentry)
1189 {
1190         return dentry->d_inode && !d_unhashed(dentry);
1191 }
```

1190 Returns true if the dentry has a valid inode and is currently hashed.

L.5   Page Faulting Within a Virtual File

Contents

L.5.1   Reading Pages During Page Fault

L.5.1.1   Function: shmem_nopage()   *(mm/shmem.c)*

This is the top-level `nopage()` function that is called by `do_no_page()` when faulting in a page. This is called regardless of the fault being the first fault or if it is being faulted in from backing storage.

```
763 struct page * shmem_nopage(struct vm_area_struct *vma,
                               unsigned long address,
                               int unused)
764 {
765     struct inode *inode = vma->vm_file->f_dentry->d_inode;
766     struct page *page = NULL;
767     unsigned long idx;
768     int error;
769
770     idx = (address - vma->vm_start) >> PAGE_SHIFT;
771     idx += vma->vm_pgoff;
772     idx >>= PAGE_CACHE_SHIFT - PAGE_SHIFT;
773
774     error = shmem_getpage(inode, idx, &page, SGP_CACHE);
775     if (error)
776         return (error == -ENOMEM)? NOPAGE_OOM: NOPAGE_SIGBUS;
777
778     mark_page_accessed(page);
779     flush_page_to_ram(page);
780     return page;
781 }
```

763 The two parameters of relevance are the VMA the fault occurred in and the faulting address.

765 Records the inode that the fault occurred in.

770-772 Calculates the `idx` as the offset in counts of `PAGE_SIZE` within the virtual file.

772 This adjustment takes into account the possibility that an entry in the page cache is a different size to a page. At the moment, there is no difference.

774-775 `shmem_getpage()` (See Section L.5.1.2) is responsible for locating the page at `idx`.

775-776 If an error occurred, this decides whether to return an OOM error or an invalid faulting address error.

778 Marks the page accessed so that it will be moved to the top of the LRU lists.

779 `flush_page_to_ram()` is responsible for avoiding dcache aliasing problems.

780 Returns the faulted-in page.

L.5.1.2   Function: `shmem_getpage()`   *(mm/shmem.c)*

```
583 static int shmem_getpage(struct inode *inode,
                                unsigned long idx,
       struct page **pagep,
       enum sgp_type sgp)
584 {
585     struct address_space *mapping = inode->i_mapping;
586     struct shmem_inode_info *info = SHMEM_I(inode);
587     struct shmem_sb_info *sbinfo;
588     struct page *filepage = *pagep;
589     struct page *swappage;
590     swp_entry_t *entry;
591     swp_entry_t swap;
592     int error = 0;
593
594     if (idx >= SHMEM_MAX_INDEX)
595         return -EFBIG;
596     /*
597      * Normally, filepage is NULL on entry, and either found
598      * uptodate immediately, or allocated and zeroed, or read
599      * in under swappage, which is then assigned to filepage.
600      * But shmem_readpage and shmem_prepare_write pass in a locked
601      * filepage, which may be found not uptodate by other callers
602      * too, and may need to be copied from the swappage read in.
603      */
604 repeat:
605     if (!filepage)
606         filepage = find_lock_page(mapping, idx);
607     if (filepage && Page_Uptodate(filepage))
608         goto done;
609
610     spin_lock(&info->lock);
```

```
611     entry = shmem_swp_alloc(info, idx, sgp);
612     if (IS_ERR(entry)) {
613         spin_unlock(&info->lock);
614         error = PTR_ERR(entry);
615         goto failed;
616     }
617     swap = *entry;
```

583 The parameters are the following:

- **inode** is the inode that the fault is occurring in.

- **idx** is the index of the page within the file that is being faulted.

- **pagep** if NULL will become the faulted page if successful. If a valid page is passed in, this function will make sure it is up to date.

- **sgp** indicates what type of access this is, which determines how a page will be located and returned.

586 SHMEM_I() returns the shmem_inode_info contained with the filesystem-specific information within the superblock information.

594-595 Makes sure the index is not beyond the end of the file.

605-606 If no page was passed in with the pagep parameter, then this tries and locates the page and locks it with find_lock_page() (See Section J.1.4.4).

607-608 If the page was found and is up to date, goto done because this function has nothing more to do.

610 Locks the inode private information struct.

611 Searches for the swap entry for this idx with shmem_swp_alloc(). If one did not previously exist, it will be allocated.

612-616 If an error occurred, this releases the spinlock and returns the error.

```
619     if (swap.val) {
620         /* Look it up and read it in.. */
621         swappage = lookup_swap_cache(swap);
622         if (!swappage) {
623             spin_unlock(&info->lock);
624             swapin_readahead(swap);
625             swappage = read_swap_cache_async(swap);
626             if (!swappage) {
627                 spin_lock(&info->lock);
628                 entry = shmem_swp_alloc(info, idx, sgp);
629                 if (IS_ERR(entry))
630                     error = PTR_ERR(entry);
631                 else if (entry->val == swap.val)
```

```
632                    error = -ENOMEM;
633                spin_unlock(&info->lock);
634                if (error)
635                    goto failed;
636                goto repeat;
637            }
638            wait_on_page(swappage);
639            page_cache_release(swappage);
640            goto repeat;
641        }
642
643        /* We have to do this with page locked to prevent races */
644        if (TryLockPage(swappage)) {
645            spin_unlock(&info->lock);
646            wait_on_page(swappage);
647            page_cache_release(swappage);
648            goto repeat;
649        }
650        if (!Page_Uptodate(swappage)) {
651            spin_unlock(&info->lock);
652            UnlockPage(swappage);
653            page_cache_release(swappage);
654            error = -EIO;
655            goto failed;
656        }
```

In this block, a valid swap entry exists for the page. The page will be first searched for in the swap cache, and, if it does not exist there, it will be read in from backing storage.

619-690 This set of lines deals with the case where a valid swap entry exists.

612 Searches for `swappage` in the swap cache with `lookup_swap_cache()` (See Section K.2.4.1).

622-641 If the page does not exist in the swap cache, this reads it in from backing storage with `read_swap_cache_async()`. In line 638, `wait_on_page()` is called to wait until the I/O completes. After the I/O completes, the reference to the page is released, and the `repeat` label is jumped to reacquire the spinlocks and try again.

644-649 Tries and locks the page. If it fails, it waits until it can be locked and jumps to `repeat` to try again.

650-656 If the page is not up to date, the I/O failed for some reason, so this returns the error.

```
658        delete_from_swap_cache(swappage);
```

```
659        if (filepage) {
660            entry->val = 0;
661            info->swapped--;
662            spin_unlock(&info->lock);
663            flush_page_to_ram(swappage);
664            copy_highpage(filepage, swappage);
665            UnlockPage(swappage);
666            page_cache_release(swappage);
667            flush_dcache_page(filepage);
668            SetPageUptodate(filepage);
669            SetPageDirty(filepage);
670            swap_free(swap);
671        } else if (add_to_page_cache_unique(swappage,
672            mapping, idx, page_hash(mapping, idx)) == 0) {
673            entry->val = 0;
674            info->swapped--;
675            spin_unlock(&info->lock);
676            filepage = swappage;
677            SetPageUptodate(filepage);
678            SetPageDirty(filepage);
679            swap_free(swap);
680        } else {
681            if (add_to_swap_cache(swappage, swap) != 0)
682                BUG();
683            spin_unlock(&info->lock);
684            SetPageUptodate(swappage);
685            SetPageDirty(swappage);
686            UnlockPage(swappage);
687            page_cache_release(swappage);
688            goto repeat;
689        }
```

At this point, the page exists in the swap cache.

658 Deletes the page from the swap cache so that we can attempt to add it to the pagecache.

659-670 If the caller supplied a page with the `pagep` parameter, this updates `pagep` with the data in `swappage`.

671-680 If not, this tries and adds `swappage` to the pagecache. Note that `info→swapped` is updated, and the page is marked up to date before the swap entry is freed, with `swap_free()`.

681-689 If we failed to add the page to the page cache, this adds it back to the swap cache with `add_to_swap_cache()`. The page is marked up to date before being unlocked and goto `repeat` to try again.

```
690        } else if (sgp == SGP_READ && !filepage) {
691            filepage = find_get_page(mapping, idx);
692            if (filepage &&
693                (!Page_Uptodate(filepage) || TryLockPage(filepage))) {
694                spin_unlock(&info->lock);
695                wait_on_page(filepage);
696                page_cache_release(filepage);
697                filepage = NULL;
698                goto repeat;
699            }
700            spin_unlock(&info->lock);
```

In this block, a valid swap entry does not exist for the `idx`. If the page is being read and the `pagep` is NULL, this locates the page in the pagecache.

691 Calls `find_get_page()` (See Section J.1.4.1) to find the page in the pagecache.

692-699 If the page was found, but was not up to date or could not be locked, this releases the spinlock and waits until the page is unlocked. Then goto `repeat` to reacquire the spinlock and try again.

700 Releases the spinlock.

```
701        } else {
702            sbinfo = SHMEM_SB(inode->i_sb);
703            spin_lock(&sbinfo->stat_lock);
704            if (sbinfo->free_blocks == 0) {
705                spin_unlock(&sbinfo->stat_lock);
706                spin_unlock(&info->lock);
707                error = -ENOSPC;
708                goto failed;
709            }
710            sbinfo->free_blocks--;
711            inode->i_blocks += BLOCKS_PER_PAGE;
712            spin_unlock(&sbinfo->stat_lock);
713
714            if (!filepage) {
715                spin_unlock(&info->lock);
716                filepage = page_cache_alloc(mapping);
717                if (!filepage) {
718                    shmem_free_block(inode);
719                    error = -ENOMEM;
720                    goto failed;
721                }
722
723                spin_lock(&info->lock);
724                entry = shmem_swp_alloc(info, idx, sgp);
```

```
725              if (IS_ERR(entry))
726                   error = PTR_ERR(entry);
727              if (error || entry->val ||
728                   add_to_page_cache_unique(filepage,
729                   mapping, idx, page_hash(mapping, idx)) != 0) {
730                   spin_unlock(&info->lock);
731                   page_cache_release(filepage);
732                   shmem_free_block(inode);
733                   filepage = NULL;
734                   if (error)
735                       goto failed;
736                   goto repeat;
737              }
738          }
739
740          spin_unlock(&info->lock);
741          clear_highpage(filepage);
742          flush_dcache_page(filepage);
743          SetPageUptodate(filepage);
744      }
```

If not, a page that is not in the page cache is being written to. It will need to be allocated.

702 Gets the superblock info with SHMEM_SB().

703 Acquires the superblock info spinlock.

704-709 If no free blocks are left in the filesystem, this releases the spinlocks, sets the return error to -ENOSPC and goto failed.

710 Decrements the number of available blocks.

711 Increments the block usage count for the inode.

712 Releases the superblock private information spinlock.

714-715 If a page was not supplied by pagep, this allocates a page and swap entry for the new page.

715 Releases the info spinlock because page_cache_alloc() may sleep.

716 Allocates a new page.

717-721 If the allocation failed, this frees the block with shmem_free_block() and sets the return error to -ENOMEM before goto failed.

723 Reacquires the info spinlock.

724 shmem_swp_entry() locates a swap entry for the page. If one does not already exist (which is likely for this page), one will be allocated and returned.

725-726 If no swap entry was found or allocated, this sets the return error.

728-729 If no error occurred, this adds the page to the pagecache.

730-732 If the page was not added to the pagecache (because we raced and another process inserted the page while we had the spinlock released, for example), this drops the reference to the new page and frees the block.

734-735 If an error occurred, goto `failed` to report the error.

736 Otherwise, goto `repeat` where the desired page will be searched for within the pagecache again.

740 Releases the info spinlock.

741 Zero-fills the new page.

742 Flushes the dcache to avoid possible CPU dcache aliasing.

743 Marks the page as being up to date.

```
745 done:
746     if (!*pagep) {
747         if (filepage) {
748             UnlockPage(filepage);
749             *pagep = filepage;
750         } else
751             *pagep = ZERO_PAGE(0);
752     }
753     return 0;
754
755 failed:
756     if (*pagep != filepage) {
757         UnlockPage(filepage);
758         page_cache_release(filepage);
759     }
760     return error;
761 }
```

746-752 If a page was not passed in by `pagep`, this decides what to return. If a page was allocated for writing, this unlocks and returns `filepage`. Otherwise, the caller is just a reader, so if returns the global zero-filled page.

753 Returns success.

755 This is the failure path.

756 If a page was allocated by this function and stored in `filepage`, this unlocks it and drops the reference to it, which will free it.

760 Returns the error code.

L.5.2   Locating Swapped Pages

L.5.2.1   Function: `shmem_alloc_entry()`   *(mm/shmem.c)*

This function is a top-level function that returns the swap entry corresponding to a particular page index within a file. If the swap entry does not exist, one will be allocated.

```
183 static inline swp_entry_t * shmem_alloc_entry (
                                struct shmem_inode_info *info,
                                unsigned long index)
184 {
185     unsigned long page = 0;
186     swp_entry_t * res;
187
188     if (index >= SHMEM_MAX_INDEX)
189         return ERR_PTR(-EFBIG);
190
191     if (info->next_index <= index)
192         info->next_index = index + 1;
193
194     while ((res = shmem_swp_entry(info,index,page)) ==
                ERR_PTR(-ENOMEM)) {
195         page = get_zeroed_page(GFP_USER);
196         if (!page)
197             break;
198     }
199     return res;
200 }
```

188-189 SHMEM_MAX_INDEX is calculated at compile time, and it indicates the largest possible virtual file in pages. If the **var** is greater than the maximum possible sized file, this returns -EFBIG.

191-192 next_index records the index of the page at the end of the file. inode→i_size alone is insufficient because the **next_index** field is needed for file truncation.

194-198 Calls `shmem_swp_entry()` to locate the **swp_entry_t** for the requested index. While searching, `shmem_swp_entry()` may need a number of pages. If it does, it returns -ENOMEM, which indicates that `get_zeroed_page()` should be called before trying again.

199 Returns the **swp_entry_t**.

L.5.2.2   Function: `shmem_swp_entry()`   *(mm/shmem.c)*

This function uses information within the inode to locate the **swp_entry_t** for a given index. The inode itself is able to store SHMEM_NR_DIRECT swap vectors. After that, indirect blocks are used.

```
127 static swp_entry_t *shmem_swp_entry (struct shmem_inode_info *info,
                                         unsigned long index,
                                         unsigned long page)
128 {
129     unsigned long offset;
130     void **dir;
131
132     if (index < SHMEM_NR_DIRECT)
133         return info->i_direct+index;
134     if (!info->i_indirect) {
135         if (page) {
136             info->i_indirect = (void **) *page;
137             *page = 0;
138         }
139         return NULL;
140     }
141
142     index -= SHMEM_NR_DIRECT;
143     offset = index % ENTRIES_PER_PAGE;
144     index /= ENTRIES_PER_PAGE;
145     dir = info->i_indirect;
146
147     if (index >= ENTRIES_PER_PAGE/2) {
148         index -= ENTRIES_PER_PAGE/2;
149         dir += ENTRIES_PER_PAGE/2 + index/ENTRIES_PER_PAGE;
150         index %= ENTRIES_PER_PAGE;
151         if (!*dir) {
152             if (page) {
153                 *dir = (void *) *page;
154                 *page = 0;
155             }
156             return NULL;
157         }
158         dir = ((void **)*dir);
159     }
160
161     dir += index;
162     if (!*dir) {
163         if (!page || !*page)
164             return NULL;
165         *dir = (void *) *page;
166         *page = 0;
167     }
168     return (swp_entry_t *) *dir + offset;
169 }
```

132-133 If the `index` is below `SHMEM_NR_DIRECT`, then the swap vector is contained within the direct block, so this returns it.

134-140 If a page does not exist at this indirect block, this installs the page that was passed in with the `page` parameter and returns NULL. This tells the called to allocate a new page and calls the function again.

142 Treats the indirect blocks as starting from index 0.

143 `ENTRIES_PER_PAGE` is the number of swap vectors contained within each page in the indirect block. `offset` is now the index of the desired swap vector within the indirect block page when it is found.

144 `index` is now the directory number within the indirect block list that must be found.

145 Gets a pointer to the first indirect block we are interested in.

147-159 If the required directory (`index`) is greater than `ENTRIES_PER_PAGE/2`, then it is a triple-indirect block, so the next block must be traversed.

148 Pointers to the next set of directory blocks are in the second half of the current block, so this calculates `index` as an offset within the second half of the current block.

149 Calculates `dir` as a pointer to the next directory block.

150 `index` is now a pointer within `dir` to a page containing the swap vectors we are interested in.

151-156 If `dir` has not been allocated, this installs the page supplied with the `page` parameter and returns NULL so that the caller will allocate a new page and call the function again.

158 `dir` is now the base of the page of swap vectors containing the one we are interested in.

161 Moves `dir` forward to the entry we want.

162-167 If an entry does not exist, this installs the `page` supplied as a parameter if available. If not, it returns NULL so that one will be allocated, and the function will be called again.

168 Returns the found swap vector.

L.6 Swap Space Interaction

Contents

L.6.1   Function: `shmem_writepage()`   *(mm/shmem.c)*

This function is responsible for moving a page from the page cache to the swap cache.

```
522 static int shmem_writepage(struct page *page)
523 {
524     struct shmem_inode_info *info;
525     swp_entry_t *entry, swap;
526     struct address_space *mapping;
527     unsigned long index;
528     struct inode *inode;
529
530     BUG_ON(!PageLocked(page));
531     if (!PageLaunder(page))
532         return fail_writepage(page);
533
534     mapping = page->mapping;
535     index = page->index;
536     inode = mapping->host;
537     info = SHMEM_I(inode);
538     if (info->flags & VM_LOCKED)
539         return fail_writepage(page);
```

This block is the function preamble to make sure the operation is possible.

522 The parameter is the page to move to the swap cache.

530 It is a bug if the page is already locked for I/O.

531-532 If the launder bit has not been set, this calls `fail_writepage()`. `fail_writepage()` is used by in-memory filesystems to mark the page dirty and reactivates it so that the page reclaimer does not repeatadly attempt to write the same page.

534-537 Records variables that are needed as parameters later in the function.

538-539 If the inode filesystem information is locked, this fails.

```
540 getswap:
541     swap = get_swap_page();
```

```
542     if (!swap.val)
543         return fail_writepage(page);
544
545     spin_lock(&info->lock);
546     BUG_ON(index >= info->next_index);
547     entry = shmem_swp_entry(info, index, NULL);
548     BUG_ON(!entry);
549     BUG_ON(entry->val);
550
```

This block is responsible for allocating a swap slot from the backing storage and a swp_entry_t within the inode.

541-543 Locates a free swap slot with get_swap_page() (See Section K.1.1). If fails, it calls fail_writepage().

545 Locks the inode information.

547 Gets a free swp_entry_t from the filesystem-specific private inode information with shmem_swp_entry().

```
551     /* Remove it from the page cache */
552     remove_inode_page(page);
553     page_cache_release(page);
554
555     /* Add it to the swap cache */
556     if (add_to_swap_cache(page, swap) != 0) {
557         /*
558          * Raced with "speculative" read_swap_cache_async.
559          * Add page back to page cache, unref swap, try again.
560          */
561         add_to_page_cache_locked(page, mapping, index);
562         spin_unlock(&info->lock);
563         swap_free(swap);
564         goto getswap;
565     }
566
567     *entry = swap;
568     info->swapped++;
569     spin_unlock(&info->lock);
570     SetPageUptodate(page);
571     set_page_dirty(page);
572     UnlockPage(page);
573     return 0;
574 }
```

This block moves from the pagecache to the swap cache and updates statistics.

552 `remove_inode_page()`(See Section J.1.2.1) removes the page from the inode and hash lists the page is a member of.

553 `page_cache_release()` drops the local reference to the page taken for the `writepage()` operation.

556 Adds the page to the swap cache. After this returns, the `page→mapping` will now be `swapper_space`.

561 The operation failed, so this adds the page back to the pagecache.

562 Unlocks the private information.

563-564 Frees the swap slot and tries again.

567 Here, the page has successfully become part of the swap cache. This updates the inode information to point to the swap slot in backing storage.

568 Increments the counter recording the number of pages belonging to this inode that are in swap.

569 Frees the private inode information.

570-571 Moves the page to the `address_space` dirty pages list so that it will be written to backing storage.

573 Returns success.

L.6.2   Function: `shmem_unuse()`   *(mm/shmem.c)*

This function will search the `shmem_inodes` list for the inode that holds the information for the requested `entry` and `page`. It is a very expensive operation, but it is only called when a swap area is being deactivated, so it is not a significant problem. On return, the swap entry will be freed, and the page will be moved from the swap cache to the pagecache.

```
498 int shmem_unuse(swp_entry_t entry, struct page *page)
499 {
500     struct list_head *p;
501     struct shmem_inode_info * nfo;
502
503     spin_lock(&shmem_ilock);
504     list_for_each(p, &shmem_inodes) {
505         info = list_entry(p, struct shmem_inode_info, list);
506
507         if (info->swapped && shmem_unuse_inode(info, entry, page))
508             /* move head to start search for next from here */
509             list_move_tail(&shmem_inodes, &info->list);
510             found = 1;
511             break;
```

```
512            }
513        }
514        spin_unlock(&shmem_ilock);
515        return found;
516 }
```

503 Acquires the `shmem_ilock` spinlock, protecting the inode list.

504 Cycles through each entry in the `shmem_inodes` list searching for the inode holding the requested `entry` and `page`.

509 Moves the inode to the top of the list. In the event that we are reclaiming many pages, the next search will find the inode of interest at the top of the list.

510 Indicates that the page was found.

511 This `page` and `entry` have been found to break out of the loop.

514 Releases the `shmem_ilock` spinlock.

515 Returns if the page was found or not by `shmem_unuse_inode()`.

L.6.3   Function: `shmem_unuse_inode()`   *(mm/shmem.c)*

This function searches the inode information in `info` to determine if the `entry` and `page` belong to it. If they do, the `entry` will be cleared, and the page will be removed from the swap cache and moved to the pagecache instead.

```
436 static int shmem_unuse_inode(struct shmem_inode_info *info,
                                  swp_entry_t entry,
  struct page *page)
437 {
438     struct inode *inode;
439     struct address_space *mapping;
440     swp_entry_t *ptr;
441     unsigned long idx;
442     int offset;
443
444     idx = 0;
445     ptr = info->i_direct;
446     spin_lock(&info->lock);
447     offset = info->next_index;
448     if (offset > SHMEM_NR_DIRECT)
449         offset = SHMEM_NR_DIRECT;
450     offset = shmem_find_swp(entry, ptr, ptr + offset);
451     if (offset >= 0)
452         goto found;
453
```

```
454        for (idx = SHMEM_NR_DIRECT; idx < info->next_index;
455            idx += ENTRIES_PER_PAGE) {
456            ptr = shmem_swp_entry(info, idx, NULL);
457            if (!ptr)
458                continue;
459            offset = info->next_index - idx;
460            if (offset > ENTRIES_PER_PAGE)
461                offset = ENTRIES_PER_PAGE;
462            offset = shmem_find_swp(entry, ptr, ptr + offset);
463            if (offset >= 0)
464                goto found;
465        }
466        spin_unlock(&info->lock);
467        return 0;
468 found:
470        idx += offset;
471        inode = info->inode;
472        mapping = inode->i_mapping;
473        delete_from_swap_cache(page);
474
475        /* Racing against delete or truncate?
       * Must leave out of page cache */
476        limit = (inode->i_state & I_FREEING)? 0:
477            (inode->i_size + PAGE_CACHE_SIZE - 1) >> PAGE_CACHE_SHIFT;
478
479        if (idx >= limit || add_to_page_cache_unique(page,
480                mapping, idx, page_hash(mapping, idx)) == 0) {
481            ptr[offset].val = 0;
482            info->swapped--;
483        } else if (add_to_swap_cache(page, entry) != 0)
484            BUG();
485        spin_unlock(&info->lock);
486        SetPageUptodate(page);
487        /*
488         * Decrement swap count even when the entry is left behind:
489         * try_to_unuse will skip over mms, then reincrement count.
490         */
491        swap_free(entry);
492        return 1;
493 }
```

445 Initializes `ptr` to start at the beginning of the direct block for the inode being searched.

446 Locks the inode private information.

447 Initializes `offset` to be the last page index in the file.

448-449 If `offset` is beyond the end of the direct block, this sets it to the end of the direct block for the moment.

450 Uses `shmem_find_swap()` (See Section L.6.4) to search the direct block for the `entry`.

451-452 If the entry was in the direct block, goto `found`. Otherwise, we have to search the indirect blocks.

454-465 Searches each of the indirect blocks for the `entry`.

456 `shmem_swp_entry()` (See Section L.5.2.2) returns the swap vector at the current `idx` within the inode. As `idx` is incremented in `ENTRIES_PER_PAGE`-sized strides, this will return the beginning of the next indirect block being searched.

457-458 If an error occurred, the indirect block does not exist, so it continues, which probably will exit the loop.

459 Calculates how many pages are left in the end of the file to see if we only have to search a partially filled indirect block.

460-461 If `offset` is greater than the size of an indirect block, this sets offset to `ENTRIES_PER_PAGE`, so this full indirect block will be searched by `shmem_find_swp()`.

462 Searches the entire of the current indirect block for `entry` with `shmem_find_swp()` (See Section L.6.4).

463-467 If the `entry` was found, goto `found`. Otherwise, the next indirect block will be searched. If the entry is never found, the `info` struct will be unlocked, and 0 will be returned, indicating that this inode did not contain the `entry` and `page`.

468 The `entry` was found, so perform the necessary tasks to free it with `swap_free()`.

470 Moves `idx` to the location of the swap vector within the block.

471-472 Gets the inode and mapping.

473 Deletes the page from the swap cache.

476-477 Checks if the inode is currently being deleted or truncated by examining `inode→i_state`. If it is, this sets `limit` to the index of the last page in the adjusted file size.

479-482 If the page is not being truncated or deleted, this adds it to the pagecache with `add_to_page_cache_unique()`. If successful, this clears the swap entry and decrement `info→swapped`.

483-484 If not, this adds the page back to the swap cache where it will be reclaimed later.

485 Releases the `info` spinlock.

486 Marks the page up to date.

491 Decrements the swap count.

492 Returns success.

L.6.4 Function: `shmem_find_swp()` *(mm/shmem.c)*

This function searches an indirect block between the two pointers `ptr` and `eptr` for the requested `entry`. Note that the two pointers must be in the same indirect block.

```
425 static inline int shmem_find_swp(swp_entry_t entry,
                                     swp_entry_t *dir,
                                     swp_entry_t *edir)
426 {
427     swp_entry_t *ptr;
428
429     for (ptr = dir; ptr < edir; ptr++) {
430         if (ptr->val == entry.val)
431             return ptr - dir;
432     }
433     return -1;
434 }
```

429 Loops between the `dir` and `edir` pointers.

430 If the current `ptr` entry matches the requested `entry`, then this returns the offset from `dir`. Because `shmem_unuse_inode()` is the only user of this function, this will result in the offset within the indirect block being returned.

433 Returns indicating that the `entry` was not found.

L.7   Setting Up Shared Regions

Contents

L.7.1   Function: shmem_zero_setup()   *(mm/shmem.c)*

This function is called to set up a VMA that is a shared region backed by anonymous pages. The call graph that shows this function is in Figure 12.5. This occurs when mmap() creates an anonymous region with the MAP_SHARED flag.

```
1664 int shmem_zero_setup(struct vm_area_struct *vma)
1665 {
1666     struct file *file;
1667     loff_t size = vma->vm_end - vma->vm_start;
1668
1669     file = shmem_file_setup("dev/zero", size);
1670     if (IS_ERR(file))
1671         return PTR_ERR(file);
1672
1673     if (vma->vm_file)
1674         fput(vma->vm_file);
1675     vma->vm_file = file;
1676     vma->vm_ops = &shmem_vm_ops;
1677     return 0;
1678 }
```

1667 Calculates the size.

1669 Calls shmem_file_setup() (See Section L.7.2) to create a file called dev/zero and of the calculated size. We will see in the functions code commentary why the name does not have to be unique.

1673-1674 If a file already exists for this virtual area, this calls fput() to drop its reference.

1675 Records the new file pointer.

1676 Sets the vm_ops so that shmem_nopage() (See Section L.5.1.1) will be called when a page needs to be faulted in for this VMA.

L.7.2   Function: shmem_file_setup()   *(mm/shmem.c)*

This function is called to create a new file in shmfs, the internal filesystem. Because the filesystem is internal, the supplied name does not have to be unique within each directory. Hence, every file that is created by an anonymous region with shmem_zero_setup() will be called "dev/zero," and regions created with shmget() will be called "SYSVNN" where NN is the key that is passed as the first argument to shmget().

```
1607 struct file *shmem_file_setup(char *name, loff_tsize)
1608 {
1609     int error;
1610     struct file *file;
1611     struct inode *inode;
1612     struct dentry *dentry, *root;
1613     struct qstr this;
1614     int vm_enough_memory(long pages);
1615
1616     if (IS_ERR(shm_mnt))
1617         return (void *)shm_mnt;
1618
1619     if (size > SHMEM_MAX_BYTES)
1620         return ERR_PTR(-EINVAL);
1621
1622     if (!vm_enough_memory(VM_ACCT(size)))
1623         return ERR_PTR(-ENOMEM);
1624
1625     this.name = name;
1626     this.len = strlen(name);
1627     this.hash = 0; /* will go */
```

1607 The parameters are the `name` of the file to create and its expected `size`.

1614 `vm_enough_memory()` (See Section M.1.1) checks to make sure there is enough memory to satisify the mapping.

1616-1617 If there is an error with the mount point, this returns the error.

1619-1620 Do not create a file greater than `SHMEM_MAX_BYTES`, which is calculated at top of `mm/shmem.c`.

1622-1623 Makes sure there is enough memory to satisify the mapping.

1625-1627 Populates the `struct qstr`, which is the string type used for dnodes.

```
1628     root = shm_mnt->mnt_root;
1629     dentry = d_alloc(root, &this);
1630     if (!dentry)
1631         return ERR_PTR(-ENOMEM);
1632
1633     error = -ENFILE;
1634     file = get_empty_filp();
1635     if (!file)
1636         goto put_dentry;
1637
1638     error = -ENOSPC;
1639     inode = shmem_get_inode(root->d_sb, S_IFREG | S_IRWXUGO, 0);
```

```
1640      if (!inode)
1641          goto close_file;
1642
1643      d_instantiate(dentry, inode);
1644      inode->i_size = size;
1645      inode->i_nlink = 0;      /* It is unlinked */
1646      file->f_vfsmnt = mntget(shm_mnt);
1647      file->f_dentry = dentry;
1648      file->f_op = &shmem_file_operations;
1649      file->f_mode = FMODE_WRITE | FMODE_READ;
1650      return file;
1651
1652 close_file:
1653      put_filp(file);
1654 put_dentry:
1655      dput(dentry);
1656      return ERR_PTR(error);
1657 }
```

1628 root is assigned to be the dnode representing the root of shmfs.

1629 Allocates a new dentry with d_alloc().

1630-1631 Returns -ENOMEM if one could not be allocated.

1634 Gets an empty struct file from the filetable. If one could not be found, -ENFILE will be returned, indicating a filetable overflow.

1639-1641 Creates a new inode, which is a regular file (S_IFREG) and globally readable, writable and executable. If it fails, it returns -ENOSPC, indicating no space is left in the filesystem.

1643 d_instantiate() fills in the inode information for a dentry. It is defined in fs/dcache.c.

1644-1649 Fills in the remaining inode and file information.

1650 Returns the newly created struct file.

1653 The error path when an inode could not be created. put_filp() fill free up the struct file entry in the filetable.

1655 dput() will drop the reference to the dentry, which destroys it.

1656 Returns the error code.

L.8   System V IPC

Contents

L.8.1   Creating a SYSV Shared Region

L.8.1.1   Function: `sys_shmget()`   *(ipc/shm.c)*

```
229 asmlinkage long sys_shmget (key_t key, size_t size, int shmflg)
230 {
231     struct shmid_kernel *shp;
232     int err, id = 0;
233
234     down(&shm_ids.sem);
235     if (key == IPC_PRIVATE) {
236         err = newseg(key, shmflg, size);
237     } else if ((id = ipc_findkey(&shm_ids, key)) == -1) {
238         if (!(shmflg & IPC_CREAT))
239             err = -ENOENT;
240         else
241             err = newseg(key, shmflg, size);
242     } else if ((shmflg & IPC_CREAT) && (shmflg & IPC_EXCL)) {
243         err = -EEXIST;
244     } else {
245         shp = shm_lock(id);
246         if(shp==NULL)
247             BUG();
248         if (shp->shm_segsz < size)
249             err = -EINVAL;
250         else if (ipcperms(&shp->shm_perm, shmflg))
251             err = -EACCES;
252         else
253             err = shm_buildid(id, shp->shm_perm.seq);
254         shm_unlock(id);
255     }
256     up(&shm_ids.sem);
257     return err;
258 }
```

234 Acquires the semaphore protecting shared memory IDs.

235-236 If `IPC_PRIVATE` is specified, most of the flags are ignored, and the region is created with `newseg()`. This flag is intended to provide exclusive access to a shared region, but Linux does not guarantee exclusive access.

237 If not, this searches to see if the key already exists with `ipc_findkey()`.

238-239 If it does not and `IPC_CREAT` was not specified, then this returns `-ENOENT`.

241 If not, this creates a new region with `newseg()`.

242-243 If the region already exists and the process requested a new region that did not previously exist to be created, this returns `-EEXIST`.

244-255 If not, we are accessing an existing region, so it locks it, makes sure we have the required permissions, builds a segment identifier with `shm_buildid()` and unlocks the region again. The segment identifier will be returned back to userspace.

256 Releases the semaphore protecting IDs.

257 Returns either the error or the segment identifier.

L.8.1.2   Function: `newseg()`   *(ipc/shm.c)*
This function creates a new shared segment.

```
178 static int newseg (key_t key, int shmflg, size_t size)
179 {
180     int error;
181     struct shmid_kernel *shp;
182     int numpages = (size + PAGE_SIZE -1) >> PAGE_SHIFT;
183     struct file * file;
184     char name[13];
185     int id;
186
187     if (size < SHMMIN || size > shm_ctlmax)
188         return -EINVAL;
189
190     if (shm_tot + numpages >= shm_ctlall)
191         return -ENOSPC;
192
193     shp = (struct shmid_kernel *) kmalloc (sizeof (*shp), GFP_USER);
194     if (!shp)
195         return -ENOMEM;
196     sprintf (name, "SYSV%08x", key);
```

This block allocates the segment descriptor.

182 Calculates the number of pages the region will occupy.

187-188 Ensures the size of the region does not break limits.

190-191 Makes sure the total number of pages required for the segment will not break limits.

193 Allocates the descriptor with `kmalloc()`(See Section H.4.2.1).

196 Prints the name of the file to be created in `shmfs`. The name is `SYSVNN` where NN is the key identifier of the region.

```
197      file = shmem_file_setup(name, size);
198      error = PTR_ERR(file);
199      if (IS_ERR(file))
200          goto no_file;
201
202      error = -ENOSPC;
203      id = shm_addid(shp);
204      if(id == -1)
205          goto no_id;
206      shp->shm_perm.key = key;
207      shp->shm_flags = (shmflg & S_IRWXUGO);
208      shp->shm_cprid = current->pid;
209      shp->shm_lprid = 0;
210      shp->shm_atim = shp->shm_dtim = 0;
211      shp->shm_ctim = CURRENT_TIME;
212      shp->shm_segsz = size;
213      shp->shm_nattch = 0;
214      shp->id = shm_buildid(id,shp->shm_perm.seq);
215      shp->shm_file = file;
216      file->f_dentry->d_inode->i_ino = shp->id;
217      file->f_op = &shm_file_operations;
218      shm_tot += numpages;
219      shm_unlock (id);
220      return shp->id;
221
222 no_id:
223      fput(file);
224 no_file:
225      kfree(shp);
226      return error;
227 }
```

197 Creates a new file in `shmfs` with `shmem_file_setup()`(See Section L.7.2).

198-200 Makes sure no error occurred with the file creation.

202 By default, the error to return indicates that no shared memory identifiers are available or that the size of the request is too large.

Shared Memory
Virtual Filesystem

206-213 Fills in fields in the segment descriptor.

214 Builds a segment identifier, which is what is returned to the caller of `shmget()`.

215-217 Sets the file pointers and file operations structure.

218 Updates `shm_tot` to the total number of pages used by shared segments.

220 Returns the identifier.

L.8.2   Attaching a SYSV Shared Region

L.8.2.1   Function: sys_shmat()   *(ipc/shm.c)*

```
568 asmlinkage long sys_shmat (int shmid, char *shmaddr,
                               int shmflg, ulong *raddr)
569 {
570     struct shmid_kernel *shp;
571     unsigned long addr;
572     unsigned long size;
573     struct file * file;
574     int    err;
575     unsigned long flags;
576     unsigned long prot;
577     unsigned long o_flags;
578     int acc_mode;
579     void *user_addr;
580
581     if (shmid < 0)
582         return -EINVAL;
583
584     if ((addr = (ulong)shmaddr)) {
585         if (addr & (SHMLBA-1)) {
586             if (shmflg & SHM_RND)
587                 addr &= ~(SHMLBA-1);         /* round down */
588             else
589                 return -EINVAL;
590         }
591         flags = MAP_SHARED | MAP_FIXED;
592     } else {
593         if ((shmflg & SHM_REMAP))
594             return -EINVAL;
595
596         flags = MAP_SHARED;
597     }
598
599     if (shmflg & SHM_RDONLY) {
600         prot = PROT_READ;
```

```
601          o_flags = O_RDONLY;
602          acc_mode = S_IRUGO;
603      } else {
604          prot = PROT_READ | PROT_WRITE;
605          o_flags = O_RDWR;
606          acc_mode = S_IRUGO | S_IWUGO;
607      }
```

This section ensures the parameters to shmat() are valid.

581-582 Negative identifiers are not allowed, so this returns -EINVAL if one is supplied.

584-591 If the caller supplied an address, this makes sure it is ok.

585 SHMLBA is the segment boundary address multiple. In Linux, this is always PAGE_SIZE. If the address is not page aligned, this checks if the caller specified SHM_RND, which allows the address to be changed. If specified, it rounds the address down to the nearest page boundary. Otherwise, it returns -EINVAL.

591 Sets the flags to use with the VMA to create a shared region (MAP_SHARED) with a fixed address (MAP_FIXED).

593-596 If an address was not supplied, this makes sure the SHM_REMAP was specified and only uses the MAP_SHARED flag with the VMA. This means that do_mmap() (See Section D.2.1.1) will find a suitable address to attach the shared region.

```
613      shp = shm_lock(shmid);
614      if(shp == NULL)
615          return -EINVAL;
616      err = shm_checkid(shp,shmid);
617      if (err) {
618          shm_unlock(shmid);
619          return err;
620      }
621      if (ipcperms(&shp->shm_perm, acc_mode)) {
622          shm_unlock(shmid);
623          return -EACCES;
624      }
625      file = shp->shm_file;
626      size = file->f_dentry->d_inode->i_size;
627      shp->shm_nattch++;
628      shm_unlock(shmid);
```

This block ensures the IPC permissions are valid.

613 shm_lock() locks the descriptor corresponding to shmid and returns a pointer to the descriptor.

Shared Memory Virtual Filesystem

614-615 Makes sure the descriptor exists.

616-620 Makes sure the ID matches the descriptor.

621-624 Makes sure the caller has the correct permissions.

625 Gets a pointer to the `struct file`, which `do_mmap()` requires.

626 Gets the size of the shared region, so `do_mmap()` knows what size of VMA to create.

627 Temporarily increments `shm_nattach()`, which normally indicates how many VMAs are using the segment. This is to prevent the segment being freed prematurely. The real counter will be incremented by `shm_open()`, which is the `open()` callback used by the `vm_operations_struct` used for shared regions.

628 Releases the descriptor.

```
630    down_write(&current->mm->mmap_sem);
631    if (addr && !(shmflg & SHM_REMAP)) {
632        user_addr = ERR_PTR(-EINVAL);
633        if (find_vma_intersection(current->mm, addr, addr + size))
634            goto invalid;
635        /*
636         * If shm segment goes below stack, make sure there is some
637         * space left for the stack to grow (at least 4 pages).
638         */
639        if (addr < current->mm->start_stack &&
640            addr > current->mm->start_stack - size - PAGE_SIZE * 5)
641            goto invalid;
642    }
643
644    user_addr = (void*) do_mmap (file, addr, size, prot, flags, 0);
```

This block is where `do_mmap()` will be called to attach the region to the calling process.

630 Acquires the semaphore protecting the `mm_struct`.

632-634 If an address was specified, calls `find_vma_intersection()` (See Section D.3.1.3) to ensure no VMA overlaps the region we are trying to use.

639-641 Makes sure there is at least a four-page gap between the end of the shared region and the stack.

644 Calls `do_mmap()`(See Section D.2.1.1), which will allocate the VMA and map it into the process address space.

```
646 invalid:
647     up_write(&current->mm->mmap_sem);
648
649     down (&shm_ids.sem);
650     if(!(shp = shm_lock(shmid)))
651         BUG();
652     shp->shm_nattch--;
653     if(shp->shm_nattch == 0 &&
654         shp->shm_flags & SHM_DEST)
655         shm_destroy (shp);
656     else
657         shm_unlock(shmid);
658     up (&shm_ids.sem);
659
660     *raddr = (unsigned long) user_addr;
661     err = 0;
662     if (IS_ERR(user_addr))
663         err = PTR_ERR(user_addr);
664     return err;
665
666 }
```

647 Releases the `mm_struct` semaphore.

649 Releases the region IDs semaphore.

650-651 Locks the segment descriptor.

652 Decrements the temporary `shm_nattch` counter. This will have been properly incremented by the `vm_ops`→`open` callback.

653-655 If the users reach 0 and the `SHM_DEST` flag has been specified, the region is destroyed because it is no longer required.

657 Otherwise, this just unlocks the segment.

660 Sets the address to return to the caller.

661-663 If an error occured, this sets the error to return to the caller.

664 Returns.

Shared Memory
Virtual Filesystem

Out of Memory Management

Contents

M.1   Determining Available Memory

Contents

M.1.1   Function: `vm_enough_memory()`   *(mm/mmap.c)*

```
53 int vm_enough_memory(long pages)
54 {
65     unsigned long free;
66
67     /* Sometimes we want to use more memory than we have. */
68     if (sysctl_overcommit_memory)
69         return 1;
70
71     /* The page cache contains buffer pages these days.. */
72     free = atomic_read(&page_cache_size);
73     free += nr_free_pages();
74     free += nr_swap_pages;
75
76     /*
77      * This double-counts: the nrpages are both in the page-cache
78      * and in the swapper space. At the same time, this compensates
79      * for the swap-space over-allocation (ie "nr_swap_pages" being
80      * too small.
81      */
82     free += swapper_space.nrpages;
83
84     /*
85      * The code below doesn't account for free space in the inode
86      * and dentry slab cache, slab cache fragmentation, inodes and
87      * dentries which will become freeable under VM load, etc.
88      * Lets just hope all these (complex) factors balance out...
89      */
90     free += (dentry_stat.nr_unused * sizeof(struct dentry)) >> PAGE_SHIFT;
91     free += (inodes_stat.nr_unused * sizeof(struct inode)) >> PAGE_SHIFT;
92
93     return free > pages;
94 }
```

68-69 If the system administrator has specified through the proc interface that overcommit is allowed, this returns immediately saying that the memory is available.

72 Starts the free pages count with the size of the pagecache because these pages may be easily reclaimed.

73 Adds the total number of free pages in the system.

74 Adds the total number of available swap slots.

82 Adds the number of pages managed by `swapper_space`. This double-counts free slots in swaps, but is balanced by the fact that some slots are reserved for pages, but are not being currently used.

90 Adds the number of unused pages in the dentry cache.

91 Adds the number of unused pages in the inode cache.

93 Returns if more free pages are available than the request.

Out of Memory
Management

M.2   Detecting and Recovering From OOM

Contents

M.2.1   Function: out_of_memory()   *(mm/oom_kill.c)*

```
202 void out_of_memory(void)
203 {
204        static unsigned long first, last, count, lastkill;
205        unsigned long now, since;
206
210        if (nr_swap_pages > 0)
211                return;
212
213        now = jiffies;
214        since = now - last;
215        last = now;
216
221        last = now;
222        if (since > 5*HZ)
223                goto reset;
224
229        since = now - first;
230        if (since < HZ)
231                return;
232
237        if (++count < 10)
238                return;
239
245        since = now - lastkill;
246        if (since < HZ*5)
247                return;
248
252        lastkill = now;
253        oom_kill();
254
255 reset:
256        first = now;
257        count = 0;
258 }
```

210-211 If there are available swap slots, the system has no OOM.

213-215 Records what time it is now in jiffies and determines how long it has been since this function was last called.

222-223 If it has been more than 5 seconds since this function was last called, this resets the timer and exits the function.

229-231 If it has been longer than a second since this function was last called, this exits the function. It is possible that I/O is in progress, which will complete soon.

237-238 If the function has not been called 10 times within the last short interval, the system is not yet OOM.

245-247 If a process has been killed within the last 5 seconds, this exits the function because the dying process is likely to free memory.

253 Ok, the system really is OOM, so it calls oom_kill() (See Section M.2.2) to select a process to kill.

M.2.2 Function: oom_kill() *(mm/oom_kill.c)*

This function first calls select_bad_process() to find a suitable process to kill. Once found, the task list is traversed, and the oom_kill_task() is called for the selected process and all its threads.

```
172 static void oom_kill(void)
173 {
174         struct task_struct *p, *q;
175
176         read_lock(&tasklist_lock);
177         p = select_bad_process();
178
179         /* Found nothing?!?! Either we hang forever, or we panic. */
180         if (p == NULL)
181                 panic("Out of memory and no killable processes...\n");
182
183         /* kill all processes that share the ->mm (i.e. all threads) */
184         for_each_task(q) {
185                 if (q->mm == p->mm)
186                         oom_kill_task(q);
187         }
188         read_unlock(&tasklist_lock);
189
190         /*
191          * Make kswapd go out of the way, so "p" has a good chance of
192          * killing itself before someone else gets the chance to ask
193          * for more memory.
```

```
194          */
195          yield();
196          return;
197 }
```

176 Acquires the read-only semaphore to the task list.

177 Calls `select_bad_process()`(See Section M.2.3) to find a suitable process to kill.

180-181 If one could not be found, this panics the system because otherwise the system will deadlock. In this case, it is better to deadlock and have a developer solve the bug than have a mysterious hang.

184-187 Cycles through the task list and calls `oom_kill_task()` (See Section M.2.5) for the selected process and all its threads. Remember that threads will all share the same `mm_struct`.

188 Releases the semaphore.

195 Calls `yield()` to allow the signals to be delivered and the processes to die. The comments indicate that **kswapd** will be the sleeper, but it is possible that a process in the direct-reclaim path will be executing this function, too.

M.2.3 Function: `select_bad_process()`   *(mm/oom_kill.c)*
   This function is responsible for cycling through the entire task list and returning the process that scored highest with the `badness()` function.

```
121 static struct task_struct * select_bad_process(void)
122 {
123     int maxpoints = 0;
124     struct task_struct *p = NULL;
125     struct task_struct *chosen = NULL;
126
127     for_each_task(p) {
128         if (p->pid) {
129             int points = badness(p);
130             if (points > maxpoints) {
131                 chosen = p;
132                 maxpoints = points;
133             }
134         }
135     }
136     return chosen;
137 }
```

127 Cycles through all tasks in the task list.

128 If the process is the system idle task, this skips over it.

129 Calls `badness()`(See Section M.2.4) to score the process.

130-133 If this is the highest score so far, this records it.

136 Returns the `task_struct`, which scored highest with `badness()`.

M.2.4 Function: `badness()` *(mm/oom_kill.c)*

This calculates a score that determines how suitable the process is for killing. The scoring mechanism is explained in detail in Chapter 13.

```
58 static int badness(struct task_struct *p)
59 {
60          int points, cpu_time, run_time;
61
62          if (!p->mm)
63              return 0;
64
65          if (p->flags & PF_MEMDIE)
66              return 0;
67
71          points = p->mm->total_vm;
72
79          cpu_time = (p->times.tms_utime + p->times.tms_stime)
                                            >> (SHIFT_HZ + 3);
80          run_time = (jiffies - p->start_time) >> (SHIFT_HZ + 10);
81
82          points /= int_sqrt(cpu_time);
83          points /= int_sqrt(int_sqrt(run_time));
84
89          if (p->nice > 0)
90                  points *= 2;
91
96          if (cap_t(p->cap_effective) & CAP_TO_MASK(CAP_SYS_ADMIN) ||
97                          p->uid == 0 || p->euid == 0)
98                  points /= 4;
99
106          if (cap_t(p->cap_effective) & CAP_TO_MASK(CAP_SYS_RAWIO))
107                  points /= 4;
108 #ifdef DEBUG
109          printk(KERN_DEBUG "OOMkill: task %d (%s) got %d points\n",
110          p->pid, p->comm, points);
111 #endif
112          return points;
113 }
```

62-63 If there is no `mm`, this returns 0 because this is a kernel thread.

65-66 If the process has already been marked by the OOM killer as exiting, this returns 0 because there is no point trying to kill it multiple times.

71 The total VM used by the process is the base starting point.

79-80 cpu_time is calculated as the total runtime of the process in seconds. run_time is the total runtime of the process in minutes. Comments indicate that there is no basis for this other than it works well in practice.

82 Divides the points by the integer square root of cpu_time.

83 Divides the points by the cube root of run_time.

89-90 If the process has been niced to be of lower priority, double its points because it is likely to be an unimportant process.

96-98 On the other hand, if the process has superuser privileges or has the CAP_SYS_ADMIN capability, it is likely to be a system process, so it divides the points by 4.

106-107 If the process has direct access to hardware, then this divides the process by 4. Killing these processes forcibly could potentially leave hardware in an inconsistent state. For example, forcibly killing X is never a good idea.

112 Returns the score.

M.2.5   Function: oom_kill_task()   *(mm/oom_kill.c)*

This function is responsible for sending the appropriate kill signals to the selected task.

```
144 void oom_kill_task(struct task_struct *p)
145 {
146     printk(KERN_ERR "Out of Memory: Killed process %d (%s).\n",
                                             p->pid, p->comm);
147
148     /*
149      * We give our sacrificial lamb high priority and access to
150      * all the memory it needs. That way it should be able to
151      * exit() and clear out its resources quickly...
152      */
153     p->counter = 5 * HZ;
154     p->flags |= PF_MEMALLOC | PF_MEMDIE;
155
156     /* This process has hardware access, be more careful. */
157     if (cap_t(p->cap_effective) & CAP_TO_MASK(CAP_SYS_RAWIO)) {
158             force_sig(SIGTERM, p);
159     } else {
160             force_sig(SIGKILL, p);
161     }
162 }
```

146 Prints an informational message on the process being killed.

153 This gives the dying process lots of time on the CPU so that it can kill itself off quickly.

154 These flags will tell the allocator to give favorable treatment to the process if it requires more pages before cleaning itself up.

157-158 If the process can directly access hardware, this sends it the `SIGTERM` signal to give it a chance to exit cleanly.

160 Otherwise, sends it the `SIGKILL` signal to force the process to be killed.

References

[BA01] Jeff Bonwick and Jonathan Adams. Magazines and vmem: Extending the slab allocator to many CPUs and arbitrary resources. In *Proceedings of the 2001 USENIX Annual Technical Conference (USENIX-01)*, pages 15–34, Berkeley, CA, June 25–30 2001. The USENIX Association.

[BC00] D. (Daniele) Bovet and Marco Cesati. *Understanding the Linux Kernel.* Cambridge, MA: O'Reilly, 2000.

[BC03] D. (Daniele) Bovet and Marco Cesati. *Understanding the Linux Kernel 2nd Edition.* Cambridge, MA: O'Reilly, 2003.

[BL89] R. Barkley and T. Lee. A lazy buddy system bounded by two coalescing delays. In *Proceedings of the Twelfth ACM Symposium on Operating Systems Principles.* ACM Press, 1989.

[Bon94] Jeff Bonwick. The slab allocator: An object-caching kernel memory allocator. In *USENIX Summer*, pages 87–98, 1994.

[Car84] Rickard W. Carr. *Virtual Memory Management.* UMI Research Press, 1984.

[CD80] E. G. Coffman and P. J. Denning. *Operating Systems Theory.* Englewood Cliffs, NJ: Prentice-Hall, 1980.

[CP99] Charles D. Cranor and Gurudatta M. Parulkar. The UVM virtual memory system. In *Proceedings of the 1999 USENIX Annual Technical Conference (USENIX-99)*, pages 117–130, Berkeley, CA, 1999. USENIX Association.

[CS98] Kevin Dowd and Charles Severance. *High Performance Computing, 2nd Edition.* Newton, MA: O'Reilly, 1998.

[Den70] Peter J. Denning. Virtual memory. *ACM Computing Surveys (CSUR)*, 2(3):153–189, 1970.

[FF02] Joseph Feller and Brian Fitzgerald. *Understanding Open Source Software Development.* Pearson Education Ltd., 2002.

[GAV95] A. Gonzalez, C. Aliagas and M. Valero. A data cache with multiple caching strategies tuned to different types of locality. In ACM, *Conference Proceedings of the 1995 International Conference on Supercomputing, Barcelona, Spain, July 3–7, 1995*, pages 338–347, New York, 1995. ACM Press.

[GC94] Berny Goodheart and James Cox. *The Magic Garden Explained: The Internals of UNIX System V Release 4, an Open Systems Design.* Prentice-Hall, 1994.

[Hac] Various Kernel Hackers. *Kernel 2.4.18 Source Code.* ftp://ftp.kernel.org/pub/linux/kernel/v2.4/linux-2.4.18.tar.gz, February 25, 2002.

[Hac00] Random Kernel Hacker. How to get your change into the linux kernel. *Kernel Source Documentation Tree (SubmittingPatches)*, 2000.

[Hac02] Various Kernel Hackers. *Kernel 2.2.22 Source Code.* ftp://ftp.kernel.org/pub/linux/kernel/v2.2/linux-2.2.22.tar.gz, 2002.

[HK97] Amir H. Hashemi and David R. Kaeli. Efficient procedure mapping using cache line coloring. In *Proceedings of the ACM SIGPLAN Conference on Programming Language Design and Implementation (PLDI-97)*, 32(5) of *ACM SIGPLAN Notices*, pages 171–182, New York, June 15–18 1997. ACM Press.

[JS94] Theodore Johnson and Dennis Shasha. 2q: a low overhead high performance buffer management replacement algorithm. In *Proceedings of the Twentieth International Conference on Very Large Databases*, pages 439–450, Santiago, Chile, 1994.

[JW98] Mark S. Johnstone and Paul R. Wilson. The memory fragmentation problem: solved? In *Proceedings of the First International Symposium on Memory Management.* ACM Press, 1998.

[KB85] David G. Korn and Kiem-Phong Bo. In search of a better malloc. In *Proceedings of the Summer 1985 USENIX Conference*, pages 489–506, Portland, OR, 1985.

[Kes91] Richard E. Kessler. Analysis of multi-megabyte secondary CPU cache memories. *Technical Report CS-TR-1991-1032*, University of Wisconsin, Madison, July 1991.

[KMC02] Scott Kaplan, Lyle McGeoch and Megan Cole. Adaptive caching for demand prepaging. In David Detlefs, editor, *ISMM'02 Proceedings of the Third International Symposium on Memory Management*, ACM SIGPLAN Notices, pages 114–126, Berlin, Germany, June 2002. ACM Press.

[Kno65] Kenneth C. Knowlton. A fast storage allocator. *Communications of the ACM*, 8(10):623–624, 1965.

[Knu68] D. Knuth. *The Art of Computer Programming, Fundamental Algorithms, Volume 1.* Reading, MA: Addison-Wesley, 1968.

[Lev00] Check Lever. *Linux Kernel Hash Table Behavior: Analysis and Improvements.* http://www.citi.umich.edu/techreports/reports/citi-tr-00-1.pdf, 2000.

[McK96] Marshall Kirk McKusick. *The Design and Implementation of the 4.4BSD Operating System.* Addison-Wesley, 1996.

[Mil00] David S. Miller. *Cache and TLB Flushing Under Linux.* Kernel Source Documentation Tree, 2000.

[MM87] Rodney R. Oldehoeft, Maekawa Mamoru and Arthur E. Oldehoeft. *Operating Systems, Advanced Concepts.* Benjamin/Cummings Publishing, 1987.

[MM01] Richard McDougall and Jim Mauro. *Solaris Internals.* Menlo Park, CA: Sun Microsystems Press, 2001.

[PN77] James L. Peterson and Theodore A. Norman. Buddy systems. *Communications of the ACM*, 20(6):421–431, 1977.

[Ray02] Eric S. Raymond. *The Cathedral and the Bazaar (Revised Edition).* O'Reilly, 2002.

[RC01] Alessandro Rubini and Jonathan Corbet. *Linux Device Drivers, 2nd Edition.* Sebastopol, CA: O'Reilly, 2001.

[RM01] Eric S. Raymond and Rick Moen. *How to Ask Questions the Smart Way.* www.catb.org/~esr/faqs/smart-questions.html, 2001.

[Sea00] Chris B. Sears. The elements of cache programming style. In *Proceedings of the 4th Annual Showcase and Conference*, pages 283–298, Berkeley, CA, October 2000. The USENIX Association.

[Tan01] Andrew S. Tanenbaum. *Modern Operating Systems, 2nd Edition.* Upper Saddle River, NJ: Prentice-Hall, 2001.

[Vah96] Uresh Vahalia. *UNIX Internals.* Upper Saddle River, NJ: Prentice-Hall, 1996.

[WJNB95] P. R. Wilson, M. S. Johnstone, M. Neely and D. Boles. Dynamic storage allocation: A survey and critical review. *Lecture Notes in Computer Science*, 986, 1995.

Code Commentary Index

Index

About the Author

MEL GORMAN earned B.Sc. and M.Sc. degrees in Computer Science from the University of Limerick, Ireland. He has worked on a wide variety of applications ranging from web development to real-time display systems for cameras. His toughest projects have been those he figured could not possibly be as hard as they were made out to be, like the Linux VM. He has also worked as a system administrator, mainly with Linux but also with Solaris and Windows. Currently Mel is a Java applications developer for IBM in Santry, Dublin.

Mel developed most of his skills through a healthy combination of college experience, exposure to the UL Computer Society and real-world work. It was the Computer Society that introduced him to Linux and convinced him that it was useful for more than a nice email address. The society developed his interest in Open Source software and particularly in the Linux kernel. He is eternally grateful to UL for providing the platform, the people and the time to work on the VM for two years.

When not pushing buttons, Mel enjoys spending time with his girlfriend, Karen, playing the guitar (badly), reading anything he can get his hands on, hanging out with friends and family (who, for some reason, avoid conversations about the VM), developing plans of dubious merit (sometimes implementing them with novel results) and getting into a kayak any time Andy convinces him it is a good idea. He is still deciding whether to continue writing about Linux or get back to programming with it, which was his original intention.

The GNU General Public License (GPL)

Version 2, June 1991

Copyright (C) 1989, 1991 Free Software Foundation, Inc.
59 Temple Place, Suite 330, Boston, MA 02111-1307 USA

Everyone is permitted to copy and distribute verbatim copies
of this license document, but changing it is not allowed.

Preamble

The licenses for most software are designed to take away your freedom to share and change it. By contrast, the GNU General Public License is intended to guarantee your freedom to share and change free software--to make sure the software is free for all its users. This General Public License applies to most of the Free Software Foundation's software and to any other program whose authors commit to using it. (Some other Free Software Foundation software is covered by the GNU Library General Public License instead.) You can apply it to your programs, too.

When we speak of free software, we are referring to freedom, not price. Our General Public Licenses are designed to make sure that you have the freedom to distribute copies of free software (and charge for this service if you wish), that you receive source code or can get it if you want it, that you can change the software or use pieces of it in new free programs; and that you know you can do these things.

To protect your rights, we need to make restrictions that forbid anyone to deny you these rights or to ask you to surrender the rights. These restrictions translate to certain responsibilities for you if you distribute copies of the software, or if you modify it.

For example, if you distribute copies of such a program, whether gratis or for a fee, you must give the recipients all the rights that you have. You must make sure that they, too, receive or can get the source code. And you must show them these terms so they know their rights.

We protect your rights with two steps: (1) copyright the software, and (2) offer you this license which gives you legal permission to copy, distribute and/or modify the software.

Also, for each author's protection and ours, we want to make certain that everyone understands that there is no warranty for this free software. If the software is modified by someone else and passed on, we want its recipients to know that what they have is not the original, so that any problems introduced by others will not reflect on the original authors' reputations.

Finally, any free program is threatened constantly by software patents. We wish to avoid the danger that redistributors of a free program will individually obtain patent licenses, in effect making the program proprietary. To prevent this, we have made it clear that any patent must be licensed for everyone's free use or not licensed at all.

The precise terms and conditions for copying, distribution and modification follow.

TERMS AND CONDITIONS FOR COPYING, DISTRIBUTION AND MODIFICATION

0. This License applies to any program or other work which contains a notice placed by the copyright holder saying it may be distributed under the terms of this General Public License. The "Program", below, refers to any such program or work, and a "work based on the Program" means either the Program or any derivative work under copyright law: that is to say, a work containing the Program or a portion of it, either verbatim or with modifications and/or translated into another language. (Hereinafter, translation is included without limitation in the term "modification".) Each licensee is addressed as "you".

Activities other than copying, distribution and modification are not covered by this License; they are outside its scope. The act of running the Program is not restricted, and the output from the Program is covered only if its contents constitute a work based on the Program (independent of having been made by running the Program). Whether that is true depends on what theProgram does.

1. You may copy and distribute verbatim copies of the Program's source code as you receive it, in any medium, provided that you conspicuously and appropriately publish on each copy an appropriate copyright notice and disclaimer of warranty; keep intact all the notices that refer to this License and to the absence of any warranty; and give any other recipients of the Program a copy of this License along with the Program.

You may charge a fee for the physical act of transferring a copy, and you may at your option offer warranty protection in exchange for a fee.

2. You may modify your copy or copies of the Program or any portion of it, thus forming a work based on the Program, and copy and distribute such modifications or work under the terms of Section 1 above, provided that you also meet all of these conditions:

> a) You must cause the modified files to carry prominent notices stating that you changed the files and the date of any change.
>
> b) You must cause any work that you distribute or publish, that in whole or in part contains or is derived from the Program or any part thereof, to be licensed as a whole at no charge to all third parties under the terms of this License.
>
> c) If the modified program normally reads commands interactively when run, you must cause it, when started running for such interactive use in the most ordinary way, to print or display an announcement including an appropriate copyright notice and a notice that there is no warranty (or else, saying that you provide a warranty) and that users may redistribute the program under these conditions, and telling the user how to view a copy

of this License. (Exception: if the Program itself is interactive but does not normally print such an announcement, your work based on the Program is not required to print an announcement.)

These requirements apply to the modified work as a whole. If identifiable sections of that work are not derived from the Program, and can be reasonably considered independent and separate works in themselves, then this License, and its terms, do not apply to those sections when you distribute them as separate works. But when you distribute the same sections as part of a whole which is a work based on the Program, the distribution of the whole must be on the terms of this License, whose permissions for other licensees extend to the entire whole, and thus to each and every part regardless of who wrote it.

Thus, it is not the intent of this section to claim rights or contest your rights to work written entirely by you; rather, the intent is to exercise the right to control the distribution of derivative or collective works based on the Program.

In addition, mere aggregation of another work not based on the Program with the Program (or with a work based on the Program) on a volume of a storage or distribution medium does not bring the other work under the scope of this License.

3. You may copy and distribute the Program (or a work based on it, under Section 2) in object code or executable form under the terms of Sections 1 and 2 above provided that you also do one of the following:

> a) Accompany it with the complete corresponding machine-readable source code, which must be distributed under the terms of Sections 1 and 2 above on a medium customarily used for software interchange; or,
>
> b) Accompany it with a written offer, valid for at least three years, to give any third party, for a charge no more than your cost of physically performing source distribution, a complete machine-readable copy of the corresponding source code, to be distributed under the terms of Sections 1 and 2 above on a medium customarily used for software interchange; or,
>
> c) Accompany it with the information you received as to the offer to distribute corresponding source code. (This alternative is allowed only for noncommercial distribution and only if you received the program in object code or executable form with such an offer, in accord with Subsection b above.)

The source code for a work means the preferred form of the work for making modifications to it. For an executable work, complete source code means all the source code for all modules it contains, plus any associated interface definition files, plus the scripts used to control compilation and installation of the executable. However, as a special exception, the source code distributed need not include anything that is normally distributed (in either source or binary form) with the major components (compiler, kernel, and so on) of the operating system on which the executable runs, unless that component itself accompanies the executable.

If distribution of executable or object code is made by offering access to copy from a designated place, then offering equivalent access to copy the source code from the same place counts as distribution of the source code, even though third parties are not compelled to copy the source along with the object code.

4. You may not copy, modify, sublicense, or distribute the Program except as expressly provided under this License. Any attempt otherwise to copy, modify, sublicense or distribute the Program is void, and will automatically terminate your rights under this License. However, parties who have received copies, or rights, from you under this License will not have their licenses terminated so long as such parties remain in full compliance.

5. You are not required to accept this License, since you have not signed it. However, nothing else grants you permission to modify or distribute the Program or its derivative works. These actions are prohibited by law if you do not accept this License. Therefore, by modifying or distributing the Program (or any work based on the Program), you indicate your acceptance of this License to do so, and all its terms and conditions for copying, distributing or modifying the Program or works based on it.

6. Each time you redistribute the Program (or any work based on the Program), the recipient automatically receives a license from the original licensor to copy, distribute or modify the Program subject to these terms and conditions. You may not impose any further restrictions on the recipients' exercise of the rights granted herein. You are not responsible for enforcing compliance by third parties to this License.

7. If, as a consequence of a court judgment or allegation of patent infringement or for any other reason (not limited to patent issues), conditions are imposed on you (whether by court order, agreement or otherwise) that contradict the conditions of this License, they do not excuse you from the conditions of this License. If you cannot distribute so as to satisfy simultaneously your obligations under this License and any other pertinent obligations, then as a consequence you may not distribute the Program at all. For example, if a patent license would not permit royalty-free redistribution of the Program by all those who receive copies directly or indirectly through you, then the only way you could satisfy both it and this License would be to refrain entirely from distribution of the Program.

If any portion of this section is held invalid or unenforceable under any particular circumstance, the balance of the section is intended to apply and the section as a whole is intended to apply in other circumstances.

It is not the purpose of this section to induce you to infringe any patents or other property right claims or to contest validity of any such claims; this section has the sole purpose of protecting the integrity of the free software distribution system, which is implemented by public license practices. Many people have made generous contributions to the wide range of software distributed through that system in reliance on consistent application of that system; it is up to the author/donor to decide if he or she is willing to distribute software through any other system and a licensee cannot impose that choice.

This section is intended to make thoroughly clear what is believed to be a consequence of the rest of this License.

8. If the distribution and/or use of the Program is restricted in certain countries either by patents or by copyrighted interfaces, the original copyright holder who places the Program under this License may add an explicit geographical distribution limitation excluding those countries, so that distribution is permitted only in or among countries not thus excluded. In such case, this License incorporates the limitation as if written in the body of this License.

9. The Free Software Foundation may publish revised and/or new versions of the General Public License from time to time. Such new versions will be similar in spirit to the present version, but may differ in detail to address new problems or concerns.

Each version is given a distinguishing version number. If the Program specifies a version number of this License which applies to it and "any later version", you have the option of following the terms and conditions either of that version or of any later version published by the Free Software Foundation. If the Program does not specify a version number of this License, you may choose any version ever published by the Free Software Foundation.

10. If you wish to incorporate parts of the Program into other free programs whose distribution conditions are different, write to the author to ask for permission. For software which is copyrighted by the Free Software Foundation, write to the Free Software Foundation; we sometimes make exceptions for this. Our decision will be guided by the two goals of preserving the free status of all derivatives of our free software and of promoting the sharing and reuse of software generally.

NO WARRANTY

11. BECAUSE THE PROGRAM IS LICENSED FREE OF CHARGE, THERE IS NO WARRANTY FOR THE PROGRAM, TO THE EXTENT PERMITTED BY APPLICABLE LAW. EXCEPT WHEN OTHERWISE STATED IN WRITING THE COPYRIGHT HOLDERS AND/OR OTHER PARTIES PROVIDE THE PROGRAM "AS IS" WITHOUT WARRANTY OF ANY KIND, EITHER EXPRESSED OR IMPLIED, INCLUDING, BUT NOT LIMITED TO, THE IMPLIED WARRANTIES OF MERCHANTABILITY AND FITNESS FOR A PARTICULAR PURPOSE. THE ENTIRE RISK AS TO THE QUALITY AND PERFORMANCE OF THE PROGRAM IS WITH YOU. SHOULD THE PROGRAM PROVE DEFECTIVE, YOU ASSUME THE COST OF ALL NECESSARY SERVICING, REPAIR OR CORRECTION.

12. IN NO EVENT UNLESS REQUIRED BY APPLICABLE LAW OR AGREED TO IN WRITING WILL ANY COPYRIGHT HOLDER, OR ANY OTHER PARTY WHO MAY

MODIFY AND/OR REDISTRIBUTE THE PROGRAM AS PERMITTED ABOVE, BE LIABLE TO YOU FOR DAMAGES, INCLUDING ANY GENERAL, SPECIAL, INCIDENTAL OR CONSEQUENTIAL DAMAGES ARISING OUT OF THE USE OR INABILITY TO USE THE PROGRAM (INCLUDING BUT NOT LIMITED TO LOSS OF DATA OR DATA BEING RENDERED INACCURATE OR LOSSES SUSTAINED BY YOU OR THIRD PARTIES OR A FAILURE OF THE PROGRAM TO OPERATE WITH ANY OTHER PROGRAMS), EVEN IF SUCH HOLDER OR OTHER PARTY HAS BEEN ADVISED OF THE POSSIBILITY OF SUCH DAMAGES.

END OF TERMS AND CONDITIONS

How to Apply These Terms to Your New Programs

If you develop a new program, and you want it to be of the greatest possible use to the public, the best way to achieve this is to make it free software which everyone can redistribute and change under these terms.

To do so, attach the following notices to the program. It is safest to attach them to the start of each source file to most effectively convey the exclusion of warranty; and each file should have at least the "copyright" line and a pointer to where the full notice is found.

> one line to give the program's name and a brief idea of what it does.
> Copyright (C)
>
> This program is free software; you can redistribute it and/or modify it under the terms of the GNU General Public License as published by the Free Software Foundation; either version 2 of the License, or (at your option) any later version.
>
> This program is distributed in the hope that it will be useful, but WITHOUT ANY WARRANTY; without even the implied warranty of MERCHANTABILITY or FITNESS FOR A PARTICULAR PURPOSE. See the GNU General Public License for more details.
>
> You should have received a copy of the GNU General Public License along with this program; if not, write to the Free Software Foundation, Inc., 59 Temple Place, Suite 330, Boston, MA 02111-1307 USA

Also add information on how to contact you by electronic and paper mail.

If the program is interactive, make it output a short notice like this when it starts in an interactive mode:

> Gnomovision version 69, Copyright (C) year name of author Gnomovision comes with ABSOLUTELY NO WARRANTY; for details type 'show w'. This is free

software, and you are welcome to redistribute it under certain conditions; type 'show c' for details.

The hypothetical commands 'show w' and 'show c' should show the appropriate parts of the General Public License. Of course, the commands you use may be called something other than 'show w' and 'show c'; they could even be mouse-clicks or menu items--whatever suits your program.

You should also get your employer (if you work as a programmer) or your school, if any, to sign a "copyright disclaimer" for the program, if necessary. Here is a sample; alter the names:

Yoyodyne, Inc., hereby disclaims all copyright interest
in the program 'Gnomovision' (which makes passes at compilers)
written by James Hacker.

signature of Ty Coon, 1 April 1989
Ty Coon, President of Vice

This General Public License does not permit incorporating your program into proprietary programs. If your program is a subroutine library, you may consider it more useful to permit linking proprietary applications with the library. If this is what you want to do, use the GNU Library General Public License instead of this License.

About the CD-ROM

The CD-ROM that accompanies *Understanding the Linux Virtual Memory Manager* contains software and tools that aid code comprehension of the kernel. The CD-ROM includes the following:

- An installation of Apache that is usable with any GNU/Linux system. Mount the CD with the command `mount /dev/cdrom /cdrom -o exec`; start the server with the command `/cdrom/start_server`.

- A web-browsable copy of the Linux 2.4.22 and 2.6.0-test4 kernels. This allows code to be browsed and identifiers to be searched for.

- A searchable index for functions that have a code commentary available. If a function is searched for that does not have a commentary, the browser will be automatically redirected to a web-browsable version of the source.

- A live version of CodeViz, the tool used to generate call graphs for the book. The generated graphs may be clicked upon to bring the browser to that function in the source code.

- The VMRegress, CodeViz and PatchSet packages. gcc-3.0.4 is also provided because it is required for building CodeViz.

The CD-ROM can be used on the GNU/Linux or Windows 95/98/NT/2000/Me/XP platforms. The web server and site require that a GNU/Linux system is used and has been tested with Debian Woody and Red Hat 7.3. It is strongly recommended that you use a GNU/Linux system to access the CD.

License Agreement

Use of the software accompanying *Understanding the Linux Virtual Manager* is subject to the terms of the License Agreement and Limited Warranty found on the previous pages.

Technical Support

Prentice Hall does not offer technical support for any of the programs on the CD-ROM. However, if the CD-ROM is damaged, you may obtain a replacement copy by sending an email that describes the problem to: disc_exchange@prenhall.com